1 B.C.

STRABO

HIPPARCHUS

ARCHIMEDES

ARISTOTLE   ARISTARCHUS

ANAXAGORAS   SOCRATES   EPICURUS .

THALES   HERODOTUS   EUCLID

XENOPHANES   DEMOCRITUS   ERATOSTHENES

ANAXIMANDER   ZENO   PLATO   STRATO

PYTHAGORAS   HERACLIDES

            HERACLITUS   THEOPHRASTUS

                ANAXIMENES

                    LEUCIPPUS

The Museum at
Alexandria

J. CAESAR

HANNIBAL

Great Wall
of China

ALEXANDER

CONFUCIUS

BUDDHA   Parthenon
built

CROESUS

Greeks defeat Persians
at Marathon

Rome
founded

Carthage
founded

100   200   300   400   500   600   700   800   900

1 THOUSAND B.C.

TIME AND MAN · (5 BILLION B.C.–1 B.C.)

PHYSICAL SCIENCE: MEN AND CONCEPTS

PHYSICAL SCIENCE: Men and Concepts

GUY C. OMER, JR.

HAROLD L. KNOWLES

BELVEY W. MUNDY

W. HERBERT YOHO

UNIVERSITY OF FLORIDA

D. C. **HEATH** AND COMPANY BOSTON

6577-8765

CHEMISTRY

Portraits by Richard F. Bartlett

Diagrams by William Beyer Associates

LIBRARY OF CONGRESS CATALOG CARD NUMBER: 62–8591

PREFACE

This book was developed in a general education course in the physical sciences at the University of Florida. There is no pretense at coverage in astronomy, physics, chemistry, or geology. Instead it is hoped that each unit is treated with sufficient depth to be true to the ideas of science. While there is considerable history in the text, this is not a history of science. Neither is it a philosophy of science, although some philosophical concepts will be found herein. It is a general education text in the physical sciences with emphasis on the human side of the story. This human emphasis has two aspects. There are, of course, biographical materials about the actors in the drama. But the stronger feature is that they speak in their own words through copious excerpts from original writings.

The origin and growth of fundamental problems are presented in chronological order. The time-sequential arrangement makes a better human story which should be read as simply one thread of the tangled skein that makes up our culture. The end-papers of this book display some simplified schematics which may help the student to keep his place in the story as he follows this thread from earliest times to the present. Even more important is the temporal relatedness of our particular story of science to the other events of political, artistic, religious, or literary history. Only a few of the important markers are given on the end-paper schematics, but they should relate our players in the drama to the wider stage of the world itself. Our story is concerned with many instances of the interactions of the several sciences and the wider culture. It is felt that the particular problems chosen are of fundamental importance in astronomy, physics, chemistry, and geology. Their solutions, except possibly in geology, have been sufficiently validated so that they form an integral part of our modern scientific structure. Geology, because of less maturity and greater complexity, may very well be a case apart. This is considered in Chapter 37 which features Chamberlin's views as to the scientific method in geology but is also concerned with the fundamental differences between the various physical sciences and the corresponding differences in scientific methods which result. This is merely one episode out of many in this book where a deeper analysis of methodology is attempted.

This is a textbook and it contains problems for class use. Many of the problems offer five alternate choices. In each case, one choice is the best, although the others may contain some elements of truth. This is particularly true when the question is concerned with methodology or philosophy. In other cases, such as the numerical problems, there is only one correct answer. Numerical problems are important since mathematics provides the language and the tools of much of physical science. A historical perspective, some appreciation for method and philosophy, and an integration of the physical sciences with the other elements of our culture are all important to one who would understand the world into which he has been born. But a textbook in the physical sciences would be fraudulent if it attempted to treat the physical world without number.

The entire book may be used for a one-year course, or by restricting the material covered, it may also be used for a one-semester course.

The authors, two physicists, a chemist, and a geologist, originally, approached our common task with somewhat different points of view, although each of us has devoted most of his teaching life to general education. One man was conditioned by the several years which he spent teaching in the "old College" of the University of Chicago. Another man was strongly influenced by the year that he spent at Harvard College as a Ford Foundation Fellow. The other two authors were inclined towards the philosophy of general education in science which was first formulated at the University of Florida by the late Dr. L. W. Gaddum. Each of us has been changed by our mutual toil, and we believe that we have now reached a strong and effective synthesis out of our disparate beginnings.

We are indebted to many people. We should like to thank particularly Dr. E. C. Pirkle who made substantial contributions to the section on geology and Dr. L. H. Roberts who prepared Chapter 3. Certain materials in Chapters 36 and 37 were included at the suggestion of Dr. C. I. Cross, the art work was suggested by Dr. J. R. Dunkle, and Dr. A. A. Broyles contributed to the concluding chapter. We should like also to express our appreciation of the helpful criticisms offered by Dr. F. C. Haber, University of Florida, on Parts I and II; by Dr. William Bertozzi, Massachusetts Institute of Technology, on Parts III and IV; by Dr. Allen Debus, University of Chicago, on Part V; by Dr. Kirtley Mather, Harvard Geological Museum, on Part VI; and by Mr. Malcolm K. Smith, Educational Services Incorporated, on Part VII. If errors still appear, only the authors are to blame. We are also appreciative of the helpful criticism offered by our other colleagues of the staff of the Department of Physical Sciences and the suggestions made by the many students who have used this material in its various mimeographed metamorphoses.

The Authors

Contents

PHYSICAL SCIENCE: MEN AND CONCEPTS

".... In the sciences the authority of thousands of opinions is not worth as much as one tiny spark of reason in an individual man."

GALILEO: *Letters on Sunspots*

Introduction

We live in revolutionary times. The world that we know today is not the world of our grandfathers' youth, nor even of the boyhood of our fathers. The tempo of change is a rapidly accelerating one, as evidenced by the events which have occurred within one's own lifetime. Almost while we watch, the world becomes both essentially smaller and more highly compartmentalized; both healthier to live in and more menacing. The accelerative factor is science and technology. This is the characteristic quality of our age. The Middle Ages ceased and Modern Times began when science and technology once more began to spread over Europe in the 16th century.

Therefore, as citizens of this world, we should understand something of the nature of science. It is part of our inheritance, part of our present, and part of that which is yet to come. Writers of advertisements in selling cars, radios, or refrigerators have helped to instill in the public mind the concept of a scientist as a man in a white coat who finds eternal truths within his laboratory by the application of something called " the scientific method." The working scientist not only knows the picture to be false but is made uncomfortable at being cast in the modern day equivalent of the medicine man of savage civilizations. The scientist does not necessarily wear a white coat, nor does he need to work in a laboratory filled with boiling retorts and flashing lights. Perhaps it is more important to say that the scientist finds relative truths instead of eternal verities and that there is no unique " scientific method."

What then is science? It is easier to tell what it is not than it is to define it precisely. Most definitions of science end in a perfect circle. Science is what scientists do. Scientists are those who do science. And the circle closes. Science, we recognize, has to do with our physical environment. It treats of stars in their courses, falling bodies, chemical changes, and the slow unceasing series of geological processes. But the phenomena have always been with us, while science is a relatively recent

1

creation. Thus, science is a creation of the minds of men which has to do with the phenomena.

While it is difficult to frame an exact definition of science, it is not difficult to name the scientists and to recognize their work as being science. This simple pragmatic course of choosing a few well-known scientists and examining the procedures they employed as explained in their own words is the purpose of this book. Fundamental problems have been chosen within four different areas of physical science. No attempt has been made to have complete coverage of physics, astronomy, chemistry, and geology. It would obviously be impossible in a single book. The problems selected are not only fundamental to the physical sciences, but are thoroughly representative of their particular areas of physical science. The sum total of physical science is a collection of interrelated problems entirely similar to the sample problems presented here.

Since we wish to emphasize the human aspects of science, the actual published work of the scientists will be used as much as possible. This, admittedly, makes for difficulties. We could, for example, study Shakespeare in at least two different fashions. We could read the learned commentary written by some modern specialist who tells us *ex cathedra* about the impact of Shakespeare on the English language, on his time and place, and on the world's literature. The method we usually adopt, however, is to read Shakespeare's works directly and draw many of our own conclusions. This requires footnotes and appendices to translate the language which has become archaic, to explain the differences between the stage of Shakespeare and our modern stages, and to give other background information so that we can read the drama with understanding. It also takes considerable effort on our part. We must try to put ourselves into the frame of mind of the 17th century. We must continually remember the differences in language and stage usages. But we usually count our personal experience of the beauty and power of Shakespeare's drama as being well worth the added effort which it cost us.

We hope that it will be the same here. The prose of a Galileo, who was a master of Italian literature as well as of world science, is easy and fluid to read. But the prose of a Newton is dense and filled with thorns. Nevertheless, Newton towers over all of the other physical scientists. The acknowledged difficulty of his prose must be tempered by the importance of what he has to say. We hope that we have provided enough explanatory material to make your task fruitful. We do not pretend that it will be easy, but we do hope that you will enjoy it.

PART ONE

THE BEGINNINGS

Prehistoric man appeared on the scene approximately two million years ago. He was not as big, nor as strong, nor even as swift as many other animals. But he did have hands that were freed from the demands of loco-motion. His thumbs opposed his fingers so that he could manipulate objects. Most important of all, he could reason to a greater or lesser degree. These talents were not many, but they were to prove sufficient.

STONE AGE MAN

Early man, like many primitive people today, was undoubtedly a food gatherer. His was a feast today and a famine tomorrow. Approximately a hundred thousand years ago an ancestor of ours saw a rock naturally shaped to fit within the palm of his hand. He picked it up to open a coconut, found it useful, and kept it. With that simple tool of all work, the Old Stone Age opens. Other rocks were picked up and perhaps chipped a bit here and there to bring them into shape. Some rocks were tied to handles to make axes and hoes. Some long narrow teeth of hard stone were used as awls. And the invention and usage of tools proliferated.

We must give our Stone Age forebears their proper due. Some of the most important human inventions of all were made by them. Consider the invention of language, the domestication of fire, the use of the wheel, social groupings into clans and tribes, and the greater security of the food supply through the evolution of herding and agriculture.

Perhaps about ten thousand years ago, man had developed a consider-able skill with rock working. His tools and other rock objects were now polished and beautifully made. This is the Neolithic Age when agriculture must have evolved. The grass seeds, which are our cereals, were planted in holes in the ground, given varying degrees of care, and harvested the following season for food.

The primitive food gatherers could be single families who wandered

3

afar seeking wild fruits and grains, following the game, or fishing in many localities. The care of herds of animals, however, required more people, so the enlarged family, the clan, or even many related families, the tribe, came into being. The tribes were nomadic, driving their herds from pasture land to pasture land as the grass was exhausted. Agricultural fields on the other hand were not portable. The early farmers established villages in the river valleys where they could tend and guard their crops.

RIVER VALLEY CULTURES

Our written history begins in the Indus, Tigris, Euphrates, and Nile river valleys. These young civilizations were contemporary and apparently in touch with each other. Many identical items, such as cylinder seals, are found at all of these sites. The newly discovered techniques of one city were carried to the others by trade. It is not possible to point to any one city as the " inventor " of civilization. In fact the city culture could well have been perfected by a people as yet unknown to us, whose ruined cities have not yet been disturbed by the shovels of archeologists.

The relatively recent discovery of the Indus valley culture in 1924 by Sir John Marshall on the western bank of the lower Indus is a case in point. Here were found solidly built brick houses and shops with bathrooms and sewer systems that their discoverer thought were eminently superior to those of the coexistent city of Ur. Here were found pottery thrown on a wheel, the first known coinage, and jewelry of those earliest of the metals — gold and silver. Mohenjo-daro, like most archeological sites, is several ruined cities piled one above the other. In the lowest levels we find the polished stone of the New Stone Age. As we rise in the ruins to later times we find a transition from stone to copper and then to bronze. The art of the smelter, the foundryman, the metalsmith, was born in the river valleys. They had a high level of well-ordered life, a blossoming technology, and a linear script which we cannot as yet read. Mohenjo-daro and the other Indus valley cities belong to prehistory where tentative conclusions about the life of the people are reached by sifting over the village dumps. We cannot read in their own words of their deeds or of their hopes and fears.

THE SUMERIAN CULTURE

The Tigris and the Euphrates rivers run parallel to each other for hundreds of miles and then join to empty into the Persian Gulf as a single river. Here in the land between the rivers lived a people known as the Sumerians. Here are located the buried cities of Ur, Eridu, Uruk (Erech), Larsa, Lagash, Nippur, and Isin. Further northward are Babylon, Kish, Agade (Akkad) — cities whose names have a Biblical ring. Ur is one of the oldest cities, being a civilized village perhaps as early as 4500 B.C. We are not certain as to the race of the early Sumerians except that they were not Semites. Some authorities have even suggested that they might be of remote Mongolian origin. But whoever they were, they began a culture which was to continue for nearly four thousand years; a culture based on irrigated fields fed from the river through irrigation canals; a culture in which writing was invented. The system of writing was a picture method like the rebus puzzles of our childhood. Each picture stood for the sound of a syllable and a group of such pictures could allow the sounds of the desired word to be approximated. This is better than the picture writing of the Chinese in which each character stands for a complete concept, but it is less efficient than our own alphabetic system where 26 symbols are sufficient to form any word whatever. This last great step was apparently taken by unknown Semites on the Sinai peninsula. The Semites did not write their vowels but fitted the proper vowels into a purely consonant-written text apparently by instinct. Thus they only needed a few of the Egyptian pictures, and these symbols, after further simplication, came to stand for only the initial sound of the picture involved.

With the invention of writing comes the beginning of recorded history. Now we can read the texts of ancient people and need not guess the entire nature of their lives. Most of the texts are dull, concerned with buying and selling and the private correspondence of individuals who lived thousands of years ago, but some of the writing is startlingly vivid across the gulf of time. The Sumerians wrote on clay with a stylus, giving us the cuneiform characters adopted by all of their successors in the Near East. The earliest Sumerians counted in tens, as most men with ten fingers and shoes on their feet tend to do, making the numerical character with the other round end of their stylus. Thus the decimal system may be as old as man himself.

The Sumerian culture continued and grew for thousands of years as an almost homogeneous whole. The people, however, had a heterogeneous and a thoroughly checkered career. Sumeria lay in the open plain and almost any warlike nation passing by managed to conquer them and become their rulers. First the Sumerians fought each other, then came the Akkadians, the Elamites, the Medes, the Persians, and the Assyrians. Life must have seemed fickle to the Mesopotamians where events were to be explained more by the caprices of the gods than by the workings of any discernible natural law. Perhaps the Babylonians did not develop a science since they may not have believed that cause and effect could possibly be linked together inexorably. Instead they tried to foresee the acts of their inconstant gods by augury and astrology.

The Babylonian priesthood observed and recorded the appearances in their skies for the thousands of years of their history. By sheer numbers of observations they discovered the saros, the period of 6585⅓ days after which the eclipses of the sun and moon repeat themselves. They had no theory for why this should be so — this was only the doings of the gods. The world was created by the gods. As the Babylonian mythos runs, "All the lands were sea — Marduk bound a rush mat upon the face of the waters, he made dirt and piled it beside the rush mat," and so on until the world was complete. Then the gods ran the world as they pleased without the hindrance of natural laws of any type whatever.

But in spite of a life filled and directed by superstition, technology continued to grow. The Hittites introduced iron into the Near East. Metal working proliferated. Great public works were planned and carried out. The Hanging Gardens of Babylonia were one of the seven wonders of the Ancient World. This rich fund of technology was inherited by the Greeks and our other intellectual ancestors and still forms part of the foundation of our own culture. As just one example of a Babylonian survival down to our own times, let us take a quick look at their number system.

The Babylonians oscillated awhile between counting in the Sumerian units of ten or using the more convenient unit of the dozen—more convenient because of the simpler fractions involved. They finally compromised and used sixty as their unit for counting. Thus instead of writing 121 as we do, meaning by the positions of the numbers, one hundred, two tens, and one unit, they wrote the cuneiform equivalent of (2)(1) meaning, again by the positions of their numbers, two sixties and one unit. The Babylonian day was divided into six parts. Each part of the day was further divided into sixty smaller parts and each of these into sixty still smaller parts. The Egyptians divided the daylight portion of the day into twelve hours and the nighttime into another twelve hours. The eventual blending of these two practices gives us our present hours, minutes, and seconds of time. The Babylonians also divided the circle into 360 parts (6 × 60), each part of which we call the degree and use as a measure of angle. Each degree is further divided into sixty minutes of angle and each minute into sixty seconds of angle. In this and many other ways we are the heirs of Babylonia.

THE CULTURE OF THE NILE VALLEY

In some ways the Egyptians, the people who lived in the river valley of the Nile, were more fortunate. They had the Mediterranean Sea to their north, formidable deserts to their east and west, and high mountains shielding them to the south. Theirs was a long narrow land well insulated from the migrant savage tribes. Except for their conquest by the Hyksos around 1700 B.C., Egypt existed as a single people under their own kings from the very earliest of times down to the sixth century before the Christian Era. Egypt is better known than the other early civilizations since the first Egyptologists came into Egypt with Napoleon in 1798, and they have been industriously digging away in increasing numbers ever since. Remains are found from the earliest Old Stone Age down to the present time. The first village economy appeared at about 4000 B.C. contemporaneous with other river valley cultures. Apparently they obtained the wheel, the chariot, and the potter's wheel from Sumeria. The most important annual event in rainless Egypt was the rising of the Nile. The Nile, in flooding, fertilized and irrigated the crop land. It also forced the art of land mensuration and surveying so that the lands could be redistributed after the river subsided — and insured the tax collector his inevitable portion.

One of the oldest mathematical texts known is the Rhind Papyrus dating from about 2000 B.C. This is a mathematical handbook, telling how to multiply and divide with the cumbersome Egyptian number system which was structured like the later Roman numeral system. Ahmose, the author, gave good rules for finding the areas of many figures including rectangles and circles (with the constant pi taken as $\frac{256}{81}$ which is nearly 3.16), as well as the volumes of cylinders and spheres and other solids. This Papyrus shocks our modern sensibilities by simply stating that the areas or the volumes are such and such *without proving the relationships* or even giving any hint as to how the relationship offered may have been evolved.

Several papyri from about the same time have been discovered that deal with medicine. These documents show careful observations and much logical treatment. However, it would appear from some that the carefully stated incantations were accounted as more efficacious than the medications! There was some astronomical observation, since the Nile usually reached its greatest height on the day of the " heliacal rising " of the star Sirius called Sothis by the Egyptians. This is the date at which Sirius can first be seen in the eastern sky just before sunrise. However, the astronomy of the Egyptians seems to be more primitive than that of the Babylonians. One belief was that the world was shaped like a great rectangular box, running north and south and being, in fact, merely their own secure Nile valley made large. The sky was supported on four pillars or mountains and the sun was a god who circled the southern sky in a boat. The moon was another god who was attacked monthly by a sow, causing the moon to wane and produce the phases. Sometimes the sow actually swallowed the moon for a while producing the observed eclipses!

This was a culture of unquestioned technical skill. One has only to look at the pyramids, the Winter Palace of Luxor, or the City of the Dead to acknowledge the 5000-year-old competence of its technicians. This was also a culture of great stability. What other culture has had a longevity of nearly 4000 years? It was also a culture firmly based in superstition. The Pharaoh with a small class of nobility was on the top and a great mass of slaves and bedeviled workingmen were on the bottom with a priestly class in the middle to make it all go. A sophisticated

Greek during the latter dynasties noted the social utility of a system
which promised the workers peace and contentment after death if they
were docile in life — and which threatened them with nameless horrors
in the afterlife if they rebelled in life. There are other ways of organizing
monolithic societies than the use of secret police!

1

The Greeks: from Homer to Socrates

● The Greeks first appear in history at about 1600 B.C. as just another savage horde from the north who conquered with bronze weapons the ancient civilizations of Crete and Mycenae. This is the Achaean invasion by the people of whom Homer sang in the *Iliad* and the *Odyssey*. These are the "long-haired Greeks" who worshipped the gods of Olympus — the gods with quite human passions and conceits who came to earth to fight on both sides of the Trojan war and who kept interfering with its natural course by many an uncalled-for miracle. Near the close of the Heroic Age about 1100 B.C. another horde of Greek-speaking savages came down from the north, this time with iron weapons, and swept all before them. This was the Dorian invasion explained by the later Greeks as being merely the merited "return of the Heracleidae," who as the descendants of Heracles were claiming that part of the Aegean which was rightly due them.

Perhaps the Dorian invaders were long-lost brethren, but the Achaean Greeks spread out over the Asiatic coast and into Italy and Sicily to escape them. Many of the Greeks did not bother to take their own women with them. They captured pre-existent cities in the pursuit of their own liberty, killed the native men, and took over the ladies. The Greeks were not as concerned with racial purity as certain latter-day states. Any one who spoke good Greek was a Greek and those who spoke bad Greek were barbarians (literally, "babblers"). Many historians ascribe the intellectual vitality of the Greeks to "hybrid vigor."

THALES AND THE IONIAN SCHOOL

So, the twelve cities of Ionia were founded on the Asiatic side of the Aegean. Southernmost among the twelve was Miletus (Fig. 1-1) which in 700–600 B.C. was the most dynamic of all the Greek cities. Here with the energy of a frontier town, they imported raw materials from Asia Mi-

9

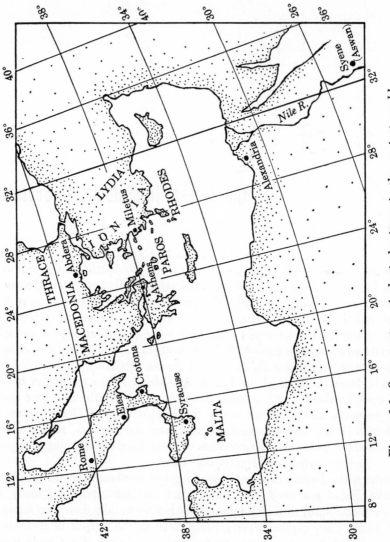

Figure 1-1. Some centers of physical science in the ancient world.

nor and exported manufactured products for sale all over the civilized world. The workers were predominantly freeborn. The arts and crafts were highly regarded as the worthy pursuit of proud men. After all, the wealth of the city was derived from these arts and crafts!

Here, about 620 B.C., Thales was born, possibly of partially Phoenician parentage. He traveled and studied in Babylonia and Egypt. While he was in Egypt he measured the heights of the pyramids by measuring the lengths of their shadows at the time of day when he observed that a man's shadow was equal to his height. On his return to Miletus he founded Greek geometry by demonstrating and proving several theorems now found in Euclid. He is usually credited with proving that a circle is bisected by a diameter; that the angles at the base of any isosceles triangle are equal; that any angle inscribed in a semicircle is a right angle; that the opposite angles formed by two intersecting straight lines are equal; and that two triangles having two angles and one side equal are themselves equal. All of this is only elementary geometry, but the important thing that Thales did was to *prove* his propositions. Remember that the Egyptians, who were highly skilled in land measure, which is the original meaning of the word geometry, merely stated the propositions without proof. With Thales' invention of the proof, mathematical science began.

Beginning with Thales, geometry became the preferred form of Greek mathematics, continuing to the times of Galileo and Newton. This geometrical thinking seems alien to us today, since the characteristic of our times is algebraic thinking, including the techniques of the calculus and differential equations as being merely logical extensions of algebra. An explanation might be found in the awkward Greek numerical system in which the letters of the alphabet were used for numbers with 10, 100, 1000, and the other decimal units requiring special letters. It is easier for us to think in terms of arithmetic or algebra because we have a better number system, which stems back through the Arabians to the Hindus.

Thales taught that primary matter was water. When suitably condensed, water would become earth. When rarified, water would become vapor (air). When incandescent, water became fire. Moreover, he believed that all matter was more or less alive. Thus the soul did not come into a material universe from outside but had always been there with the constituent matter. A little of this type of thinking was current in mining technology in nearly recent times. We still talk about " veins " of an " ore body " as though it had grown from the " mother lode." This, of course, was exactly what was thought up through the Middle Ages.

Thales pictured the world as a flat disk floating on top of water with the sun and stars as incandescent bodies of " water " moving around it. This cosmology is just as primitive as that of the Babylonians. The important element here, however, is that Thales *left Marduk out of the explanation!* The living matter was simply doing what was natural to it. No god was required. This hypothesis of rigorous cause and effect in the physical world is the second great contribution of Thales to newly born science. In latter days when the Greeks named their Seven Wise Men, Thales' name headed their list.

Thales acquired fame throughout Ionia by successfully predicting a solar eclipse for May 28, 585 B.C. This was possibly from his knowledge of the Babylonian astronomy and the long series of Babylonian records. For all of his wisdom, however, he was accused of being "impractical" by his fellow citizens. How modern this all sounds! Thales' rejoinder is well-told by Aristotle [1]:

There is the anecdote of Thales the Milesian and his financial device, which involves a principle of universal application, but is attributed to him on account of his reputation for wisdom. He was reproached for his poverty, which was supposed to show that philosophy was of no use. According to the story, he knew by his skill in the stars while it was yet winter that there would be a great harvest of olives in the coming year; so, having a little money, he gave deposits for the use of all the olive-presses in Chios and Miletus, which he hired at a low price because no one bid against him. When the harvest-time came, and many were wanted all at once and of a sudden, he let them out at any rate which he pleased, and made a quantity of money. Thus he showed the world that philosophers can easily be rich if they like, but that their ambition is of another sort.

The Greek idea of the "four elements" of fire, earth, air (or earlier, *mist*), and water (which we first meet in incipient form in Thales) was to continue to nearly modern times at the close of the 18th century. These were not thought of in the same sense as we conceive "elements" today. These four were considered the basic attributes of matter. They did not occur in nature in the pure form. Naturally occurring water, for instance, was obviously a compound containing some earth since if you boiled away a pot-full of well-water you would find a residue remaining in the pot. Thus, obviously to the Greeks, the water out of the well contained earth as an impurity. It might also contain air (or mist to earlier Greek thinkers) since bubbles could be seen rising from some containers of water. Moreover, if the water was hot, it must also contain some of the "element" fire. Thus the four elements were the basic characteristics of matter and real matter was produced by varying mixtures of these fundamental idealized four. The opposite properties of hot and cold or of wet and dry were produced by mixing the elements as shown in the diagram (Fig. 1-2).

As we have seen, Thales thought that all materials were simply different states of his primary element, water. His pupil, Anaximander, who lived from 611 to 549 B.C. thought otherwise. To him the primary element was an indeterminate and infinite, in both time and space, "substratum" from

---

[1] *The Works of Aristotle Translated into English*, Vol. X, translated by Benjamin Jowett, by permission of Oxford University Press, London, 1921, p. 1259.

which the materials arose. Only scraps of the works of Greek thinkers before Plato exist. We have to search for the ideas of men like Anaximander in the works of later Greeks. Such an author is Simplicius (fl. 530 A.D.) who reports [2]:

Anaximander of Miletos, son of Praxiades, a fellow-citizen and associate of Thales, said that the material cause and first element of things was the Infinite, he being the first to introduce this name of the material cause. He says it is neither water nor any other of the so-called elements, but a substance different from them which is infinite, from which arise all the heavens and the worlds within them.

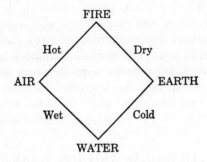

Figure 1-2. *The four elements and the four properties.*

Anaximander thought that the fire heated the water, producing mist and dry land. When the volume of mist reached the breaking point, the universe burst and the fire was contained in whirling tubes of mist. Thus the sun, moon and stars were holes in the tubes through which the enclosed fire glows. This ingenious explanation accounted for eclipses of the sun or moon as simply partial closings of the holes!

Anaximander's pupil was Anaximenes (ca. 550 B.C.). Anaximenes felt that Anaximander's creation of materials by "separation out of the substratum" was too vague. Anaximenes took mist as his primary element and formed the other materials by condensation or rarefaction. Once more to quote Simplicius [3]:

Anaximenes of Miletos, son of Eurystratos, who had been an associate of Anaximander, said, like him, that the underlying substance was one and infinite. He did not, however, say it was indeterminate, like Anaximander, but determinate; for he said it was Air.

When it is dilated so as to be rarer, it becomes fire; while winds, on the other hand, are condensed Air. Cloud is formed from Air by felting; and this, still further condensed, becomes water. Water, condensed still more, turns to earth; and when condensed as much as it can be, to stones.

[2] John Burnet, *Early Greek Philosophy*, by permission of A. & C. Black, Ltd., London, and The Macmillan Co., New York, 1920, p. 52.
[3] *Ibid.*, p. 73.

Thales had urged that the twelve cities of Ionia should form a tight alliance with a common citizenship for mutual defense. His pleas fell on the deaf ears of intense individualism, which was typical of the Greeks. Croesus of Lydia conquered the Ionian cities one by one. Miletus bought continued independence by abandoning her sister cities. This was also, unfortunately, typically Greek. Croesus was a mild overlord and the arts and sciences continued to flourish.

In Ephesus, north of Miletus, Heraclitus the Obscure was born in 530 B.C. He withdrew to the mountains as a hermit-sage, finally depositing his collection of cryptic sayings, "On Nature," in the temple of Artemis for preservation. Heraclitus proposed fire as the primary element. He found the universe in continual change and endless transformation. As he says, "You cannot step twice into the same river, for other waters are ever flowing on to you." The continual changes are the products of the tension in the world between the opposites, such as hot and cold, wet and dry, and so forth. In fact, the opposites are necessary to define the states. How could one speak of "wet" if there were no "dry"; or of "hot" if there were no "cold" to serve as a reference?

PYTHAGORAS AND HIS SCHOOL

In 546 B.C. Cyrus conquered Lydia and added the Ionic cities to the Persian Empire. The great days of the Asiatic Greeks were now over. Pythagoras was born in Samos about 580 B.C., but not caring for the political situation in Ionia, he emigrated to Crotona, on the "instep" of the Italian peninsula. Here at the age of fifty he established his school. Perhaps it might better be described as a religious brotherhood since the students bound themselves with vows to their master and to each other and to a series of strict regulations governing their diet, dress, and deportment.

The Pythagoreans were unique among the Greeks, since they delighted in number. They were the first to classify numbers as odd and even, or as *triangular, square,* or *cubic* (see Fig. 1-3).

Among the many possible geometrical classifications of number, the last two, square and cubic, are still meaningful to us today. Pythagoras and his followers built their world out of number. Since their points had bulk, a finite series of points would make a line having breadth. A series of lines would make a plane with depth. A sequence of planes would make a solid. Hence from a study of number they hoped to find the secrets of the world. Here in their bulky points we may find the genesis of our atoms.

They were also skilled in geometry, like good Greek theoreticians. Pythagoras is famous for his Pythagorean theorem in which he proved that the square of the length of the hypotenuse of a right triangle is equal to the sum of the squares of the lengths of the other two sides. This theorem

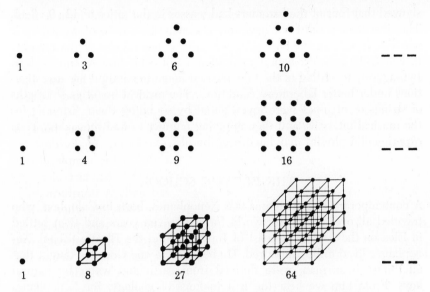

Figure 1-3. *The Pythagorean geometrical classifications of numbers.*

not only delighted the Master so that he sacrificed a hundred oxen to the gods, but it also scandalized him since he could construct a line of length $\sqrt{2}$ units by simply drawing the hypotenuse of a right triangle with sides of unit length. The ratio of this hypotenuse to one of its sides could not be expressed as a whole fraction and thereby could not be made up from a finite number of bulky points! Such numbers, being unthinkable, were called "irrational," while numbers which could properly be expressed as exact fractions were called "rational."

This feeling for number and geometry led the Pythagoreans to propose that the earth, sun, moon, and planets were spheres and moved in circular orbits within a spherical universe. The sphere and the circle were "perfect" figures and thus were fitting to celestial bodies. A Pythagorean aberration was the hypothesis of the "central fire" which burned at the center of the universe and was never seen on earth. The earth moved in a circular orbit about the central fire as did the sun and the planets, but since the inhabited side of the earth was always turned away from the central fire, it went unseen by men! This curious doctrine was hailed by Copernicus and Kepler in a later age as the progenitor of their own views.

We find the first appearance of the experimental method in the School of Pythagoras. According to Boethius, Pythagoras was struck by the musical intervals heard in a blacksmith's shop. Perhaps the difference in pitch of the tones from the hammer blows was determined by the strength of the men? He asked the men to exchange hammers, but the tones were unchanged. Then the pitch must be inherent in the hammers. Weighing showed that four of the hammers had masses in the ratios of $12 : 9 : 8 : 6$. The fifth hammer did not have any commensurate ratio of weight so it was excluded from the choir. Ah, now a true musical chord was sounded in which the heaviest hammer sounded a full octave below the lightest! Pythagoras, according to the tale, hurried home to continue his investigations under better laboratory conditions. The musical qualities of lengths of strings or of pipes were investigated by sounding them, listening for the musical intervals, and then applying number to find the secret. Thus experimental physics may have been born!

THE ELEATIC SCHOOL

A contemporary of Pythagoras was Xenophanes, born in Colophon, who traveled all over the Greek world for sixty-seven years and then settled in Elea on the southwest coast of Italy to found the Eleatic School. Xenophanes lived to be a hundred. He believed in one God. He taught that all things, even man, were derived from earth and water by natural laws. From him we hear the first inklings of geology, for Xenophanes pointed out that fossils are found on land and in the mountains; that in the quarries of Syracuse the imprints of a fish and of seals have been found; and at Paros the imprint of a sardine deep in stone; and at Malta traces of all sorts of things of the sea. Xenophanes proposed that once the ocean covered all when these fossils were laid down. He also believed that the earth would fall once more below the waves and with the disappearance of man, a new creation would begin.

His most famous pupil was Parmenides who rejected the Pythagorean approach in part as putting entirely too much reliance on the validity of the senses. It is obvious that one's physical senses can mislead. Among the amusements of adolescence are those geometric constructions in which straight lines appear bent and lines of equal length appear unequal. Hence Parmenides wrote in verse a clarion call to reject the misleading evidences of the senses and to see the truth through the mind alone, even though the consequences of pure thought might seem a bit ajar with the observed physical world. His own intellectual model for the world is considerably ajar! Grant me, he says, two simple hypotheses:

(1) That-which-is *is,* and (2) That-which-is-not *is not.*

Now it follows from strict logic that motion is impossible in the world. A body cannot move from A to B. If it exists at A, then that state is. Hence it does not yet exist at B and that state is-not. Now it cannot move from A to B since that would require an admixture of state A which is with state B which-is-not! Parmenides thought that Reality was a hard, smooth, uniform sphere existing forever without change. This is indeed a strong contrast to Heraclitus who on the other shore of the Mediterranean was insisting that all is change and flux!

The difficulty lies in the second hypothesis denying the existence of that-which-is-not. The argument as to the existence of vacuum or of empty space was to continue down to the times of Galileo two thousand years later. Certainly a vacuum is the very epitome of that-which-is-not, since it obviously consists of nothing at all. But other Greeks were to insist on the reality of the vacuum to permit the very motion which Parmenides refused.

The successor to Parmenides in the school at Elea was Zeno who was active in 465 B.C. He wrote a book of paradoxes to show that space does not exist and that motion is impossible. Nine of his paradoxes have survived to our times. Perhaps it will be sufficient to paraphrase a single one of them into modern terms. Zeno would prove to you that it was impossible to walk out of the door of your room. Before reaching your door, you must first reach that point which is halfway between you and the door. But having achieved that point, there is still another halfway point yet to be reached. And throughout your journey to the door, there will always be a point halfway between yet to be reached. Hence, obviously, you cannot leave your room by way of your door! Zeno's paradoxes are by no means solved to this day. They are concerned with the nature of infinity and of infinite processes. Some modern mathematicians avoid this difficulty by rejecting infinity and infinite processes from proper and rational mathematics. This rejection, of course, also casts the calculus and similar fields of mathematics into the outer darkness!

Empedocles of Agrigentum in Sicily studied in the Pythagorean school and was reputed to have been expelled for revealing some of their religious secrets. Nevertheless, he did not find the Eleatic school to his taste. He admitted the fallibility of the senses but insisted that their evidence could be critically evaluated and used. It was he who proposed that all materials were ultimately composed of the four elements air, fire, water, and earth. He carried out a series of experiments to show that air was matter, although it cannot be perceived by the senses. Wind, then, becomes a good example of an unseen agency at work in the universe.

About 435 B.C. Leucippus of Miletus came to Elea and studied under Zeno. He settled in Abdera on the shores of the Aegean Sea and established a school there. He proposed that the universe consisted of atoms with empty space between and nothing else. Democritus was his pupil and developed his atomic theory still further. Democritus met Parmenides part way by dividing properties up into primary and secondary. The primary qualities were those that existed independently of the senses, such as mass in a later day. The illusory secondary qualities were those which were provided by the senses themselves, such as sweet and sour, and harmonious or dissonant musical intervals. It is a well-known trick in psychology classes to pass around certain substances which taste sweet to part of the class but react as sour for the rest. A little study of the history of music will also show us that certain intervals which sound harmonious enough to us today were violently rejected by our forefathers as just so much noise.

Thus the atoms of the four elements, according to Democritus, differed from each other in primary qualities, such as shape, size, and weight. The individual atoms had been in existence forever and unchanged within themselves, thus satisfying the demands of Parmenides. However the world as we see it is made up of constantly changing configurations of the atoms — thus also satisfying the concepts of Heraclitus. This is a brilliant solution to a philosophical difficulty, but note that all of this has nothing directly to do with the chemical transformations of matter which will concern Dalton. Honor is due both Democritus and Dalton for their differing atomic theories.

ATHENS AND THE SOPHISTS

We have now described several hundred years of Greek science and philosophy. We have touched nearly every shore of the Grecian seas. But we have not yet mentioned Athens. This is the Athens of Pericles, rapidly approaching her golden age of power and wealth. Zeno had visited Athens in 450 B.C., perhaps with Parmenides as a traveling companion. Anaxagoras of Clazomenae settled in Athens at about 480 B.C., perhaps at the invitation of Pericles. At least Pericles was his close friend and defender. Anaxagoras taught that [4]:

> The sun and the moon and all the stars are fiery stones carried round by the rotation of the aether. . . . We do not feel the heat of the stars because of the greatness of their distance from the earth. . . . The moon is below the sun, and nearer us. The sun surpasses the Peloponnesos in size. The moon has not a light of her own, but gets it from the sun. The course of the stars goes under the earth. The moon is eclipsed by the earth screening the sun's light from it, . . . The sun is eclipsed at the new moon, when the moon screens it from us. . . . the moon was of earth and had plains and ravines in it.

For these impious statements, a formal indictment was brought against him. Pericles managed to save Anaxagoras from prison. Not having a taste for hemlock, he left Athens for exile in Asia Minor. As a further indication of the temper of these times, the Athenian Assembly passed a law forbidding the teaching or the study of astronomy!

Attracted by the wealth of Athens, a group of wandering scholars called the Sophists came and established their schools. They were much like private schools today. The Sophists rented halls and gave courses of lectures to students who paid fees to attend. Socrates defended his ignorance of grammar because he could not afford the fifty-drachma course

---

[4] John Burnet, *Early Greek Philosophy*, by permission of A. & C. Black, Ltd., London, and The Macmillan Co., New York, 1920, p. 271.

of Prodicus, but only the elementary one-drachma course. One of the most famous of the Sophists was Protagoras, of whom Plato wrote in a dialogue named for him. Protagoras gave courses over many fields, but he might be best remembered as the founder of grammar and philology. At a meeting in the home of the dramatist Euripides, Protagoras read an essay which began: "With regard to the gods I know not whether they exist or not, or what they are like. Many things prevent our knowing: the subject is obscure, and brief is the span of our mortal life." This was enough. The Athenian Assembly once more detected impiety and banished Protagoras from Athens and burned all of his books that they could find.

Gorgias of Leontini was wise enough to spend most of his time outside of Athens, although he drew most of his paying students from that city. Nothing of his teaching survived except for three propositions which he sought to prove in his lost book, *On Nature:*

1. Nothing exists beyond the senses.
2. If anything did exist outside of the senses, it would not be knowable, since all knowledge comes through the senses.
3. If something suprasensual were known, it could not be made known to another, since all communication is through the senses.

The last Sophist which we shall consider among the many who taught in Athens in Periclean times is Hippias of Elis who undertook to teach all of the arts and sciences. It was the pride of Hippias to attend the Olympian games attired in festive garb every item of which was made by his own hands. Hippias was an old-fashioned gentleman for his age, since he gave full respect to the arts. It was characteristic of the old Ionian Greeks to give honor to their great inventors such as Anacharsis who invented the bellows, or Glaucus of Chios who invented the soldering iron, or Theodorus of Samos who invented the level and the lathe, or Zopyrus who invented the crossbow. These men were remembered and honored by the early Greeks along with Thales, Anaximander, and Anaximenes. But this was not so in the Athens of 400 B.C. Here the arts were the province of the slaves. Free men avoided all manual labor as though it would contaminate. In so far as philosophy or science was to be pursued, it must be as entirely a matter for the mind alone.

SOCRATES

With so many interesting foreigners in town, some native-born Athenians were bound to take up philosophy. Such a man was Socrates, a stonecutter by trade and a philosophical gadfly by choice. He had studied physics under the Sophist Archelaus, but in his mature years he turned from astronomy to morality, from physics to ethics, and from geometry to logic. He himself claimed to know nothing, but by his adroit questioning quickly showed that more pretentious men also knew very little. Such a man, always asking embarrassing questions but never answering them himself, is likely to be either intensely loved or hated. Plato, who was one of his disciples, said that he "was truly the wisest, and justest, and best of all the men whom I have ever known." Aristophanes, on the other hand, poked fun at him in his comedy *The Clouds*. It is said that Socrates stood during the entire performance in good nature so that the people could see him the better.

In 399 B.C. an indictment against Socrates was entered before the Athenian Assembly charging: "Socrates is a public offender in that he does not recognize the gods that the state recognizes, but introduces new demoniacal beings. He has also offended by corrupting the youth." He was found guilty by a jury of five hundred citizens in a popular court and condemned to death. Although his escape from Athens had been prepared by the bribes of his wealthy friends, Socrates chose to hold true to his ethics and remained to drink the hemlock as told dramatically by Plato in his " Phaedo."

2

The Greeks: from the Academy to the Museum

THE ACADEMY

● According to the account of Diogenes Laërtius, Plato, named Aristocles by his parents, was of aristocratic lineage. He was a many-talented young man. When he wrestled at the Isthmian games he acquired his lifelong nickname " Platon " (" The Broad ") from his healthy and sturdy physique. He was trying to decide between the pursuit of poetry or of politics when he met Socrates and was completely charmed by his vivid personality. He burned his verse and followed his new master. When he was in his early twenties, his uncle Charmides, who had been one of the leaders of the aristocratic revolution of 404 B.C., was put to death by the victorious democrats. This was followed shortly by Socrates' cup of hemlock. Plato fled from Athens to tour the civilized world. While visiting Dionysius I, the tyrant of Syracuse, he was sold into slavery, ransomed by Anniceris and restored to Athens. Here his friends purchased a grove of trees in suburban Athens which was called the Academy from the name of its local god, Academus. Here Plato established his school. His students paid no fees, but since they were the children of the aristocrats, their parents made suitable contributions to the school. We know very little of what he taught in his oral lectures, but we do have the complete corpus of his *Dialogues*. These were written in semipopular form to instruct the educated layman in the elements of philosophy. The fortunate blending of poet and philosopher in Plato makes the *Dialogues* delightful reading. Perhaps their literary charm accounts for their survival. Plato is the first of the Greek thinkers whose work came down to us in substance. Only scraps and hearsay evidence now exist for the work of his predecessors.

Plato was an idealist. A well-known simile of his is that of the cave. We are, he says, like men in a cave, constrained to sit always with our backs to the mouth of the cave and able to see only the shadows that the real world casts on the walls. From these shadows our minds must

deduce the true nature of the real world. Plato, the proud aristocrat, rejects the experimental method. The evidence of the senses can deceive
and manual labor is for slaves! He has scorn for the Pythagorean musi-
cians who listen closely for the harmonies as they twang their strings.
He declares that one will never learn of astronomy by observing the
stars. No, true conclusions are to be reached with the mind alone. For
him, the true realities are the ideas which exist within the mind. Let us
consider the idea of "tree." This is purely a concept which is entirely
within our minds. The concept covers tall trees and short trees, broad-
leaved or needle-leaved trees, and so on in the infinite variety of observed
trees. Any observed tree is only a partial fulfillment of our concept
"tree." The observed tree will grow, die, and fall; but the concept "tree"
goes on forever. Here again is a compromise between Parmenides and
Heraclitus.

Idealism has had its followers in physics. Only recently, the English
physicist Eddington has argued for both Pythagoras and Plato. Like a
good modern-day Pythagorean, Eddington believed that the basic structure of the physical world was to be revealed in number — numbers such
as the " fine-structure constant " and the total number of electrons in the
universe. Moreover, like a good follower of Plato, Eddington believed
that these numbers could be arrived at by pure processes of thought
without doing any laboratory experiments if one were only intelligent
enough. This seems a curious echo within the 20th century by one of our
own leading physical scientists of the Greek thought of 2500 years before.

Plato's influence on astronomy was immediate. Before his time, the
study of astronomy was forbidden by the Athenian Assembly as impious.
The sun and the planets might be deities, but anyone who cared to watch
could see that they moved about the sky in a most irregular manner. It
had been suspected by the Pythagoreans that they must really move in
some system of regular circles, but they could not devise a proper system. A later Greek, Geminus (fl. 70 B.C.) wrote [1]:

> It is a fundamental assumption in all astronomy that the sun, the moon, and
> the five planets move in circular orbits at uniform speed in a sense contrary to
> that of the universe. For the Pythagoreans, who were the first to apply them-
> selves to investigations of this kind, assumed the movements of the sun, the
> moon, and the five planets to be circular and uniform. They would not admit,
> with reference to things divine and eternal, any disorder such as would make
> them move at one time more swiftly, at one time more slowly, and at another
> time stand still, as the five planets do at their so-called *stationary points.* For
> such irregularity of motion would not even be expected of a decent and orderly
> man in his journeys. With men, of course, the necessities of life are often causes
> of slowness and swiftness; but with the imperishable stars it is not possible to

[1] T. L. Heath, *Aristarchus of Samos,* Oxford at the Clarendon Press, London, 1913,
p. 269.

adduce any cause of swiftness or slowness. Accordingly, they proposed the problem, how the phenomena could be accounted for by means of circular and uniform movements.

According to one story, Plato discovered two of his students, Eudoxus and Callippus, using geometry to devise new machines for worldly use. He upbraided them for having sullied the intellectual purity of mathematics by using it to create something practical — and then assigned them the astronomical task at which the Pythagoreans had failed. They delighted Plato and the Grecian world by showing that a combination of approximately thirty uniformly rotating circles would account for the irregular appearances.

The altered view of astronomy can be shown by quoting a bit of Plutarch's " Life of Nicias." Nicias, the richest slave owner in all Athens, was in command of a fleet attacking Syracuse. The war went badly, and on the one night when Nicias and his fleet could have escaped they were frightened by an eclipse of the moon. In the following days they were slaughtered and Athens never did recover her former power. But let us quote from the ancient historian [2]:

And when all were in readiness, and none of the enemy had observed them, not expecting such a thing, the moon was eclipsed in the night, to the great fright of Nicias and others, who, for want of experience, or out of superstition, felt alarm at such appearances. That the sun might be darkened about the close of the month, this even ordinary people now understood pretty well to be the effect of the moon; but the moon itself to be darkened, how that could come about, and how, on the sudden, a broad full moon should lose her light, and show such various colours, was not easy to be comprehended; they concluded it to be ominous, and a divine intimation of some heavy calamities. For he who the first, and the most plainly of any, and with the greatest assurance committed to writing how the moon is enlightened and overshadowed, was Anaxagoras; and he was as yet but recent, nor was his argument much known, but was rather kept secret, passing only amongst a few, under some kind of caution and confidence. People would not then tolerate natural philosophers, and theorists, as they then called them, about celestial things; as lessening the divine power, by explaining away its agency into the operation of irrational causes and senseless forces acting by necessity, without anything of Providence, or a free agent. Hence it was that Protagoras was banished, and Anaxagoras cast in prison, so that Pericles had much difficulty to procure his liberty; and Socrates, though he had no concern whatever with this sort of learning, yet was put to death for philosophy. It was only afterwards that the reputation of Plato, shining forth by his life, and because he subjected natural necessity to divine and more excellent principles, took away the obloquy and scandal that had attached to such contemplations, and obtained these studies currency among all people.

[2] A. H. Clough, *Plutarch's Lives*, Vol. 3, Little Brown & Co., 1875, pp. 321–322.

THE LYCEUM

Aristotle was born in Thrace, the son of the physician to Amyntas II, the father of Philip of Macedonia. His father may have trained him in medicine, before sending him to Athens to study in Plato's Academy. Aristotle remained in Athens for twenty years studying at the Academy and elsewhere. It may have been while he was at the Academy that he began his twenty-seven popular dialogues, which Cicero tells us were fully as excellent as Plato's. Unfortunately they did not survive for us to read.

He left Athens after the death of Plato. He married and spent some time at Lesbos where he studied the natural history of the island. In 343 B.C. Philip invited him to come to Macedonia to teach the young Alexander. In 334 he returned to Athens and opened his school in one of the most elegant sets of buildings in Athens, a group dedicated to the god Apollo Lyceus, from which came the school's name of the Lyceum. He gave advanced lectures to his students in the mornings and popular lectures to the people in the afternoons. It is his lecture notes, rough and unpolished, that come down to us today as the published work of Aristotle. Like any professor's lecture notes, they do not make easy reading.

Aristotle was a logician whose work in logic is just as valid today as it was 2300 years ago. Every element of discourse is analyzed under his ten "categories": substance, quantity, quality, relation, place, time, position, possession, activity, and passivity. Every definition is carefully drawn. He is under the influence of Plato's theory of ideas, which he called the "forms." But he holds that the evidence of the senses has validity and that the forms cannot exist apart from matter. Matter is made up of five elements. There are the classic four — fire, earth, air, and water — which make up the earth on which we live. Out beyond the orbit of the moon, the heavenly bodies, the sun, the planets, and the stars are made up of a perfect celestial element — the quintessence. The physics of the two domains, the terrestrial and the celestial, are quite different, as befitting their different elements. In the terrestrial domain, matter is in continual flux, flowing into and out of the various forms. Thus our tree, of earlier example, draws its elements from other forms in its neighborhood while it is growing and returns its elements to still other forms when it decays. Flux, quite in the fashion of Heraclitus, is the keynote of terrestrial matter. The celestial matter, however, is single and perfect, so the sun, planets, and stars continue unchanged forever.

All of this terrestrial flux is not senseless but has its origins in God, who is defined as the Unmoved Mover. Aristotle hopes to understand the causes of the observed effects, which he classifies as material, efficient, formal, and final causes. His definitions may be illustrated by considering a class-room building. The material cause of such a building was the stone, steel, plaster, and other materials which comprise the building. The efficient cause of the building was the workmen who laid the stone, steel, and plaster. The formal cause of the building was the set of blueprints from which the structure was built, and the final cause of the building was that it was needed as a place to hold classes. Aristotle holds that the final causes are the most important, and it is these which he seeks in his world.

Thus, among Aristotle's predecessors, Democritus with his atoms was seeking the material cause; Heraclitus with his tensions of the opposites was seeking the efficient cause; the Pythagoreans with number as the basis of all were seeking the formal cause; while Aristotle sought only the final cause. This is quite contrary to modern-day science. Today we seek material, efficient, and even formal causes in our science but leave the final causes to the metaphysicists.

The final cause of motion to Aristotle was natural place. Every element had its natural place to which it sought to return " like a lover seeking his beloved," and the closer that it approached its natural place the more that it " exulted " and hence accelerated. A stone held in the hand has its natural place in the earth, since the stone is presumed to be predominately earth. Thus if the stone is simply released from the hand, its natural motion will be straight downward, moving more rapidly as it approaches the earth. Of course the stone can be thrown sideways, but this is to do violence to it and such sideward motions were called " violent motions." The air, on the other hand, has a natural motion of straight upwards, if it were released at the bottom of a swimming pool. Thus, in the beginning Aristotle thought that all of the elements could have been mixed together, but each would seek its natural place — earth at the center of the universe, water on top of that, air on top of that, and fire above the others. Then the celestial bodies would be formed into perfect spheres, since the sphere was the natural shape of the celestial element, and would move in circular paths about the earth, since circular motions were the natural motions of celestial matter because they are the only motions which can continue forever without change. It was a system of considerable logical consistency, but of little observational validity. It was to dominate man's thinking for two thousand years and to require an almost violent revolution of thought in the 17th century to overthrow it.

Since the problem of falling bodies was so important to Galileo, let us read two short excerpts from Aristotle's " On the Heavens " [3]:

A given weight moves a given distance in a given time; a weight which is as great and more moves the same distance in a less time, the times being in inverse proportion to the weights. For instance, if one weight is twice another, it will take half as long over a given movement.

Whenever bodies are moving with their proper motion, the larger moves quicker.

[3] *The Works of Aristotle Translated into English*, Vol. II DeCaelo, translated by J. L. Stocks, Oxford University Press, London, 1922, pp. 273b, 290a.

And in addition, a longer excerpt from Aristotle's *Physics* giving his opinions as to how bodies fall through different media [4]:

Further, the truth of what we assert is plain from the following considerations. We see the same weight or body moving faster than another for two reasons, either because there is a difference in what it moves through, as between water, air, and earth, or because, other things being equal, the moving body differs from the other owing to excess of weight or of lightness.

Now the medium causes a difference because it impedes the moving thing, most of all if it is moving in the opposite direction, but in a secondary degree even if it is at rest; and especially a medium that is not easily divided, i.e., a medium that is somewhat dense.

A, then, will move through B in time C, and through D, which is thinner, in time E (if the length of B is equal to D), in proportion to the density of the hindering body. For let B be water and D air; then by so much as air is thinner and more incorporeal than water, A will move through D faster than through B. Let the speed have the same ratio to the speed, then, that air has to water. Then if air is twice as thin, the body will transverse B in twice the time that it does D, and the time C will be twice the time E. And always, by so much as the medium is more incorporeal and less resistant and more easily divided, the faster will be the movement.

Reread these quotations again after reading Galileo's *Two New Sciences*.

Although Aristotle's physics and astronomy seem to be almost entirely logic, careful definitions, and metaphysics, in biology he applied the experimental method and sounds quite modern. Note how he reports his observations of the development of the chicken embryo [5]:

Generation from the egg proceeds in an identical manner with all birds, but the full periods from conception to birth differ, as has been said. With the common hen after three days and three nights there is the first indication of the embryo; . . . the heart appears, like a speck of blood, in the white of the egg. This point beats and moves as though endowed with life, and from it two vein-ducts with blood in them trend in a convoluted course; and a membrane carrying bloody fibers now envelops the yolk, leading off from the vein-ducts. A little afterwards the body is differentiated, at first very small and white. . . .

When the egg is now ten days old the chick and all its parts are distinctly visible. The head is still larger than the rest of its body, and the eyes larger than the head, but still devoid of vision. . . .

About the twentieth day, if you open the egg and touch the chick, it moves inside and chirps; and it is already coming to be covered with down, when, after the twentieth day is past, the chick begins to break the shell. . . . So much as to the generation from the egg in the case of birds.

Here is a carefully detailed observation of nature which is fully modern.

---

[4] *The Students' Oxford Aristotle*, Vol. II Physica Book IV–8, edited by W. D. Ross, Oxford University Press, London, 1942, p. 215a.

[5] *The Works of Aristotle Translated into English*, Vol. IV, Historia Animatium, translated by D. W. Thompson, University of Oxford, Clarendon Press, London, 1910, pp. 561a-562a.

The schools which Plato and Aristotle founded continued long after their deaths. Plato willed his Academy to his nephew Speusippus, who was a biologist without much taste for metaphysics. Nor was he a very great biologist either. He left the school to Xenocrates of whom it has been said "He was an amiable moralist who out of piety taught Plato's philosophy but did not understand it." The Academy continued for nearly nine hundred years with a repute for teaching but with no further originality.

Aristotle was perhaps more fortunate in the subsequent history of his school. Hearing that the Athenian Assembly was talking of indicting him for impiety, he gave his school over to Theophrastus and retired outside the city limits, saying that he would not give the Athenians the opportunity to sin twice against philosophy. Apparently this did not satisfy the Athenians, for Theophrastus, hearing that the Assembly might indict him for impiety, moved the entire school outside the city limits also. Athens, feeling sharply the financial loss of several thousand students, begged him to return the school to Athens. Theophrastus brought the Lyceum back to its original locale and we read nothing further in the annals of Athens about indictments for impiety against philosophers.

Theophrastus was born on the island of Lesbos about 373 B.C. and lived for eighty-five years, surviving his teacher by some thirty-five years. Both he and his own successor, Strato, were men of very great attainments. Sarton has said that if Aristotle had never lived, this historic period would have been known as "the age of Theophrastus." This is a very modern appraisal. While Theophrastus wrote enough to fill fifty good sized modern books, less than ten percent of it survived the ages. This small fraction we have collated and appreciated only within recent years. It was his teacher, Aristotle, who so completely dominated men's thinking for over two thousand years. Yet we can now see that Theophrastus criticized and extended Aristotle's work. He is not as certain as Aristotle that everything in the world exists for a purpose; he doubts whether fire should be considered a primary element; he draws better distinctions in the biological world, and so on throughout the Aristotelian corpus.

THE MUSEUM

Strato of Lampsacus had studied under Theophrastus at the Lyceum. Following graduation from the Lyceum he went to Alexandria to become the tutor of the second Ptolemy. While he held this royal post, he suggested the establishment of the Museum of Alexandria to the first Ptolemy, his royal patron. The Museum, in a way, was the logical continuation of Aristotle's Lyceum. It was from Alexandria that Strato was summoned back to Athens in 287 B.C. to take over the headship of the Lyceum. While we know from contemporaneous accounts the names of the books which he wrote, none of them has survived. We have only fragments to judge the man. His interest was seemingly in physics and he is one of the first men known in history to devise and construct special equipment to carry on experiments. This is an essential part of physics today as any physics department shop will testify. His will, strangely enough, was kept while his books were lost. We read in his will, " I leave the school to Lyco, since the others are either too old or too busy. It would be well if the others would co-operate with him. I bequeath to him all my books, except those of which I am the author." Lyco turned the interest of the Lyceum from natural science to ethics and rhetoric. He attempted to revive the more popular aspects of the old Lyceum under Aristotle, such as the public afternoon lectures. We hear little about the school after Lyco. The torch had been handed on to the new Museum in Alexandria.

The Alexandrian Museum was not a collection of pictures and sculpture. The original meaning of the word is a temple to the Muses. Although the head of the Museum at Alexandria was technically the high priest, in practice he became the librarian. The Museum was a group of buildings erected near the royal palaces. There was a mess hall where the scholars must have eaten in common, as they still do in Oxford and Cambridge. There was a lecture hall, a botanical garden, an astronomical observatory, and there was the great library soon to number more than a half million rolls. Resident in the Museum were hundreds of scholars divided into four groups: astronomers, mathematicians, physicians, and followers of the liberal arts. In later years, formal lectures were given to students, but the primary task of the Museum was not that of a university but rather that of an institute for advanced studies. The universities of Athens, such as the Lyceum and the Academy, were private institutions. The Museum, like a modern state university, was supported by the state. As far as we know it was the first such institution in history.

Heraclides of Pontus (388–310 B.C.) was a student of Speusippus in the Academy at Athens. From the fragmentary references to him in the works of other men we conclude that he proposed two rather revolutionary ideas:

1. that the planets Venus and Mercury moved in circular orbits about the sun instead of about the earth, and
2. that the earth rotated on its axis to give the appearance of the stars moving from east to west.

Among the almost infinite variety of Grecian thought was that of Aristarchus of Samos (310–230 B.C.), a student of Strato whom Copernicus acknowledged to be the inventor of the heliocentric theory. Living in a less fanatic city, Alexandria, and in a more enlightened age, Aristarchus escaped prosecution for impiety. Society was content to simply destroy his books. Fragments of his ideas survive in the books of others. Archimedes in his "Sand-Reckoner" gives the following account of the ideas of Aristarchus [6]:

Now you are aware that 'universe' is the name given by most astronomers to the sphere whose centre is the centre of the earth and whose radius is equal to the straight line between the centre of the sun and the centre of the earth. This is the common account, as you have heard from astronomers. But Aristarchus of Samos brought out a book consisting of some hypotheses, in which the premisses lead to the result that the universe is many times greater than that now so called. His hypotheses are that the fixed stars and the sun remain unmoved, that the earth revolves about the sun in the circumference of a circle, the sun lying in the middle of the orbit, and that the sphere of the fixed stars, situated about the same centre as the sun, is so great that the circle in which he supposes the earth to revolve bears such a proportion to the distance of the fixed stars as the centre of the sphere bears to its surface. Now it is easy to see that this is impossible; for, since the centre of the sphere has no magnitude, we cannot conceive it to bear any ratio whatever to the surface of the sphere. We must however take Aristarchus to mean this: since we conceive the earth to be, as it were, the centre of the universe, the ratio which the earth bears to what we describe as the 'universe' is the same as the ratio which the sphere containing the circle in which he supposes the earth to revolve bears to the sphere of the fixed stars. For he adapts the proofs of his results to a hypothesis of this kind, and in particular he appears to suppose the magnitude of the sphere in which he represents the earth as moving to be equal to what we call the 'universe.'

An excerpt from Plutarch's book *On the Face in the Disk of the Moon,* reads [7]:

Only do not, my good fellow, enter an action against me for impiety in the style of Cleanthes, who thought it was the duty of Greeks to indict Aristarchus of Samos on the charge of impiety for putting in motion the Hearth of the Universe, this being the effect of his attempt to save the phenomena by supposing the heaven to remain at rest and the earth to revolve in an oblique circle, while it rotates, at the same time, about its own axis.

The third man to head the Alexandrian Museum was the astronomer Eratosthenes of Cyrene, whom we remember for his measurement of the circumference of the earth. He had observed that in the city of Syene (the modern Aswan near the head of the Nile, which is the site of the modern Egyptian high dam) the sun was directly overhead (Fig. 2-1) at noon on the day of the summer solstice, June 21 on our modern calendar, while at Alexandria it was $7\frac{1}{2}°$ south from the vertical. As $7\frac{1}{2}°$ is approximately one-fiftieth of $360°$, Eratosthenes estimated that the distance of 5000 stadia (570 miles) between Alexandria and Syene must

---

[6] T. L. Heath, *The Works of Archimedes,* "The Sand-Reckoner," Cambridge University Press, 1897, pp. 221–222.

[7] T. L. Heath, *Aristarchus of Samos,* Oxford at the Clarendon Press, London, 1913, p. 304.

be one-fiftieth of the circumference of the world. If we give him the benefit of the doubt, since the stadium (being actually the length of a stadium where the word means the same thing today) was a very variable unit, then his estimate was close to the presently accepted value.

Archimedes. The greatest of all Greek scientists was Archimedes, born in Syracuse about 287 B.C., the son of an astronomer and the cousin of Hieron II, the ruler of Syracuse. Hieron ruled for fifty-four years, accord-

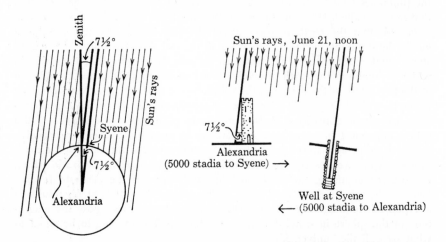

Figure 2-1. *Eratosthenes' observations used in determining the circumference of the earth. Since the angle between the vertical and sun's rays on June 21 was one-fiftieth of a circle at Alexandria when the sun was straight overhead at Syene, Eratosthenes reasoned that the circumference of the earth was fifty times the distance from Alexandria to Syene.*

ing to Polybius, "without killing, exiling, or injuring a single citizen, which indeed is the most remarkable of all things." Archimedes prided himself on his mathematical achievements above all else. Of his ten books which survive, eight treat of pure mathematics. In these mathematical books, he comes very close to inventing calculus. Only two books deal with physics. *On Plane Equilibriums* makes a science of weighing, balancing, and the lever. *On Floating Bodies* is the beginning of the science of hydrostatics. All of us have heard the story of how Archimedes discovered the principle of specific gravity in his bath and dashed through the streets of Syracuse shouting "Eureka! Eureka!" ("I've found it! I've found it!") What he had found was the solution to his cousin Hieron's problem as to whether his new crown was pure gold or had been fraudulently alloyed. Archimedes comes so close to Galileo in physics and to Newton in mathematics that one wonders why he did not go just one step further and usher in modern science two thousand years before the Renaissance.

Archimedes was also an ingenious inventor of machines. Syracuse, as all of the Greek cities at one time or another, was involved in war with Rome. The Roman general, Marcellus, attacked by both land and sea. Archimedes was now seventy-five years of age, but he undertook the defense of the city. He invented and had constructed catapults, grappling hooks, large metal mirrors to serve as "burning glasses" to set Roman ships on fire at a distance, and so many other devices that the historian Polybius said [8]:

Having got ready their . . . siege material, they were in high hopes owing to their large numbers that in five days their works would be much more advanced than those of the enemy, but in this they did not reckon with the ability of Archimedes, or foresee that in some cases the genius of one man accomplishes much more than any number of hands.

*   *   *   *   *   *   *

Such a great and marvellous thing does the genius of one man show itself to be when properly applied to certain matters. The Romans at least, strong as they were both by sea and land, had every hope of capturing the town at once if one old man of Syracuse were removed; but as long as he was present, they did not venture even to attempt to attack in that fashion in which the ability of Archimedes could be used in the defence. On the contrary, thinking that owing to the large population of the town the best way to reduce it was by famine, they placed their hope in this, cutting off supplies from the sea by their fleet and those from the land by their army.

They had lost too many ships to his "burning glasses" and grappling hooks, and too many men to superstition aroused by his machinery. Marcellus finally starved the city out after an eight month siege. During the sack of the city after its fall, Archimedes was killed by a Roman soldier.

Hipparchus. Hipparchus of Nicaea lived and worked in Rhodes, still a flourishing Greek state, somewhere about 140 B.C. Claudius Ptolemy gives him full credit as his predecessor in his *Almagest*. Again, very little of his work survives except one slight book and the fragments which we find in Ptolemy's text. Ptolemy tells that Hipparchus worked with the various combinations of circles, eccentric and epicyclic, which both Ptolemy and Hipparchus used to model the solar system. Quoting from the *Almagest* [9]:

And so I consider Hipparchus to have been most zealous after the truth, both because of all these things and especially because of his having left us more examples of accurate observations than he ever got from his predecessors.

[8] "Polybius," Vol. III, translated by W. R. Paton, by permission of William Heineman, London, and The Loeb Classical Library, Harvard University Press, Cambridge, 1923, pp. 453, 461.
[9] Claudius Ptolemy, "The Almagest," *Great Books of the Western World*, Vol. 16, Encyclopædia Britannica, Inc., Chicago, 1955, p. 272.

He sought out the hypotheses of the sun and moon, and demonstrated as far as possible and by every available means that they were accomplished through uniform circular movements, but he did not attempt to give the principle of the hypotheses of the five planets, as far as we can tell from those memoirs of his which have come down to us, but only arranged the observations in a more useful way and showed the appearances to be inconsistent with the hypotheses of the mathematicians of that time.

By comparing star positions as given by Alexandrian records of 150 years and the earlier Babylonian records, Hipparchus found a real change had taken place in the celestial latitudes and longitudes of the stars. To serve the similar needs of those who would come after him, he made a careful catalog of the positions of nearly 1000 fixed stars. From careful numerical records of this type come important discoveries in later ages.

During the change from the pre-Christian to the Christian era, the Roman legions had conquered one Greek state after another. Henceforth, the arts and sciences would have to speak two languages.

PART TWO

THE GRECO-ROMAN WORLD

Beginning at about 280 B.C. Rome began to expand rapidly. Over the next two centuries she had conquered all of the Greek cities and most of the civilized world. Some of the Greek cities, such as Syracuse, resisted their conquerors bravely. Others, such as once proud Sparta, torn by the class struggle, actually invited their Roman overlords into their cities.

One after another, all of the Greek cities fell to Roman domination. Why did they fall? The Greeks were always violently divisive. We have seen how even the cities of Ionia, of common blood and language, could not unite in a common defense against the obvious danger of Lydia. But against the greater danger of Persia, most of the Greeks did unite and for the first time in history stopped the previously all-conquering Persian power. But they found no such commonness of purpose against the Romans.

The franchise in the Greek city states was always limited. Of course neither slaves nor women could vote, but neither could life-long residents, whether Greek or barbarian, if they were born in some other city. To the restrictions to male, native-born, and free Greeks were often added various property qualifications. In many of the Greek city-states only a small number of the "haves" had any voice in the city affairs. The overwhelming number of the "have-nots" were left with only duties and resentments. As the economic differences sharpened, social conflict was bound to arise. For example, Nabis, a slave, led a slave revolt at Sparta, freed all the slaves, gave Spartan citizenship to everyone, canceled all debts, and redistributed the land. The poor of the Greek cities on all sides of Sparta acclaimed Nabis and cast in their lots with him. The oligarchs called in the Romans who were fought to a standstill by Nabis' formerly slave army. The oligarchs finally arranged the assassination of Nabis, but by then the Romans were firmly in control.

What kind of man was the Roman? In early republican days, at least, he was a solid citizen with all of the sturdy virtues. He was honest, public-spirited, and thoroughly practical-minded; substantial qualities which sometimes appear a bit pedantic compared to the more mercurial Greeks. An Athenian embassy to republican Rome in 155 B.C. included the Sophist Carneades of Cyrene. Carneades lectured in Rome one day in defense of justice, proving positively that it was the best goal of a state. The next day in another lecture he took exactly the opposite view and proved, also conclusively, that justice was an impracticable dream. Why, if Rome were to follow a just course, she would have to restore to the various nations of the Mediterranean all that she had plundered from them! The Greeks were amused by this sort of antic, but the Romans were horrified to the very depths of their Puritan souls. The embassy was expelled from Rome on the following day by Cato as posing a threat to public morals.

The Roman was also completely practical in his outlook. Consider the public-spirited life of Sextus Julius Frontinus. He served first as a consul of Rome, then was appointed governor of Britain. Here he fought some successful campaigns against the Silures who preferred their liberty to Roman civilization. Having become an expert in the art of war, he wrote two books about these skills after his return to Rome. Then in A.D. 78 Nerva put him in charge of Rome's water supply. Typically, he studied his new subject and became technically skilled in the engineering and administrative problems involved. These form the subject of his book *De Aquis*. Frontinus plainly feels that the useful Roman aqueducts, impressive even today in their ruins, are more beautiful than the Greek temples. As he says in his book, " With such an array of indispensable structures carrying so many waters compare, if you will, the idle pyramids or the useless though famous works of the Greeks."

The Roman could also work very hard trying to assimilate the Greek culture. Pliny the Elder (Caius Plinius Secundus) was a soldier, lawyer, traveler, administrator, admiral of the western Roman fleet, and an advisor to the Emperor Vespasian. He was also a busy scholar and author of numerous books on oratory, grammar, the javelin, a history of Rome, a history of Rome's German wars, and an encyclopedia of all knowledge which survived through the Middle Ages as a bit of flotsam within the seas of the classical ruin. How he packed all of these activities into a lifetime of fifty-five years is explained by his nephew, Pliny the Younger (Caius Plinius Caecilius Secundus) [1]:

You will wonder how a man so engaged as he was, could find time to compose such a number of books; and some of them too upon abstruse subjects. But your surprise will rise still higher, when you hear, that for some time he engaged in the profession of an advocate, that he died in his fifty-sixth year,

---

[1] William Melmoth, *Pliny Letters*, Vol. I, by permission of William Heineman Ltd., London, and The Loeb Classical Library, Harvard University Press, Cambridge, 1940, pp. 199, 201, 203.

that from the time of his quitting the bar to his death he was engaged and trammelled by the execution of the highest posts, and by the friendship of his sovereigns. But he had a quick apprehension, incredible zeal, and a wakefulness beyond compare. He always began to work at midnight when the August festival of Vulcan came round; not for the good omen's sake, but for the sake of study; in winter generally at one in the morning, but never later than two, and often at midnight. No man ever slept more readily, insomuch that he would sometimes, without retiring from his book, take a short sleep, and then pursue his studies.

Before day-break he used to wait upon Vespasian; who likewise chose that season to transact business. When he had finished the affairs which that emperor committed to his charge, he returned home again to his studies. After a short and light repast at noon (agreeably to the good old custom of our ancestors) he would frequently in the summer, if he was disengaged from business, repose himself in the sun; during which time some author was read to him, from whence he made extracts and observations, as indeed this was his constant method whatever book he read: for it was a maxim of his, that "no book was so bad but some profit might be gleaned from it." When this basking was over, he generally went into the cold bath, and as soon as he came out of it, just took a slight refreshment, and then reposed himself for a little while. Then, as if it had been a new day, he immediately resumed his studies till dinner-time, when a book was again read to him, upon which he would make some running notes. I remember once, his reader having pronounced a word wrong, somebody at the table made him repeat it again; upon which my uncle asked his friend if he understood it? Who acknowledging that he did; "why then," said he, "would you make him go back again? We have lost by this interruption of yours above ten lines: " so chary was this great man of time! In summer he always rose from supper by day-light; and in winter as soon as it was dark: and this was a sort of binding law with him.

Such was his manner of life amidst the noise and hurry of the town; but in the country his whole time was devoted to study without intermission, excepting only while he bathed. But in this exception I include no more than the time he was actually in the bath; for all the while he was rubbed and wiped, he was employed either in hearing some book read to him, or in dictating himself. In his journeys, as though released from all other cares, he found leisure for this sole pursuit. A shorthand writer, with book and tablets, constantly attended him in his chariot, who, in the winter, wore a particular sort of warm gloves, that the sharpness of the weather might not occasion any interruption to his studies; and for the same reason my uncle always used a sedan chair in Rome. I remember he once reproved me for walking; "You might," said he, "not have lost those hours: " for he thought all was time lost that was not given to study. By this extraordinary application he found time to write so many volumes, besides one hundred and sixty which he left me, consisting of a kind of common-place, written on both sides, in a very small character; so that one might fairly reckon the number considerably more. I have heard him say that when he was comptroller of the revenue in Spain, Larcius Licinus offered him four hundred thousand sesterces for these manuscripts: and yet they were not then quite so numerous.

When you reflect upon the books he has read, and the volumes he has written, are you not inclined to suppose that he never was an official or a courtier? On the other hand, when you are informed how painstaking he was in his studies, are you not disposed to think that he read and wrote too little? For, on one side, what obstacles would not the business of a court throw in his way? And on the other, what is it that such intense application might not perform? I cannot but smile therefore when I hear myself called a studious man, who in comparison to him am a mere loiterer. But why do I mention myself, who am diverted from these pursuits by numberless duties both public and private? Where is he, among those whose whole lives are spent in study, who must not blush under the consciousness of being but a sluggard and a dreamer, compared with this great scholar?

With such industry he read over 2000 volumes (in the ancient sense) by some 473 authors to produce one of the most durable of all one-man encyclopedias. He died A.D. 79 while observing the eruption of Vesuvius from too close a vantage point.

Some Romans, such as Lucretius, produced very good Latin transcriptions of Greek thought. But there are no important Roman contributions to mathematics or to the physical sciences. The Roman talent was elsewhere. They were first-rate engineers as remains over half of Europe attest today. Vitruvius, for instance, left us a thoroughly competent handbook on architecture showing a sound pragmatic knowledge of building methods as well as an orderly outline of the various architectural styles. He was a good applied scientist and showed a lively appreciation of the experimental method. But neither he nor any other Roman made a worthwhile contribution to science as such. The Roman genius was found in law and the science of government. Our two-house representative system, our system of checks and balances, our idea of a written constitution, and much of our law are all of Roman origin. Many of the devices of power politics which we may think are typical of recent European history were known and used cynically by the Romans.

The Romans are indeed our intellectual ancestors as much as the Greeks, but not in the area of the physical sciences. The Greeks carried on under Roman rule. Young Romans learned Greek and went to study in the universities at Athens. Greeks, who wished to sell their intellectual wares, learned Latin and set up schools in Roman cities. The later Roman philosophers even wrote their own books in Greek. Greek became the official language of the Eastern Roman Empire. Thus the conquered eventually conquered the conquerors!

The Museum at Alexandria continued. When Julius Caesar wished to reform the calendar, he sent to Alexandria for his expert. Sosigenes did an excellent job of it and except for a small change in the leap-year rule, it is the same calendar that we use today. Geminus of Rhodes who lived at about 70 B.C. wrote an excellent introductory textbook in astronomy. Strabo who was born in Amasia in Greek Pontus on about 63 B.C. was a geographer of merit. He used a reference system which was closely akin to our lines of latitude and longitude. He considered the facts of physical geography as any modern would. Moreover he anticipated our modern geologists in seeing that the great orogenic changes in the earth's surface might arise from the very small observed changes within our own time. Then there was Ptolemy, mathematician, astronomer, geographer, and physicist who worked in Alexandria at about A.D. 150. We shall hear more about him in this section since we will excerpt part of his great book, known to us as the *Almagest*.

These excerpts may sound curiously modern after 1800 years. Most Greek and Latin authors strike a responsive chord with us in contrast to ancient Chinese or Indian books. And why shouldn't they? They are our intellectual ancestors. Our technical terms are drawn straight from their two languages. Their very books are the patterns which later authors emulated. Their thought is the beginning of our thought.

3

The Heavens Above Us

● In this age of extensive urban development with its city lights, industrial " smog," television, night-time sports and other distractions, modern man has lost that intimate touch with the sky which is so frequently associated with the ancients. The sun and the moon he knows. Perhaps he has also observed the planet Venus as a bright evening or morning star and he may even recognize one or two constellations, but this is probably the extent of his astronomical observations. Therefore in order to form a perspective for the chapters which immediately follow, it will be desirable to review here the principal apparent celestial motions which are observable to the naked eye and upon which ancient theories of the universe were based.

Inasmuch as the reader is probably acquainted with one or two proofs of the earth's spherical shape, and since several arguments for its curvature will be mentioned in Chapter 4, we shall tentatively assume the earth's sphericity at this time and confine our attention largely to the phenomena and appearances of our sky. With few minor exceptions this is the same sky which Thales, Ptolemy, Copernicus, and Galileo saw. This is the beginning of astronomy.

THE CELESTIAL SPHERE

To even the most casual observer, stars seem to be points of light of varying brightness and color affixed to the inner surface of an immense hollow sphere in which the immobile earth is centered. This impression is very readily acquired if one will isolate himself from extraneous lights on some clear dark night and observe the hemispherical sky above his horizon.

It is common knowledge that stars do not possess any perceptible motion relative to each other and hence are seen in fixed groups or constellations, most of which were named by the ancients. An important movement relative to the observer's horizon can be detected, however, if one will but watch the sky for a short time — say an hour or so. Suppose an observer in a middle northern latitude carefully plots the path of a star in the northern sky — that is, a star or group of stars is chosen which can be seen somewhere above the northern horizon. As an alternative the use of a camera would be more convincing, but in either case the results would resemble that shown in Figure 3-1. We note that above the northern horizon

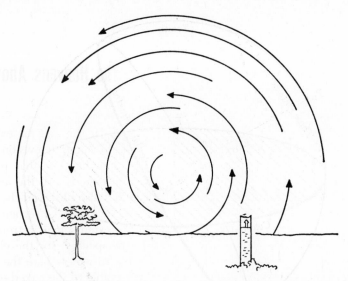

Figure 3-1. *Apparent paths of stars in the northern sky during an eight-hour exposure with a camera located in middle northern latitudes, aligned with its optical axis parallel to the axis of the celestial sphere.*

one point of the sky remains stationary and all celestial objects seem to move in circles concentric to this point.

Results produced by repeating the same procedure as the observer faces south suggest another point in the sky below the southern horizon about which the stars are concentrically in motion.

Continued observations of this nature show the sky apparently turning as a whole about two opposite points and hence lead us to accept the concept of a *celestial sphere* in daily rotation about an axis passing through the two stationary *celestial poles*. Figure 3-2 illustrates the earth-centered sphere for an observer at 30°N latitude. The great circle of the celestial sphere halfway between its poles is known as the *celestial equator,* and the plane of the celestial equator intersects the earth's surface along the earth's equator. The *diurnal* (daily) *motions* of all natural celestial bodies are now seen to be in circles parallel to the celestial equator, those bodies near the poles traveling in smaller diurnal circles than those near the equator. The *pole star* Polaris remains relatively stationary for any observer since it lies approximately at the north celestial pole.

In locating celestial objects we shall necessarily require the use of basic concepts such as direction and angular distance. Accordingly, *west* on the celestial sphere is defined as that direction parallel to the celestial equator toward which the sphere rotates; *east*, the opposite direction, and *north* and *south* toward the north and south celestial poles respectively. *Declination* of a celestial body, like latitude on the earth's surface, is its angular

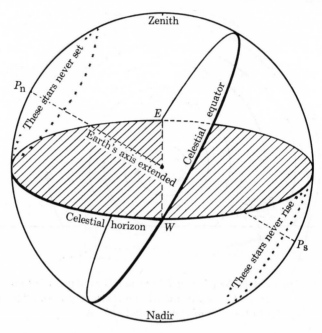

Figure 3-2. *Celestial sphere with horizon for an observer at 30°N latitude.*

distance north or south of the celestial equator. Since Polaris is nearly overhead at the north geographic pole, its declination is about 90°N; an object overhead at Columbus, Ohio (latitude 40°N) would have a declination 40°N.

Because the celestial sphere has an "infinite" radius relative to the earth's dimensions, extending one's horizontal plane to intersect the sky produces a great circle on the sphere, known as the *celestial horizon*, which cuts the sphere equally in two parts — half above the horizon and half below. It is significant to note that two diametrically opposite observers, such as one at the north geographic pole and the other at the south geographic pole, would each have the same celestial horizon (Fig. 3-3). The *zenith*, which is that point in the sky directly overhead of an observer, and the opposite point, the *nadir*, are each 90° from the horizon. By extending one's meridian plane to intersect the sky, a *celestial meridian* is produced which contains the zenith, nadir, celestial poles, and *north* and *south points.* The *east* and *west points* of the horizon are found 90° from the north and south points.

Figures 3-2, 3-3, and 3-4 illustrate the effect of one's latitude on the appearance of diurnal motions of various parts of the celestial sphere. Except when an observer is located at one of the geographic poles, we note that the celestial equator always intersects the horizon at the east and west points, and crosses the meridian at an angular distance from the zenith,

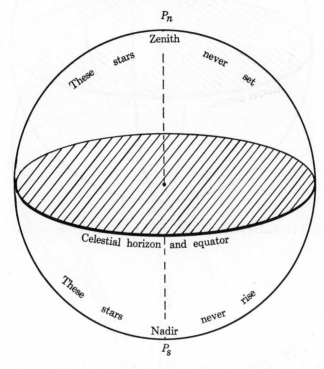

Figure 3-3. *Celestial sphere with horizon for observer at the north pole.*

the *zenith distance*, equal to the latitude of the observer (Fig. 3-5). This latter statement also implies that the celestial pole will be elevated above the horizon (have an altitude) by an amount equal to the observer's latitude. Hence, we see that the region of stars which are *circumpolar*, those stars which never set, depends upon the observer's latitude.

THE SUN

As previously noted, the apparent rotation of the celestial sphere carries heavenly bodies such as the sun and stars in an east-west direction across the observer's meridian each day. The instant when the sun is on the upper branch of one's celestial meridian (that part containing the zenith)

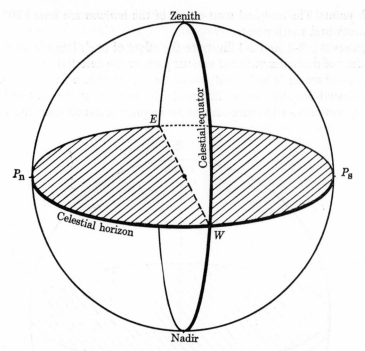

Figure 3-4. *Celestial sphere with horizon for observer at the equator.*

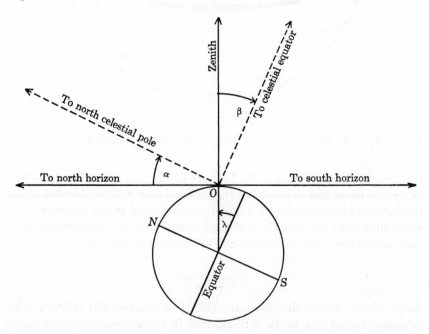

Figure 3-5. *Meridian section of earth through observer at 0 showing the altitude (α) of celestial pole equal to observer's latitude (λ). Zenith distance (β) of celestial equator also equal to latitude (λ).*

is known as *local noon,* and the interval of time between successive *transits* (crossings) of the same branch of the meridian by the sun is called an *apparent solar day.* This interval is arbitrarily divided in 24 hours and the hours further subdivided into minutes and seconds. The interval between successive transits of the same branch of the meridian by a given star is known as a *sidereal day.* The average solar day exceeds the sidereal day by 3 minutes and 56 seconds; so that if one locates a star exactly on his meridian this evening at 9:00 P.M., tomorrow evening that same star

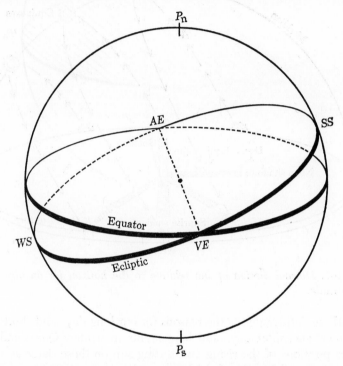

Figure 3-6. *Celestial sphere with equator, ecliptic, solstices, equinoxes, and celestial poles.*

will cross his meridian at about 8:56 P.M. This difference between the solar and sidereal days results from a general west-east progression of the sun around the celestial sphere independent of any diurnal motions.

To determine the sun's path against the background of stars, the ancients observed the eastern sky before sunrise and the western sky just after sunset in order to identify constellations just west and east of the sun. Continued bracketing observations of this type show that the sun annually moves along a great circle of the celestial sphere, called the *ecliptic,* which is inclined about 23.5° to the celestial equator (Fig. 3-6). The two points on opposite sides of the celestial sphere where the ecliptic cuts the equator are known as the *vernal* and *autumnal equinoxes.* When the sun is at either of these points on about March 21 and September 21 respectively, daylight and night will be of equal length. Between the equinoxes are two points where equator and ecliptic are farthest apart; these are known as the *summer* and *winter solstices* and indicate the sun's positions about June 21 and December 21. At the solstices the midday altitude of the sun reaches its highest and lowest values for an observer in middle or high latitudes. Figure 3-7 illustrating the diurnal paths of the

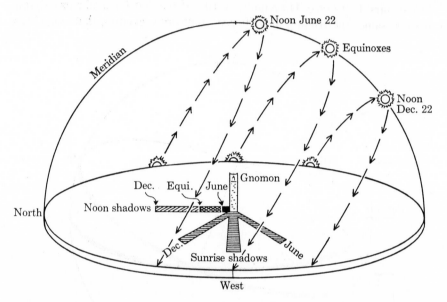

Figure 3-7. *Diurnal motion of sun relative to the horizon for an observer at 30°N latitude.*

sun on these dates suggests the reasons for our long days and short nights in summer, and short days and long nights in winter. One should also note the positions of the rising and setting sun on these dates as well as the directions and lengths of shadows cast by the gnomon.

The sun's motion along the ecliptic, though steady, is not uniform. This is responsible for variation in the lengths of our seasons — in the northern hemisphere spring lasting 92.9 days, summer 93.7 days, autumn 89.6 days, and winter 89 days. This variable motion of the sun along the ecliptic also causes the "apparent" (true) sun to cross our meridian at unequal intervals of time so that we generally regulate our daily activities by "mean solar time," using a fictitious sun which crosses our meridian in uniform time intervals, instead of "apparent solar time."

The belt of the sky extending 8° either side of the ecliptic and called the *zodiac* has been divided into twelve equal parts identified by the twelve "*zodiacal constellations.*" [1] In primitive times, the beginning of the

[1] In this and succeeding sections the reader will find it beneficial to refer frequently to the zodiacal band shown in Figure 3-9.

year was recorded from the start of the vernal equinox, the day when the
sun crossed the celestial equator from south to north in its motion along
the ecliptic. The year of the seasons or *tropical year* is now known as the
interval of time (365^d 5^h 48^m 46^s) between two successive arrivals of the
sun at the vernal equinox, while the *sidereal year* is defined by the interval between the sun's return to exactly the same point in the sky relative
to the stars. In 125 B.C. Hipparchus had noted that the two intervals were
not the same, the tropical year being about 20 minutes shorter than the

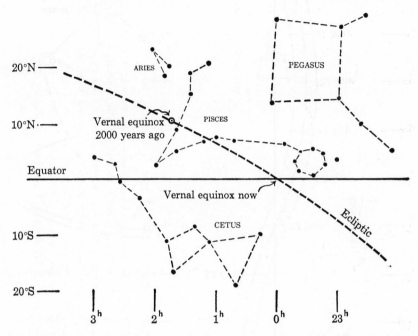

Figure 3-8. *Precession of the vernal equinox; compare with Figure 3-9.*

sidereal year. A westward motion of the equinoxes and solstices to meet
the sun (which travels eastward around the ecliptic) known as *precession of the equinoxes* (Fig. 3-8) accounts for this 20 minutes difference.
Fragmentary historical records from the Euphrates valley suggest that the
vernal equinox may have been in the constellation Taurus around
2450 B.C.; in the days of Hipparchus it had moved into Aries; today it is
in Pisces and is moving steadily westward through the zodiacal constellations.

THE MOON

The second most conspicuous object in the sky is the moon, and a few
minutes observation each night, or day, for a month will reveal the main
characteristics of its motion and varying appearance.

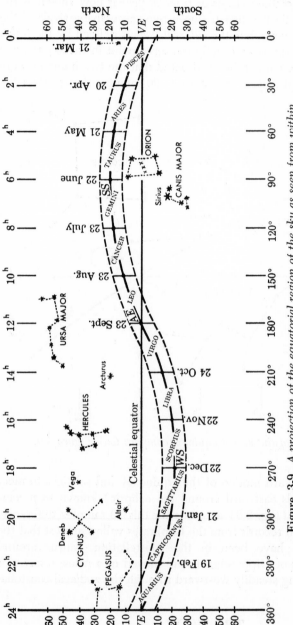

Figure 3-9. *A projection of the equatorial region of the sky as seen from within the celestial sphere (observer facing south) showing zodiacal band, ecliptic, equinoxes, solstices and sun's positions near certain dates. Declination is indicated along vertical margins and angular distance eastward from the vernal equinox shown along bottom of map. The eastward distance (right ascension) can also be expressed in hours, minutes, and seconds from a relationship in which one hour corresponds to 15 degrees. Compare with Figure 3-6.*

First, the moon possesses the same east-west diurnal motion as the sun, for it rises in the east, crosses the meridian, sets in the west, and rises in the east again a little more than a day later.

Secondly, with careful observation, the moon is seen to travel eastward through the zodiac in a circular path which is inclined about 5° to the ecliptic. At a rate of some 13° each day, the time required for it to pass through all twelve zodiacal constellations amounts to approximately 27⅓ days and is known as its *sidereal period.*

Since the moon moves eastward around the celestial sphere faster than the sun (which travels about 1° per day), it will frequently overtake and pass the sun in the zodiacal band (Fig. 3-10). The interval of time for the moon to "lap" the sun averages about 29½ days and is known as its *synodic period.* Owing to the differential of motions between the two bodies, the moon advances approximately 12° further east of the sun and hence crosses one's meridian roughly 50 minutes later each day. Concurrent with this daily eastward progression of the moon relative to the sun, the moon exhibits changing shape or *phases* which are repeated each synodic month.

A brief description of the cycle of phases follows.

New.   Occurs when moon is passing the sun. Moon generally not visible (unless eclipsing the sun); rises and sets with the sun.

Waxing crescent.   Moon east of sun becoming visible about two days after new phase; seen in western sky after sundown.

First quarter.   Occurs about a week after new phase when moon is 90° east of ("one-quarter" of the way from) the sun; moon is seen as a half-illuminated disk; rises about noon.

Waxing gibbous.   Bulging or lopsided appearance when moon is found more than 90°, but less than 180°, east of the sun; rises between noon and sunset.

Full.   Full round illuminated disk; seen about two weeks after new phase when moon is 180° around zodiac from the sun; moon rises about sunset.

During the above two-week period the moon has been waxing or increasing in girth as it moved away from the eastern side of the sun. For the next two-week period as it moves eastward toward the western side of the sun, the moon wanes or decreases as it exhibits similar phases in reverse order — waning gibbous, last quarter, waning crescent to new phase again.

To illustrate the relationship between relative position of sun and moon to the lunar phases, Figure 3-11 indicates the appearances of phases with position of moon to sun plotted during a "lunar month."

Since the paths of the moon and sun are two distinct, intersecting great circles on the celestial sphere, the moon will be on the north side of the ecliptic for half of a lunar month and on the south side the other half, and must cross the ecliptic at two points known as the *ascending* (moon mov-

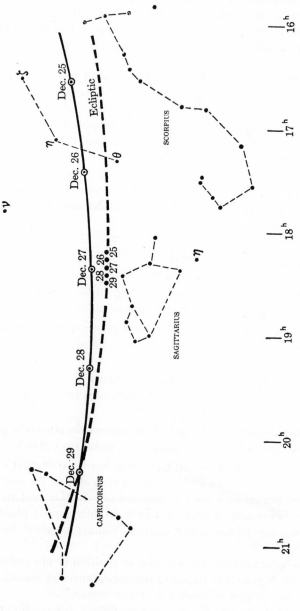

Figure 3-10. *Plot of moon's and sun's paths relative to the ecliptic for the period December 25, 1962 to December 29, 1962. Dots on ecliptic represent the sun's positions on dates indicated. Observer facing south.*

ing from south to north) and *descending nodes* (N and N', Fig. 3-12).
When the sun and moon are at opposite nodes simultaneously, the earth
will lie directly between them since the nodes are 180° apart; in this case
a lunar eclipse will occur which is visible from any point on the earth's
surface where the moon is above the horizon. The lunar eclipse begins
on the eastern side of the full moon's disk as it enters the earth's shadow.
On the other hand a solar eclipse, which at a given instant is visible from

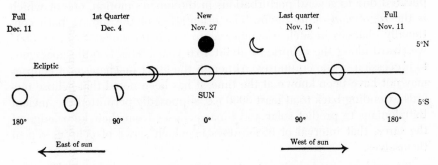

Figure 3-11. *Moon's positions relative to sun and ecliptic for the period
November 11, 1962 to December 11, 1962. Angular distance north or south
of ecliptic indicated along vertical margin; angular distance east or west of
sun along bottom of figure. Observer facing south.*

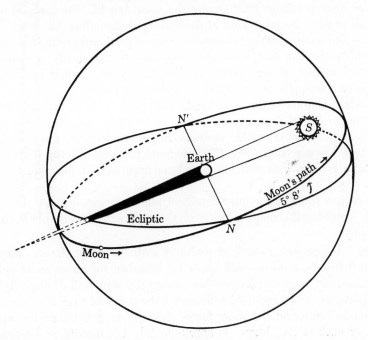

Figure 3-12. *Apparent paths of sun and moon on celestial sphere illustrating
that eclipses may occur only when sun and moon are near a node N or N'.*

a relatively small area of the earth's surface, begins on the west side of the sun's disk as the new moon interposes itself between earth and sun. In order for a solar eclipse to occur the moon must be at the same node as the sun.

Calculation of the time of occurrence of a particular eclipse is not difficult in principle since the moon must be at one of the nodes when in new or full phase. In practice, however, this calculation becomes rather complicated due to several perturbations in the moon's motion, one of which is the *regression* of its nodes. The orientation of the moon's path continually changes in such a manner as to cause the nodes to move 360° westward along the ecliptic in about 18.6 years. This is quite analogous to precession of the equinoxes. Although the exact mechanism of eclipses may not have been known at the time, it has been noted that eclipse records extending back to at least 3000 B.C. supposedly permitted the ancient Babylonians to predict solar and lunar eclipses from their knowledge of the saros, that interval of 6585⅓ days in which series of eclipses repeat themselves.

PLANETS

Unlike the moon and the sun which show sizeable disks of about ½ degree each, the five planets (or "wanderers") recognized by the ancients appear as mere points of light among the stars, but like the sun and moon they all possess the same kind of diurnal revolution about the earth. Like the sun and moon also they normally progress eastward around the zodiac but unlike the sun and moon their motions are not steady. The normal eastward motion of each planet is occasionally interrupted by brief intervals of retrograde westward motion through the stars.

Another characteristic associated with planets is their variation in brightness. All planets exhibit some variation which correlates quite closely with their retrograde motions; in general, planets are seen to be brightest when retrograding. The ancients properly interpreted this increase in brilliance as indicating a closer approach of the planet to the earth.

To review some of the finer details of planetary motions, we shall now briefly consider the major aspects of those planets discernable with the naked-eye.

Saturn. Unless one is well acquainted with the constellations through which it travels, Saturn could easily be mistaken for an ordinary yellow star. Carefully mapping its position among the stars will disclose its motion, however, and Figure 3-13 illustrates the result of such a process.

Extended observations show firstly that the time between the occurrence of each of its "loops" is approximately 12½ months and secondly, that this westward motion occurs shortly before, during, and after opposition when the planet is in the opposite part of the zodiac from the sun

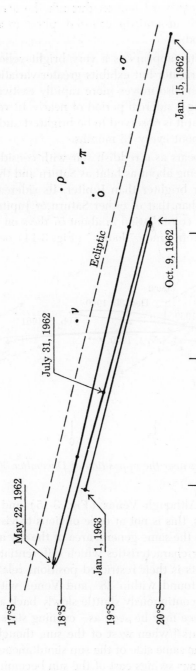

Figure 3-13. *Plot of Saturn's retrograde motion through Capricornus within the period January 15, 1962 to January 1, 1963.*

(Fig. 3-9). This interval of 12½ months (about 378 days) is known as the synodic period of Saturn.

By extrapolating its eastward motion through the stars, we find that Saturn travels completely around the celestial sphere in about 29½ years. This is its sidereal period.

Jupiter. Visually, Jupiter appears as a very bright yellow, star-like object which is not only brighter but exhibits greater variation in its brightness than Saturn. Jupiter also moves more rapidly eastward through the stars than Saturn, having a sidereal period of nearly 12 years. Its synodic period is 399 days so that it is observed to be brightest and simultaneously in retrograde motion about every 13 months.

Mars. This planet appears as a reddish star with considerable variation in brilliance, at times being about as faint as Saturn and then, when at opposition, as bright as or brighter than Jupiter. Its sidereal period of 687 days, which is shorter than that of either Saturn or Jupiter, permits it to pass through a zodiacal constellation in about 57 days on the average. Its oppositions and hence retrograde "loops" (Fig. 3-14) occur at intervals of about 780 days.

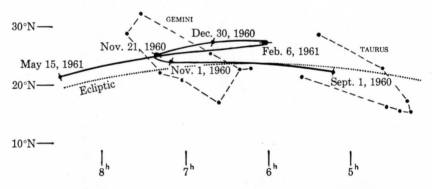

Figure 3-14. *Path of Mars near the opposition of December 30, 1960.*

Venus and Mercury. Although Venus (Fig. 3-15) and Mercury both have retrograde motions, this is not at once obvious to visual observation since the sun is found in the same general area of the sky as these planets. In fact one of the major characteristics which differentiate Mercury and Venus from other planets is their restricted positions relative to the sun, Mercury always being found within 28° and Venus within 47° of the sun's disk. Both planets continuously shuttle slowly back and forth across the moving sun and hence may be seen as "evening stars" when east of the sun or "morning stars" when west of the sun, though they will not necessarily be seen on the same side of the sun simultaneously.

As an evening star Venus swings east of the sun becoming brighter and brighter as it reaches its greatest (47°) angular distance 220 days after emergence from behind the sun's disk. It then turns westward toward the sun attaining its maximum yellow-white brilliance (brighter than any planet or star) when still 39° east of the sun. From here on it rapidly decreases in brightness to disappear into the sun's glare 292 days from the time of initial emergence. In another 72 days it reaches its maximum angular distance west of the sun during which time it is seen as a morn-

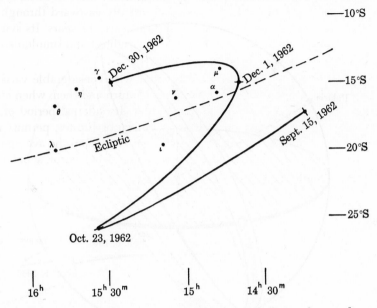

Figure 3-15. *Plot of Venus' motion relative to the ecliptic during the period September 15, 1962 to December 30, 1962.*

ing star, and gradually becoming fainter it disappears into the sun's glare 220 days later to reappear again as an evening star.

Mercury, though much fainter and nearer to the sun, goes through the same motions, completing its cycle in 116 days as compared with the 584-day synodic period of Venus.

SUMMARY

The present chapter outlines the main characteristics of the celestial motions of the stars, sun, moon, and planets as discerned from naked-eye observations. Some of the leading observational facts are summarized below.

1. The celestial sphere, upon which stars are seen as fixed points of light, apparently rotates as a coherent body between two celestial poles, one of which is now near the star Polaris.

2. In about twenty-four hours, every natural celestial object makes one complete east-west circuit around the axis of the celestial sphere along a circular path parallel to the celestial equator; this is the diurnal rotation.

3. In addition to its diurnal motion, the sun completes a west-east circuit of the sphere in one year; the path of the sun (ecliptic) is inclined to the celestial equator by about 23½°.

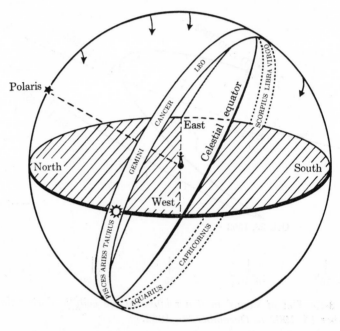

Figure 3-16. *Sunset, June 22 for an observer at 30°N latitude.*

4. The moon and planets travel eastward around the celestial sphere in paths that are roughly confined to the zodiacal band, a strip which extends 8° to either side of the ecliptic.

5. The moon describes more than a complete west-east circuit around the zodiacal band in about one month during which it exhibits a cycle of phases.

6. In their motions around the zodiac,

(a) Mars, Jupiter, and Saturn periodically "retrograde," and

(b) Venus and Mercury oscillate from one side of the sun to the other.

To review the system further, let us look at the four drawings (Figs. 3-16, 3-17, 3-18, 3-19) showing the celestial stages settings at four different times on June 21 for an observer at 30°N latitude.

On this date the sun is located at the summer solstice between the constellations Gemini and Taurus and rotates daily around on the celestial

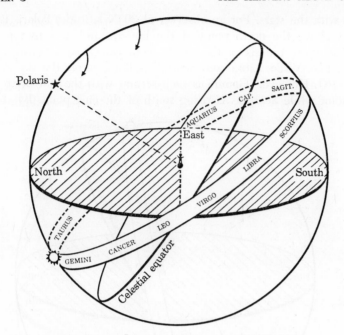

Figure 3-17. *Midnight, June 22 for an observer at 30°N latitude.*

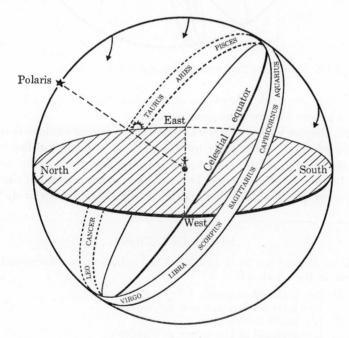

Figure 3-18. *Sunrise, June 22 for an observer at 30°N latitude.*

sphere with the stars. For an observer at 30°N latitude, Polaris is thirty degrees above the north point of the horizon and at sunset at about 7:00 P.M. there are six of the twelve zodiacal constellations — Gemini, Cancer, Leo, Virgo, Libra, and Scorpius — flung across the sky in a belt (Fig. 3-16). However, Gemini is seen setting with the sun north of the west point while Scorpius is rising south of the east point. By studying

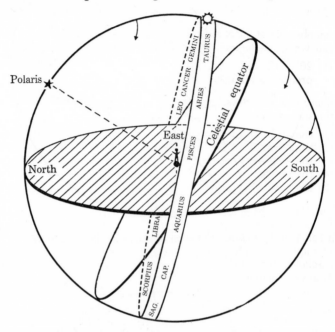

Figure 3-19. *Noon, June 22 for an observer at 30°N latitude.*

these figures the reader should be able to visualize the appearance of the celestial sphere for any other time or date.

In this chapter we have briefly outlined the *apparent* motions in the sky. It is the job of the astronomer to explain them in a rational fashion and not simply as the erratic behavior of irresponsible gods. In the material which follows we shall see how Ptolemy, the most successful of the Greek astronomers, put it all together and tried to make sense out of it.

STUDY QUESTIONS

1. For an observer at 30°N latitude, a star which crosses his meridian 30° south of the zenith will

    (1) set in the southwest
    (2) be above the horizon just 12 hours
    (3) rise in the southeast
    (4) be overhead at the tropic of Cancer
    (5) set in the northwest.

2. Select the correct statement or statements concerning circumpolar stars.
   a. Observers at any location on the earth can see some circumpolar stars.
   b. For an observer at the earth's north pole, all of the stars in the northern celestial hemisphere would appear to be circumpolar.
   c. An observer at 40°N latitude would see more circumpolar stars than would an observer at 30°N latitude.
   The correct answer is
       (1) a   (2) b   (3) c   (4) b and c   (5) a, b, and c.

3. For an observer at 30°N latitude, what would be the altitude of a circumpolar star whose declination is 80°N when it crosses the meridian?
       (1) 20°   (2) 30°   (3) 40°   (4) 50°   (5) It could be two of the preceding choices.

4. Ordinary calendar days begin at midnight. This instant of time is marked by the sun crossing
       (1) that branch of the meridian which is above the horizon
       (2) that branch of the meridian which is below the horizon
       (3) the eastern horizon
       (4) the western horizon
       (5) the zenith.

5. Choose the correct statement or statements.
   a. The apparent daily path of the sun across the sky is always essentially parallel to the celestial equator.
   b. The apparent daily path of the sun across the sky is always essentially parallel to the ecliptic.
   c. At any particular time the sun lies in the ecliptic.
   The correct answer is
       (1) a   (2) b   (3) c   (4) a and c   (5) b and c.

6. The time required for the sun to make one apparent complete revolution about the ecliptic is
       (1) 1 solar day   (2) 1 sidereal day   (3) about $29\frac{1}{2}$ days   (4) $365\frac{1}{4}$ solar days   (5) $366\frac{1}{4}$ solar days.

7. If you observed that the sun's noon shadow never vanished during the year and always pointed to the south, you would be
       (1) at the south pole
       (2) at the north pole
       (3) between the tropic of Capricorn and the Antarctic circle
       (4) between the tropics of Capricorn and Cancer
       (5) north of the tropic of Cancer but not at 90°N.

8. Select the correct statement or statements concerning the number of hours of daylight.
   a. An observer on the tropic of Cancer would have 12 hours of daylight on June 21.
   b. An observer at 60°N would have 12 hours of daylight on March 21.
   c. An observer on the equator would have 12 hours of daylight on December 21.
   The correct answer is
       (1) a   (2) b   (3) c   (4) b and c   (5) a, b, and c.

9. On March 21 at 6 A.M. local time, the ecliptic crosses the observer's meridian

    (1) at the same place as the celestial equator
    (2) 23½° south of the celestial equator
    (3) 23½° north of the celestial equator
    (4) 53½° south of the celestial equator
    (5) 53½° north of the celestial equator.

10. On March 21 at local noon, the ecliptic crosses the observer's meridian

    (1) at the same place as the celestial equator
    (2) 23½° south of the celestial equator
    (3) 23½° north of the celestial equator
    (4) 53½° south of the celestial equator
    (5) 53½° north of the celestial equator.

11. On December 21 at local midnight, an observer at 30° north latitude would observe the ecliptic crossing his meridian

    (1) at his zenith
    (2) about 6° south of his zenith
    (3) 23½° south of his zenith
    (4) 30° south of his zenith
    (5) 53½° south of his zenith.

12. For an observer in New York, which one of the following zodiacal constellations will remain above the horizon for the greatest length of time in any one 24-hour period?

    (1) Aquarius (2) Scorpius (3) Taurus (4) Virgo (5) Capricornus.

13. Does the orientation of the zodiacal band at a particular time on a certain day represent the path followed by the sun across the sky on that particular day?

14. Choose the correct statement or statements.
    a. If on a certain day the sun is observed to rise about 10°N of east, then on that same day it would set about 10°N of west as seen by the same observer.
    b. If on a certain day at a certain time the zodiacal band is about 10°N of east on the eastern horizon, then at the same time to the same observer the position of the zodiacal band on the western horizon would be about 10°N of west.
    c. If on a certain day at noon the zodiacal band is observed to be 10°N of west on the western horizon, it follows that for the same observer the sun will set on that day at approximately 10°N of west.
    The correct answer is

    (1) a   (2) b   (3) c   (4) a and c   (5) a, b, and c.

15. At 6:00 P.M. (local solar time) on October 1st, the zodiacal constellation most nearly on our meridian is

    (1) Gemini   (2) Leo   (3) Pisces   (4) Virgo   (5) Sagittarius.

16. The moon's orbit is inclined about 5° to the ecliptic. Therefore its declination varies approximately from

    (1) 5°N to 5°S
    (2) 28½°N to 18½°S
    (3) 28½°N to 28½°S

(4) 28½°S to 23½°S

(5) 23½°N to 23½°S.

17. Select the correct statement or statements.
    a. The twelve zodiacal constellations lie along the celestial equator.
    b. The sun stays in a particular zodiacal constellation for about thirty days.
    c. The moon (as seen from the earth) stays in a particular zodiacal constellation for about thirty days.
    The correct answer is

    (1) a   (2) b   (3) c   (4) a and b   (5) b and c.

18. Select the correct statement or statements concerning the full moon.
    a. The full moon always lies within the zodiacal band.
    b. The full moon always lies on the celestial equator.
    c. The full moon, earth, and sun are always approximately in a straight line.
    The correct answer is

    (1) a   (2) b   (3) c   (4) a and c   (5) a, b, and c.

19. On a given day, is the apparent path of the sun across the sky the same as the apparent path of the full moon?

20. For an observer at 30°N latitude on June 21, would the number of hours that the sun is above the horizon be approximately equal to the number of hours that a full moon is above the horizon? About how many hours?

21. At what time of the year does the full moon pass nearest the zenith in middle southern latitudes?

22. A last quarter moon occurring on March 21 would be seen in or near the constellation.

    (1) Virgo   (2) Pisces   (3) Gemini   (4) Sagittarius   (5) Leo.

23. If the moon were in last quarter phase on March 21, its approximate declination would be between

    (1) 18½°N and 28½°N
    (2) 18½°S and 28½°S
    (3) 5°N and 5°S
    (4) 15°N and 25°S
    (5) 7°S and 17°S.

24. Select the true statement or statements.
    a. During a total solar eclipse, the apparent diameter of the sun is greater than the apparent diameter of the moon.
    b. The moon is at or near one of its nodal points during a lunar eclipse.
    c. The western edge of the moon is the first to be eclipsed.
    The correct answer is

    (1) a   (2) a and b   (3) b   (4) b and c   (5) a, b, and c.

25. The precession of the equinoxes causes the vernal equinox to move 360° westward relative to the stars in approximately

    (1) 23½ days   (2) 1 month   (3) 1 year   (4) 10 years   (5) 26,000 years.

26. The star Sirius crosses the meridian at a certain place at about 9:30 P.M. (EST) on February 15th. At about what time (EST) does the star Sirius cross the same meridian 30 days later?

    (1) 10:30 P.M.   (2) 10:00 P.M.   (3) 9:30 P.M.   (4) 8:30 P.M.
    (5) 7:30 P.M.

27. Which of the following celestial bodies could never be on your meridian at the same time as a full moon?

    (1) Mars   (2) Venus   (3) Jupiter   (4) Saturn   (5) none of the preceding.

28. During the opposition of Mars indicated in Figure 3-14, the sun was in or near the constellation

    (1) Gemini   (2) Cancer   (3) Leo   (4) Sagittarius   (5) Aries.

29. In any given 24-hour period during the opposition of Mars (Fig. 3-14), an observer in middle northern latitudes could

    (1) observe the sun above his horizon longer than Mars
    (2) see the sun set in the northwest
    (3) see Mars rise in the northeast
    (4) observe the constellation Virgo above his horizon longer than Gemini
    (5) see Mars as an extremely faint object.

30. The maximum number of hours that Mercury can remain above the horizon after sunset is about

    (1) 1 hour   (2) 2 hours   (3) 3 hours   (4) 4 hours   (5) none of the preceding.

31. Under what circumstances can Venus be visible at local midnight?

    32–34. The sketch below represents the moon rising near the horizon. Refer to it in answering the following items.

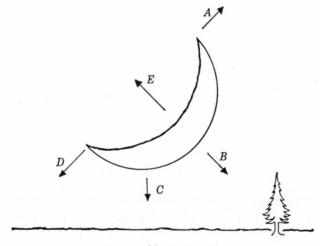

For problems 32–34.

32. The moon's phase in this diagram is

    (1) waxing crescent
    (2) waxing gibbous
    (3) first quarter
    (4) waning gibbous
    (5) waning crescent.

33. The direction to the sun is indicated by

     (1) A   (2) B   (3) C   (4) D   (5) E.

34. Select the true statement or statements.
   a. The observer is probably in the southern hemisphere.
   b. The local time is approximately 2:00 P.M.
   c. The observer is probably in the northern hemisphere.

   The correct answer is

     (1) a   (2) a and b   (3) b   (4) b and c   (5) c.

4

Ptolemy: the Postulates of the Almagest

● Claudius Ptolemy was born at Ptolemais on the
Nile and hence his name. Not much is known about his life. He made
astronomical observations in Alexandria from about A.D. 127 to 151. According to one tradition, he worked for 40 years in Alexandria and lived
to the age of 78. His great work was titled by him *Mathematike Syntaxis*
but was dubbed by the Arabian astronomers who admired the work intensely as the *Al-megiste*. This is a pidgin word, being the Arabic article
" Al " but the Greek superlative " megiste," making the affectionate bi-
lingual Arabic-Greek title " The Greatest." The scholars of Europe at the
end of the Middle Ages further corrupted it into the *Almagest* and that is
the title by which we call it today. In the pages to follow less than four
per cent of the original text is reproduced. It is a very large book and this
is only a small taste. Only Ptolemy's system for explaining the observed
celestial motions will be given. All of the other interesting things in his
book will be omitted.

Like Euclid's *Elements* and the other textbooks of the later Alexandrian
era, Ptolemy's book is not entirely his own work. Ptolemy is quite frank
to give proper credit to his predecessors, particularly to Hipparchus. The
Ptolemaic system is one of eminent common sense. The heavens are assumed to move exactly as they appear to move. The earth appears to be
stationary in space, so it is assumed to be motionless. The stars, the sun,
the moon, and the planets, retrograde motions and all, are assumed to
move exactly as they appear to move. This is all hard-headed logic of the
highest order. We moderns who insist that all is illusion and that the
heavens do not move as they appear to do, but in quite a different way,
need to reexamine our own premises to be certain that we are without
error.

Ptolemy's solution to the planetary problem is to take a combination
of circles, both eccentric and epicyclic, to account for the apparent motions. This system works rather well if one takes enough circles. In fact

the gearing of the planetary projectors in a Zeiss planetarium is epicyclic, and it gives the planetary positions for thousands of years in the past or in the future within visual accuracy. The current Newtonian scheme with its many perturbations is just as complicated mathematically as the Ptolemaic system with its many different circles. We must not make too quick a judgment on the grounds of either simplicity or greater accuracy for any theory of the celestial appearances.

Ptolemy's introduction is not included in this excerpt. In his introduction Ptolemy gives his reasons for picking the mathematics of astronomy for his treatise. He considers that the subject is nicely located between the realms of theology and physics. He agrees with most of the Greek thinkers in accepting God as the first and the final cause of the universe. But God, the Infinite, must always be incomprehensible to finite man. Theology, then, is beyond man's understanding. Physics, on the other hand, deals with unstable corruptible matter in a continual Heraclitean flux. Then there is no predictable uniformity in physics. Therefore neither subject is suitable for agreement among philosophers. But mathematics applied to astronomy is based on observation and is certain. The celestial bodies are less than the gods and being composed of the perfect quintessence move eternally in a predictable system of circles.

It is actually his second section, " On the Order of the Theorems," which opens this excerpt. He begins the study of astronomy as Euclid began his book on geometry. He proposes five postulates or axioms which in a mathematical work would be accepted without proof. Here, however, he tries to justify his assumed postulates from the observed phenomena.

In the following section he argues for the existence of the celestial sphere from the apparent circular motions of the stars. In particular, the circumpolar stars suggest the idea of a pole of rotation. Moreover, other proposals by other Greeks are considered and disproven. Heraclitus thought that the stars were illuminated upon rising and extinguished upon setting. But this is at variance with the observation that the stars which rise and set at some latitudes never drop below the horizon at more northern latitudes. The final argument is " physical considerations " in the sense of Aristotle's physics. It is inferred that the universe *must* be spherical since it is filled with spheres!

In the last section for this chapter, Ptolemy argues that the earth must be spherical in form. Although this is 1300 years before Columbus, his reasons are essentially those given today. Observers along an east-west line do not see an eclipse of the moon at the same local time. Observers along a north-south line see a continuous change in the circumpolar stars as they move to other latitudes. It must be remembered that Thales and his pupil Anaximenes thought that the earth was flat, and Anaximander pictured the earth as a cylinder whose height was a third of its diameter. However, about four centuries before the time of Ptolemy, Eratosthenes had calculated the circumference of a supposedly spherical earth.

THE ALMAGEST [1]
by Claudius Ptolemy
BOOK ONE

  ❖   ❖   ❖   ❖   ❖   ❖   ❖

2. On the Order of the Theorems

A view, therefore, of the general relation of the whole earth to the whole of the heavens will begin this composition of ours. And next, of things in particular, there will first be an account of the ecliptic's position and of the places of that part of the earth inhabited by us, and again of the difference, in order, between each of them according to the inclinations of their horizons. For the theory of these, once understood, facilitates the examination of the rest. And, secondly, there will be an account of the solar and lunar movements and of their incidents. For without a prior understanding of these one could not profitably consider what concerns the stars. The last part, in view of this plan, will be an account of the stars. Those things having to do with the sphere of what are called the fixed stars would reasonably come first, and then those having to do with what are called the five planets. And we shall try and show each of these things using as beginnings and foundations for what we wish to find, the evident and certain appearances from the observations of the ancients and our own, and applying the consequences of these conceptions by means of geometrical demonstrations.

And so, in general, we have to state that the heavens are spherical and move spherically; that the earth, in figure, is sensibly spherical also when taken as a whole; in position, lies right in the middle of the heavens, like a geometrical centre; in magnitude and distance, has the ratio of a point with respect to the sphere of the fixed stars, having itself no local motion at all. And we shall go through each of these points briefly to bring them to mind.

3. That the Heavens Move Spherically

It is probable the first notions of these things came to the ancients from some such observation as this. For they kept seeing the sun and moon and other stars always moving from rising to setting in parallel circles, beginning to move upward from below as if out of the earth itself, rising little by little to the top, and then coming around again and going down in the same way until at last they would disappear as if falling into the earth. And then again they would see them, after remaining some time invisible, rising and setting as if from another beginning; and they saw that the times and also the places of rising and setting generally corresponded in an ordered and regular way.

But most of all the observed circular orbit of those stars which are always visible, and their revolution about one and the same centre led them to this spherical notion. For necessarily this point became the pole of the heavenly sphere; and the stars nearer to it were those that spun around in smaller cir-

---

[1] Claudius Ptolemy, "The Almagest," *Great Books of the Western World*, Vol. 16, Encyclopædia Britannica, Inc., Chicago, 1955, pp. 6–14, 86–88, 270, 292–293.

cles, and those farther away made greater circles in their revolutions in proportion to the distance, until a sufficient distance brought one to the disappearing stars. And then they saw that those near the always-visible stars disappeared for a short time, and those farther away for a longer time proportionately. And for these reasons alone it was sufficient for them to assume this notion as a principle, and forthwith to think through also the other things consequent upon these same appearances, in accordance with the development of the science. For absolutely all the appearances contradict the other opinions.

If, for example, one should assume the movement of the stars to be in a straight line to infinity, as some have opined, how could it be explained that each star will be observed daily moving from the same starting point? For how could the stars turn back while rushing on to infinity? Or how could they turn back without appearing to do so? Or how is it they do not disappear with their size gradually diminishing, but on the contrary seem larger when they are about to disappear, being covered little by little as if cut off by the earth's surface? But certainly to suppose that they light up from the earth and then again go out in it would appear most absurd. For if anyone should agree that such an order in their magnitudes and number, and again in the distances, places, and times is accomplished in this way at random and by chance, and that one whole part of the earth has an incandescent nature and another a nature capable of extinguishing, or rather that the same part lights the stars up for some people and puts them out for others, and that the same stars happen to appear to some people either lit up or put out and to others not yet so — even if anyone, I say, should accept all such absurdities, what could we say about the always-visible stars which neither rise nor set? Or why don't the stars which light up and go out rise and set for every part of the earth, and why aren't those which are not affected in this way always above the earth for every part of the earth? For in this hypothesis the same stars will not always light up and go out for some people, and never for others. But it is evident to everyone that the same stars rise and set for some parts, and do neither of these things for others.

In a word, whatever figure other than the spherical be assumed for the movement of the heavens, there must be unequal linear distances from the earth to parts of the heavens, wherever or however the earth be situated, so that the magnitudes and angular distances of the stars with respect to each other would appear unequal to the same people within each revolution, now larger now smaller. But this is not observed to happen. For it is not a shorter linear distance which makes them appear larger at the horizon, but the steaming up of the moisture surrounding the earth between them and our eyes, just as things put under water appear larger the farther down they are placed.

The following considerations also lead to the spherical notion: the fact that instruments for measuring time cannot agree with any hypothesis save the spherical one; that, since the movement of the heavenly bodies ought to be the least impeded and most facile, the circle among plane figures offers the easiest path of motion, and the sphere among solids; likewise that, since of different figures having equal perimeters those having the more angles are the greater, the circle is the greatest of plane figures and the sphere of solid figures, and the heavens are greater than any other body.

Moreover, certain physical considerations lead to such a conjecture. For example, the fact that of all bodies the ether has the finest and most homogeneous parts; but the surfaces of homogeneous parts must have homogeneous parts, and only the circle is such among plane figures and the sphere among solids. And since the ether is not plane but solid, it can only be spherical. Likewise the fact that nature has built all earthly and corruptible bodies wholly out of rounded figures but with heterogeneous parts, and all divine bodies in the ether out of spherical figures with homogeneous parts, since if they were plane or disc-like they would not appear circular to all those who see them from different parts of the earth at the same time. Therefore it would seem reasonable that the ether surrounding them and of a like nature be also spherical, and that because of the homogeneity of its parts it moves circularly and regularly.

4. That also the Earth, Taken as a Whole, Is Sensibly Spherical

Now, that also the earth taken as a whole is sensibly spherical, we could most likely think out in this way. For again it is possible to see that the sun and moon and the other stars do not rise and set at the same time for every observer on the earth, but always earlier for those living towards the orient and later for those living towards the occident. For we find that the phenomena of eclipses taking place at the same time, especially those of the moon, are not recorded at the same hours for everyone — that is, relatively to equal intervals of time from noon; but we always find later hours recorded for observers towards the orient than for those towards the occident. And since the differences in the hours is found to be proportional to the distances between the places, one would reasonably suppose the surface of the earth spherical, with the result that the general uniformity of curvature would assure every part's covering those following it proportionately. But this would not happen if the figure were any other, as can be seen from the following considerations.

For, if it were concave, the rising stars would appear first to people towards the occident; and if it were flat, the stars would rise and set for all people together and at the same time; and if it were a pyramid, a cube, or any other polygonal figure, they would again appear at the same time for all observers on the same straight line. But none of these things appears to happen. It is further clear that it could not be cylindrical with the curved surface turned to the risings and settings and the plane bases to the poles of the universe, which some think more plausible. For then never would any of the stars be always visible to any of the inhabitants of the curved surface, but either all the stars would both rise and set for observers or the same stars for an equal distance from either of the poles would always be invisible to all observers. Yet the more we advance towards the north pole, the more the southern stars are hidden and the northern stars appear. So it is clear that here the curvature of the earth covering parts uniformly in oblique directions proves its spherical form on every side. Again, whenever we sail towards mountains or any high places from whatever angle and in whatever direction, we see their bulk little by little increasing as if they were arising from the sea, whereas before they seemed submerged because of the curvature of the water's surface.

STUDY QUESTIONS

1. At the time of Ptolemy, the political world was dominated by the
   (1) Greeks   (2) Romans   (3) Egyptians   (4) Arabians   (5) Babylonians.

2. At the time of Ptolemy, the intellectual world was dominated by the contributions of the
   (1) Greeks   (2) Romans   (3) Egyptians   (4) Arabians   (5) Babylonians.

3. At the time of Ptolemy, scientific thought was probably most deeply influenced by the contributions of
   (1) Thales   (2) Pythagoras   (3) Archimedes   (4) Aristotle
   (5) Ptolemy.

4. Which of the following are arguments proposed by Ptolemy for the sphericity of the sky?
   a. The observed paths traveled by circumpolar stars.
   b. Only with a spherical sky could the moon be eclipsed.
   c. The constant brightness of stars as they travel across the sky.
   The correct answer is
   (1) a   (2) b   (3) c   (4) a and c   (5) a, b, and c.

5. Which of the following Ptolemaic arguments for a spherically-shaped sky, if accepted, would refute the idea that the sky is cubical in shape and rotates on an axis with the celestial objects attached to the inner surface of the cube?
   a. Distances to the celestial objects, and hence their brightness would vary.
   b. The appearances of the circumpolar stars.
   c. The most favorable shape for three-dimensional motion is the sphere.
   The correct answer is
   (1) a   (2) b   (3) c   (4) a, b, and c   (5) none of them.

6–8. *Following are three of Ptolemy's arguments for the spherical shape of the earth:*
   a. *Two observers at the same latitude but in different longitudes will not see a given celestial object rise at the same instant; the one to the east will see the object first.*
   b. *Lunar eclipses do not occur at the same local time for observers located on an east-west line, with the western observer seeing the eclipse at an earlier local time, the differences in hours being proportional to the distances between places.*
   c. *As one travels northward more stars in the northern sky become circumpolar while, in the same proportion, fewer stars of the southern sky are seen at all.*

   Which one or ones of these arguments would refute the following possible shapes of the earth?

6. The earth shaped as a flat disc.
   (1) a   (2) a and b   (3) b and c   (4) a, b, and c   (5) c.

7. The earth shaped as a football, with the poles at the ends.
   (1) a   (2) b   (3) c   (4) a, b, and c   (5) none of them.

8. The earth shaped as a concave dish.

    (1) a   (2) a and b   (3) b and c   (4) a, b, and c   (5) c.

9. Which of the following are valid reasons that a north-south path along the earth's surface is an arc of a circle?
    a. As one travels north, a given star to the north on the observer's meridian gets higher by the same angle that a star to the south on the observer's meridian gets lower.
    b. Equal successive distances traveled toward the north cause a star to the north on the observer's meridian to rise by equal angles.
    c. For a given distance traveled toward the north the number of new northern circumpolar stars that appear is equal to the number of southern circumpolar stars that disappear.
    The correct answer is

    (1) a   (2) b   (3) c   (4) a, b, and c   (5) none of them.

10. Why is it that " instruments for measuring time cannot agree with any hypothesis save the spherical one "?
11. Why should the earth be spherical and not pear-shaped or some similar rounded form?
12. Did Eratosthenes' calculation of the circumference of the earth show that the earth is spherical?

5

The Geocentric Universe

● In his fifth section which
opens this chapter, Ptolemy presents arguments for his third postulate
that the earth lies in the middle of the heavens by using the method of
reductio ad absurdum. His reasoning consists of assuming the earth to be
at possible locations other than the center of the universe, and then showing that the observations from these other locations would not agree with
the actual observations of the sky. If the earth is not in the middle of the
universe, then it might be in one of three possible locations. First, it might
be equidistant from the poles of the celestial sphere, but not at the center.
Second, it might be on the north-south axis of the celestial sphere but not
at the center. The arguments against these two classes of locations might
be more easily followed with the aid of the explanations and drawings
which are interpolated into Ptolemy's text. The third possibility of the
earth off-axis and closer to one pole than to the other is quickly disposed
of as a simple combination of the first two situations.

In the next section he argues that the dimensions of the celestial sphere
must be infinitely great as compared to the radius of the earth, since observations made anywhere on the face of the earth are essentially the same
as if taken at the center of the earth.

In the last section of this chapter, Ptolemy argues that the earth must
be stationary at the center of the celestial sphere. His reasons here are
twofold: if the earth moved in an orbit of appreciable size as compared
to the celestial sphere, the observations of the type discussed in the opening section of this chapter would have been found for at least part of each
year; the other half of his argument is based upon Aristotelian mechanics.
Aristotelian concepts of all natural and violent motions on the earth require a stationary earth, for after all, the enormous weight of a moving
earth would cause it to easily outdistance all objects of lesser weights,
leaving "animals and other weights" hanging in the air.

THE ALMAGEST
by Claudius Ptolemy
BOOK ONE

✿   ✿   ✿   ✿   ✿   ✿   ✿

5. That the Earth Is in the Middle of the Heavens

Now with this done, if one should next take up the question of the earth's position, the observed appearances with respect to it could only be understood if we put it in the middle of the heavens as the centre of the sphere. If this were not so, then the earth would either have to be off the axis but equidistant from the poles, or on the axis but farther advanced towards one of the poles, or neither on the axis nor equidistant from the poles.

The following considerations are opposed to the first of these three positions — namely, that if the earth were conceived as placed off the axis either above or below in respect to certain parts of the earth, those parts, in the right sphere, would never have any equinox since the section above the earth and the section below the earth would always be cut unequally by the horizon. Again, if the sphere were inclined with respect to these parts, either they would have no equinox or else the equinox would not take place midway between the summer and winter solstices. The distances would be unequal because the equator which is the greatest of those parallel circles described about the poles would not be cut in half by the horizon; but one of the circles parallel to it, either to the north or to the south, would be so cut in half. It is absolutely agreed by all, however, that these distances are everywhere equal because the increases from the equinox to the longest day at the summer tropic are equal [1] to the decreases to the least days at the winter tropic. And if the deviation for certain parts of the earth were supposed either towards the orient or the occident, it would result that for these parts neither the sizes and angular distances of the stars would appear equal and the same at the eastern and western horizons, nor would the time from rising to the meridian be equal to the time from the meridian to setting. But these things evidently are altogether contrary to the appearances.

The "right sphere" for case I is the special case wherein the observer's horizon is parallel to the axis; that is, when the observer is on the earth's equator as shown in Figure 5-1. Ptolemy argues that there would be no equal days and nights in this case.

The oblique or "inclined sphere" for case I is the more general case where the observer's horizon is not parallel to the axis, as shown in Figure 5-2. Ptolemy argues that in this case, (a) there would be unequal intervals from spring to midsummer and from fall to midwinter, and (b) the celestial equator would not cut the horizon in two equal halves.

As to the second position where the earth would be on the axis but farther advanced towards one of the poles, one could again object, that if this were so,

---

[1] This is an approximate statement as has been seen in an earlier chapter.

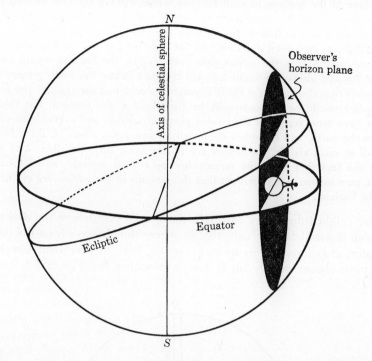

Figure 5-1. *The earth off the axis of the celestial sphere and equidistant from the poles. The case of the right sphere with the observer on the equator and the horizon parallel to the celestial axis.*

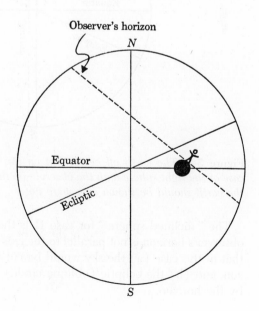

Figure 5-2. *The earth off the axis of the celestial sphere and equidistant from the poles. The case of the oblique sphere with the observer north of the earth's equator.*

the plane of the horizon in each latitude would always cut into uneven parts the sections of the heavens below the earth and above, different with respect to each other and to themselves for each different deviation. And the horizon could cut into two even parts only in the right sphere. But in the case of the inclined sphere with the nearer pole ever visible, the horizon would always make the part above the earth less and the part below the earth greater with the result that also the great circle through the centre of the signs of the zodiac (ecliptic) would be cut unequally by the plane of the horizon. But this has never been seen, for six of the twelve parts are always and everywhere visible above the earth, and the other six invisible; and again when all these last six are all at once visible, the others are at the same time invisible. And so — from the fact that the same semicircles are cut off entirely, now above the earth, now below — it is evident that the sections of the zodiac are cut in half by the horizon.

The " right sphere " for case II is the special case where the observer's horizon is parallel to the axis; that is, where the observer is on the earth's equator, as before. In this special case, the horizon would cut the sky in two parts almost equally, on Ptolemy's reasoning. See Figure 5-3.

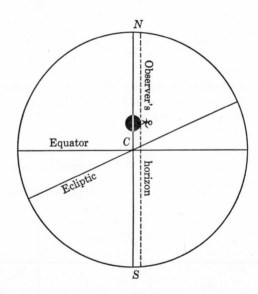

Figure 5-3. *The earth off center but on the axis of the celestial sphere. The case of the right sphere with the observer on the equator. According to Ptolemy, the earth should be shown as a mere dot.*

The " inclined sphere " for case II is the more general case where the observer's horizon is not parallel to the axis (see Fig. 5-4). Ptolemy argues that in this case (a) the sky would be cut into unequal parts by the horizon, and (b) the ecliptic (oblique circle) would be cut in unequal parts by the horizon.

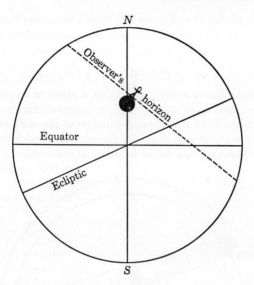

Figure 5-4. *The earth off center but on the axis of the celestial sphere. The case of the oblique sphere with the observer north of the earth's equator.*

And, in general, if the earth did not have its position under the equator but lay either to the north or south nearer one of the poles, the result would be that, during the equinoxes, the shadows of the gnomons at sunrise would never perceptibly be on a straight line with those at sunset in planes parallel to the horizon. But the contrary is everywhere seen to occur. And it is immediately clear that it is not possible to advance the third position since each of the obstacles to the first two would be present here also.

The gnomon of a sundial is the central pin or finger which casts a shadow on the dial, from which time can be read. In the simplest form of sundial, consisting of a vertical gnomon in the center of a horizontal plate, the shadow falls due west at dawn and due east at sunset on March 21 and September 21 (the equinoxes). This straight line formed by the dawn and sunset shadows is used by Ptolemy to support his contention that the earth is in the middle of the sky. The relative positions of the shadows of the gnomon which had been actually observed and were known to Ptolemy are shown in Figure 3-7.

In brief, all the observed order of the increases and decreases of day and night would be thrown into utter confusion if the earth were not in the middle. And there would be added the fact that the eclipses of the moon could not take place for all parts of the heavens by a diametrical opposition to the sun, for the earth would often not be interposed between them in their diametrical oppositions, but at distances less than a semicircle.

In section 5 Ptolemy uses the fact that the eclipsed moon is at the opposite point in the sky from the sun, to support his contention that the earth is in the middle of the sky. Figure 5-5 shows his concept of how the off-center earth would be between the sun and moon when they are not at opposite points in the sky. The arc θ is less than 180°.

6. That the Earth Has the Ratio of a Point to the Heavens

Now, that the earth has sensibly the ratio of a point to its distance from the sphere of the so-called fixed stars gets great support from the fact that in all parts of the earth the sizes and angular distances of the stars at the same times appear everywhere equal and alike, for the observations of the same stars in the different latitudes are not found to differ in the least.

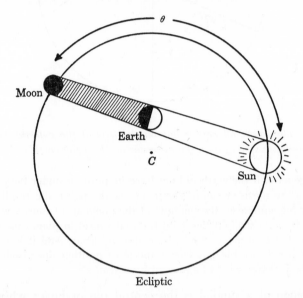

Ecliptic

Figure 5-5. *Relative positions on the ecliptic of the sun, earth, and moon for an eclipse of the moon with the earth off center. The moon and sun would not be separated by six zodiacal constellations.*

Moreover, this must be added: that sundials placed in any part of the earth and the centres of armillary spheres can play the role of the earth's true centre for the sightings and the rotations of the shadows, as much in conformity with the hypotheses of the appearances as if they were at the true midpoint of the earth.

And the earth is clearly a point also from this fact: that everywhere the planes drawn through the eye, which we call horizons, always exactly cut in half the whole sphere of the heavens. And this would not happen if the magnitude of the earth with respect to its distance from the heavens were perceptible; but only the plane drawn through the point at the earth's centre would exactly cut the sphere in half, and those drawn through any other part of the earth's surface would make the sections below the earth greater than those above.

7. That the Earth Does Not in any Way Move Locally

By the same arguments as the preceding it can be shown that the earth can neither move in any one of the aforesaid oblique directions, nor ever change at all from its place at the centre. For the same things would result as if it had another position than at the centre. And so it also seems to me superfluous to look for the causes of the motion to the centre when it is once for all clear from the very appearances that the earth is in the middle of the world and all weights move towards it. And the easiest and only way to understand this is to see that, once the earth has been proved spherical considered as a whole and in the middle of the universe as we have said, then the tendencies and movements of heavy bodies (I mean their proper movements) are everywhere and always at right angles to the tangent plane drawn through the falling body's point of contact with the earth's surface. For because of this it is clear that, if they were not stopped by the earth's surface, they too would go all the way to the centre itself, since the straight line drawn to the centre of a sphere is always perpendicular to the plane tangent to the sphere's surface at the intersection of that line.

All those who think it paradoxical that so great a weight as the earth should not waver or move anywhere seem to me to go astray by making their judgment with an eye to their own affects and not to the property of the whole. For it would not still appear so extraordinary to them, I believe, if they stopped to think that the earth's magnitude compared to the whole body surrounding it is in the ratio of a point to it. For thus it seems possible for that which is relatively least to be supported and pressed against from all sides equally and at the same angle by that which is absolutely greatest and homogeneous. For there is no " above " and " below " in the universe with respect to the earth, just as none could be conceived of in a sphere. And of the compound bodies in the universe, to the extent of their proper and natural motion, the light and subtle ones are scattered in flames to the outside and to the circumference, and they seem to rush in the upward direction relative to each one because we too call " up " from above our heads to the enveloping surface of the universe; but the heavy and coarse bodies move to the middle and centre and they seem to fall downwards because again we all call " down " the direction from our feet to the earth's centre. And they properly subside about the middle under the everywhere-equal and like resistance and impact against each other. Therefore the solid body of the earth is reasonably considered as being the largest relative to those moving against it and as remaining unmoved in any direction by the force of the very small weights, and as it were absorbing their fall. And if it had some one common movement, the same as that of the other weights, it would clearly leave them all behind because of its much greater magnitude. And the animals and other weights would be left hanging in the air, and the earth would very quickly fall out of the heavens. Merely to conceive such things makes them appear ridiculous.

Now some people, although they have nothing to oppose to these arguments, agree on something, as they think, more plausible. And it seems to them there is nothing against their supposing, for instance, the heavens immobile and the earth as turning on the same axis from west to east very nearly one revolution a day; or that they both should move to some extent, but only on the same axis as we said, and conformably to the overtaking of the one by the other.

But it has escaped their notice that, indeed, as far as the appearances of the stars are concerned, nothing would perhaps keep things from being in accordance with this simpler conjecture, but that in the light of what happens around us in the air such a notion would seem altogether absurd. For in order for us to grant them what is unnatural in itself, that the lightest and subtlest bodies either do not move at all or no differently from those of contrary nature, while those less light and less subtle bodies in the air are clearly more rapid than all the more terrestrial ones; and to grant that the heaviest and most compact bodies have their proper swift and regular motion, while again these terrestrial bodies are certainly at times not easily moved by anything else — for us to grant these things, they would have to admit that the earth's turning is the swiftest of absolutely all the movements about it because of its making so great a revolution in a short time, so that all those things that were not at rest on the earth would seem to have a movement contrary to it, and never would a cloud be seen to move toward the east nor anything else that flew or was thrown into the air. For the earth would always outstrip them in its eastward motion, so that all other bodies would seem to be left behind and to move towards the west.

For if they should say that the air is also carried around with the earth in the same direction and at the same speed, none the less the bodies contained in it would always seem to be outstripped by the movement of both. Or if they should be carried around as if one with the air, neither the one nor the other would appear as outstripping, or being outstripped by, the other. But these bodies would always remain in the same relative position and there would be no movement or change either in the case of flying bodies or projectiles. And yet we shall clearly see all such things taking place as if their slowness or swiftness did not follow at all from the earth's movement.

STUDY QUESTIONS

1. Which of the following were observational facts known to Ptolemy?
   a. Six and only six zodiacal constellations are always above the horizon.
   b. The moon is always in the zodiac on or near the ecliptic.
   c. The full moon rises as the sun sets.
   The correct answer is

        (1) a   (2) b   (3) c   (4) a and c   (5) a, b, and c.

2. Which of the following were observational facts known to Ptolemy?
   a. The shadows of a vertical post fall due east and west at sunrise and sunset on June 21.
   b. Alexandria, Egypt has twelve hours of daylight at the vernal equinox.
   c. The elapsed time between sunrise and meridian crossing is equal to the elapsed time between meridian crossing and sunset.
   The correct answer is

        (1) a   (2) b   (3) c   (4) b and c   (5) a, b, and c.

3. Consistent with Ptolemy's assumptions concerning the earth and celestial sphere, the particular observer shown whose horizon is parallel to the celestial axis (right sphere)
   a. would always have equal daylight and darkness
   b. would never see the sun north of his zenith
   c. would see the sun rise 90° along the horizon east of north on March 21.

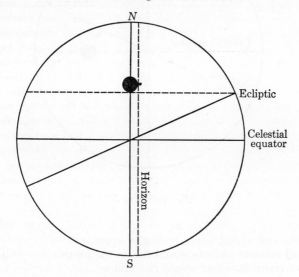

For problem 3.

The correct answer is

   (1) a   (2) b   (3) c   (4) a and b   (5) a, b, and c.

4. Those items in question 3 which are *consistent* with *observation* for an actual observer on the earth's equator are

   (1) a   (2) b   (3) c   (4) a and b   (5) a and c.

5. Consistent with Ptolemy's assumptions concerning the earth and celestial sphere, the particular observer shown whose horizon is not parallel to the celestial axis (the oblique sphere, see page 78)
   a. would never have equal days and nights
   b. would never see an eclipse of the moon
   c. would see the sun rise due east on March 21.
   The correct answer is

   (1) a   (2) b   (3) c   (4) a and b   (5) b and c.

6. Those items in question 5 which are *consistent* with *observation* for an actual observer at, say, 60°N are

   (1) a   (2) b   (3) c   (4) a and b   (5) b and c.

7. Ptolemy argued that the earth had no movement of translation (such as revolving about the sun) because if it did, then

   (1) planets would rise in the west
   (2) the earth would move away from the center of the celestial sphere

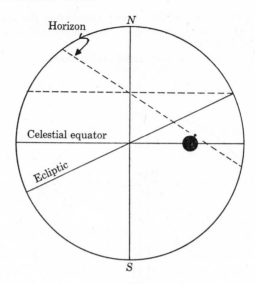

For problem 5.

(3) the sun would never cross the equator
(4) all massive objects would fall to the earth
(5) circumpolar stars would rise and set.

8. Which one of the following statements best describes Ptolemy's approach in attempting to prove that the earth is at the middle of the celestial sphere?

 (1) Ptolemy noted the consequences of having the earth at a position other than the center of the celestial sphere and compared the consequences with actual observations.
 (2) Ptolemy measured the distance to the celestial sphere in three different directions and found the same value for each measurement.
 (3) Ptolemy noted the length of time between lunar eclipses and from this calculated the radius of the celestial sphere.
 (4) Socrates and Pythagoras, employing the Pythagorean theorem, had determined the position of the earth relative to the celestial sphere. Ptolemy merely recounted their calculations.
 (5) Ptolemy offered no proof that the earth is at the center of the celestial sphere. Instead, he merely assumed this to be true.

9. Which of the following seems to you to be the best statement about the nature of Ptolemy's " physical considerations " (philosophical but not observational)?

 (1) It is logical and careful reasoning based upon the known physical sciences.
 (2) It is purely "wishful thinking" indulged in by Ptolemy when he cannot prove an intensely desired opinion logically.
 (3) It is an attempt to reason honestly from certain purely philosophical views about nature.
 (4) It is an appeal to "revealed knowledge" and is nonscientific and it is not rational.

(5) It is fraudulent and false material which adds bulk but no merit to Ptolemy's text.

10. Which of the following seems to you to be the best statement about the nature of Ptolemy's book *The Almagest?*

    (1) It is simply the work of other men assembled and edited by Ptolemy.

    (2) It is purely the work of Ptolemy, who, after all, was one of the great men of the ages.

    (3) Its long period of authority (nearly 1600 years) was based on the fact that it was accepted as the official dogma of the Catholic Church.

    (4) It, like Homer's epic poems, is the work of many men and it is ascribed to Ptolemy purely as a tradition.

    (5) Its long period of authority was based on the fact that it was a sound work based upon widely-held assumptions and supported by a great deal of actual observational work. It was compatible with the predominant philosophies of its time, and the predictions as to celestial appearances calculated from it were found to be reasonably accurate.

11. Would not all of Ptolemy's arguments be satisfied if the celestial sphere were replaced with a celestial cube turning around an axis from the north celestial pole to the south celestial pole?

12. What do you make of Ptolemy's " physical considerations "? Are these the arguments of a rational man?

13. How could Ptolemy tell whether the horizon cut the sky into two equal halves, or is this simply a figure of speech?

14. Is Ptolemy's argument for the earth being in the center of the universe because of the eclipses of the moon correct?

15. Ptolemy rejects the views of Aristarchus of Samos in toto, even the simple suggestion that the diurnal motions could be best explained by the rotation of the tiny earth rather than the daily rotation of the immense celestial sphere. Just what are Ptolemy's reasons for insisting on a fixed and immovable earth?

6

The Ptolemaic Planetary System

● After justifying his five postulates, Ptolemy says that he is now ready to take up the details of the heavens. The daily movement of the celestial sphere is the first of his prime movements in the sky. While this accounts roughly for the appearances of one day, continued observation for many days shows that the sun, moon, and planets move slowly about on the celestial sphere. This additional slow motion eastwards, which is contrary to the apparent daily westward rotation of the celestial sphere, is nearly in the plane of the ecliptic (Ptolemy's oblique circle) and is the second prime movement in the sky. The foregoing, he says in the beginning of his section 9, completes his presentation of his general principles. The remainder of the *Almagest* is devoted to the details.

Portions of Ptolemy's Book Three and Book Nine are excerpted here to show his epicyclic system in his own words.[1] The motion of the sun is not uniform along the ecliptic but is at slightly different rates each day during the year. It was known from observation to Hipparchus that it took the sun 94½ days [2] to pass from the vernal equinox to the summer solstice but only 92½ days in the next season for the sun to reach the autumnal equinox. Similarly it took the sun only 88⅛ days to move on to the winter solstice and a further 90⅛ days to return to the vernal equinox of the next year. Thus the apparent times required for the sun to move through successive

---

[1] " Book Three " or " Book Nine " is not the best translation. Ptolemy, like all of the Greek, Roman, or other writers of his period, wrote on long rolls of writing material such as papyrus or vellum. The entire *Almagest* is one connected work, but it was too long for one roll of material. It is the contents of any particular roll that is referred to here as a " book." The Latin term for it was " volume," meaning " rolled up." Today, books are printed on folded sheets of paper which are sewn together at the folds and then bound. There is considerably more wordage in each single hand-held unit which is today's book or volume.

[2] Note the reasonably close agreement between the lengths of the seasons as given by Hipparchus and the modern values given on page 44.

90° intervals of its annual path varied noticeably. In the part of Ptolemy's Book Three which is presented here, he shows that two different geometrical constructions of circles could each account for the observed irregular motion of the sun. In the first, which is the eccentric hypothesis, the sun moves uniformly on a circle which is not centered on the earth. In the second, which is the epicyclic hypothesis, the sun moves on a combination of two circles. One circle, the deferent, is centered on the earth and bears another rotating circle, the epicycle, on its circumference. The apparent motions of the sun in the sky can be reproduced by placing the sun on the epicycle and adjusting properly the periods of revolution and the diameters of the two circles. This necessary tailoring of theory to observation was termed by the Greeks " saving the appearances."

Several technical terms appear in this section which may be of strange appearance but are really of simple meaning. The terms *apogee* and *perigee* mean respectively, "farthest from the earth" and "closest to the earth." The etymology of these two words may be apparent when it is recalled that *geos* is the Greek term for the earth. The term *anomaly* means an apparent irregularity of motion — that is, departure from an otherwise uniform motion in a circle centered on the observer. The differing lengths of the four seasons represent the anomaly of the sun's motion on the ecliptic.

In the excerpt from Ptolemy's Book Nine, his system for the moon and for the fixed planets which are visible to the unaided eye is presented. These objects along with the sun are the sum total of all that was known about our solar system before 1781. By the "spheres" of the sun, the moon, and the planets, Ptolemy means their orbits. Some philosophers conceived them as actual "crystalline" spheres which carried the sun, moon, and the planets and were worked by some sort of celestial clockwork driven off the daily motion of the celestial sphere.

The term *parallax* which occurs in this section means a method of determining a distance without actually taping it off. It can be a method of very high precision. Triangulation, as it is also called, is actually the basic procedure of our fundamental land survey in the United States. Consider a baseline AB of known measured length (Fig. 6-1). With a transit, or other suitable instrument, the angle BAC at A and the angle ABC at point B are measured to the point C. Now with one side and the two angles, it is possible by trigonometry to calculate the lengths of the other two sides AC and BC. Thus, one can determine a distance to an otherwise inaccessible point, such as the moon. Ptolemy determined the distance to the moon in this fashion using a known baseline measured upon the surface of the earth. The planets, however, were so far away that no baseline upon the earth was sufficiently long to determine their distances.

Ptolemy accounts for the planetary appearances by a combination of his eccentric circles and epicycles along with a new hypothesis of the "equants." This proposal that a circle does not turn uniformly about its

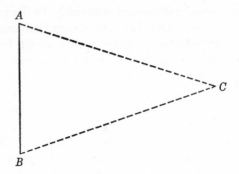

Figure 6-1. *The distance* AC *or* BC *may be calculated if the distance* AB *and the angles at* A *and* B *are measured.*

center but about quite a different point, the equant, was particularly offensive to Copernicus. An explanatory note is added at the end of the Ptolemy excerpt to help to clarify his proposed mechanism.

THE ALMAGEST
by Claudius Ptolemy
BOOK ONE

❧   ❧   ❧   ❧   ❧   ❧   ❧

8. That There Are Two Different Prime Movements in the Heavens

It will be sufficient for these hypotheses, which have to be assumed for the detailed expositions following them, to have been outlined here in such a summary way since they will finally be established and confirmed by the agreement of the consequent proofs with the appearances. In addition to those already mentioned, this general assumption would also be rightly made that there are two different prime movements in the heavens. One is that by which everything moves from east to west, always in the same way and at the same speed with revolutions in circles parallel to each other and clearly described about the poles of the regularly revolving sphere. Of these circles the greatest is called the equator, because it alone is always cut exactly in half by the horizon which is a great circle of the sphere, and because everywhere the sun's revolution about it is sensibly equinoctial. The other movement is that according to which the spheres of the stars make certain local motions in the direction opposite to that of the movement just described and around other poles than those of that first revolution. And we assume that it is so because, while, from each day's observation, all the heavenly bodies are seen to move generally in paths sensibly similar and parallel to the equator and to rise, culminate, and set (for such is the property of the first movement), yet from subsequent and more continuous observation, even if all the other stars appear to preserve their angular distances with respect to each other and their properties as regards their places within the first movement, still the sun and moon and planets make certain complex movements unequal to each other, but all contrary to the general movement, towards the east opposite to the movement of the fixed stars which preserve their respective angular distances and are moved as if by one sphere.

If, then, this movement of the planets also took place in circles parallel to the equator — that is, around the same poles as those of the first revolution — it would be sufficient to assume for them all one and the same revolving movement in conformity with the first. For it would then be plausible to suppose that their movement was the result of a lag and not of a contrary movement. But they always seem, at the same time they move towards the east, to deviate towards the north and south poles without any uniform magnitude's being observed in this deviation, so that this seems to befall them through impulsions. But although this deviation is irregular on the hypothesis of one prime movement, it is regular when effected by a circle oblique to the equator. And so such a circle is conceived one and the same for, and proper to, the planets, quite exactly expressed and as it were described by the motion of the sun, but traveled also by the moon and planets which ever turn about it with every deviation from it on the part of any planet either way, a deviation within a prescribed distance and governed by rule. And since this is seen to be a great circle also because of the sun's equal oscillation to the north and south of the equator, and since the eastward movements of all the planets (as we said) take place on one and the same circle, it was necessary to suppose a second movement different from the general one, a movement about the poles of this oblique circle or ecliptic in the direction opposite to that of the first movement.

Then if we think of a great circle described through the poles of both the circles just mentioned, which necessarily cuts each of them — that is, the equator and the circle inclined to it — exactly in half and at right angles, there will be four points on the oblique circle or ecliptic: the two made by the equator diametrically opposite each other and called the equinoxes of which the one guarding the northern approach is called spring, and the opposite one autumn. And the two made by the circle drawn through both sets of poles, also clearly diametrically opposite each other, are called the tropics, of which the one to the south of the equator is called winter, and the one to the north summer. [See Fig. 6-2.]

The one first movement which contains all the others will be thought of then as described and as if defined by the great circle, through both sets of poles, which is carried around and carries with it all the rest from east to west about the poles of the equator. And these poles are as if they were on what is called the meridian, which differs from the circle through both sets of poles in this alone: that it is not always drawn through the poles of the ecliptic, but is conceived as continuously at right angles to the horizon and therefore called the meridian, since such a position cutting in half as it does each of the two hemispheres, that below the earth and that above, provides midday and midnight. But the second movement, consisting of many parts and contained by the first, and embracing itself all the planetary spheres, is carried by the first as we said, and revolves about the poles of the ecliptic in the opposite direction. And these poles of the ecliptic being on the circle effecting the first revolution — that is, on the circle drawn through all four poles together — are carried around with it as one would expect; and, moving therefore with a motion opposite to the second prime movement, in this way keep the position of the great circle which is the ecliptic ever the same with respect to the equator.

The celestial coordinates referred to in section 8 are essentially the same as those in use today (Fig. 6-2).

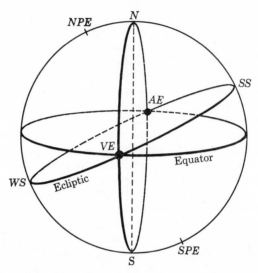

Figure 6-2. *The celestial coordinates:*

N, S .... *North and south celestial poles*
NPE .... *North pole of the ecliptic*
SPE .... *South pole of the ecliptic*
Ecliptic .... *The " inclined circle "*
Equator .... *The " equinoctial circle "*
VE .... *Vernal equinox*
SS .... *Summer solstice*
AE .... *Autumnal equinox*
WS .... *Winter solstice*

BOOK THREE

❀   ❀   ❀   ❀   ❀   ❀   ❀

3. On the Hypotheses concerning Regular and Circular Movement

Since the next thing is to explain the apparent irregularity of the sun, it is first necessary to assume in general that the motions of the planets in the direction contrary to the movement of the heavens are all regular and circular by nature, like the movement of the universe in the other direction. That is, the straight lines, conceived as revolving the stars or their circles, cut off in equal times on absolutely all circumferences equal angles at the centres of each; and their apparent irregularities result from the positions and arrangements of the circles on their spheres through which they produce these movements, but no departure from their unchangeableness has really occurred in their nature in regard to the supposed disorder of their appearances.

But the cause of this irregular appearance can be accounted for by as many as two primary simple hypotheses. For if their movement is considered with respect to a circle in the plane of the ecliptic concentric with the cosmos so that our eye is the centre, then it is necessary to suppose that they make their regular movements either along circles not concentric with the cosmos, or along concentric circles; not with these simply, but with other circles borne upon

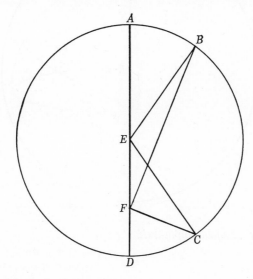

Figure 6-3. *The eccentric hypothesis.*

them called epicycles. For according to either hypothesis it will appear possible for the planets seemingly to pass, in equal periods of time, through unequal arcs of the ecliptic circle which is concentric with the cosmos.

For if, in the case of the hypothesis of eccentricity [Fig. 6-3], we conceive the eccentric circle ABCD on which the star moves regularly, with E as center and with diameter AED, and the point F on it as your eye so that the point A becomes the apogee and the point D the perigee; and if, cutting off equal arcs AB and DC, we join BE, BF, CE, and CF, then it will be evident that the star moving through each of the arcs AB and CD in an equal period of time will seem to have passed through unequal arcs on the circle described around F as a centre. For since

angle BEA = angle CED,

therefore angle BFA is less than either of them, and angle CFD greater (Eucl. I, 16).

And if in the hypothesis of the epicycle [Fig. 6-4] we conceive the circle ABCD concentric with the ecliptic with centre E and diameter AEC, and the epicycle FGHK borne on it on which the star moves, with its centre at A, then it will be immediately evident also that as the epicycle passes regularly along the circle ABCD, from A to B for example, and the star along the epicycle, the

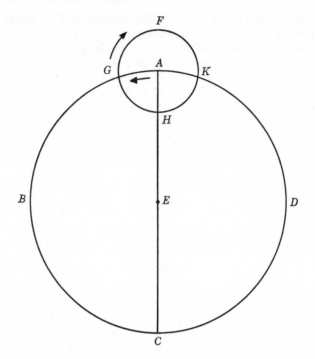

Figure 6-4. *The epicyclic hypothesis.*

star will appear indifferently to be at A the centre of the epicycle when it is at F or H; but when it is at other points, it will not. But having come to G, for instance, it will seem to have produced a movement greater than the regular movement by the arc AG; and having come to K, likewise less by the arc AK.

Then with the hypothesis of eccentricity it is always the case that the least movement belongs to the apogee and the greatest movement to the perigee, since angle AFB is always less than angle DFC. But both cases can come about with the hypothesis of the epicycle. For when the epicycle moves contrary to the heavens (from west to east), for example from A to B, if the star so moves on the epicycle that it goes from the apogee again contrary to the heavens (that is, from F in the direction of G), there will result at the apogee the greatest advance, because the epicycle and the star are moving the same way. But if the movement of the star on the epicycle is in the direction of that of the heavens (from east to west), that is, from F towards K, conversely the least advance will be effected at the apogee because the star is then moving contrary to the movement of the epicycle.

With these things established, it must next be understood that, in the case of those planets which effect two anomalies,[3] it is possible to combine both of these hypotheses, as we shall show in the chapters concerning them. But, in the case of those planets subject to only one anomaly, one of the hypotheses

---

[3] Retrograde motion and nonuniform motion in the orbit would be *two* anomalies.

will suffice. And it must be understood that all the appearances can be cared for interchangeably according to either hypothesis, when the same ratios are involved in each. In other words, the hypotheses are interchangeable when, in the case of the hypothesis of the epicycle, the ratio of the epicycle's radius to the radius of the circle carrying it is the same as, in the case of the hypothesis of eccentricity, the ratio of the line between the centres (that is, between the eye and the centre of the eccentric circle), to the eccentric circle's radius; with the added conditions that the star move on the epicycle from the apogee in the direction of the movement of the heavens with the same angular velocity as the epicycle moves on the circle concentric with the eye in the direction opposite to that of the heavens, and that the star move regularly on the eccentric circle with the same angular velocity also and in the direction opposite to the movement of the heavens.

And we shall briefly show in a systematic way, first by reasoning and secondly by the numbers discovered in the appearances of the sun's anomaly, that with the above assumptions the same appearances agree with either hypothesis.

✿   ✿   ✿   ✿   ✿   ✿   ✿

BOOK NINE

1. Concerning the Order of the Spheres of the Sun and Moon and Five Planets

Now, certainly whatever one could say in general about the fixed stars, to the extent that the appearances up until now fall under our apprehension, would be pretty much like this. But since this Composition still lacks a treatment of the five planets, we shall give an exposition of them, going as far as possible with what they have in common to avoid repetition, and then adding on the plan of each one in particular.

First, then, concerning the order of their spheres, all of which have their positions about the poles of the ecliptic, we see the foremost mathematicians agree that all these spheres are nearer the earth than the sphere of the fixed stars, and farther from the earth than that of the moon; that the three — of which Saturn's is the largest, Jupiter's next earthward, and Mars' below that — are all farther from the earth than the others and that of the sun. On the other hand, the spheres of Venus and Mercury are placed by the earlier mathematicians below the sun's, but by some of the later ones above the sun's because of their never having seen the sun eclipsed by them. But this judgment seems to us unsure since these planets could be below the sun and never yet have been in any of the planes through the sun and our eye but in another, and therefore not have appeared in a line with it; just as in the case of the moon's conjunctive passages there are for the most part no eclipses.

Since there is no other way of getting at this because of the absence of any sensible parallax in these stars,[4] from which appearance alone linear distances are gotten, the order of the earlier mathematicians seems the more trustworthy, using the sun as a natural dividing line between those planets which can be any angular distance from the sun and those which cannot but which always move near it. Besides, it does not place them far enough at their perigees to produce a sensible parallax.

[4] " Stars " here and in section 6 obviously refers to planets.

2. On the Aim of the Planetary Hypotheses

So much, then, for the orders of the spheres. Now, since our problem is to demonstrate, in the case of the five planets as in the case of the sun and moon, all
their apparent irregularities as produced by means of regular and circular motions (for these are proper to the nature of divine things which are strangers to
disparities and disorders) the successful accomplishment of this aim as truly
belonging to mathematical theory in philosophy is to be considered a great
thing, very difficult and as yet unattained in a reasonable way by anyone.

❀   ❀   ❀   ❀   ❀   ❀   ❀

6. On the Mode and Difference of these Hypotheses

The mode of the hypotheses just derived would be more easy to understand in
this way:

In the case of the hypothesis of all the planets except Mercury, first let there
be conceived the eccentric circle ABC about the centre D, and the diameter
ADC through D and the centre of the ecliptic. And on this diameter let E be
made the centre of the ecliptic, the point A the apogee, and C the perigee.
And let DE be bisected at F; and with F as centre and DA as radius, let circle
GHK be drawn, equal of course to circle ABC. And with H as centre let the
epicycle LM be drawn, and let the straight line LHMD be joined.

Then first we suppose the plane of the eccentric circles to be inclined to that
of the ecliptic, and again the plane of the epicycle to that of the eccentric, because of the latitudinal passage of the stars to be demonstrated by us hereafter.
But to make things easy as far as the longitudinal passages are concerned, we
suppose that they are all conceived in the one plane of the ecliptic, since there
will be no appreciable difference in longitude resulting from such inclinations
as will be found for each of the stars.

Then we say that the whole plane revolves eastward in the direction of the
signs about centre E, moving the apogees and perigees one degree in a hundred years; that the epicycle's diameter LHM in turn is revolved regularly by
centre D eastward in the direction of the signs at the rate of the star's longitudinal return; and that at the same time it revolves the points of the epicycle L
and M, its centre H always borne on the eccentric GHK, and the star itself. And
the star in turn moves on the epicycle LM, regularly with respect to the diameter always pointing to centre D, and makes its returns at the rate of the mean
cycle of the anomaly with respect to the sun, moving eastward in the order of
the signs at the apogee L.

Lest the reader be lost in the welter of circles, the proposed motions
will be recapitulated. The earth (Fig. 6-5) is assumed to be located at the
fixed point *E* ("the center of the ecliptic" circle which is not shown).
The planet is carried on the epicycle *ML* rotating at a constant rate with
respect to the radial line *DMHL*, thereby producing the observed retrograde motion. The epicycle is carried on the deferent *GBK* ("the sphere
of the planet") but does not move uniformly with respect to the center
F of the deferent — but instead moves uniformly with respect to the sym-
metrically offset point *D*, which is called the equant. Then the whole sys-

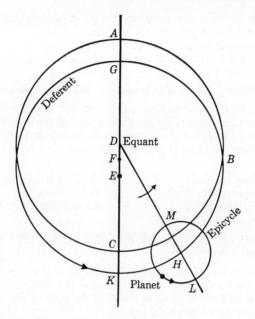

Figure 6-5. *Ptolemaic planetary motion.*

tem built around the line $AGDFECK$ moves slowly eastward at the rate of about a degree per century. This last motion was necessary since it was known that the vernal equinox (the position of the sun among the fixed stars on the first day of spring) was slowly moving westward. The motion proposed for Mercury by Ptolemy was even more complicated since the equant itself moved upon a small circle. However it can be seen that with a suitable combination of enough circles, almost any observed apparent motion could be accounted for. The reader is referred to the highly simplified drawing of the Ptolemaic system, Figure 7-2, page 108.

STUDY QUESTIONS

1. Days are equinoctial when the sun
   a. rises due east of an observer on the equator
   b. rises due east of an observer 30°N of the equator
   c. is situated on the celestial equator.
   The correct answer is

       (1) a   (2) b   (3) c   (4) a and c   (5) a, b, and c.

2. The observed contrary movement of the planets
   a. is along the celestial equator
   b. is at the same rate for the different planets
   c. is at a constant but different rate for each planet.
   The correct answer is

       (1) a   (2) b   (3) c   (4) a and c   (5) none of them.

3. According to Ptolemy, any meridian is a great circle which
   a. passes through the poles of the ecliptic
   b. is perpendicular to the plane of the horizon
   c. cuts in half the hemisphere below the horizon.
   The correct answer is

   (1) a   (2) b   (3) c   (4) b and c   (5) a, b, and c.

4. Ptolemy noted two prime movements in the sky. All celestial objects could
   have their motions essentially parallel to one of the two common circles.
   Match each of the celestial objects of List I with its common circle from
   List II. Choices from List II may be used more than once.

I	II
a. Sun (annual)	A. Celestial equator
b. Moon (monthly)	B. Horizon
c. Sirius (daily)	C. Ecliptic

   The correct matching is

   (1) aA bB cC   (2) aA bA cB   (3) aC bA cC   (4) aC bC cA
   (5) aC bB cA.

5. Ptolemy was aware of the relationship between the number of hours of
   daylight in the longest day of the year and the observer's latitude. What
   would be the latitude of an observer if, at the time of the summer solstice,
   he experienced 12 hours of daylight?

   (1) 0°   (2) 23½°N   (3) 60°N   (4) 45°S   (5) 90°N or S.

   *6–7. The second, or contrary, motion of the planets, Ptolemy notes,
   ". . . is different from the general movement of the universe, and
   . . . it is made around the poles of the oblique circle . . ."*

6. The oblique circle to which Ptolemy refers is known today as the

   (1) equator   (2) meridian   (3) hour circle   (4) ecliptic   (5) vernal
   equinox.

7. How far are the poles of the oblique circle from the celestial poles?

   (1) 0°   (2) 23½°   (3) 30°   (4) 66⅔°   (5) 90°.

8. Ptolemy notes four conditions which must be satisfied in making an explanation of the observed movements of the sun and planets. Which one
   of the following is *not* a condition set forth by Ptolemy?

   (1) The celestial objects move in paths which are generated by
       combinations of circular motions.
   (2) The earth is stationary.
   (3) The earth is located nearly at the center of the orbits of the
       celestial objects.
   (4) The celestial objects move around their various circles at an-
       gular speeds that are constant with respect to specified points
       of reference.
   (5) The sun moves on an epicycle.

9. The eccentric hypothesis of Ptolemy was used to explain

   (1) the nonuniform motion of the sun
   (2) the diurnal paths of the stars
   (3) the retrograde motion of the planets
   (4) the formation of craters on the moon
   (5) the occurrence of circumpolar stars.

10–13. Refer to the diagram below. It represents Ptolemy's idea of the circular orbit of the sun in its contrary motion. Six points on this orbit have been labelled by the numbers 1 through 6. The following questions are to be answered by referring to one of these six orbital positions.

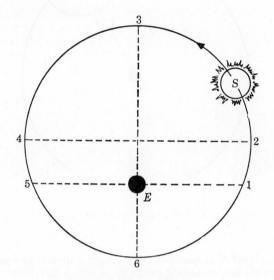

For problems 10–13.

10. The point of the sun's orbit where the sun is farthest from the earth is

     (1) 1   (2) 2   (3) 3   (4) 4   (5) 5.

11. The point of the sun's orbit where its movement relative to the stars is fastest is

     (1) 1   (2) 2   (3) 6   (4) 4   (5) 5.

12. The point of the sun's orbit where its movement relative to the stars is slowest is

     (1) 1   (2) 6   (3) 3   (4) 4   (5) 5.

13. The point of the sun's orbit known as perigee is

     (1) 1   (2) 2   (3) 3   (4) 6   (5) 5.

14. Ptolemy's explanation of the retrograde motion of the planets was based on which hypothesis?

     (1) eccentric.   (2) equinoctial.   (3) epicycle.   (4) equatorial.
     (5) equant.

15–17. Refer to the diagram on page 92. It represents a simplified version of the Ptolemaic scheme of epicycles as viewed from Polaris. Two possible positions of the planet (P) are indicated by the numbers 1 and 2. The following questions refer to those two orbital positions. Assume the linear speed of P around the epicycle is four times the linear speed of C along the deferent.

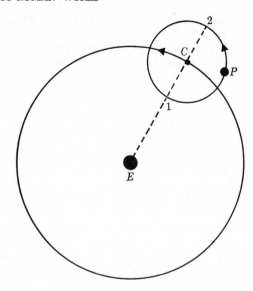

For problems 15–17.

15. When the planet is at position 1 its apparent motion as viewed from the earth *E* would be proceeding primarily in which direction?

 (1) north   (2) east   (3) south   (4) west   (5) northeast.

16. When the planet is at position 2 its apparent motion viewed from the earth *E* would be proceeding primarily in which direction?

 (1) south   (2) northwest   (3) east   (4) west   (5) north.

17. Which of the following terms is correctly associated with the type of motion the planet apparently undergoes when it is at position 1?

 (1) absolute motion   (2) retrograde motion   (3) vertical motion
 (4) direct motion   (5) perpetual motion.

18. Can it be inferred whether Ptolemy believes that the moon, sun, planets, and the stars are made of material like the earth, or whether he assumes that they are completely different in composition?

19. Are the poles of the " spheres of the planets " the same as the ecliptic poles?

20. Might there be any connection between theories of mechanics (physics) and theories about astronomy?

21. If Ptolemy did not know the radii of his deferents, just what could he determine about the dimensions of his system?

22. We have seen how Ptolemy's theories reflect the philosophy of his age. Can you list any similar items of the philosophy of our own times which mold every opinion which we might form of the physical universe? These basic concepts are often so much a part of us that we are not really aware of them.

23. How did Ptolemy know that the sun made " equal oscillation to the north and south of the equator "?

PART THREE

THE MEDIEVAL PERIOD AND ITS SEQUEL

In the 3rd century of our epoch the Hsiung-nu, known to us as the Huns, feeling the pressure of the Chinese and the Mongols to their east, drove westward with horse, bow, and dagger. The Huns conquered and destroyed the Alani, crossed the Volga, and defeated the Ostrogoths in the Ukraine. The Ostrogoths fled westwards into the lands of the Visigoths north of the Danube. The Visigoths were forced westward into the lands of the Thuringians, Burgundians, Angles, Saxons, Jutes, Frisians, Gepidee, Quadi, Vandals, Alemanni, Suevi, Lombards, Franks, et al. Like a gigantic game of falling dominoes the tribes were in motion. Being pushed by fiercer people on their east, they fell in turn upon the people to the west.

THE DECLINE OF ROME

For nearly two hundred years the tribes pressed upon the Roman borders. Rome withdrew troops from quiet areas to rush them to threatened areas. Here and there the Germanic tribes were admitted to the border regions of the Empire as colonists. More and more of the Germans were hired as mercenaries to fill out the Roman Army. Parts of the Western Empire — Gaul, Spain, Africa — fell to Franks, Visigoths, Vandals, and Ostrogoths. Finally in 455 Gaiseric sacked Rome itself. This, however, was not the death of the Roman Empire. The Empire died slowly. At the beginning of the 4th century, Constantine had moved the capital of the Empire to his new city of Nova Roma, or Constantinople as it was to become. As the Byzantine Empire it still contained Egypt, Asia Minor, and the Grecian peninsula. This remnant of Imperial Rome shrank under Moslem assault and finally fell to the Christian West in 1204 as the ignoble culmination of the Fourth Crusade! The Christian West conquered the Christian East and succeeded where the Moslem had failed. But even the final fall of Constantinople to the Turks in 1453 did not end the ancient Empire. As the Holy Roman Empire, it survived in concept to almost our own day.

This period of about a thousand years during which the Roman Empire steadily lost ground in both authority and territory was the Medieval period — the Middle Ages. Knowledge did not vanish overnight anymore than did the Roman Empire. While Gaiseric was sacking Rome, the universities in Athens were in full operation as was the Museum at Alexandria. But the Athenian universities, the Alexandrian Museum, and most of the custodians of the ancient classical culture were pagan. Perhaps this is why they were resented by the newly converted Christian population. Some were like Theophilus, Patriarch of Alexandria, who may have loved God, as indicated by his name, but did not always love men. It was Theophilus who burned to the ground the pagan temple and the library of Serapis in 389. The library was one of the most important in the classical world. The Archbishop Cyril of Alexandria is thought to have instigated in 415 the murder of Hypatia, one of the last professors of the Museum. She was pulled from her carriage, carried into a nearby Christian church and torn into pieces by a mob. We are rightly shocked by the burning of the Library at Alexandria in 641 by the Moslems, but contemporary evidence indicates that most of the library had been destroyed long before 641 by a fanaticism which feared paganism far more than it did ignorance.

To a great degree the classic culture killed itself. The people in their enthusiasm for their newly acquired Christianity destroyed pagan temples and idols, which were sometimes the highest works of Greek art; burned the pagan books, which were often the accumulated heritage of Greek learning; and persecuted the surviving pagans, who included some of the Greek scholars. They were equally abusive to each other. The expulsion of successive waves of heretics from the Christian world is responsible in part for the transmission of the Greek learning to the Arabian world. Nor did the Germanic tribes eating away at the remains of the Roman Empire help the preservation of knowledge. Burning, looting, and killing are not the best environment for the pursuit of learning. By the 8th century very little of the classic culture was left in Western Europe. Pliny's *Natural History* was one of the few books that survived from classical times. Parts of Aristotle's logical works were translated into Latin with commentaries by Boethius in the 6th century. These along with a collection of popular writings by Cassiodorus and the " Etymologies " of Isidore, both written in the 6th century, made up the " scientific " book-shelf of the Medieval monastery. There was more to be had in Byzantium, but differences in language and religion locked it away from Europe. There was a rich and active culture in Arabian lands, but there was even a higher wall between Christendom and Islam.

THE HIATUS IN SCIENCE

In retrospect there seems but a short distance from Archimedes to Galileo. Galileo reads like the direct continuation of Archimedes' thought, but the step forward which Galileo took opened the doors to modern science. However Galileo published his *Two New Sciences* in 1638, whereas Archimedes died in 212 B.C. Why the hiatus of nearly two thousand years? The Greco-Roman world had continued in full vigor for at least another six hundred years. Why didn't some Greek or Roman take that one small additional step which would have initiated the modern world so many centuries earlier? While any answer that we might give to this tantalizing question can only be supposition, the reason might well have been the wide-spread institution of slavery in the classical world. Ancient society was carried on the back of a slave. All of the work of the classical world, the building, the baking, the hewing of wood, and the carrying of water, was done by a great multitude of slaves who outnumbered the free citizenry by a factor of four or five. An ancient Greek publicly bewailed his poverty, pointing out that he had only five slaves to do his work for him! Under these social conditions it is little wonder that the work-a-day world came to be regarded as demeaning and fit only for slaves. The true life of a gentleman was to be lived entirely in the mind without soiling the hands. Archimedes was an excellent engineer almost in spite of himself. In the stress of the Roman attack on his native Syracuse he invented enough new machines of war to keep the invaders at bay until hunger itself reduced his city. But Archimedes appears to have been ashamed of his inventions and refused to publish any account of them. He wished to be remembered instead for his work in pure geometry.

Science, then, in the ancient world, came to be a purely intellectual activity which served to amuse the privileged classes and had no immediate relationship to the work-a-day world. This is in contrast to our current extremely close pairing of science and engineering, which is so typical of our modern world that most people are not even aware that there is a difference between the two! One of the goals of our modern world is to replace all of the cruder sorts of human labor with machinery. There was a different point of view in the Greco-Roman world since slaves were plentiful. The Emperor Vespasian had no interest in using the labor-saving hoisting machine offered him by its inventor for use in his building program. Vespasian said that he had plenty of man power and had no use for the machine!

On the contrary, Europe had a shortage of man power toward the close of the Middle Ages. The windmill and the water wheel served as two of the first machine replacements for human muscle. The use of the Saxon wheeled plow spread over Europe during the very depth of the Middle Ages. This plow allowed a deeper culture and a more intensive agriculture than the Roman plow which it replaced. The prosaic invention of the horse collar allowed the faster horse to be used for pulling the plow without choking him to death as with the Roman harness. All in all, medieval agriculture was many times more efficient and intensive than the Roman agriculture had been. The work was done in the main by serfs, who were not freemen, nor were they slaves. The serf had rights and some privileges and expected a few services from his liege lord. Moreover the growing cities with their beginning mercantile system needed more and ever more man power. Most of the young cities offered freedom to any serf who left his manor and sought them out. This continuing replacement of human muscle by wind, animal, and water power marks the beginning of both the scientific and the industrial revolutions, whose symbiotic relationship makes modern times. On the other hand, the Greco-Roman world, after achieving some very admirable intellectual heights, was content to slumber on for many centuries while the slaves dealt with the real world.

THE FLOWERING OF THE ARABIC WORLD

Mohammed was born in 570 in the Arabian peninsula near the Red Sea. With Mohammed was born one of the newest of the great universal religions. Soon Arabian armies poured out of their deserts with fast horse, sword, and Koran to conquer nearly all before them. Syria, Persia, part of India, Egypt, North Africa, and nearly all of Spain fell to them. Having turned the Mediterranean into a Moslem lake, Sicily and other islands fell to the followers of the Prophet. Finally they were stopped just short of the Pyrenees by the Franks and just at the edge of the Black Sea by Byzantium. The high point in territorial expansion was reached by about 750 with all of Islam under the Caliph at Baghdad.

With Empire, wealth, and stability came culture. The proven efficacy of the Greek medicine developed an interest in the other aspects of the Greek culture. By 830 al-Mamun established at Baghdad a " House of Wisdom " which was a combination scientific academy, astronomical observatory, public library, and a translation bureau busily at work translating every available Greek book into Arabic. At the head of the translating service was a Nestorian Christian, one of the "heretic" groups expelled from the Christian world, who was paid for his translated books by their weight in gold. By 850 most of the standard Greek works had been translated into Arabic. Now the Moslem, with his new leisure, discovered the same intoxication with things of the mind as had the ancient Greeks. In fact, the Arab regarded himself as the direct successor of the Greek. Ptolemy was translated. Further observations of the skies were made in well equipped observatories. New combinations of deferents and epicycles were calculated to better fit the observed phenomena. Galen was translated. The Arabic medicine was vigorous and practical-minded. Further case histories were compiled. Additional diseases and cures were carefully recorded. Strabo was translated and the Arabs wrote new and large geographies of their own travels over the immense spaces of Islam. Euclid was translated and the Moslems proved new theorems concerning the higher curves.

Yet the Arabian was not a servile imitator of the Greek culture. We are deeply indebted to him for introducing algebraic thinking into science rather than the geometric thinking which was characteristic of the Greeks. We remember Omar Khayyám as a poet. The Arabians honor him as a mathematician who solved quadratic equations. We are indebted to al-Khwarizmi for introducing us to the Hindu numerals. His treatise, *Al-Khwarizmi on the Numerals of the Indians* was translated eventually into Latin as *Algoritmi de numero Indorum,* from which Latin rendering of his name came our words algorithm and algorism which mean any arithmetical system based upon the decimal notation. The very essential zero may well have been a purely Arabic invention. The Arabic word " sifr " corresponds to our " cipher " and through a devious Latin and Italian route became our " zero." Our very word algebra is the Arabic " al-jabr." We can only take notice of a few Arabian scientists in this short summary. The great multitude of deserving men must pass without mention. Al-Biruni was a universal scholar. He wrote books about philosophy, history, geography, mathematics, astronomy, physics, and even found the time to compose a bit of verse. In astronomy he wrote that all of the appearances in the sky could be explained equally well by assuming that the earth rotates daily on its axis and moves annually in an orbit about the sun as by assuming the more generally accepted Ptolemaic system.

One of the two greatest Moslem thinkers was abu-Ali al-Husein ibn-Sina, or Avicenna, to give him the Latin name assigned to him by the European scholars who turned his works into Latin and studied them mightily. He wrote a hundred books on medicine and nearly every field of science and philosophy, as well as some excellent verse. Consider the following fragment from his hundred books, this portion dealing with the formation of mountains [1] :

Mountains may be due to two different causes. Either they are effects of upheavals of the crust of the earth, such as might occur during a violent earthquake, or they are the effect of water, which, cutting for itself a new route, has denuded the valleys, the strata being of different kinds, some soft, some hard. The winds and waters disintegrate the one, but leave the other intact. Most of the eminences of the earth have had this latter origin. It would require a long period of time for all such changes to be accomplished, during which the mountains themselves might be somewhat diminished in size. But that water has been the main cause of these effects is proved by the existence of fossil remains of aquatic and other animals on many mountains.

Avicenna tells us that he read Aristotle's *Metaphysics* forty times without understanding it until he came across a commentary by al-Farabi. Understanding came with a rush and he ran down into the streets and gave money to the poor in thanksgiving. One is reminded of Pythagoras and his sacrifice of one hundred oxen to the gods. He adopted the complete

---

[1] John William Draper, *History of the Intellectual Development of Europe,* Vol. 1, Harper & Brothers, Publishers, New York, 1918, p. 411.

Aristotelian system and adapted it to the needs of Mohammedanism, defining God as the First Cause and the Prime Mover of the Universe. His commentary was both brilliant and in excellent literary style. Roger Bacon accounted him as "the chief authority in philosophy after Aristotle" and St. Thomas Aquinas equated him with Plato.

The last great Moslem figure that we shall introduce is abu-al-Walid Muhammad-ibn-Rushd, or Averroës as his name was translated into Latin. Avicenna lived in the extreme eastern part of the Moslem Empire at the time of its greatest intellectual activity (ca. 1000). Averroës lived in Moslem Spain at the close of the 12th century when the Christian forces were slowly but surely reconquering the Iberian Peninsula. Averroës served as chief justice of Seville and Cordova and then was called to Morocco by the Emir as his court physician. At the request of Emir abu-Yaqub, Averroës undertook to write a clear exposition of Aristotle. For each major work of Aristotle he wrote (1) a summary, (2) a brief commentary, and finally (3) a detailed commentary for the advanced student. When science and religion did not entirely agree, he had no hesitancy in tailoring his Mohammedanism to fit the Procrustean bed of Aristotle. Averroës certainly implied the useful doctrine later proposed by certain Christian Scholastics that a given proposition might be true in philosophy but false in religion, a most excellent way of having one's cake and consuming it as well! Averroës adopted the Neoplatonic idea of the active and the passive intellect. The active intellect was the capacity to feel and to reason and was part of the body and perished with it. On the other hand, the passive intellect was a fragment of the divine and was common to all men but had no individuality of its own. Thus Averroës argued against individual immortality and placed himself outside of the orthodox Mohammedan pale. Although his works were rejected by the latter-day Moslem world, he was treasured in Europe. Roger Bacon ranked Averroës third in line after Aristotle and Avicenna. St. Thomas Aquinas was ordered by his Dominican superior to write his *Summae* as a Christian rejoinder to the alluring attractiveness of Averroës' *Commentaries*. Aquinas adopted much of Averroës' work into his own system but made the necessary exceptions to fit a more orthodox Christianity.

Our deep and variegated debt to the Arabian culture can be sensed by listing just a few of the words in our language which came from the Arabic: orange, lemon, sugar, syrup, sherbert, julep, elixir, jar, azure, arabesque, mattress, sofa, muslin, satin, fustian, bazaar, caravan, check, tariff, traffic, magazine, risk, sloop, barge, cable, admiral, azimuth, alembic, zenith, almanac, and many, many more. Most of these words entered our language when the original Latin translators of Arabic books could not find a Latin equivalent for a given term so they simply transliterated it into a pseudo-Latin form. Then why did such a dynamic culture which was so far ahead of the European for the four hundred years between 800 and 1200 slack off into stagnation?

It is again dangerous to give too pat an answer to this vital question. Certainly the Crusades hurt the Moslem world, but this was merely a bee sting as compared to the fury of Mongols in the first half of the 13th century. The Mongols came to destroy, not to conquer. They fell upon the eastern part of Islam, and swept through to Baghdad itself. They left behind them irrigation canals ruined, cities burned to the ground, and inhabitants of all ages and sexes slaughtered. Only pyramids of skulls remained to survey the ravished land. This part of the world, the former homeland of Avicenna, has never fully recovered even down to our day. Again, it is possible that the Arabian world destroyed itself much as did the Greco-Roman world at an earlier time. Seventy years before the Mongols came, the Caliph Mustanjid in 1140 at Baghdad ordered that all of the philosophical books of Avicenna and other free-thinking philosophers should be burned. At the other end of the Moslem Empire in 1194 this action was echoed by the Emir abu-Yusuf Yaqub al-Mansur at Seville who ordered the burning of all the books of Averroës except a few harmless ones on natural science. Furthermore, he made the study of philosophy illegal and urged his subjects to burn all books of philosophy irrespective of author. The scholar ibn-Habib was put to death under this Emir for the crime of studying philosophy! This represented the complete triumph of thorough orthodoxy in religious thought and the corresponding utter suppression of all independent thought. In this particular denouement, science also perished.

THE AWAKENING OF EUROPE

Shortly after A.D. 1000, Europe began to come to life. It is a bit frustrating to look over history and not to find a unique event or a specific cause which might be alleged to be the beginning of the awakening. About 1103 Abélard came to Paris as a young man obsessed with logic and taught in the cathedral school of Notre Dame. His intellectual resources were the scraps of Aristotle, Plato, Boethius, Cassiodorus, et al. which his medieval predecessors had fed upon for the previous five hundred years. But Abélard gloried in the power of reason and was not willing to accept anything on faith. His lectures must have been brilliant, for students followed him about, even into remote rural areas, during his troubled life. His students in turn became great teachers, and so did their students for many academic generations. Abélard might be considered the intellectual founder of the University of Paris. He also found time for his bittersweet romance with Héloïse so well-known to all romantics.

Certainly the Crusades can be credited with helping to prepare the ground so that the new European intellectualism would continue to grow. Jerusalem was a holy city for three great faiths. Until 1070 Christians were free to make their pilgrimages to the Holy Land with every encouragement from the authorities. But in 1070 Jerusalem was captured by the

Turks who with the fanaticism of new converts to Islam began to persecute the Christians. Pope Urban II issued a call to all Christians to unite and expel the infidels from the Holy Land. The First Crusade from 1095 to 1099 went rather well. Jerusalem and most of the coastal cities were taken by the European army. In true medieval style, the conquered land was divided up into semi-independent dukedoms, and feudalism was imposed upon the inhabitants, Moslem and Christian alike. The Arabian world regrouped to win back its lost provinces and the Second Crusade was launched in 1146 to shore up the weak Latin Kingdom of Jerusalem. It was a fiasco with great losses due to both climate and Moslems. The Third Crusade, begun in 1189 and led by Richard the Lion-Hearted against Saladin, was a bright page in medieval chivalry but a military failure. The Fourth Crusade of 1202 was venially turned by Venice into assaults upon the Christian cities of Zara, Hungary's only seaport, and Constantinople. Not one Moslem was killed. The Holy Land was never sighted. There were further Crusades which were minor. The heart had gone out of the cause. Finally in 1228, Frederick II, Holy Roman Emperor, King of Sicily, landed in Syria and negotiated in Arabic an extremely favorable treaty with the Saracen commander, al-Kamil. Frederick had grown up in the polyglot island of Sicily and knew and appreciated Arabic both as a language and as a culture. Pope Gregory IX was furious. Frederick was under a ban of excommunication. The Pope refused to ratify the treaty. This was unfortunate since the proffered treaty contained everything that the West had desired. The European holdings in the Holy Land were slowly eroded away and in a few more years nothing remained of the united efforts of all of Europe.

The failure of the Crusades was a shock to Europe and a defeat for orthodoxy. The Christians had lost and the Moslems had won. The people began to wonder whether the Crusades had actually been blessed by God. Moreover Saladin, al-Kamil, and other Moslems were seen to be gentlemen of the highest type. How could a religion that was so wrong produce such admirable personalities? Furthermore, it was obvious that the Arabian medicine was superior to the European. With the absorption of Moslem medical arts and physicians into Europe came the other elements of Arabic culture. The failure of the Crusades made impossible the continued unthinking acceptance of medieval orthodoxy. The need for a rethinking was apparent. The new ideas introduced from Islam gave material for the rethinking.

The translation of first Arabic and then Greek books into Latin was another step into the modern world. As Christian armies drove the Moslems out of Spain and Sicily, the newly conquered areas were found to be filled with Arabic books and scholars. Soon translating projects were under way in both lands. Toledo in Spain was a center for translations from the Arabic with Gerard of Cremona translating al-Khwarizmi, al-Kindi, Rhazes, Alfarabi, Avicenna, Aristotle, Euclid, Archimedes, Ptolemy, and many others from Arabic to Latin. While Gerard's was probably the greatest single-handed translation effort, others were at work in Spain and Sicily translating all available books both from Arabic and directly from the Greek into the Latin which was then read all over Europe. This flood of new books into Europe in the 12th and 13th centuries was the fuse which kindled the Renaissance in the 14th century.

Still another factor in the spreading of the enlightenment was the founding and growth of European universities. There had always been schools in Europe to train a literate clergy. Beginning with the 11th and 12th centuries we begin to hear of the cathedral schools of Notre Dame, Chartres, Canterbury, and elsewhere. In the 12th and 13th centuries the students increased in number and could no longer be accommodated in the naves of the cathedrals. Additional lecture halls were rented in the student areas of the cities. Guilds of teachers were formed. Students were organized into colleges with deans and rectors. The University of Paris was the simple outgrowth of the cathedral school of Notre Dame and both were under the same bishop at first. In 1240 Robert Grosseteste was at once the leading physical scientist in Europe, " Master of the Oxford Schools," and Bishop of Lincoln. The young universities became increasingly more secular, particularly when the towns began paying the salaries of the professors, finding as ever that the presence of students is a definite economic advantage! With increasing freedom from both hierarchical and political control, scholars became free to think.

Thus slowly and hesitantly modern times began in Europe. The thought of Aristotle was once more vital in Europe. St. Thomas Aquinas forged a workable union of Aristotle and orthodox Christianity. It was a complete system which undertook to explain all of life. In broad outline it was the same beguiling system which had so completely charmed the Greeks, the Romans, the Moslems, and our own European forbears. But in the height of the Renaissance, Aristotelianism was successfully attacked for the first time in two thousand years and overthrown part by part. In the section which follows we shall see the attack on the Ptolemaic astronomy by Copernicus, Kepler, and Galileo. In Part IV of this book we shall see the successful attack on Aristotle's mechanics by Galileo and Newton. Never again would the world be explained by a single unified system. Today within a single field of science, closely related phenomena are often explained by differing and even contradictory theories. The empiricism of today is esthetically ugly, but it works!

7

The Copernican Revolution

● Nicholas Copernicus (Fig. 7-1) was born on February 19, 1473 in the city of Thorn on the Vistula, somewhere in the no-man's land between Prussia and Poland. His uncle was the Bishop of Ermland, and was essentially an independent princeling. Copernicus had a long and variegated education both at the University of Cracow and at the University of Bologna, Europe's leading university at that time. He returned home with the degree of Doctor of Canon Law and with considerable study in medicine and in "mathematics." He was appointed canon at the Cathedral of Frauenburg by his uncle and was thereby well fixed for life.

Between attending to his ecclesiastical duties, which were light, and helping his uncle govern the principality, he found ample time for astronomical observations and speculation. According to his disciple, Rheticus, Copernicus became affronted at the Ptolemaic idea of equants and, accordingly, sought a better geometry to explain the appearances. Copernicus wished his circles to turn on their centers rather than eccentrically. He was able to eliminate the equants by placing the sun at the center of the system, and in his early work to make do with only 34 circles for the solar system as compared to 79 circles required by Fracastoro to fit the Ptolemaic system.

Copernicus was a wise man who knew the age in which he lived. He quietly worked on his new system without making himself obvious to the authorities. Word about his work was bruited about Europe, notwithstanding. As the result of a direct inquiry, Copernicus wrote a letter, now known as the *Commentariolus* outlining his system. This letter was copied by hand by interested people which included Kepler and circulated to a small audience around Europe. The first half of the *Commentariolus* is reproduced here. In it Copernicus starts by objecting to the Ptolemaic equant, and then he sets forth a "more reasonable" system in his list of seven assumptions.

Figure 7-1. *Niklas Kippernigk, better known as Nicholas Copernicus (1473–1543).*

THE COMMENTARIOLUS [1]

Nicholas Copernicus

Sketch of his Hypotheses for the Heavenly Motions

Our ancestors assumed, I observe, a large number of celestial spheres for this reason especially, to explain the apparent motion of the planets by the principle of regularity. For they thought it altogether absurd that a heavenly body, which is a perfect sphere, should not always move uniformly. They saw that by connecting and combining regular motions in various ways they could make any body appear to move to any position.

Callippus and Eudoxus, who endeavored to solve the problem by the use of concentric spheres, were unable to account for all the planetary movements; they had to explain not merely the apparent revolutions of the planets but also the fact that these bodies appear to us sometimes to mount higher in the heavens, sometimes to descend; and this fact is incompatible with the principle of concentricity. Therefore it seemed better to employ eccentrics and epicycles, a system which most scholars finally accepted.

Yet the planetary theories of Ptolemy and most other astronomers, although consistent with the numerical data, seemed likewise to present no small difficulty. For these theories were not adequate unless certain equants were also conceived; it then appeared that a planet moved with uniform velocity neither on its deferent nor about the center of its epicycle. Hence a system of this sort seemed neither sufficiently absolute nor sufficiently pleasing to the mind.

Having become aware of these defects, I often considered whether there could perhaps be found a more reasonable arrangement of circles, from which

[1] Nicholas Copernicus, *The Commentariolus* from *Three Copernican Treatises*, translated by Edward Rosen, Columbia University Press, New York, 1939, pp. 57–68.

every apparent inequality would be derived and in which everything would move uniformly about its proper center, as the rule of absolute motion requires. After I had addressed myself to this very difficult and almost insoluble problem, the suggestion at length came to me how it could be solved with fewer and much simpler constructions than were formerly used, if some assumptions (which are called axioms) were granted me. They follow in this order.

Assumptions

1. There is no one center of all the celestial circles or spheres.
2. The center of the earth is not the center of the universe, but only of gravity and of the lunar sphere.
3. All the spheres revolve about the sun as their mid-point, and therefore the sun is the center of the universe.
4. The ratio of the earth's distance from the sun to the height of the firmament is so much smaller than the ratio of the earth's radius to its distance from the sun that the distance from the earth to the sun is imperceptible in comparison with the height of the firmament.
5. Whatever motion appears in the firmament arises not from any motion of the firmament, but from the earth's motion. The earth together with its circumjacent elements performs a complete rotation on its fixed poles in a daily motion, while the firmament and highest heaven abide unchanged.
6. What appear to us as motions of the sun arise not from its motion but from the motion of the earth and our sphere, with which we revolve about the sun like any other planet. The earth has, then, more than one motion.
7. The apparent retrograde [2] and direct motion of the planets arises not from their motion but from the earth's. The motion of the earth alone, therefore, suffices to explain so many apparent inequalities in the heavens.

Having set forth these assumptions, I shall endeavor briefly to show how uniformity of the motions can be saved in a systematic way. However, I have thought it well, for the sake of brevity, to omit from this sketch mathematical demonstrations, reserving these for my larger work. But in the explanation of the circles I shall set down here the lengths of the radii; and from these the reader who is not unacquainted with mathematics will readily perceive how closely this arrangement of circles agrees with the numerical data and observations.

Accordingly, let no one suppose that I have gratuitously asserted, with the Pythagoreans, the motion of the earth; strong proof will be found in my exposition of the circles. For the principal arguments by which the natural philosophers attempt to establish the immobility of the earth rest for the most part on the appearances; it is particularly such arguments that collapse here, since I treat the earth's immobility as due to an appearance.

The Order of the Spheres

The celestial spheres are arranged in the following order. The highest is the immovable sphere of the fixed stars, which contains and gives position to all things. Beneath it is Saturn, which Jupiter follows, then Mars. Below Mars is

---

[2] See Galileo's Copernican explanation of retrograde motion which is excerpted from his *Dialogue Concerning the Two Chief World Systems* in Chapter 10.

the sphere on which we revolve; then Venus; last is Mercury. The lunar sphere revolves about the center of the earth and moves with the earth like an epicycle. In the same order also, one planet surpasses another in speed of revolution, according as they trace greater or smaller circles. Thus Saturn completes its revolution in thirty years, Jupiter in twelve, Mars in two and one-half, and the earth in one year; Venus in nine months, Mercury in three.

The Apparent Motions of the Sun

The earth has three motions. First, it revolves annually in a great circle about the sun in the order of the signs, always describing equal arcs in equal times; the distance from the center of the circle to the center of the sun is 1/25 of the radius of the circle. The radius is assumed to have a length imperceptible in comparison with the height of the firmament; consequently the sun appears to revolve with this motion, as if the earth lay in the center of the universe. However, this appearance is caused by the motion not of the sun but of the earth, so that, for example, when the earth is in the sign of Capricornus, the sun is seen diametrically opposite in Cancer, and so on. On account of the previously mentioned distance of the sun from the center of the circle, this apparent motion of the sun is not uniform, the maximum inequality being 2 1/6°. The line drawn from the sun through the center of the circle [3] is invariably directed to-

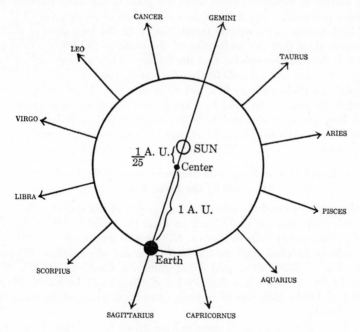

For footnote 3.

---

[3] The meaning of this passage is not too clear. To agree with the astronomical observations, the line from the center of the earth's orbit through the sun would have to point in the direction of Gemini. The sun is seen in Gemini during the summer when the sun is furthest from the earth.

ward a point of the firmament about 10° west of the more brilliant of the two bright stars in the head of Gemini; therefore when the earth is opposite this point, and the center of the circle lies between them, the sun is seen at its greatest distance from the earth. In this circle, then, the earth revolves together with whatever else is included within the lunar sphere.

The second motion, which is peculiar to the earth, is the daily rotation on the poles in the order of the signs, that is, from west to east. On account of this rotation the entire universe appears to revolve with enormous speed. Thus does the earth rotate together with its circumjacent waters and encircling atmosphere.

The third is the motion in declination. For the axis of the daily rotation is not parallel to the axis of the great circle, but is inclined to it at an angle that intercepts a portion of a circumference, in our time about 23½°. Therefore, while the center of the earth always remains in the plane of the ecliptic, that is, in the circumference of the great circle, the poles of the earth rotate, both of them describing small circles about centers equidistant from the axis of the great circle. The period of this motion is not quite a year and is nearly equal to the annual revolution on the great circle. But the axis of the great circle is invariably directed toward the points of the firmament which are called the poles of the ecliptic. In like manner the motion in declination, combined with the annual motion in their joint effect upon the poles of the daily rotation, would keep these poles constantly fixed at the same points of the heavens, if the periods of both motions were exactly equal. Now with the long passage of time it has become clear that this inclination of the earth to the firmament changes. Hence it is the common opinion that the firmament has several motions in conformity with a law not yet sufficiently understood. But the motion of the earth can explain all these changes in a less surprising way. I am not concerned to state what the path of the poles is. I am aware that, in lesser matters, a magnetized iron needle always points in the same direction. It has nevertheless seemed a better view to ascribe the changes to a sphere, whose motion governs the movements of the poles. This sphere must doubtless be sublunar.

Equal Motion Should Be Measured Not by the Equinoxes but by the Fixed Stars

Since the equinoxes and the other cardinal points of the universe shift considerably, whoever attempts to derive from them the equal length of the annual revolution necessarily falls into error. Different determinations of this length were made in different ages on the basis of many observations. Hipparchus computed it as 365¼ days, and Albategnius the Chaldean as 365^d 5^h 46^m, that is, 13⅗^m or 13⅓^m less than Ptolemy. Hispalensis increased Albategnius's estimate by the 20th part of an hour, since he determined the tropical year as 365^d 5^h 49^m.

Lest these differences should seem to have arisen from errors of observation, let me say that if anyone will study the details carefully, he will find that the discrepancy has always corresponded to the motion of the equinoxes. For when the cardinal points moved 1° in 100 years, as they were found to be moving in the age of Ptolemy, the length of the year was then what Ptolemy stated it to be. When however in the following centuries they moved with greater rapidity, being opposed to lesser motions, the year became shorter; and this decrease corresponded to the increase in precession. For the annual motion was completed in a shorter time on account of the more rapid recurrence of the equinoxes. Therefore the derivation of the equal length of the year from the fixed stars is more accurate. I used Spica Virginis and found that the year has always been 365 days, 6 hours, and about 10 minutes, which is also the estimate of the ancient Egyptians. The same method must be employed also with the other motions of the planets, as is shown by their apsides, by the fixed laws of their motion in the firmament, and by heaven itself with true testimony.

The third motion of the earth (motion in declination) requires some explanation. Copernicus thought that a planet should move in its orbit like the bob of a conical pendulum. Thus if the north pole of the axis of the earth is inclined toward the sun by 23½° as it is in midsummer, then without a "motion in declination," it would always be inclined toward the sun by 23½°. Since the angle of inclination toward the sun changes throughout the year, there must be a third motion. Moreover, since the advance of the equinoxes was well-known to Copernicus, he assumed that the period of this third motion was just a little less than a year, for if the third motion had a period of exactly one year, the direction of the earth's axis would be unchanging in space and there would be no motion of the ecliptic poles and precession of the equinoxes.

Ptolemy's great authority, even over Copernicus, is evident in the discussion of the length of the year of the seasons which is the time from the sun's passage from one vernal equinox to the next. Copernicus measured this tropical year as 365 days, 6 hours, and 10 minutes. However, Ptolemy had reported a considerably different value. Copernicus does not conclude that Ptolemy's value was faulty, but that the actual length of the year is changing. Copernicus had been invited by the Pope to revise the existing calendar, since he was recognized as the leading astronomer of his time, but for the preceding reason had concluded that calendar revision was impossible until the "variability" of the year's duration could be ascertained.

Ptolemy's authority is also evident in the last portion of the *Commentariolus* which will not be quoted. In this last part, he describes the presumed motions of the various planets. Copernicus, like a good Ptolemaic disciple, assumes that the planets move in some combination of circles, namely a deferent and several epicycles. Figure 7-3, page 108, is a simplified drawing of the Copernican system (compare Fig. 7-2). The exterior planets — Mars, Jupiter, and Saturn — are assumed to move in deferents having various centers with none centering on the sun. The planets move on epicycles which are themselves carried on other epicycles. The systems actually proposed by Copernicus were something like that one actually drawn for our moon, but have been simplified down to a single epicycle in the illustration. The systems proposed for the interior planets Venus and Mercury are even more complicated since there are now central circles upon which the centers of the deferents run. The actual theoretical paths produced by these various combinations of circles are oval orbits not centered upon the sun. It was Kepler, not Copernicus, who took the next step away from Ptolemy.

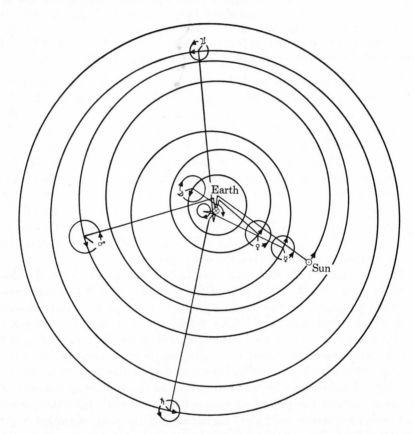

Figure 7-2. *The Ptolemaic System. This drawing and Figure 7-3 are designed to point out how similar in complexity were the Ptolemaic and Copernican systems. Even a cursory glance convinces one that neither system is essentially simpler geometrically than its competitor. Drawings cannot be made accurate in radial dimensions, but special care has been taken properly to orient the centers of the planetary orbits relative to the zodiac. Thus, if one traces in the Ptolemaic diagram the radial line from the sun to the point under "A" in the word "Earth," the point which is the center of the sun's orbit, it is seen to be between the centers of rotation of Venus and Mars, precisely as Ptolemy's geocentric theory requires. The relative senses of rotation of the epicycles on their deferent circles and the planets on the epicycles are indicated by the arrows. The planetary distances remain arbitrary, which is not so in the Copernican system. Reprinted from "Dialogue on the Great World Systems" by Giorgio de Santillana (trans.), by permission of The University of Chicago Press. Drawings by William D. Stahlman. Copyright 1955 by The University of Chicago. All rights reserved. Copyright 1955 under the International Copyright Union.*

This explanation of the orbits of the planets as produced by various combinations of circles is thoroughly in the Ptolemaic mold. There are only two departures from the system which had reigned for over a thousand years:

(1) The sun, rather than the earth, was placed near the center of the planetary system. This important change of viewpoint made the earth simply another planet along with Mercury, Venus, Mars, Jupiter, and Saturn.

(2) There were no equants in the scheme of Copernicus. This was ap-

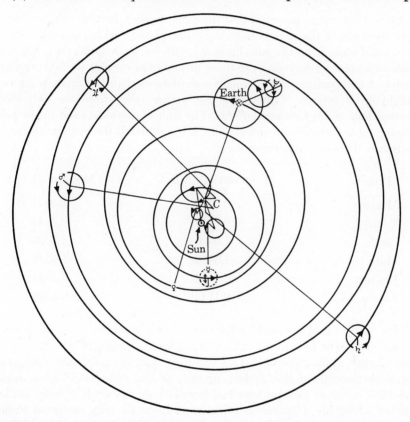

Figure 7-3. *The Heliocentric System as Conceived by Copernicus. In Copernicus' system the sun appears in the center of the stage, but the actual momentary centers of rotation of the planets cluster around the momentary center C of the earth's orbit. In this system, Mercury was handled in a unique fashion, librating on the center of an epicycle instead of traveling on the epicycle. The planetary symbols are as follows:*

| ☉ *Sun* | ♀ *Venus* | ⊕ *Earth* | ♃ *Jupiter* |
| ☿ *Mercury* | ☾ *Moon* | ♂ *Mars* | ♄ *Saturn* |

The epicycles preserved in the system accounted for the actual eccentricities of the orbits and could be discarded only after Kepler showed that the true orbits were elliptical.

parently the most important advantage in the mind of its creator. An argument could also have been made for the relative simplicity of the Copernican system. The concluding paragraph of his *Commentariolus* reads:

Then Mercury runs on seven circles in all; Venus on five; the earth on three, and round it the moon on four; finally Mars, Jupiter, and Saturn on five each. Altogether, therefore, thirty-four circles suffice to explain the entire structure of the universe and the entire ballet of the planets.

Since Copernicus assumed that the earth moved, he was able to calculate the radii of the deferents to the other planets, which is to say, their mean distances from the sun. Ptolemy, with his stationary earth, was not able to reach any decision as to these distances or even as to their relative order. A comparison of Copernicus' calculations with the modern figures might be of interest. Copernicus' figures are taken from the unquoted second half of his *Commentariolus*. The unit of distance used in the following table is the astronomical unit (A.U.) which is the average distance between the earth and the sun.

Planet	Copernicus (A.U.)	Modern (A.U.)
Mercury	0.3763	0.3871
Venus	0.7193	0.7233
Earth	1.0000	1.0000
Mars	1.5198	1.5237
Jupiter	5.2192	5.2028
Saturn	9.1743	9.5388

The second astronomical " publication " of Copernicus was also a personal letter sent to a former classmate. This document is now known as the " Letter against Werner." This was the extent of his astronomical publications throughout his lifetime, in spite of the strongest of pleas from scientists all over Europe who had heard about his work. Finally at the end of a long life, Copernicus relented and sent his manuscript off to his disciple Rheticus to be printed. The first copy of his book reached him on the day that he died, May 24, 1543. This was highly adroit timing. For publicly teaching similar views, Giordano Bruno was burned at the stake (1600), and Galileo was condemned by the Inquisition (1633).

Copernicus' book carried the short title of *De Revolutionibus Orbium Coelestium Libri VI* which is to say *Six Books Concerning the Revolutions of the Heavenly Spheres*. It is nearly as large a work as Ptolemy's book, and only a small part of Book I is reproduced here. This is the part which gives a general outline of his system and is peculiarly adapted to a direct comparison with Ptolemy's text. Of the five short sections given here, the first gives his proof that the universe is spherical. His proof is of the same nature as that of Ptolemy, except that it is probably not as good! In the next section he reasons correctly that the earth is spherical in form — but so did Ptolemy by nearly the same reasoning. In the third section he departs from Ptolemy by asking whether the daily motion observed is real or apparent. He decides that it is more plausible to conclude that the heavens are at rest while the earth is in motion, for " should not the motion be ascribed to the thing contained rather than the container? " In the fourth section on the basis of the physics and the philosophy of his day, he attempts to show that it is more logical for the earth than the celestial sphere to rotate. For if the celestial sphere were infinite in radius, its daily rotation would be at infinite linear speed, which is impossible. If the celestial sphere were finite in radius, then what lies outside this finite sphere and why? It is simpler to assume an infinite celestial sphere and " acknowledge the *appearance* of a daily revolution belongs to the heavens, its *actuality* to the earth." In the final section is an interesting suggestion that gravity may act in all celestial bodies and not only on the earth. Actually until the time of Newton, gravity was defined as that mysterious agency which caused bodies to fall toward the earth and only toward the earth. The Greek ideas as to the natural places of the four elements should be recalled in this connection.

Copernicus changed many details of his planetary system in his *De Revolutionibus*. There are now many more than thirty-four circles in his ballet of the planets. But these are detailed changes only and need not concern us. The *De Revolutionibus* is built on the same broad principles as the *Commentariolus*.

ON THE REVOLUTIONS OF THE HEAVENLY SPHERE [4]
Nicholas Copernicus

1. The World is Spherical

In the beginning we should remark that the world is globe-shaped; whether because this figure is the most perfect of all, as it is an integral whole and needs no joints; or because this figure is the one having the greatest volume and thus is especially suitable for that which is going to comprehend and conserve all things; or even because the separate parts of the world i.e., the sun, moon, and stars are viewed under such a form; or because everything in the world tends to be delimited by this form, as is apparent in the case of drops of water and other liquid bodies, when they become delimited of themselves. And so no one would hesitate to say that this form belongs to the heavenly bodies.

2. The Earth is Spherical Too

The Earth is globe-shaped too, since on every side it rests upon its centre. But it is not perceived straightway to be a perfect sphere, on account of the great

[4] Nicholas Copernicus, *Revolutions of Heavenly Spheres*, I, Great Books of the Western World, Vol. 16, Encyclopædia Britannica, Inc., pp. 511–512, 514–515, 518–519, 520–521.

height of its mountains and the lowness of its valleys, though they modify its universal roundness to only a very small extent.

That is made clear in this way. For when people journey northward from anywhere, the northern vertex of the axis of daily revolution gradually moves overhead, and the other moves downward to the same extent; and many stars situated to the north are seen not to set, and many to the south are seen not to rise any more. So Italy does not see Canopus, which is visible to Egypt. And Italy sees the last star of Fluvius, which is not visible to this region situated in a more frigid zone. Conversely, for people who travel southward, the second group of stars becomes higher in the sky; while those become lower which for us are high up.

Moreover, the inclinations of the poles have everywhere the same ratio with places at equal distances from the poles of the Earth and that happens in no other figure except the spherical. Whence it is manifest that the Earth itself is contained between the vertices and is therefore a globe.

Add to this the fact that the inhabitants of the East do not perceive the evening eclipses of the sun and moon; nor the inhabitants of the West, the morning eclipses; while of those who live in the middle region — some see them earlier and some later.

Furthermore, voyagers perceive that the waters too are fixed within this figure; for example, when land is not visible from the deck of a ship, it may be seen from the top of the mast, and conversely, if something shining is attached to the top of the mast, it appears to those remaining on the shore to come down gradually, as the ship moves from the land, until finally it becomes hidden, as if setting.

Moreover, it is admitted that water, which by its nature flows, always seeks lower places — the same way as earth — and does not climb up the shore any farther than the convexity of the shore allows. That is why the land is so much higher where it rises up from the ocean.

    ✻   ✻   ✻   ✻   ✻   ✻   ✻

5. Does The Earth Have a Circular Movement? And of Its Place

Now that it has been shown that the Earth too has the form of a globe, I think we must see whether or not a movement follows upon its form and what the place of the Earth is in the universe. For without doing that it will not be possible to find a sure reason for the movements appearing in the heavens. Although there are so many authorities for saying that the Earth rests in the centre of the world that people think the contrary supposition inopinable and even ridiculous; if however we consider the thing attentively, we will see that the question has not yet been decided and accordingly is by no means to be scorned. For every apparent change in place occurs on account of the movement either of the thing seen or of the spectator, or on account of the necessarily unequal movement of both. For no movement is perceptible relatively to things moved equally in the same directions — I mean relatively to the thing seen and the spectator. Now it is from the Earth that the celestial circuit is beheld and presented to our sight. Therefore, if some movement should belong to the Earth it will appear, in the parts of the universe which are outside, as the same movement but in the opposite direction, as though the things outside were passing over. And the daily revolution in especial is such a movement. For the daily revolution appears to carry the whole universe along, with the exception of the Earth and the things around it. And if you admit that the heavens possess none of this movement but that the Earth turns from west to east, you will find — if you make a serious examination — that as regards the apparent rising and setting of the sun, moon, and stars the case is so. And since it is the heavens which contain and embrace all things as the place common to the universe, it will not be clear at once why movement should not be assigned to the contained rather than to the container, to the thing placed rather than to the thing providing the place.

As a matter of fact, the Pythagoreans Herakleides and Ekphantus were of this opinion and so was Hicetas the Syracusan in Cicero; they made the Earth to revolve at the centre of the world. For they believed that the stars set by reason of the interposition of the Earth and that with cessation of that they rose again.

❀   ❀   ❀   ❀   ❀   ❀   ❀

8. Answer to the Aforesaid Reasons and Their Inadequacy

For these and similar reasons they say that the Earth remains at rest at the middle of the world and that there is no doubt about this. But if someone opines that the Earth revolves, he will also say that the movement is natural and not violent. Now things which are according to nature produce effects contrary to those which are violent. For things to which force or violence is applied get broken up and are unable to subsist for a long time. But things which are caused by nature are in a right condition and are kept in their best organization. Therefore Ptolemy had no reason to fear that the Earth and all things on the Earth would be scattered in a revolution caused by the efficacy of nature, which is greatly different from that of art or from that which can result from the genius of man. But why didn't he feel anxiety about the world instead, whose movement must necessarily be of greater velocity, the greater the heavens are than the Earth? Or have the heavens become so immense, because an unspeakably vehement motion has pulled them away from the centre, and because the heavens would fall if they came to rest anywhere else?

Surely if this reasoning were tenable, the magnitude of the heavens would extend infinitely. For the farther the movement is borne upward by the vehement force, the faster will the movement be, on account of the ever-increasing circumference which must be traversed every twenty-four hours: and conversely, the immensity of the sky would increase with the increase in movement. In this way, the velocity would make the magnitude increase infinitely, and the magnitude the velocity. And in accordance with the axiom of physics that *that which is infinite cannot be traversed or moved in any way*, then the heavens will necessarily come to rest.

But they say that beyond the heavens there isn't any body or place or void or anything at all; and accordingly it is not possible for the heavens to move outward: in that case it is rather surprising that something can be held together by nothing. But if the heavens were infinite and were finite only with respect to a hollow space inside, then it will be said with more truth that there is nothing outside the heavens, since anything which occupied any space would be in

them; but the heavens will remain immobile. For movement is the most powerful reason wherewith they try to conclude that the universe is finite.

But let us leave to the philosophers of nature the dispute as to whether the
world is finite or infinite, and let us hold as certain that the Earth is held together between its two poles and terminates in a spherical surface. Why therefore should we hesitate any longer to grant to it the movement which accords
naturally with its form, rather than put the whole world in a commotion — the
world whose limits we do not and cannot know? And why not admit that the
appearance of daily revolution belongs to the heavens but the reality belongs
to the Earth? And things are as when Aeneas said in Virgil: " We sail out of
the harbor, and the land and the cities move away." As a matter of fact, when
a ship floats on over a tranquil sea, all the things outside seem to the voyagers
to be moving in a movement which is the image of their own, and they think
on the contrary that they themselves and all the things with them are at rest.
So it can easily happen in the case of the movement of the Earth that the whole
world should be believed to be moving in a circle.

      ✻   ✻   ✻   ✻   ✻   ✻   ✻

9. Whether Many Movements Can Be Attributed to the Earth, and Concerning the Centre of the World

Therefore, since nothing hinders the mobility of the Earth, I think we should
now see whether more than one movement belongs to it, so that it can be regarded as one of the wandering stars. For the apparent irregular movement of
the planets and their variable distances from the Earth — which cannot be understood as occurring in circles homocentric with the Earth — make it clear
that the Earth is not the centre of their circular movements. Therefore, since
there are many centres, it is not foolhardy to doubt whether the centre of gravity of the Earth rather than some other is the centre of the world. I myself think
that gravity or heaviness is nothing except a certain natural appetency im-
planted in the parts by the divine providence of the universal Artisan, in order
that they should unite with one another in their oneness and wholeness and
come together in the form of a globe. It is believable that this affect is present
in the sun, moon, and the other bright planets and that through its efficacy
they remain in the spherical figure in which they are visible, though they nevertheless accomplish their circular movements in many different ways. Therefore if the Earth too possesses movements different from the one around its
centre, then they will necessarily be movements which similarly appear on the
outside in the many bodies; and we find the yearly revolution among these
movements. For if the annual revolution were changed from being solar to being terrestrial, and immobility were granted to the sun, the risings and settings
of the signs and of the fixed stars — whereby they become morning or evening
stars — will appear in the same way; and it will be seen that the stoppings,
retrogressions, and progressions of the wandering stars are not their own, but
are a movement of the Earth and that they borrow the appearances of this
movement. Lastly, the sun will be regarded as occupying the centre of the
world. And the ratio of order in which these bodies succeed one another and
the harmony of the whole world teaches us their truth, if only — as they say —
we would look at the thing with both eyes.

STUDY QUESTIONS

1. Select the correct statement or statements.
   a. Greek science was introduced into Europe by the return of the Crusaders from the Holy Lands.
   b. The expansion of the Arabian world to encompass the Mediterranean put an end to scientific advancement about the 8th century A.D.
   c. Much scientific knowledge was introduced into Europe from the Arabs in Spain.
   The correct answer is

   (1) a   (2) b   (3) c   (4) b and c   (5) none of them.

2. It seems probable that the effect of slavery in the Greco-Roman world upon the development of science was to
   a. accelerate it through providing more leisure time
   b. restrict it by discouraging the application of scientific ideas to everyday living.
   c. encourage it by the invention of labor-saving machinery which would replace expensive slaves whom only the rich could afford.
   The best answer is

   (1) a   (2) b   (3) c   (4) a and c   (5) none of them.

3. Which of the following Ptolemaic concepts did Copernicus discard?
   a. Circular motion.
   b. Revolving spheres (crystalline).
   c. Epicycles.
   The correct answer is

   (1) a   (2) b   (3) c   (4) a, b, and c   (5) none of them.

4. Copernicus outlined his explanations of observed planetary motions in his

   (1) *Commentariolus*   (2) *Almagest*   (3) *Worlds in Collision*
   (4) *Elements*   (5) *Principia*.

5. Which of the following best describes the extent of Copernicus' published writings?

   (1) He wrote many books and pamphlets.
   (2) He wrote several books and nothing else.
   (3) He wrote but one book and some letters.
   (4) He wrote no books but published many articles in magazines.
   (5) He wrote nothing at all.

6. According to Copernicus, Callippus and Eudoxus attempted to explain planetary motions by means of

   (1) elliptical orbits   (2) concentric spheres   (3) epicyclic circles
   (4) cubic orbits   (5) none of the foregoing.

7. Which one of the following statements do you regard as the best?

   (1) Copernicus assumed that the planets moved about the sun in elliptical orbits with the sun at one focus.
   (2) Copernicus assumed that the planets moved about the sun in elliptical orbits with the sun at the center.
   (3) Copernicus used epicycles to account for the observed retrograde motion of the planets.

(4) Copernicus used epicycles to account for the observed ovalness of the orbital motion of the planets.

(5) Copernicus did not use epicycles in his system.

8. Retrograde motion of planets

(1) could be approximately accounted for by the system of Copernicus but not by the Ptolemaic system

(2) could be approximately accounted for by the Ptolemaic system but not by the Copernican system

(3) could be approximately accounted for by neither the Ptolemaic system nor the Copernican system

(4) could be approximately accounted for by both the Ptolemaic and the Copernican systems

(5) was not observed until after the time of Copernicus.

9. Choose the most accurate statement.

(1) Copernicus had a fairly accurate concept of the order and distances of six planets from the sun, and also of their periods of revolution.

(2) Copernicus had a fairly accurate concept of the distances of the planets from the sun, but he presumed them all to have equal periods of revolution.

(3) Copernicus offered no explanation of motion of the moon which might account for observed phases of the moon.

(4) Copernicus observed no relation between the distance of a planet from the sun and its speed of revolution.

(5) Copernicus believed the earth to be the closest to the sun of all the planets.

10. In the Ptolemaic system observed movements of planets were approximately accounted for by the concepts of deferents and epicycles. Copernicus' accounting for observed planetary motions employed

(1) deferents but no epicycles   (2) epicycles but no deferents
(3) neither deferents nor epicycles   (4) both deferents and epicycles
(5) more circles than did the Ptolemaic system.

11. Following are three arguments Copernicus used to prove the spherical shape of the earth.

a. Travel to the north results in the north celestial pole being seen at a greater altitude while the south pole sinks an equal amount farther below the horizon.

b. Eclipses are not seen at the same local time for people living east and west of each other.

c. Observations at sea indicate the convex curvature of the ocean's surface.
Which of the Copernican arguments were also used by Ptolemy?

(1) a   (2) a and b   (3) b and c   (4) a, b, and c   (5) c.

12. Copernicus offers evidence that the earth is spherical. But the observations mentioned by Copernicus, considered together, could also be observed if the earth were a

(1) plane (2) cube (3) cylinder (4) disk (5) none of the preceding.

13. Which one of the following do you regard as best?

(1) Copernicus' proof that the earth is spherical is not as good as Ptolemy's since Copernicus did not disprove the possibility that

the earth might be cylindrical or made up of facets as did Ptolemy.

(2) Copernicus' proof that the earth is spherical is fully equivalent to Ptolemy's.

(3) Copernicus' proof that the earth is spherical in form is superior to Ptolemy's since Copernicus cited additional phenomenological data to support his assumption.

(4) Copernicus was concerned with the motions of the earth and not with its shape.

(5) The arguments of both Copernicus and Ptolemy about the form of the earth are invalid since they did not have the necessary evidence of large-scale land survey.

14. Which one of the following do you regard as the strongest (and best) argument made by Copernicus for the daily rotation of the earth?

(1) The rising of the sun, moon, planets, and stars in the east and their setting in the west is in a regular and predictable manner.

(2) "Since the heavens which contain and retain all things are the common home of all things, it is not at once comprehensible why a motion is not rather ascribed to the thing contained than to the containing, to the located rather than to the locating."

(3) The rotation of the earth is a natural motion and is not violent. Whatever happens in the course of nature remains in good conditions and in its best arrangements.

(4) It is easier and more plausible to assume the motion of the small earth rather than the corresponding motion of the very large (or even infinite) celestial sphere.

(5) All motion of celestial bodies as viewed from the North Star must be counterclockwise.

15. Which one of the following statements might best summarize Copernicus' views about gravity?

(1) It is a force acting only upon the earth and accounts for the spherical shape.

(2) It is a force acting upon the earth, moon, sun, and planets and accounts for their spherical shapes.

(3) It is a force acting between the earth, moon, sun, and the planets and accounts for their orbits.

(4) It is an universal force between any two material bodies acting as the products of their masses and inversely as the square of the distance between them.

(5) Copernicus makes no statements about gravity.

16. Which one of the following statements do you regard as the best?

(1) Copernicus had no better proof that the earth moved about the sun than Ptolemy had for the earth being stationary. Both men were doing some wishful thinking.

(2) If anything, Copernicus had a weaker case than Ptolemy, since he did not offer any observational evidence which was not known to Ptolemy. Actually, Ptolemy's principle of assuming the apparent motions to be the real motions unless compelled to the contrary is more "scientific" than Copernicus' flat statement that the earth moves without offering any observational proof whatsoever.

(3) Copernicus had the better proof since he pointed out that the apparent motions of the planets cannot be explained by a system of concentric circles with the earth at the center.
(4) Copernicus had the better proof since his construction eliminated the equants.
(5) Copernicus had the better proof since stellar parallaxes show that the earth does move in an orbit about the sun.

17. The maximum angular displacement from the sun of a hypothetical planet is observed from the earth to be 30°. By the method of computation available to Copernicus, its distance from the sun would be

(1) one-half the earth's distance from the sun
(2) equal to the earth's distance from the sun
(3) twice the earth's distance from the sun
(4) three times the earth's distance from the sun
(5) undeterminable.

18. How may have Copernicus calculated " the radii of the planets' deferents "?
19. Many of the Greeks thought of the celestial sphere containing all of the stars as being located just a bit beyond the orbit of Saturn. How big does Copernicus make his celestial sphere? What is outside his celestial sphere?
20. Ptolemy apparently held that the sun, moon, planets, and the stars were different from the earth, being divine and celestial rather than terrestrial and corruptible. Does Copernicus assume that the other celestial bodies are like or unlike the earth?
21. What is the nature of gravity in the Copernican scheme?
22. Neugebauer wrote in 1946 that " the Copernican theory is by no means so different from or superior to the Ptolemaic theory as is customarily asserted in anniversary celebrations." Are we justified in regarding it as " The Copernican Revolution "?
23. Why does Copernicus rule out the celestial sphere rotating with infinite speed?
24. What modern concepts of mechanics are hinted at by Copernicus?

8

Kepler, the Bridge Between Medieval
and Modern Astronomy

● Johannes Kepler (Fig. 8-1) was born a
premature and sickly child on December 27, 1571 in the Swabian imperial
city of Weil der Stadt in southwest Germany. Thus began in full character a life of brilliance, but also of grinding poverty, continuing sick-
ness, and repeated frustration. His father was of the minor nobility.
In modern terms he would have been lower middle class. But in the
16th century, he was a soldier of fortune who retired from the wars to
run the village tavern. He also signed a note for a friend. In the 16th
century, even as in our own time, this could bankrupt a man. Kepler
was withdrawn from school and sent to labor in the fields to help, in a
slight way, to support the family's now-fallen fortunes. Fortunately, he
was eventually able to attend the Protestant seminary at Adelberg as a
charity student. Two years later he transferred to the college at Maul-
bronn. Here he took his bachelor's degree in 1588, writing a brilliant examination which opened the doors for him to the University of Tuebingen.
There he took his master's degree in philosophy, studying astronomy
under Maestlin, who converted his student to Copernicus. Apparently
Kepler wished to enter the Lutheran ministry, but the first job offered
to him was as professor of mathematics and astronomy at Graz, the capital
city of the south Austrian province of Styria. Astronomy was then a minor
science, much like meteorology is today.

At Graz, in the course of giving his lectures on astronomy, he began
to wonder why there were just the six planets, Mercury, Venus, Earth,
Mars, Jupiter, and Saturn, in the Copernican scheme. Then he remembered that Euclid had proven that only five Platonic solids exist. The
Platonic solids (Fig. 8-2) are regular figures having identical faces, and
consist of the tetrahedron, cube, octahedron, dodecahedron, and the
icosahedron. The tetrahedron has four faces made up of identical equi-

119

Figure 8-1. *Johannes Kepler (1571–1630).*

lateral triangles; the cube has six faces of squares; the octahedron has eight faces of equilateral triangles; the dodecahedron has twelve faces of equilateral pentagons; while the twenty faces of the icosahedron are all equilateral triangles. There are no other regular solid figures. Kepler

Figure 8-2. *The Platonic solids: tetrahedron, cube, octahedron, dodecahedron, icosahedron.*

found that the radii of the spheres which were successively inscribed and circumscribed about these five solids were nearly proportional to the planetary distances in the Copernican system if they were arranged concentrically as shown in Figure 8-3.

There are only five Platonic solids and there were only six planets in Kepler's universe. It seemed to Kepler that he had miraculously found a bit of the Divine order of the world. This is "number magic" but it is exactly of the same nature as the modern "Bode's law" (which is neither a law nor was it discovered by Bode) by which present day astronomy students learn the approximate distances of the planets by taking the sum of four plus a series of successively doubled numbers and then dividing by ten, viz.:

Planet	Series	Sum/10	Known Distance
Mercury	4 + 0	0.4	0.39
Venus	4 + 3	0.7	0.72
Earth	4 + 6	1.0	1.00
Mars	4 + 12	1.6	1.52
Asteroids	4 + 24	2.8	2.65 (Av.)
Jupiter	4 + 48	5.2	5.20
Saturn	4 + 96	10.0	9.54
Uranus	4 + 192	19.6	19.19
Neptune	....	30.0	30.07
Pluto	4 + 384	38.8	39.52

which is not a bad rule of thumb, if one remembers Neptune as a case apart and as being about 30 A.U. from the sun.

Kepler carried his new discovery back to Tuebingen in triumph. His old teacher, Maestlin, saw it through the press. In the spring of 1597 Kepler's first book, the *Mysterium Cosmographicum* appeared. He distributed free copies of his little pamphlet widely. One copy went to the best observational astronomer of his age, Tycho Brahe (1546–1601), a Danish nobleman and a close friend of the Danish king, and the opposite

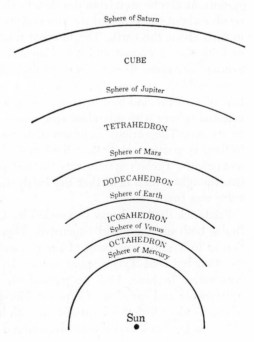

Figure 8-3. *The six planetary spheres circumscribing and inscribing the five regular solids.*

of Kepler in many ways. Tycho had health, wealth, leisure, and ample opportunity. His friend King Frederick II gave him the entire island of Hven for his observatory and supplied him with copious funds for staff and equipment. The telescope had not been invented yet, so Tycho's observatory equipment consisted of large and accurate quadrants with open rifle-type sights for measuring the angles to the planets and the stars. Tycho's accuracy of measurement was of the order of 1' of arc. He corrected for the effects of atmospheric refraction as would any modern. His observational work was good — and it is still good today.

Tycho was familiar with the theory of Copernicus but rejected it for good observational reasons. First, if the earth moved in an orbit, then a parallax of the nearest stars should be observed. None was found to within his observational accuracy of better than 1' of arc. Consequently the best assumption was that the earth did not move. Moreover, he had visually measured the apparent diameter of the brighter stars and thought that they were several minutes of arc in size. Now if a star the size of the sun were to be seen with an angular diameter of a few minutes of arc, then it could not be very far away in space. Accordingly, Tycho's observational results seemed to call for a stationary earth and stars just a bit beyond the orbit of Saturn.

On the other hand, Tycho was not willing to accept the older system of Ptolemy. Thus, he invented his own system, the Tychonic system (Fig. 8-4), which is nearly relativistically equivalent to the Copernican system. As can be seen from the sketch, all of the planets except the earth revolve about the sun, and the sun and its attendant planets then revolve in turn about the earth. The internal relationships are exactly the same in both the Tychonic and the Copernican systems. In particular, the average distances from the sun to the various planets are precisely the same in both systems. His system is a sort of halfway point between that of Ptolemy and that of Copernicus. Tycho's earth is unmoving. The celestial sphere with attendant sun, moon, and planets rotates once daily on its axis. The various members of the solar system move more slowly in their respective orbits than the celestial sphere, causing their contrary movements. Tycho's system was the last rallying point of that conservative thought which held that the earth was unmoving and that the universe was small.

Frederick died and was succeeded by Christian IV who found Tycho Brahe both arrogant and expensive. There remains a continuing question as to Tycho's treatment of the peasants on his island. There is little question but that Tycho spent money lavishly and did not propose to economize. In June, 1597 he packed his observational records and his instruments and sailed for Germany. He spent the winter in Wittenberg where Kepler's little book caught up with him. Kepler's worth was apparent from his book and Tycho determined to add Kepler to his retinue.

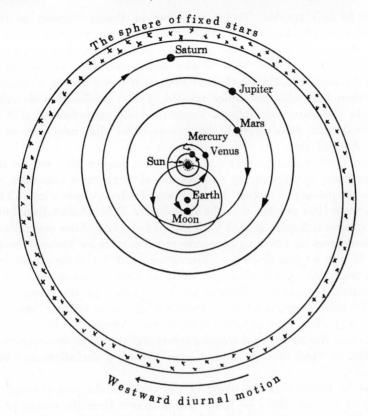

Figure 8-4. *The Tychonic system. The earth is stationary at the center of the celestial sphere. The planets revolve around the sun and the sun in turn revolves about the earth.*

He wrote Kepler a warm letter of both appreciation and reasoned criticism and invited the young man to join him.

In the meantime Kepler had returned to Graz with honor and had married the daughter of a rich miller. Kepler may have felt reasonably secure as a teacher in the Protestant school in a province where most of the middle class and the minor nobility were Protestants. However a few months before Kepler's wedding, the Catholic Archduke Ferdinand ascended the throne and began to reclaim his Province of Styria for the Catholic Church. Within only a few years the people of Styria had the choice of either becoming Catholics or leaving the province. Kepler tried desperately to find another job. He begged his old university of Tuebingen for a post, any post whatever. But no aid was offered. He wrote to his acquaintances all over Germany, but nothing was found. Fate, which must have seemed cold and relentless, forced Kepler into

Tycho Brahe's employ. Tycho was now at Prague serving as court mathematician to Rudolph II, Holy Roman Emperor. Tycho wrote another friendly letter to Kepler and once more invited him to come to Prague. On February 4, 1600, Kepler and Tycho met face to face for the first time in Benatky Castle near Prague. It was a historic association. Each man had what the other needed. Tycho possessed a wealth of accurate planetary observations. Kepler had the mathematical skill and the intellectual drive to seek the cosmic order that might lie within these observations.

Upon Tycho's death a year and a half later, Kepler inherited his position as court mathematician and continued work on a compilation of tables of planetary motion based upon Tycho's observations. These tables were later published as the *Rudolphine Tables* (after Rudolph II, their sponsor). Kepler started with the planet Mars. After several years of calculations he fitted an eccentric circular orbit to Tycho's observations. It was a good fit to the observations, but it did depart by 8' of arc at one point. For Ptolemy, or even for Copernicus, this 8' discrepancy would have been nothing at all, near perfection. But Kepler knew that Tycho's observations were considerably more reliable than that. Thus for the first time in man's history and solely on the basis of an 8' divergence, Kepler rejected circular orbits and started to determine what the orbit of Mars must be purely from Tycho's observations and nothing more.

First he found that the plane of the orbit would pass through the center of the sun. Then he found a line drawn from the center of the sun to the planet (Fig. 8-5) would move through the same area of space

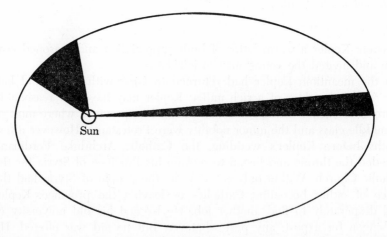

Figure 8-5. *The radius vector of Kepler's second law is the line from the sun at one focus to the planet. This line sweeps across equal areas in equal times. Thus a planet travels fastest in its orbit when nearest the sun.*

every day. Hence the planet would move most rapidly when near the sun and move more slowly when it was furthest from the sun. This is now known as Kepler's second law. At this time he knew that Mars moved in an "oval" orbit, but what was the exact form of the curve? After more years he recognized the curve as being an ellipse (Fig. 8-6) with the sun at one of the focal points, and so circles and combinations of circles were relegated to the ideological trash pile for all time. This

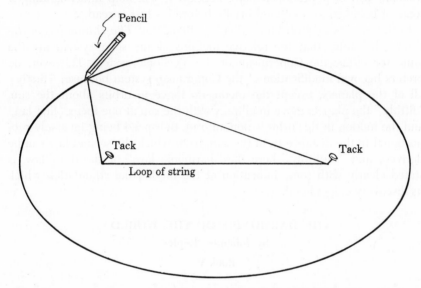

Figure 8-6. *An ellipse is easily drawn with two thumbtacks, a loop of string and a pencil. The points occupied by the thumbtacks are the foci of the ellipse.*

discovery is now known as Kepler's first law. His third law, or "harmonic" law, came towards the close of his life and relates the time of revolution in an orbit to the dimensions of the orbit.

Kepler is usually disposed of in astronomy texts by simply quoting his three laws:

1. *The planets move in ellipses, with the sun at one focus.*
2. *The radius vector sweeps out equal areas in equal times.*
3. *The square of the time of revolution is proportional to the cube of the mean distance.*

This is all in good textbook form. Kepler's work was not that simple. It is not even simple to excerpt his printed works. Nowhere does he state his "three laws" in textbook form and with conciseness. Kepler is trying the much harder job of finding out how the solar system is put together directly from the raw data of observations and without any theoretical bias whatsoever. His language is unfamilar and even smacks of "number magic." Yet his intellectual method is fully akin to the compulsive seeking of numerical relationships which characterizes much of physical science today.

Kepler wrote many books. Some of his critics feel that he wrote entirely too many. Perhaps his subsequent fame would have been greater if he had not been so wordy. Out of his large printed output, a few parts of his *The Harmonies of the World* and his *Epitome of Copernican Astronomy* will be reproduced here. Perhaps it will help understanding if some of his ideas are outlined briefly before his text is read.

In the excerpt taken from section 3 of Book V of *The Harmonies of the World*, he states that the relative motions of the solar system are the same for either the Copernican or the Tychonic system. However, he prefers his own modification of the Copernican system because: " firstly," all of the planets, except the moon, do move in orbits about the sun, " fifthly," the planets move in ellipses with the sun at one focus (first law) and the motion in this orbit is nonuniform, the speed being inversely proportional to the distance from the sun, from which the second law can be derived, and " eighthly," here the " harmonic law," or the third law, is stated clearly with some indication of the intellectual stimulation which its discovery engendered.

<h3 style="text-align:center">THE HARMONIES OF THE WORLD [1]</h3>

by Johannes Kepler

Book V

❊   ❊   ❊   ❊   ❊   ❊   ❊

3. A Summary of Astronomical Doctrine Necessary for Speculation into the Celestial Harmonies

First of all, my readers should know that the ancient astronomical hypotheses of Ptolemy, in the fashion in which they have been unfolded in the *Theoricae* of Peurbach and by the other writers of epitomes, are to be completely removed from this discussion and cast out of the mind. For they do not convey the true lay out of the bodies of the world and the polity of the movements.

Although I cannot do otherwise than to put solely Copernicus' opinion concerning the world in the place of those hypotheses and, if that were possible, to persuade everyone of it; but because the thing is still new among the mass of the intelligentsia, and the doctrine that the Earth is one of the planets and moves among the stars around a motionless sun sounds very absurd to the ears of most of them: therefore those who are shocked by the unfamiliarity of this opinion should know that these harmonical speculations are possible even with the hypotheses of Tycho Brahe — because that author holds, in common with Copernicus, everything else which pertains to the lay out of the bodies and the tempering of the movements, and transfers solely the Copernican annual move-

[1] Johannes Kepler, *The Harmonies of the World*, Great Books of the Western World, Vol. 16, Encyclopædia Britannica, Inc., pp. 1014–1016, 1018, 1019–1020.

ment of the Earth to the whole system of planetary spheres and to the sun, which occupies the centre of that system, in the opinion of both authors. For after this transference of movement it is nevertheless true that in Brahe the Earth occupies at any time the same place that Copernicus gives it, if not in the very vast and measureless region of the fixed stars, at least in the system of the planetary world. And accordingly, just as he who draws a circle on paper makes the writing-foot of the compass revolve, while he who fastens the paper or tablet to a turning lathe draws the same circle on the revolving tablet with the foot of the compass or stylus motionless; so too, in the case of Copernicus the Earth, by the real movement of its body, measures out a circle revolving midway between the circle of Mars on the outside and that of Venus on the inside; but in the case of Tycho Brahe the whole planetary system (wherein among the rest the circles of Mars and Venus are found) revolves like a tablet on a lathe and applies to the motionless Earth, or to the stylus on the lathe, the midspace between the circles of Mars and Venus; and it comes about from this movement of the system that the Earth within it, although remaining motionless, marks out the same circle around the sun and midway between Mars and Venus, which in Copernicus it marks out by the real movement of its body while the system is at rest. Therefore, since harmonic speculation considers the eccentric movements of the planets, as if seen from the sun, you may easily understand that if any observer were stationed on a sun as much in motion as you please, nevertheless for him the Earth, although at rest (as a concession to Brahe), would seem to describe the annual circle midway between the planets and in an intermediate length of time. Wherefore, if there is any man of such feeble wit that he cannot grasp the movement of the earth among the stars, nevertheless he can take pleasure in the most excellent spectacle of this most divine construction, if he applies to their image in the sun whatever he hears concerning the daily movements of the Earth in its eccentric — such an image as Tycho Brahe exhibits, with the Earth at rest.

And nevertheless the followers of the true Samian philosophy have no just cause to be jealous of sharing this delightful speculation with such persons, because their joy will be in many ways more perfect, as due to the consummate perfection of speculation, if they have accepted the immobility of the sun and the movement of the earth.

Firstly, therefore, let my readers grasp that today it is absolutely certain among all astronomers that all the planets revolve around the sun, with the exception of the moon, which alone has the Earth as its centre: the magnitude of the moon's sphere or orbit is not great enough for it to be delineated in this diagram in just ratio to the rest. Therefore, to the other five planets, a sixth, the Earth, is added, which traces a sixth circle around the sun, whether by its own proper movement with the sun at rest, or motionless itself and with the whole planetary system revolving.

*   *   *   *   *   *   *

Fifthly: To arrive at the movements between which the consonances have been set up, once more I impress upon the reader that in the *Commentaries on Mars* I have demonstrated from the sure observations of Brahe that daily arcs, which are equal in one and the same eccentric circle, are not traversed with equal speed; but that these differing delays in equal parts of the eccentric ob-

serve the ratio of their distances from the sun, the source of movement; and
conversely, that if equal times are assumed, namely, one natural day in both
cases, the corresponding true diurnal arcs of one eccentric orbit have to one
another the ratio which is the inverse of the ratio of the two distances from the
sun. Moreover, I demonstrated at the same time that the planetary orbit is elliptical and the sun, the source of movement, is at one of the foci of this ellipse;
and so, when the planet has completed a quarter of its total circuit from its
aphelion, then it is exactly at its mean distance from the sun, midway between
its greatest distance at the aphelion and its least at the perihelion. . . .

    ❊   ❊   ❊   ❊   ❊   ❊   ❊

Eighthly: So far we have dealt with the different delays or arcs of one and
the same planet. Now we must also deal with the comparison of the movements
of two planets. Here take note of the definitions of the terms which will be
necessary for us. We give the name of the nearest apsides of two planets to the
perihelion of the upper and the aphelion of the lower, notwithstanding that
they tend not towards the same region of the world but towards distinct and
perhaps contrary regions. By extreme movements understand the slowest and
the fastest of the whole planetary circuit; by converging or converse extreme
movements, those which are at the nearest apsides of two planets — namely, at
the perihelion of the upper planet and the aphelion of the lower; by diverging
or diverse, those at the opposite apsides — namely, the aphelion of the upper
and the perihelion of the lower. Therefore again, a certain part of my *Mysterium Cosmographicum*, which was suspended twenty-two years ago, because it
was not yet clear, is to be completed and herein inserted. For after finding the
true intervals of the spheres by the observations of Tycho Brahe and continuous labour and much time, at last, at last the right ratio of the periodic times
to the spheres

> though it was late, looked to the unskilled man,
> yet looked to him, and, after much time, came,

and, if you want the exact time, was conceived mentally on the 8th of March in
this year One Thousand Six Hundred and Eighteen but unfelicitously submit-
ted to calculation and rejected as false, finally, summoned back on the 15th of
May, with a fresh assault undertaken, outfought the darkness of my mind by
the great proof afforded by my labor of seventeen years on Brahe's observations and meditation upon it uniting in one concord, in such fashion that I
first believed I was dreaming and was presupposing the object of my search
among the principles. But it is absolutely certain and exact that the ratio which
exists between the periodic times of any two planets is precisely the ratio of
the 3/2th power of the mean distances, i.e., of the spheres themselves; provided, however, that the arithmetic mean between both diameters of the ellip-
tic orbit be slightly less than the longer diameter. And so if any one take the
period, say, of the Earth, which is one year, and the period of Saturn, which is
thirty years, and extract the cube roots of this ratio and then square the ensuing
ratio by squaring the cube roots, he will have as his numerical products the
most just ratio of the distances of the Earth and Saturn from the sun. For the

cube root of 1 is 1, and the square of it is 1; and the cube root of 30 is greater than 3, and therefore the square of it is greater than 9. And Saturn, at its mean distance from the sun is slightly higher than nine times the mean distance of the Earth from the sun. Further on, in Chapter 9, the use of this theorem will be necessary for the demonstration of the eccentricities.

In the Introduction of Book IV of his *Epitome of Copernican Astronomy*, Kepler lists the specifications of the Copernican system as (1) the sun at the center and immovable, (2) the planets moving in orbits about the sun in a combination of perfect circles including epicycles, (3) the earth in an orbit between Mars and Venus, (4) a very large celestial sphere, and (5) the moon moving in an orbit about the earth. Tycho's system changed the first and third principles. Tycho took the earth stationary and the sun moving, but with all relative motions unchanged. He also assumed a small celestial sphere which lay just beyond Saturn's orbit. Kepler's modifications of the Copernican system were to replace circular orbits with ellipses and to accept the rotation of the sun. He quotes the observations of the sunspots as evidence for the solar rotation.

In Part II of Book IV he describes the various rotations of the sun, earth, and planets. He states the information of his third law in his discussion of the relations between the periods of the various planets and in his calculations of their linear speeds in their orbits. He thinks that the sun is the cause of the motion of the planets since (1) the "harmonic law" of $P^2 = D^3$ applies to the relations between planetary periods and distances from the sun, (2) by his second law an individual planet moves faster in its orbit near the sun, (3) the sun is beautiful, et cetera, and (4) the sun's direction of rotation is the same as the direction of revolution of the planets.

In a subsequent portion of his book, Kepler attempts to give a theoretical explanation of his three laws. His theory is interesting as one of the many such attempts before Newton achieved his own grand synthesis of physics and astronomy. Kepler's theory is not reproduced here because of the prolixity of his text. Perhaps it can be summarized. As stated in the beginning of Book IV, Part III, Kepler believes that it is the rotation of the sun which causes the motion of the planets. Whatever this agency may be, its effectiveness must fall off with distance since the more distant planets move more slowly than the closer ones. Thus both the second and the third laws could be explained, but not the first law which states that the orbits are ellipses with the sun at one focus. Kepler reminded his readers about the observed facts of magnetism and suggested that there might be some sort of similar polarized agency in the planets. The drawing (Fig. 8-7) is an attempt to illustrate Kepler's theory. Suppose that the "magnet-like" agency, whatever it might be, would be polarized as shown by the arrow drawn in the planet. Assume

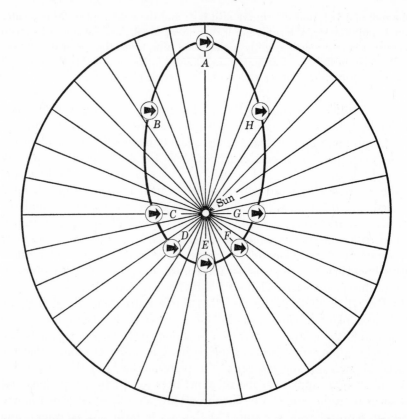

Figure 8-7. *Kepler's diagram of planetary motion, showing alternate effects of attraction and repulsion of the sun on the planet.*

that the head of the arrow is attractive to the sun while the tail of the arrow is repulsive to the sun. Now starting with the planet at a place such as C, it is attracted toward the sun and starts to move in closer as shown in subsequent positions D and E. Of course it also moves faster in its orbit since the effect of the sun's rotation, shown by rays, is greater and the second law of equal areas in equal times is thereby explained. In positions F and G the planet is presenting its repulsive side to the sun and is pushed out to a greater distance as shown in positions H and A, where it now moves more slowly since it is further from the sun. Then in moving through the positions B and C we have completed the orbit. Kepler does not give any mathematical development to his ideas but feels that this varying force of attraction and repulsion along with the regular agency of the rotating sun, which he called its "virtue," might explain the facts which he observed empirically. Note that there is no thought that gravitation might be responsible for the organization of the solar system. This was to be Newton's contribution.

EPITOME OF COPERNICAN ASTRONOMY [2]
by Johannes Kepler
Book IV

First Book on the Doctrine of the Schemata
On the Position, Order, and Movement of the Parts of the World;
or, on the System of the World

❋   ❋   ❋   ❋   ❋   ❋   ❋

What are the hypotheses or principles wherewith Copernican astronomy saves the appearances in the proper movements of the planets?

They are principally: (1) that the sun is located at the centre of the sphere of the fixed stars — or approximately at the centre — and is immovable in place; (2) that the single planets move really around the sun in their single systems, which are compounded of many perfect circles revolved in an absolutely uniform movement; (3) that the Earth is one of the planets, so that by its mean annual movement around the sun it describes its orbital circle between the orbital circles of Mars and Venus; (4) that the ratio of its orbital circle to the diameter of the sphere of the fixed stars is imperceptible to sense and therefore, as it were, exceeds measurements; (5) that the sphere of the moon is arranged around the Earth as its centre, so that the annual movement around the sun — and so the movement from place to place — is common to the whole sphere of the moon and to the Earth.

Do you judge that these principles should be held to in this Epitome?

Since astronomy has two ends, to save the appearances and to contemplate the true form of the edifice of the world — of which I have treated in Book I, folia 4 and 5 — there is no need of all these principles in order to attain the first end: but some can be changed and others can be omitted; however, the second principle must necessarily be corrected: and even though most of these principles are necessary for the second end, nevertheless they are not yet sufficient.

Which of these principles can be changed or omitted and the appearances still be saved?

Tycho Brahe demonstrates the appearances with the first and third principles changed: for he, like the ancients, places the Earth immobile, at the centre of the world; but the sun — which even for him is the centre of the orbital circles of the five planets — and the system of all the spheres he makes to go around the Earth in the common annual movement, while at the same time in this common system any planet completes its proper movements. Moreover, he omits the fourth principle altogether and exhibits the sphere of the fixed stars as not much greater than the sphere of Saturn.

What in turn do you substitute for the second principle and what else do you add to the true form of the dwelling of the world or to what belongs to the nature of the heavens?

Even though the true movements are to be left singly to the single planets,

[2] Johannes Kepler, *Epitome of Copernican Astronomy*, Great Books of the Western World, Vol. 16, Encyclopædia Britannica, Inc., pp. 852–853, 887, 888, 895–896.

nevertheless these movements do not move by themselves nor by the revolutions of spheres — for there are no solid spheres — but the sun in the centre of the world, revolving around the centre of its body and around its axis, by this revolution becomes the cause of the single planets going around.

Further, even though the planets are really eccentric to the centre of the sun: nevertheless there are no other smaller circles called epicycles, which by their revolution vary the intervals between the planet and the sun; but the bodies themselves of the planets, by an inborn force (vi insite), furnish the occasion for this variation.

    ✿   ✿   ✿   ✿   ✿   ✿   ✿

Book IV

Part II — On the Movement of the Bodies of the World

1. How Many and of What Sort Are the Movements?

What was the opinion of Copernicus concerning the movement of bodies? For him, what was in motion and what was at rest?

There are two species of local movement: for either the whole thing turns, while remaining in its place, but with its parts succeeding one another. This movement can be called . . . — lathe-movement, or cone-movement — from the resemblance; or rotation from a rotating pole. Or else the whole thing is borne from place to place circularly. The Greeks . . . [and] the Latins . . . call both movements generally revolution.

Accordingly Copernicus lays down that the sun is situated at the centre of the world and is motionless as a whole, viz., with respect to its centre and axis. Only a few years ago, however, we grasped by sense that the sun turns with respect to the parts of its body, i.e., around its centre and axis — as reasons had led me to assert for a long time — and with such great speed that one rotation is completed in the space of 25 or 26 days.

Now according as each of the primary bodies is nearer the sun, so it is borne around the sun in a shorter period, under the same common circle of the zodiac, and all in the same direction in which the parts of the solar body precede them — Mercury in the space of three months, Venus in seven and one-half months, the Earth with the lunar heaven in twelve months, Mars in twenty-two and one-half months or less than two years, Jupiter in twelve years, Saturn in thirty years. But for Copernicus the sphere of the fixed stars is utterly immobile.

The Earth meanwhile revolves around its own axis too, and the moon around the Earth — still in the same direction (if you look towards the outer parts of the world) as all the primary bodies.

Now for Copernicus all these movements are direct and continuous, and there are absolutely no stations or retrogradations in the truth of the matter.

    ✿   ✿   ✿   ✿   ✿   ✿   ✿

How is the ratio of the periodic times, which you have assigned to the mobile bodies, related to the aforesaid ratio of the spheres wherein those bodies are borne?

The ratio of the times is not equal to the ratio of the spheres, but greater than it, and in the primary planets exactly the ratio of the 3/2th powers. That is to say, if you take the cube roots of the 30 years of Saturn and the 12 years of Jupiter and square them, the true ratio of the spheres of Saturn and Jupiter will exist in these squares. This is the case even if you compare spheres which are not next to one another. For example, Saturn takes 30 years; the Earth takes one year. The cube root of 30 is approximately 3.11. But the cube root of 1 is 1. The squares of these roots are 9.672 and 1. Therefore the sphere of Saturn is to the sphere of the Earth as 9,672 is to 1,000. And a more accurate number will be produced, if you take the times more accurately.

What is gathered from this?

Not all the planets are borne with the same speed, as Aristotle wished, otherwise their times would be as their spheres, and as their diameters; but according as each planet is higher and farther away from the sun, so it traverses less space in one hour by its mean movement: Saturn — according to the magnitude of the solar sphere believed in by the ancients — traverses 240 German miles (in one hour), Jupiter 320 German miles, Mars 600, the centre of the Earth 740, Venus 800, and Mercury 1,200. And if this is to be according to the solar interval proved by me in the above, the number of miles must everywhere be tripled.

    ✿   ✿   ✿   ✿   ✿   ✿   ✿

3. On the Revolution of the Solar Body Around its Axis and its Effect in the Movement of the Planets

By what reasons are you led to make the sun the moving cause or the source of movement for the planets?

1. Because it is apparent that in so far as any planet is more distant from the sun than the rest, it moves the more slowly — so that the ratio of the periodic times is the ratio of the 3/2th powers of the distances from the sun. Therefore we reason from this that the sun is the source of movement.

2. Below we shall hear the same thing come into use in the case of the single planets — so that the closer any one planet approaches the sun during any time, it is borne with an increase of velocity in exactly the ratio of the square.

3. Nor is the dignity or the fitness of the solar body opposed to this, because it is very beautiful and of a perfect roundness and is very great and is the source of light and heat, whence all life flows out into the vegetables: to such an extent that heat and light can be judged to be as it were certain instruments fitted to the sun for causing movement in the planets.

4. But in especial, all the estimates of probability are fulfilled by the sun's rotation in its own space around its immobile axis, in the same direction in which all the planets proceed: and in a shorter period than Mercury, the nearest to the sun and fastest of all the planets.

For as regards the fact that it is disclosed by the telescope in our time and can be seen every day that the solar body is covered with spots, which cross the disk of the sun or its lower hemisphere within 12 or 13 or 14 days, slowly at the beginning and at the end, but rapidly in the middle, which argues that they are stuck to the surface of the sun and turn with it; I proved in my *Commentaries on Mars*, Chapter 34, by reasons drawn from the very movement of the planets, long before it was established by the sun-spots, that this movement necessarily had to take place.

    ✦   ✿   ✿   ✿   ✿   ✿   ✿

STUDY QUESTIONS

1. Which of the following statements are applicable to Bode's law?
   a. The "law" was not discovered by Bode.
   b. The "law" is accurate for all planets.
   c. The "law" is not a law.
   The applicable statement(s) is/are

   (1) a   (2) b   (3) c   (4) a and b   (5) a and c.

2. According to Bode's law of planetary distances, the distance from Mars to the sun in astronomical units, is

   (1) 0.7   (2) 1.6   (3) 2.8   (4) 5.2   (5) 10.0.

3. Select the true statement or statements.
   a. In the Ptolemaic system the distance of a planet from the earth remained fixed.
   b. The Ptolemaic system accounted approximately but not exactly for apparent planetary motions.
   c. The Ptolemaic system included an effort to explain the retrograde motion of planets.
   The correct selection includes only

   (1) a   (2) b   (3) c   (4) a and b   (5) b and c.

4. Which of the following Ptolemaic concepts did Kepler discard?
   a. Circular motion.
   b. Revolving spheres (crystalline).
   c. Epicycles.
   The correct answer is

   (1) a   (2) b   (3) c   (4) a, b, and c   (5) none of them.

5. Comparing the speeds with which two planets revolve about the sun, the outer planet has
   a. a longer period of revolution.
   b. a smaller angular speed.
   c. a smaller linear speed.
   The correct answer is

   (1) a   (2) b   (3) c   (4) a and b   (5) a, b, and c.

6. Select from the following list those statements which describe Kepler's laws of planetary motion.
   a. All planets revolve about the sun at uniform rates.
   b. Each planet moves in its orbit in such a fashion that its radius vector sweeps across equal areas of space in equal lengths of time.
   c. All planets revolve about the sun in elliptical orbits.
   d. As viewed from a position near the south ecliptic pole, all planets revolve about the sun in a counterclockwise direction.
   e. The ratio of the cubes of the average distances from the sun of any two planets is equal to the ratio of the squares of those planets' periods.
   f. The ratio of the squares of the average distances from the sun of any two planets is equal to the ratio of the cubes of those planets' periods.
   The correct selection includes only

   (1) a, b, and c   (2) b, c, and f   (3) c, d, and e   (4) b, c, and e
   (5) a, c, and e.

7. Kepler's third law may be written as $P^2 = D^3$, or $P = D\sqrt{D}$ where P is the planet's period in years and D is the ratio of the planet's distance from the sun to the earth's distance from the sun. What would be the period of a planet that was nine times as far from the sun as the earth?

(1) 9 years (2) 81 years (3) 3 years (4) 243 years (5) 27 years.

8–11. Consider an imaginary planet with a sidereal period of revolution about the sun equal to 1½ years.

8. About how many degrees would the planet move each year?

(1) 120 (2) 180 (3) 240 (4) 360 (5) 540.

9. About how many degrees would the earth gain on the planet in a year?

(1) 120 (2) 180 (3) 240 (4) 270 (5) none of the preceding.

10. How long is the synodic [3] period of the planet?

(1) 1 year (2) 2 years (3) 3 years (4) 4 years (5) 18 months.

11. The interval from one opposition of the planet to the next would be

(1) 1 year (2) 2 years (3) 3 years (4) 4 years (5) 18 months.

12. Which of the following is the best statement about the excerpts that were quoted?

(1) Kepler stated his second law in its usual form.
(2) Kepler did not state his second law.
(3) The second law is not stated in its usual form, but it can be derived from other statements which were made.
(4) The second law is not stated in its usual form and it cannot be derived from other statements which were made.
(5) The second law can be derived from the first and third laws.

13. According to Kepler, the paths of the planets about the sun are determined by

(1) a gravitational attraction of the planet's mass by the mass of the sun
(2) only a "virtue" produced by the rotation of the sun
(3) only a magnetic-like attraction and repulsion
(4) a combination of the "virtue" of the sun's rotation and a magnetic-like attraction and repulsion
(5) a curvature of space produced by the mass of the sun.

14. If there were a planet beyond Pluto which obeyed Bode's law, then it would probably have a period of about

(1) 15 years   (2) 77.2 years   (3) 247.7 years   (4) 410 years
(5) 680 years.

15. Is there any basis for choosing between the Tychonic and the Keplerian systems?

---

[3] The synodic period of another planet as viewed from the earth is the time required for the planet to move from one geometric relation to the sun (such as being directly opposite to the sun in the sky, called an "opposition") to the following repetition of that geometric relation.

16. How do you evaluate the relative merits of the work of Copernicus and that of Kepler? Which was the greater innovator?
17. According to Kepler, what would be the motion of the moon if the earth did not rotate?
18. Why did Tycho assume that, if the earth moved, parallax of the stars should be observable?

9

Galileo and the Invention of the Telescope

● Galileo Galilei (Fig. 9-1) was born at Pisa on February 15, 1564 in the year that Michelangelo died and Shakespeare was born. He was born into an old and distinguished Florentine family whose family name had been changed to Galilei five generations earlier in honor of an earlier Galileo who had been a famous physician of the 15th century. Galileo's father, Vincenzio Galilei, was a cloth merchant who had moved his family from Florence to Pisa in the hopes of greater trade. Vincenzio was an accomplished amateur musician. While he had lived in Florence he was a member of a group of musical radicals who proposed to overthrow the older forms of music and create completely new forms in their place. Vincenzio and his friends invented the recitative, a musical device found in nearly every modern opera. In fact, many historians of music credit this Florence group with the origination of opera. In 1581, Vincenzio published a very good book on musical theory entitled *Dialogue on Ancient and Modern Music*. It is an obvious predecessor to his son's books in form and literary style, differing only in subject matter. Both Galileis wrote lively books which display a love for learning, a skill in mathematics, a strong distaste for classical authority, a startling polemic ability, and a graceful literary style. Vincenzio taught his son music, and Galileo found pleasure in playing his lute throughout his life. It is also thought that the father taught his son drawing, as Galileo's artistic skill was respected by the artists of his day.

Galileo's early instruction was at home by his remarkable father and at the day school of a local Jesuit monastery. At the age of seventeen he enrolled in the University of Pisa. It was his father's hope that he would become a physician like his illustrious namesake. Medical instruction at Pisa at that time was predominately based upon the classic texts of Aristotle and Galen. Galileo did not find this to his liking. He soon acquired a reputation among his professors as being an extremely argumentative youth. Galileo's interests turned to mathematics in which he

137

Figure 9-1. *Galileo Galilei (1564–1642).*

received instruction from Ostilio Ricci, a practical mathematician attached to the Tuscan court and not to the university. Galileo left the university without taking a degree. However at the age of twenty-five he was appointed professor of mathematics at the University of Pisa as the result of an intercession in his behalf by the nobleman Guidobaldo dal Monte. The post had honor but little money, and even the honor lasted for only three years. Here at Pisa he began his work on mechanics and may or may not have dropped the two balls from the Leaning Tower. However, he certainly did discover the time-keeping properties of the pendulum by watching a swinging lamp during a dull sermon at the Cathedral of Pisa.

He left Pisa in 1592 to become professor of mathematics at the University of Padua at the age of twenty-eight, a post that he held for eighteen years. His career as a public servant of the Republic of Venice would have been a happy one except for his continual homesickness for his native Tuscany. He had a great and good friend in Marina Gamba, a woman of Venice, who presented him with two daughters and one son. Here at Padua, he later recalled, were the happiest and most productive years of his life. Here he did the bulk of the work in astronomy and mechanics which he would clarify and publish later. Here he published his first book, a small instruction manual in Italian on the use of a mathematical instrument which he had invented. This manual was subsequently translated into scholarly Latin by Baldassar Capra, a student at Padua, who passed off Galileo's invention as being his own. Galileo successfully brought action against Capra with the university faculty, and to be certain that the facts were properly known about Europe, published the entertaining *Defense against the Calumnies and Impostures of Baldassar Capra* which demolished Capra as thoroughly as a sharpened pen could.

Galileo was an early, but cautious, convert to Copernicism. In a letter to Kepler, he wrote: [1]

> I adopted the teaching of Copernicus many years ago, and his point of view enables me to explain many phenomena of nature which certainly remain inexplicable according to the more current hypotheses. I have written many arguments in support of him and in refutation of the opposite view — which, however, so far I have not dared to bring into the public light, frightened by the fate of Copernicus himself, our teacher, who, though he acquired immortal fame with some, is yet to an infinite multitude of others (for such is the number of fools) an object of ridicule and derision. I would certainly dare to publish my reflections at once if more people like you existed; as they don't, I shall refrain from doing so.

He remained discretely silent until he heard that a Dutch spectacle-maker had created an instrument with two lenses which magnified distant objects. Apparently with only the rumor to go on, he sat down and worked out the theory of the telescope within a single day and then started making them. After a series of small instruments, he built his " great " telescope with an objective lens of about an inch in diameter mounted in a tube about eighteen inches in length. This telescope, nothing but a " spy-glass " held in the hand, was in its time " the world's largest telescope." Galileo probably made as many important discoveries with it as has any modern astronomer using instruments approaching 200 inches in aperture.

Galileo, with his telescope, discovered: the spots on the sun which appeared to rotate around it in about 27 days and horrified the philosophers by insisting that the spotted sun, a celestial body, was " corruptible " like the earth; the mountains, craters and plains on the moon; the planets were disks of light of appreciable size and not points of light like the fixed stars; the phases of Venus which run through the complete gamut from new to full and back as do those of our moon; four satellites circulating around Jupiter like a miniature Copernican system; Saturn with its rings seen poorly and appearing like a triple body jointed together; the " libration " of the moon, that apparent tipping motion which allows us to see 59% of its surface; 36 stars in the Pleiades where the unaided eye sees only 6 or 7; 40 stars in the Praesepe cluster which looks like three " nebulous stars " to our eye; that the Milky Way was actually made up of myriads of stars. What other telescope can claim so many important discoveries?

With his telescope at hand, Galileo became a publicly professing Copernican. Did not the moons of Jupiter display a small model of the

[1] Arthur Koestler, *The Sleepwalkers,* by permission of Macmillan, New York, 1959, p. 356.

Copernican system for any eye to see? Did not the four Medicean planets (named by Galileo for his former pupil, Cosimo II de' Medici, soon to become Grand Duke of Tuscany) revolve about Jupiter exactly as Copernicus proposed for the planets about the sun? Did not the periods of revolution increase for the more remote satellites as Copernicus had insisted for the planets from Mercury through Saturn? Did not the planet Venus show phases which were quite impossible under the Ptolemaic dispensation? Did not that most perfect of celestial objects, the sun, show spots on its face, spots which continually changed? Verily, the sun was " corruptible " in the same sense that the Aristoteleans charged the earth. This evidence to support the Copernican theory was there for any one to see, who would only look.

But, only a year after his first flush of discoveries, Galileo wrote to Kepler: [2]

We will laugh at the extraordinary stupidity of the crowd, my Kepler. What do you say to the main philosophers of our school, who, with the stubbornness of vipers, never wanted to see the planets, the moon or the telescope although I offered them a thousand times to show them the planets and the moon. Really, as some have shut their ears, these have shut their eyes towards the light of truth. This is an awful thing, but it does not astonish me. This sort of person thinks that philosophy is a book like the Aeneid or Odyssey and that one has not to search for truth in the world of nature, but in the comparisons of texts (to use their own words).

In another important letter which he wrote to Kepler he described his discovery of the phases of the planet Venus. An inspection of the drawings for the Ptolemaic and the Copernican systems (See Chap. 7) will show that Venus should show only new and crescent phases under the Ptolemaic system but should show the complete range of phases under the Copernican arrangement. This test of the two systems was well known to the Greeks who regretted that human eyesight was not sufficiently acute to apply the obvious test. Galileo in inventing a new instrument was extending the range of human senses and the test was now possible. Galileo sent his conclusions to Kepler at first in the form of a puzzle — an anagram which read, " Haec Immatura a me jam frustra leguntur, o.y.", which he now translates and explains. It is noteworthy that he ignores the Tychonic system which would have also predicted all the phases of Venus (see the drawing in the preceding chapter).[3]

It is time for me to disclose the method of reading the letters which some weeks since I sent you as an anagram. It is time now, I mean, after I have become quite certain about the matter, so much so that I have no longer even a

[2] Carola Baumgardt, *Johannes Kepler; Life and Letters,* Philosophical Library, New York, 1951, p. 86.

[3] E. S. Carlos, *The Sidereal Messenger of Galileo Galilei,* Rivingtons, London, 1880, pp. 99–102.

shadow of doubt. You must know then that about three months ago, when the star of Venus could be seen, I began to look at it through a telescope with great attention, so that I might grasp with my physical senses an idea which I was entertaining as certain. At first then you must know the planet Venus appeared of a perfectly circular form, accurately so, and bounded by a distinct edge, but very small; this figure Venus kept until it began to approach its greatest distance from the sun, and meanwhile the apparent size of its orb kept on increasing. From that time it began to lose its roundness on the eastern side, which was turned away from the sun, and in a few days it contracted its visible portion into an exact semicircle; that figure lasted without the smallest alteration until it began to return towards the sun where it leaves the tangent drawn to its epicycle. At this time it loses the semi-circular form more and more, and keeps on diminishing that figure until its conjunction, when it will wane to a very thin crescent. After completing its passage past the sun, it will appear to us, at its appearance as a morning star, as only sickle-shaped, turning a very thin crescent away from the sun; afterwards the crescent will fill up more and more until the planet reaches its greatest distance from the sun, in which position it will appear semicircular, and that figure will last for many days without appreciable variation. Then by degrees, from being semicircular it will change to a full orb, and will keep that perfectly circular figure for several months; but at this instant the diameter of the orb of Venus is about five times as large as that which it showed at its first appearance as an evening star.

From the observation of these wonderful phenomena we are supplied with a determination most conclusive, and appealing to the evidence of our senses, of two very important problems, which up to this day were discussed by the greatest intellects with different conclusions. One is that the planets are bodies not self-luminous (if we may entertain the same views about Mercury as we do about Venus). The second is that we are absolutely compelled to say that Venus (and Mercury also) revolves round the sun, as do also all the rest of the planets. A truth believed indeed by the Pythagorean school, by Copernicus, and by Kepler, but never proved by the evidence of our senses, as it is now proved in the case of Venus and Mercury. Kepler therefore and the rest of the school of Copernicus have good reason for boasting that they have shown themselves good philosophers, and that their belief was not devoid of foundation; however much it has been their lot, and may even hereafter be their lot, to be regarded by the philosophers of our times, who philosophise on paper, with an universal agreement, as men of no intellect, and little better than absolute fools.

The words which I sent with their letters transposed, and which said,

Haec immatura a me jam frustra leguntur, o.y.

when reduced to their proper order, read thus,

Cynthiae figuras aemulatur mater amorum:
The mother of the Loves rivals the phases of Cynthia:

that is,

Venus imitates the phases of the Moon.

In 1610, at Venice, Galileo published in Latin his *Sidereus Nuncius*, or as usually translated into English, *The Sidereal Messenger*. This small book of seventy-odd pages reported to the learned world his invention of the astronomical telescope and the important astronomical discoveries that he had made with it. We reproduce here only a few pages of his book in which he describes his invention of the telescope and his discovery of the four moons of Jupiter.

THE SIDEREAL MESSENGER [4]
by Galileo Galilei

❀   ❀   ❀   ❀   ❀   ❀   ❀

About ten months ago a report reached my ears that a Dutchman had constructed a telescope, by the aid of which visible objects, although at a great distance from the eye of the observer, were seen distinctly as if near; and some proofs of its most wonderful performances were reported, which some gave credence to, but others contradicted. A few days after, I received confirmation of the report in a letter written from Paris by a noble Frenchman, Jaques Badovere, which finally determined me to give myself up first to inquire into the principle of the telescope, and then to consider the means by which I might compass the invention of a similar instrument, which a little while after I succeeded in doing, through deep study of the theory of Refraction; and I prepared a tube, at first of lead, in the ends of which I fitted two glass lenses, both plane on one side, but on the other side one spherically convex, and the other concave.[5] Then bringing my eye to the concave lens I saw objects satisfactorily large and near, for they appeared one-third of the distance off and nine times larger than when they are seen with the natural eye alone. I shortly afterwards constructed another telescope with more nicety, which magnified objects more than sixty times. At length, by sparing neither labour nor expense, I succeeded in constructing for myself an instrument so superior that objects seen through it appear magnified nearly a thousand times, and more than thirty times nearer than if viewed by the natural powers of sight alone.

It would be altogether a waste of time to enumerate the number and importance of the benefits which this instrument may be expected to confer, when used by land or sea. But without paying attention to its use for terrestrial objects, I betook myself to observations of the heavenly bodies; and first of all, I viewed the Moon as near as if it was scarcely two semidiameters of the Earth distant. After the Moon, I frequently observed other heavenly bodies, both fixed stars and planets, with incredible delight. . . .

Discovery of Jupiter's Satellites

There remains the matter, which seems to me to deserve to be considered the most important in this work, namely, that I should disclose and publish to the

---

[4] E. S. Carlos, *The Sidereal Messenger of Galileo Galilei*, Rivingtons, London, 1880, 10–11, 44–48, 68–70, 72.

[5] The lenses in Galileo's telescope were arranged as shown in the figure. Inexpensive opera glasses and toy " spy-glasses " are still manufactured with this optical arrangement.

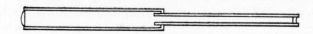

world the occasion of discovering and observing four planets, never seen from the very beginning of the world up to our own times, their positions, and the observations made during the last two months about their movements and their changes of magnitude; . . .

On the 7th day of January in the present year, 1610, in the first hour of the following night, when I was viewing the constellations of the heavens through a telescope, the planet Jupiter presented itself to my view, and as I had prepared for myself a very excellent instrument, I noticed a circumstance which I had never been able to notice before, owing to want of power in my other telescope, namely, that three little stars, small but very bright, were near the planet; and although I believed them to belong to the number of the fixed stars, yet they made me somewhat wonder, because they seemed to be arranged exactly in a straight line, parallel to the ecliptic, and to be brighter than the rest of the stars, equal to them in magnitude. The position of them with reference to one another and to Jupiter was as follows (Fig. 1) [Plate 9-1, page 144].

On the east side there were two stars, and a single one towards the west. The star which was furthest towards the east, and the western star, appeared rather larger than the third.

I scarcely troubled at all about the distance between them and Jupiter, for, as I have already said, at first I believed them to be fixed stars; but when on January 8th, led by some fatality, I turned again to look at the same part of the heavens, I found a very different state of things, for there were three little stars all west of Jupiter, and nearer together than on the previous night, and they were separated from one another by equal intervals, as the accompanying illustration (Fig. 2) shows.

At this point, although I had not turned my thoughts at all upon the approximation of the stars to one another, yet my surprise began to be excited, how Jupiter could one day be found to the east of all the aforesaid fixed stars when the day before it had been west of two of them; and forthwith I became afraid lest the planet might have moved differently from the calculation of astronomers, and so had passed those stars by its own proper motion. I therefore waited for the next night with the most intense longing, but I was disappointed of my hope, for the sky was covered with clouds in every direction.

But on January 10th the stars appeared in the following position with regard to Jupiter; there were two only, and both on the east side of Jupiter, the third, as I thought, being hidden by the planet (Fig. 3). They were situated just as before, exactly in the same straight line with Jupiter, and along the Zodiac.

When I had seen these phenomena, as I knew that corresponding changes of position could not by any means belong to Jupiter, and as, moreover, I perceived that the stars which I saw had been always the same, for there were no others either in front or behind, within a great distance, along the Zodiac — at length, changing from doubt into surprise, I discovered that the interchange of position which I saw belonged not to Jupiter, but to the stars to which my attention had been drawn, and I thought therefore that they ought to be observed henceforward with more attention and precision.

Accordingly, on January 11th I saw an arrangement of the following kind (Fig. 4), namely, only two stars to the east of Jupiter, the nearer of which was distant from Jupiter three times as far as from the star further to the east; and the star furthest to the east was nearly twice as large as the other one; whereas

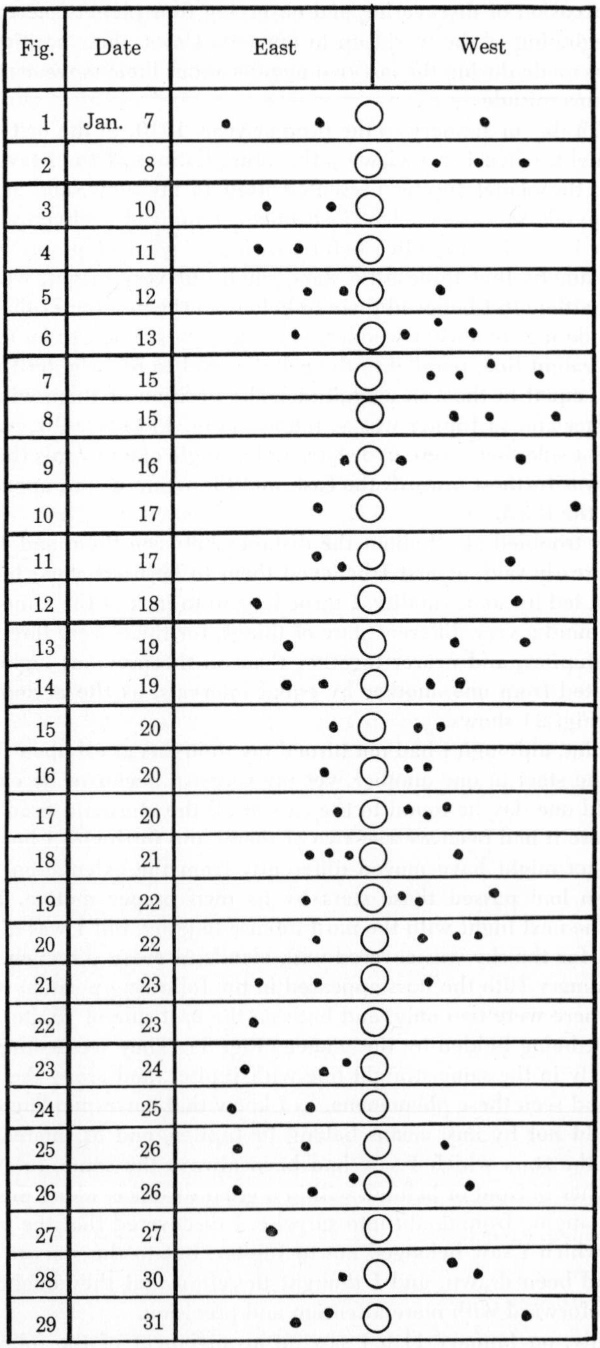

Fig.	Date	East	West
1	Jan. 7	• • ○	•
2	8	○	• • •
3	10	• • ○	
4	11	• • ○	
5	12	• •○	•
6	13	• ○	• • •
7	15	○	• • • •
8	15	○	• • •
9	16	•○•	•
10	17	• ○	•
11	17	•• ○	•
12	18	• ○	•
13	19	• ○	• •
14	19	• • ○	• •
15	20	• ○	• •
16	20	• ○	• •
17	20	• ○	•• •
18	21	• • •○	•
19	22	○ ••	•
20	22	• ○	• • •
21	23	• • ○	•
22	23	• ○	
23	24	• •○	
24	25	• • ○	
25	26	• • ○	•
26	26	• • •○	•
27	27	• ○	
28	30	•○	••
29	31	• • ○	•

Plate 9-1. *Configurations of Jupiter's satellites observed by Galileo in the month of January, 1610. From E. S. Carlos, " The Sidereal Messenger of Galileo Galilei," Rivingtons, London, 1880.*

on the previous night they had appeared nearly of equal magnitude. I therefore concluded, and decided unhesitatingly, that there are three stars in the heavens moving about Jupiter, as Venus and Mercury round the Sun; which at length was established as clear as daylight by numerous other subsequent observations. These observations also established that there are not only three, but four, erratic sidereal bodies performing their revolutions round Jupiter, . . .

Orbits and Periods of Jupiter's Satellites

And, in the first place, since they are sometimes behind, sometimes before Jupiter, at like distances, and withdraw from this planet towards the east and towards the west only within very narrow limits of divergence, and since they accompany this planet alike when its motion is retrograde and direct, it can be a matter of doubt to no one that they perform their revolutions about this planet, while at the same time they will accomplish together orbits of twelve years' length about the centre of the world. Moreover, they revolve in unequal circles, which is evidently the conclusion to be drawn from the fact that I have never been permitted to see two satellites in conjunction when their distance from Jupiter was great, whereas near Jupiter two, three, and sometimes all (four), have been found closely packed together. Moreover, it may be detected that the revolutions of the satellites which describe the smallest circles round Jupiter are the most rapid, for the satellites nearest to Jupiter are often to be seen in the east, when the day before they have appeared in the west, and contrariwise. Also the satellite moving in the greatest orbit seems to me, after carefully weighing the occasions of its returning to positions previously noticed, to have a periodic time of half a month. Besides, we have a notable and splendid argument to remove the scruples of those who can tolerate the revolution of the planets round the Sun in the Copernican system, yet are so disturbed by the motion of one Moon about the Earth, while both accomplish an orbit of a year's length about the Sun, that they consider that this theory of the constitution of the universe must be upset as impossible; for now we have not one planet only revolving about another, while both traverse a vast orbit about the Sun, but our sense of sight presents to us four satellites circling about Jupiter, like the Moon about the Earth, while the whole system travels over a mighty orbit about the Sun in the space of twelve years.

STUDY QUESTIONS

1. Galileo's first astronomical telescope used

    (1) lenses   (2) concave mirrors   (3) both lenses and mirrors
    (4) plain mirrors   (5) prisms.

2. Select from the following list the feature or object which Galileo did *not* discover with his telescope.

    (1) The phases of Venus.
    (2) Four of Jupiter's moons.

(3) Spots on the sun.
(4) The two moons of Mars.
(5) "Librations" of the earth's moon.

3. Which of the following are true?
   a. Galileo thought of the Medicean planets (moons of Jupiter) as being planets grouped with Jupiter in its orbit but not necessarily revolving about Jupiter.
   b. Galileo saw only three of Jupiter's moons.
   c. Galileo assumed the objects he named the Medicean planets revolved around Jupiter and hence traveled with it in its orbit.
   The correct answer is

   (1) a   (2) b   (3) c   (4) a and b   (3) b and c.

4. Fortified by his telescopic discoveries, Galileo became a publicly professing Copernican. Which of the following statements describes best the way in which his discoveries were received?

   (1) No one accepted his statements. Everyone considered him a crackpot.
   (2) A few people accepted his findings as tentative evidence for the Copernican system, but none completely rejected the Ptolemaic system.
   (3) A few people accepted his discoveries as strong evidence for the Copernican system and as definite disproof of the Ptolemaic system.
   (4) Most people accepted the discoveries as a proof of the Copernican system.
   (5) Everyone adopted the Copernican system and rejected the Ptolemaic system because of his discoveries.

5. Which of the following are true?
   a. Previous observers had noted Jupiter's moons and Galileo only checked these observations.
   b. It was mostly chance that Galileo observed Jupiter on two consecutive nights and from his memory of the first observation decided several changes had been made in the star configuration around Jupiter.
   c. In the process of observing the moons of Jupiter, Galileo obtained an approximate period for at least one of Jupiter's moons.
   The correct answer is

   (1) a and b   (2) b   (3) c   (4) b and c   (5) a and c.

6. Reproduced below are two observations by Galileo of the moons of Jupiter during January 1610. The most probable reason for the fourth moon not being shown on the drawing of January 12 is that

   (1) it was eclipsed by Jupiter
   (2) Galileo wasn't a careful observer
   (3) it was really a star, not a moon

East   West

Jan. 12   • •○   •

Jan. 13   •   ○ • • •

(4) it was outside the field of his telescope

(5) it was eclipsed by another moon.

7. Galileo noted that the satellites of Jupiter did not all move with the same speed. He found that the smaller the radius of a satellite's orbit the faster the satellite moved. This observation could be considered evidence which supports

(1) Bode's law   (2) Kepler's 3rd law   (3) the Pythagorean rule
(4) the eccentric hypothesis   (5) the epicyclic theory.

8. Which of the following statements concerning the appearance of Venus are correct?

a. When in the full phase, Venus appears to have the greatest diameter.

b. When in the quarter phase, the curved side of Venus is toward the sun.

c. After passing through the new phase and approaching the first quarter, Venus appears to move westward from the sun.

The correct answer is

(1) a   (2) b   (3) c   (4) b and c   (5) a, b, and c.

9. Which of the following do you believe to be the best statement about the importance of Galileo's discovery of Jupiter's satellites?

(1) Galileo's discovery was important since it answered a criticism of the Copernican system. Copernicus' system had been criticized since all of the bodies moved in orbits about the sun except for the moon which moved in an orbit about the earth. Galileo was able to show that four satellites moved about Jupiter and that the entire system then moved about the sun. Thus the earth-moon system was not unique.

(2) Galileo's discovery was important since it demonstrated that Jupiter and its satellites were a miniature Copernican system. Thus, the planets could revolve about the sun just as plausibly as the evident revolutions of Jupiter's satellites about Jupiter.

(3) Galileo's discovery was important since it showed that there was more of the solar system yet to be discovered.

(4) Galileo's discovery was important since it enabled him to calculate the mass of Jupiter by observing the periods of Jupiter's satellites.

(5) Galileo's discovery was important since it showed that Jupiter did not shine by its own light. That is, the satellites were eclipsed when they came into the shadow of Jupiter. If Jupiter shone with its own light, there would be no such eclipses.

10. Which of the following phases of Venus did Galileo observe?

(1) full (2) crescent (3) quarter (4) gibbous (5) all of the above.

11. Which of the following correctly completes the sentence?

Galileo's observations of Venus proved to him that

a. Venus revolved about the earth and hence, like the moon, showed all phases

b. Venus revolved about the sun because it showed phases and changed in apparent size

c. Venus was definitely not self-luminous.

The correct answer is

(1) a   (2) b   (3) c   (4) a and b   (5) b and c.

12. Which of the following are true?
    a. All of Galileo's work was recorded for posterity through the letters he wrote to his contemporaries.
    b. Galileo was a recluse and his work was recorded for posterity through his diaries.
    c. Galileo recorded none of his work; our only knowledge of his work is through the writings of his contemporaries.
    The correct answer is

    (1) a　　(2) b　　(3) c　　(4) all　　(5) none of them.

13. Tycho Brahe claimed that the earth was stationary in space, just as Ptolemy had done. However, he held that Venus revolved around the sun as the sun went around the earth. Which, if any, of Galileo's observations disproved this idea?

    (1) The motion of Jupiter's satellites.　　(2) The phases of Venus.
    (3) The "librations" of the moon.　　(4) The spots on the sun.
    (5) None of the observations disproved the theory.

14. Which of the following do you believe to be the best statement about the importance of Galileo's discovery of the phases of Venus?

    (1) Referring to the drawings at the end of Chapter 7, we see that in the Ptolemaic system (Fig. 7-2) Venus would show only new and crescent phases while in the Copernican system (Fig. 7-3) Venus would show all of the phases to the earth. Hence the importance of Galileo's observations was that they disproved the Ptolemaic system and proved the Copernican system.
    (2) The importance of Galileo's observations was that they showed that Venus moved completely around the sun as seen from the earth, but they did not prove that the earth moved. Thus the Ptolemaic system is incorrect, but the Copernican system is not proven.
    (3) The importance of Galileo's observations was that they showed that Venus shone by reflected light from the sun and was not self-luminous.
    (4) The importance of Galileo's observations was that they produced new and previously unknown data about the solar system.
    (5) The importance of Galileo's observations was that they showed that Venus, another planet, was much like the earth. Hence the other planets were no more "celestial and perfect" than the earth.

15. Galileo could not prove the motion of the earth yet believed in it very strongly even though this meant personal danger. Why do you suppose he took this unpopular stand?

    (1) Because he knew that progress is made only by scientists who refuse to conform to any established standards.
    (2) Because the comparative simplicity of the Copernican system appealed to him.
    (3) Because he liked to be different and to live recklessly.
    (4) Because Copernicus offered the only theory consonant with his observations.
    (5) Because it gave him great prestige with the Church.

16. What significance did Galileo's discovery of the satellites of Jupiter have on theories of the planetary system? Could Galileo's observations be accom-

modated by the Ptolemaic theory? Was the discovery of Jupiter's satellites proof of the Copernican scheme?

17. What effect did Galileo's discovery of the phases of Venus have on the Ptolemaic system? Study the earlier diagram of the Ptolemaic system (Fig. 7-2) and decide which phases should have been shown to the earth if that system were true.

18. What effect did Galileo's discovery of the phases of Venus have on the Copernican construction?

19. Galileo says in his foreword " To the Diligent Reader " in his *Dialogue* that: " I shall try to show that all experiments practicable upon the earth are insufficient measures for proving its mobility, since they are indifferently adaptable to an earth in motion or at rest." Can Galileo's observations of the phases of Venus be adapted to the postulate of a stationary earth?

20. If it was not possible for Galileo to prove the motion of the earth, why do you think he believed so fervently (and with such personal dangers) in the Copernican system?

10

Galileo and the Copernican System

● Both the telescope and the *Sidereal Messenger* were immediate successes. The Republic of Venice granted Galileo life-time tenure in his appointment as a professor at the University of Padua and doubled his salary. But Galileo was a homesick Florentine. He had sought the private post of tutor to the young Cosimo. He had dedicated his book to Cosimo II de' Medici now newly elevated to be the Fourth Grand Duke of Tuscany. He had named his newly discovered satellites of Jupiter after the Medici family. While the acclaim of the world was still loud in his ears, he journeyed to Pisa during the Easter vacation of 1610 and applied to Belisario Vinta, Secretary of State to the Grand Duke of Tuscany, for the position of court mathematician. In July of that year Galileo was appointed chief mathematician and philosopher to the Grand Duke of Tuscany and head mathematician of the University of Pisa (without any teaching duties) at the same annual salary which the Republic of Venice had paid him.

Venice was annoyed, even angry, at Galileo's unceremonious leave-taking. After all, Venice had welcomed Galileo to the university at Padua after he had been ejected from the Tuscan university at Pisa. Venice had sheltered and honored him for eighteen years. Perhaps he would never have left if his good friend and politically powerful associate, Giovan Francesco Sagredo, had been in Venice at the time. But Sagredo was absent from Venice on a diplomatic mission. Upon his return a year later, Sagredo wrote Galileo a very astute letter pointing out that Galileo was beyond the reach of the Inquisition at Venice, but not at Florence. History was to bear Sagredo out!

In 1611 Galileo made a triumphal visit to Rome where he was hailed as the discoverer of the age and feted by the Jesuit mathematicians at the Roman College. Here he was elected to the Accademia dei Lincei, one of the first of the scientific societies which characterize our own age. This academy was organized and financially supported by the young

150

nobleman Federigo Cesi, the son of the powerful Duke of Aquasparta. At first, the academy had consisted of only Cesi, his teacher, Giambattasta Porta, and three friends. Galileo was the sixth member to be elected. The Academy went on to expand further and to become important in the Italian scientific scene. Galileo prized his own election highly and added the designation " Linceo " to his own name on the frontispieces of his books. But as a small omen of the future, shortly after Galileo's return to Florence, Cardinal Bellarmine sent a secret letter to the chief inquisitor at Padua to see if Galileo's name had been mentioned in the proceedings against Cesare Cremonino. Cremonino, head of the philosophy department of the University of Padua, had long been sought by the Inquisition for trial for heresy, but was protected by the Republic of Venice and never surrendered to the Church.

Galileo published a book on floating bodies in which the experimental refutation of certain classic Aristotelian views was displayed for all to see. Then he moved to the suburban Villa delle Selve owned by his friend Filippo Salviati, where he wrote his " Letter on Sunspots." Galileo was a publicly avowed Copernican by this time and found himself under ecclesiastical attack for espousing a new and different arrangement of the heavens. His friends suggested that he make the tactical compromise of proposing the Copernican system as being only mathematically convenient while holding the Ptolemaic as theologically true. Galileo did not propose to compromise but to meet the issues head-on. His stubbornness here does not appear to have been a hardheaded insistence on his own views, but instead to have been a genuine concern that the Church should not appear foolish in an area in which clerics were not competent to judge.

In December of 1615, Galileo journeyed to Rome to lay his case directly before the Church. At first he seemed to have success. He had many friends among the high hierarchy of the Church. Most of the important Cardinals seemed to want to avoid the issue by one compromise or another. But Pope Paul V wished to end the discussion for all time. Accordingly, Paul asked the Congregation of the Index to decide the issue. The decision was against Copernicus. Galileo was instructed not to teach the Copernican system from that time hence. Galileo returned to Florence broken-hearted and worked quietly at noncontroversial matters.

In 1623 Galileo's old friend, Cardinal Maffeo Barberini, became Pope Urban VIII. Galileo dedicated his new book *The Assayer* to him. This was a polemic about astronomical questions aimed against the Jesuit Horatio Grassi. The new Pope was amused by the book and appreciative of the dedication. Galileo began to work again on his *Dialogue Concerning the Two Chief World Systems.* He discussed his forthcoming book with the new and friendly Pope. It was agreed that he could present as hypotheses only both the Copernican and the Ptolemaic systems as long as he was impartial to both. He completed his book in 1630, but another year was to pass in gaining permissions to print and in making the changes suggested by the Church. His book finally appeared in February, 1632 under the full imprimatur of the Church.

We present here three excerpts from his book. The first is the all-important foreword "To the Diligent Reader" in which he hoped to propitiate the Church while still presenting his true views to his reading public. Here he outlines his literary form of a dialogue between three participants who presumably meet to discuss the questions on four successive days. He was to adopt the same form and same cast of interlocutors in his last great book, *Dialogues Concerning Two New Sciences*. The two textual excerpts are both from the Third Day of the Dialogue and pertain to the arrangements of the planetary orbits and to the Copernican explanation of the observed retrograde motion of the planets.

DIALOGUE CONCERNING THE TWO CHIEF WORLD SYSTEMS [1]
by Galileo Galilei
To the Diligent Reader

A salutary edict was published in Rome a few years ago which — to prevent the dangerous searchings of the present age — imposed an appropriate silence on the Pythagorean opinion that the earth moves. Some people asserted rashly that this edict has not been the product of judicious inquiry, but of an ill-informed passion, and complaints were heard that advisors who were completely inexpert regarding astronomical observations ought not to clip the wings of speculative intellects by means of sudden prohibitions. My zeal could not allow me to remain silent upon hearing the boldness of such complaints. I decided, being fully instructed regarding that very wise determination, to appear publicly in the theater of the world, as a witness of sincere truth. I was at that time in Rome; I obtained not only hearings but also approval by the most eminent prelates of that court; the publication of this decree eventually followed, but not without my previous knowledge. Therefore, it is my intention in the present work to show foreign nations that more is known about this matter in Italy and especially in Rome, than could ever be imagined by intellectuals beyond the Alps; and to let them know that notice of all of it had been brought before the Roman censorship, and that not only dogmas for the salvation of the soul come out of this climate, but also ingenious discoveries which delight the mind.

For this purpose in the discourse, I took the Copernican part, proceeding as with a pure mathematical hypothesis and trying in every artful way to represent it as superior, not absolutely to that of an immovable earth, but in the manner maintained by some who carry the name of professional Peripatetics and are content, without taking walks, to adore the shadows, philosophizing

[1] Galileo Galilei — *Due Massima Sistemi Del Mondo, Le Opere di Galileo Galilei* Vol. VII Firenge, 1897, pp. 29–31, 350–354, 370–372. Adapted from a translation by A. Moskovic, 1960.

not with proper wisdom, but only with the recollection of the misunderstood four principles (elements).

A three-fold treatment will be presented. At first I shall try to show that all practicable experiments performed on the earth are insufficient measures to prove its mobility, since they can be equally explained by a movable or immovable earth. I hope in this case to reveal many observations unknown to the ancients. In the second place, celestial phenomena will be examined, strengthening the Copernican hypothesis, as if it would emerge absolutely victorious, adding new ideas which are astronomically probable but are not necessarily proven by nature. In the third place, I shall make an ingenious proposal. Many years ago I happened to assert that the unexplained phenomenon of the ocean tides could be partially clarified by the assumption that the earth moves. This assertion of mine, transmitted by word of mouth, found charitable fathers who adopted it as the offspring of their own minds. Hence to make it impossible that some stranger, having fortified himself with our weapons, take advantage of us in a matter of such importance, I have revealed those hypotheses which would make the explanation plausible assuming the earth moves. I hope that, by way of these considerations, the world will learn that if other nations have navigated more, we have not speculated less, and that again asserting the immobility of the earth and taking the contrary view solely as a mathematical whim, does not come from not knowing what others may have thought about it, but if not from anything else, from those reasons which are supplied by devotion, by religion, by the knowledge of Divine Omnipotence, and by the realization of the weakness of the human mind.

Moreover, I have thought it advisable to explain these concepts in the form of a dialogue which, not limited by the rigor of mathematical laws, gives opportunity for digressions which are sometimes no less interesting than the principal topic.

I often found myself, many years ago, in the marvelous city of Venice in conversation with Signor Giovan Francesco Sagredo, illustrious by birth and of the sharpest intuition. Signor Filippo Salviati came there from Florence. The least of his glories were his distinction of blood and the magnificence of his wealth. His was a sublime intellect which fed on no delicacy more avidly than on exquisite speculation. I often found myself discussing these subjects with both of them, with the intervention of a certain Peripatetic philosopher whose greatest obstacle to understanding the truth was the renown he had acquired through his interpretations of Aristotle.

Today, as Venice and Florence have been deprived of both of these brilliant men through their unfortunate deaths in the prime of their lives, I have decided to prolong — as much as possible with my weak forces — their fame in these dialogues of mine by introducing them as interlocutors in the present controversy. Nor will the good Peripatetic lose his place; however, it seemed appropriate — because of his overpowering affection for the commentaries of Simplicius — to give him the name of that revered writer rather than mentioning his own. These two great souls, always venerable to my heart, may accept this public monument of my undying love, and may the memory of their eloquence help me to explain the promised discussions to posterity.

Various discussions occurred casually at different times between these gentlemen, in whose minds the thirst to learn was kindled. Thereby they made the wise decision to meet together on certain days on which, by banishing other business, they would dedicate themselves to orderly discussions of God's marvels in heaven and on earth.

After meeting in the palace of the illustrious Sagredo, following brief compliments, Salviati began in this manner.

The Third Day

✢   ✢   ✢   ✢   ✢   ✢   ✢

Salv. Returning now to the first general ideas, I reply that the sun is the center of the celestial revolutions of the five planets: Saturn, Jupiter, Mars, Venus, and Mercury; and it will also be of the movement of the earth, if we succeed in putting the earth in the heavens. As for the moon, it has a circular movement around the earth, from which it cannot separate itself by any means. However, the moon and the earth together move around the sun as a consequence of the annual revolution of the earth.

Simp. I am not convinced of this arrangement. Perhaps it can be better understood by making a diagram on which the discussion can be based.

Salv. That shall be done. Furthermore I wish that for your greater satisfaction as well as astonishment you yourself draw it, and that you see, although not believing to understand it, you do comprehend it perfectly and will draw it perfectly simply by answering my questions. Take, therefore, a sheet of paper and a compass, and let this white sheet be the immense expanse of the universe, in which you have to distribute and arrange its parts as reason dictates. And first, since without my saying so you suppose the earth to be standing still in this universe, mark a point at which you intend to place the earth and designate it with a letter.

Simp. Let the terrestrial globe be at this place marked A [Fig. 10-1].

Salv. All right. I am aware, moreover, that you know perfectly well that the earth is not inside the body of the sun nor adjacent to it, but at a certain distance; assign to the sun another place that suits you best, at a convenient distance from the earth, and mark this also.

Simp. Here, that's done: let the place of the sun be designated by O.

Salv. After having placed both of these, I desire that we place Venus in such a manner that its position and movement agree with visual observations; however, limit yourself to what you have learned, in former discussions or by your own observations, takes place with this star; and hence assign to it any position that seems suitable.

Simp. I assume that the appearances as told by you and which I have also read in the " booklet of conclusions " are correct, namely, that this star never gets more than 40 degrees or so from the sun, so that it is never in opposition to the sun, nor even in quadrature, nor even at the sextile aspect.[2] Moreover, sometimes it looks nearly 40 times bigger than at other times; biggest when it

---

[2] The aspects of the planets with respect to the sun are related to the angle measured from the sun to the particular planet concerned as viewed from the earth. If this angle is zero the aspect is conjunction; if 60°, sextile aspect; if 90°, quadrature; and if 180°, opposition. (See diagram for footnote 2 on opposite page.)

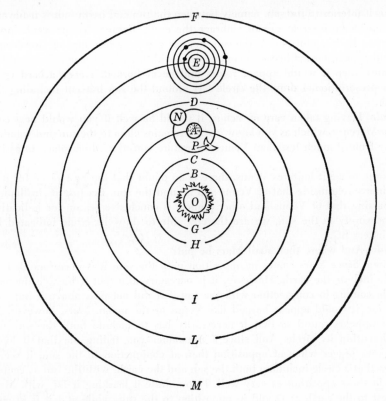

Figure 10-1. *Galileo's Copernican system.*

is retrograde, standing in evening conjunction with the sun, and smallest when with direct movement it comes to morning conjunction. Furthermore, it actually shows a horned form when it appears largest, and when it seems smallest it is perfectly round. Assuming such appearances as real, I do not see how the conclusion can be avoided that this star revolves in a circle around the sun. It can also be said that such a circle in no way contains the earth within itself,

For footnote 2.

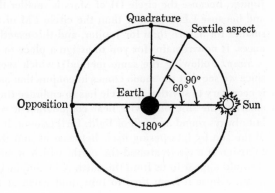

nor is it inferior to the sun, namely between the sun and earth, nor is it beyond the sun. Such a circle cannot embrace the earth, because Venus would upon occasion be in opposition to the sun; neither can it be inferior, because Venus would appear horned between conjunctions with the sun. It cannot be superior, because then it would appear round and never horned. Hence according to your prescription, I draw the circle CH around the sun but not including the earth.

Salv. Having taken care of Venus, it would be well if you would next consider Mercury, which as you know always remains close to the sun and wanders away from it much less than Venus. Therefore consider which place to assign to it.

Simp. Since it imitates Venus, there is no doubt that the best place for it is a minor circle inside that of Venus and around the sun. Because its brilliancy, surpassing that of Venus and other planets is conclusive reason for indicating its proximity to the sun, we are thereby able to draw its circle indicated by the letters BG.

Salv. And where then shall Mars be put?

Simp. Since Mars comes in opposition with the sun, it is necessary that its circle include the earth. However, it is necessary also that it include the sun, for in coming in conjunction with the sun if it did not pass above it but was inferior, it would appear horned like Venus or the moon. Mars, however, always appears round so that it necessarily has to include both the sun and earth within its circle. And since I remember you telling me that it looks 60 times bigger when at opposition than at conjunction to the sun, it seems to me that a circle including both the sun and the earth, with the sun as center, will fit these appearances very well. I now draw it marking it DI, with Mars closest to the earth at D and in opposition to the sun, while at I it is in conjunction with the sun and most distant from the earth. And since the same appearances are observed in Jupiter and Saturn, although with less change in apparent size in Jupiter than in Mars and still less in Saturn than in Jupiter, I conclude that we shall satisfy both these planets with two circles around the sun, marking the first one for Jupiter EL and the second larger one for Saturn FM.

Salv. So far you have behaved remarkably. And since the approach and recession of the three outer planets is twice as great as the distance between the earth and the sun, this distance makes a greater difference for Mars than for Jupiter, because the circle DI of Mars is smaller than the circle EL of Jupiter; and because EL is smaller than the circle FM of Saturn, the difference is still smaller for Saturn than for Jupiter, and this exactly corresponds to the appearances. It now remains for you to assign a place to the moon.

Simp. Following the same method (which seems most conclusive to me), since we see that the moon comes in conjunction and opposition with the sun, it is necessary to say that its circle has to embrace the earth. However, it need not embrace the sun, otherwise near conjunction it would not show itself horned but always round and full of light; furthermore, it could never cause an eclipse of the sun by interposing itself between us and the sun. Hence it is necessary to assign it a circle around the earth, which would be NP, so that when at P it would appear to us from the earth A in conjunction with the sun from where it can eclipse it from time to time, and when at N it is seen in opposition to the sun and in such position can pass into the shadow of the earth and become obscured.

Salv. Now, Simplicio, what shall we do with the fixed stars? Are we going to disperse them throughout the immense abyss of the universe at different distances from any pre-determined point, or else located on one spherical surface around a given center, so that each of them would be equally distant from that center?

Simp. I would rather keep a middle course and assign them an orb described around a definite center and between two spherical surfaces, the outer concave and the inner convex, containing between them the innumerable multitude of stars, but at different distances. This could be called the sphere of the universe, containing on the inside the orbits of the planets as designed by ourselves.

Salv. Thus, Simplicio, we have arranged the celestial bodies according to the distribution by Copernicus, and this has been done by your own hand. Moreover, you have assigned their own movements to all of them, except to the sun, the earth, and the sphere of the stars. You attributed to Mercury and to Venus circular movements around the sun, not embracing the earth. You made the three superior planets, Mars, Jupiter, and Saturn, move around the same sun, assuming the earth inside of their circles, while the moon cannot move in any other manner but around the earth, without embracing the sun. In these motions you quite agree with Copernicus himself. Now three things remain to be decided concerning the sun, the earth, and the stellar sphere, namely, the state of rest which seems to characterize the earth, the annual movement which seems to be that of the sun, and the diurnal movement which seems to belong to the stellar sphere, shared by the entire remainder of the universe with the exception of the earth. And since it is true that all the orbits of the planets, namely of Mercury, Venus, Mars, Jupiter, and Saturn are moving around the sun as their center, it seems much more reasonable that the state of rest belong to the same sun rather than to the earth, because it is much more reasonable that the center of the moving spheres remain at rest than any other place distant from that center. Hence to the earth which is placed in the midst of the moving parts, I say between Venus and Mars, the first of which makes its revolution in nine months and the second in two years, the movement of one year can be attributed very suitably, leaving rest to the sun. And assuming this, the diurnal rotational movement of the earth follows as a necessary consequence, because if, by the sun standing motionless, and if the earth did not rotate (about itself) but only had an annual movement around the sun, our year would be only one day and one night, namely six months of day and six months of night, as stated previously. Thus you see how nicely the extremely precipitous movement of each 24 hours is taken away from the universe, and how the fixed stars which are all suns enjoy perpetual rest in conformity with our sun. You see, moreover, with what simplicity this outline explains such great phenomena in the celestial bodies.

    ✿   ✿   ✿   ✿   ✿   ✿   ✿

Sagr. I would like to understand better how these stations, retrogressions and forward motions, which had always appeared highly improbable to me, take place in the Copernican system.

Salv. Sagredo, you will see them explained in such manner that this hypothesis alone should be sufficient to cause anyone who is not stubborn and unteachable to agree with the entire remaining part of this doctrine. I tell you, consequently, that there has been no change in the movement of Saturn in 30 years, in that of Jupiter in 12 years, in that of Mars in 2, in that of Venus in 9 months, and in that of Mercury in about 80 days. The annual movement of the earth between Mars and Venus is the sole cause of the apparent inequalities in the motions of all five stars mentioned, and to help you understand everything easily and completely, I wish to diagram [3] it. Let us suppose the sun located at the center O [Fig. 10-2], around which we indicate the orbit described by the earth with an annual movement BGM, and let *bgm* be the circle described by Jupiter around the sun in 12 years, and let us assume the zodiac *pua* in the stellar space. Moreover, we divide the annual orbit of the earth into several equal arcs BC, CD, DE, EF, FG, GH, HI, IK, KL, LM, and we indicate on Jupiter's circle other arcs passed over in the same times as those passed over by the earth. Let these be *bc, cd, de, ef, fg, gh, hi, ik, kl, lm,* each of which is proportionally smaller than those marked on the earth's orbit since Jupiter's motion in its circle is slower than that of the earth. Let us now suppose that when the earth is at B, Jupiter is at *b* and will appear to us to be in the zodiac at *p* along the straight line B*bp*. Now assume the earth moves from B to C and Jupiter moves from *b* to *c* in the same time. To us Jupiter will appear to have arrived at *q* in the zodiac, moving forward in the direction of the signs from *p* to *q*. As the earth moves forward to D, Jupiter will move to *d* and appear in the zodiac at *r*, and with the earth at E, Jupiter at *e* will appear at *s* continuing to move in the same direction. However, as the earth begins to move more nearly in a direct line between Jupiter and the sun, arriving at F, Jupiter at *f* will appear in the zodiac at *t* and is now ready to start the appearance of moving backward along the zodiac. In the time required for the earth to have traveled along the arc EF, Jupiter will appear to us to be almost standing still between the points *s* and *t*. Upon the arrival of the earth at G and Jupiter at *g* in opposition to the sun, Jupiter will be seen in the zodiac at *u*, having returned backward by the arc *tu*, but actually, Jupiter always following its uniform course has advanced not only in its own orbit but also could have been seen to advance among the stars if viewed from the sun. The earth and Jupiter continuing their motion, the earth having come to H and Jupiter to *h*, it will be seen that Jupiter has returned along the zodiac by the whole arc *ux*; the earth having arrived at I and Jupiter at *i* will have moved apparently the small distance *xy* in the zodiac and will appear there as almost stationary. When the earth arrives at K and Jupiter at *k*, it will advance the arc *yn* along the zodiac. Continuing, Jupiter at *l* will be seen at *z* from the earth at L, and finally Jupiter at *m* will be seen at *a* from the earth at M, still in direct motion. The entire apparent retrograde motion of Jupiter will be not more than the arc *tx* along the zodiac, made while Jupiter is traveling along its own circle from *f* to *h* and the earth along its circle from F to H.

What has been said about Jupiter is also valid for Saturn and Mars, whereby retrogressions are somewhat more frequent with Saturn than with Jupiter,

---

[3] The diagram as shown here has been reversed from that given by Galileo who looked at the solar system from the south rather than the north side. The arc traveled by Jupiter in one year has also been expanded for clarity.

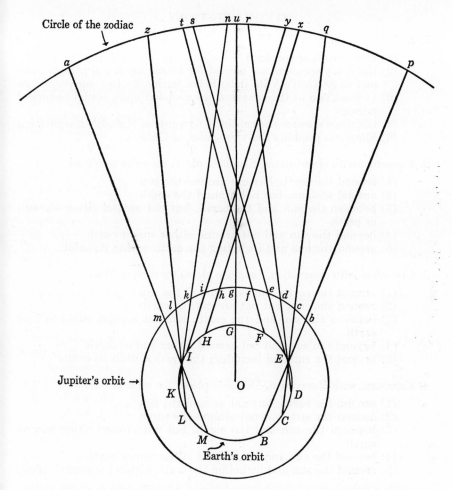

Figure 10-2. *Retrograde motion of Jupiter. As the earth moves from F to G, Jupiter appears to start to move westward against the background of stars.*

since its movement is slower than that of Jupiter and the earth catches up with it in a shorter time. In Mars the retrogressions are rarer, since its movement is faster than that of Jupiter and the earth requires more time to catch up with it.

As to Venus and Mercury with their circles inside that of the earth, their positions and regressions do not appear to be caused by their own motions but by the annual motion of the earth, as Copernicus acutely demonstrates with Apollonius of Perga in Chapter 35 of Book 5 of his *Revolutions.*

You see, gentlemen, with how much ease and simplicity the assumed annual motion of the earth is able to explain the apparent anomalies observed in the movements of the five planets, Saturn, Jupiter, Mars, Venus, and Mercury, abolishing all of them and reducing them to regular motions, and it was Nicolas Copernicus who first made apparent the reasons for this marvelous effect.

STUDY QUESTIONS

1. In Galileo's *Dialogue,*

   (1) there are four speakers
   (2) the three speakers are named for actual historical persons who met in Salviati's Villa delle Selve for intellectual conversations
   (3) at least two of the speakers are modeled upon actual historical persons
   (4) the three speakers are entirely figments of Galileo's imagination
   (5) Simplicio presents the view-point of Galileo.

2. Consistent with observations, Simplicio places the orbit of Venus

   (1) around the earth, but not around the sun
   (2) around the sun, but not around the earth
   (3) between the sun and the earth, but not around either the sun or earth
   (4) beyond the sun and not around either sun or earth
   (5) around the sun and including the earth within its orbit.

3. Consistent with observation, Simplicio places the orbit of Mars

   (1) around the earth, but not around the sun
   (2) around the sun, but not around the earth
   (3) between the sun and the earth, but not around either sun or earth
   (4) beyond the sun and not around either sun or earth
   (5) around the sun and including the earth within its orbit.

4. Consistent with observation, Simplicio places the orbit of the moon

   (1) around the earth, but not around the sun
   (2) around the sun, but not around the earth
   (3) between the sun and the earth, but not around either sun or earth
   (4) beyond the sun and not around either sun or earth
   (5) around the sun and including the earth within the moon's orbit.

5. Simplicio chose his particular orbit for Venus because

   (1) Venus when seen in conjunction with the sun was apparently 40 times larger when in the new phase than it was when in the full phase
   (2) Venus was observed in quarter phase when in opposition to the sun
   (3) Venus never approached closer than 40° to the sun
   (4) Venus was observed to have only the phases of new — crescent — new
   (5) Venus was observed to go through all of the phases of the moon, being new when in conjunction with the sun and full when in opposition.

6. Simplicio chose his particular orbit for Mars because

   (1) Mars when seen in conjunction with the sun was apparently 40 times larger when in the new phase than it was when in the full phase

(2) Mars when seen in opposition to the sun was in the full phase and apparently 60 times larger than when it was in conjunction with the sun and also appeared in the full phase

(3) Mars never approached closer than 40° to the sun

(4) Mars was observed to have only the phases of new — crescent — new

(5) Mars was observed to go through all of the phases of the moon, being new when in conjunction with the sun and full when in opposition.

7. Simplicio chose his particular orbit for the moon because

(1) the moon when seen in conjunction with the sun was apparently 80 times larger when in the new phase than it was when in the full phase

(2) the moon was observed in quarter phase when in opposition to the sun

(3) the moon never approached closer than 40° to the sun

(4) the moon was observed to have only the phases of new — crescent — new

(5) the moon was observed to go through all of the phases, new — quarter — full — quarter — new, being in full phase when in opposition to the sun and new phase when in conjunction with the sun.

8. Simplicio placed the fixed stars

(1) on a celestial sphere at a great but finite distance from the earth

(2) on a celestial sphere at an infinite distance from the earth

(3) between two spheres; one was of very great radius while the second sphere was closer at hand

(4) uniformly throughout all space

(5) on a celestial sphere located between the orbits of Jupiter and Saturn.

9. In the excerpt quoted, Galileo

(1) proved that the state of rest belonged to the sun, the annual motion to the earth moving in its orbit, and the diurnal movement to the rotation of the earth

(2) proved that the state of rest belonged to the earth; the annual motion to the sun; and the diurnal movement to the celestial sphere

(3) did not prove either proposition (1) or (2), but indicated a preference for (1)

(4) did not prove either proposition (1) or (2), but indicated a preference for (2)

(5) proved that the sun moved among the stars and that all motion was purely relative.

10. The observed retrograde motion of the planets is explained by Galileo by

(1) the uniform motions of all the planets including the earth in circular orbits about the sun

(2) the use of epicycles

(3) a variable motion of the planets within the orbits

    (4) the earth moving more slowly in its orbit than the planet Jupiter

    (5) a projection of the relative motions of the earth and Jupiter upon a celestial sphere just a little beyond the orbit of Jupiter.

11. Galileo states in his foreword that " I shall try to show that all experiments practicable upon the earth are insufficient measures for proving its mobility, since they are indifferently adaptable to an earth in motion or at rest." Why then does Galileo state so positively in the excerpts which we have read that it is the earth which is in motion?

12. It is very curious that Galileo should have ignored the Tychonic system. How would his various arguments for the motion of the earth and the arrangement of the solar system have applied to the Tychonic system?

13. Precisely what are the advances (if any) in astronomy between the time of Ptolemy and that of Galileo as seen in their texts?

14. Can you deduce the approximate radius of the orbit of Venus from the observations which Galileo quotes in his text?

PART FOUR

THE REVISION OF MECHANICS

The appearance of *The Dialogue Concerning the Two Chief World Systems* in February of 1632 aroused widespread interest. By the time that the Church learned that Ptolemy and Aristotle fared badly in it, hardly a copy remained unsold in all of Italy. In August of that year the printer was ordered to cease the sale of the book. The Church swiftly listed the *Dialogue* and Kepler's *Epitome of Copernican Astronomy* on the Index along with Copernicus' *De Revolutionibus,* and all three books remained under ban until 1835.

Galileo was ordered to Rome for trial under the Inquisition. He pleaded age and ill health, but to no avail. He surrendered to the Holy Office in Rome on April 12, 1633 and was imprisoned in the Inquisition Building. His trial proceeded slowly, through April, May, and into June. Finally on June 22, 1633 he was brought to a large hall in the Dominican convent of Santa Maria sopra Minerva which stands on the site of the old Roman temple to the goddess of wisdom. Here, dressed in the white shirt of penitence, he knelt before his judges while the sentence was read to him: [1]

We say, pronounce, sentence, and declare that you, the said Galileo, . . . have rendered yourself in the judgment of this Holy Office vehemently suspected of heresy, namely, of having believed and held the doctrine — which is false and contrary to the sacred and divine Scriptures — that the Sun is the center of the world and does not move from east to west and that the Earth moves and is not the center of the world; . . . From which we are content that you be absolved, provided that, first, with a sincere heart and unfeigned faith, you abjure, curse, and detest before us the aforesaid errors and heresies and every other error and heresy contrary to the Catholic and Apostolic Roman Church in the form to be prescribed by us for you.

And, in order that this your grave and pernicious error and transgression may not remain altogether unpunished and that you may be more cautious in

----

[1] Giorgia De Santillana, *The Crime of Galileo,* The Univ. of Chicago Press, pp. 310, 312. Copyright 1955 by the University of Chicago.

the future and an example to others that they may abstain from similar delinquencies we ordain that the book of the " Dialogue of Galileo Galilei " be prohibited by public edict.

We condemn you to the formal prison of this Holy Office during our pleasure, and by way of salutary penance we enjoin that for three years to come you repeat once a week the seven penitential Psalms. Reserving to ourselves liberty to moderate, commute, or take off, in whole or in part, the aforesaid penalties and penance.

And so we say, pronounce, sentence, declare, ordain, and reserve in this and in any other better way and form which we can and may rightfully employ.

In accordance with this sentence, Galileo made his abjuration in the form prescribed to him:

I, Galileo, son of the late Vincenzo Galilei, Florentine, aged seventy years, arraigned personally before this tribunal and kneeling before you, Most Eminent and Reverend Lord Cardinals Inquisitors-General against heretical pravity throughout the entire Christian commonwealth, having before my eyes and touching with my hands the Holy Gospels, swear that I have always believed, do believe, and by God's help will in the future believe all that is held, preached, and taught by the Holy Catholic and Apostolic Church. But, whereas — after an injunction had been judicially intimated to me by this Holy Office to the effect that I must altogether abandon the false opinion that the Sun is the center of the world and immovable and that the Earth is not the center of the world and moves and that I must not hold, defend, or teach in any way whatsoever, verbally or in writing, the said false doctrine, and after it had been notified to me that the said doctrine was contrary to Holy Scripture — I wrote and printed a book in which I discuss this new doctrine already condemned and adduce arguments of great cogency in its favor without presenting any solution of these, I have been pronounced by the Holy Office to be vehemently suspected of heresy, that is to say, of having held and believed that the Sun is the center of the world and immovable and that the Earth is not the center and moves:

Therefore, desiring to remove from the minds of your Eminences, and of all faithful Christians, this vehement suspicion justly conceived against me, with sincere heart and unfeigned faith, I abjure, curse, and detest the aforesaid errors and heresies and generally every other error, heresy, and sect whatsoever contrary to the Holy Church, . . .

It was the intent of the Inquisition that Galileo should spend a long period of penitence in the monastery of Santa Croce in Gerusalemme. However, Ascario Piccolomini, Archbishop of Siena, with the help of Cardinal Barberini, had Galileo committed to his care for five months, although the provision was imposed that Galileo was to see no one. Nevertheless, as soon as Piccolomini received custody of Galileo, he lodged him in his archiepiscopal palace in Siena and opened the doors to all who wanted to see him. Here he began to work energetically on the theory of mechanics. After the five months in Siena, it was intended that Galileo be committed to the Charterhouse of Florence. This sentence was later commuted and Galileo was allowed to return to his own farm at Arcetri in the suburbs of Florence to live out his life under perpetual house arrest.

It was thoroughly pertinent that Galileo should spend the last years of his life working on the theory of mechanics. Part of the sentence read to Galileo by the Judges of the Inquisition was: [2]

The proposition that the Sun is the center of the world and does not move from its place is absurd and false philosophically and formally heretical, because it is expressly contrary to the Holy Scripture.

The proposition that the Earth is not the center of the world and immovable but that it moves, and also with a diurnal motion, is equally absurd and false philosophically and theologically considered at least erroneous in faith.

These two propositions were false according to the philosophy of Aristotle. If the earth were made of the four terrestrial elements, earth, water, fire, and air, whose natural place was at the center of the universe, the earth and not the sun would be at the center of the world. If the sun, moon, planets, and stars were made of the fifth element, the quintessence, whose natural motions were some combinations of circles, the Ptolemaic system is almost a logical necessity. A new astronomy demanded a new mechanics.

The Aristotelian physics had had its critics even in classical times. For example, John Philoponus, who lived in the 6th century, held that bodies did not fall as alleged by Aristotle with speeds which were directly proportional to their weights and inversely proportional to the resistance of the medium. He held more than a thousand years before Galileo that a body would fall through a vacuum at a finite speed and would require a greater time to fall through a resisting medium. It would also appear that John Philoponus had experimentally disproven Aristotle by actually dropping bodies of different weights and finding that they fell with nearly the same speeds through air.

Projectile motion was controversial in Greek thought. Aristotle held that violent motion was the direct result of an extraneous force. The violent motion would continue as long as the force was applied and would cease when the force vanished. Thus it was held that an arrow flew through the air because the air in front of the arrow was forced aside to regroup and push on the back of the arrow. Thus the violent motion of the arrow resulted first from the force of the bowstring and then continued because of the pushing of the flowing air on the back of the arrow. This mechanism did not seem plausible to John Philoponus. He proposed that some sort of incorporeal motive force was imparted to the projectile by the projector. This incorporeal force was used up in overcoming the resistance of the air during the flight of the arrow.

The Arabian scholars continued the Greek controversies. Avempace

---

[2] Giorgia De Santillana, *The Crime of Galileo,* The Univ. of Chicago Press, p. 307. Copyright 1955 by The University of Chicago.

agreed with Philoponus as to the speed of falling bodies. Averroës, however, defended Aristotle. Avicenna felt that the projectile received something which he called "mail" from the mover. It was this something which made the body move.

With the revival of learning in Europe four mathematical logicians at Merton College in Oxford in 1328 began the study of kinematics, the description of motion. These four men were Thomas Bradwardine, later to be Archbishop of Canterbury; William Heytesbury, who may have become chancellor of Oxford in his later days; Richard Swineshead; and John Dumbleton. These four men sharpened the terminology of mechanics. Aristotle and his later commentators had spoken loosely about speed and motion. The Merton College men were careful logicians and knew that space and time were completely different logical categories. Therefore their measure of uniform velocities was the comparison of the spaces traversed in a particular given time. A uniform velocity was recognized as one traversing equal spaces in all equal time intervals. They recognized several different types of motion. Instantaneous velocity would be proportional to the space which would have been traversed in a given interval of time if the motion had continued on as uniform. Accelerated motion was motion in which the instantaneous velocity varied with time. If the instantaneous velocity was proportional to the time, then the motion was uniformly accelerated. They stated and proved the important theorem that the distance covered by a point moving with uniform acceleration during a stated time interval was equal to the distance which this point would have moved with the mean velocity, the instantaneous velocity of the point at the middle of the time interval, during this given time interval.

The ideas of the Merton school crossed the Channel to Nicole Oresme at the University of Paris. Oresme presented quantities and motion by geometrical figures. While Oresme probably did not invent this technique, he did make the relations between the various kinds of motion more graphic and hence more easily assimilated. Symbolization is an important step toward modern science. It is true that ideas are basic and that ideas should be representable by words, but symbols, whether geometric or algebraic, allow the mind to grasp complicated interrelationships at one glance.

The genius of the Paris school was not in kinematics but in dynamics. It was Oresme's teacher, John Buridan, who was the principal exponent of impetus dynamics. Buridan thought of "impetus" as something put into a body by a force. The impetus increased directly with the weight of the body and with its velocity. Thus the concept is suggestive of Newton's "quantity of motion" or of our modern "momentum." But Buridan thought of impetus as a kind of force which kept the body moving with its violent motion until the impetus was expended against the resistance to the motion. If there were no resistance, the motion would continue forever. Thus Buridan thought of the celestial bodies, the stars, planets, sun, and moon, as moving in an empty outer space without resistance and hence moving forever with the original impetus which was given to them in the beginning by God.

These ideas spread throughout all of Europe, although with some modification of terms and meanings. We find them, for instance, in the notebooks of Leonardo da Vinci. Leonardo, however, like many other scholars of his time, would use the Merton definition of uniform acceleration as equal changes in velocities during equal time intervals on one page, but would use the idea of uniform acceleration as being equal changes in velocities during equal distances of motion on another page, without being aware of the logical contradiction involved.

From this brief account we must not conclude that Aristotle's physics was overthrown in the 6th century and that a new mechanics was modeled over its grave. For every John Philoponus there was a Simplicius who was a greater authority and a firm Aristotelian. An Avempace was overshadowed by the greater fame of an Averroës. The Merton school, John Buridan, and Oresme were completely overwhelmed by the universal respect paid to St. Thomas Aquinas. St. Thomas created a monumental system by the synthesis of Aristotle and the Holy Scriptures which accounted for all aspects of life. No, a truer statement of the situation at the beginning of the 17th century was that Aristotelianism reigned well nigh supreme with only a few dissident voices raised here and there. On the other hand, we can see that Galileo did not begin his revision of mechanics in an intellectual vacuum. He had predecessors and they had ideas which Galileo and Newton were able to bring into full flower.

11

Galileo and the Refutation of Aristotle's Mechanics

● Galileo wrote his greatest book *Discourses and Mathematical Demonstrations Concerning Two New Sciences* in the years which remained to him at Arcetri. He completed most of the manuscript for this book in 1634, but found that it was difficult for a man under sentence from the Inquisition to find a publisher. His friends tried to arrange publication at Venice, but the Church intervened. He sent part of his manuscript to his former student, Giovanni Battista Pieroni, who was in the service of the Holy Roman Emperor, hoping for publication in Germany. Here, too, difficulties, real or imagined, arose. So when the Dutch publisher Louis Elzevir visited Italy in 1636, Galileo turned his manuscript over to him for publication in Holland, a Protestant country. The book appeared at Leyden in July of 1638 carrying a foreword by Galileo denying all knowledge as to how his manuscript might have ever fallen into Elzevir's hands. After all, part of the sentence imposed upon Galileo forbade him from publishing any of his work!

This last great book of Galileo is concerned with the strength of materials and with problems in motion. Here in the refutation of Aristotle's mechanics and its reformulation into modern mechanics begins this modern scientific age. The book opens with the three friends, Salviati, Sagredo, and Simplicio, visiting a shipyard in Venice. The question arises as to why a large boat needs copious scaffolding to hold it together during erection while a small boat can be built on the floor without any added supports whatever. The reason must reside in the nature of matter and the source of its ultimate strength. Since Galileo believes that matter can be infinitely divided, it must be made up of an infinite number of mathematical point atoms. Then the final source of the strength of material must be some sort of nonmaterial force acting between the atoms. The only nonmaterial force which Galileo can suggest is "the power of the vacuum" which, while small, could accumulate to any required total when acting between an infinite number of atoms.

But in the opening statement of the excerpt which follows, Simplicio objects that as a logical conclusion of Aristotle's mechanics a vacuum cannot exist. Galileo, in the roles of his two old friends, Salviati and Sagredo, shows experimentally that Aristotle's mechanics fails to account for nature as observed.

DIALOGUES CONCERNING TWO NEW SCIENCES [1]
by Galileo Galilei

Simp. So far as I remember, Aristotle inveighs against the ancient view that a vacuum is a necessary prerequisite for motion and that the latter could not occur without the former. In opposition to this view Aristotle shows that it is precisely the phenomenon of motion, as we shall see, which renders untenable the idea of a vacuum. His method is to divide the argument into two parts. He first supposes bodies of different weights to move in the same medium; then supposes, one and the same body to move in different media. In the first case, he supposes bodies of different weight to move in one and the same medium with different speeds which stand to one another in the same ratio as the weights; so that, for example, a body which is ten times as heavy as another will move ten times as rapidly as the other. In the second case he assumes that the speeds of one and the same body moving in different media are in inverse ratio to the densities of these media; thus, for instance, if the density of water were ten times that of air, the speed in air would be ten times greater than in water. From this second supposition, he shows that, since the tenuity of a vacuum differs infinitely from that of any medium filled with matter however rare, any body which moves in a plenum through a certain space in a certain time ought to move through a vacuum instantaneously; but instantaneous motion is an impossibility; it is therefore impossible that a vacuum should be produced by motion.

Salv. The argument is, as you see, ad hominem, that is, it is directed against those who thought the vacuum a prerequisite for motion. Now if I admit the argument to be conclusive and concede also that motion cannot take place in a vacuum, the assumption of a vacuum considered absolutely and not with reference to motion, is not thereby invalidated. But to tell you what the ancients might possibly have replied and in order to better understand just how conclusive Aristotle's demonstration is, we may, in my opinion, deny both of his assumptions. And as to the first, I greatly doubt that Aristotle ever tested by experiment whether it be true that two stones, one weighing ten times as much as the other, if allowed to fall, at the same instant, from a height of, say, 100 cubits,[2] would so differ in speed that when the heavier had reached the ground, the other would not have fallen more than 10 cubits.

---

[1] Galileo Galilei, *Dialogues Concerning Two New Sciences,* Translated by Henry Crew and Alfonso De Salvio, Northwestern University, Chicago, 1939, pp. 61–68.

[2] The "cubit" is a unit of length equal to the length of the forearm from elbow to outstretched finger tips.

Simp. His language would seem to indicate that he had tried the experiment, because he says: " We see the heavier "; now the word " see " shows that he had made the experiment.

Sagr. But I, Simplicio, who have made the test can assure you that a cannon ball weighing one or two hundred pounds, or even more, will not reach the ground by as much as a span ahead of a musket ball weighing only half a pound, provided both are dropped from a height of 200 cubits.

Salv. But, even without further experiment, it is possible to prove clearly, by means of a short and conclusive argument, that a heavier body does not move more rapidly than a lighter one provided both bodies are of the same material and in short such as those mentioned by Aristotle. But tell me, Simplicio, whether you admit that each falling body acquires a definite speed fixed by nature, a velocity which cannot be increased or diminished except by the use of force or resistance.

Simp. There can be no doubt but that one and the same body moving in a single medium has a fixed velocity which is determined by nature and which cannot be increased except by the addition of momentum or diminished except by some resistance which retards it.

Salv. If then we take two bodies whose natural speeds are different, it is clear that on uniting the two, the more rapid one will be partly retarded by the slower, and the slower will be somewhat hastened by the swifter. Do you not agree with me in this opinion?

Simp. You are unquestionably right.

Salv. But if this is true, and if a large stone moves with a speed of, say, eight while a smaller moves with a speed of four, then when they are united, the system will move with a speed less than eight; but the two stones when tied together make a stone larger than that which before moved with a speed of eight. Hence the heavier body moves with less speed than the lighter; an effect which is contrary to your supposition. Thus you see how, from your assumption that the heavier body moves more rapidly than the lighter one, I infer that the heavier body moves more slowly.

Simp. I am all at sea because it appears to me that the smaller stone when added to the larger increases its weight and by adding weight I do not see how it can fail to increase its speed or, at least, not to diminish it.

Salv. Here again you are in error, Simplicio, because it is not true that the smaller stone adds weight to the larger.

Simp. This is, indeed, quite beyond my comprehension.

Salv. It will not be beyond you when I have once shown you the mistake under which you are laboring. Note that it is necessary to distinguish between heavy bodies in motion and the same bodies at rest. A large stone placed in a balance not only acquires additional weight by having another stone placed upon it, but even by the addition of a handful of hemp its weight is augmented six to ten ounces according to the quantity of hemp. But if you tie the hemp to the stone and allow them to fall freely from some height, do you believe that the hemp will press down upon the stone and thus accelerate its motion or do you think the motion will be retarded by a partial upward pressure? One always feels the pressure upon his shoulders when he prevents the motion of a load resting upon him; but if one descends just as rapidly as the load would fall how can it gravitate or press upon him? Do you not see that this would be the same as trying to strike a man with a lance when he is running away from you with a speed which is equal to, or even greater, than that with which you are following him? You must therefore conclude that, during free and natural fall, the small stone does not press upon the larger and consequently does not increase its weight as it does when at rest.

Simp. But what if we should place the larger stone upon the smaller?

Salv. Its weight would be increased if the larger stone moved more rapidly; but we have already concluded that when the small stone moves more slowly it retards to some extent the speed of the larger, so that the combination of the two, which is a heavier body than the larger of the two stones, would move less rapidly, a conclusion which is contrary to your hypothesis. We infer therefore that large and small bodies move with the same speed provided they are of the same specific gravity.[3]

Simp. Your discussion is really admirable; yet I do not find it easy to believe that a bird-shot falls as swiftly as a cannon ball.

Salv. Why not say a grain of sand as rapidly as a grindstone? But, Simplicio, I trust you will not follow the example of many others who divert the discussion from its main intent and fasten upon some statement of mine which lacks a hair's-breadth of the truth and, under this hair, hide the fault of another which is as big as a ship's cable. Aristotle says that " an iron ball of one hundred pounds falling from a height of one hundred cubits reaches the ground before a one-pound ball has fallen a single cubit." I say that they arrive at the same time. You find, on making the experiment, that the larger outstrips the smaller by two finger-breadths, that is, when the larger has reached the ground, the other is short of it by two finger-breadths; now you would not hide behind these two fingers the ninety-nine cubits of Aristotle, nor would you mention my small error and at the same time pass over in silence his very large one. Aristotle declares that bodies of different weights, in the same medium, travel (in so far as their motion depends upon gravity) with speeds which are proportional to their weights; this he illustrates by use of bodies in which it is possible to perceive the pure and unadulterated effect of gravity, eliminating other considerations, for example, figure as being of small importance, influences which are greatly dependent upon the medium which modifies the single effect of gravity alone. Thus we observe that gold, the densest of all substances, when beaten out into a very thin leaf, goes floating through the air; the same thing happens with stone when ground into a very fine powder. But if you wish to maintain the general proposition you will have to show that the same ratio of speeds is preserved in the case of all heavy bodies, and that a stone of twenty pounds moves ten times as rapidly as one of two; but I claim that this is false and that, if they fall from a height of fifty or a hundred cubits, they will reach the earth at the same moment.

Simp. Perhaps the result would be different if the fall took place not from a few cubits but from some thousands of cubits.

Salv. If this were what Aristotle meant you would burden him with another error which would amount to a falsehood; because, since there is no such sheer height available on earth, it is clear that Aristotle could not have made the ex-

---

[3] The " specific gravity " of a body is the ratio of its weight to the weight of the same volume of some standard substance, usually water.

periment; yet he wishes to give us the impression of his having performed it when he speaks of such an effect as one which we see.

Simp. In fact, Aristotle does not employ this principle, but uses the other one which is not, I believe, subject to these same difficulties.

Salv. But the one is as false as the other; and I am surprised that you yourself do not see the fallacy and that you do not perceive that if it were true that, in media of different densities and different resistances, such as water and air, one and the same body moved in air more rapidly than in water, in proportion as the density of water is greater than that of air, then it would follow that any body which falls through air ought also to fall through water. But this conclusion is false inasmuch as many bodies which descend in air not only do not descend in water, but actually rise.

Simp. I do not understand the necessity of your inference; and in addition I will say that Aristotle discusses only those bodies which fall in both media, not those which fall in air but rise in water.

Salv. The arguments which you advance for the Philosopher are such as he himself would have certainly avoided so as not to aggravate his first mistake. But tell me now whether the density of the water, or whatever it may be that retards the motion, bears a definite ratio to the density of air which is less retardative; and if so fix a value for it at your pleasure.

Simp. Such a ratio does exist; let us assume it to be ten; then, for a body which falls in both these media, the speed in water will be ten times slower than in air.

Salv. I shall now take one of those bodies which fall in air but not in water, say a wooden ball, and I shall ask you to assign to it any speed you please for its descent through air.

Simp. Let us suppose it moves with a speed of twenty.

Salv. Very well. Then it is clear that this speed bears to some smaller speed the same ratio as the density of water bears to that of air; and the value of this smaller speed is two. So that really if we follow exactly the assumption of Aristotle we ought to infer that the wooden ball which falls in air, a substance ten times less-resisting than water, with a speed of twenty would fall in water with a speed of two, instead of coming to the surface from the bottom as it does; unless perhaps you wish to reply, which I do not believe you will, that the rising of the wood through the water is the same as its falling with a speed of two. But since the wooden ball does not go to the bottom, I think you will agree with me that we can find a ball of another material, not wood, which does fall in water with a speed of two.

Simp. Undoubtedly we can; but it must be of a substance considerably heavier than wood.

Salv. That is it exactly. But if this second ball falls in water with a speed of two, what will be its speed of descent in air? If you hold to the rule of Aristotle you must reply that it will move at the rate of twenty; but twenty is the speed which you yourself have already assigned to the wooden ball; hence this and the other heavier ball will each move through air with the same speed. But now how does the Philosopher harmonize this result with his other, namely, that bodies of different weight move through the same medium with different speeds — speeds which are proportional to their weights? But without going into the matter more deeply, how have these common and obvious properties escaped your notice? Have you not observed that two bodies which fall in water, one with a speed a hundred times as great as that of the other, will fall in air with speeds so nearly equal that one will not surpass the other by as much as one hundredth part? Thus, for example, an egg made of marble will descend in water one hundred times more rapidly than a hen's egg, while in air falling from a height of twenty cubits the one will fall short of the other by less than four finger-breadths. In short, a heavy body which sinks through ten cubits of water in three hours will traverse ten cubits of air in one or two pulse-beats; and if the heavy body be a ball of lead it will easily traverse the ten cubits of water in less than double the time required for ten cubits of air. And here, I am sure, Simplicio, you find no ground for difference or objection. We conclude, therefore, that the argument does not bear against the existence of a vacuum; but if it did, it would only do away with the vacua of considerable size which neither I nor, in my opinion, the ancients ever believed to exist in nature, although they might possibly be produced by force as may be gathered from various experiments whose description would here occupy too much time.

Sagr. Seeing that Simplicio is silent, I will take the opportunity of saying something. Since you have clearly demonstrated that bodies of different weights do not move in one and the same medium with velocities proportional to their weights, but that they all move with the same speed, understanding of course that they are of the same substance or at least of the same specific gravity; certainly not of different specific gravities, for I hardly think you would have us believe a ball of cork moves with the same speed as one of lead; and again since you have clearly demonstrated that one and the same body moving through differently resisting media does not acquire speeds which are inversely proportional to the resistances, I am curious to learn what are the ratios actually observed in these cases.

Salv. These are interesting questions and I have thought much concerning them. I will give you the method of approach and the result which I finally reached. Having once established the falsity of the proposition that one and the same body moving through differently resisting media acquires speeds which are inversely proportional to the resistances of these media, and having also disproved the statement that in the same medium bodies of different weight acquire velocities proportional to their weights (understanding that this applies also to bodies which differ merely in specific gravity), I then began to combine these two facts and to consider what would happen if bodies of different weight were placed in media of different resistances; and I found that the differences in speed were greater in those media which were more resistant, that is, less yielding. This difference was such that two bodies which differed scarcely at all in their speed through air would, in water, fall the one with a speed ten times as great as that of the other. Further, there are bodies which will fall rapidly in air, whereas if placed in water not only will not sink but will remain at rest or will even rise to the top: for it is possible to find some kinds of wood, such as knots and roots, which remain at rest in water but fall rapidly in air.

In the foregoing excerpt, it is seen that Galileo uses the terms velocity or speed quite loosely, even vaguely. He speaks of individual bodies having characteristic speeds and compares these speeds by comparing distances fallen in equal time intervals, quite in the Merton tradition. In subsequent excerpts, Galileo will clarify the use of terms as he develops the modern concepts of velocity and acceleration.

To see if Galileo's method of comparing speeds by comparing distances is valid, it will be necessary to anticipate Galileo's later clarifications by defining here the terms speed and velocity in their modern forms. *Average speed* is the distance traveled divided by the time required. It may be written as

$$\text{average speed} = \frac{\text{distance}}{\text{time}},$$

or in symbols as

$$\bar{v} = \frac{d}{t}.$$

As an example, the speedometer on a car may indicate a speed of 60 miles per hour. This means that if the car continues to travel at a constant rate it will cover a distance of 60 miles in one hour. While traveling at this rate, a distance of about 90 feet is covered each second, since 1 mile per hour is equivalent to approximately 1.5 feet per second. But cars and other objects generally do not travel at constant speed, and the speedometer reading of the car is generally changing. Thus the speedometer reading indicates neither a constant nor an average speed but instead an instantaneous speed. The *instantaneous speed* at a point may be regarded as the limit of a series of average speeds taken over ever smaller intervals of distance. As the distance intervals approach zero, so the series of average speeds approach a limiting value which might be called the instantaneous speed at that point.

Galileo compares speeds of two bodies by comparing the distances they fall in equal time intervals. Thus it is seen that it is their average speeds which he is comparing. In the next chapter, it will be seen that their final speeds are also being compared.

In considering the motion of bodies, another aspect besides speed is often of importance; that aspect is the direction in which the motion is taking place. In the foregoing excerpt, Galileo was concerned only with vertical motion, but in subsequent chapters we shall be concerned with motions which are the result of independent motions in different directions.

When both speed and direction are to be considered, the term "velocity" is used. A given *velocity* is a given speed in a given direction. Direction, too, can be important. Certainly it makes a difference in our weather whether that 30 mile per hour wind is blowing from the north or from the south! A velocity is an example of a *vector* quantity in which both a numerical magnitude and a direction must be stated.

Velocities, being vector quantities, must be added with due regard to their directions. Thus an airplane heading east (Fig. 11-1) at the rate of 100 miles per hour in a north wind of 50 miles per hour will in one hour travel east 100 miles, and also simultaneously be carried south 50 miles. Thus the actual resultant velocity of the airplane with respect to the ground can be found by making a careful scale drawing — or by calculating the same results by the Pythagorean theorem for right triangles.

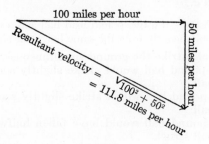

Figure 11-1. *Addition of vector quantities.*

Not only may two velocities be added vectorially to obtain the resultant, but a reverse process of resolving a given velocity, or any other vector, into two components may be carried out. To illustrate (Fig. 11-2), assume a boat is traveling at a constant speed of 20 miles per hour in a direction 30° north of east. How fast is it traveling toward the north? Again the approximate answer may be obtained by a scale drawing. Starting at the point O on the east-west line and using any convenient scale, say 5 miles per hour to the inch, a line OA 4 inches long is drawn

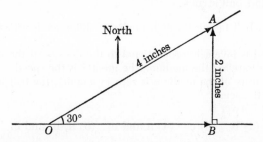

Figure 11-2. *Resolution of vector OA into two components at right angles to each other.*

in a direction 30° north of east. A perpendicular is dropped from A to the east-west line at B. Then BA represents the northward component of velocity of the boat. Measurement will show BA to be 2 inches long representing a northward velocity of 10 miles per hour. In a 30°–60° right triangle as shown, it can readily be demonstrated that the ratios of the lengths of the sides $AB : OA : OB$ are $1 : 2 : \sqrt{3}$.

STUDY QUESTIONS

1. The determination of a velocity requires the measurement of which of the following quantities?
a. Distance. b. Time. c. Acceleration. d. Force. e. Direction. f. Mass.
The correct answer is

   (1) a, b, and c   (2) d, e, and f   (3) a, c, and e   (4) b, d, and f
   (5) a, b, and e.

2. According to Aristotle, if a two-pound lead ball and a one-pound lead ball are dropped simultaneously from the same height in air

   (1) they would strike the ground simultaneously
   (2) the two-pound ball would strike slightly sooner than the one-pound ball
   (3) the one-pound ball would strike slightly sooner than the two-pound ball
   (4) the one-pound ball would have fallen halfway when the two-pound ball struck
   (5) the two-pound ball would have fallen halfway when the one-pound ball struck.

3. According to Galileo, if a two-pound lead ball and a one-pound lead ball are dropped simultaneously from the same height in air

   (1) they would strike the ground simultaneously
   (2) the two-pound ball would strike slightly sooner than the one-pound ball
   (3) the one-pound ball would strike slightly sooner than the two-pound ball
   (4) the one-pound ball would have fallen halfway when the two-pound ball struck
   (5) the two-pound ball would have fallen halfway when the one-pound ball struck.

4. For a given ball falling through media of different densities, according to Aristotle
a. the speed is inversely proportional to the density of the medium
b. the more rarefied the medium, the greater is the speed
c. if the density of the medium is zero (vacuum), the ball would fall with an infinite speed.
The correct answer is

   (1) a   (2) b   (3) c   (4) a and c   (5) a, b, and c.

5. Galileo rejects Aristotle's conceptions as to how bodies fall because

   (1) they would have denied the existence of the vacua which Galileo required for his theory for the cohesion of solid matter
   (2) Aristotle did not actually make the experiments which he is alleged to have done
   (3) Aristotle's conclusions were in contradiction to experiments which Galileo performed
   (4) Aristotle's conclusions were in logical contradiction as shown by Galileo in his discussion of the two falling bodies which could be tied together
   (5) they would not have served as the basis of modern mechanics.

6. Why would Galileo conclude that instantaneous motion was an impossibility?

    (1) Instantaneous motion would be at infinite velocity and an infinite velocity is impossible.
    (2) Actual material bodies cannot move faster than the velocity of light.
    (3) Instantaneous motion would require that a given body be in two different places at the same time, which is logically impossible.
    (4) An instantaneous motion could only occur in a vacuum which logically cannot exist since space must be filled with something in order to exist, even conceptually.
    (5) No body could accelerate to an infinite velocity within a finite length of time.

7. Which of the following is the best statement of Aristotle's conception as to how bodies fall?

    (1) All bodies would fall at the same finite speed if the effect of the medium could be eliminated.
    (2) The greater the resistance of the medium, the faster is the speed of fall.
    (3) In the first case, he supposes bodies of different weight to move in one and the same medium with different speeds which stand to one another in the same ratio as the weights; and in the second case he assumes that the speeds of one and the same body moving in a different media are in the ratio of the densities of these media.
    (4) In the first case, he supposes bodies of different weight to move in one and the same medium with different speeds which stand to one another in the same ratio as the weights; and in the second case he assumes that the speeds of one and the same body moving in different media are in inverse ratio to the densities of these media.
    (5) In the first case, he supposes bodies of different weight to move in one and the same medium with different speeds which stand to one another in the same ratio as the weights, if it is possible to eliminate all other considerations (shape of body, etc.) which modify the single effect of gravity alone. In the second case, he assumes that the speeds of one and the same body moving in different media are in inverse ratio to the densities of these media.

8. Galileo concludes that

    (1) two bodies will fall through the air at exactly the same speed
    (2) two bodies of the same geometric shape will fall through the air with exactly the same speed
    (3) two bodies composed of the same material will fall through the air with exactly the same speed
    (4) two bodies of the same geometric shape will fall through the air with nearly the same speed, but the difference between them will become greater as the medium becomes denser
    (5) two bodies of different weights would fall through a vacuum with different speeds.

9. Actually, it is not Aristotle's first postulate that different bodies fall through the same medium with speeds which are proportional to their weights which forbids the existence of the vacuum. It is Aristotle's second postulate that the speed of fall of a given body is inversely proportional to the density of the medium which Galileo must disprove. Galileo was able to disprove this second postulate of Aristotle's by observing

(1) that not all bodies which will fall in air will fall in water
(2) that a wooden ball which falls in air with a speed of twenty should fall in water with a speed of two, but doesn't
(3) that corresponding to the previous wooden ball, it is possible to find another heavier ball which will fall through water with a speed of two and which then should fall through the air with a speed of twenty. Thus two balls of different weight would fall through the air with the same speed
(4) that it is possible to find some objects which fall rapidly in air but which will remain at rest in water, neither floating nor sinking
(5) that two bodies which differed scarcely at all in their speed through air would, in water, fall the one with a speed ten times as great as that of the other.

10. Judging from the preceding excerpts, which of the following do you think might be the best statement as to the relation between theory and experiment?

(1) Since Galileo was limited to pulse-beats and finger-breadths, his experiments were not accurate enough to disprove any theory whatsoever.
(2) Since theories deal with abstractions which have no real existence, but experiments deal with the real world, the one has no bearing on the other.
(3) Aristotle's mechanics could be disproved only recently with the development of highly accurate timing and measuring devices for use in the laboratory.
(4) Although theories deal with abstractions which have no real existence and experiments are never precise, it is often possible to devise experiments which will indicate which theory among several might be best.
(5) Although theories deal with abstractions which have no real existence and experiments are never precise, it is possible to devise experiments which will indicate which theory among several might be true.

11. Select the correct statement or statements.
a. Average speed is defined as being equal to one-half of the final speed.
b. Velocity and speed are synonymous.
c. The speedometer reading of a car gives the instantaneous speed.
The correct selection includes only

(1) a   (2) b   (3) c   (4) a and c   (5) b and c.

12. If a trip between two cities which are 420 miles apart is made in 10½ hours, the average speed for the trip is, in miles per hour,

(1) 20   (2) 21   (3) 35   (4) 40   (5) 50.

13. A car traveling 60 miles per hour will travel in one-half second a distance in feet of approximately

   (1) 45   (2) 90   (3) 22   (4) 30   (5) 60.

14. A car travels a distance of 200 miles, the first half of the distance being covered at an average speed of 25 miles per hour and the remaining distance being covered at an average speed of 50 miles per hour. The average speed for the entire trip is (in miles per hour)

   (1) 27½   (2) 30   (3) 33⅓   (4) 37½   (5) 42½.

15. Two trains A and B, starting simultaneously from stations 100 miles apart, travel toward each other. If A travels at an average speed of 20 miles per hour, and the trains meet 3 hours after leaving the stations, the average speed of train B in miles per hour is

   (1) 10   (2) 13½   (3) 15   (4) 25   (5) 40.

16. A motor boat which can normally do 6 mi/hr in still water is headed directly across a stream which is flowing at the rate of 2 mi/hr. What is the velocity of the motor boat with respect to the starting point on the bank of the river?

   (1) 2.3 mi/hr   (2) 4 mi/hr   (3) 6.3 mi/hr   (4) 8 mi/hr
   (5) impossible to determine.

17. Referring to the example on page 175 concerning resolution of velocities, what is the eastward velocity of the boat?

18. Which of the experiments quoted by Galileo do you think that he might have actually performed? Why?

19. Is it possible for purely " arm-chair reasoning," such as Galileo's " short and conclusive argument " about the two falling stones tied together, to disprove a physical theory?

20. Since theories deal with abstractions which exist only in the mind and not in the real external world, what possible relationship can they have to experiments performed in the real world?

21. Galileo says that the one-pound iron ball lags behind the hundred-pound iron ball by only two finger-breadths when both are dropped from a height of a hundred cubits. How do you think he may have measured this quantity? Any smashed fingers in the process?

22. The preceding experiment was supposed (by many people) to have actually been performed from the leaning tower of Pisa. Consider all of the possible experimental errors which might have arisen (if the experiment was performed). How accurate would it have been and would it have been crucial in the theory of falling bodies?

12

How Bodies Fall

● Having destroyed
Aristotle's ideas as to how bodies fall, Galileo is now obligated to state
his own ideas of the matter. He proposes that all bodies would fall
through a vacuum with exactly the same speed. As is typical of Galileo,
this is a concept which cannot be directly tested but was derived as a
limiting case from phenomena which could be observed. Since perfect
vacua were not to be had, Galileo considers the factors in the fall of real
bodies through real media which would slow the ideal motion. Two
factors are mentioned, to wit: the force of buoyancy in the medium and
the fluid resistance offered by the medium to the falling body. In the following excerpt from the "First Day" of his *Dialogues,* he shows how
these two factors can be used to explain the observed facts of real bodies
falling through real media. Note that Galileo assumes that the fluid resistance increases as the speed increases. When the fluid resistance exactly balances the weight of the falling body, the acceleration ceases and
the motion becomes uniform. This is revolutionary thinking. The older
point of view in mechanics was that motion would cease when the net
force vanished.

DIALOGUES CONCERNING TWO NEW SCIENCES [1]
by Galileo Galilei

❀   ❀   ❀   ❀   ❀   ❀   ❀

Salv. . . . let us again take up our problem. We have already seen that
the difference of speed between bodies of different specific gravities is most
marked in those media which are the most resistant: thus, in a medium of quicksilver, gold not merely sinks to the bottom more rapidly than lead but it is
the only substance that will descend at all; all other metals and stones rise to

[1] Ibid., pp. 71–77.

the surface and float. On the other hand the variation of speed in air between balls of gold, lead, copper, porphyry, and other heavy materials is so slight that in a fall of 100 cubits a ball of gold would surely not outstrip one of copper by as much as four fingers. Having observed this I came to the conclusion that in a medium totally devoid of resistance all bodies would fall with the same speed.

Simp. This is a remarkable statement, Salviati. But I shall never believe that even in a vacuum, if motion in such a place were possible, a lock of wool and a bit of lead can fall with the same velocity.

Salv. A little more slowly, Simplicio. Your difficulty is not so recondite nor am I so imprudent as to warrant you in believing that I have not already considered this matter and found the proper solution. Hence for my justification and for your enlightenment hear what I have to say. Our problem is to find out what happens to bodies of different weight moving in a medium devoid of resistance, so that the only difference in speed is that which arises from inequality of weight. Since no medium except one entirely free from air and other bodies, be it ever so tenuous and yielding, can furnish our senses with the evidence we are looking for, and since such a medium is not available, we shall observe what happens in the rarest and least resistant media as compared with what happens in denser and more resistant media. Because if we find as a fact that the variation of speed among bodies of different specific gravities is less and less according as the medium becomes more and more yielding, and if finally in a medium of extreme tenuity, though not a perfect vacuum, we find that, in spite of great diversity of specific gravity, the difference in speed is very small and almost inappreciable, then we are justified in believing it highly probable that in a vacuum all bodies would fall with the same speed. Let us, in view of this, consider what takes place in air, where for the sake of a definite figure and light material imagine an inflated bladder. The air in this bladder when surrounded by air will weigh little or nothing, since it can be only slightly compressed; its weight then is small being merely that of the skin which does not amount to the thousandth part of a mass of lead having the same size as the inflated bladder. Now, Simplicio, if we allow these two bodies to fall from a height of four or six cubits, by what distance do you imagine the lead will anticipate the bladder? You may be sure that the lead will not travel three times, or even twice, as swiftly as the bladder, although you would have made it move a thousand times as rapidly.

Simp. It may be as you say during the first four or six cubits of the fall; but after the motion has continued a long while, I believe that the lead will have left the bladder behind not only six out of twelve parts of the distance but even eight or ten.

Salv. I quite agree with you and doubt not that, in very long distances, the lead might cover one hundred miles while the bladder was traversing one; but, my dear Simplicio, this phenomenon which you adduce against my proposition is precisely the one which confirms it. Let me once more explain that the variation of speed observed in bodies of different specific gravities is not caused by the difference of specific gravity but depends upon external circumstances and, in particular, upon the resistance of the medium, so that if this is removed all bodies would fall with the same velocity; and this result I deduce mainly from the fact which you have just admitted and which is very true, namely, that, in the case of bodies which differ widely in weight, their velocities differ more and more as the spaces traversed increase, something which would not occur if the effect depended upon differences of specific gravity. For since these specific gravities remain constant, the ratio between the distances traversed ought to remain constant whereas the fact is that this ratio keeps on increasing as the motion continues. Thus a very heavy body in a fall of one cubit will not anticipate a very light one by so much as the tenth part of this space; but in a fall of twelve cubits the heavy body would outstrip the other by one-third, and in a fall of one hundred cubits by 90/100, etc.

Simp. Very well: but, following your own line of argument, if differences of weight in bodies of different specific gravities cannot produce a change in the ratio of their speeds, on the ground that their specific gravities do not change, how is it possible for the medium, which also we suppose to remain constant, to bring about any change in the ratio of these velocities?

Salv. This objection with which you oppose my statement is clever; and I must meet it. I begin by saying that a heavy body has an inherent tendency to move with a constantly and uniformly accelerated motion toward the common center of gravity, that is toward the center of our earth, so that during equal intervals of time it receives equal increments of momentum and velocity. This, you must understand, holds whenever all external and accidental hindrances have been removed; but of these there is one which we can never remove, namely, the medium which must be penetrated and thrust aside by the falling body. This quiet, yielding, fluid medium opposes motion through it with a resistance which is proportional to the rapidity with which the medium must give way to the passage of the body; which body, as I have said, is by nature continuously accelerated so that it meets with more and more resistance in the medium and hence a diminution in its rate of gain of speed until finally the speed reaches such a point and the resistance of the medium becomes so great that, balancing each other, they prevent any further acceleration and reduce the motion of the body to one which is uniform and which will thereafter maintain a constant value. There is, therefore, an increase in the resistance of the medium, not on account of any change in its essential properties, but on account of the change in rapidity with which it must yield and give way laterally to the passage of the falling body which is being constantly accelerated.

Now seeing how great is the resistance which the air offers to the slight momentum of the bladder and how small that which it offers to the large weight of the lead, I am convinced that, if the medium were entirely removed, the advantage received by the bladder would be so great and that coming to the lead so small that their speeds would be equalized. Assuming this principle, that all falling bodies acquire equal speeds in a medium which, on account of a vacuum or something else, offers no resistance to the speed of the motion, we shall be able accordingly to determine the ratios of the speeds of both similar and dissimilar bodies moving either through one and the same medium or through different space-filling, and therefore resistant, media. This result we may obtain by observing how much the weight of the medium detracts from the weight of the moving body, which weight is the means employed by the falling body to open a path for itself and to push aside the parts of the medium, something which does not happen in a vacuum where, therefore, no difference of speed is to be expected from a difference of specific gravity. And since it is known that the effect of the medium is to diminish the weight of the body by the weight of the medium displaced,[2] we may accomplish our purpose by diminishing in just this proportion the speeds of the falling bodies, which in a non-resisting medium we have assumed to be equal.

Thus, for example, imagine lead to be ten thousand times as heavy as air while ebony is only one thousand times as heavy. Here we have two substances whose speeds of fall in a medium devoid of resistance are equal: but, when air is the medium, it will subtract from the speed of the lead one part in ten thousand, and from the speed of the ebony one part in one thousand, i.e., ten parts in ten thousand. While therefore lead and ebony would fall from any given height in the same interval of time, provided the retarding effect of the air were removed, the lead will, in air, lose in speed one part in ten thousand; and the ebony, ten parts in ten thousand. In other words, if the elevation from which the bodies start be divided into ten thousand parts, the lead will reach the ground leaving the ebony behind by as much as ten, or at least nine, of these parts. Is it not clear then that a leaden ball allowed to fall from a tower two hundred cubits high will outstrip an ebony ball by less than four inches? Now ebony weighs a thousand times as much as air but this inflated bladder only four times as much; therefore air diminishes the inherent and natural speed of ebony by one part in a thousand; while that of the bladder which, if free from hindrance, would be the same, experiences a diminution in air amounting to one part in four. So that when the ebony ball, falling from the tower, has reached the earth, the bladder will have traversed only three-quarters of this distance. Lead is twelve times as heavy as water; but ivory is only twice as heavy. The speeds of these two substances which, when entirely unhindered, are equal will be diminished in water, that of lead by one part in twelve, that of ivory by half. Accordingly when the lead has fallen through eleven cubits of water the ivory will have fallen through only six. Employing this principle we shall, I believe, find a much closer agreement of experiment with our computation than with that of Aristotle.

In a similar manner we may find the ratio of the speeds of one and the same body in different fluid media, not by comparing the different resistances of the media, but by considering the excess of the specific gravity of the body above those of the media. Thus, for example, tin is one thousand times heavier than air and ten times heavier than water; hence, if we divide its unhindered speed into 1000 parts, air will rob it of one of these parts so that it will fall with a speed of 999, while in water its speed will be 900, seeing that water diminishes its weight by one part in ten while air by only one part in a thousand.

Again take a solid a little heavier than water, such as oak, a ball of which will weigh let us say 1000 drachms; suppose an equal volume of water to weigh 950, and an equal volume of air, 2; then it is clear that if the unhindered speed of the ball is 1000, its speed in air will be 998, but in water only 50, seeing that the water removes 950 of the 1000 parts which the body weighs, leaving only 50.

Such a solid would therefore move almost twenty times as fast in air as in water, since its specific gravity exceeds that of water by one part in twenty. And here we must consider the fact that only those substances which have a specific gravity greater than water can fall through it — substances which

---

[2] This principle was discovered by Archimedes.

must, therefore, be hundreds of times heavier than air; hence when we try to obtain the ratio of the speed in air to that in water, we may, without appreciable error, assume that air does not, to any considerable extent, diminish the free weight, and consequently the unhindered speed of such substances. Having thus easily found the excess of the weight of these substances over that of water, we can say that their speed in air is to their speed in water as their free weight is to the excess of this weight over that of water. For example, a ball of ivory weighs 20 ounces; an equal volume of water weighs 17 ounces; hence the speed of ivory in air bears to its speed in water the approximate ratio of 20 : 3.

Just as velocity may be defined as the time rate of change of the distance traveled, so may acceleration be defined as the time rate of change of velocity. That is, the change in velocity divided by the time required to make this change defines the new term *acceleration*. An algebraic statement of this definition would be even more concise. If we let the letter a represent the constant acceleration of a body for which v is its final velocity and v_0 its initial velocity where the velocity change has taken place during the time t, then

$$a = (v - v_0)/t$$

or, if the initial velocity were zero,

$$a = v/t.$$

A body freely falling near the earth without any air resistance or buoyancy would accelerate at the rate of $a = 32$ feet per second each second. This is called "the acceleration of gravity" and is often designated by g.

We can manipulate our algebraic relation for acceleration, starting from rest, to give

$$v = at.$$

This velocity is the instantaneous final velocity and not the average velocity. The average velocity would be

$$\bar{v} = d/t$$

where d is the distance traveled in the time t. Thus also,

$$d = \bar{v}t$$

and, of course, the average velocity for a body which accelerated uniformly from an initial speed of zero to the final velocity of v would be

$$\bar{v} = \tfrac{1}{2}v.$$

A simple combination of these two ideas gives

$$d = \bar{v}t = \tfrac{1}{2}vt = \tfrac{1}{2} \cdot at \cdot t$$

and

$$d = \tfrac{1}{2}at^2.$$

Perhaps the time required to accelerate to the final velocity is not immediately known. This time, of course, can be found from $t = v/a$. If this is substituted in the previous equation, a little algebra shows that

$$v^2 = 2ad.$$

These relations are all simple common sense. A little work with actual numbers instead of symbols may help to make them more understandable. While Galileo used geometrical reasoning instead of algebra, the results of the preceding relations were all known to him. His geometric derivations have been largely omitted in the excerpts which have been quoted.

STUDY QUESTIONS

1–4. Consider five spheres of identical dimensions but composed of
    a. gold   b. lead   c. copper   d. ivory   e. plastic, a ping-pong ball.

1. Which sphere will fall the fastest in water?
    (1) a   (2) b   (3) c   (4) d   (5) e.

2. Which sphere will fall the slowest in water?
    (1) a   (2) b   (3) c   (4) d   (5) e.

3. Which sphere will fall the fastest in air?
    (1) a   (2) b   (3) c   (4) d   (5) e.

4. Which sphere will fall the slowest in air?
    (1) a   (2) b   (3) c   (4) d   (5) e.

5. To put one of Galileo's arguments into modern terms, consider a ping-pong ball and a glass ball of the same diameter. According to Galileo, both balls will fall nearly together through a height of two or three yards, but the ping-pong ball will fall appreciably slower through a height of a hundred yards. According to Galileo, the reason for the final behavior of the balls

    (1) cannot lie within the medium, since the ratio of the speeds changes with the length of fall, while all properties of the medium remain constant
    (2) must be due to the differing densities of the two balls, since the heavier ball falls the faster
    (3) is to be found in the "buoyancy" of the ping-pong ball. As Galileo points out, the net force acting on the ball is the difference between the weight of the ball and the weight of the same volume of air. This net force is a smaller fraction of the weight in the case of the ping-pong ball than for the glass ball, hence the ping-pong ball falls appreciably slower
    (4) is to be found in the amount of the "air resistance," which is the effect of the quiet, yielding, fluid medium which must be pushed aside by the falling ball. This air resistance is obviously much higher for the more rapidly falling glass ball
    (5) is to be found in the "terminal velocity" reached by each ball. This terminal velocity is achieved when the air resistance on the ball is exactly equal to its net force of gravity and hence there is no further acceleration.

6. In the preceding case, the glass ball falls somewhat faster than the ping-pong ball through the first two or three yards of fall. The fact that the difference was not greater, according to Galileo, was to be expected,

(1) since the glass ball is appreciably more dense than the ping-pong ball

(2) since the glass ball weighs appreciably more than the ping-pong ball

(3) since the air resistance for the ping-pong ball was greater than that for the glass ball

(4) since the air would take away, say, one-tenth of the speed of the ping-pong ball, while taking away only about one part in one thousand of the speed of the glass ball

(5) since the glass ball will reach its terminal velocity within this distance.

7–8. *Consider two balls of the same diameter where ball A has twice the density of water while ball B has three times the density of water. Then if these two balls were dropped simultaneously into water and their instantaneous positions were measured after a short lapse of time, they might have fallen the following amounts:*

	A	B
(1)	2 in.	3 in.
(2)	6 in.	12 in.
(3)	6 in.	8 in.
(4)	8 in.	8 in.
(5)	8 in.	6 in.

7. Following Galileo's reasoning, which of the above answers would be obtained?

8. Following Aristotle's reasoning, which of the above answers would be obtained?

9. Identical aluminum balls of specific gravity 3 are dropped simultaneously in water and in air of specific gravity .001. The initial ratio of speed in air to speed in water is

(1) $3:2$ (2) $2.999:2$ (3) $2:3$ (4) $2:2.999$ (5) $3:1.999$.

10. Galileo states (plausibly) that as the medium becomes more and more yielding the difference in speeds of fall between identically sized spheres of materials of different densities would become less and less. Hence, as the medium becomes one of extreme tenuity, though not a perfect vacuum, this difference in speed is very small and almost inappreciable. Therefore, he is justified in believing that in a vacuum all bodies would fall with the same speed, which would be

(1) finite, since infinite velocities are impossible

(2) infinite, since the speed steadily increases as the medium becomes more and more yielding

(3) finite, as illustrated by the fact that the speed of a lead ball in air would differ only by about one part in ten thousand from its speed in a vacuum

(4) finite, since if the measured speeds of fall are plotted against the reciprocals of the densities of the media, a straight line should be obtained

(5) infinite, since in a vacuum there will be no "quiet, yielding, fluid medium" which must be pushed away by the motion of the spheres.

11. A motorboat travels at a speed of 5 miles per hour in still water. Suppose the boat is headed straight across a river 1 mile wide that has a current of 2 miles per hour. The boat will land at the opposite bank at a point

(1) directly opposite the starting point   (2) 2 miles downstream
(3) ⅖ mile downstream   (4) ⅘ mile downstream
(5) 2½ miles downstream.

12. A river boat can travel 15 miles per hour in still water. The river current has a speed of 5 miles per hour. How many hours will be required for a round trip between two points one of which is 40 miles upstream from the other?

(1) 5⅓   (2) 6   (3) 3   (4) 4   (5) 8.

13. Select the correct statement or statements among those below.
    a. If two velocities are imposed on a body simultaneously, the resultant velocity may have a magnitude greater than that of either component velocity.
    b. If two accelerations are imposed on a body simultaneously, the magnitude of the resultant acceleration can be found by adding the two accelerations vectorially, since acceleration is a vector quantity.
    c. Velocity is a vector quantity, but speed is not a vector quantity.
    The correct selection of statements includes

(1) only a   (2) only b   (3) only c   (4) only a and b
(5) a, b, and c.

14. A stone is dropped from a bridge 144 feet above the water. Neglecting air resistance, what is the elapsed time in seconds for the stone to fall to the water?

(1) 6   (2) 2.1   (3) 3   (4) 4.5   (5) 8.

15. For a given falling body, how will the air resistance vary with the speed of fall of the body?

16. Why should a hundred-pound iron ball fall faster than a one-pound iron ball?

17. Specifically, why is Galileo's theory as to how bodies fall a better theory than that proposed by Aristotle?

18. Would it be possible from Galileo's theory to calculate how rapidly a cork would rise in water?

19. Galileo refused to accept the differing densities of the two falling balls as the explanation of their varying ratios of speeds of fall. His reason was that a varying effect could not have a constant cause. How does Galileo get around his own logical principles in ascribing the varying effect to the action of the medium — which is certainly constant?

13

Uniform and Accelerated Motions

● The *Dialogues* is a large book and only a small part of it is reproduced here. The "Second Day" of the *Dialogues* is concerned with the strength of beams and columns. Galileo reached good modern conclusions, but we are more interested in his development of modern mechanics. Therefore the next excerpt will be from his "Third Day" in which Galileo first develops the ideas of velocity and uniform motion. To keep the length of text within bounds, only his definition of uniform motion and his caution will be given. Galileo developed the properties of uniform motion in a long series of theorems which he proved by geometry. The essential results have already been stated at the end of a previous chapter in modern shortened algebraic form.

After treating uniform motion, Galileo introduces the idea of acceleration and defines it as did the Merton College men three hundred years earlier. The alternate form suggested by Sagredo that uniformly accelerated motion should be such that speed increases in proportion to the space traversed is one that had bothered Galileo himself in his earlier *Dialogue Concerning the Two Chief World Systems.* In this last particular cul-de-sac, Galileo had lots of distinguished company which included Leonardo da Vinci, Descartes, and Albert of Saxony. However, here in his last book he has finally successfully defined acceleration in the form in which we still use it today.

Note Sagredo's introduction of the impetus theory "that we may obtain a proper solution of the problem discussed by philosophers, namely, what causes the acceleration in the natural motion of heavy bodies?" Galileo obviously feels that this line of inquiry is sterile and rejects the metaphysical "why do bodies move?" in favor of a very pragmatic "how do bodies move?" This is one of the historic turning points of science. Until this time men had sought the Aristotelian final causes. Here, beginning with Galileo, men turned to formal, efficient, or material causes and ceased emphasizing the metaphysical "why?" Perhaps the strength of

188

modern science lies in its intensely pragmatic manner of thinking which is always asking " how? "

It is also noteworthy that Galileo's proof of his law of falling bodies is experimental and not based upon some all-inclusive philosophical system. However he was unable to time and measure the distances traveled by freely falling bodies. Therefore he performed his famous inclined plane experiment which 'did lie within his technical resources and reasoned that the limit as the plane became more and more nearly perpendicular would be free-fall. With his own description of this important experiment this excerpt is concluded.

DIALOGUES CONCERNING TWO NEW SCIENCES [1]
by Galileo Galilei

❖   ❖   ❖   ❖   ❖   ❖   ❖

Third Day — Change of Position

My purpose is to set forth a very new science dealing with a very ancient subject. There is, in nature, perhaps nothing older than motion, concerning which the books written by philosophers are neither few nor small; nevertheless I have discovered by experiment some properties of it which are worth knowing and which have not hitherto been either observed or demonstrated. Some superficial observations have been made, as, for instance, that the free motion of a heavy falling body is continuously accelerated; but to just what extent this acceleration occurs has not yet been announced; for so far as I know, no one has yet pointed out that the distances traversed, during equal intervals of time, by a body falling from rest, stand to one another in the same ratio as the odd numbers beginning with unity.

It has been observed that missiles and projectiles describe a curved path of some sort; however no one has pointed out the fact that this path is a parabola. But this and other facts, not few in number or less worth knowing, I have succeeded in proving; and what I consider more important, there have been opened up to this vast and most excellent science, of which my work is merely the beginning, ways and means by which other minds more acute than mine will explore its remote corners.

This discussion is divided into three parts; the first part deals with motion which is steady or uniform; the second treats of motion as we find it accelerated in nature; the third deals with the so-called violent motions and with projectiles.

Uniform Motion

In dealing with steady or uniform motion, we need a single definition which I give as follows:

Definition

By steady or uniform motion, I mean one in which the distances traversed by the moving particle during any equal intervals of time, are themselves equal.

[1] Op. cit., pp. 153, 160–165, 166–172, 178–179.

Caution

We must add to the old definition (which defined steady motion simply as one in which equal distances are traversed in equal times) the word " any," meaning by this, all equal intervals of time; for it may happen that the moving body will traverse equal distances during some equal intervals of time and yet the distances traversed during some small portion of these time-intervals may not be equal, even though the time-intervals be equal.

    *   *   *   *   *   *   *

Naturally Accelerated Motion

The properties belonging to uniform motion have been discussed in the preceding section; but accelerated motion remains to be considered.

And first of all it seems desirable to find and explain a definition best fitting natural phenomena. For anyone may invent an arbitrary type of motion and discuss its properties; thus, for instance, some have imagined helices and conchoids as described by certain motions which are not met with in nature, and have very commendably established the properties which these curves possess in virtue of their definitions; but we have decided to consider the phenomena of bodies falling with an acceleration such as actually occurs in nature and to make this definition of accelerated motion exhibit the essential features of observed accelerated motions. And this, at last, after repeated efforts we trust we have succeeded in doing. In this belief we are confirmed mainly by the consideration that experimental results are seen to agree with and exactly correspond with those properties which have been, one after another, demonstrated by us. Finally, in the investigation of naturally accelerated motion we were led, by hand as it were, in following the habit and custom of nature herself, in all her various other processes, to employ only those means which are most common, simple and easy.

For I think no one believes that swimming or flying can be accomplished in a manner simpler or easier than that instinctively employed by fishes and birds.

When, therefore, I observe a stone initially at rest falling from an elevated position and continually acquiring new increments of speed, why should I not believe that such increases take place in a manner which is exceedingly simple and rather obvious to everybody? If now we examine the matter carefully we find no addition or increment more simple than that which repeats itself always in the same manner. This we readily understand when we consider the intimate relationship between time and motion; for just as uniformity of motion is defined by and conceived through equal times and equal spaces (thus we call a motion uniform when equal distances are traversed during equal time-intervals), so also we may, in a similar manner, through equal time-intervals, conceive additions of speed as taking place without complication; thus we may picture to our mind a motion as uniformly and continuously accelerated when, during any equal intervals of time whatever, equal increments of speed are given to it. Thus if any equal intervals of time whatever have elapsed, counting from the time at which the moving body left its position of rest and began to descend, the amount of speed acquired during the first two time-intervals will be double that acquired during the first time-interval alone; so the amount added during three of these time-intervals will be treble; and that in four, quadruple that of the first time-interval. To put the matter more clearly, if a body were to continue its motion with the same speed which it had acquired during the first time-interval and were to retain this same uniform speed, then its motion would be twice as slow as that which it would have if its velocity had been acquired during two time-intervals.

And thus, it seems, we shall not be far wrong if we put the increment of speed as proportional to the increment of time; hence the definition of motion which we are about to discuss may be stated as follows: A motion is said to be uniformly accelerated, when starting from rest, it acquires, during equal time-intervals, equal increments of speed.

Sagr. Although I can offer no rational objection to this or indeed to any other definition, devised by any author whomsoever, since all definitions are arbitrary, I may nevertheless without offense be allowed to doubt whether such a definition as the above, established in an abstract manner, corresponds to and describes that kind of accelerated motion which we meet in nature in the case of freely falling bodies. And since the Author apparently maintains that the motion described in his definition is that of freely falling bodies, I would like to clear my mind of certain difficulties in order that I may later apply myself more earnestly to the propositions and their demonstrations.

Salv. It is well that you and Simplicio raise these difficulties. They are, I imagine, the same which occurred to me when I first saw this treatise, and which were removed either by discussion with the Author himself, or by turning the matter over in my own mind.

Sagr. When I think of a heavy body falling from rest, that is, starting with zero speed and gaining speed in proportion to the time from the beginning of the motion; such a motion as would, for instance, in eight beats of the pulse acquire eight degrees of speed; having at the end of the fourth beat acquired four degrees; at the end of the second, two; at the end of the first, one: and since time is divisible without limit, it follows from all these considerations that if the earlier speed of a body is less than its present speed in a constant ratio, then there is no degree of speed however small (or, one may say, no degree of slowness however great) with which we may not find this body travelling after starting from infinite slowness, i.e., from rest. So that if that speed which it had at the end of the fourth beat was such that, if kept uniform, the body would traverse two miles in an hour, and if keeping the speed which it had at the end of the second beat, it would traverse one mile an hour, we must infer that, as the instant of starting is more and more nearly approached, the body moves so slowly that, if it kept on moving at this rate, it would not traverse a mile in an hour, or in a day, or in a year or in a thousand years; indeed, it would not traverse a span in an even greater time; a phenomenon which baffles the imagination, while our senses show us that a heavy falling body suddenly acquires great speed.

Salv. This is one of the difficulties which I also at the beginning, experienced, but which I shortly afterwards removed; and the removal was effected by the very experiment which creates the difficulty for you. You say the experiment appears to show that immediately after a heavy body starts from rest it acquires a very considerable speed: and I say that the same experiment makes clear the fact that the initial motions of a falling body, no matter how heavy, are very slow and gentle. Place a heavy body upon a yielding material, and leave it there without any pressure except that owing to its own weight; it is clear that if one lifts this body a cubit or two and allows it to fall upon the same material, it will, with this impulse, exert a new and greater pressure than that caused by its mere weight; and this effect is brought about by the (weight of the) falling body together with the velocity acquired during the fall, an effect which will be greater and greater according to the height of the fall, that is according as the velocity of the falling body becomes greater. From the quality and intensity of the blow we are thus enabled to accurately estimate the speed of a falling body. But tell me, gentlemen, is it not true that if a block be allowed to fall upon a stake from a height of four cubits and drives it into the earth, say, four finger-breadths, that coming from a height of two cubits it will drive the stake a much less distance, and from the height of one cubit a still less distance; and finally if the block be lifted only one finger-breadth how much more will it accomplish than if merely laid on top of the stake without percussion? Certainly very little. If it be lifted only the thickness of a leaf, the effect will be altogether imperceptible. And since the effect of the blow depends upon the velocity of this striking body, can any one doubt the motion is very slow and the speed more than small whenever the effect (of the blow) is imperceptible? See now the power of truth; the same experiment which at first glance seemed to show one thing, when more carefully examined, assures us of the contrary.

But without depending upon the above experiment, which is doubtless very conclusive, it seems to me that it ought not to be difficult to establish such a fact by reasoning alone. Imagine a heavy stone held in the air at rest; the support is removed and the stone set free; then since it is heavier than the air it begins to fall, and not with uniform motion but slowly at the beginning and with a continuously accelerated motion. Now since velocity can be increased and diminished without limit, what reason is there to believe that such a moving body starting with infinite slowness, that is, from rest, immediately acquires a speed of ten degrees rather than one of four, or of two, or of one, or of a half, or of a hundredth; or, indeed, of any of the infinite number of small values (of speed)? Pray listen. I hardly think you will refuse to grant that the gain of speed of the stone falling from rest follows the same sequence as the diminution and loss of this same speed when, by some impelling force, the stone is thrown to its former elevation: but even if you do not grant this, I do not see how you can doubt that the ascending stone, diminishing in speed, must before coming to rest pass through every possible degree of slowness.

Simp. But if the number of degrees of greater and greater slowness is limitless, they will never be all exhausted, therefore such an ascending heavy body will never reach rest, but will continue to move without limit always at a slower rate; but this is not the observed fact.

Salv. This would happen, Simplicio, if the moving body were to maintain its speed for any length of time at each degree of velocity; but it merely passes each point without delaying more than an instant: and since each time-interval however small may be divided into an infinite number of instants, these will always be sufficient (in number) to correspond to the infinite degrees of diminished velocity.

That such a heavy rising body does not remain for any length of time at any given degree of velocity is evident from the following: because if, some time-interval having been assigned, the body moves with the same speed in the last as in the first instant of that time-interval, it could from this second degree of elevation be in like manner raised through an equal height, just as it was transferred from the first elevation to the second, and by the same reasoning would pass from the second to the third and would finally continue in uniform motion forever.

Sagr. From these considerations it appears to me that we may obtain a proper solution of the problem discussed by philosophers, namely, what causes the acceleration in the natural motion of heavy bodies? Since, as it seems to me, the force impressed by the agent projecting the body upwards diminishes continuously, this force, so long as it was greater than the contrary force of gravitation, impelled the body upwards; when the two are in equilibrium the body ceases to rise and passes through the state of rest in which the impressed impetus is not destroyed, but only its excess over the weight of the body has been consumed — the excess which caused the body to rise. Then as the diminution of the outside impetus continues, and gravitation gains the upper hand, the fall begins, but slowly at first on account of the opposing impetus, a large portion of which still remains in the body; but as this continues to diminish it also continues to be more and more overcome by gravity, hence the continuous acceleration of motion.

Simp. The idea is clever, yet more subtle than sound; for even if the argument were conclusive, it would explain only the case in which a natural motion is preceded by a violent motion, in which there still remains active a portion of the external force; but where there is no such remaining portion and the body starts from an antecedent state of rest, the cogency of the whole argument fails.

*   *   *   *   *   *   *

Salv. The present does not seem to be the proper time to investigate the cause of the acceleration of natural motion concerning which various opinions have been expressed by various philosophers, some explaining it by attraction to the center, others to repulsion between the very small parts of the body, while still others attribute it to a certain stress in the surrounding medium which closes in behind the falling body and drives it from one of its positions to another. Now, all these fantasies, and others too, ought to be examined; but it is not really worth while. At present it is the purpose of our Author merely to investigate and to demonstrate some of the properties of accelerated motion (whatever the cause of this acceleration may be) — meaning thereby a motion, such that the momentum of its velocity goes on increasing after departure from rest, in simple proportionality to the time, which is the same as saying that in equal time-intervals the body receives equal increments of velocity; and if we find the properties (of accelerated motion) which will be demonstrated later are realized in freely falling and accelerated bodies, we may conclude that the assumed definition includes such a motion of falling bodies and that their speed goes on increasing as the time and the duration of the motion.

Sagr. So far as I see at present, the definition might have been put a little more clearly perhaps without changing the fundamental idea, namely, uniformly accelerated motion is such that its speed increases in proportion to the space traversed; so that, for example, the speed acquired by a body in falling four cubits would be double that acquired in falling two cubits and this latter speed would be double that acquired in the first cubit. Because there is no doubt but that a heavy body falling from the height of six cubits has, and strikes with, a momentum double that it had at the end of three cubits, triple that which it would have if it had fallen from two, and sextuple that which it would have had at the end of one.

Salv. It is very comforting to me to have had such a companion in error; and moreover let me tell you that your proposition seems so highly probable that our Author himself admitted, when I advanced this opinion to him, that he had for some time shared the same fallacy. But what most surprised me was to see two propositions so inherently probable that they commanded the assent of everyone to whom they were presented, proven in a few simple words to be not only false, but impossible.

Simp. I am one of those who accept the proposition, and believe that a falling body acquires force in its descent, its velocity increasing in proportion to the space, and that the momentum of the falling body is doubled when it falls from a doubled height; these propositions, it appears to me, ought to be conceded without hesitation or controversy.

Salv. And yet they are as false and impossible as that motion should be completed instantaneously; and here is a very clear demonstration of it.[2] If the velocities are in proportion to the spaces traversed, or to be traversed, then these spaces are traversed in equal intervals of time; if, therefore, the velocity with which the falling body traverses a space of eight feet were double that with which it covered the first four feet (just as the one distance is double the other) then the time-intervals required for these passages would be equal. But for one and the same body to fall eight feet and four feet in the same time is possible only in the case of instantaneous (discontinuous) motion; but observation shows us that the motion of a falling body occupies time, and less of it in covering a distance of four feet than of eight feet; therefore it is not true that its velocity increases in proportion to the space.

The falsity of the other proposition may be shown with equal clearness. For if we consider a single striking body the difference of momentum in its blows can depend only upon difference of velocity; for if the striking body falling from a double height were to deliver a blow of double momentum, it would be necessary for this body to strike with a doubled velocity; but with this doubled speed it would traverse a doubled space in the same time-interval; observation however shows that the time required for fall from the greater height is longer.

Sagr. You present these recondite matters with too much evidence and ease; this great facility makes them less appreciated than they would be had they been presented in a more abstruse manner. For, in my opinion, people esteem more lightly that knowledge which they acquire with so little labor than that acquired through long and obscure discussion.

---

[2] The argument presented here contains a fallacy because Galileo assumed in this case ($v \propto d$) that the average velocity was one-half the final velocity. For a critical analysis see I. B. Cohen, " Galileo's Rejection of the Possibility of Velocity Changing Uniformly with Respect to Distance," *Isis* (1956), Vol. 47, p. 291.

Salv. If those who demonstrate with brevity and clearness the fallacy of many popular beliefs were treated with contempt instead of gratitude the injury would be quite bearable; but on the other hand it is very unpleasant and annoying to see men, who claim to be peers of anyone in a certain field of study, take for granted certain conclusions which later are quickly and easily shown by another to be false. I do not describe such a feeling as one of envy, which usually degenerates into hatred and anger against those who discover such fallacies; I would call it a strong desire to maintain old errors, rather than accept newly discovered truths. This desire at times induces them to unite against these truths, although at heart believing in them, merely for the purpose of lowering the esteem in which certain others are held by the unthinking crowd. Indeed, I have heard from our Academician many such fallacies held as true but easily refutable; some of these I have in mind.

Sagr. You must not withhold them from us, but, at the proper time, tell us about them even though an extra session be necessary. But now, continuing the thread of our talk, it would seem that up to the present we have established the definition of uniformly accelerated motion which is expressed as follows:

A motion is said to be equally or uniformly accelerated when, starting from rest, its momentum receives equal increments in equal times.

Salv. This definition established, the Author makes a single assumption, namely,

The speeds acquired by one and the same body moving down planes of different inclinations are equal when the heights of these planes are equal.

By the height of an inclined plane we mean the perpendicular let fall from the upper end of the plane upon the horizontal line drawn through the lower end of the same plane. Thus, to illustrate, [see Fig. 13-1] let the line AB be

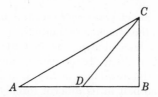

Figure 13-1. *Balls rolling down different inclines of the same height CB attain the same velocity at the foot of the incline.*

horizontal, and let the planes CA and CD be inclined to it; then the Author calls the perpendicular CB the " height " of the planes CA and CD; he supposes that the speeds acquired by one and the same body, descending along the planes CA and CD to the terminal points A and D are equal since the heights of these planes are the same, CB; and also it must be understood that this speed is that which would be acquired by the same body falling from C to B.

Sagr. Your assumption appears to me so reasonable that it ought to be conceded without question, provided of course there are no chance or outside resistances, and that the planes are hard and smooth, and that the figure of the moving body is perfectly round, so that neither plane nor moving body is rough. All resistance and opposition having been removed, my reason tells me at once that a heavy and perfectly round ball descending along the lines CA, CD, CB would reach the terminal points A, D, B, with equal momenta.

Salv. Your words are very plausible; but I hope by experiment to increase the probability to an extent which shall be little short of a rigid demonstration.

Imagine this page to represent a vertical wall, with a nail driven into it; and from the nail let there be suspended a lead bullet of one or two ounces by means of a fine vertical thread, AB [see Fig. 13-2], say from four to six feet long, on this wall draw a horizontal line DC, at right angles to the vertical

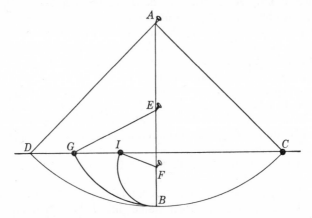

Figure 13-2. *Galileo's demonstration with the pendulum to show that the velocity attained by the bob at the bottom of the swing depends only on the vertical height through which it descends.*

thread AB, which hangs about two finger-breadths in front of the wall. Now bring the thread AB with the attached ball into the position AC and set it free; first it will be observed to descend along the arc CBD, to pass the point B, and to travel along the arc BD, till it almost reaches the horizontal CD, a slight shortage being caused by the resistance of the air and the string; from this we may rightly infer that the ball in its descent through the arc CB acquired a momentum on reaching B, which was just sufficient to carry it through a similar arc BD to the same height. Having repeated this experiment many times, let us now drive a nail into the wall close to the perpendicular AB, say at E or F, so that it projects out some five or six finger-breadths in order that the thread, again carrying the bullet through the arc CB, may strike upon the nail E when the bullet reaches B, and thus compel it to traverse the arc BG, described about E as center. From this we can see what can be done by the same momentum which previously starting at the same point B carried the same body through the arc BD to the horizontal CD. Now, gentlemen, you will observe with pleasure that the ball swings to the point G in the horizontal, and you would see the same thing happen if the obstacle were placed at some lower point, say at F, about which the ball would describe the arc BI, the rise of the ball always terminating exactly on the line CD. But when the nail is placed so low that the remainder of the thread below it will not reach to the height CD (which would happen if the nail were placed nearer B than to the intersection of AB with the horizontal CD) then the thread leaps over the nail and twists itself about it.

This experiment leaves no room for doubt as to the truth of our supposition; for since the two arcs CB and DB are equal and similarly placed, the momentum acquired by the fall through the arc CB is the same as that gained by fall through the arc DB; but the momentum acquired at B, owing to fall through CB, is able to lift the same body through the arc BD; therefore, the momentum acquired in the fall BD is equal to that which lifts the same body through the same arc from B to D; so, in general, every momentum acquired by fall through an arc is equal to that which can lift the same body through the same arc. But all these momenta which cause a rise through the arcs BD, BG, and BI are equal, since they are produced by the same momentum, gained by fall through CB, as experiment shows. Therefore all the momenta gained by fall through the arcs DB, GB, IB are equal.

Sagr. The argument seems to me so conclusive and the experiment so well adapted to establish the hypothesis that we may, indeed, consider it as demonstrated.

Salv. I do not wish, Sagredo, that we trouble ourselves too much about this matter, since we are going to apply this principle mainly in motions which occur on plane surfaces, and not upon curved, along which acceleration varies in a manner greatly different from that which we have assumed for planes.

So that, although the above experiment shows us that the descent of the moving body through the arc CB confers upon it momentum just sufficient to carry it to the same height through any of the arcs BD, BG, BI, we are not able, by similar means, to show that the event would be identical in the case of a perfectly round ball descending along planes whose inclinations are respectively the same as the chords of these arcs. It seems likely, on the other hand, that, since these planes form angles at the point B, they will present an obstacle to the ball which has descended along the chord CB, and starts to rise along the chords BD, BG, BI.

In striking these planes some of its momentum will be lost and it will not be able to rise to the height of the line CD; but this obstacle, which interferes with the experiment, once removed, it is clear that the momentum (which gains in strength with descent) will be able to carry the body to the same height. Let us then, for the present, take this as a postulate, the absolute truth of which will be established when we find that the inferences from it correspond to and agree perfectly with experiment. The author having assumed this single principle passes next to the propositions which he clearly demonstrates; the first of these is as follows:

❋   ❋   ❋   ❋   ❋   ❋   ❋

Salv. The request which you, as a man of science, make, is a very reasonable one; for this is the custom — and properly so — in those sciences where mathematical demonstrations are applied to natural phenomena, as is seen in the case of perspective, astronomy, mechanics, music, and others where the principles, once established by well-chosen experiments, become the foundations of the entire superstructure. I hope therefore it will not appear to be a waste of time if we discuss at considerable length this first and most fundamental question upon which hinge numerous consequences of which we have in this book only a small number, placed there by the Author, who has done so much to open a pathway hitherto closed to minds of speculative turn. So far as experiments go they have not been neglected by the Author; and often, in his company, I have attempted in the following manner to assure myself that the acceleration actually experienced by falling bodies is that above described.

A piece of wooden molding or scantling, about 12 cubits long, half a cubit wide, and three finger-breadths thick, was taken; on its edge was cut a channel a little more than one finger in breadth; having made this groove very straight, smooth, and polished, and having lined it with parchment, also as smooth and polished as possible, we rolled along it a hard, smooth, and very round bronze ball. Having placed this board in a sloping position, by lifting one end some one or two cubits above the other, we rolled the ball, as I was just saying, along the channel, noting, in a manner presently to be described, the time required to make the descent. We repeated this experiment more than once in order to measure the time with an accuracy such that the deviation between two observations never exceeded one-tenth of a pulse-beat. Having performed this operation and having assured ourselves of its reliability, we now rolled the ball only one-quarter the length of the channel; and having measured the time of its descent, we found it precisely one-half of the former. Next we tried other distances, comparing the time for the whole length with that for the half, or with that for two-thirds, or three-fourths, or indeed for any fraction; in such experiments, repeated a full hundred times, we always found that the spaces traversed were to each other as the squares of the times, and this was true for all inclinations of the plane, i.e., of the channel, along which we rolled the ball. We also observed that the times of descent, for various inclinations of the plane, bore to one another precisely that ratio which, as we shall see later, the Author had predicted and demonstrated for them.

For the measurement of time, we employed a large vessel of water placed in an elevated position; to the bottom of this vessel was soldered a pipe of small diameter giving a thin jet of water, which we collected in a small glass during the time of each descent, whether for the whole length of the channel or for a part of its length; the water thus collected was weighed, after each descent, on a very accurate balance; the differences and ratios of these weights gave us the differences and ratios of the times, and this with such accuracy that although the operation was repeated many, many times, there was no appreciable discrepancy in the results.

In the preceding excerpts, Galileo has advanced the hypothesis that the motion of a freely falling body is such that in equal time intervals the body acquires equal increments of velocity. That this hypothesis is consistent with the way bodies actually do fall he is unable to show by direct experiment since his timing devices are not sufficiently precise. However, he concludes from his experiments with the pendulum and with inclined planes that the velocity attained by a ball rolling down any incline depends only on the height of the incline and not on the slope. Thus he reasons that if the motion down an incline agrees with his description of uniformly accelerated motion so also will the limiting case of free fall when the plane becomes vertical.

At the end of the preceding chapter it was shown algebraically that Galileo's definition of uniformly accelerated motion led to the conclusion that starting from rest, the distance traveled at a given acceleration should be proportional to the square of the time. Thus

$$\frac{d_1}{d_2} = \frac{t_1^2}{t_2^2}.$$

Now if d_1 is the distance covered the first unit of time and d_2 is the distance covered the first two units of time,

$$\frac{d_1}{d_2} = \frac{1^2}{2^2} = \frac{1}{4},$$

and for two and three units of time

$$\frac{d_2}{d_3} = \frac{2^2}{3^2} = \frac{4}{9}, \quad \text{etc.}$$

Thus the total distance traveled in total elapsed times of 1, 2, 3, etc. units would be 1, 4, 9, etc. and the distances covered during successive equal time intervals would be 1, 3, 5, etc. as Galileo states in the opening paragraph of his "Third Day" (p. 189).

It then remained for Galileo to demonstrate that this is the way a ball actually does move down an incline, which he describes in his two concluding paragraphs above. Thus his hypothesis concerning uniformly accelerated motion has been substantiated by experiment.

Although Galileo's experiments with the inclined plane led him to the conclusion that freely falling bodies would fall with uniform acceleration that would be the same for all bodies, there is no indication that he actually evaluated this acceleration which we now know to be about 32 feet per second per second. In fact, if he had attempted to arrive at the acceleration of a freely falling body from values determined from inclined planes, he would have been led into some error since he dealt with balls rolling rather than sliding down the planes. It may be shown that a ball rolling down an incline will not attain quite as much velocity as it would if it were sliding down a smooth plane of the same height.

STUDY QUESTIONS

1. Galileo proposed his definition of uniformly accelerated motion — " in equal time-intervals the body receives equal increments of velocity " — because

   (1) this is the way freely falling bodies fall when all other factors except gravity are removed
   (2) it was the simplest kind of changing motion he could conceive
   (3) it was a hypothesis which he could verify for freely falling bodies by measuring the increments of velocity that occurred in equal intervals of time

(4) it was a guess that freely falling bodies would move this way and the consequences of this type of motion could be checked experimentally in terms of measured distances and times

(5) it is a definition, and as a definition he could propose anything he wished.

2. Consider a body moving with a given constant acceleration as defined by Galileo. Which of the following statements are true?

   a. The increment of velocity attained between an elapsed time of 2.0 seconds and 2.1 seconds is equal to that attained between an elapsed time of 1.0 seconds and 1.1 seconds.

   b. The increment of velocity attained between an elapsed time of 2.0 seconds and 2.1 seconds is greater than that attained between an elapsed time of 1.0 seconds and 1.1 seconds.

   c. The increment of velocity attained between an elapsed time of 1.0 seconds and 1.2 seconds is double that attained between an elapsed time of 2.0 seconds and 2.1 seconds.

The correct answer is

   (1) a   (2) b   (3) c   (4) a and c   (5) none of them.

3. Assume a ball, starting from rest, rolls a distance of 1 cubit down an inclined plane while 9 weight-measures of water flow from a Galilean water clock. Which of the following would also be true for the same incline if the ball each time starts from rest?

   a. The ball would roll a distance of 2 cubits while 18 weight-measures of water flow from the clock.

   b. The ball would roll a distance of 4 cubits while 18 weight-measures of water flow from the clock.

   c. If the ball rolls down the incline until 27 weight-measures of water have flowed from the clock, the distance traveled while the last 9 weight-measures were being collected was 3 cubits.

The correct answer is

   (1) a   (2) b   (3) c   (4) a and c   (5) b and c.

4–8. The instantaneous velocity of a ball at any point while rolling down an inclined plane may be determined by allowing the ball to roll from the incline onto a horizontal plane. The constant velocity along the horizontal is thus equal to the instantaneous velocity acquired along the incline. Assume a ball rolls from the incline onto the horizontal after traveling down the incline for 2 seconds. The ball rolls a distance of 40 inches along the horizontal in 1 second.

4. The instantaneous velocity of the ball at the foot of the incline in inches per second is

   (1) 10   (2) 20   (3) 40   (4) 80   (5) 5.

5. The acceleration of the ball down the incline in inches per second per second is

   (1) 10   (2) 20   (3) 40   (4) 80   (5) 5.

6. The distance traveled down the incline in inches during the 2 seconds is

   (1) 10   (2) 20   (3) 40   (4) 80   (5) 5.

7. The distance traveled down the incline in inches during the first second is

   (1) 10   (2) 20   (3) 40   (4) 80   (5) 5.

8. If the ball had continued down the incline a total time of 4 seconds, it would have rolled a total distance in inches of

   (1) 10   (2) 20   (3) 40   (4) 80   (5) 160.

9. A problem which concerned Galileo in the "Third Day" was whether a body in falling begins moving abruptly with a finite velocity or whether the body began moving with zero velocity and then "went through all degrees of slowness" in reaching its final velocity. Galileo referred to his "pile driver" experiment in which he dropped a weight from varying heights upon a stake or onto "a yielding substance" and studied the effects of dropping the weight from different heights.

   (1) This experiment has no relation to Galileo's problem.
   (2) This experiment does not prove that a falling body began moving with an infinitesimally small velocity.
   (3) This experiment proves that any body reaches a higher velocity in falling from a great height than in falling from a somewhat lesser height.
   (4) This experiment proves that the velocity of a falling body is always finite.
   (5) This experiment proves that a body falls with constant acceleration.

10. Galileo was not able to directly measure falling bodies since he did not have satisfactory timing devices. Instead, his experiments are of balls rolling relatively slowly down long inclined planes. He reasons that under perfect conditions a ball would have the same velocity at the foot of the inclined plane as though it had fallen the vertical distance CB (see Fig. 13-1).

    (1) The pendulum experiments mentioned have no bearing on the problem of the inclined plane since the motion of the bob in a pendulum is a circular arc and not a straight line (as in the plane).
    (2) The pendulum experiments mentioned have no bearing on the problem of the inclined plane since the bob moves through the air on the end of a light cord and does not roll down an inclined plane.
    (3) The pendulum experiments (Fig. 13-2) do not have a bearing on the problem of the inclined plane but show that the velocity of the bob at point B at the end of the half-swing CB is sufficient to lift the bob up the other arcs BD, BG, or BI.
    (4) The pendulum experiments do have a bearing on the problem of the inclined plane and show that the velocities which the bob would have had at the end of any of the half-swings GB, DB, or IB would have been equal.
    (5) Even if a relation could be established between the pendulum experiments and the inclined plane experiments, this would have had no bearing on the problem of freely falling bodies, since, most obviously, neither pendulum nor ball on an inclined plane is a freely falling body.

11–13. *A car coasting up an incline is slowed down at the rate of 3 feet per second per second until its speed drops from an initial value of 45 feet per second to 15 feet per second.*

11. The elapsed time is, in seconds,

    (1) 30   (2) 20   (3) 15   (4) 10   (5) 5.

12. The average speed of the car while slowing down is, in feet per second,

    (1) 30   (2) 20   (3) 15   (4) 10   (5) 5.

13. The distance traveled by the car is, in feet,

    (1) 100   (2) 300   (3) 225   (4) 600   (5) 50.

14. Galileo points out for the first time in history that " the distances traversed, during equal intervals of time, by a body falling from rest, stand to one another in the same ratio as the odd numbers beginning with unity." The proof, by geometry, is not included in the quoted material. Prove it algebraically.

15. What is the significance of Galileo's " Caution " following his definition of Uniform Motion?

16. The nature of infinity and of infinite processes seems to haunt Galileo. We see it in the question as to whether a body starts to fall from rest (that is, from zero velocity) and then " passes through all degrees of velocity in attaining a given velocity." For instance, " the number of degrees of greater and greater slowness is limitless, they will never be all exhausted, therefore an ascending heavy body will never reach rest, but will continue to move without limit always at a slower rate; but this is not the observed fact." What are the logical problems and how does Galileo solve them?

17. The inclined plane experiment described by Galileo is a very famous one. Exactly what does it presume to prove? What might have been the principal experimental difficulties? How accurate do you think the experiment might have been?

14

Projectile Motion

● In the concluding portion of his book, the "Fourth Day," Galileo is concerned with projectile motion. In the short excerpt which follows there are at least two ideas which are important. One idea is that the motions in the vertical and the horizontal directions are mutually independent of each other. One of the older conjectures, for example, was that if two different impeti were given to a body the first impetus would have to be fully expended before the second impetus would become effective. The second idea is the assumption that the horizontal motion will continue on forever at constant velocity if nothing occurs to alter it. This is very close to Newton's first law of motion which appeared in his *Principia* in 1687.

It is also possible to show from the theorems on inclined planes that Galileo derived in his "Third Day" that the accelerations produced on a body sliding down one of the smooth planes are proportional to the forces acting upon the body. This is another turning point in the development of modern science. The earlier opinion had been that motion was proportional to the applied force. Even the impetus was thought of as a sort of force placed within the body and pushing on it to make it move. Here, for the first time, Galileo proposes that it is the change of motion which is proportional to the force acting. Newton and others were worthy successors who carried Galileo's ideas on to fruition as the modern mechanics which underlies all of modern physics.

DIALOGUES CONCERNING TWO NEW SCIENCES [1]
by Galileo Galilei

Fourth Day

Salviati. Once more, Simplicio is here on time; so let us without delay take up the question of motion. The text of our Author is as follows:

[1] Op. cit., pp. 244–245, 248–253.

The Motion of Projectiles

In the preceding pages we have discussed the properties of uniform motion and of motion naturally accelerated along planes of all inclinations. I now propose to set forth those properties which belong to a body whose motion is compounded of two other motions, namely, one uniform and one naturally accelerated; these properties, well worth knowing, I propose to demonstrate in a rigid manner. This is the kind of motion seen in a moving projectile; its origin I conceive to be as follows:

Imagine any particle projected along a horizontal plane without friction; then we know, from what has been more fully explained in the preceding pages, that this particle will move along this same plane with a motion which is uniform and perpetual, provided the plane has no limits. But if the plane is limited and elevated, then the moving particle, which we imagine to be a heavy one, will on passing over the edge of the plane acquire, in addition to its previous uniform and perpetual motion, a downward propensity due to its own weight; so that the resulting motion which I call projection, is compounded of one which is uniform and horizontal and of another which is vertical and naturally accelerated. We now proceed to demonstrate some of its properties, the first of which is as follows:

    ❀   ❀   ❀   ❀   ❀   ❀   ❀

Let us imagine an elevated horizontal line [Fig. 14-1] or plane *ab* along which a body moves with uniform speed from *a* to *b*. Suppose this plane to end abruptly at *b;* then at this point the body will, on account of its weight, acquire also a natural motion downwards along the perpendicular *bn.* Draw the line *be* along the plane *ba* to represent the flow, or measure, of time; divide

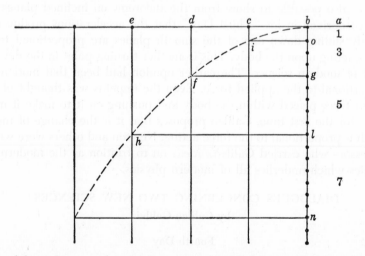

Figure 14-1. *Motion of a projectile given an initial horizontal velocity along* ab. *During subsequent equal time intervals, the horizontal distances traveled are equal and the vertical distances fallen are proportional to the successive odd integers.*

this line into a number of segments, bc, cd, de, representing equal intervals of time; from the points b, c, d, e, let fall lines which are parallel to the perpendicular bn. On the first of these lay off any distance ci, on the second a distance four times as long, df; on the third, one nine times as long, eh; and so on, in proportion to the squares of cb, db, eb, or, we may say, in the squared ratio of these same lines. Accordingly we see that while the body moves from b to c with uniform speed, it also falls perpendicularly through the distance ci, and at the end of the time-interval bc finds itself at the point i. In like manner at the end of the time-interval bd, which is the double of bc, the vertical fall will be four times the first distance ci; for it has been shown in a previous discussion that the distance traversed by a freely falling body varies as the square of the time; in like manner the space eh traversed during the time be will be nine times ci; thus it is evident that the distances eh, df, ci will be to one another as the squares of the lines be, bd, bc. Now from the points i, f, h draw the straight lines io, fg, hl parallel to be; these lines hl, fg, io are equal to eb, db and cb, respectively; so also are the lines bo, bg, bl respectively equal to ci, df, and eh. The square of hl is to that of fg as the line lb is to bg; and the square of fg is to that of io as gb is to bo; therefore the points i, f, h, lie on one and the same parabola. In like manner it may be shown that, if we take equal time-intervals of any size whatever, and if we imagine the particle to be carried by a similar compound motion, the positions of this particle, at the ends of these time-intervals, will lie on one and the same parabola.[2]

Salv. This conclusion follows from the converse of the first of the two propositions given above. For, having drawn a parabola through the points b and h, any other two points, f and i, not falling on the parabola must lie either within or without; consequently the line fg is either longer or shorter than the line which terminates on the parabola. Therefore the square of hl will not bear to the square of fg the same ratio as the line lb to bg, but a greater or smaller;

[2] The parabola is one of the conic sections. A conic section is any curve produced by cutting a cone with a plane. If the cut is made parallel to the base of the cone, the section is a circle. If the cut is made parallel to one side of the cone, the section is a parabola. An ellipse lies between the circle and the parabola, while hyperbolas result from sections which exceed the parabola. See diagram below.

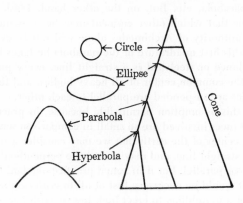

For footnote 2.

the fact is, however, that the square of *hl* does bear this same ratio to the square of *fg*. Hence the point *f* does lie on the parabola, and so do all the others.

Sagr. One cannot deny that the argument is new, subtle and conclusive, resting as it does upon this hypothesis, namely, that the horizontal motion remains uniform, that the vertical motion continues to be accelerated downwards in proportion to the square of the time, and that such motions and velocities as these combine without altering, disturbing, or hindering each other, so that as the motion proceeds the path of the projectile does not change into a different curve: but this, in my opinion, is impossible. For the axis of the parabola along which we imagine the natural motion of a falling body to take place stands perpendicular to a horizontal surface and ends at the center of the earth; and since the parabola deviates more and more from its axis no projectile can ever reach the center of the earth or, if it does, as seems necessary, then the path of the projectile must transform itself into some other curve very different from the parabola.

Simp. To these difficulties, I may add others. One of these is that we suppose the horizontal plane, which slopes neither up nor down, to be represented by a straight line as if each point on this line were equally distant from the center, which is not the case; for as one starts from the middle (of the line) and goes toward either end, he departs farther and farther from the center (of the earth) and is therefore constantly going uphill. Whence it follows that the motion cannot remain uniform through any distance whatever, but must continually diminish. Besides, I do not see how it is possible to avoid the resistance of the medium which must destroy the uniformity of the horizontal motion and change the law of acceleration of falling bodies. These various difficulties render it highly improbable that a result derived from such unreliable hypotheses should hold true in practice.

Salv. All these difficulties and objections which you urge are so well founded that it is impossible to remove them; and, as for me, I am ready to admit them all, which indeed I think our Author would also do. I grant that these conclusions proved in the abstract will be different when applied in the concrete and will be fallacious to this extent, that neither will the horizontal motion be uniform nor the natural acceleration be in the ratio assumed, nor the path of the projectile a parabola, etc. But, on the other hand, I ask you not to begrudge our Author that which other eminent men have assumed even if not strictly true. The authority of Archimedes alone will satisfy everybody. In his Mechanics and in his first quadrature of the parabola he takes for granted that the beam of a balance or steelyard is a straight line, every point of which is equidistant from the common center of all heavy bodies, and that the cords by which heavy bodies are suspended are parallel to each other.

Some consider this assumption permissible because, in practice, our instruments and the distances involved are so small in comparison with the enormous distance from the center of the earth that we may consider a minute of arc on a great circle as a straight line, and may regard the perpendiculars let fall from its two extremities as parallel. For if in actual practice one had to consider such small quantities, it would be necessary first of all to criticise the architects who presume, by use of a plumbline, to erect high towers with parallel sides. I may add that, in all their discussions, Archimedes and the others considered them-

selves as located at an infinite distance from the center of the earth, in which
case their assumptions were not false, and therefore their conclusions were absolutely correct. When we wish to apply our proven conclusions to distances
which, though finite, are very large, it is necessary for us to infer, on the basis
of demonstrated truth, what correction is to be made for the fact that our distance from the center of the earth is not really infinite, but merely very great
in comparison with the small dimensions of our apparatus. The largest of these
will be the range of our projectiles — and even here we need consider only the
artillery — which, however great, will never exceed four of those miles of
which as many thousand separate us from the center of the earth; and since
these paths terminate upon the surface of the earth only very slight changes
can take place in their parabolic figure which, it is conceded, would be greatly
altered if they terminated at the center of the earth.

As to the perturbation arising from the resistance of the medium this is more
considerable and does not, on account of its manifold forms, submit to fixed
laws and exact description. Thus if we consider only the resistance which the
air offers to the motions studied by us, we shall see that it disturbs them all
and disturbs them in an infinite variety of ways corresponding to the infinite
variety in the form, weight, and velocity of the projectiles. For as to velocity,
the greater this is, the greater will be the resistance offered by the air; a resistance which will be greater as the moving bodies become less dense. So that although the falling body ought to be displaced in proportion to the square of
the duration of its motion, yet no matter how heavy the body, if it falls from a
very considerable height, the resistance of the air will be such as to prevent
any increase in speed and will render the motion uniform; and in proportion
as the moving body is less dense this uniformity will be so much the more
quickly attained and after a shorter fall. Even horizontal motion which, if no
impediment were offered, would be uniform and constant is altered by the resistance of the air and finally ceases; and here again the less dense the body
the quicker the process. Of these properties of weight, of velocity, and also of
form, infinite in number, it is not possible to give any exact description; hence,
in order to handle this matter in a scientific way, it is necessary to cut loose
from these difficulties; and having discovered and demonstrated the theorems,
in the case of no resistance, to use them and apply them with such limitations
as experience will teach. And the advantage of this method will not be small;
for the material and shape of the projectile may be chosen, as dense and round
as possible, so that it will encounter the least resistance in the medium. Nor
will the spaces and velocities in general be so great but that we shall be easily
able to correct them with precision.

In the case of those projectiles which we use, made of dense material and
round in shape, or of lighter material and cylindrical in shape, such as arrows,
thrown from a sling or crossbow, the deviation from an exact parabolic path
is quite insensible. Indeed, if you will allow me a little greater liberty, I can
show you, by two experiments, that the dimensions of our apparatus are so
small that these external and incidental resistances, among which that of the
medium is the most considerable, are scarcely observable.

Galileo continued the theory of projectile motion at length in the remainder of the " Fourth Day " of his *Two New Sciences*. It is indicative

of his intellectual outlook that he sought practical ballistic results. He proved, for instance, that a cannon would have a maximum range when fired at an elevation of 45°, a result which had been obtained experimentally by Tartaglia nearly a hundred years before.

In 1639 the Pope flatly refused to free Galileo, now seventy-five years old and blind. On January 8, 1642 Galileo died at Arcetri, still under the ban of the Inquisition. The Pope forbade the Grand Duke of Tuscany to erect any monument to Galileo if any word on it would " offend the reputation of the Holy Office." Galileo's body was laid away in the basement of the bell tower of Santa Croce for nearly a hundred years. His body is now interred under a proper monument in the Church of Santa Croce in Florence, his beloved city. The modern world is indebted to Galileo as one of those courageous and great men who broke down the barriers of medieval thought and laid the foundations of our modern scientific age.

STUDY QUESTIONS

1. Choose the statements that are consistent with Galileo's beliefs concerning projectile motion.
   a. The horizontal motion of a projectile does not affect its vertical motion.
   b. Two bullets, one fired horizontally and one dropped simultaneously from the same height, would hit the ground approximately simultaneously.
   c. Two bullets, one fired horizontally and the other fired up simultaneously at an elevation of 45° from the same height, would hit the ground approximately simultaneously.
   The correct answer is

   (1) a   (2) b   (3) c   (4) a and b   (5) a, b, and c.

2. Two bullets are fired simultaneously from ground level with the same muzzle speeds. Bullet A is fired vertically upward and bullet B is fired at an angle of 45° with the ground. (Neglect air resistance.)
   a. A and B will stay in the air the same time and hit the ground nearly simultaneously.
   b. A and B will rise to the same maximum height above the ground.
   c. A and B will hit the ground with the same speeds.
   The correct answer is

   (1) a   (2) b   (3) c   (4) a and b   (5) none of them.

3. A bullet is fired horizontally from a given elevation. After a certain length of time t, it has dropped 8 inches below its original horizontal path. After twice as long a time ($= 2t$), the distance it will drop from its original path is in inches

   (1) 8   (2) 16   (3) 24   (4) 32   (5) 64.

4. With regard to projectile motion, Galileo concludes that
   a. his theories fully account for and accurately agree with the observed motions of real projectiles

   b. the center of the earth is so distant that the departure from a plane, the lack of parallelness, and the departure from a parabolic path cannot be discerned within the few miles in which a real experiment can be conducted

   c. experiments can be designed whose results will agree quite closely with his theories.

The correct answer is

   (1) a   (2) b   (3) c   (4) a and b   (5) a, b, and c.

5. Two bullets A and B are fired horizontally and simultaneously from the same elevation. The muzzle speed of bullet A is twice that of bullet B. (Neglect air resistance.) At the end of 1 second,

   a. bullet A will have traveled twice the horizontal distance that B has

   b. bullet A will have dropped 16 feet below its original line of flight

   c. bullet B will have dropped 8 feet below its original line of flight.

The correct answer is

   (1) a   (2) b   (3) c   (4) a and b   (5) a, b, and c.

6–8. A heavy streamlined object dropped from an airplane flying horizontally attains a final vertical velocity of 960 feet per second when it hits the ground. (Neglect air resistance.)

6. The time in seconds for the object to drop is

   (1) 10   (2) 20   (3) 30   (4) 40   (5) 60.

7. The average vertical velocity of the falling object is, in feet per second,

   (1) 32   (2) 320   (3) 480   (4) 960   (5) 1920.

8. The distance in feet which the object falls vertically is

   (1) 3200   (2) 6400   (3) 9200   (4) 11,200   (5) 14,400.

9–14. A flare dropped from an airplane flying horizontally at a speed of 300 feet per second requires 20 seconds to fall. (Neglect air resistance.)

9. The final vertical velocity of the flare is, in feet per second,

   (1) 80   (2) 160   (3) 320   (4) 480   (5) 640.

10. The final horizontal speed of the flare just before impact in feet per second is

   (1) 150   (2) 6000   (3) 300   (4) 940   (5) 640.

11. The average vertical velocity is, in feet per second,

   (1) 80   (2) 160   (3) 320   (4) 480   (5) 640.

12. The average horizontal speed of the flare in feet per second is

   (1) 150   (2) 15   (3) 300   (4) 470   (5) 320.

13. The vertical distance the flare falls is, in feet,

   (1) 1600   (2) 3200   (3) 6400   (4) 9600   (5) 12,800.

14. The horizontal distance the flare travels in feet between release and impact is

   (1) 3000   (2) 300   (3) 6000   (4) 9400   (5) 6400.

15. A stone is dropped from a bridge 400 feet high. Neglecting air resistance, the elapsed time in seconds before the stone hits the ground is

    (1) 7.5   (2) 25   (3) 3.8   (4) 12.5   (5) 5.

16. How would you design an experiment to test Galileo's theory for the perfect motion of projectiles in parabolic trajectories? In other words, what factors must be carefully controlled (and in what way) so that the experiment does not disagree with the theory?

17. Since theories are always about ideal worlds of the mind and never about the real work-a-day world of observed phenomena, what practical value can they have?

18. How would it be possible today to improve upon Galileo's experiments to determine phenomenologically the way in which bodies really fall?

19. What modifications to Galileo's theory on projectile motion would be necessary when applied to an ICBM of 6000 mile range?

15

Isaac Newton; the Principia

● Newton entered the Scientific Revolution at a time that was ripe for his prodigious powers. Galileo's study of the motion of bodies had laid the foundations for dynamics, and the testing of ideas by experiment had become an accepted procedure.[1] There had been an awakening in mathematics, and the essential part that mathematical reasoning was beginning to play in the development of physical science was well recognized. Concurrently with these developments, attention had been focused on astronomy by the work of Copernicus, Galileo, Brahe, and Kepler, and there was a need for an all-embracing theory of dynamics.

Into this picture stepped Newton, and his analytical ability and mathematical skill were such that, combined with his great powers of intuition, he was able to establish a framework of dynamics to which little was added in the following two hundred years.

The theory of gravitation, of course, did not originate with Newton. Aristotle conceived of the four elements seeking their places. This was superseded during the 16th century by the idea of similar matter tending to coalesce, with each of the heavenly bodies being held together by the mutual attraction of its similar parts. Thus the earth attracted terrestrial objects but would not attract parts of other planets or the moon. But even after Galileo suggested the similar composition of the planets, mutual attraction of the planets for each other was not considered since such an assumption, without knowledge of centripetal forces, would lead to the conclusion that the planets and moon would all come together. For Galileo, motion of planets did not involve centripetal force,

---

[1] The Scientific Revolution with its emphasis on experiment did not immediately revolutionize the pattern of thinking, however. Galileo complained of the " scientists " who would not even look through his telescope to see the answers to questions they were disputing, and as late as the beginning of the 18th century Newton's critics on the nature of white light resorted to argumentation instead of accepting the results of simple experiments.

since he considered their motion in circular orbits to be inertial and natural. Kepler, however, extended the idea of terrestrial gravitation by concluding that gravitational forces are mutual in that not only is a stone attracted toward the earth but the earth in turn is pulled by the stone. He extended this idea to explain the tides as being due to the attraction of the moon, and further assumed that the sun exerted both driving and attractive forces on the planets. Descartes, being aware that circular motion required an explanation, suggested that the planets were held in their orbits about the sun by the increasing density of the solar vortex with increasing distance from the sun. Borelli, like Kepler, considered that the solar system was driven, and while realizing that a centripetal tendency was required to hold the planets in their paths, did not attribute this tendency to gravitation.

Thus the stage was set for the synthesis of a solar system embracing the ideas of inertial motion, centripetal force, and universal gravitation. This synthesis was performed by Hooke and Newton. Each arrived at the conclusion that gravitational attraction decreased inversely as the square of the distance from the attracting body, but while Hooke's conclusion was an educated guess, Newton's was arrived at with mathematical precision. By 1666 Newton had shown that the motion of the moon could be accounted for approximately by considering that there was an inverse square attraction between the moon and earth, but his calculations were laid aside probably because at the time he was unable to prove mathematically that the attractive force of a spherical mass could be considered as acting from the geometric center of the mass. This proof, however, he supplied to Halley in 1684. Halley was so impressed by the importance of Newton's work that he prevailed upon him to publish his findings, and the result was the *Principia* in 1687. While the epitome of this book is the Newtonian system of the world, its significance in establishing a firm foundation for dynamics cannot be overestimated. The explanation of the solar system was just one application of the basic principles concerning moving matter laid down by Newton. Today, our modern technological age rests firmly on Newtonian mechanics.

Isaac Newton (Fig. 15-1) was born Christmas Day, 1642 in a farmhouse near Grantham, England. His father had died before Isaac was born. Unlike the boyhoods of some other geniuses, his seemed not unusual and there were few signs of the intellectual flowering to come. As a boy he was ingenious at constructing mechanical devices and did sufficiently well with his books that it was decided he should go to the university instead of becoming a farmer. Accordingly, in 1661 he entered Trinity College at Cambridge.

The signs of Newton's budding genius were probably first noticed by Isaac Barrow, Professor of Mathematics, who encouraged him in his studies of mathematics and optics. In 1665 Newton graduated as virtually an unknown, except to Barrow, and with the closing of the university due

Figure 15-1. *Isaac Newton (1642–1727).*

to the Great Plague, returned to his home where he spent the next two years. These two years of uninterrupted work were probably the most productive of his life.

It is difficult to fix dates for many of Newton's discoveries, as he was a solitary individual who made little or no attempt to publish his findings. In fact, most of his publications were made years after the concepts had been developed, and then only under pressure from his associates. However, it appears that during the two years at home he formulated his three laws of motion and the law of gravitation and became convinced that they could be used to explain the motion of the moon and planets; he developed the basic principles of the differential and integral calculus; he determined the nature of white light. It was not until 1669 that Newton gave Barrow a written account of a part of his work and it was years later before it was published.

In 1667, Newton returned to Cambridge and successively became a Minor Fellow, a Major Fellow, a Senior Fellow and, following Barrow's resignation, was appointed Lucasian Professor of Mathematics at the age of twenty-six. Much of his work in optics followed, and at the request of the Royal Society, he sent them a reflecting telescope which he had designed and constructed. The first published account of any of Newton's discoveries followed in 1672 when the *Transactions of the Royal Society* published Newton's explanation and description of the telescope. The controversy concerning the nature of light which this and a subsequent paper evoked were very distasteful to Newton, and his enthusiasm for scientific investigation waned. This interest was revived a short time later by Halley, who questioned Newton concerning the path that a planet would follow if attracted toward the sun by a gravitational force that varied inversely as the square of the distance. This question had been raised earlier by Hooke, with whom Newton had had a number of controversies. Newton's answer to Halley that the path would be an ellipse and his subsequent mathematical proofs convinced Halley of the importance of Newton's work and the need for publication. As a consequence, the *Mathematical Principles of Natural Philosophy*, or the *Principia* as it is usually called, was written and published in less than two years.

In 1689 Newton was elected a Member of Parliament by the university. His disinterest in science returned, and he tried to obtain a government position, initially without success. He became despondent and in 1692 suffered a nervous breakdown but recovered within a year. In 1696 he was made Warden of the Mint and in 1699 became Master of the Mint, thus entering a completely new phase of life. The Mastership was held by Newton until his death and was a well-paid position.

In London, Newton's home was cared for by his niece Catherine Barton, and he had many social and business contacts. His work with the mint was of considerable importance and was carried out with characteristic imagination and efficiency.

Although Newton's work in science after moving to London was sporadic, he became President of the Royal Society in 1703, a position which he held until his death in 1727. In 1704, with the probability of controversy lessened due to Hooke's death, he published *Opticks*. This work was written in English, rather than the Latin which was usual at the time and in which the *Principia* had been written. By this time Newton had become renowned throughout the scientific world and was knighted by Queen Anne in 1705 for his contributions to science.

The last two decades of Newton's life were filled with many activities. Although he did little further work in science, his abilities were still great. A number of books were published, grudgingly, based on the work he had accomplished years before. During this period, Newton continued work along the theological lines that he had spent much time on previously. In all, well over a million words in his own handwriting remain on historical and religious subjects. While based on sound scholarship, much of this is considered by many to be of a magical or mystical nature in which Newton was seeking to unlock the secrets of the universe, as he had those of the solar system.

Newton's influence upon the development of man's thought and culture has been profound, and his leaps in the evolution of scientific thought have seldom if ever been equalled. Perhaps his preeminence lay in his powers of intuition and concentration which allowed him to hold a problem before himself continuously until its solution was revealed. At the time of his death in 1727, Newton was revered throughout Europe, and the honors bestowed upon him at his burial in Westminster Abbey were greater than those accorded most nobility.

The *Principia*, as Newton himself said, is not an easy book to read. It was written reluctantly under pressure from Halley and was not intended for lay readers. It is a compilation of work which in many cases had been done twenty years previously, and it is quite improbable that the mathematical proofs follow Newton's original line of reasoning. In fact, Newton's powers of intuition were so great that it is felt by many that the proofs were often developed after he became convinced of the validity of the concepts. As the complete title indicates, the *Principia* is a mathematical treatment and uses geometric proof far more extensively than geometry is customarily employed at the present time. In the following selections, nearly all of the geometric proofs are omitted, but one should peruse a complete copy of the *Principia* if he wishes to get some idea of the magnitude of this work.

In the following excerpts, the reader is not expected to understand completely everything that he is asked to read. However, with the help of the study questions at the end of each chapter, one should be able to get an understanding and appreciation of the basic principles set forth by Newton. One cannot hope to have much understanding of present-day physical science without some familiarity with the basic laws of mechanics as formulated by Newton. These laws concerning force, mass, acceleration, and momentum (quantity of motion) form the groundwork on which are built our present concepts of work and energy, and thus are fundamental in the fields of mechanics, heat, radiant energy, and electricity. Energy transformations permeate the whole field of physical science.

The material in the following chapters taken from the *Principia* gives the basic laws of motion and the law of gravitation and shows how these principles were used by Newton to explain the motions within the solar system. In considering the motion of bodies, Newton's definitions and statements of the laws relate the concepts of force, mass, quantity of motion (momentum), and acceleration. The particular case of a centripetal (acting toward the center) force is developed, and the motion of a body acted upon by a centripetal force which varies inversely as the square of the distance from the center of rotation is studied. By calculations on the motion of the moon, this force on the moon is shown to be the force of gravity. Further calculations show the motions of the planets as described by Kepler's laws to be mathematically consistent with the laws of motion and the law of gravitation.

Thus the heliocentric system of Copernicus, being inconsistent with the Aristotelian principles of mechanics based on bodies seeking their places, called for a new system of mechanics. This new system, fashioned largely by Galileo and Newton, for the first time explained qualitatively and quantitatively how all bodies, both terrestrial and celestial, move.

MATHEMATICAL PRINCIPLES OF NATURAL PHILOSOPHY [2]
by Isaac Newton
DEFINITIONS
Definition I

The quantity of matter is the measure of the same, arising from its density and bulk conjunctly.

Thus air of a double density, in a double space, is quadruple in quantity; in a triple space, sextuple in quantity. The same thing is to be understood of snow, and fine dust or powders, that are condensed by compression or liquefaction, and of all bodies that are by any causes whatever differently condensed. I have no regard in this place to a medium, if any such there is, that freely pervades the interstices between the parts of bodies. It is this quantity that I mean hereafter everywhere under the name of body or mass. And the same is known by the weight of each body; for it is proportional to the weight, as I have found by experiments on pendulums, very accurately made, which shall be shown hereafter.

To define quantity of matter (mass) as the product of density and bulk (volume) may appear to be circular reasoning, since density in turn is currently defined as mass per unit volume. However, in Newton's time, density probably was synonymous with specific gravity which compares the density of a substance to that of a standard substance, generally water. Thus a unit volume of a substance having a specific gravity ("density") of 8 has a quantity of matter of 8 mass units if the quantity of matter in unit volume of water is arbitrarily taken as unity. Then 3 units of volume of the substance would have a quantity of matter of 24 mass units.

Here in introducing the concept of mass as being an invariable property of any body, Newton is making a step which is essential to his system of mechanics. In defining any quantity, that quantity is described in terms of known previously-defined quantities. While Newton in Definition I is attempting to describe mass in terms of volume and specific gravity, the present-day practice is to use mass as one of three so-called fundamental quantities, the other two being length and time, in terms of which other physical quantities are described. Thus if mass is taken as one of these three, it becomes a starting point for other definitions but is not itself definable. This does not mean, however, that it is not measurable.

As we shall see, mass has two properties, inertia and gravitational attraction for other masses. Either of these properties may be used for comparing two masses, and if one of these masses is arbitrarily established as a standard mass, say 1 pound-mass, then the mass of the other may be obtained. It is usually easier to compare masses by weighing, using gravitation, than by comparing their inertias. That the ratio of the weights of

[2] Isaac Newton, *The Mathematical Principles of Natural Philosophy*, with minor adaptations from the trans. by Andrew Motte, Daniel Adee, New York, 1848, pp. 73–77.

two bodies at any given place is the same as the ratio of their masses was proven by Newton in the pendulum experiments referred to in Definition I and discussed in Chapter 19. This is in no way inconsistent, however, with the concept that the mass or inertia of a body is a constant, while the weight of a body is a quantity which varies with the distance of the body from the center of the earth. Thus two masses can be compared by weighing only if they are weighed at the same place, that is, at the same distance from the center of the earth.

Definition II

The quantity of motion is the measure of the same, arising from the velocity and quantity of matter conjunctly.

The motion of the whole is the sum of the motions of all the parts; and therefore in a body double in quantity, with equal velocity, the motion is double; with twice the velocity, it is quadruple.

Definition III

The vis insita, *or innate force of matter, is a power of resisting, by which every body, as much as in it lies endeavors to persevere in its present state, whether it be of rest, or of moving uniformly forward in a right line.*

This force is ever proportional to the body whose force it is and differs nothing from the inactivity of the mass, but in our manner of conceiving it. A body, from the inertness of matter, is not without difficulty put out of its state of rest or motion. Upon which account, this *vis insita* may, by a most significant name, be called inertia (*vis inertiae*) or force of inactivity. But a body exerts this force only when another force, impressed upon it, endeavors to change its condition; and the exercise of this force may be considered both as resistance and impulse; it is resistance in so far as the body, for maintaining its present state, opposes the force impressed; it is impulse in so far as the body, by not easily giving way to the impressed force of another, endeavors to change the state of that other. Resistance is usually ascribed to bodies at rest, and impulse to those in motion; but motion and rest, as commonly conceived, are only relatively distinguished; nor are those bodies always truly at rest, which commonly are taken to be so.

Definition IV

An impressed force is an action exerted upon a body, in order to change its state, either of rest, or of moving uniformly forward in a right line.

This force consists in the action only and remains no longer in the body when the action is over. For a body maintains every new state it acquires, by its inertia only. Impressed forces are of different origins, as from percussion, from pressure, from centripetal force.

Definition V

A centripetal force is that by which bodies are drawn or impelled, or any way tend, towards a point as to a centre.

Of this sort is gravity, by which bodies tend to the centre of the earth; magnetism, by which iron tends to the loadstone; and that force, whatever it is, by which the planets are perpetually drawn aside from the rectilinear motions, which otherwise they would pursue, and made to revolve in curvilinear orbits.[3] A stone, whirled about in a sling, endeavors to recede from the hand that turns it; and by that endeavor, distends the sling, and that with so much the greater force, as it is revolved with the greater velocity, and as soon as it is let go, flies away. That force which opposes itself to this endeavor, and by which the sling perpetually draws back the stone towards the hand, and retains it in its orbit, because it is directed to the hand as the centre of the orbit, I call the centripetal force. And the same thing is to be understood of all bodies, revolved in any orbits. They all endeavor to recede from the centres of their orbits; and were it not for the opposition of a contrary force which restrains them to, and detains them in their orbits, which I therefore call centripetal, would fly off in right lines, with an uniform motion. A projectile, if it was not for the force of gravity, would not deviate towards the earth, but would go off from it in a right line, and that with an uniform motion, if the resistance of the air was taken away. It is by its gravity that it is drawn aside perpetually from its rectilinear course, and made to deviate towards the earth, more or less, according to the force of its gravity, and the velocity of its motion. The less its gravity is, or the quantity of its matter, or the greater the velocity with which it is projected, the less will it deviate from a rectilinear course, and the farther it will go. If a leaden ball, projected from the top of a mountain by the force of gunpowder, with a given velocity, and in a direction parallel to the horizon, is carried in a curved line to the distance of two miles before it falls to the ground; the same, if the resistance of the air were taken away, with a double or decuple velocity, would fly twice or ten times as far. And by increasing the velocity, we may at pleasure increase the distance to which it might be projected, and diminish the curvature of the line which it might describe, till at last it should fall at the distance of 10, 30, or 90 degrees, or even might go quite round the whole earth before it falls; or lastly, so that it might never fall to the earth, but go forwards into the celestial spaces, and proceed in its motion in infinitum. And after the same manner that a projectile, by the force of gravity, may be made to revolve in an orbit, and go round the whole earth, the moon also, either by the force of gravity, if it is endued with gravity, or by any other force, that impels it towards the earth, may be perpetually drawn aside towards the earth, out of the rectilinear way which by its innate force it would pursue; and would be made to revolve in the orbit which it now describes; nor could the moon without some such force be retained in its orbit. If this force was too small, it would not sufficiently turn the moon out of a rectilinear course; if it was too great, it would turn too much, and draw down the moon from its orbit towards the earth. It is necessary that the force be of a just quantity, and it belongs to the mathematicians to find the force that may serve exactly to retain a body in a given orbit with a given velocity; and vice versa, to determine the curvilinear

[3] Note the completion of the break, started by Kepler, with the idea which had been accepted for about two thousand years that circular motion was " natural " for celestial bodies. Newton here is stating the idea that the natural thing for any body, celestial or terrestrial, to do is to continue moving in a straight line. The observed motion along a curved path thus calls for a centripetal force. It will be recalled that Kepler also felt the need for a force between the sun and a planet to account for the variable distance of the planet from the sun.

way into which a body projected from a given place with a given velocity may be made to deviate from its natural rectilinear way, by means of a given force.

The quantity of any centripetal force may be considered as of three kinds: absolute, accelerative, and motive.[4]

❖   ❖   ❖   ❖   ❖   ❖   ❖

Definition VIII

The motive quantity of a centripetal force is the measure of the same, proportional to the motion which it generates in a given time.

Thus the weight is greater in a greater body, less in a less body; and, in the same body, it is greater near to the earth, and less at remoter distances. This sort of quantity is the centripetency, or propension of the whole body towards the centre, or, as I may say, its weight [5]; and it is always known by the quantity of an equal and contrary force just sufficient to hinder the descent of the body.

❖   ❖   ❖   ❖   ❖   ❖   ❖

Scholium

Hitherto I have laid down the definitions of such words as are less known, and explained the sense in which I would have them to be understood in the following discourse. I do not define time, space, place, and motion, as being well known to all. Only I must observe, that ordinary people conceive those quantities under no other notions but from the relation they bear to sensible objects. And thence arise certain prejudices, for the removing of which, it will be convenient to distinguish them into absolute and relative, true and apparent, mathematical and common.

❖   ❖   ❖   ❖   ❖   ❖   ❖

The scholium continues at some length to develop the ideas of relative and absolute time, space, and motion. Newton felt that while relative time is measured by motion (rotation of the earth on its axis, revolution about the sun, etc.) absolute time existed entirely apart from motion. He felt that an absolute immovable space also existed, but that since all bodies in the universe which come under our observation move with respect to each other, we have no way of setting up a frame of reference in absolute space. Absolute motion would be the transfer of a body from one place in absolute space to another, and relative motion of two bodies would be the difference in their absolute motions. The question of abso-

---

[4] Definitions VI and VII of absolute and accelerative centripetal force are omitted as they are not emphasized in modern usage. The necessary results may all be obtained from motive centripetal force.

[5] It should not be inferred from this statement that the centripetal force acting on a body is always equal to its weight. Since Newton is calling any force that acts toward a center a centripetal force, the weight of a body which acts toward the center of the earth he calls a centripetal force. However, only a small fraction of this weight is necessary to prevent the spin of the earth from throwing an object on its surface out into space. According to present usage, we would refer only to the unbalanced force required to hold a body in a circular path as the centripetal force. Thus a two-pound mass whirled in a sling might require a centripetal force of many times the weight, depending on the speed of rotation and the length of the sling.

lute time, space, and motion is thus a philosophical one since these quantities cannot be measured, and physical science confines itself to relative time, space, and motion. However, we are continuously confronted by the necessity of choosing a suitable frame of reference with respect to which our measurements of time, space, and motion can be made. Thus if we are making measurements of a ball rolling down an inclined plane, we shall take the surface of the earth as being our frame of reference and the only motion considered will be that of the ball with respect to the surface of the earth. However if one were interested in the motion of the ball with respect to the center of the sun as the ball rolls down the incline, both the rotation of the earth on its axis and its revolution about the sun would need to be considered. In this case, the center of the sun would be considered stationary and would determine our frame of reference. The problem becomes even more complex if the motion of the ball with respect to the center of our galaxy is to be considered, because the sun itself is moving with respect to our galaxy. In each case before Newton's laws can be applied for calculating such quantities as forces and changes in momentum, a frame of reference must be established.

STUDY QUESTIONS

1. Newton's Definition I states that the quantity of matter is the measure of the same arising from both its density and bulk. From his discussion it may be inferred that

    (1) mass and weight are the same
    (2) Newton is using circular reasoning, since density is defined in terms of mass and volume
    (3) the masses of two bodies can be compared by comparing their weights
    (4) the luminiferous ether that pervades the interstices has no mass
    (5) pendulum experiments prove that the ratio of the weight of a given body to its mass is a constant, regardless of the elevation of the body above sea level.

2. From Newton's Definition II of quantity of motion, it may always be inferred that
    a. " quantity of motion " has the same meaning as " quantity of matter "
    b. doubling the velocity of a body quadruples its quantity of motion
    c. if the velocity of A is twice the velocity of B, the quantity of motion of A must be twice the quantity of motion of B.
    The correct answer is

    (1) a   (2) b   (3) c   (4) a and b   (5) none of them.

3. In Definition III concerning *vis insita*, or innate force of matter, Newton considers that inertia
    a. opposes changes in the motion of a body

    b. acts in a different manner in a body at rest and in the same body when in motion

    c. is always equal and opposite to the applied force acting on a given body.

The correct answer is

    (1) a   (2) b   (3) c   (4) a and c   (5) none of them.

4. Newton's Definition IV concerning an impressed force implies that

    a. force may be defined as that action which tends to accelerate a body

    b. when the applied force acting on a body is removed, the inertia of the body simultaneously disappears

    c. the inertia of a body is an accelerating force on that body.

The correct answer is

    (1) a   (2) b   (3) c   (4) a and c   (5) none of them.

5. Newton makes the statement in Definition V that, " If a leaden ball, projected . . . parallel to the horizon, is carried . . . two miles . . . , with a double or decuple velocity, would fly twice or ten times as far." Explain how this statement is or is not consistent with Galileo's work on projectile motion.

6. Select the correct statement concerning Definition V of a centripetal force.

    (1) Centripetal force acting on a body depends only on the speed of the body.

    (2) Centripetal force acts outward from the center of rotation.

    (3) Centripetal force acting on a body acts tangentially to the circular path of the body.

    (4) Centripetal force acting on the moon causes it to maintain a constant (nearly) speed in its orbit.

    (5) The centripetal force acting on a body moving in a circular path does not affect the speed of the body.

7. Does Newton's statement in Definition V that " a projectile, by the force of gravity, may be made to revolve in an orbit, and go round the whole earth " have any experimental verification in his or the present time?

8. Select the correct statement or statements concerning Definition VIII of the motive quantity of a centripetal force.

    a. The centripetal force acting on a body is always equal to its weight.

    b. The motive quantity of a centripetal force is proportional to the change of momentum which it causes in a given time.

    c. The motive quantity of a centripetal force is twice as large for double the mass traveling with the same circular motion.

The correct answer is

    (1) a   (2) b   (3) c   (4) b and c   (5) none of them.

9. Select the correct statement or statements.

    a. By absolute time, Newton referred to sidereal instead of solar time.

    b. True or absolute time is not measured by motion.

    c. Modern methods of measuring time depend on motion.

The correct answer is

    (1) a   (2) b   (3) c   (4) a and b   (5) b and c.

10–12. A passenger walks toward the rear of a train with a speed of 2 miles per hour. The train is traveling due east along the equator on December 21 at a speed of 60 miles per hour. Due to the earth's rotation, a point on the equator is moving 1000 miles per hour, and the earth is traveling in its orbit 66,660 miles per hour.

10. If it is midnight on the train, the relative speed of the man with respect to the solar system as calculated from the above data is, in miles per hour,

    (1) 67,720 toward the east [6]   (2) 67,718 toward the east
    (3) 67,718 toward the west   (4) 65,602 toward the west
    (5) none of the above.

11. If it is noon on the train, the relative speed of the man with respect to the solar system as calculated from the above data is in miles per hour

    (1) 67,722 toward the west   (2) 67,718 toward the east
    (3) 65,602 toward the east   (4) 65,602 toward the west
    (5) none of the above.

12. With respect to the above data, select the correct statement or statements.
    a. The correct answers in the two previous questions give the absolute velocities also.
    b. The correct answers are independent of the date.
    c. It is not possible to calculate the absolute motion of the passenger.
    The correct answer is

    (1) a   (2) b   (3) c   (4) b and c   (5) none of them.

13. Is it possible to determine if any place in space is immovable (absolute rest)?
14. Can the relative motion of a body be changed without applying an accelerating force to that body?
15. Compare the concepts of inertia and impetus.

   [6] When applied to the whole solar system, the term " east " may be interpreted as the direction of counterclockwise motion as viewed from the North Star side.

16

Laws of Motion

● Galileo had shown
by means of several experiments with inclined and horizontal planes
that continued motion at constant speed in a straight line is as natural as
rest when there is no cause of change of motion. Galileo thus associated
force (cause) and change of motion (effect) and paved the way for
Newton's first two laws of motion. Even though Galileo had essentially
demonstrated that on an inclined plane the acceleration produced is proportional to the force producing it, he failed to develop the idea and there
is no indication that the concept of mass occurred to him.

Newton, in his "Definitions" and "Laws of Motion," introduced the
concept of mass and thus was able to develop the idea of measuring forces
by the changes of motion or accelerations which they produced.

MATHEMATICAL PRINCIPLES OF NATURAL PHILOSOPHY [1]

by Isaac Newton

Axioms, or Laws of Motion

Law I

Every body perseveres in its state of rest, or of uniform motion in a right line,
unless it is compelled to change that state by forces impressed upon it.

Projectiles persevere in their motions, so far as they are not retarded by the
resistance of the air, or impelled downwards by the force of gravity. A top,
whose parts by their cohesion are perpetually drawn aside from rectilinear motions, does not cease its rotation, otherwise than as it is retarded by the air.
The greater bodies of the planets and comets, meeting with less resistance in
freer spaces, preserve their motions both progressive and circular for a much
longer time.

Law II

The alteration of motion is always proportional to the motive force impressed,
and is made in the direction of the right line in which that force is impressed.

[1] Newton, op. cit., pp. 83–84, 86–87.

If any force generates a motion, a double force will generate double the motion, a triple force triple the motion, whether that force be impressed altogether and at once, or gradually and successively. And this motion (being always directed the same way with the generating force), if the body moved before, is added to or deducted from the former motion, according as they directly conspire with or are directly contrary to each other; or obliquely joined, when they are oblique, so as to produce a new motion compounded from the determination of both.

It seems probable that Newton had a rather flexible concept of force and did not always use it in the restricted sense that it is used today.[2, 3] Newton associated change of momentum (effect) with force (cause), stating that the change in momentum is proportional to the applied force. In present day usage, force is defined as being proportional to the *rate of* change of momentum or to the change in momentum per unit of time. That Newton on occasion used the term force in the restricted sense it is used today seems obvious from Proposition XXIV of Book II which states:

For the velocity which a given force can generate in a given matter in a given time is directly as the force and the time, and inversely as the matter. The greater the force or the time is, or the less the matter, the greater the velocity that will be generated. This is manifest from the second Law of Motion.

His later calculations with centripetal force also show that his concept of force was essentially the same as that used today. It is possible that in the initial statement of the second law the term force was used to designate what we now call impulse, where *impulse* is the product of the force and the time. This interpretation would give meaning to the statement, "whether that force be impressed altogether and at once, or gradually and successively." The total change in momentum is proportional to the impulse, but the rate of change of momentum is proportional to the applied force.

Law III

To every action there is always opposed an equal reaction: or the mutual actions of two bodies upon each other are always equal, and directed to contrary parts.

Whatever draws or presses another is as much drawn or pressed by that other. If you press a stone with your finger, the finger is also pressed by the stone. If a horse draws a stone tied to a rope, that horse (if I may so say) will be equally drawn back towards the stone; for the distended rope, by the same endeavor to relax or unbend itself, will draw the horse as much towards the stone as it does the stone towards the horse, and will obstruct the progress of the one as much as it advances that of the other. If a body impinge upon another, and by its force change the motion of the other, that body also (because

---

[2] J. W. Herivel, " Newton's Discovery of the Law of Centrifugal Force," *Isis* (1960) Vol. 51, p. 546.

[3] For a different explanation, see Max Jammer, *Concepts of Force*, Harvard University Press, 1957, p. 124.

of the equality of the mutual pressure) will undergo an equal change, in its own motion, towards the contrary part. The changes made by these actions are equal, not in the velocities but in the motions of bodies; that is to say, if the bodies are not hindered by any other impediments. For, because the motions are equally changed, the changes of the velocities made towards contrary parts are inversely proportional to the bodies. This law takes place also in attractions, as will be proved in the next Scholium.

Corollary I

A body by two forces impressed simultaneously, will describe the diagonal of a parallelogram in the same time that it would describe the sides by those forces separately.

If a body in a given time, by the force M impressed apart in the place A [Fig. 16-1], should with an uniform motion be carried from A to B, and by

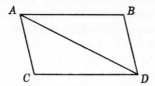

Figure 16-1. *Vector addition of velocities.*

the force N impressed apart in the same place, should be carried from A to C, complete the parallelogram ABCD, and, by both forces acting together, it will in the same time be carried in the diagonal from A to D. For since the force N acts in the direction of the line AC, parallel to BD, this force (by the second law) will not at all alter the velocity generated by the other force M, by which the body is carried towards the line BD. The body therefore will arrive at the line BD in the same time, whether the force N be impressed or not; and therefore at the end of that time it will be found somewhere in the line BD. By the same argument, at the end of the same time it will be found somewhere in the line CD. Therefore it will be found in the point D, where both lines meet. But it will move in a right line from A to D, by Law I.

❊   ❊   ❊   ❊   ❊   ❊   ❊

Corollary III

The quantity of motion, which is obtained by taking the sum of the motions directed towards the same parts, and the difference of those that are directed to contrary parts, suffers no change from the action of bodies among themselves.

For action and its opposite reaction are equal, by Law III, and therefore, by Law II, they produce in the motions equal changes towards opposite parts. Therefore if the motions are directed towards the same parts, whatever is added to the motion of the preceding body will be deducted from the motion of that which follows; so that the sum will be the same as before. If the bodies meet, with contrary motions, there will be an equal deduction from the motions of both; and therefore the difference of the motions directed towards opposite parts will remain the same.

Thus if a spherical body A with two parts of velocity is triple of a spherical body B which follows in the same right line with ten parts of velocity, the motion of A will be to that of B as 6 to 10. Suppose, then, their motions to be of 6 parts and of 10 parts, and the sum will be 16 parts. Therefore, upon the meeting of the bodies, if A acquire 3, 4, or 5 parts of motion, B will lose as many; and therefore after reflection A will proceed with 9, 10, or 11 parts, and B with 7, 6, or 5 parts; the sum remaining always of 16 parts as before. If the body A acquire 9, 10, 11, or 12 parts of motion, and therefore after meeting proceed with 15, 16, 17, or 18 parts, the body B, losing so many parts as A has got, will either proceed with 1 part, having lost 9, or stop and remain at rest, as having lost its whole progressive motion of 10 parts; or it will go back with 1 part, having not only lost its whole motion, but (if I may so say) one part more; or it will go back with 2 parts, because a progressive motion of 12 parts is taken off. And so the sums of the conspiring motions 15 + 1, or 16 + 0, and the differences of the contrary motions 17 − 1 and 18 − 2, will always be equal to 16 parts, as they were before the meeting and reflection of the bodies. But, the motion being known with which the bodies proceed after reflection, the velocity of either will be also known, by taking the velocity after to the velocity before reflection, as the motion after is to the motion before. As in the last case, where the motion of the body A was of 6 parts before reflection, and of 18 parts after, and the velocity was of 2 parts before reflection, the velocity thereof after reflection will be found to be of 6 parts; by saying, as the 6 parts of motion before to 18 parts after, so are 2 parts of velocity before reflection to 6 parts after.

But if the bodies are either not spherical, or; moving in different right lines, impinge obliquely one upon the other; and their motions after reflection are required, in those cases we are first to determine the position of the plane that touches the concurring bodies in the point of contact, then the motion of each body (by Cor. II) is to be resolved into two, one perpendicular to that plane, and the other parallel to it. This done, because the bodies act upon each other in the direction of a line perpendicular to this plane, the parallel motions are to be retained the same after reflection as before; and to the perpendicular motions we are to assign equal changes towards the contrary parts; in such manner that the sum of the conspiring and the difference of the contrary motions may remain the same as before. From such kind of reflections also sometimes arise the circular motions of bodies about their own centres. But these are cases which I do not consider in what follows; and it would be too tedious to demonstrate every particular one that relates to this subject.

STUDY QUESTIONS

1–2. A car is traveling east on a flat, straight east-west street with a constant speed of 20 miles per hour.

1. If the motion of the earth is neglected, the unbalanced force acting on the car is

> (1) directed toward the west   (2) directed toward the east
> (3) vertically up   (4) vertically down   (5) zero.

2. If the rotation of the earth is not neglected, with respect to the earth's axis the unbalanced force acting on the car is

     (1) directed toward the east   (2) directed toward the west
     (3) vertically up   (4) vertically down
     (5) down and perpendicular to the earth's axis.

3–4. A car is parked on a level east-west street.

3. If the motion of the earth is neglected, the unbalanced force acting on the car is

     (1) directed toward the west   (2) directed toward the east
     (3) vertically up   (4) vertically down   (5) zero.

4. If the rotation of the earth is not neglected, with respect to the earth's axis the unbalanced force acting on the car is

     (1) directed toward the east   (2) directed toward the west
     (3) vertically up   (4) vertically down
     (5) down and perpendicular to the earth's axis.

5. From Newton's second law as used today, it follows that
     a. an accelerating force of 5 pounds-force applied to a given body for 2 seconds would produce the same change in momentum as an accelerating force of 10 pounds-force applied for 1 second
     b. an accelerating force of 5 pounds-force applied to a given body for 2 seconds would produce half the change in momentum that it would if applied for 1 second
     c. an accelerating force of 10 pounds-force applied to a given body for 2 seconds would produce twice the change in momentum that a 10 pound-force applied for 1 second would produce.
The correct answer is

     (1) a   (2) b   (3) c   (4) a and c   (5) a, b, and c.

6. Select the correct statement or statements.
     a. If two equal forces act for equal times on two unequal masses, the changes in momentum produced are equal.
     b. If two equal forces act for unequal times on two equal masses, the changes in momentum produced are equal.
     c. If two unequal forces act for unequal times on two unequal masses, the changes in momentum produced may be equal.
The correct answer is

     (1) a   (2) b   (3) c   (4) a and c   (5) none of them.

7. Select the correct statement or statements.
     a. Since the mass of the earth is much greater than the mass of the moon, the gravitational attraction of the earth for the moon is much greater than the attraction of the moon for the earth.
     b. For a horse to start a wagon, the horse must pull with a greater force on the wagon than the wagon pulls back on the horse.
     c. Action and reaction are equal only when the bodies acting upon each other are in equilibrium (that is, not accelerated).
The correct answer is

     (1) a   (2) b   (3) c   (4) a, b, and c   (5) none of them.

8. Car A of mass 2000 pounds traveling 30 miles per hour runs head-on into car B of mass 4000 pounds traveling 15 miles per hour. Select the correct statement or statements.
   a. The force exerted on B by A is equal to the force exerted on A by B during the collision.
   b. The change in momentum of car A during the collision is equal to the change in momentum of car B.
   c. Assuming the two cars stick together, they will be stationary immediately after the collision.
   The correct answer is

       (1) a   (2) b   (3) c   (4) a and b   (5) a, b, and c.

9–12. *Car A of mass 2000 pounds traveling 20 feet per second overtakes and bumps into the rear of car B of mass 3000 pounds traveling 10 feet per second.*

9. The total momentum of the two cars before impact in pounds-mass feet per second is

       (1) 10,000   (2) 20,000   (3) 30,000   (4) 40,000   (5) 70,000.

10. The total momentum of the two cars immediately after impact, assuming they stick together, is in pounds-mass feet per second

       (1) 10,000   (2) 20,000   (3) 30,000   (4) 40,000   (5) 70,000.

11. The total momentum of the two cars immediately after impact, assuming they bounce apart, is in pounds-mass feet per second

       (1) 10,000   (2) 20,000   (3) 30,000   (4) 40,000   (5) 70,000.

12. If the original direction of motion of car B is reversed so that the two cars collide head-on, then the total momentum of the two cars before impact in pounds-mass feet per second is

       (1) 10,000   (2) 20,000   (3) 30,000   (4) 40,000   (5) 70,000.

17

Experimental Verification of the Third Law: Conservation of Momentum

● In the concluding part of the previous chapter, Newton discussed the fact that when two bodies impinge on each other, the momentum lost by one is always equal to the momentum gained by the other. In the present chapter, he describes experiments in which two balls hung as pendulums are displaced and then released and allowed to collide. The experimental results show that in all cases, irrespective of the materials of which the balls are made and of their relative motions before impact, the loss of momentum of one ball always is equal to the gain in momentum of the other. From these results it follows that action and reaction are equal and the third law of motion is experimentally verified.

MATHEMATICAL PRINCIPLES OF NATURAL PHILOSOPHY [1]

by Isaac Newton

Axioms, or Laws of Motion

Scholium

Hitherto I have laid down such principles as have been received by mathematicians, and are confirmed by abundance of experiments. By the first two Laws and the first two Corollaries, Galileo discovered that the descent of bodies varied directly as the square of the time and that the motion of projectiles was in the curve of a parabola; experience agreeing with both, unless so far as these motions are a little retarded by the resistance of the air. When a body is falling, the uniform force of its gravity acting equally, impresses, in equal intervals of time, equal forces [2] upon that body, and therefore generates equal velocities; and in the whole time impresses a whole force, and generates a whole velocity proportional to the time. And the spaces described in proportional times are as the product of the velocities and the times; that is, as the

---

[1] Newton, op. cit., pp. 89–93.
[2] "Force" here may be considered to mean impulse. See previous discussion of the second law, p. 224.

squares of the times. And when a body is thrown upwards, its uniform gravity impresses forces and takes off velocities proportional to the times; and the times of ascending to the greatest heights are as the velocities to be taken off, and those heights are as the product of the velocities and the times, or as the squares of the velocities. And if a body be projected in any direction, the motion arising from its projection is compounded with the motion arising from its gravity. If the body A [Fig. 17-1] by its motion of projection alone could de-

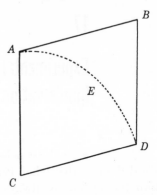

Figure 17-1. *Projectile motion, with initial velocity directed at an angle above the horizontal.*

scribe in a given time the right line AB, and with its motion of falling alone could describe in the same time the altitude AC; complete the parallelogram ABCD, and the body by that compounded motion will at the end of the time be found in the place D; and the curved line AED, which that body describes, will be a parabola, to which the right line AB will be a tangent at A; and whose ordinate BD will be as the square of the line AB. On the same Laws and Corollaries depend those things which have been demonstrated concerning the times of the vibration of pendulums, and are confirmed by the daily experiments of pendulum clocks. By the same, together with the third Law, Sir Christopher Wren, Dr. Wallis, and Mr. Huygens, the greatest geometers of our times, did severally determine the rules of the impact and reflection of hard bodies, and much about the same time communicated their discoveries to the Royal Society, exactly agreeing among themselves as to those rules. Dr. Wallis, indeed, was somewhat earlier in the publication; then followed Sir Christopher Wren, and, lastly, Mr. Huygens. But Sir Christopher Wren confirmed the truth of the thing before the Royal Society by the experiments on pendulums, which M. Mariotte soon after thought fit to explain in a treatise entirely upon that subject. But to bring this experiment to an accurate agreement with the theory, we are to have a due regard as well to the resistance of air to the elastic force of the concurring bodies. Let the spherical bodies A, B, be suspended [Fig. 17-2] by the parallel and equal strings AC, BD, from the centres C, D. About these centres, with those lengths describe the semicircles EAF, GBH, bisected by the radii CA, DB. Bring the body A to any point R of the arc EAF, and (withdrawing the body B) let it go from thence, and after one oscillation suppose it to return to the point V: then RV will be the retardation arising from the resistance of air. . . . And in like manner, when two bodies are let go together from different places, we are to find the motion of each, as well before as after reflection; and then we may compare the motions between themselves,

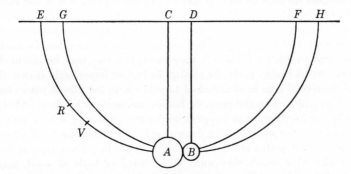

Figure 17-2. *Impact experiment with two pendulums to demonstrate conservation of momentum.*

and collect the effects of the reflection. Thus trying the thing with pendulums of 10 feet, in unequal as well as equal bodies, and making the bodies to concur after a descent through large spaces, as of 8, 12, or 16 feet, I found always, without an error of 3 inches, that when the bodies concurred together directly, equal changes towards the contrary parts were produced in their motions, and, of consequence, that the action and reaction were always equal. As if the body A impinged upon the body B at rest with 9 parts of motion, and losing 7, proceeded after reflection with 2, the body B was carried backwards with those 7 parts. If the bodies concurred with contrary motions, A with 12 parts of motion, and B with 6, then if A receded with 2, B receded with 8; to wit, with a deduction of 14 parts of motion on each side. For from the motion of A deducting 12 parts, nothing will remain; but deducting 2 parts more, a motion will be generated of 2 parts towards the contrary way; and so, from the motion of the body B of 6 parts, deducting 14 parts, a motion is generated of 8 parts towards the contrary way. But if the bodies were made both to move towards the same way, A, the swifter, with 14 parts of motion, B, the slower, with 5, and after reflection A went on with 5, B likewise went on with 14 parts; 9 parts being transferred from A to B. And so in other cases. By the collision of bodies, the quantity of motion, obtained from the sum of the motions directed towards the same way, or from the difference of those that were directed towards contrary ways, was never changed. For the error of an inch or two in measures may be easily ascribed to the difficulty of executing everything with accuracy. It was not easy to let go two pendulums so exactly together that the bodies should impinge one upon the other in the lowermost place AB; nor to mark the places s, and k, to which the bodies ascended after collision. Nay, and some errors, too, might have happened from the unequal density of the parts of the pendulous bodies themselves, and from the irregularity of the texture proceeding from other causes.

But to prevent an objection that may perhaps be alleged against the rule, for the proof of which this experiment was made, as if this rule did suppose that the bodies were either absolutely hard, or at least perfectly elastic (whereas no such bodies are to be found in Nature), I must add, that the experiments we have been describing, by no means depending upon that quality of hardness, do succeed as well in soft as in hard bodies. For if the rule is to be tried in bodies not perfectly hard, we are only to diminish the reflection in such a certain proportion as the quantity of the elastic force requires. By the theory of Wren and Huygens, bodies absolutely hard return one from another with the same velocity with which they meet. But this may be affirmed with more certainty of bodies perfectly elastic. In bodies imperfectly elastic the velocity of the return is to be diminished together with the elastic force; because that force (except when the parts of bodies are bruised by their collision, or suffer some such extension as happens under the strokes of a hammer) is (as far as I can perceive) certain and determined, and makes the bodies to return one from the other with a relative velocity, which is in a given ratio to that relative velocity with which they met. This I tried in balls of wool, made up tightly, and strongly compressed. For, first, by letting go the pendulous bodies, and measuring their reflection, I determined the quantity of their elastic force; and then, according to this force, estimated the reflections that ought to happen in other cases of collision. And with this computation other experiments made afterwards did accordingly agree; the balls always receding one from the other with a relative velocity, which was to the relative velocity with which they met as about 5 to 9. Balls of steel returned with almost the same velocity; those of cork with a velocity something less; but in balls of glass the proportion was as about 15 to 16. And thus the third Law, so far as it regards percussions and reflections, is proved by a theory exactly agreeing with experience.

In attractions, I briefly demonstrate the thing after this manner. Suppose an obstacle is interposed to hinder the approach of any two bodies A, B, mutually attracting one another: then if either body, as A, is more attracted towards the other body B, than that other body B is towards the first body A, the obstacle will be more strongly urged by the pressure of the body A than by the pressure of the body B, and therefore will not remain in equilibrio: but the stronger pressure will prevail, and will make the system of the two bodies, together with the obstacle, to move directly towards the parts on which B lies; and in free spaces, to go forwards in infinitum with a motion perpetually accelerated; which is absurd and contrary to the first Law. For, by the first Law, the system ought to persevere in its state of rest, or of moving uniformly forwards in a right line; and therefore the bodies must equally press the obstacle, and be equally attracted one by the other. I made the experiment on the loadstone and iron. If these, placed apart in proper vessels, are made to float by one another in standing water, neither of them will propel the other; but, by being equally attracted, they will sustain each other's pressure, and rest at last in equilibrium.

So the gravitation between the earth and its parts is mutual. Let the earth FI [Fig. 17-3] be cut by any plane EG into two parts EGF and EGI, and their weights one towards the other will be mutually equal. For if by another plane HK, parallel to the former EG, the greater part EGI is cut into two parts EGKH and HKI, whereof HKI is equal to the part EFG, first cut off, it is evident that the middle part EGKH will have no propension by its proper weight towards either side, but will hang as it were, and rest in an equilibrium between both. But the one extreme part HKI will with its whole weight bear upon and press the middle part towards the other extreme part EGF; and therefore the force with which EGI, the sum of the parts HKI and EGKH,

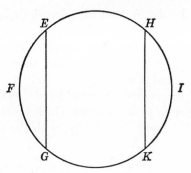

Figure 17-3. *Newton's diagram for demonstrating equal gravitational pulls between unequal parts of the earth.*

tends towards the third part EGF, is equal to the weight of the part HKI; that is, to the weight of the third part EGF. And therefore the weights of the two parts EGI and EGF, one towards the other, are equal, as I was to prove. And indeed if those weights were not equal, the whole earth floating in the nonresisting ether would give way to the greater weight, and, retiring from it, would be carried off in infinitum.

Although Newton previously had invented his mathematical method of fluxions (the calculus) and had written on algebra under the title of universal arithmetic, the mathematics employed in the *Principia* is geometry. This was because Newton had a great liking for geometry and because he wished the material of the *Principia* to be readily available to his contemporaries who were not familiar with the calculus. Thus his definition of force and the laws of motion are written in terms of proportions rather than algebraic equations as we use them today.

Let us put the second law in algebraic form. The statement that the rate of change [3] of motion is proportional to the motive force impressed may be written

$$F \propto \frac{\Delta(mv)}{t}$$

where $\propto$ stands for "is proportional to," mv is the quantity of motion or momentum, the Greek letter Δ means "the change of," and t represents the time during which the force is applied.

Since it is more convenient to work with an equation than a proportionality, the second law may be put in equation form by introducing a constant of proportionality.[4] Thus

$$F = k \frac{\Delta(mv)}{t}.$$

---

[3] See note on second law, p. 224.
[4] This procedure may be illustrated as follows:
The cost (C) of apples is obviously proportional to the number (N) of apples purchased. Thus one could write

$$C \propto N.$$

(Continued on page 234.)

The value of k may be determined experimentally by applying a known force for a known time to a given mass and measuring the change in momentum. Such experiments show that the value of k is always the same, regardless of what body is used, provided that the same units of measurement are used for F, t, and $\Delta(mv)$.

In the cases that are commonly considered (autos, balls, projectiles, planets, etc.), the change in momentum which takes place when a force is applied is due to a change in velocity, with the mass remaining constant. Thus

$$\Delta(mv) = m\,\Delta v$$

and the second law may be written

$$F = k\,\frac{m\,\Delta v}{t}\,.$$

But Galileo has already defined acceleration as being the change in velocity per unit of time;

$$a = \frac{\Delta v}{t}\,.$$

The second law of motion then becomes

$$F = kma.$$

To return to a consideration of the units, there are a number of combinations in use today. The one with which we probably are most familiar measures F in pounds-force, m in pounds-mass, and a in feet per second per second. One pound-mass is defined as a mass equal to that of the standard pound-mass kept at the Bureau of Standards. To define a unit of force, let us make use of experimentally determined information which is available. A one pound-mass when freely falling near sea level is known to have an acceleration of about 32 feet per second per second under the action of the gravitational pull of the earth. We could then arbitrarily define a one *pound-force* [5] as the force with which the earth pulls a one

---

This may be written as an equation by introducing a constant of proportionality (p).

$$C = pN$$

In this case, p is the price per apple.

[5] In Part VII, we shall have occasion to refer to two other units of force, the dyne and the newton. These units are used in the metric system where the arbitrary unit of length is the meter, or its submultiple the centimeter, and the arbitrary unit of mass is the kilogram, or its submultiple the gram. The dyne is defined from Newton's second law $F = kma$ by arbitrarily setting k equal to unity and defining the dyne as that force that will give a one gram-mass which is free to move an acceleration of one centimeter per second per second. Thus since $k = 1$, $m = 1$, and $a = 1$,

$$F = kma = 1 \cdot 1 \cdot 1 = 1$$

and this force of unity is called the dyne.

In a similar manner, the force which will give a one kilogram-mass which is free to move an acceleration of one meter per second per second is defined as the newton.

pound-mass near sea level or more generally as any force that will give a one pound-mass which is free to move [6] an acceleration of 32 feet per second per second. Using these arbitrarily defined units of force and mass and considering a one pound-mass, the value of k in the second law may be determined.

$$k = \frac{F}{ma} = \frac{1}{1 \cdot 32} = \frac{1}{32}.$$

Obviously the value of k is independent of the mass used, since a 3 pound-force acting on a 3 pound-mass would still produce an acceleration of 32.

If we agree to use the system of units discussed above, Newton's second law of motion can be written in the two following forms:

$$F = \frac{1}{32} \cdot \frac{\Delta(mv)}{t}$$

$$F = \frac{1}{32} \, ma.$$

Let us now consider the collision of two bodies, such as that of the balls hung as pendulums which are described by Newton. His experimental results showed that in all cases studied the momentum loss of one ball was always equal to the momentum gain of the other. This was true whether the balls were originally moving in the same or opposite directions before impact and whether the impact was between hard elastic balls or softer balls with less elasticity. This proved that the forces exerted by the balls on each other were equal. If $\Delta(mv)_A$ and $\Delta(mv)_B$ represent the changes in momentum of balls A and B during the impact, Newton found by experiment that

$$\Delta(mv)_A = -\Delta(mv)_B.$$

Obviously the time t of impact, which is the time that each ball pushes on the other, is equal for the two balls. Dividing each side of the above equation by t and multiplying by k

$$k \frac{\Delta(mv)_A}{t} = -k \frac{\Delta(mv)_B}{t}.$$

But by Newton's second law, the term on the left is the force acting on ball A and the term on the right is the force acting on ball B. Thus during the collision, action and reaction are equal and opposite, and

$$F_A = -F_B.$$

Then in the metric system the two following combinations of units may be used in Newton's second law:

F(dynes) $= m$(grams-mass) $\cdot a$(centimeters per second per second)
F(newtons) $= m$(kilograms-mass) $\cdot a$(meters per second per second)

It may be easily shown that

1 newton = 100,000 dynes,

and

1 newton = .22 pounds-force.

[6] By " free to move " is meant that there is no obstruction or resistance to motion,

Furthermore it follows that since the momentum gained by one ball was equal to the momentum lost by the other, the change in momentum of the *system of two balls* during collision was zero. In other words, the total momentum of a system which is not acted upon by any forces from the outside is conserved and remains constant. (The force exerted by each ball on the other is an internal force within the two-ball system, and these forces are not exerted on the two-ball system from the outside.) Since the total momentum of two colliding objects is not changed by the collision, it follows that the algebraic sum of the momentums of the two objects before impact is equal to the algebraic sum of the momentums after impact. Thus if V_A and v_A represent the velocities of mass m_A before and after impact, with mass m_B having velocities V_B and v_B before and after impact, then

$$m_A V_A + m_B V_B = m_A v_A + m_B v_B.$$

It should be noted of course that if velocities, say to the right, are considered positive those to the left must be taken as negative.

STUDY QUESTIONS

1. Select the correct statement or statements concerning Newton's experiments with the pendulums.
   a. He neglected the slight effects due to air resistance.
   b. The loss of velocity of one pendulum bob during impact was always equal to the gain in velocity of the other.
   c. The total momentum is conserved (remains unchanged) during collision only if the two bobs are perfectly elastic.
   The correct answer is

       (1) a   (2) b   (3) c   (4) b and c   (5) none of them.

2. An unbalanced force of 5 pounds-force acting on a 10 pounds-mass for 3 seconds will produce what change in momentum in pounds-mass feet per second?

       (1) 15   (2) 480   (3) $\frac{1}{2}$ (4) 150   (5) 30.

3. To produce an acceleration of 8 feet per second per second on a 3200 pounds-mass car, the unbalanced force required is, in pounds-force,

       (1) 25,600   (2) 800   (3) $\frac{1}{400}$ (4) 400   (5) 3200.

   4–6. The maximum braking force that can be exerted on a certain 3200 pounds-mass car is 1600 pounds-force. Assume the car traveling 60 miles per hour (approximately 90 feet per second).

4. The maximum negative acceleration of the car while being stopped is, in feet per second per second,

       (1) 53   (2) $\frac{1}{2}$ (3) 16   (4) 4   (5) 32.

5. The time in seconds required to bring the car to rest is

       (1) 22   (2) 2.7   (3) 1.6   (4) 44   (5) 5.5.

6. The distance in feet traveled by the car after the brakes are applied before coming to rest is
   (1) 968   (2) 120   (3) 70.4   (4) 242   (5) 484.

7. Select the correct statement or statements.
   a. If two equal accelerating forces act for unequal times on two equal masses, the accelerations produced will be equal.
   b. If two equal accelerating forces act for equal times on two unequal masses, the accelerations produced will be equal.
   c. If two equal accelerating forces act for equal times on two unequal masses, the changes in momentum produced are unequal.
   The correct answer is
   (1) a   (2) b   (3) c   (4) a and c   (5) none of them.

   8–12. Car A of 3200 pounds-mass traveling 40 feet per second toward the east runs into the rear of truck B of 4800 pounds-mass traveling 20 feet per second toward the east. The time of impact is 1/5 second.

8. If the car and truck stick together, immediately after the impact they would be traveling at a velocity in feet per second of
   (1) 0   (2) 28 toward the east   (3) 28 toward the west
   (4) 4 toward the east   (5) 4 toward the west.

9. The change in momentum of car A is, in pounds-mass feet per second,
   (1) 38,400   (2) 128,000   (3) 115,200   (4) 96,000   (5) 89,600.

10. The change in momentum of truck B is, in pounds-mass feet per second,
    (1) 38,400   (2) 128,000   (3) 115,200   (4) 96,000   (5) 89,600.

11. The impulse exerted on truck B in pounds-force seconds is
    (1) 38,400   (2) 1200   (3) 4000   (4) 3000   (5) 6000.

12. The force in pounds-force exerted on truck B during the impact is
    (1) 240   (2) 1200   (3) 4000   (4) 3000   (5) 6000.

13. Car A of 3200 pounds-mass traveling 40 feet per second toward the east collides head-on with truck B of 4800 pounds-mass traveling 20 feet per second in the opposite direction. If the car and truck stick together, immediately after the impact they would be traveling at a speed in feet per second of
    (1) 0   (2) 28 toward the east   (3) 28 toward the west
    (4) 4 toward the east   (5) 4 toward the west.

    14–17. A 1 pound wax ball and a 2 pound wax ball are hung as simple pendulums from the same support by strings 6 feet long. They are pulled apart in opposite directions until they have been raised through a vertical height of 4 feet. They are then released simultaneously and stick together when they collide.

14. Calculate the speed of the 1 pound ball at the bottom of the swing in feet per second.
    (1) 32   (2) 8   (3) 16   (4) 4   (5) 64.

15. Calculate the speed of the 2 pound ball at the bottom of the swing in feet per second.

    (1) 32   (2) 8   (3) 16   (4) 4   (5) 64.

16. Calculate the velocity of the two balls (stuck together) immediately after the collision in feet per second.

    (1) 5⅓   (2) 2⅔   (3) 16   (4) 10⅔   (5) 4.

17. How high vertically would they rise in feet?

    (1) 4/9   (2) 2   (3) 3   (4) 4   (5) ¾.

18–20. A model airplane of 4 pounds-mass is powered by a tiny gasoline motor which gives it an air speed of 40 feet per second. It is made to fly in a horizontal circle of 50 foot radius by a wire held by the operator at the center of the circle. The tension in the wire is measured by a spring balance held by the operator as being 4 pounds-force.

18. The acceleration of the plane in feet per second per second is

    (1) 1   (2) 0   (3) 32   (4) 4   (5) 128.

19. The direction of the acceleration is

    (1) toward the operator   (2) away from the operator
    (3) vertically up   (4) vertically down   (5) no direction, since the plane travels with constant speed and has no acceleration.

20. By experimenting, it is found that if the plane flies faster in the circle of 50 foot radius, the tension in the wire increases, and if the plane continues to fly at 40 feet per second when the length of the wire is increased, the tension in the wire is decreased. Consistent with all the information given, the relationship between the acceleration a of the plane, the speed v, and the radius R is found by trial and error to be

$$(1)\ a = 0 \quad (2)\ a = \frac{v}{R} \quad (3)\ a = \frac{v}{R^2} \quad (4)\ a = \frac{v^2}{R} \quad (5)\ a = vR$$

18

Centripetal Force

● Galileo and Copernicus, as had the Greeks centuries before, assumed that circular motion was natural for heavenly bodies and consequently required no explanation. Kepler, however, made an attempt to break with the past by explaining the motions of the planets as being due to virtues and attractions and repulsions emanating from the sun. He had also shown that in fact the celestial motions were in general not circular!

Newton assumed that his laws of motion applied equally to either terrestrial or celestial bodies. He showed, as had others, that uniform circular motion is an accelerated motion and therefore due to an unbalanced force acting toward the center of rotation. By his Rules of Reasoning,[1] he assumed that since a centripetal force (see Definition V) is required to maintain a ball whirling on a string in a circular path, a centripetal force is also required to maintain the moon or a planet in a circular orbit. To demonstrate that for the moon this centripetal force is gravity, the same cause that made the apple fall, it was necessary for him to show that a consistent numerical relationship existed between the "fall" of the moon and of the apple. To do this, it became necessary to prove that the distances between gravitating spherical bodies must be measured between centers, a proof which took Newton some time to work out. Newton's calculations showing the agreement between the fall of the moon and that of an object at the earth's surface will be given later in Chapter 21.

The present chapter outlines how centripetal forces are to be calculated. In the following short excerpts, the propositions and corollaries have been stated but the geometric proofs as usual have been largely omitted. In the Scholium, Newton outlines an alternate method of determining centripetal force.

---

[1] See Chapter 20.

MATHEMATICAL PRINCIPLES OF NATURAL PHILOSOPHY [2]
by Isaac Newton
Book I
The Motion of Bodies
Section II Centripetal Forces
Proposition I. Theorem I.

The areas, which revolving bodies describe by radii drawn to an immovable centre of force do lie in the same immovable planes, and are proportional to the times in which they are described.

❖   ❖   ❖   ❖   ❖   ❖   ❖

Proposition II. Theorem II.

Every body that moves in any curved line described in a plane, and by a radius, drawn to a point either immovable, or moving forwards with an uniform rectilinear motion, describes about that point areas proportional to the times, is urged by a centripetal force directed to that point.

❖   ❖   ❖   ❖   ❖   ❖   ❖

Kepler had shown that the planets travel about the sun in elliptical orbits in such a manner that a line joining the sun and a planet, called a radius vector, sweeps across equal areas in equal times. The sun is situated at one focus of the elliptical orbit. In Proposition II, Theorem II, Newton proves that under these conditions the planet is pulled toward the sun by a centripetal force.

Proposition III. Theorem III.

Every body, that by a radius drawn to the centre of another body, howsoever moved, describes areas about that centre proportional to the times, is urged by a force compounded out of the centripetal force tending to that other body, and of all the accelerative force by which that other body is impelled.

❖   ❖   ❖   ❖   ❖   ❖   ❖

Proposition IV. Theorem IV.

The centripetal forces of bodies, which by equable motions describe different circles, tend to the centres of the same circles; and are one to the other as the squares of the arcs described in equal times divided respectively by the radii of the circles.

❖   ❖   ❖   ❖   ❖   ❖   ❖

Cor. 1. Therefore, since those arcs are as the velocities of the bodies, the centripetal forces are directly proportional to the squares of the velocities and inversely proportional to the radii.

❖   ❖   ❖   ❖   ❖   ❖   ❖

[2] Newton, op. cit., pp. 103–109.

Cor. 6.[3] If the periodic times are as the 3/2th powers of the radii, and therefore the velocities inversely as the square roots of the radii, the centripetal forces will be inversely as the squares of the radii; and conversely.

❁   ❁   ❁   ❁   ❁   ❁   ❁

Cor. 9. From the same demonstration it likewise follows, that the arc which a body, uniformly revolving in a circle by means of a given centripetal force, describes in any time, is a mean proportional between the diameter of the circle, and the space which the same body falling by the same given force would descend through in the same given time.

Scholium

The case of the sixth Corollary obtains in the celestial bodies (as Sir Christopher Wren, Dr. Hooke, and Dr. Halley have severally observed); and therefore in what follows, I intend to treat more at large of those things which relate to centripetal force decreasing as the squares of the distances from the centres.

Moreover, by means of the preceding Proposition and its Corollaries, we may discover the proportion of a centripetal force to any other known force, such as that of gravity. For if a body by means of its gravity revolves in a circle concentric to the earth, this gravity is the centripetal force of that body. But from the descent of heavy bodies, the time of one entire revolution, as well as the arc described in any given time, is given (by Cor. 9 of this Prop.). And by such propositions, Mr. Huygens, in his excellent book *De Horologio Oscillatorio*, has compared the force of gravity with the centrifugal forces of revolving bodies.

The preceding Proposition [IV] may be likewise demonstrated after this manner. In any circle suppose a polygon to be inscribed of any number of sides. And if a body, moved with a given velocity along the sides of the polygon, is reflected from the circle at the several angular points, the force,[4] with which at every reflection it strikes the circle, will be as its velocity: and therefore the sum of the forces, in a given time, will be as that velocity multiplied by the number of reflections; that is (if the species of the polygon be given), as the length described in that given time, and increased or diminished in the ratio of the same length to the radius of the circle; that is, as the square of that length divided by the radius; and therefore the polygon, by having its sides diminished in infinitum, coincides with the circle, as the square of the arc described in a given time divided by the radius. This is the centrifugal force, with which the body impels the circle; and to which the contrary force, wherewith the circle continually repels the body towards the centre, is equal.

In Corollary 1, and again in the last paragraph of the Scholium, Newton arrives at the conclusion that a body traveling with constant speed in a circular path is acted upon by a centripetal (toward the center) force which is directly proportional to the square of the speed and inversely proportional to the radius of the circle. The geometric proof for this rela-

---

[3] Cor. 6 and Cor. 9 will be discussed in subsequent chapters.
[4] "Force" here may be interpreted to mean impulse.

tionship developed by Newton in Propositions I–IV is involved and has been omitted. In the Scholium, Newton uses a combination of physical intuition and geometry to arrive at the same result. The following derivation is essentially parallel to the line of reasoning followed in the Scholium.

Consider a mass m moving at a constant speed v along a many-sided polygon inscribed in a circle (Fig. 18-1). Then at each corner of the poly-

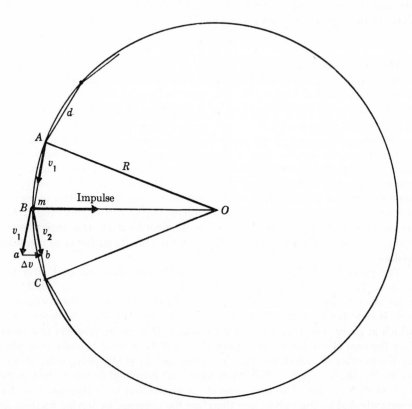

Figure 18-1. *A smooth ball of mass m moving at constant speed v around a polygon inscribed in a circular smooth hoop.*

gon the mass m bumps against the circle (is reflected) and the smooth circle pushes the mass toward the center of the circle, changing the velocity (but producing no net change in the speed) and hence the momentum of the mass. (If the circle is smooth, the impact force must be perpendicular to it, since a sideways push cannot be exerted on a frictionless surface, and therefore the force exerted on the body, being perpendicular to the circle, is toward the center of the circle.) The change in velocity Δv of the mass m due to the impact at point B is indicated in the velocity triangle abB. This velocity triangle is obtained in the following manner. Referring to the polygon, m has a velocity represented by the vector v_1 as it leaves the point A and approaches B. As it leaves B, the velocity is represented by v_2, which is equal in length to v_1 (constant speed) but has a different direction. To find how much the velocity changes during impact at B, draw v_1 from point B to a, keeping the direction the same as that traveled in going from A to B on the polygon. It is seen that to the velocity v_1 before impact, a velocity Δv must be added to give a resultant velocity v_2 after impact. Thus Δv represents the change in velocity which took place during impact; it is the amount that must be added to v_1 to give v_2.

During the actual time of impact at B, an impulse (force × time) is exerted on the mass m which, by the second law, is given by the expression:

Impulse during one impact $= km \, \Delta v$.

The time for the mass m to travel one side of the polygon and hence the time between impacts is

$$t = \frac{d}{v}$$

and the number of impacts per second is the reciprocal of this time;

$$n = \frac{v}{d}.$$

Therefore the change in momentum per second, which by Newton's second law is the average force,[5] is

$$F = km \, \Delta v \cdot n = km \, \Delta v \cdot \frac{v}{d}.$$

Now the angles of the isosceles triangle abB are equal respectively [6] to the angles of the isosceles triangle OAB, so the triangles are similar and their corresponding sides are proportional.

$$\frac{\Delta v}{v} = \frac{d}{R} \quad \text{and} \quad \Delta v = \frac{vd}{R}.$$

Substituting this value of Δv in the expression for the average force

$$F = km \frac{vd}{R} \cdot \frac{v}{d} = km \frac{v^2}{R}.$$

---

[5] The tacit assumption is being made here that a very small fraction of the path around the circle is being traversed in the one second of time, and that each side of the polygon is very short, so that the successive impulses during the one second of time are essentially parallel and may be added arithmetically.

[6] $\angle OAB = \angle ABO$ and $\angle a = \angle b$ because they are opposite equal sides.

$\angle ABO = \angle CBO$ from the symmetry of the way m bounces from the smooth surface or from the symmetry of the polygon.

$\angle aBb + \angle CBO + \angle OBA = 180°$ because they form a straight angle.

$\angle AOB + \angle OAB + \angle OBA = 180°$, the sum of the angles of a triangle.

$\angle AOB + \angle CBO + \angle OBA = 180°$, and $\angle aBb = \angle AOB$

It then follows that the equal angles at the bases of the isosceles triangles are equal and the triangles are similar.

Now as the number of sides of the polygon increases indefinitely, the polygon approaches a circle, and the mass m moves in a circular path. The average force $F = k \dfrac{mv^2}{R}$ in the case of the polygon thus becomes a force of constant magnitude pushing (or pulling) the mass m toward the center of the circle. It is the centripetal force acting on a mass m traveling with a constant speed v in a circular path of radius R.

The foregoing mathematical derivation of the expression for centripetal force, while using algebraic rather than the geometric reasoning of Newton, illustrates the essential part played by mathematics since the time of Galileo in the development of the physical sciences. Not all phases of science lend themselves to mathematical treatment, as for instance certain phases of meteorology and geology. However, it is in those phases of science, the exact sciences which are subject to mathematical treatment, that advances have been most rapid and far-reaching.

STUDY QUESTIONS

1. A satellite is observed to move around the earth so that its radius vector from the center of the earth sweeps across equal areas in equal times. According to Newton,
   a. the satellite must be traveling in a circular orbit
   b. a centripetal force of constant magnitude acts on the satellite
   c. the earth may not be at the geometric center of the orbit.
   The correct answer is
   >   (1) a   (2) b   (3) c   (4) a and b   (5) none of them.

2. A soft ball of putty is thrown with a velocity of 50 feet per second against a wall. What is the change in the velocity of the ball in feet per second as it strikes the wall?
   >   (1) 0   (2) 25   (3) 50   (4) 100   (5) insufficient data.

   3–5. A ¼ pound-mass perfectly elastic ball is thrown with a velocity of 50 feet per second against a hard smooth wall. The ball is in contact with the wall for .01 second.

3. What is the change in the velocity of the ball in feet per second while it is in contact with the wall?
   >   (1) 0   (2) 25   (3) 50   (4) 100   (5) insufficient data.

4. What is the average acceleration of the ball while in contact with the wall in feet per second per second?
   >   (1) 0   (2) 2500   (3) 5000   (4) 10,000   (5) insufficient data.

5. What is the approximate average force exerted on the ball by the wall in pounds-force?
   >   (1) 0   (2) 80   (3) 2500   (4) 100   (5) ¼.

6–7. A car traveling north 100 feet per second rounds a curve at constant speed, continuing toward the east at 100 feet per second.

6. What is the approximate change in the velocity of the car in feet per second?

    (1) 0   (2) 50   (3) 100   (4) 140   (5) 200.

7. This change in velocity is directed toward the

    (1) north   (2) northeast   (3) east   (4) southeast   (5) south.

8–10. A ball of 2 pounds-mass fastened to a string is whirled in a horizontal circle on a smooth table at a constant speed of 10 feet per second. The tension in the string is 10/32 pounds-force.

8. What is the centripetal force acting on the ball in pounds-force?

    (1) 0   (2) 2   (3) 10   (4) $\frac{10}{32}$ (5) 5.

9. What is the average acceleration of the ball in feet per second per second?

    (1) 0   (2) 2   (3) 10   (4) $\frac{10}{32}$ (5) 5.

10. What is the radius of the circle in feet?

    (1) 10   (2) 2   (3) 500   (4) 20   (5) 5.

11–13. A car of 3200 pounds-mass rounds a curve of 100 feet radius at a speed of 30 miles per hour.

11. Calculate the centripetal acceleration of the car in feet per second per second.

    (1) 9   (2) 20   (3) 3.3   (4) .4   (5) .05.

12. Calculate the centripetal force on the car in pounds-force.

    (1) 2000   (2) 64,000   (3) 40   (4) 900   (5) 5.

13. If the turn is not banked, will the car get around safely?

14. Sputnik I had a mass of about 180 pounds-mass and traveled in an orbit roughly 300 miles above the earth. Make a rough calculation of the necessary orbital speed in miles per hour of this satellite.

    (1) 25,000   (2) 18,000   (3) 350   (4) 10,000   (5) 700,000,000.

15. Compare the methods by which Kepler and Newton arrived at the equal-areas-equal-times principle.

16. To what use did Newton put the equal-areas-equal-times principle?

19

Inverse Square Law

● Corollary 6 in Chapter eighteen stated that if the periodic times are as the 3/2th powers of the radii, the centripetal forces will be inversely as the squares of the radii. This corollary is obviously related to Kepler's third law of planetary motion which was based on the observed fact that the periods of the planets are proportional to the 3/2th powers of their radii. Reasoning from the three-halves power law and using the relationship for centripetal force derived in Proposition IV, Newton showed that the planets must be pulled toward the sun with a force (gravity) varying inversely as the square of the distance. The reasoning may be shown as follows.

From Kepler's third law, the period P of a planet is related to its mean radius R from the sun as follows:

$$P \propto R^{3/2}$$

But the period or time for one revolution is the circumference of the orbit divided by the average speed v along the orbit.

$$P = \frac{2\pi R}{v} \propto \frac{R}{v}$$

$$\therefore \quad \frac{R}{v} \propto R^{3/2}$$

Dividing both sides by R

$$\frac{1}{v} \propto R^{1/2}$$

Inverting and squaring

$$v^2 \propto \frac{1}{R}.$$

In the previous chapter it was shown that the centripetal force acting on a given mass m is directly proportional to the square of the speed and inversely proportional to the radius of the path followed.

$$F \propto \frac{v^2}{R}$$

$$\therefore \quad F \propto \frac{1}{R} \cdot v^2 \propto \frac{1}{R} \cdot \frac{1}{R} \propto \frac{1}{R^2}$$

Thus Newton showed that planets obeying Kepler's third law must be pulled toward the sun with forces (gravity) which vary inversely as the squares of the distances of the planets from the sun.

Now gravitational attraction for a given mass depends not only on the distance but also on the mass being attracted, as Newton showed by comparing the weights of two masses here on the earth.

MATHEMATICAL PRINCIPLES OF NATURAL PHILOSOPHY [1]
by Isaac Newton

Book II
Section VI
Of the Motion and Resistance of Pendulous Bodies
Proposition XXIV. Theorem XIX.

The quantities of matter in pendulus bodies, whose centres of oscillation are equally distant from the centre of suspension, are in a ratio compounded of the ratio of the weights and the squared ratio of the times of the oscillations in a vacuum.

For the velocity which a given force can generate in a given matter in a given time varies directly as the force and the time, and inversely as the matter. The greater the force or the time is, or the less the matter, the greater the velocity that will be generated. This is manifest from the second Law of Motion. Now if pendulums are of the same length, the motive forces in places equally distant from the perpendicular are as the weights: . . . and therefore the quantities of matter are . . . as the motive forces and the squares of the times, that is, as the weights and the squares of the times. Q. E. D.

Cor. 1. Therefore if the times are equal, the quantities of matter in each of the bodies are as the weights.

Newton, as did Galileo, used pendulums instead of freely falling bodies to illustrate and prove certain principles, since the motion of a pendulum may be made much slower than that of a freely falling body. However, it is simpler for us to set up the relation given above by Newton for the case of freely falling bodies rather than for pendulums.

Consider two freely falling bodies having masses m_1 and m_2. When released, they accelerate toward the earth, showing that accelerating forces F_1 and F_2 respectively act on them. Now from Newton's second law of motion

$$F_1 = km_1a_1$$
$$\text{and} \quad F_2 = km_2a_2.$$

---

[1] Newton, op. cit., p. 303.

Dividing equations,

$$\frac{F_1}{F_2} = \frac{m_1 a_1}{m_2 a_2}.$$

Since the bodies started from rest, the accelerations are related to the distances and times of fall by the relation

$$d = \frac{1}{2} at^2 \quad \text{or} \quad a = \frac{2d}{t^2}.$$

Substituting for a in the previous equation for forces,

$$\frac{F_1}{F_2} = \frac{m_1 \dfrac{2d_1}{t_1^2}}{m_2 \dfrac{2d_2}{t_2^2}} = \frac{m_1 d_1 t_2^2}{m_2 d_2 t_1^2}.$$

If the two bodies fall equal distances so that $d_1 = d_2$,

$$\frac{F_1}{F_2} = \frac{m_1 t_2^2}{m_2 t_1^2}.$$

But the forces accelerating the falling bodies are their weights, so

$$\frac{W_1}{W_2} = \frac{m_1 t_2^2}{m_2 t_1^2}$$

and

$$\frac{m_1}{m_2} = \frac{W_1 t_1^2}{W_2 t_2^2}.$$

This expression for freely falling bodies is the same as that arrived at above by Newton for two masses oscillating as pendulums.

Galileo had concluded that for two freely falling bodies the times t_1 and t_2 of free fall through equal distances would be equal and hence their accelerations would be equal. This equality of times was determined with far greater accuracy, however, by Newton by comparing the periods of the pendulums. Thus it was shown that

$$\frac{W_1}{W_2} = \frac{m_1}{m_2}$$

which means that *here on the earth* the gravitational force pulling a body (its weight) is proportional to the mass of that body:

$$F \propto m.$$

Thus far in following the line of reasoning used by Newton in arriving at the law of gravitation, several steps have been completed. First, it has been shown that any body of mass m traveling along the arc of a circle is acted upon by a centripetal force at right angles to its motion such that the force is directly proportional to the mass and the square of the speed and inversely proportional to the radius. Second, if a mass traveling in a curved path obeys Kepler's three-halves power law, the mass must be pulled toward the center of the arc along which it is traveling with a force inversely proportional to the square of the radius. Third, the gravitational pull (weight) on any body near the earth is proportional to the mass of that body.

In the following chapter, Newton cites data to show that the motions of the satellites of Jupiter and Saturn, as well as those of the planets about the sun, obey Kepler's third law. The moon also obeys Kepler's second law, its radius vector sweeping across equal areas in equal times. Thus the planets and satellites must be attracted towards their centers of revolution with forces proportional to their masses and inversely proportional to the squares of the radii of their circles.

In Chapter 20 it will be shown that a body (satellite) traveling around the earth out as far as the orbit of the moon is attracted toward the earth with a force directly proportional to the mass of the body and inversely proportional to the square of its distance from the center of the earth.

The concluding Chapter 22 of this section then synthesizes these findings into the universal law of gravitation, thus explaining the observed motions of bodies within the solar system.

STUDY QUESTIONS

1. The weight in pounds-force of a 1 pound-mass at an elevation of 8000 miles above the surface of the earth is approximately

    (1) 1   (2) ½   (3) ¼   (4) ⅑   (5) 1/16.

    2–4. A satellite traveling about the earth in an elliptic orbit is four times as far from the earth at apogee as it is at perigee.

2. The ratio of the speed of the satellite at perigee to the speed at apogee is

    (1) 2 to 1   (2) 4 to 1   (3) 16 to 1   (4) 1 to 2   (5) 1 to 4.

3. The ratio of the gravitational force on the satellite at perigee to that at apogee is

    (1) 2 to 1   (2) 4 to 1   (3) 16 to 1   (4) 1 to 2   (5) 1 to 4.

4. If the area swept across in one hour by the radius vector to the satellite is A when the satellite is at apogee, the area swept across in one hour when the satellite is at perigee is

    (1) A   (2) 2A   (3) $\dfrac{A}{2}$ (4) 4A   (5) $\dfrac{A}{4}$.

    5–7. A ball whirled with a speed v in a horizontal circle of radius R requires a centripetal force of 4 pounds-force.

5. If the speed of the ball is doubled, the radius remaining the same, the new centripetal force in pounds-force is

    (1) 1   (2) 2   (3) 16   (4) 4   (5) 8.

6. If the speed remains v and the radius of the circle is doubled, the new centripetal force in pounds-force is

    (1) 1   (2) 2   (3) 16   (4) 4   (5) 8.

7. If the speed of the ball is doubled to $2v$ and the radius is also doubled to $2R$, the new centripetal force in pounds-force is

    (1) 1   (2) 2   (3) 16   (4) 4   (5) 8.

8. An artificial satellite is launched in such a manner as to circle the earth halfway between the earth and the moon. The approximate time in months for the satellite to make one revolution is

    (1) 1   (2) .35   (3) .12   (4) 4   (5) .5.

9. At sea level on an equal-arm balance, a sack of sugar is just balanced by a standard 5 pound-mass. Would the two still balance if taken to the top of Pikes Peak? If the sugar were weighed with a spring balance, would it weigh the same at both places?

> *10–12. Two satellites of equal mass are traveling in concentric circular orbits about the earth. The outer orbit has a radius twice that of the inner orbit.*

10. If the centripetal force on the inner satellite is 1000 pounds-force, the centripetal force in pounds-force on the outer satellite is

    (1) 500   (2) 250   (3) 1000   (4) 2000   (5) 40,000.

11. If the speed of the inner satellite is 26,000 feet per second, the speed of the outer satellite in feet per second is

    (1) 13,000   (2) 52,000   (3) 26,000   (4) $26,000\sqrt{2}$ (5) $\dfrac{26,000}{\sqrt{2}}$.

12. Is the answer in question 10 above consistent with the expression for centripetal force in which the radius of the orbit to the first power appears in the denominator?

20

The Solar System

● In the *Principia,*
Book I: The Motion of Bodies, Newton developed the basic principles of mechanics and determined the geometry of motion of bodies being acted upon by various forces. A particular proof of vital importance to the establishment of the law of gravitation was also included. This proof demonstrated that if two spheres were composed of particles which attracted each other with forces varying inversely as the squares of the distances between the particles, the total attracting force of one sphere upon the other varied inversely as the square of the distance between the centers of the spheres.

In Book II, Newton considered the motions of bodies through fluids which resisted their motions. He also considered the motions of fluids themselves, and of wave motions through fluids.

All creative scientists have a philosophy about the world, either consciously held or perhaps deeply ingrained in their subconscious minds. However, this working philosophy is rarely publicly stated. Newton again is exceptional and states frankly his basic philosophic views about the physical world in the opening pages of his Book III. He believes that Nature is fundamentally simple. He believes that the relation between cause and effect is unalterable by changes in either time or space. He believes that the essential properties such as mass or extension of the limited number of bodies that he can actually handle and sense are likewise properties of all bodies anywhere and at anytime even though they may be beyond the reach of his senses. And finally he believes in the validity of induction. One can reach a general conclusion after performing a necessarily limited number of experiments. Then this conclusion is to be held, even though an infinite number of further experiments could be performed. A rethinking of this conclusion would be necessary only if a new experiment should prove contradictory. With these highly pragmatic Rules of Reasoning, Newton is ready to cast the world into a mathematical formulation generalized from the relatively few experiments which mankind has performed.

The Rules of Reasoning are followed by Phenomena which are summarizations of extensive observational data concerning the solar system which were available to Newton. These include data concerning the positions and motions of the moon, planets, satellites, and even the tides.

In the remainder of Book III are an extensive series of propositions in which Newton explained the various phenomena of the solar system in terms of his laws of motion and the inverse square law of gravitation.

MATHEMATICAL PRINCIPLES OF NATURAL PHILOSOPHY [1]

by Isaac Newton
Book III
System of the World

In the preceding books I have laid down the principles of philosophy; principles not philosophical, but mathematical: such, to wit, as we may build our reasonings upon in philosophical inquiries. These principles are the laws and conditions of certain motions, and powers of forces, which chiefly have respect to philosophy; but, lest they should have appeared of themselves dry and barren, I have illustrated them here and there with some philosophical scholiums, giving an account of such things as are of more general nature, and which philosophy seems chiefly to be founded on; such as the density and the resistance of bodies, spaces void of all bodies, and the motion of light and sounds. It remains that, from the same principles, I now demonstrate the frame of the System of the World. Upon this subject I had, indeed, composed the third Book in a popular method, that it might be read by many; but afterwards, considering that such as had not sufficiently entered into the principles could not easily discern the strength of the consequences, nor lay aside the prejudices to which they had been many years accustomed, therefore, to prevent the disputes which might be raised upon such accounts, I chose to reduce the substance of this Book into the form of Propositions (in the mathematical way), which should be read by those only who had first made themselves masters of the principles established in the preceding Books: not that I would advise anyone to the previous study of every Proposition of those Books; for they abound with such as might cost too much time, even to readers of good mathematical learning. It is enough if one carefully reads the Definitions, the Laws of Motion, and the first three sections of the first Book. He may then pass on to this Book, and consult such of the remaining Propositions of the first two Books, as the references in this, and his occasions, shall require.

Rules of Reasoning in Philosophy
Rule I

We are to admit no more causes of natural things than such as are both true and sufficient to explain their appearances.

To this purpose the philosophers say that Nature does nothing in vain, and

---

[1] Newton, op. cit., pp. 383–389.

more is in vain when less will serve; for Nature is pleased with simplicity, and affects not the pomp of superfluous causes.

Rule II

Therefore to the same natural effects we must, as far as possible, assign the same causes.

As to respiration in a man and in a beast; the descent of stones in Europe and in America; the light of our culinary fire and of the sun; the reflection of light in the earth, and in the planets.

Rule III

The qualities of bodies, which admit neither intensification nor remission of degrees, and which are found to belong to all bodies within the reach of our experiments, are to be esteemed the universal qualities of all bodies whatsoever.

For since the qualities of bodies are only known to us by experiments, we are to hold for universal all such as universally agree with experiments; and such as are not liable to diminution can never be quite taken away. We are certainly not to relinquish the evidence of experiments for the sake of dreams and vain fictions of our own devising; nor are we to recede from the analogy of Nature, which tends to be simple, and always consonant to itself. We no other way know the extension of bodies than by our senses, nor do these reach it in all bodies; but because we perceive extension in all that are sensible, therefore we ascribe it universally to all others also. That abundance of bodies are hard, we learn by experience; and because the hardness of the whole arises from the hardness of the parts, we therefore justly infer the hardness of the undivided particles not only of the bodies we feel but of all others. That all bodies are impenetrable, we gather not from reason, but from sensation. The bodies which we handle we find impenetrable, and thence conclude impenetrability to be an universal property of all bodies whatsoever. That all bodies are movable, and endowed with certain powers (which we call the inertia) of persevering in their motion, or in their rest, we only infer from the like properties observed in the bodies which we have seen. The extension, hardness, impenetrability, mobility, and inertia of the whole, result from the extension, hardness, impenetrability, mobility, and inertia of the parts; and thence we conclude the least particles of all bodies to be also all extended, and hard, and impenetrable, and movable, and endowed with their proper inertia. And this is the foundation of all philosophy. Moreover, that the divided but contiguous particles of bodies may be separated from one another, is matter of observation; and, in the particles that remain undivided, our minds are able to distinguish yet lesser parts, as is mathematically demonstrated. But whether the parts so distinguished, and not yet divided, may, by the powers of Nature, be actually divided and separated from one another, we cannot certainly determine. Yet, had we the proof of but one experiment that any undivided particle, in breaking a hard and solid body, suffered a division, we might by virtue of this rule conclude that the undivided as well as the divided particles may be divided and actually separated to infinity.

Lastly, if it universally appears, by experiments and astronomical observations, that all bodies about the earth gravitate towards the earth, and that in proportion to the quantity of matter which they severally contain; that the moon likewise, according to the quantity of its matter, gravitates towards the earth; that, on the other hand, our sea gravitates towards the moon; and all the planets mutually one towards another; and the comets in like manner towards the sun; we must, in consequence of this rule, universally allow that all bodies whatsoever are endowed with a principle of mutual gravitation. For the argument from the appearances concludes with more force for the universal gravitation of all bodies than for their impenetrability; of which, among those in the celestial regions, we have no experiments, nor any manner of observation. Not that I affirm gravity to be essential to bodies: by their vis insita I mean nothing but their inertia. This is immutable. Their gravity is diminished as they recede from the earth.

Rule IV

In experimental philosophy we are to look upon propositions obtained by general induction from phenomena as accurately or very nearly true, notwithstanding any contrary hypotheses that may be imagined, till such time as other phenomena occur, by which they may either be made more accurate, or liable to exceptions.

This rule we must follow, that the argument of induction may not be evaded by hypotheses.

Phenomena, or Appearances.

Phenomenon I

That the circumjovial planets, by radii drawn to Jupiter's centre, describe areas proportional to the times of description; and that their periodic times, the fixed stars being at rest, are as the 3/2th power of their distances from its centre.

This we know from astronomical observations. For the orbits of these planets differ but insensibly from circles concentric to Jupiter; and their motions in those circles are found to be uniform. And all astronomers agree that their periodic times are as the 3/2th power of the semidiameters of their orbits; and so it manifestly appears from the following table.

The periodic times of the satellites of Jupiter.
$1^d.18^h.27'.34''., 3^d.13^h.13'.42''., 7^d.3^h.42'.36''., 16^d.16^h.32'.9''.$
The distances of the satellites from Jupiter's centre.

From the observations of:	1	2	3	4	
Borelli	5⅔	8⅔		24⅔	
Townly by the micrometer	5.52	8.78	13.47	24.72	Semi-
Cassini by the telescope	5	8	13	23	diameter
Cassini by the eclipse of the satellites	5⅔	9	14 23/60	25 3/10	of Jupiter
From the periodic times	5.667	9.017	14.384	25.299	

Mr. Pound hath determined, by the help of excellent micrometers, the diameters of Jupiter and the elongation of its satellites after the following manner. The greatest heliocentric elongation of the fourth satellite from Jupiter's centre was taken with a micrometer in a 15-foot telescope and at the mean distance of Jupiter from the earth was found about 8′16″. The elongation of the third satellite was taken with a micrometer in a telescope of 123 feet,[2] and at the same distance of Jupiter from the earth was found 4′42″. The greatest elongations of the other satellites, at the same distance of Jupiter from the earth, are found from the periodic times to be 2′56″47‴, and 1′51″6‴.

The diameter of Jupiter taken with the micrometer in a 123-foot telescope several times, and reduced to Jupiter's mean distance from the earth, proved always less than 40″, never less than 38″, generally 39″. This diameter in shorter telescopes is 40″ or 41″; for Jupiter's light is a little dilated by the unequal refrangibility of the rays, and this dilation bears a less ratio to the diameter of Jupiter in the longer and more perfect telescopes than in those which are shorter and less perfect. The times in which two satellites, the first and the third, passed over Jupiter's body, were observed, from the beginning of the ingress to the beginning of the egress, and from the complete ingress to the complete egress, with the long telescope. And from the transit of the first satellite, the diameter of Jupiter at its mean distance from the earth came forth 37⅛″, and from the transit of the third 37⅜″. There was observed also the time in which the shadow of the first satellite passed over Jupiter's body, and thence the diameter of Jupiter at its mean distance from the earth came out about 37″. Let us suppose its diameter to be 37¼″, very nearly, and then the greatest elongations of the first, second, third, and fourth satellite will be respectively equal to 5.965, 9.494, 15.141, and 26.63 semidiameters of Jupiter.

Phenomenon II.

That the circumsaturnal planets, by radii drawn to Saturn's centre, describe areas proportional to the times of description; and that their periodic times, the fixed stars being at rest, are as the 3/2th power of their distances from its centre.

    ✿   ✿   ✿   ✿   ✿   ✿   ✿

Phenomenon II.

That the five primary planets, Mercury, Venus, Mars, Jupiter, and Saturn, with their several orbits, encompass the sun.

That Mercury and Venus revolve about the sun, is evident from their moonlike appearances. When they shine out with a full face, they are, in respect of us, beyond or above the sun; when they appear half full, they are about the same height on one side or other of the sun; when horned, they are below or between us and the sun; and they are sometimes, when directly under, seen like spots traversing the sun's disk. That Mars surrounds the sun, is as plain from its full face when near its conjunction with the sun, and from the gibbous figure which it shows in its quadratures. And the same thing is demonstrable of Jupiter and Saturn, from their appearing full in all situations; for the shadows

---

[2] The 123 feet refers to the length. The longer the telescope barrel, the longer is the focal length of the objective lens. A long focal length means only slight curvature of the lens surfaces thus causing minimum aberration. The longer telescope also gives greater magnification.

of their satellites that appear sometimes upon their disks make it plain that the light they shine with is not their own but borrowed from the sun.

Phenomenon IV.

That the fixed stars being at rest, the periodic times of the five primary planets, and (whether of the sun about the earth, or) of the earth about the sun, are as the 3/2th power of their mean distances from the sun.

This proportion, first observed by Kepler, is now received by all astronomers; for the periodic times are the same, and the dimensions of the orbits are the same, whether the sun revolves about the earth, or the earth about the sun. And as to the measures of the periodic times, all astronomers are agreed about them. But for the dimensions of the orbits, Kepler and Bullialdus, above all others, have determined them from observations with the greatest accuracy; and the mean distances corresponding to the periodic times differ but insensibly from those which they have assigned, and for the most part fall in between them; as we may see from the following table.

The periodic times with respect to the fixed stars, of the planets and earth revolving about the sun, in days and decimal parts of a day.

Saturn	Jupiter	Mars	Earth	Venus	Mercury
10759.275	4332.514	686.9785	365.2565	224.6176	87.9692

The mean distances of the planets and of the earth from the sun.

	Saturn	Jupiter	Mars
According to Kepler	951000	519650	152350
" " Bullialdus	954198	522520	152350
" " the periodic times	954006	520096	152369

	Earth	Venus	Mercury
According to Kepler	100000	72400	38806
" " Bullialdus	100000	72398	38585
" " the periodic times	100000	72333	38710

As to Mercury and Venus, there can be no doubt about their distances from the sun; for they are determined by the elongations of those planets from the sun; and for the distances of the superior planets, all dispute is cut off by the eclipses of the satellites of Jupiter. For by those eclipses the position of the shadow which Jupiter projects is determined; whence we have the heliocentric longitude of Jupiter.[3] And from its heliocentric and geocentric longitudes compared together, we determine its distance.

---

[3] A method of calculating the distance from the sun to Jupiter may be seen from the figure on page 257. Let M and M' respectively be the positions of one of Jupiter's moons when it is hidden from the earth and when it is in Jupiter's shadow. If the time for the moon to travel from M to M' is observed, and the moon's period is also known, the angle B can be readily determined. The observed angle A between the sun and Jupiter can be measured, and thus angle C can be determined.

Taking the distance from the earth to the sun as 1 astronomical unit, the distance R_j in astronomical units from the sun to Jupiter can be calculated since the triangle has one side and all angles known.

Phenomenon V.

Then the primary planets, by radii drawn to the earth describe areas in no wise proportional to the times; but the areas which they describe by radii drawn to the sun are proportional to the times of description.

For to the earth they appear sometimes direct, sometimes stationary, nay, and sometimes retrograde. But from the sun they are always seen direct, and to proceed with a motion nearly uniform, that is to say, a little swifter in the perihelion and a little slower in the aphelion distances, so as to maintain an equality in the description of the areas. This is a noted proposition among astronomers, and particularly demonstrable in Jupiter, from the eclipses of his satellites; by the help of these eclipses, as we have said, the heliocentric longitudes of that planet, and its distances from the sun, are determined.

Phenomenon VI.

That the moon, by a radius drawn to the earth's centre, describes an area proportional to the time of description.

This we gather from the apparent motion of the moon, compared with its apparent diameter. It is true that the motion of the moon is a little disturbed by the action of the sun: but in laying down these Phenomena, I neglect those small and inconsiderable errors.

STUDY QUESTIONS

1. Select the inference(s) consistent with Newton's Rules of Reasoning.
   a. The smallest particles of matter should be hard and impenetrable.
   b. Since ordinary objects can be divided, and these smaller parts further subdivided, it follows that any object can be subdivided into an infinite number of particles.
   c. It is more logical to assume the property of impenetrability holds for a distant planet than to assume the planet has the property of gravitation.
   The correct answer is

       (1) a   (2) b   (3) c   (4) a and b   (5) none of them.

For footnote 3.

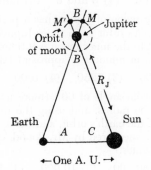

2. Taking the period of Mars as 1.9 years, the radius of Mars' orbit in astro-nomical units is approximately

    (1) 1.5   (2) 1.9   (3) 3.6   (4) ⅔   (5) ½.

3. That Jupiter is not self-luminous can be determined from
    a. the shadows cast by its moons
    b. its series of phases from full to new
    c. the fact that it appears full in all relative positions with respect to the earth and sun.
    The correct answer is

    (1) a   (2) b   (3) c   (4) a and b   (5) a and c.

4. Select the correct statement or statements.
    a. A radius vector drawn from the earth to Jupiter sweeps across equal areas in equal times.
    b. No appreciable change during the month can be detected in the appar-ent diameter of the moon thus showing the moon's orbit to be essen-tially circular.
    c. If the motion of Mars could be observed from the sun, it would periodi-cally appear to retrograde.
    The correct answer is

    (1) a   (2) b   (3) c   (4) a, b, and c   (5) none of them.

5. Select the correct statement or statements.
    a. When Mars is in quadrature with the sun it appears in the gibbous phase.
    b. When Venus rises just before sunrise, it always appears to be near the full phase.
    c. When Mercury is visible just after sunset, it never appears to be near the full phase.
    The correct answer is

    (1) a   (2) b   (3) c   (4) a and b   (5) a, b, and c.

6. According to the Rules of Reasoning,
    a. there is no justification for believing that the laws of motion apply on another planet until they can be tested on that planet
    b. there is only one true explanation of any given phenomena
    c. it may be inferred that if one body could be subdivided until point par-ticles were obtained all other bodies could also be subdivided to obtain point particles.
    The correct answer is

    (1) a   (2) b   (3) c   (4) b and c   (5) none of them.

7. If the next to the inner moon of Jupiter has a period of 5000 minutes, the radius of the inner moon's orbit is 5⅜ times Jupiter's radius, and the radius of the orbit of the next to the inner moon is 9 times Jupiter's radius, the pe-riod of the inner moon in minutes is approximately

    (1) 2500   (2) 3700   (3) 1250   (4) 1000   (5) 10,000.

8. Using the fact that for an angle of 60° (more nearly 57°), the arc is ap-proximately equal to the radius, and using the radius of Jupiter's orbit as about 5.2 times that of the earth's orbit, and the approximate angular diam-eter of Jupiter as 40″ as measured by Mr. Pound, calculate the approximate diameter of Jupiter in miles.

    (1) 500,000   (2) 80,000   (3) 10,000   (4) 15,000   (5) 25,000.

9–11. *The distance between Jupiter and the sun is to be determined by observations on the next-to-inner moon of Jupiter which has a period of 5000 minutes. Assume that the angle A between Jupiter and the sun is measured to be 79° and the elapsed time for the moon to pass behind Jupiter and continue until it enters Jupiter's shadow is 153 minutes. Refer to the diagram in the text.*

9. The angle B is in degrees

    (1) 11   (2) 32   (3) .03   (4) 18   (5) 5.

10. The angle C is in degrees

    (1) 90   (2) 69   (3) 83   (4) 79   (5) 96.

11. A drawing to scale gives approximately what distance in astronomical units for R_J, the distance from the sun to Jupiter?

12. What significance would Newton attach to the fact that Jupiter's satellites obey the three-halves power law?

21

The Moon and the Apple

● The story that Newton was led to the theory of gravitation by seeing the falling apple is, like the story of Galileo and the leaning tower of Pisa, without direct documentary verification. However, one of Newton's associates related many years later that Newton had told him that while pondering one day as to what action held the moon in its orbit, the fall of an apple set him to thinking that the same gravitational attraction which caused the apple to fall might also explain the orbital motion of the moon. To show that both actions could be due to the same cause it was necessary to show that the fall of an object near the earth, when modified by the inverse square law, was numerically consistent with the "fall" of the moon toward the earth. This calculation is made in Proposition IV, Theorem IV.

MATHEMATICAL PRINCIPLES OF NATURAL PHILOSOPHY [1]

by Isaac Newton

Book III
Propositions
Proposition I.   Theorem I.

That the forces by which the circumjovial planets are continually drawn off from rectilinear motions, and retained in their proper orbits, tend to Jupiter's centre; and are inversely as the squares of the distances of the places of those planets from that centre.

    ❀   ❀   ❀   ❀   ❀   ❀   ❀

Proposition II.   Theorem II.

That the forces by which the primary planets are continually drawn off from rectilinear motions, and retained in their proper orbits, tend to the sun; and are inversely as the squares of the distances of the places of those planets from the sun's centre.

    ❀   ❀   ❀   ❀   ❀   ❀   ❀

[1] Newton, op. cit., pp. 390–397.

Proposition III.   Theorem III.

That the force by which the moon is retained in its orbit tends to the earth; and is inversely as the square of the distance of its place from the earth's centre.

❀   ❀   ❀   ❀   ❀   ❀   ❀

Proposition IV.   Theorem IV.

That the moon gravitates towards the earth, and by the force of gravity is continually drawn off from a rectilinear motion, and retained in its orbit.

The mean distance of the moon from the earth in the syzygies in semi-diameters of the earth, is, according to Ptolemy and most astronomers, 59; according to Vendelin and Huygens, 60; to Copernicus, 60⅓; to Street, 60⅖; and to Tycho, 56½. But Tycho, and all that follow his tables of refraction, making the refractions of the sun and moon (altogether against the nature of light) to exceed the refractions of the fixed stars, and that by four or five minutes near the horizon, did thereby increase the moon's horizontal parallax by a like number of minutes, that is, by a twelfth or fifteenth part of the whole parallax. Correct this error, and the distance will become about 60½ semi-diameters of the earth, near to what others have assigned. Let us assume the mean distance of 60 diameters in the syzygies; and suppose one revolution of the moon, in respect of the fixed stars, to be completed in 27^d.7^h.43^m., as astronomers have determined; and the circumference of the earth to amount to 123249600 Paris feet, as the French have found by mensuration. And now if we imagine the moon, deprived of all motion, to be let go, so as to descend towards the earth with the impulse of all that force by which (by Cor. Prop. III) it is retained in its orb, it will in the space of one minute of time, describe in its fall 15 1/12 Paris feet. This we gather by a calculus, founded either upon Prop. XXXVI, Book I, or (which comes to the same thing) upon Cor. IX, Prop. IV, of the same Book.[2] For the versed sine of that arc, which the

---

[2] Note on Proposition IV, Theorem IV, Cor. IX (see diagram, p. 262).

Consider a body m, such as the moon, traveling with constant speed around the circular path of radius R. In a short unit interval of time, say one minute, it will travel along the arc from A to B a distance v. However, if after leaving A, it had not been pulled from its straight line path (Newton's first law), it would have traveled to B'. Thus it is seen to have been pulled from its straight-line path a distance BB'. If the arc v is a very small fraction of the circumference of the circle, as it would be for the distance traveled by the moon in one minute, the line BB' is essentially parallel to and equal to h. Thus h, which Newton calls the versed sine, represents the distance the body m falls toward the center of the circle as it travels the relatively short arc v.

Now by geometry it may be shown that if the arc v is small, the following proportion holds:

$$\frac{h}{v} = \frac{v}{2R}.$$

Knowing the radius of the moon's orbit and its period, the distance v traveled per minute can be obtained. Then the distance h which the moon falls toward the earth each minute may be calculated from the above equation.

It should be noted that if the acceleration of the body m toward the center of

moon, in the space of one minute of time, would by its mean motion describe at the distance of 60 semidiameters of the earth, is nearly 15 1/12 Paris feet, or more accurately 15 feet, 1 inch, and 1 line 4/9. Wherefore, since that force, in approaching to the earth, increases inversely as the square of the distance, and, upon that account, at the surface of the earth, is 60 · 60 times greater

---

the circle is known, the distance h that the body will fall during any given interval of time t also may be calculated from

$$h = \tfrac{1}{2}at^2$$

where a is the centripetal acceleration given by

$$a = \frac{v^2}{R}.$$

Thus

$$h = \frac{1}{2}\frac{v^2}{R}t^2$$

and the distance fallen in unit time is

$$h = \frac{v^2}{2R}$$

which is the same expression as that obtained above.

Although m is continually accelerated toward the center O, it never acquires any speed toward O because at every instant the velocity with which m is traveling is perpendicular to R and has no component along R toward O. Thus the expression

$$h = \tfrac{1}{2}at^2,$$

which is valid only when the initial velocity in the direction of h is zero, may be applied at any point along the circular path.

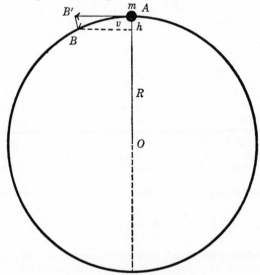

For footnote 2, page 261.

than at the moon, a body in our regions, falling with that force, ought in the space of one minute of time, to describe 60 · 60 · 15 1/12 Paris feet; and, in the space of one second of time, to describe 15 1/12 of those feet; or more accurately 15 feet, 1 inch, and 1 line 4/9. And with this very force we actually find that bodies here upon earth do really descend; . . . And therefore the force by which the moon is retained in its orbit becomes, at the very surface of the earth, equal to the force of gravity which we observe in heavy bodies there. And therefore (by Rule 1 and 2) the force by which the moon is retained in its orbit is that very same force which we commonly call gravity; for, were gravity another force different from that, then bodies descending to the earth with the joint impulse of both forces would fall with a double velocity, and in the space of one second of time would describe 30⅙ Paris feet; altogether against experience.

This calculus is founded on the hypothesis of the earth's standing still; for if both earth and moon move about the sun, and at the same time about their common centre of gravity, the distance of the centres of the moon and earth from one another will be 60½ semidiameters of the earth; as may be found by a computation from Prop. LX, Book I.

Scholium

The demonstration of this Proposition may be more diffusely explained after the following manner. Suppose several moons to revolve about the earth, as in the system of Jupiter or Saturn; the periodic times of these moons (by the argument of induction) would observe the same law which Kepler found to obtain among the planets; and therefore their centripetal forces would be inversely as the squares of the distances from the centre of the earth, by Prop. 1, of this Book. Now if the lowest of these were very small, and were so near the earth as almost to touch the tops of the highest mountains, the centripetal force thereof, retaining it in its orbit, would be very nearly equal to the weights of any terrestrial bodies that should be found upon the tops of those mountains, as may be known by the foregoing computation. Therefore if the same little moon should be deserted by its centrifugal force that carries it through its orbit, and so be disabled from going onward therein, it would descend to the earth; and that with the same velocity as heavy bodies do actually fall with upon the tops of those very mountains; because of the equality of the forces that oblige them both to descend. And if the force by which that lowest moon would descend were different from gravity, and if that moon were to gravitate towards the earth, as we find terrestrial bodies do upon the tops of mountains, it would then descend with twice the velocity, as being impelled by both these forces conspiring together. Therefore since both these forces, that is, the gravity of heavy bodies, and the centripetal forces of the moons, are directed toward the centre of the earth, and are similar and equal between themselves, they will (by Rule 1 and 2) have one and the same cause. And therefore the force which retains the moon in its orbit is that very force which we commonly call gravity; because otherwise this little moon at the top of a mountain must either be without gravity, or fall twice as swiftly as heavy bodies are wont to do.

❀   ❀   ❀   ❀   ❀   ❀   ❀

Proposition VI.   Theorem VI.

That all bodies gravitate towards every planet; and that the weights of bodies towards the same planet, at equal distances from the centre of the planet, are proportional to the quantities of matter which they severally contain.

It has been, now for a long time, observed by others, that all sorts of heavy bodies (allowance being made for the inequality of retardation which they suffer from a small power of resistance in the air) descend to the earth from equal heights in equal times; and that equality of times we may distinguish to a great accuracy, by the help of pendulums. . . . By these experiments, in bodies of the same weight, I could manifestly have discovered a difference of matter less than the thousandth part of the whole, had any such been. But, without all doubt, the nature of gravity towards the planets is the same as toward the earth. For, should we imagine our terrestrial bodies removed to the orbit of the moon, and there, together with the moon, deprived of all motion, to be let go, so as to fall together towards the earth, it is certain, from what we have demonstrated before, that, in equal times, they would describe equal spaces with the moon, and of consequence are to the moon, in quantity of matter, as their weights to its weight. Moreover, since the satellites of Jupiter perform their revolutions in times which observe the 3/2th power of the proportion of their distances from Jupiter's centre, their accelerative gravities towards Jupiter will be inversely as the squares of their distances from Jupiter's centre; that is, equal, at equal distances. And, therefore, these satellites, if supposed to fall towards Jupiter from equal heights, would describe equal spaces in equal times, in like manner as heavy bodies do on our earth. And, by the same argument, if the circumsolar planets were supposed to be let fall at equal distances from the sun, they would, in their descent towards the sun, describe equal spaces in equal times. But forces which equally accelerate unequal bodies must be as those bodies: that is to say, the weights of the planets towards the sun must be as their quantities of matter. Further, that the weights of Jupiter and of his satellites towards the sun are proportional to the several quantities of their matter, appears from the exceedingly regular motions of the satellites (by Cor. 3, Prop. LXV, Book I). For if some of those bodies were more strongly attracted to the sun in proportion to their quantity of matter than others, the motions of the satellites would be disturbed by that inequality of attraction (by Cor. 2, Prop. LXV, Book I). . . .

But further; the weights of all the parts of every planet towards any other planet are one to another as the matter of the several parts; for if some parts did gravitate more, others less, than for the quantity of their matter, then the whole planet, according to the sort of parts with which it most abounds, would gravitate more or less than in proportion to the quantity of matter in the whole. Nor is it of any moment whether these parts are external or internal; for if, for example, we should imagine the terrestrial bodies with us to be raised up to the orbit of the moon, to be there compared with its body; if the weights of such bodies were to the weights of the external parts of the moon as the quantities of matter in the one and in the other respectively, but to the weights of the internal parts in a greater or less proportion, then likewise the weights of those bodies would be to the weight of the whole moon in a greater or less proportion; against what we have shown above.

Cor. 1.   Hence the weights of bodies do not depend upon their forms and textures; for if the weights could be altered with the forms, they would be greater or less, according to the variety of forms, in equal matter; altogether against experience.

Cor. 2.   Universally, all bodies about the earth gravitate towards the earth; and the weights of all, at equal distances from the earth's centre, are as the quantities of matter which they severally contain. This is the quality of all bodies within the reach of our experiments; and therefore (by Rule 3) to be affirmed of all bodies whatsoever.

If the ether, or any other body, were either altogether void of gravity, or were to gravitate less in proportion to its quantity of matter, then, because (according to Aristotle, Descartes, and others) there is no difference between that and other bodies but in mere form of matter, by a successive change from form to form, it might be changed at last into a body of the same condition with those which gravitate most in proportion to their quantity of matter; and, on the other hand, the heaviest bodies, acquiring the first form of that body, might by degrees quite lose their gravity. And therefore the weights would depend upon the forms of bodies, and with those forms, might be changed: contrary to what was proved in the preceding Corollary.

Cor. 3.   All spaces are not equally full; for if all spaces were equally full, then the specific gravity of the fluid which fills the region of the air, on account of the extreme density of the matter, would fall nothing short of the specific gravity of quicksilver, or gold, or any other the most dense body; and, therefore, neither gold, nor any other body, could descend in air; for bodies do not descend in fluids, unless they are specifically heavier than the fluids. And if the quantity of matter in a given space can, by any rarefaction, be diminished, what should hinder a diminution to infinity?

Cor. 4.   If all the solid particles of all bodies are of the same density, and cannot be rarefied without pores, a void, space, or vacuum must be granted. By bodies of the same density, I mean those whose inertias are in the proportion of their bulks.

Cor. 5.   The power of gravity is of a different nature from the power of magnetism; for the magnetic attraction is not as the matter attracted. Some bodies are attracted more by the magnet; others less; most bodies not at all. The power of magnetism in one and the same body may be increased and diminished; and is sometimes far stronger, for the quantity of matter, than the power of gravity; and in receding from the magnet decreases not at the square but almost as the cube of the distance, as nearly as I could judge from some rude observations.

In Proposition IV, Newton showed that, assuming the inverse square law, an object taken out from the earth to the distance of the moon and then released would have the same acceleration toward the earth which the moon has. But as pointed out in Proposition VI, bodies having equal accelerations must be acted on by forces which are proportional to the masses of those bodies. Thus not only on the earth but out to the distance of the moon, the gravitational pull of the earth is proportional to the mass of the object being attracted. Thus for gravitational attraction toward the earth out as far as the moon

$$F \propto \frac{m}{R^2}$$

where m is the mass being attracted and R is the distance of that mass from the center of the earth.

It has been previously shown (Chap. 19) that for planets about the sun or satellites about Jupiter which have been seen to obey Kepler's three-halves power law the centripetal forces maintaining them in their orbits vary inversely with the squares of the distances from the center of revolution. Furthermore, the centripetal force is always proportional to the mass of the body being pulled toward the center. Therefore for any planet or satellite the gravitational attraction that pulls it toward the center of its orbit must be directly proportional to the mass attracted and inversely proportional to the square of the distance from the center of revolution.

In completing the formulation of the law of gravitation there remains but to find the effect of the size of the mass exerting the attraction.

STUDY QUESTIONS

1–3. At a certain distance from the earth the acceleration of a body falling toward the earth is 2 feet per second per second.

1. When released, how far in feet would the body fall toward the earth the first second?

   (1) 1   (2) 2   (3) $\frac{1}{2}$ (4) 4   (5) 16.

2. How far would the body fall in feet the first minute?

   (1) 60   (2) 3600   (3) 7200   (4) 30   (5) 16.

3. How far in miles above the surface of the earth was the body released?

   (1) 1000   (2) 4000   (3) 8000   (4) 12,000   (5) 16,000.

4–14. Refer to Proposition IV.

4. The distance in feet traveled by the moon in making one revolution about the earth is approximately

   (1) 123,000,000   (2) 60 × 123,000,000   (3) 2π × 123,000,000

   (4) 2π × 123,000,000 × 60   (5) $\dfrac{60 \times 123,000,000}{2\pi}$.

5. The time in minutes for the moon to make one revolution about the earth is approximately

   (1) 39,600   (2) 2,200   (3) 648   (4) 691   (5) 2,400,000.

6. The speed of the moon in its orbit in feet per minute is approximately

   (1) 3100   (2) 11,160,000   (3) 186,000   (4) 15   (5) 18.

7. Let v be the distance traveled by the moon in one minute, h the distance in feet the moon would fall toward the earth the first minute if it were " de-

prived of all motion, to be let go, so as to descend — " and r the radius of the earth. Then h could be calculated from the proportion.

(1) $\dfrac{h}{v} = \dfrac{v}{r}$ (2) $\dfrac{h}{v} = \dfrac{v}{2r}$ (3) $\dfrac{v}{h} = \dfrac{h}{2r}$ (4) $\dfrac{h}{v} = \dfrac{v}{120r}$ (5) $\dfrac{h}{r} = \dfrac{r}{v}$.

8. The distance in feet that the moon would fall toward the earth in one minute, if it were " deprived of all motion, to be let go, so as to descend towards the earth — ," can be approximately obtained from which one of the following?

(1) $\dfrac{h}{186{,}000} = \dfrac{186{,}000}{123{,}000{,}000/\pi}$ (2) $\dfrac{h}{186{,}000} = \dfrac{186{,}000}{60 \times 123{,}000{,}000/\pi}$

(3) $\dfrac{h}{3100} = \dfrac{3100}{60 \times 123{,}000{,}000/\pi}$

(4) $\dfrac{h}{123{,}000{,}000/\pi} = \dfrac{123{,}000{,}000/\pi}{186{,}000}$

(5) $\dfrac{h}{18} = \dfrac{18}{123{,}000{,}000/\pi}$.

9. The distance h in feet that the moon would fall toward the earth in one minute is from the previous problem approximately

(1) 15   (2) 30   (3) ¼   (4) ¹⁄₂₄₀   (5) 900.

10. According to the inverse square law, if the gravitational force of the earth on a 1 pound-mass on the earth's surface is 1 pound-force, the gravitational force in pounds-force of the earth for a 1 pound-mass at the distance of the moon is

(1) 1   (2) 60   (3) 3600   (4) ¹⁄₆₀   (5) ¹⁄₃₆₀₀.

11. If the acceleration of a freely falling body at the earth's surface is 32 feet per second per second, the acceleration of a body freely falling toward the earth at the distance of the moon in feet per second per second is

(1) 32   (2) 60 × 32   (3) 3600 × 32   (4) ³²⁄₆₀   (5) ³²⁄₃₆₀₀.

12. The distance in feet a freely falling body falls the first second at the earth's surface is

(1) 16   (2) 32   (3) 32 × 60   (4) ³²⁄₆₀   (5) ¹⁵⁄₃₆₀₀.

13. The distance in feet a freely falling body at the distance of the moon falls toward the earth the first second is

(1) 16   (2) 32   (3) 32 × 60   (4) ³²⁄₆₀   (5) ¹⁶⁄₃₆₀₀.

14. The distance in feet a freely falling body at the distance of the moon falls toward the earth the first minute is

(1) 16   (2) ¹⁶⁄₆₀   (3) 16 × 60   (4) 32 × 60   (5) 32.

22

The Law of Gravitation

● The law of gravitation as we currently use it states that every particle of matter attracts every other particle with a force which is directly proportional to the product of the masses of the particles and inversely proportional to the square of the distance between them. Mathematically, the law of gravitation may be written

$$F \propto \frac{m_1 m_2}{d^2}$$

or

$$F = G \frac{m_1 m_2}{d^2}$$

where F is the force of attraction of either mass m_1 or m_2 on the other when the particles, or spheres, are separated a distance d between centers and G is a constant of proportionality which is experimentally determined.

Nowhere does Newton state the law of gravitation in the algebraic form given above. In fact, he shows a reluctance to speak of bodies at a distance exerting forces on each other and instead at times speaks of them as gravitating toward each other. The law of gravitation makes no attempt to tell us why bodies attract and gravitate toward each other, but it does furnish a means by which future motions of bodies can be calculated from known masses, present distances, and present motions.

In arriving at the law of gravitation, Newton used his Rules of Reasoning to extend his laws of motion to apply to the motions of the heavenly bodies. These laws, when combined with Kepler's empirically determined three-halves power law for planets and satellites, led to a gravitational force proportional to the masses of the attracting bodies and inversely proportional to the square of the distance between their centers. The development of the law of gravitation is completed in this chapter, with excerpts from Book III of the *Principia*.

268

MATHEMATICAL PRINCIPLES OF NATURAL PHILOSOPHY [1]
by Isaac Newton
Book III
Proposition VII.   Theorem VII.

That there is a power of gravity tending to all bodies, proportional to the several quantities of matter which they contain.

That all the planets mutually gravitate one towards another, we have proved before; as well as that the force of gravity towards every one of them, considered apart, is inversely as the square of this distance of places from the centre of the planet. And thence (by Prop. LXIX, Book I, and its Corollaries) [2] it follows, that the gravity tending towards all the planets is proportional to the matter which they contain.

Moreover, since all the parts of any planet A gravitate towards any other planet B; and the gravity of every part is to the gravity of the whole as the matter of the part to the matter of the whole; and (by Law III) to every action corresponds an equal reaction; therefore the planet B will, on the other hand, gravitate towards all the parts of the planet A; and its gravity towards any one part will be to the gravity towards the whole as the matter of the part to the matter of the whole. Q.E.D.

Cor. 1.   Therefore the force of gravity towards any whole planet arises from, and is compounded of, the forces of gravity towards all its parts. Magnetic and electric attractions afford us examples of this; for all attraction towards the whole arises from the attractions towards the several parts. The thing may be easily understood in gravity, if we consider a greater planet, as formed of a number of lesser planets, meeting together in one globe; for hence it would appear that the force of the whole must arise from the forces of the component parts. If it is objected, that, according to this law, all bodies with us must naturally gravitate one towards another, whereas no such gravitation anywhere appears, I answer, that since the gravitation towards these bodies is to the gravitation towards the whole earth as these bodies are to the whole earth, the gravitation towards them must be far less than to fall under the observation of our senses.

Cor. 2.   The force of gravity towards the several equal particles of any body is inversely as the square of the distance of places from the particles; as appears from Cor. 3, Prop. LXXIV, Book I.

If body A attracts body B with a force which is proportional to the mass of B, by the Rules of Reasoning and by the third law of motion, body B will attract body A with an equal force which is proportional to the mass

---

[1] Newton, op. cit., pp. 397; 504; 506–7.

[2] Book I. Proposition LXIX. Theorem XXIX.

" In a system of several bodies A, B, C, D, etc., if any one of those bodies, as A, attract all the rest, B, C, D, etc., with accelerative forces that are inversely as the squares of the distances from the attracting body; and another body, as B, attracts also the rest, A, C, D, etc., with forces that are inversely as the squares of the distances from the attracting body; the absolute forces of the attracting bodies A and B will be to each other as those very bodies A and B to which those forces belong."

The term " absolute force " may be interpreted as the force on a unit mass.

of A. Thus the force of attraction of one body on the other must be proportional to the size of each mass and hence to the product of the masses. Furthermore it has been shown previously that this force is inversely proportional to the square of the distance between their centers. Algebraically the foregoing may be summarized to give

$$F \propto \frac{m_1 m_2}{d^2}$$

or

$$F = G \frac{m_1 m_2}{d^2}.$$

At the end of the *Principia* is a section entitled "The System of the World" in which is given a résumé of the motions of the planets, satellites, and tides within the solar system. The following additional statement on gravitation is contained in this section [3]:

> Wherefore the absolute force of every globe is as the quantity of matter which the globe contains; but the motive force by which every globe is attracted towards another, and which, in terrestrial bodies, we commonly call their weight, is as the content under the quantities of matter in both globes divided by the square of the distance between their centres (by Cor. 4, Prop. LXXVI, Book I), to which force the quantity of motion, by which each globe in a given time will be carried towards the other, is proportional. . . . And from these principles well understood, it will now be easy to determine the motions of the celestial bodies among themselves.

In summary, the steps as given in the *Principia* by which Newton arrived at the law of gravitation are briefly as follows:

1. Any mass m_A moving in a curved path about a point so that the radius vector sweeps across equal areas in equal times (Kepler's second law) is pulled toward the point by centripetal force (Prop. II, p. 240).
2. The centripetal force acting on a revolving mass m_A is proportional to the product of the mass m_A and the square of the speed and inversely proportional to the distance of m_A from the center (p. 240).
3. A body A of mass m_A which is one of two or more planets or satellites obeying Kepler's third law is acted upon by a centripetal force which is directly proportional to the mass m_A of the body and inversely proportional to the square of the distance from the attracting body B (Cor. 6, p. 246).
4. By Newton's third law, the attractive force on body A due to B is equal and opposite to the force on B due to A so this force is proportional to both the attracted mass m_A and the attracting mass m_B (Prop. LXIX, p. 269).

[3] Newton, op. cit., p. 529.

5. Combining 3 and 4, the force exerted on A by B, is

$$F \propto \frac{m_A m_B}{d^2}.$$

By using his axioms of motion and the law of gravitation, Newton was able to explain the motions of the various bodies within the solar system. Since the observed motions of the planets are described by Kepler's three laws of planetary motion, these laws should be mathematically derivable from Newton's axioms and the law of gravitation. Concerning the first two of Kepler's laws, Newton summarizes as follows:

Book III

Proposition XIII.　Theorem XIII.

The planets move in ellipses which have their common focus in the centre of the sun; and, by radii drawn to that centre, they describe areas proportional to the times of description.

We have discoursed above on these motions from the Phenomena. Now that we know the principles on which they depend, from those principles we deduce the motions of the heavens a priori. Because the weights of the planets towards the sun are inversely as the squares of their distances from the sun's centre, if the sun were at rest, and the other planets did not act upon one another their orbits would be ellipses, having the sun in their common focus; and they would describe areas proportional to the times of description, by Prop. I and XI, and Cor. 1, Prop. XIII, Book I.

Proposition I is stated in Chapter 18 and Proposition XI demonstrates that a body traveling in an elliptical path is acted upon by an inverse square centripetal force directed toward one focus of the ellipse.

Kepler's third law may also be derived by using the expressions for centripetal force and for gravitational attraction to show that satellites or planets whose elliptical motions are determined by these forces should move in orbits with periods proportional to the three-halves power of the radii.[4]

Consider the motion of a planet around the sun. The planet is held in this orbit by being pulled toward the sun with a centripetal force given by

$$F = k\, \frac{m_p v^2}{R}$$

where m_p is the mass of the planet, v its speed in its orbit, and R the radius of the orbit. As shown by Newton, this force F is the gravitational pull of the sun on the planet, and

$$F = G\, \frac{m_s m_p}{R^2}$$

where m_s is the mass of the sun.

---

[4] Note that this is the reverse procedure to that previously employed by Newton where the three-halves power law was used to show that the centripetal force was an inverse square relationship.

Equating these expressions for the force

$$G \frac{m_s m_p}{R^2} = k \frac{m_p v^2}{R}$$

and

$$G \frac{m_s}{R} = k v^2.$$

But

$$v = \frac{2\pi R}{P}$$

where P is the time required for the planet to make one revolution about the sun. Then

$$G \frac{m_s}{R} = \frac{4\pi^2 R^2}{P^2} k$$

and

$$P^2 = \frac{4\pi^2 k}{G m_s} R^3.$$

Since $\dfrac{4\pi^2 k}{G m_s}$ is a constant which is the same for any of the planets,

$$P^2 \propto R^3 \quad \text{or} \quad P \propto R^{3/2}$$

which is Kepler's third law. Kepler arrived at his third law by a study of observational data on the positions of the planets at various times. Newton showed that the observed motions would be expected if each planet were attracted to the sun by a force proportional to the product of the masses concerned and inversely proportional to the square of the distance between their centers.

General Scholium

❋   ❋   ❋   ❋   ❋   ❋   ❋

Bodies projected in our air suffer no resistance but from the air. Withdraw the air, as is done in Mr. Boyle's vacuum, and the resistance ceases; for in this void a bit of fine down and a piece of solid gold descend with equal velocity. And the same reasoning must hold in the celestial spaces above the earth's atmosphere; in which spaces, where there is no air to resist their motions, all bodies will move with the greatest freedom; and the planets and comets will constantly pursue their revolutions in orbits given in kind and position, according to the laws above explained; but though these bodies may, indeed, persevere in their orbits by the mere laws of gravity, yet they could by no means have at first derived the regular position of the orbits themselves from those laws.

The six primary planets are revolved about the sun in circles concentric with the sun, and with motions directed towards the same parts, and almost in the same plane. Ten moons are revolved about the earth, Jupiter, and Saturn, in circles concentric with them, with the same direction of motion, and nearly in the planes of the orbits of those planets; but it is not to be conceived that mere mechanical causes could give birth to so many regular motions, since the comets range over all parts of the heavens in very eccentric orbits; for by that kind of motion they pass easily through the orbs of the planets, and with great rapidity; and in their aphelions, where they move the slowest, and are detained the longest, they recede to the greatest distances from each other, and thence suffer the least disturbance from their mutual attractions. This most beautiful system of the sun, planets, and comets, could only proceed from the counsel and dominion of an intelligent and powerful Being. And if the fixed stars are the centres of other like systems, these, being formed by the like wise counsel, must be all subject to the dominion of One; especially since the light of the fixed stars is of the same nature with the light of the sun, and from every system light passes into all the other systems: and lest the systems of the fixed stars should, by their gravity, fall mutually on each other, he hath placed those systems at immense distances one from another.

＊   ＊   ＊   ＊   ＊   ＊   ＊

Hitherto we have explained the phenomena of the heavens and of our sea by the power of gravity, but have not yet assigned the cause of this power. This is certain, that it must proceed from a cause that penetrates to the very centres of the sun and planets, without suffering the least diminution of its force; that operates not according to the quantity of the surfaces of the particles upon which it acts (as mechanical causes used to do), but according to the quantity of the solid matter which they contain, and propagates its virtue on all sides to immense distances, decreasing always as the inverse square of the distances. Gravitation towards the sun is made up out of the gravitations towards the several particles of which the body of the sun is composed; and in receding from the sun decreases accurately as the inverse square of the distances as far as the orbit of Saturn, as evidently appears from the quiescence of the aphelions of the planets; nay, and even to the remotest aphelions of the comets, if those aphelions are also quiescent. But hitherto I have not been able to discover the cause of those properties of gravity from phenomena, and I frame no hypotheses; for whatever is not deduced from the phenomena is to be called an hypothesis; and hypotheses, whether metaphysical or physical, whether of occult qualities or mechanical, have no place in experimental philosophy. In this philosophy particular propositions are inferred from the phenomena, and afterwards rendered general by induction. Thus it was that the impenetrability, the mobility, and the impulsive force of bodies, and the laws of motion and of gravitation, were discovered. And to us it is enough that gravity does really exist, and act according to the laws which we have explained, and abundantly serves to account for all the motions of the celestial bodies, and of our sea.

And now we might add something concerning a certain most subtle Spirit which pervades and lies hid in all gross bodies; by the force and action of which Spirit the particles of bodies mutually attract one another at near distances, and cohere, if contiguous; and electric bodies operate to greater distances, as well repelling as attracting the neighboring corpuscles; and light is emitted, reflected, refracted, inflected, and heats bodies; and all sensation is excited, and the members of animal bodies move at the command of the will, namely, by the vibrations of this Spirit, mutually propagated along the solid filaments of the nerves, from the outward organs of sense to the brain, and from the brain into the muscles. But these are things that cannot be explained in few words, nor are we furnished with that sufficiency of experiments which is required to an accurate determination and demonstration of the laws by which this electric and elastic Spirit operates.

Newton used his laws of mechanics and gravitation to explain more than just the motions of the planets about the sun or of the satellites about the planets. He was also able to account for certain departures from strict Keplerian motion of the moon, such as the precession of the plane of the moon's orbit. By making some assumptions about the elasticity of the earth, he calculated that the rotating earth should bulge around its equator by a factor of about 1/230th of its radius. Today with better knowledge of the earth's interior, we both calculate and observe an equatorial bulging of about 1/297th of the earth's radius. Since the earth is not a perfect sphere, the gravitational attraction of the moon and of the sun upon this bulge would tend to turn the earth so that its axis is perpendicular to its orbit. However, since it is like a spinning top, it precesses instead. Thus Newton was able to explain the precession of the equinoxes which had carried the vernal equinox from the constellation of Aries in the days of Hipparchus to the constellation of Pisces where it is found today. Perhaps even more striking was his explanation of the tides as due to the differences in the gravitational attractions by the moon and by the sun upon the ocean nearest to the attracting body and the lesser attraction for that part of the ocean which was on the opposite side of the earth.

By the time of Newton's death in 1727, Newton's ideas had been rather well accepted by all of the English and Scottish universities. They were not so quickly accepted on the continent. The Paris Academy in awarding prizes for essays on the planetary motions in 1730 gave the first prize to John Bernouilli for a treatment based on Descartes' vortex theory while a Newtonian essay merited only second place. Perhaps part of the trouble was the geometrical form in which Newton had cast his work. With the spread of the calculus developed by Newton and Leibnitz independently, and the invention and elaboration of new analytical methods, Newton's system came into its own. Euler, Clairaut, D'Alembert, Lagrange, Laplace, and many others used the Newtonian mechanics and the Newtonian law of universal gravitation to explain nearly all known details of celestial motions. The Newtonian system went from success to ever more success in theoretical astronomy.

A laboratory confirmation of Newton's law of gravitation was made in 1797 by Cavendish. Two small lead spheres (see Fig. 22-1) mounted on the ends of a light rod were suspended by a fine wire fastened to the center of the rod. Two large lead spheres were brought up on opposite sides of the horizontal rod until they were near the small spheres. The attraction of the large spheres for the small ones caused the fine wire suspension to be twisted through a small angle. By reversing the positions of the large spheres, the angular deflection of the rod supporting the small spheres was also reversed and the accuracy of measurement appreciably increased. From the known masses, distances, and force to twist the fine wire suspension through a given angle, the constant G in the gravitation equation could be calculated. This experiment furnished an opportunity for the direct observation of motion caused by gravitational forces.

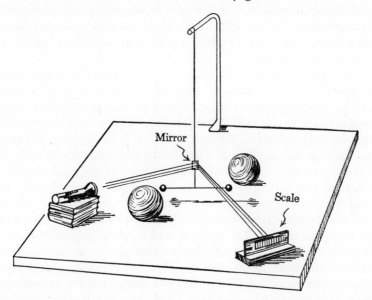

Figure 22-1. *Simplified Cavendish experiment for measuring the gravitational attraction between spheres of known masses.*

But an even more dramatic triumph of Newton's theories was in the successful prediction and subsequent discovery of a previously unknown planet. The story actually begins in 1781 when F. William Herschel, a professional musician turned amateur astronomer, was systematically searching the skies with a 6.2 inch aperture reflecting telescope of his own making. Near the constellation of Gemini he found a small star which moved eastward nearly along the ecliptic. Continued observation verified it as a newly discovered planet, now known to us as Uranus. One can imagine the excitement engendered by the discovery of the very first new planet within man's written history! One obvious result was to turn Herschel into a professional astronomer and an amateur musician by his appointment as Royal Astronomer to George III.

Herschel found Uranus purely by chance. The next new planet was discovered partly by chance and partly by mathematical design. J. E. Bode had organized a cooperative search with five other astronomers to seek out the missing planet at 2.8 astronomical units from the sun which was to be expected from "Bode's law" as was indicated in Chapter 8. However, on the opening night of the 19th century, January 1, 1801, Giuseppe

Piazzi, who was not in the group, found an eighth magnitude star in the constellation of Taurus which moved as a planet. This small object, now named Ceres, was at the expected distance but was considerably smaller than the expected size, being less than 500 miles in diameter. Thousands of small minor planets, ranging from Ceres, the largest, down to small blocks of rock only a few feet in diameter, were subsequently found at average distances of 2.8 A.U. These are called the asteroids and are often thought of as fragments of a planet, perhaps destroyed by Jupiter's gravitational field.

Planetary astronomy had obviously become fashionable in the 19th century. Continued observations of Uranus showed increasing departures from its positions calculated from Newtonian mechanics. These discrepancies reached 2′ of arc in 1844 and could no longer be disregarded. Two young men, J. C. Adams in England and U. J. J. Leverrier in France, began to work on the problem independently and unknown to each other. Each postulated the existence of another planet as yet unobserved in an orbit beyond that of Uranus. The unobserved planet would pull Uranus ahead of its calculated positions as the two planets approached and would pull Uranus behind these same calculated positions as the two planets receded from each other. The problem which Adams and Leverrier posed to themselves was to calculate the position of the as yet unobserved planet from Newton's theory and the observed departures from the first calculated ephemeris [5] of Uranus. Adams completed his calculations in October, 1845 and sent his results to G. B. Airy, the English Astronomer Royal. For reasons which are still not understandable, Airy did not assign a very high priority to Adams' project. Meanwhile in August, 1846, Leverrier had also solved the problem and without knowing of Adams' work, had written to the observatory at Berlin. J. G. Galle found the new planet (Neptune) on September 23, 1846 within a half hour after beginning the search and within a degree of the calculated position.

This spectacular achievement of finding a previously unsuspected planet purely by mathematics gave immediate and world-wide acceptance to Newton's theories. In fact the continuing successes of the Newtonian system were the principal reason for believing in the Keplerian-Copernican arrangement of the solar system rather than one of the competing schemes such as the Tychonic. As will be recalled from the previous chapters, Newton had shown that the planetary motions could be calculated if an inverse square force directed toward the sun was postulated. Moreover the earth was treated as just another planet moving in an orbit about the sun subject to this same universal gravitation. The Newtonian system worked and worked well. Therefore the Keplerian-Copernican arrangement of the solar system was accepted even though stellar parallax had not been observed.

[5] A table of calculated positions of an astronomical body for various times in the future.

The lack of a measured stellar parallax to well into the 19th century was not due to any lack of trying. Tycho had attempted a visual determination. Galileo with his telescope kept close watch on the angular separation of pairs of stars close together. The Herschels had used essentially the same method but with improvements in technique and with larger telescopes. James Bradley had observed Gamma Draconis continuously for three years with a special vertical telescope permanently bricked up into an otherwise unused chimney. Nevertheless it was not until 1838 that F. W. Bessel using Galileo's method actually measured a parallax of a third of a second of arc for the faint star 61 Cygni. The stars are very far away and the angle is extremely small. But once the technique had been developed the flood-gates were opened. T. Henderson in 1839 measured a parallax of nearly a second of arc for Alpha Centauri, still the sun's closest neighbor in space and F. G. W. Struve reported a parallax of a quarter of a second for Vega in 1840. Today we have measured parallaxes for thousands of stars determined by photographic methods with large telescopes. Thus the long-sought observational proof of the earth's orbital motion about the sun was finally found only a little over a hundred years ago!

To the proof of the earth's orbital motion was added a few years later an experimental demonstration of the earth's rotation on its axis. In 1851 the French physicist Foucault suspended a heavy iron ball by a long wire from the dome of the Pantheon in Paris. When set to oscillating back and forth in a straight north-south line, it was observed that the direction of oscillation of the pendulum seemed to slowly rotate in a clockwise direction as viewed from above. Its rate of rotation was such that it would make a complete revolution in about thirty hours. In reality of course the pendulum was continuing to oscillate in the same direction in space while the earth rotated beneath it. Perhaps the mechanism would be more apparent if the pendulum were assumed to be at the North Pole as shown in Figure 22-2. Then the pendulum continues to swing in a definite direction in space while the earth rotates under it once every 24 hours. To the observer on the earth, of course, the appearances are that the direction of the path of the pendulum is rotating, completing a cycle in 24 hours. On the other hand, a pendulum moving north and south at the equator would not rotate, since it would always be moving parallel to the earth's axis irrespective of the rotation of the earth. It is plausible, therefore, that the apparent period of the rotation of the pendulum should increase from 24 hours at the poles to infinity at the equator and constitute an observational proof of the earth's rotation.

The success of Newtonism in finding Neptune led to the prediction of a trans-Neptunian planet to account for the remaining discrepancies in Uranus' orbit. Lowell Observatory, among others, began a large scale survey of the sky in a broad band centered on the ecliptic. Early in 1930 C. W. Tombaugh found the planet Pluto. Although its existence had been

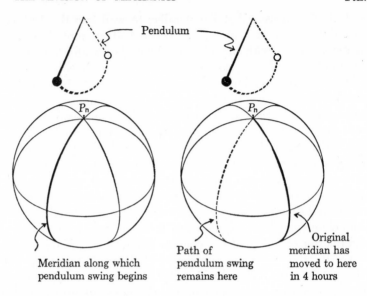

Figure 22-2. *Foucault pendulum at the North Pole.*

postulated on mathematical grounds, it was not found at a predicted position as was Neptune. Pluto was found by hard work and the strong conviction that a needle did exist in the haystack!

With Pluto in 1930, the muster of presently known planets about our sun is complete to date. Nevertheless, another planet had been predicted in the latter days of the 19th century and had been unsuccessfully sought. The long axis of Mercury's elliptical orbit is slowly turning in space. Most of this " advance of perihelion " of Mercury can be explained on Newtonian grounds as due to attractions from Venus, Earth, and the other planets. However, about 40″ of rotation each 100 years remained unexplainable. The same previously successful Newtonian methods were applied and a new planet confidently named Vulcan was predicted within Mercury's orbit. After long searching, it became apparent by the close of the 19th century that this planet did not exist.

In the first quarter of the 20th century, Einstein proposed a new law of gravitation, the general theory of relativity. In the hands of the theoretical astronomer Karl Schwarzschild, the new theory accounted for the troublesome 40″ per century and the seeming necessity for Vulcan vanished. Then is the Newtonian theory of gravitation no longer true? Perhaps the question of truth in theoretical physical science is also relative. Many theories have come and gone. It has become increasingly common not to be too concerned with the eternal " truth " of a given theory but instead with its usefulness. The Newtonian theory of gravitation remains an extremely close approximation to the results of the general theory of relativity within the solar system. Only in exceptional cases, such as Mercury, do very slight differences appear between the predictions of the two theories, and the differences between the two systems of mechanics become marked only when velocities approach that of light or when distances become extragalactic in magnitude.

The Newtonian mechanics remains today as the very cornerstone of the physical sciences. With Newton's publication of the *Principia* in 1687 we have reached one of the high points in the history of science. The astronomy of Kepler and the physics of Galileo were shown to be merely parts of the same whole. The old rigid Aristotelian division of the physical world into terrestrial and celestial was destroyed for all time. For the next two hundred years men had high hopes of explaining the entire natural world in terms of mechanism. If effect always inexorably follows cause, then the living universe is a sort of gigantic machine subject to the inanimate laws of mechanics. Free-will in ethics, consciousness in psychology, and vitalism in biology were all illusions. The individual had no real choice when faced with a decision, since his choice was foreordained by his earlier conditioning. Conscious thought was to be explained in terms of connectivity of the cells of the cerebrum, in principle similar to the large computer assemblies of today. Perhaps man creates the machine in his own image. The vital processes of the living cell were to be understood in terms of chemical transformations and physical processes such as osmosis. One logical resultant of strict mechanism is a predestination [6] much more alarming than that of Calvin! Newton, who in some ways in his thinking was really one of the last of the great medieval men, became the patron saint of the Age of Enlightenment. His impact on the 18th and 19th centuries was permanent and decisive.

STUDY QUESTIONS

1. From the law of gravitation it may be concluded that
   a. the weight of a body at an elevation of 4000 miles above the surface of the earth is essentially one-half its weight at the earth's surface
   b. the mass of a body at an elevation of 4000 miles above the surface of the earth is essentially one-half its mass at the earth's surface
   c. mass and weight in the English system of units are always numerically equal.
   The correct answer is

   (1) a   (2) b   (3) c   (4) a and c   (5) none of them.

2. The mass of the earth is about 80 times the mass of the moon. If the gravitational pull of the earth on the moon is F, the force with which the moon pulls on the earth is

   (1) 0   (2) 80F   (3) $\dfrac{F}{80}$ (4) F   (5) $\dfrac{F}{6400}$.

[6] See Chapter 41 on the theory of indeterminism.

3. The mass of the earth is about 80 times the mass of the moon. The radius of the earth is about 4 times the radius of the moon. If the weight of an object on the earth's surface is 100 pounds-force, its weight on the moon in pounds-force is approximately

    (1) 100   (2) 20   (3) 500   (4) 4   (5) 2500.

4. The acceleration of a freely falling body on the moon in feet per second per second would be approximately (using data from previous problem)

    (1) 32   (2) 6   (3) 3   (4) 8   (5) 160.

5–7. The force of attraction between two masses m and M situated a distance d between centers is F.

5. If d is doubled, the masses remaining fixed, the new force of attraction is

    (1) $\dfrac{F}{4}$ (2) $\dfrac{F}{2}$ (3) F (4) $2F$ (5) $4F$.

6. If both masses are tripled, d remaining fixed, the new force of attraction is

    (1) $\dfrac{F}{9}$ (2) $\dfrac{F}{3}$ (3) F (4) $3F$ (5) $9F$.

7. If both masses, and d are halved, the new force of attraction is

    (1) $\dfrac{F}{4}$ (2) $\dfrac{F}{2}$ (3) F (4) $2F$ (5) $4F$.

8–12. The mass of the earth is approximately 13×10^{24} pounds-mass.

8. The gravitation pull of the earth on a 1 pound-mass placed 4000 miles from the center of the earth is, in pounds-force,

    (1) 1   (2) 13×10^{24} (3) 1×10^{-24} (4) $\frac{16}{13} \times 10^{-18}$
    (5) $\frac{13}{16} \times 10^{18}$.

9. The gravitational pull of a 1 pound-mass on another 1 pound-mass at a distance of 4000 miles is, in pounds-force,

    (1) 1   (2) 13×10^{24} (3) $\frac{1}{13} \times 10^{-24}$ (4) $\frac{16}{13} \times 10^{-18}$
    (5) $\frac{13}{16} \times 10^{18}$.

10. If masses are measured in pounds-mass, forces in pounds-force, and distances in miles, calculate the value of the constant G in the law of gravitation

    (1) 1   (2) 13×10^{24} (3) $\frac{1}{13} \times 10^{-24}$ (4) $\frac{16}{13} \times 10^{-18}$
    (5) $\frac{13}{16} \times 10^{18}$.

11. What is the attractive force in pounds of a 1 pound-mass for another 1 pound-mass at a distance of 1 mile?

    (1) 1   (2) 13×10^{24} (3) $\frac{1}{13} \times 10^{-24}$ (4) $\frac{16}{13} \times 10^{-18}$
    (5) $\frac{13}{16} \times 10^{18}$

12. To obtain the attractive force between two 1 pound-masses separated a distance of 1 foot between centers, the answer in prob. 11 should be

    (1) multiplied by 5280   (2) multiplied by $(5280)^2$
    (3) divided by 5280   (4) divided by $(5280)^2$
    (5) left unchanged.

PART FIVE

THE NATURE OF MATTER

The previous section concluded with an explanation of a phenomenon concerning matter on a large scale, the solar system, based on Newton's laws of motion and his law of universal gravitation. In the present section a problem at the other end of the size spectrum will be considered. This problem is part of the atomic theory [1] of chemistry, namely, the determination of the relative weights of the atoms of different elements. This determination was made possible through the interpretation of certain laws of the science of chemistry.

CHEMICAL PROBLEMS OF THE 18TH CENTURY

The revolution in chemistry, which was a necessary prerequisite to determining relative atomic weights, did not occur until the latter part of the 18th century, over one hundred years after the publication of Newton's *Principia*. The delay was due largely to the complexity of the subject matter of chemistry, where the problem was to discover order in the almost infinite varieties of matter found in nature. Questions that concerned chemists in the 18th century were the make-up of the air and the relationship between the reactants and products of a chemical change. These called for careful and painstaking study and often the development of special laboratory techniques. Today in studying chemistry we are so quick to write an equation representing what occurs in a particular reaction that we lose sight of the fact that it often took many years of study of the reaction itself before it was possible to write the equation. This is illustrated by the fact that it took chemists the better part of the 18th century to acquire an understanding of the comparatively simple chemical change of combustion.

[1] Many sources were consulted in the preparation of this section, but special acknowledgement is due L. K. Nash, *The Atomic-Molecular Theory*, Harvard University Press, 1950.

The search for the " building blocks " of matter, the elements, was made difficult by the fact that it was first necessary to recognize the experimental criteria that elements must meet and then to develop experimental techniques so the criteria could be applied.

All three of these problems, the make-up of the air, the nature of combustion, and the problem of the elements were solved almost single-handedly by the French chemist Lavoisier in the latter part of the 18th century.

NEWTON'S INFLUENCE ON THE STUDY OF THE NATURE OF MATTER

Newton's work was influential in making possible a solution of these problems. Newton's views on the atomic constitution of matter also greatly influenced Dalton. Indeed the success of the Newtonian synthesis was all pervasive in the 18th century, and even the social sciences adopted the Newtonian method as the ideal for which to strive. Some idea of the extent of the Newtonian influence can be seen from the fact that prior to 1800 there had appeared over seventy books in six languages about the *Principia*.

Specifically Newton's explanation of the property of weight of matter was instrumental in introducing the chemical balance into the study of chemical reactions. Prior to Newton and back to and including the Greeks, it was generally believed that matter was conserved throughout the apparent changes it might undergo, but weight, associated as it was with the idea of bodies seeking their natural places, did not suggest itself as a means of checking on the conservation of matter. It was only after Newton had developed the concept of mass or inertia, had shown that the mass or inertia of a body is the sum of the masses or inertias of the particles of which it is composed, and had demonstrated that weight is proportional to mass that weight conservation became a criterion of matter conservation. The chemist began using the balance in studying chemical reactions in order to construct a " balance sheet " and make certain that all matter was accounted for in a particular reaction. If the weight of the products of a particular reaction was less than the weight of the reactants, some elusive component had escaped notice. Such studies of chemical reactions played an integral part in the solution of the three problems cited above.

The success of Newtonian mechanics established the mechanical explanation of all phenomena, an explanation in terms of bodies or particles and forces operating between them, as the objective to be strived for in all scientific explanations. Newton stated that he was " induced by many reasons to suspect that all the phenomena of nature may depend upon certain forces by which the particles of bodies, by some causes hitherto unknown, are either mutually impelled towards each other, and cohere in

regular figures or are repelled and recede from each other." In particular
in the *Principia,* Newton proposed a possible mechanistic explanation
of the physical phenomenon summarized in Boyle's law that the volume of
a gas varies inversely as the pressure:

**If a fluid [gas] be composed of particles fleeing from each other, and the
density be as the compression [that is, the density varies directly as the pressure or what is the same thing, the volume varies inversely as the pres-
sure] . . . the forces of the particles will be inversely proportional to the distances of their centres.**

This attitude continued to set the tenor of scientific explanations on into
the present century. The atomic theory of matter and the explanation of
chemical reactions in terms of combinations of atoms obviously falls
within this general trend.

THE BEGINNINGS OF THE ATOMIC THEORY

Speculations on the ultimate nature of matter on the conceptual, rather
than the observational, level have been along different lines at different
times, but the view that interests us here is the atomic. The beginning of
the atomic view goes back to two Greek philosophers of the materialistic
school, Leucippus (ca. 450 B.C.) and Democritus (ca. 420 B.C.). Leucippus
proposed the theory, which was developed more fully by Democritus, that
all matter was composed of small particles, atoms, and empty space, the
void. The atoms were believed to be indivisible (the Greek word *a-tomos*
means " without cutting " or " indivisible ") and everlasting. The similarity
of this view to the modern atomic theory, at least in the realm of ordinary
chemical change, is obvious and is apt to lead to a misconception. It will
be recalled from Chapter 1 that Democritus developed his atomic theory
in an effort to resolve the philosophical crisis that had arisen in the 5th
century B.C. due on the one hand to Parmenides' conclusion that no
change was possible and on the other hand to the reality of change in the
world. Democritus' theory was not an attempt to explain any specific
physical or chemical processes. The modern atomic theory on the other
hand did arise out of an attempt to explain certain physical and chemical
processes. Subsequently Democritus did apply his philosophical atomic
theory to explain certain processes in nature. Thus decay, disappearance
of water upon boiling, and similar processes were considered to be atoms
or groups of atoms moving apart; processes such as growth and condensation of water vapor were considered to be atoms or groups of atoms coming together.

The atomic theory was taken over by Epicurus (341–270 B.C.) and became a fundamental part of the philosophy that bears his name. It became
known in the west principally through *The Nature of the Universe,* the
work of the Roman Epicurean poet Lucretius (98–55 B.C.).

Aristotle opposed the atomic view in general on account of its materialistic aspects, and specifically he opposed it as being contrary to his views on motion. As we have already seen, he adopted the common-sense view that motion was possible only through contact, and hence all space must be filled with matter (no vacuum or void) if any motion is to occur. Aristotle did not believe, however, that the continuous matter of nature was divisible without limit.

Other opposition to the atomic view came from Jewish and Christian theologians due principally to its association with Epicurean philosophy. As a result of these two oppositions, Aristotelian and religious, the atomic theory was not popular in the West until the beginning of the Renaissance and the revival of interest in all Greek philosophers. During the 17th and 18th centuries many scientists were in the habit of thinking in terms of atoms to explain various physical phenomena. However, there was little interest in the atoms themselves, which were thought to be very much alike, until Dalton proposed a chemical method of determining their relative weights. The present section will outline the development of an unambiguous method of determining these relative weights.

23

Views on Matter Prior to Dalton

● Because of almost constant exposure to the atomic concept of matter, it is difficult for us today to appreciate the work of Dalton and his successors on determining the relative weights of atoms. This chapter will consist of a brief review of views on matter prior to Dalton, so that we can better gain a perspective of the background against which Dalton worked and an appreciation of his contributions.

Let us emphasize once again our present objectives. The essential contributions to atomic theory of Dalton and his successors that we shall consider in this section could be summarized in a few pages and can be found in most chemistry texts. The finished subject matter of science at any particular time is comparatively easy to understand, as the student is told what is important, such as mass, velocity, or law of definite proportions, and clear definitions are laid down. What is really difficult and important in the progress of science is knowing what to look for and which concepts are to be singled out. A realization and appreciation of the latter is one of our primary goals here.

In this brief review of the history of man's thoughts on matter prior to Dalton, a chronological presentation will not be attempted; rather the material will be presented under several logical heads, and within each heading the most important historical developments will be noted.

WHAT IS MATTER?

Logically the first question to be asked in discussing matter is — what is to be included under the heading? Today we recognize three states of matter — gas, liquid, and solid — and the criteria that all three meet are that they occupy space and possess weight or, to be more general, inertia.

The " occupy space " criterion was recognized as an essential property as soon as man began to think about matter. Empedocles recognized it and cited an experiment to prove that air was a form of matter. In the experiment he demonstrated that air had extension by immersing an inverted vessel in a container of water. As the water did not fill the vessel, air had extension and occupied space. The weight criterion, however, was not immediately recognized. The fact that air had weight was known by Galileo, and was later demonstrated by use of the mercury barometer invented in 1643 by Torricelli and Viviani, students of Galileo. Pascal in 1648, by ascending a mountain with a mercury barometer and observing the drop in the mercury column, proved that the mercury was supported in the barometer by the weight of the atmosphere pressing on the free surface of the mercury in the dish.

CLASSIFICATION OF MATTER

Having decided what things are to be considered as matter, we should like next to find some kind of order in the many kinds of matter that exist; that is, we should like to devise some kind of classification scheme. To do this we must have criteria on the basis of which a piece of matter can be assigned a place in the scheme. Early attempts at classification prior to the 18th century were generally on the basis of use, although some special groups of matter had been classified on the basis of properties. But the scheme of classification in which we are interested, and one used by the chemist today, is a scheme whose criteria are furnished by the make-up of matter. As a start in such a scheme, we note what can be determined about matter by direct examination. One of the first things determined visually is that it is either homogeneous or heterogeneous.

Matter is said to be *homogeneous* if any given part is visually indistinguishable from every other part and furthermore the properties are uniform throughout. For example, a piece of quartz found in nature is homogeneous. Homogeneous matter may be gaseous, liquid, or solid.

If the sample of matter has visually distinguishable parts separated by boundaries, even though a powerful microscope is required to see them, the matter is said to be *heterogeneous*. For example, some granite consists of a mixture of three visually distinguishable kinds of matter — feldspar, quartz, and mica. Each within itself is homogeneous. The like homogeneous portions of a piece of matter taken together constitute a *phase*. Thus granite is composed of three phases: mica, feldspar, and quartz.

As a first step, all matter can be classified as homogeneous or heterogeneous on the basis of the above criterion. Obviously by *mechanical* means, heterogeneous matter can be separated into its homogeneous components. Diagrammatically we then have:

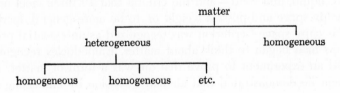

Now, can homogeneous matter be further subdivided into subclasses? Here we are confronted with a problem that was clarified only recently. In retrospect it can be seen that the problem was one of distinguishing between homogeneous pure substances and homogeneous mixtures of pure substances, called solutions.

A straightforward definition of a pure substance could specify the criteria a sample of homogeneous matter must meet in order to be so classified, but this assumes we already have matter that meets these criteria, and generally such matter does not exist in nature. The problem is graphically illustrated by the bottles of matter (pure substances) that are found on the chemist's laboratory shelves as contrasted with the matter that is found in nature. The jars of matter on the chemist's shelves came from nature, but they were derived in general by laborious and complicated processes.

Let us examine the problem first by means of an example. Consider rain water, ocean water, and river water which have been filtered to remove any solid particles so there is a single phase. They differ from one another in their properties, such as taste and perhaps color. Now is there some one component common to all these "waters"? The answer, of course, is yes. By suitable means of purification, such as distillation or freezing, a liquid called water which possesses *definite properties* can be isolated. By "definite properties" is meant that the properties, such as boiling point, freezing point, and density of the water so obtained do not depend on the source of the water, and that under constant conditions the properties are the same today as tomorrow. Moreover, further attempts at purifying this water by such methods as distillation or freezing result only in getting back the same water again, recognizable by the same definite properties.

When we have succeeded in isolating such a sample of homogeneous matter, we have an individual, a chemical individual, or a *pure substance.* An individual, in as much as it is unique, cannot be further subdivided by purification processes and possesses properties which are invariable. Such a statement cannot be made about any one of the "waters" from which the pure water is derived. The properties of river water depend on the source, and the properties of a particular source change with time; ocean water also changes with time.

The above statements apply to any chemical individual or pure substance. Once again, such substances occur only rarely in nature. Hence the development of such a concept of a pure substance, depending as it does on purity, is evidently dependent on developments in technique. Even today the decision as to what constitutes a pure substance is a relative one, as the attainment of "absolute purity" is difficult and rare for a given sample of matter.

Actually, the need for purification in medicine and other fields, the methods of purification, and the concept of pure substances developed more or less simultaneously. In other words, man did not start out with the concept of pure substances and the means of obtaining them, but having once obtained reasonably pure matter, he recognized it as such.

The next step in the classification of matter can now be taken quickly, as homogeneous matter is either a pure substance or a *solution* which is a single homogeneous phase consisting of a mixture of pure substances. In practice we differentiate between a single homogeneous phase of a pure substance and a solution by subjecting the phase to such processes as freezing and distillation, and in the case of a solid phase, melting. If by such treatment two or more phases with different properties are obtained, the original phase was a solution. For example, salt dissolved in water is a single homogeneous phase that by the process of distillation can be separated into two phases, solid salt and liquid water, and is hence a solution. If by such processes it is not possible to separate the original single phase into two or more phases with different properties, the original phase was a pure substance.

In carrying out such processes as distillation and freezing in an attempt to determine whether a sample of homogeneous matter is a solution or pure substance, care must be taken that a chemical change (to be defined shortly) does not occur. In practice this can be determined by mixing the phases together after the separation process and noting if the original homogeneous matter is obtained. If it is, then no chemical change has occurred. Thus in the example above of the solution of salt and water, if the separated phases of salt and water are mixed together the original solution is obtained. On the other hand if mixing the separated phases together does not result in the original homogeneous matter, it is generally true that a chemical change has occurred. For example, heating sugar results in the production of water vapor and a black carbonaceous mass. Upon mixing the condensed water phase and the carbonaceous mass the original sugar is not reobtained. Thus a chemical change has occurred. Processes such as distillation and freezing that do not result in chemical change are called *physical* processes, and it is only these processes that are to be used in differentiating between pure substances and solutions.

The study of one form of homogeneous matter, the gaseous state, caused particular difficulty. The gaseous or vapor state of a pure substance is, of course, homogeneous as is also any mixture of pure gaseous substances. Due to the less tangible nature of gases as compared to solids and liquids, chemists were slow to recognize the various different pure substances that existed as gases and to discover methods of separating mixtures of pure gaseous substances into their components. In particular as already noted, the problem of the composition of the air was not clarified until the latter part of the 18th century by Lavoisier.

In summary up to this point, all matter can be classified as either heterogeneous or homogeneous. Heterogeneous matter in turn is composed of homogeneous phases. Homogeneous matter can be classified as either pure substances or solutions, and solutions in turn are composed of a mixture of pure substances.

Diagrammatically our classification-composition scheme becomes:

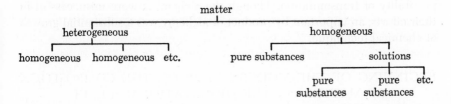

Can pure substances themselves be further subdivided into classes? Experience shows that there are a multitude of pure substances. However, the feeling that behind this apparent diversity of matter there is comparative simplicity and that all matter is composed of a comparatively few "fundamental" or elemental kinds of matter, themselves not further resolvable, dates back at least to the Greeks. Let us digress momentarily from our classification scheme to consider the development of views on the make-up of pure substances.

CONSTITUTION OF PURE SUBSTANCES ON THE OBSERVATIONAL LEVEL; EARLY VIEWS

Views on the make-up of pure substances occupy two levels, the observational, leading to the recognition of elements, and the conceptual, culminating in the atomic theory. The interplay of these two levels will concern us throughout this entire section on the atomic theory, but in this chapter it is the observational level that will be considered.

The observational level deals with what we can ascertain about the make-up of pure substances through direct examination and through experiments in which observations are made by using our senses. The information obtained on this level is objective and hence there is general agreement. The classification scheme we are constructing was of course unknown to the early Ionian Greeks who held the four-element theory of matter. However assuming that they were familiar with the above scheme and had reached pure substances in the classification-composition scheme it would be consistent with their views to consider pure substances as a "blend" of the four elements. Thus they would complete the above classification-composition by saying that all pure substances are composed of the four elements, earth, air, fire, and water, themselves not further resolvable. Most matter found in nature would be mixtures, homogeneous and heterogeneous, of the various pure substances.

The four-element theory of the Greeks underwent modifications and refinements as it passed successively to the Arabs and then to western

Europe in the Middle Ages. But the fundamental idea that the elements of matter were related to the properties of matter was retained through the various modifications and refinements.

This concept of the elements led the alchemists to the belief of the possibility of transmutation. Though the alchemists were unsuccessful in their efforts, an important by-product of alchemy was a substantial growth of chemical technique.

BEGINNING OF THE MODERN VIEW ON THE COMPOSITION OF MATTER ON THE OBSERVATIONAL LEVEL

There was considerable criticism and discussion of the four-element theory of matter and its various modifications in the 17th century. One of the chief critics was the British scientist Robert Boyle (1627–1691). His *Sceptical Chymist* published in 1661 contains the following observations on the meanings that should be attached to the word element, signifying the nonresolvable components of matter [1]:

> **I mean by elements, as those Chymists that speak plainest do by their principles, certain primitive and simple, or perfectly unmingled bodies; which not being made of any other bodies, or of one another, are the ingredients of which all those called perfectly mixt bodies are immediately compounded, and into which they are ultimately resolved. . . .**

Let us consider Boyle's definition of an element in the light of our composition-classification scheme. Consider a piece of matter that meets the criteria of a pure substance. If this pure substance is unresolvable into components or "any other bodies," it is to be classified as an *element*. On the other hand if the pure substance upon being subjected to "resolution" can be resolved into ultimate components or elements, it is to be classified as a "perfectly mixt body" which today is called a *compound*. The method of "ultimately resolving" a pure substance, which Boyle refers to, requires a procedure or technique and none is specified. The "ultimate resolution" of a particular pure substance, if it can be accomplished, is an example of a chemical change. A *chemical* change is a process whereby a certain substance or substances that are recognized by its or their properties disappear and a new substance or substances that are recognized by its or their properties appear. The changes in properties that occur are generally marked. Energy changes often accompany a chemical change. Examples of chemical changes are the burning of wood and the rusting of iron. The "ultimate resolution" above is an example of chemical decomposition in which a pure substance is resolved into two or more elements such as the decomposition of water into hydrogen and oxygen. Note also in Boyle's definition that there is no decision

---

[1] Quoted in M. M. Pattison Muir's introduction to Boyle's *Sceptical Chymist*, E. P. Dutton & Co., New York, 1911, p. XVII.

implied *a priori* as to what the number of elements may be, unlike the four-element theory.

Limited by the techniques at his disposal, the state of chemical knowledge at his time and his corpuscular view of the ultimate nature of matter, into which we cannot enter here,[2] Boyle was unable to apply the definition in a fruitful manner. The successful application of the definition by Lavoisier had to await developments in pneumatic or gas chemistry and in quantitative chemistry. To appreciate the developments needed in these two fields, let us consider what is necessary in order to be able to apply Boyle's definition successfully, and then see by whom and with what advances the requirements were supplied.

Suppose we have before us a pure substance, such as a liquid. We shall assume the means are at hand to resolve this liquid, and that in so doing a solid phase and a gaseous phase result.[3]

$$Liquid \rightarrow solid + gas.$$

The solid and gas are, of course, themselves pure substances or mixtures of pure substances, recognizable by their properties. For simplicity we shall assume that the solid and gas phase are each constituted of a single pure substance.

The solid in the above change generally presents no special problem, but it should be examined further to see if it is truly an element or is itself resolvable. On the other hand, it has already been noted that the gaseous state of matter posed a particular problem. For a long time it was thought that there was only one gaseous state, the air in which we live, and that all gases were air, but air which was slightly tainted or modified. In order to apply Boyle's definition, we must know something about gases — is only one or are there many? If there are many, how do we recognize them? Van Helmont (1577–1644), sometimes called the father of pneumatic chemistry, was the first to recognize that there existed gaseous substances distinct from the air in which we live. Among the gaseous substances prepared by Van Helmont were those known today as carbon dioxide, hydrogen, and sulfur dioxide. He recognized these gaseous substances as being unique and that they should be treated in a similar manner to the more tangible liquid and solid substances. But the view that all gases were modifications of air persisted on into the 18th century. Now if we can take a liquid and resolve it into a solid and a gas in order to specify the components into which the liquid was resolvable, we must know what the particular gas is. Is it an element, not further resolvable, or a compound? That is, we need information on the different

---

[2] See A. R. Hall, *The Scientific Revolution*, Beacon Press, Boston, 1956, pp. 320–323.

[3] The problem of resolution techniques is not a simple one, and it will not be discussed here. Suffice it to say that for a long time heating was thought to be the only method of resolution.

gases, their make-up and properties. This development was taking place in the 100 years that separated Boyle and Lavoisier.

There is the possibility that in the resolution of a liquid into a solid and a gas something has perhaps been overlooked. In particular, an elusive gas may have escaped notice, since in trying to collect this gaseous product, one or more gases may have dissolved in the water over which the gas was collected. We could be sure that such was not the case if the weight of the liquid equalled the weight of the solid plus the weight of the gas, and the law of conservation of weight were accepted; that is, a balance must be used in studying chemical reactions to make certain by weighing that all matter is accounted for.

The Scottish chemist Black (1728–1799) is largely responsible for making the balance an indispensable piece of laboratory equipment. In a paper published in 1756, he reported, along with other studies, the transformation of what we today call basic magnesium carbonate into another solid, magnesium oxide, and a gas, carbon dioxide, and the subsequent conversion of the oxide back into basic magnesium carbonate from which the oxide was initially prepared. In each step he used the balance to keep account of all matter involved. His success in studying these reactions influenced other chemists to use the balance in the same manner and to study gases.

In 1789 Lavoisier in the preface to his *Elements of Chemistry* restated Boyle's definition as follows [4]:

All that can be said upon the number and nature of elements is, in my opinion, confined to discussions entirely of a metaphysical nature. The subject only furnishes us with indefinite problems, which may be solved in a thousand different ways, not one of which, in all probability, is consistent with nature. I shall therefore only add upon this subject, that if, by the term elements, we mean to express those simple and indivisible atoms of which matter is composed, it is extremely probable we know nothing at all about them; but, if we apply the term elements, or principles of bodies, to express our idea of the last point which analysis is capable of reaching, we must admit as elements all the substances into which we are capable, by any means, to reduce bodies by decomposition. Not that we are entitled to affirm that these substances we consider as simple may not be compounded of two, or even of a greater number of principles; but, since these principles cannot be separated, or rather since we have not hitherto discovered the means of separating them, they act with regard to us as simple substances, and we ought never to suppose them compounded until experiment and observation has proved them to be so.

This is essentially the modern definition of element. Armed with such a definition and some of the techniques at hand to apply it, chemists by the end of the 18th century recognized about 23 elements. Most of these

---

[4] Antoine Lavoisier, *Elements of Chemistry*, Book I, Henry Regnery Co., Chicago, 1949, p. 11.

were also known by the ancients but were not recognized by them for what they were. At the end of the 18th century, many pure substances known to us today to be compounds had to be considered elemental because the means of separating them into their components had yet to be discovered. Notable in this group are the oxides of what are now called the alkali metals and alkaline earth metals. The means of separating these pure substances into their elemental components was discovered at the beginning of the 19th century through the use of Volta's cell.

Before returning to our classification scheme, let us consider Lavoisier's contribution to a parallel problem, that of nomenclature of pure substances. Prior to Lavoisier the names of various substances generally bore little or no relation to the composition of the substances. For example, the term " blue vitriol " applied to a substance tells us little about its composition. Lavoisier along with several other French chemists drew up a system of nomenclature that forms the basis of that used today. In this system the name of a substance indicates the elements that enter into its composition. For example, blue vitriol was renamed copper sulfate, which conveys to the initiated the information that the substance is composed of copper, sulfur, and oxygen. When Lavoisier and his associates completed their work they issued a dictionary with the old and new names of about 700 substances. Besides its convenience, the new system shows that the idea of chemical individuality had become well established.

COMPLETION OF CLASSIFICATION SCHEME OF MATTER

We have seen that pure substances are either elements, not further reducible by ordinary chemical means, or compounds, reducible into two or more irreducible elements. We can now complete our classification-composition scheme by adding

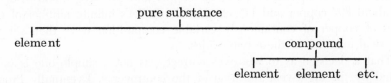

Now that we have arrived at the end of our classification scheme we note that a truly remarkable thing has occurred. Experience gained during a century or so of investigation after Lavoisier showed that among the diversity of matter encountered in nature there are hundreds of thousands of pure substances, but *all pure substances, and in turn all matter, are found to be composed of some 90 naturally occurring elements.* It is extremely fortunate that this simplification has resulted.

Before considering the conceptual level of the make-up of matter in the next chapter, there remains an experimental law relative to compounds to be considered.

THE CONTROVERSY BETWEEN BERTHOLLET AND PROUST; THE LAW OF DEFINITE PROPORTIONS

Between 1799 and 1808 there occurred a famous dispute between two French chemists, Berthollet and Proust, regarding compounds. The final resolution of this controversy resulted in the clarification of two facts regarding compounds: the number of compounds that could be produced from two pure substances (elements or compounds) and the composition of each compound produced. The discussion here for simplicity will be limited to the cases of compounds composed of two elements.

Berthollet contended from his experiments that in the case of certain pairs of elements chemical combination could result in an infinite series of compounds whose composition varied continuously within certain limits. However, if the compound was produced as a precipitate or gas, the infinite series was not obtained. Thus as one example, he claimed that copper upon being heated in the presence of oxygen combined with varying amounts of oxygen in continuous gradations by weight to form an infinite series of oxides of copper, wherein the percentage of copper varied continuously from about 80% to 89%, the remainder being oxygen. He was supported in this contention by the fact that copper upon being heated in the presence of oxygen gradually changes in appearance as more and more oxygen enters into combination with the copper.

Proust claimed in all the cases of combination of two elements cited by Berthollet that in reality only a limited number of compounds, two, were produced and that Berthollet's apparent infinite series of compounds were actually only a physical mixture of these two compounds. Thus in the case of the combination of copper and oxygen two oxides were possible, oxide I composed of about 80% copper and 20% oxygen and oxide II of about 89% copper and 11% oxygen. Berthollet's infinite number of oxides of copper of continuously variable composition were then simply physical mixtures of these two oxides.

That a decision as to who was correct was not a simple one is indicated by the eight-year duration of the controversy. Eventually Proust succeeded in convincing the majority of chemists of the correctness of his views that when two elements combine chemically the number of compounds possible is limited; in some cases it is one but quite often it is two as in the examples that caused the dispute. There are also cases where two elements can combine to produce more than two compounds, but never an infinite series. The same is also true of compounds composed of more than two elements. This is one important result of the Berthollet and Proust controversy.

Another important result was the establishment of the law of definite proportions of compounds. This law may be stated as follows: *A pure compound always has the same composition by weight for all samples of the compound regardless of the source.* For example in the case above, copper oxide I always has the composition 80% copper, 20% oxygen, whether prepared in the laboratory or found in nature. As another example pure water whether derived by such physical processes as filtration or distillation from the ocean, a river, or any other source, or chemically prepared in the laboratory, is always found to be composed of 8 parts of oxygen to 1 part of hydrogen by weight.

It is instructive to consider the Berthollet-Proust controversy in the light of our classification-composition scheme of matter. It will be recalled that the criteria a piece of matter must meet in order to be classified as a compound is that it be homogeneous, not be separable into two or more different phases by any physical process, and be composed of two or more elements. Berthollet thought he was dealing with a pure compound, whereas he was in reality dealing with a mixture of two compounds. It was first necessary to resolve the mixture into the two compounds, themselves not further resolvable by physical means, and then determine their compositions. That this clarification required eight years of effort on the part of two very able chemists indicates that the resolution of a mixture, particularly a homogeneous mixture or solution, into its components is not always easy in practice.

If Berthollet had been proven correct instead of Proust, the attack on the problem of relative atomic weights by Dalton would have been virtually impossible.

STUDY QUESTIONS

1. It is stated in the text that we recognize pure substances by their properties. Consider that you have a certain quantity of a pure substance before you. What do you understand by " the properties of the pure substance by which you recognize it "? In the following list pick out those properties that may be used in recognizing a *pure substance.*
   a. Melting point. b. Hardness. c. Mass. d. Temperature. e. Odor. The correct choice is

   (1) a and b   (2) a, c, and d   (3) a, b, and e   (4) a, b, c, d, and e
   (5) a, b, and d.

   If mass and volume are not properties that may be utilized in identifying a substance, how might a new quantity be defined in terms of these two that could be used?
   There are many properties that may serve to identify a substance. List as many as you can think of that might be used.

2. Chemical change is defined in the text. The chemical changes that a pure substance does or does not undergo constitute its chemical properties and are an aid in its identification.
   Which of the following are chemical properties?
   a. Extent of solubility of a substance in water.
   b. Substance combines readily with oxygen.
   c. Substance is a good conductor of electricity.
   d. Substance does not react with nitrogen at any temperature.
   e. Boiling point.
   The correct answer is

   (1) a and b   (2) b and c   (3) b and d   (4) b and e   (5) b.

3. Which of the following are examples of heterogeneous matter?
   a. Mixture of the gases nitrogen and oxygen.   b. " Homogenized " milk.
   c. Cast iron.   d. A sample of gneiss rock.   e. Quartz.
   The correct answer is

   (1) a, b, and c   (2) b, c, and d   (3) c, d, and e   (4) a, c, and d
   (5) b, d, and e.

   If you are unsure whether some of the above are heterogeneous, how would you go about deciding?

4. Consider a heterogeneous mixture of finely ground sand and iron. Devise at least two methods whereby the sand and iron might be quickly separated. What properties did you make use of in devising methods of separation?

5. Consider a homogeneous liquid, such as gasoline. How would you go about deciding whether the homogeneous liquid was a pure substance or a solution?

6. Consider two containers each containing a heretofore unknown, colorless, odorless, tasteless gas. How would you go about characterizing each by listing properties whereby each could be recognized?

7. Why do you think that it was only in comparatively recent times that the concept of element as we understand it today appeared?

8. Under the definition of element noted in the text, could a given substance be an element one day and a compound the next? In view of the periodic table, knowledge of atomic structure, etc., do you think this is likely to happen? In line with the above thought, can you suggest an alternate definition of element that uses the *mental* concept of the atom?

9. Refer to Lavoisier's definition of an element, " if we apply the term, elements . . . to express our idea of the last point which analysis is capable of reaching we must admit as element all the substances into which we are, *by any means*, to reduce bodies by decomposition." In view of this definition and the common knowledge that today atoms may be split to yield various other particles, how is the statement that there are only 92 naturally occurring elements to be understood?

10. Consider two elements A and B that combine to form two compounds. Compound I is 20% A and 80% B. Compound II is 80% A and 20% B. The compounds I and II form solid solutions in all proportions. Then an investigator, repeating Berthollet's mistake on the compounds of copper and oxygen, might be expected to claim that A and B do not combine in definite proportions by weight but form compounds whose composition varies over what range?

11. Consider a homogeneous solution of definite composition of sugar dissolved in water. Wherein does the solution differ from a pure substance?

24

Dalton's Atomic Theory

● John Dalton, like many others, made important contributions to science under the stimulus of the Newtonian influence. Dalton (Fig. 24-1) was born in 1766 at Eaglesfield in Cumberland, England, the son of poor Quaker parents. He received little formal education but at the age of 10 was known in the community for his intellectual competence. To help out the inadequate family income, he began to earn his own living at 12 by instructing in a school that he opened and at 15 taught in a school his brother was conducting. Throughout his life Dalton earned his living as a teacher in various positions. He devoted his spare time to research and to study.

Dalton was not initially a person whom we would classify today as a chemist. Meteorology was among his first interests, and this led him to a study of the atmosphere and gases, and these studies in turn led eventually to his atomic theory. In fact, his interest in the atmosphere was so great that he preferred to live on the meager income of a tutor so that he would have more free time to engage in weather observations. He made and recorded over two hundred thousand observations during his lifetime. His last entry in his notebook was made July 26, 1844, the day before he died at the age of 78.

A controversy exists as to the events leading up to Dalton's postulation of his atomic theory. According to one persuasive article,[1] there were probably two distinct phases in Dalton's development of his theory. He apparently first focused his attention on the particles of matter, in 1803, in an attempt to explain a physical problem, that of the variation in solubility of different gases in water. He conjectured that the variation in solubility was due to variations in the weights of the particles (atoms) that constituted different gases, the heavier the particles the more solu-

---

[1] L. K. Nash, "The Origin of Dalton's Chemical Atomic Theory," *Isis* (1956) Vol. 47, p. 101.

Figure 24-1. *John Dalton (1766–1844).*

ble the gas being in water. This conjecture in application did not prove too successful, and Dalton, confusing the theory itself with its application to this particular problem, appears to have lost interest. At this time he had had little experience in chemistry and apparently did not appreciate the possible import of his theory to chemistry.

About a year later in 1804, several events occurred which rekindled Dalton's interest in the theory. First was the interest of Thomas Thomson, an experienced Scottish chemist, in the possible applications of the theory to chemistry. Secondly, Dalton in the course of his experiments had detected an example of the law of multiple proportions (see Chap. 25) which is explainable in terms of the atomic theory. Thirdly, Dalton for several years had been concerned with the problem of the homogeneity of the atmosphere which is composed mainly of a mixture of nitrogen, oxygen, and water vapor. He saw in the atomic theory a possible explanation of this problem.

Dalton's explanation of the homogeneity of the atmosphere on the basis of the atomic theory contains an important point that bears on the later development of the theory. He pictured the gaseous state of a gas A as one in which the ultimate particles or atoms of A were surrounded by envelopes of heat, a weightless fluid called *caloric*. This envelope of heat about each individual atom was the origin of the repulsive force between the atoms which resulted in the tendency of gases to expand. He thought and demonstrated to his satisfaction that, if the atoms plus caloric envelopes were of different sizes for the different constituents of a gaseous mixture, the spheres of unequal size in contact could never come to equilibrium, and thus the heavier particles would not settle to the bottom. Thus the homogeneity of the atmosphere would be explained. This led Dalton to visualize a variation in the sizes of the atoms of gases.

Having once again become interested in the relative weights and sizes of atoms, Dalton cast about for a possible method of determining these relative weights. He at first considered the specific gravities of gases relative to air as a measure, though not completely reliable, of the relative weights of particles of a gas. The assumed variation in the size of the atom plus caloric envelope for different gases could invalidate a direct relation between specific gravities and particle weights. However, it will be noted later that Dalton does give some weight to specific gravity as a measure of particle weight.

Dalton finally seized on a chemical approach to the relative weights of atoms. He attempted to establish a link between the experimental fact that a compound is composed of elements in a definite proportion by weight and the relative weights of the atoms of the elements constituting the compound. It is chiefly the problem of effecting this linkage that we shall read about later in Dalton's text.

Let us first consider the problem of the link by means of an example. In the laboratory we have before us two substances A and B each of which satisfies Lavoisier's definition of an element. Substances A and B are observed to react to form a compound C, and the formation of 11 pounds of C is found to require 1 pound of A and 10 pounds of B (law of definite proportions). Now let us move to the imagined atomic scale, and suppose that in forming the compound C, 1 atom of A " comes together " with 1 atom of B to form the particle that constitutes the compound C. Note that no decision is made or attempted on the total number of atoms involved in any particular reaction, only the relative number; that is, 1 atom of A to 1 of B or 1 atom of A to 2 of B, et cetera. Symbolically the situation is as follows on the atomic scale,

$$\textcircled{A} + \textcircled{B} \rightarrow \textcircled{A}\textcircled{B}$$

where $\textcircled{A}$ represents an atom of A, $\textcircled{B}$ an atom of B and $\textcircled{A}\textcircled{B}$ a particle of compound C. On the laboratory scale,

$$1 \text{ lb. of } A + 10 \text{ lbs. of } B \rightarrow 11 \text{ lbs. of } C.$$

If the atomic scale picture is the correct one, then from the observed weight relations in the laboratory the atom of B must weigh 10 times as much as the atom of A, and we have determined the relative atomic weights. In making the supposition that 1 atom of A " comes together " with 1 atom of B, we have created the link by means of which the relative atomic weights can be determined from the combining weight data.

On the other hand, let us suppose 1 atom of A "comes together" with 2 atoms of B in forming the particle of the compound C. Then on the atomic scale,

$$\text{(A)} + \text{(B)} + \text{(B)} \rightarrow \begin{smallmatrix} \text{(B)} & \text{(B)} \\ & \text{(A)} \end{smallmatrix}$$

and on the laboratory scale,

1 lb. of A + 10 lbs. of B → 11 lbs. of C.

It is easily deduced that under these conditions the atom of B must weigh 5 times as much as the atom of A.

The problem is which of the two above suppositions, or any others that may be imagined, regarding the relative numbers of atoms of A and B involved is the correct one. Once the relative numbers of atoms involved are known, it is a simple step to the relative atomic weights. To repeat, the relative number of atoms involved is the connecting link whereby the observed weight relations in the laboratory can be translated into relative atomic weights. The connecting link whereby Dalton bridges the gap is contained in his seven rules on page 304. These rules furnish criteria whereby a decision can be made regarding the relative numbers of atoms involved in forming a particular compound. Eventually these rules proved to be an unsatisfactory link, but they were valuable in Dalton's initial attack on the problem.

We start our original quotations from Dalton with portions of Chapters II and III from his text *A New System of Chemical Philosophy* published in 1808. In Chapter II, after a preliminary discussion as to how it is possible for a substance to be either liquid, solid, or gas through the process of adding or subtracting heat, he seeks to justify the atomic conception of matter. In Chapter III, he first discusses the nature of chemical union and pictures it as involving atoms. The conclusion of Chapter III contains the heart of Dalton's contribution, his seven rules, which form the link whereby relative atomic weights can be determined from the observed combining weights.

A NEW SYSTEM OF CHEMICAL PHILOSOPHY [2]

by John Dalton

Chapter II

On the Constitution of Bodies

There are three distinctions in the kinds of bodies, or three states, which have more especially claimed the attention of philosophical chemists; namely, those which are marked by the terms *elastic fluids* [gases], *liquids, and solids.* A very

---

[2] John Dalton, *A New System of Chemical Philosophy*, Part I, R. Bickerstaff, London, 1808, pp. 141–144; 211–216; 219–220; Plate IV.

familiar instance is exhibited to us in water, of a body, which, in certain circumstances, is capable of assuming all the three states. In steam we recognise a perfectly elastic fluid, in water, a perfect liquid, and in ice a complete solid. These observations have tacitly led to the conclusion which seems universally adopted, that all bodies of sensible magnitude, whether liquid or solid, are constituted of a vast number of extremely small particles, or atoms of matter bound together by a force of attraction, which is more or less powerful according to circumstances, and which as it endeavours to prevent their separation, is very properly called in that view, *attraction of cohesion;* but as it collects them from a dispersed state (as from steam into water) it is called *attraction of aggregation,* or more simply, *affinity.* What ever names it may go by, they still signify one and the same power. It is not my design to call in question this conclusion, which appears completely satisfactory; but to shew that we have hitherto made no use of it, and that the consequence of the neglect, has been a very obscure view of chemical agency, which is daily growing more so in proportion to the new lights attempted to be thrown upon it.

The opinions I more particularly allude to, are those of Berthollet on the Laws of chemical affinity; such as that chemical agency is proportional to the mass, and that in all chemical unions, there exist insensible gradations in the proportions of the constituent principles.[3] The inconsistence of these opinions, both with reason and observation, cannot, I think, fail to strike every one who takes a proper view of the phenomena.

Whether the ultimate particles of a body, such as water, are all alike, that is, of the same figure, weight, etc. is a question of some importance. From what is known, we have no reason to apprehend a diversity in these particulars: if it does exist in water, it must equally exist in the elements constituting water, namely, hydrogen and oxygen. Now it is scarcely possible to conceive how the aggregates of dissimilar particles should be so uniformly the same. If some of the particles of water were heavier than others, if a parcel of the liquid on any occasion were constituted principally of these heavier particles, it must be supposed to affect the specific gravity of the mass, a circumstance not known. Similar observations may be made on other substances. Therefore we may conclude that *the ultimate particles of all homogeneous bodies are perfectly alike in weight, figure, etc.* In other words, every particle of water is like every other particle of water; every particle of hydrogen is like every other particle of hydrogen, etc.

Besides the force of attraction, which, in one character or another, belongs universally to ponderable bodies, we find another force that is likewise universal, or acts upon all matter which comes under our cognisance, namely, a force of repulsion. This is now generally, and I think properly, ascribed to the agency of heat. An atmosphere of this subtile fluid constantly surrounds the atoms of all bodies, and prevents them from being drawn into actual contact. This appears to be satisfactorily proved by the observation, that the bulk of a body may be diminished by abstracting some of its heat; but from what has been stated in the last section, it should seem that enlargement and diminution of bulk depend perhaps more on the arrangement, than on the size of the ultimate particles. Be this as it may, we cannot avoid inferring from the preceding

---

[3] See Chapter 23, discussion on Berthollet and Proust.

doctrine on heat, and particularly from the section on the natural zero of temperature, that solid bodies, such as ice, contain a large portion, perhaps 4/5 of the heat which the same are found to contain in an elastic state, as steam.

✻   ✻   ✻   ✻   ✻   ✻   ✻

Chapter III
On Chemical Synthesis

When any body exists in the elastic state, its ultimate particles are separated from each other to a much greater distance than in any other state; each particle occupies the centre of a comparatively large sphere, and supports its dignity by keeping all the rest, which by their gravity, or otherwise are disposed to encroach upon it, at a respectful distance. When we attempt to conceive the *number* of particles in an atmosphere, it is somewhat like attempting to conceive the number of stars in the universe; we are confounded with the thought. But if we limit the subject, by taking a given volume of any gas, we seem persuaded that, let the divisions be ever so minute, the number of particles must be finite; just as in a given space of the universe, the number of stars and planets cannot be infinite.

Chemical analysis and synthesis go no farther than to the separation of particles one from another, and to their reunion. No new creation or destruction of matter is within the reach of chemical agency. We might as well attempt to introduce a new planet into the solar system, or to annihilate one already in existence, as to create or destroy a particle of hydrogen. All the changes we can produce, consist in separating particles that are in a state of cohesion or combination, and joining those that were previously at a distance.

In all chemical investigations, it has justly been considered an important object to ascertain the relative *weights* of the simples which constitute a compound. But unfortunately the enquiry has terminated here; whereas from the relative weights in the mass, the relative weights of the ultimate particles or atoms of the bodies might have been inferred, from which their number and weight in various other compounds would appear, in order to assist and to guide future investigations, and to correct their results. Now it is one great object of this work, to shew the importance and advantage of ascertaining *the relative weights of the ultimate particles, both of simple and compound bodies, the number of simple elementary particles which constitute one compound particle, and the number of less compound particles which enter into the formation of one more compound particle.*

Let us pause here to examine the meanings Dalton apparently attaches to various terms, such as " ultimate particle," and " atom." The problem of the meaning or definition of terms is one of the most important and difficult that will confront us in this and following chapters. Different scientists attach different meanings to the same term or use different terms to mean the same thing. The reader must guard against attaching his own meaning to a term and must accept that of the author he is reading at a particular time. The modern definitions of such terms as atom and molecule are one of the products of the early gropings in the various papers we are considering.

Let us first examine the meaning Dalton attaches to "ultimate particle" when used in reference to elements and compounds. Imagine we have before us a certain quantity of a pure substance, either an element or a compound according to Lavoisier's definitions. This pure substance has certain chemical properties by which we recognize it. In our imagination let us cut this quantity in half, then halve one of these halves, and assume this process is continued many times. Eventually in the case of an element, according to the Daltonian view, we arrive at a quantity which cannot be further subdivided that still has the identical chemical properties of the element. And this quantity, which is a particle since it cannot be subdivided, Dalton would call the ultimate particle of the element. In the case of a compound we eventually in our subdivision process arrive at a quantity or particle which if further subdivided yields particles no longer having the chemical properties of the original substance. The last particle of subdivision having the chemical properties of the original compound is called by Dalton the "ultimate particle" of the compound. There are methods whereby this ultimate particle can be subdivided into its constituent particles, but these constituent particles no longer would have the chemical properties of the original compound. They would be the particles of the elements that make up the compound. Synonymous terms used by Dalton for the ultimate particle of an element are "atom" and "simple elementary particle." Dalton also uses the term "atom" to designate the ultimate particle of a compound, where the ultimate particle of a compound is to be understood as explained above. He also uses "compound particle" occasionally to designate the ultimate particle of a compound.

In the problems when the term "atom" is used to signify the ultimate particle of a compound, it will always be enclosed by quotation marks, since the meaning is so contrary to modern terminology. Atom without quotation marks will refer to the ultimate particles of elements in the Daltonian sense.

If there are two bodies, A and B, which are disposed to combine, the following is the order in which the combinations may take place, beginning with the most simple: namely,

1 atom	of A + 1 atom	of B = 1 atom	of C, binary.
1 atom	of A + 2 atoms	of B = 1 atom	of D, ternary.
2 atoms	of A + 1 atom	of B = 1 atom	of E, ternary.
1 atom	of A + 3 atoms	of B = 1 atom	of F, quaternary.
3 atoms	of A + 1 atom	of B = 1 atom	of G, quaternary.

etc. etc.

The following general rules may be adopted as guides in all our investigations respecting chemical synthesis.

1st. When only one combination of two bodies can be obtained, it must be presumed to be a *binary* one, unless some cause appear to the contrary.

2nd. When two combinations are observed, they must be presumed to be a *binary* and a *ternary*.

3rd. When three combinations are obtained, we may expect one to be a *binary*, and the other two *ternary*.

4th. When four combinations are observed, we should expect one *binary*, two *ternary*, and one *quaternary*, etc.

5th. A *binary* compound should always be specifically heavier than the mere mixture of its two ingredients.

6th. A *ternary* compound should be specifically heavier than the mixture of a binary and a simple, which would, if combined, constitute it; etc.

7th. The above rules and observations equally apply, when two bodies such as C and D, D and E, etc. are combined.

These seven rules are the means whereby Dalton sought to bridge the gap between that which could be demonstrated in the laboratory and the mentally imagined atom in order to be able to determine the relative weights of the atoms of the various elements.

The origin of rules 1–4 is obvious; lacking any direct knowledge of the number of atoms of A and B that combined to produce the "atoms" that make up a compound, he assumed the situation was the simplest possible. For example in rule 1, if two "bodies" (elements or compounds) combine to produce only one compound, then the "atoms" of the compound must consist of one atom of A and one atom of B, if A and B are elements and one "atom" of A and one "atom" of B if A and B are compounds.

Rules 5 and 6 stated here by Dalton are readily applicable only to gaseous reactants that produce gaseous products and have their origin in Dalton's "picture" of the gaseous state, which was the commonly accepted theory at that time. As previously noted according to this view, each atom was assumed to be surrounded by an envelope of heat which was in contact with the heat envelopes of the adjacent atoms. Dalton imagined this heat envelope about an atom to be globular in shape, the density of the heat fluid being greatest near the atom and decreasing with distance from the atom. The size of the heat envelope of a gaseous substance was considered to be many times greater than the size of the atom itself and to vary in size for different atoms. Extraction of heat resulted in a contraction of the size of the envelope and thus in the volume occupied by the gas. Addition of heat increased the size of the envelope and caused the gas to expand. Graphically an atom of A surrounded by its heat envelope is indicated in Figure 24-2. An atom of A and an atom B of another substance before reacting would appear as shown in Figure 24-3. Now if the atoms of A and B react to produce a binary compound, the atoms of A and B, in "coming together" to produce the "atom" AB of the binary compound, "squeeze out" the heat originally between the

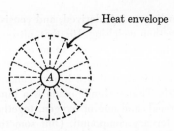

Figure 24-2. *Dalton's concept of the heat envelope about an atom A.*

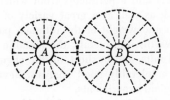

Figure 24-3. *Dalton's concept of atoms A and B before reacting.*

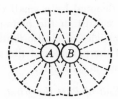

Figure 24-4. *Dalton's concept of the " atom " AB and its heat envelope.*

atoms A and B. The heat squeezed out would manifest itself as the heat evolved during the reaction. The " atom " of AB would be as illustrated in Figure 24-4. The volume of the " atom " AB would be less than the sum of the volumes of the unreacted atoms of A and B. Hence the specific gravity of the gaseous compound would be greater than the specific gravity of the mixture of the gases that yielded the compound upon reaction. Or as Dalton states it, " A binary compound should always be specifically heavier than the mere mixture of its two ingredients."

From the application of these rules, to the chemical facts already well ascertained, we deduce the following conclusions; 1st. That water is a binary compound of hydrogen and oxygen, and the relative weights of the two elementary atoms are as 1 : 7, nearly; 2d. That ammonia is a binary compound of hydrogen and azote [nitrogen], and the relative weights of the two atoms are as 1 : 5, nearly; 3d. That nitrous gas is a binary compound of azote and oxygen, the atoms of which weigh 5 and 7 respectively; that nitric acid is a binary or ternary compound according as it is derived, and consists of one atom of azote and two of oxygen, together weighing 19; that nitrous oxide is a compound similar to nitric acid, and consists of one atom of oxygen and two of azote, weighing 17; that nitrous acid is a binary compound of nitric acid and nitrous gas, weighing 31; that oxynitric acid is a binary compound of nitric acid and oxygen, weighing 26; 4th. That carbonic oxide is a binary compound, consisting of one atom of charcoal, and one of oxygen, together weighing nearly 12; that carbonic acid is a ternary compound, (but sometimes binary) consisting of one atom of charcoal, and two of oxygen, weighing 19; etc. etc. In all these cases the weights are expressed in atoms of hydrogen, each of which is denoted by unity.

In the sequel, the facts and experiments from which these conclusions are derived, will be detailed; as well as a great variety of others from which are inferred the constitution and weight of the ultimate particles of the principal acids, the alkalies, the earths, the metals, the metallic oxides and sulphurets, the long train of neutral salts, and in short, all the chemical compounds which have hitherto obtained a tolerably good analysis. Several of the conclusions will be supported by original experiments.

From the novelty as well as importance of the ideas suggested in this chapter, it is deemed expedient to give plates [Fig. 24-5], exhibiting the mode of combination in some of the more simple cases. A specimen of these accompanies this first part. The elements or atoms of such bodies as are conceived at present to be simple, are denoted by a small circle, with some distinctive mark; and the combinations consist in the juxta-position of two or more of these; when three or more particles of elastic fluids are combined together in one, it is to be supposed that the particles of the same kind repel each other, and therefore take their stations accordingly.

End of Part the First

This plate [Fig. 24-5] contains the arbitrary marks or signs chosen to represent the several chemical elements or ultimate particles.

Fig.			Fig.		
1. Hydrog. its rel. weight . .	1		11. Strontites, ...	46
2. Azote, ...	5		12. Barytes, ...	68
3. Carbone or charcoal, . .	5		13. Iron, ...	38
4. Oxygen, ...	7		14. Zinc, ...	56
5. Phosphorus, ...	9		15. Copper, ...	56
6. Sulphur, ...	13		16. Lead, ...	95
7. Magnesia, ...	20		17. Silver, ...	100
8. Lime, ...	23		18. Platina, ...	100
9. Soda, ...	28		19. Gold, ...	140
10. Potash, ...	42		20. Mercury, ...	167

21. An atom of water or steam, composed of 1 of oxygen and 1 of hydrogen, retained in physical contact by a strong affinity, and supposed to be surrounded by a common atmosphere of heat; its relative weight = ... 8

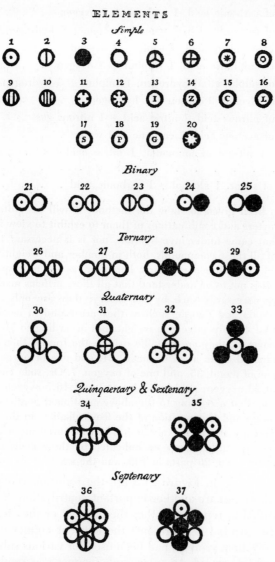

Figure 24-5. *Dalton's symbols for the elements.*

22. An atom of ammonia, composed of 1 of azote and 1 of hydrogen .   6
23. An atom of nitrous gas, composed of 1 of azote and 1 of oxygen .   12
24. An atom of olefiant gas, composed of 1 of carbone and 1 of hydrogen   6
25. An atom of carbonic oxide composed of 1 of carbone and 1 of oxygen   12
26. An atom of nitrous oxide, 2 azote + 1 oxygen   17
27. An atom of nitric acid, 1 azote + 2 oxygen   19

28. An atom of carbonic acid, 1 carbone + 2 oxygen 19
29. An atom of carburetted hydrogen, 1 carbone + 2 hydrogen . . 7
30. An atom of oxynitric acid, 1 azote + 3 oxygen 26
31. An atom of sulphuric acid, 1 sulphur + 3 oxygen 34
32. An atom of sulphuretted hydrogen, 1 sulphur + 3 hydrogen . . 16
33. An atom of alcohol, 3 carbon + 1 hydrogen 16
34. An atom of nitrous acid, 1 nitric acid + 1 nitrous gas 31
35. An atom of acetous acid, 2 carbone + 2 water 26
36. An atom of nitrate of ammonia, 1 nitric acid + 1 ammonia + 1 water 33
37. An atom of sugar, 1 alcohol + 1 carbonic acid 35

Enough has been given to shew the method; it will be quite unnecessary to devise characters and combinations of them to exhibit to view in this way all the subjects that come under investigation; nor is it necessary to insist upon the accuracy of all these compounds, both in number and weight; the principle will be entered into more particularly hereafter, as far as respects the individual results. It is not to be understood that all those articles marked as simple substances, are necessarily such by the theory; they are only necessarily of such weights. Soda and Potash, such as they are found in combination with acids, are 28 and 42 respectively in weight; but according to Mr. Davy's very important discoveries, they are metallic oxides; the former then must be considered as composed of an atom of metal, 21, and one of oxygen, 7; and the latter of an atom of metal, 35, and one of oxygen, 7. Or, soda contains 75 percent metal and 25 oxygen; potash, 83.3 metal and 16.7 oxygen. It is particularly remarkable, that according to the above-mentioned gentleman's essay on the Decomposition and Composition of the fixed alkalies, in the Philosophical Transactions (a copy of which essay he has just favoured me with) it appears that " the largest quantity of oxygen indicated by these experiments was for potash 17, and for soda, 26 parts in 100, and the smallest 13 and 19." [4]

The symbols given in Figure 24-5 are the forerunners of the modern chemical symbols and are another important contribution of Dalton. Dalton uses a symbol to represent either the element or the atom of the element. Thus the symbol © represents the element copper or the copper atom. Prior to Dalton, symbols had been used for various substances, both elementary and compound. As an example, copper was symbolized by ♀, which signified copper in any amount.

There are two advantages to Dalton's symbols. When used to represent the atoms they have a quantitative as well as a qualitative significance since © not only stands for copper, but for one atom of copper of definite weight relative to the hydrogen atom. Secondly, the symbols of atoms

---

[4] The work of Davy referred to here was his decomposition of sodium and potassium oxides by means of an electric current (electrolysis). Prior to Davy's work the compounds sodium oxide and potassium oxide were regarded as elements, as their decomposition had not been accomplished. Lavoisier suspected their compound nature but did not possess the means of resolution by an electric current.

were placed in juxtaposition to represent the "atom" of a compound, thereby indicating the elemental composition of the compound. Thus $\odot\bigcirc$ represents Dalton's binary "atom" of water composed of a hydrogen and an oxygen atom.

For convenience, Dalton's symbolism by which an atom of the element Alpha was represented by Ⓐ will be simplified by omitting the circle. Thus

$$A + B \to AB$$

means that one atom of element Alpha combines with one atom of element Beta to form one "atom" AB of the compound. Henceforth in discussing the atomic constitution of actual compounds we shall use the modern symbols, such as H for hydrogen and O for oxygen, that date from Berzelius (1814). Thus when we discuss Dalton's view that the "atom" of water is composed of one atom of hydrogen and one atom of oxygen we will symbolize the "atom" of water as HO. In the case where twice as many atoms of Alpha as of Beta are involved,

$$2A + B \to A_2B.$$

In setting up a system for determining atomic weights, Dalton arbitrarily assigned hydrogen, the lightest, a value of unity which we may call 1 atomic weight unit (1 a.w.u.). The relation between the atomic weight unit and some other unit of weight, such as the pound, was not known or necessary at that time. Hereafter, the statement that the atomic weight of an atom is 20 means that it weighs 20 times as much as a hydrogen atom or 20 a.w.u.

STUDY QUESTIONS

1. Apparently the basis on which Dalton (from his text) and others tacitly concluded that atoms exist was

   (1) the evidence stated in the writings of the ancient Greeks
   (2) that the alternate conclusion of continuously divisible matter was inconceivable
   (3) the existence of three states of matter (gas, liquid, and solid) and in particular that water could assume all three states
   (4) that the existence of the three states of matter could be explained on the basis of the assumed atoms plus the assumption of an attractive force between the atoms and a repulsive force due to heat
   (5) that the experimentally proven law of definite proportions could be readily explained by assuming the existence of atoms.

2. Dalton defines the term atom as meaning

   (1) the extremely small particles of which all bodies are constituted
   (2) the smallest particle of which an element is composed

(3) the particle which is not capable of further subdivision by ordinary chemical or physical means

(4) the ultimate particle of matter composed of neutrons, protons, and electrons

(5) those particles which constitute the molecule.

3. Bearing in mind that Dalton was aware that water could be decomposed into hydrogen and oxygen, what apparently does he mean by the conclusion that " the ultimate particles " of water and all other homogeneous bodies are alike?

4. What observations does Dalton make regarding the forces of attraction that exist between atoms?

5. Dalton believes the force of repulsion that operates between the particles that constitute a body (gas, liquid or solid) is

(1) electrical in nature

(2) due to heat, a subtle fluid that surrounds the atoms

(3) due to heat, which is a manifestation of the kinetic energy of the atoms

(4) magnetic in nature; unlike poles attract, like repel

(5) due to the actual physical contact of the atoms which occurs on compression.

6. Explain the relation that Dalton thought existed between the properties of an element and the atom of that element; the properties of a compound and the " atom " of the compound.

7. Which of the following is the probable origin of Dalton's seven rules?

(1) These rules were based on experience. For example, Dalton knew there were two compounds of carbon and oxygen; one composed of one atom of oxygen and one atom of carbon, the other of 2 atoms of oxygen and one atom of carbon, as well as similar examples. Knowing this, he formulated general rules and thought these rules would extrapolate to unknown cases.

(2) These rules are nothing more than "common-sense" — if only one compound of A and B is known then obviously it is composed of one atom of A and one atom of B, etc.

(3) In the face of the unknown, Dalton did the only thing possible at the time; he assumed the facts covering the combination of atoms were the simplest possible.

(4) These rules are in reality just another way of stating what is contained in the periodic table, which contains information on weights of atoms and valences.

(5) Knowing the relative weights of the atoms and the ratio in which the elements combined to form a compound, the formula of the compound could be deduced. These rules fit the known results.

8. According to Dalton's rules if two elements A and B combine to form four different compounds and the atomic constitution of three of the " atoms " that go to make up three of the compounds are AB, A_2B, AB_2, then the atomic constitution of the " atoms " of the fourth compound might be

(1) A_2B (2) AB_3 (3) A_3B_2 (4) A_2B_2 (5) A_4B.

9. Consider a reaction in which two gases A and B react to produce a gaseous product C. What statement can be made about the volume of the product

as compared to the volumes of the reactants A and B according to Dalton's rules 5 and 6?

10. Suppose 1 volume of gas A of specific gravity 1 reacts with 1 volume of gas B of specific gravity 3 to produce a gaseous product C. Which of the following is the most restrictive statement that can be made about the specific gravity of gas C according to Dalton's rules 5 and 6? (Assume the volumes of gases A and B are additive upon mixing.) The specific gravity of gas C is

(1) between 1 and 3   (2) greater than 1   (3) greater than 3
(4) greater than 2   (5) greater than 2 but less than 3.

11. Suppose gas A reacts with gas B to produce a gaseous compound C. Further suppose that gaseous compound C in turn reacts with gas B to produce another gaseous compound D. Atomic constitutions of AB for compound C and AB_2 for compound D would be in harmony with the above observations. What other atomic constitutions are possible? Can a decision be made among the possible atomic constitutions of C and D on the basis of the relative specific gravities of C and D?

12. If there is only one known compound of the element A with hydrogen and from analysis this compound is found to consist of 18 lbs. of A with 3 lbs. of hydrogen, then the atomic weight of A relative to hydrogen as 1 must be, according to Dalton,

(1) 3   (2) 6   (3) 9   (4) 1.5   (5) 12.

13–14. A compound from laboratory analysis is found to be composed of 1 lb. of A and 2.5 lbs. of B. The atomic weight of B is accepted as 20.

13. If this is the only known compound of A and B, then according to Dalton it must be binary and the atomic weight of A is

(1) 12   (2) 2   (3) 16   (4) 4   (5) 8.

14. If from other evidence the atomic constitution is believed to be A_2B, then the atomic weight of A is

(1) 8   (2) 2   (3) 16   (4) 4   (5) 12.

15. A compound upon analysis is found to be 60% A and 40% B. If the atomic weight of A is 15 and this is the only known compound of A and B, then the atomic weight of B is, according to Dalton,

(1) 40   (2) 30   (3) 10   (4) 20   (5) 5.

A little reflection will show that if we know any two of the items, combining weights, atomic constitution and atomic weights, the third can be determined. Above we have taken as known the combining weights and the atomic constitution and deduced the atomic weights. Problems 16–18 below illustrate the remaining two possibilities.

16. The atomic constitution of the " atoms " of a compound has been deduced to be A_2B_3. The atomic weight of A is 10 and that of B is 12. Then 5 lbs. of A would combine with how many lbs. of B?

(1) 12   (2) 24   (3) 36   (4) 6   (5) 9.

17. The elements A and B combine in the weight ratio 1.5 parts of B with 1 of A. The atomic weight of A is 12 and the atomic weight of B is 30. The atomic composition of the " atoms " of the compound is

(1) AB   (2) A_2B (3) A_2B_3 (4) A_5B_3 (5) A_3B_2.

18. Accepting Dalton's table of atomic weights and his atomic composition for carbonic acid (page 306), the number of lbs. of carbon combined with 21 lbs. of oxygen in carbonic acid is

(1) 5   (2) 10   (3) 16   (4) 7.5   (5) 3.3.

19. Imagine three substances A, B, and C, either elements or compounds, capable of reacting in pairs with each other. Further imagine the three compounds so formed are binary, AB, AC, BC. Let the weights of the atoms or " atoms " of A, B, and C be respectively 5, 10, and 15. What would be the ratio of the weight of A to the weight of B reacting with a fixed weight of C? What would be the ratio of the weight of A to the weight of B that combine with each other? (The above weight relations, deduced from the postulates of Dalton's atomic theory, can be summarized in the general statement, " When three elements A, B, and C, combine in pairs, the weights of A and B which combine with a fixed weight of C are in the same ratio as the weights of A and B that combine with each other." This is a statement of the law of equivalent or reciprocal proportions discovered experimentally by Richter between 1792 and 1802. Dalton apparently was not familiar with Richter's work, but the law is explicable in terms of Dalton's theory.)

25

Dalton: Compounds of Two Elements

● In this chapter portions of Chapter V of Dalton's text in which he discusses several groups of compounds including water, the oxides of nitrogen, and the oxides of carbon will be considered. He explains in particular the various methods of determining the quantitative compositions of these compounds and the application of his rules to this composition data in order to determine the relative weights of the atoms involved.

It will be noted that the value accepted by Dalton for the composition of water, 7 parts of oxygen to 1 of hydrogen by weight, differs from that accepted today, 8 of oxygen to 1 of hydrogen. The latter value of course is the more accurate; and the disagreement is due to various experimental errors, one of which, the presence of water vapor in a supposedly pure gas, is discussed by Dalton.

Dalton in treating the various oxides of nitrogen demonstrates that the compositions are in accord with the law of multiple proportions. Prior to Dalton the existence of the law of multiple proportions had been detected for special groups of compounds, but scientists were unaware of its general applicability to all cases where two substances react to form more than one compound. The law is discussed in detail at the conclusion of the section on the oxides of nitrogen (see page 318). Incidentally the atomic constitutions for the various oxides of nitrogen arrived at by Dalton are the ones accepted today. This is one of the few cases of agreement.

In the concluding section cited here Dalton discusses the two oxides of carbon, carbonic oxide and carbonic acid, both of which are gases. These two gases are known today as carbon monoxide and carbon dioxide respectively. The atomic constitution to be assigned to the "atoms" of these two gases gives him pause. Partly because of the fact that carbonic acid has a greater specific gravity than carbonic oxide, he concludes that the carbonic oxide "atom" has the atomic constitution CO and the carbonic acid "atom" the constitution CO_2. However he is not completely

313

satisfied with these compositions since the analytical data on relative weights could just as well be explained by C_2O for carbonic oxide and CO for carbonic acid.

Dalton is particularly hesitant in assigning atomic constitutions to these compounds of carbon because of the fact that carbon is known only in the solid state, and hence he possesses no indication of the relative atomic weight of the carbon atom from specific gravity data. Furthermore, the atom of carbon may be so light " that two atoms of it with one of oxygen (C_2O) may be specifically lighter than one with one (CO)." That is, Dalton says that if the following reaction could be made to occur,

carbonic acid (vol. V_1) + C (solid, negligible vol.)

$$\rightarrow \text{carbonic oxide (vol. } V_2),$$

that on the atomic scale we might have

$$CO + C \rightarrow C_2O.$$

And the carbonic oxide (atomic constitution C_2O) could have a smaller specific gravity than carbonic acid (atomic constitution CO) if the relative volume increase (V_2/V_1) is greater than the relative weight increase, due to the lightness of the carbon atom.

Dalton cites evidence that indicates to him that the weight of the carbon atom is of the same order of magnitude as that of the oxygen atom and adopts CO as the constitution of the " atoms " of carbonic oxide and CO_2 as the constitution of the " atoms " of carbonic acid. These are also the constitutions accepted today.

A NEW SYSTEM OF CHEMICAL PHILOSOPHY [1]

by John Dalton

Chapter 5

Compounds of Two Elements

In order to understand what is intended to be signified by binary and ternary compounds, etc. the reader is referred to pg. [303 + seq]. Some persons are used to denominate all compounds, where only two elements can be discovered, binary compounds; such, for instance, as nitrous gas, nitrous oxide, nitric acid, etc. in all of which we find only azote and oxygen. But it is more consistent with our views to restrict the term binary, to signify two atoms; ternary, to signify three atoms, etc. whether those atoms be elementary or otherwise, that is, whether they are the atoms of undecompounded bodies, as hydrogen and oxygen, or the atoms of compounded bodies, as water and ammonia.

In each of the following sections, we shall consider the compounds of some two of the elementary or undecompounded bodies; beginning each section with binary compounds, then proceeding to the ternary compounds, or at least to those which consist of *three* atoms, though they may be *binary* in the sense we use the term; and so on to the more complex forms.

[1] John Dalton, A New System of Chemical Philosophy, Part V, R. Bickerstaff, London, 1808, pp. 269–276; 316–319; 368–370.

This chapter will comprehend all the aeriform bodies that have not been considered in the last, several of the acids, the alkalies, the earths, and the metallic oxides, sulphurets, carburets, and phosphurets.

In treating of these articles, I intend to adopt the most common names for them; but it will be obvious, that if the doctrine herein contained be established, a renovation of the chemical nomenclature will in some cases be expedient.

Section 1
Oxygen with Hydrogen
1. Water

This liquid, the most useful and abundant of any in nature, is now well known both by analytic and synthetic methods, to be a compound of the two elements, oxygen and hydrogen.

Canton has proved that water is in degree compressible. The expansive effect of heat on water has been already pointed out. The weight of a cubic foot of water is very near 1000 ounces avoirdupoise. This fluid is commonly taken as the standard for comparing the specific gravities of bodies, its weight being denoted by unity.

Distilled water is the purest; next to that, rain water; then river water; and lastly, spring water. By purity in this place, is meant freedom from any foreign body in a state of solution; but in regard to transparency, and in agreeable taste, spring water generally excells the others. Pure water has the quality we call *soft*; spring and other impure water has the quality we call *hard*. Every one knows the great difference of waters in these respects; yet it is seldom that the hardest spring water contains so much as 1/1000 part of its weight of any foreign body in solution. The substances held in solution are usually carbonate and sulphate of lime.

Water usually contains about 2 per cent of its bulk of common air. This air is originally forced into it by the pressure of the atmosphere; and can be expelled again no other way than by removing that pressure. This may be done by an air-pump; or it may in great part be effected by subjecting the water to ebullition, in which case steam takes the place of the incumbent air, and its pressure is found inadequate to restrain the dilatation of the air in the water, which of course makes its escape. But it is difficult to expel all the air by either of those operations. Air expelled from common spring water, after losing 5 or 10 per cent of carbonic acid, consists of 38 per cent of oxygen and 62 of azote.

Water is distinguished for entering into combination with other bodies. To some it unites in a small definite proportion, constituting a solid compound. This is the case in its combination with the fixed alkalies, lime, and with a great number of salts; the compounds are either dry powders or crystals. Such compounds have received the name of *hydrates*. But when the water is in excess, a different sort of combination seems to take place, which is called *solution*. In this case, the compound is *liquid* and transparent; as when common salt or sugar are dissolved in water. When any body is thus dissolved in water, it may be uniformly diffused through any larger quantity of that liquid, and seems to continue so, without manifesting any tendency to subside, as far as is known.

In 1781, the composition and decomposition of water were ascertained; the former by Watt and Cavendish, and the latter by Lavoisier and Meusnier. The first experiment on the composition of water on a large scale, was made by Monge, in 1783; he procured about ¼ lb. of water, by the combustion of hydrogen gas, and noted the quantities of hydrogen and oxygen gas which had disappeared. The second experiment was made by Le Fevre de Gineau, in 1788; he obtained about 2½ lbs. of water in the same way. The third was made by Fourcroy, Vauquelin, and Seguin, in 1790, in which more than a pound of water was obtained. The general result was, that 85 parts by weight of oxygen unite to 15 of hydrogen to form 100 parts of water. Experiments to ascertain the proportion of the elements arising from the decomposition of water, were made by Le Fevre de Gineau and by Lavoisier, by transmitting steam through a red hot tube containing a quantity of soft iron wire; the oxygen of the water combined with the iron, and the hydrogen was collected in gas. The same proportion, or 85 parts of oxygen and 15 of hydrogen, were found as in the composition.

The Dutch chemists, Dieman and Troostwyk, first succeeded in decomposing water by electricity, in 1789. The effect is now produced readily by galvanism. The composition of water is easily and elegantly shewn, by means of Volta's eudiometer, an instrument of the greatest importance in researches concerning elastic fluids. It consists of a strong graduated glass tube, into which a wire is hermetically sealed, or strongly cemented; another detached wire is pushed up the tube, nearly to meet the former, so that an electric spark or shock can be sent from one wire to the other through any portion of gas, or mixture of gases, confined by water or mercury. The end of the tube being immersed in a liquid, when an explosion takes place, no communication with the external air can arise; so that the change produced is capable of being ascertained.

The component parts of water being clearly established, it becomes of importance to determine with as much precision as possible, the relative weights of the two elements constituting that liquid. The mean results of analysis and synthesis, have given 85 parts of oxygen and 15 of hydrogen, which are generally adopted. In this estimate, I think, the quantity of hydrogen is overrated. There is an excellent memoir in the 53rd vol. of the Annal. de Chemie, 1805, by Humboldt and Gay-Lussac, on the proportion of oxygen and hydrogen in water. They make it appear, that the quantity of aqueous vapor which elastic fluids usually contain, will so far influence the weight of hydrogen gas, as to change the more accurate result of Fourcroy, etc. of 85.7 oxygen and 14.3 hydrogen, to 87.4 oxygen and 12.6 hydrogen. Their reasoning appears to me perfectly satisfactory. The relation of these two numbers is that of 7 to 1 nearly. There is another consideration which seems to put this matter beyond doubt. In Volta's eudiometer, *two* measures of hydrogen require just *one* of oxygen to saturate them. Now, the accurate experiments of Cavendish and Lavoisier, have shewn that oxygen is nearly 14 times the weight of hydrogen; the exact coincidence of this with the conclusion above deduced, is a sufficient confirmation. If, however, any one chooses to adopt the common estimate of 85 to 15, then the relation of oxygen to hydrogen will be as 5⅔ to 1; this would require the weight of oxygeneous gas to be only 11⅓ times the weight of hydrogen.

The absolute weights of oxygen and hydrogen in water being determined, the relative weights of their atoms may be investigated. As only *one* compound of oxygen and hydrogen is certainly known, it is agreeable to the first rule, [pg. 304] that water should be concluded a *binary* compound; or, one atom of oxygen unites with one of hydrogen to form one of water. Hence, the relative weights of the atoms of oxygen and hydrogen are 7 to 1.

The above conclusion is strongly corroborated by other considerations. Whatever may be the proportions in which oxygen and hydrogen are mixed, whether 20 measures of oxygen to 2 of hydrogen, or 20 of hydrogen to 2 of oxygen, still when an electric spark is passed, water is formed by the union of 2 measures of hydrogen with 1 of oxygen, and the surplus gas is unchanged. Again, when water is decomposed by electricity, or by other agents, no other elements than oxygen and hydrogen are obtained. Besides, all the other compounds into which those two elements enter, will in the sequel be found to support the same conclusion.

After all, it must be allowed to be possible that water may be a ternary compound. In this case, if two atoms of hydrogen unite to one of oxygen, then an atom of oxygen must weigh 14 times as much as one of hydrogen; if two atoms of oxygen unite to one of hydrogen, then an atom of oxygen must weigh 3½ times one of hydrogen.

     ❀   ❀   ❀   ❀   ❀   ❀   ❀

Section 2
Oxygen with Azote

The compounds of oxygen with azote, hitherto discovered, are five; they may be distinguished by the following names; nitrous gas, nitric acid, nitrous oxide, nitrous acid, and oxynitric acid.[2] In treating of these, it has been usual to begin with that which contains the least oxygen, (nitrous oxide) and to take the others in order as they contain more oxygen. Our plan requires a different principle of arrangement; namely, to begin with that which is most simple, or which consists of the smallest number of elementary particles, which is commonly a binary compound, and then proceed to the ternary and other higher compounds. According to this principle, it becomes necessary to ascertain, if possible, whether any of the above, and which of them, is a binary compound. As far as the specific gravities of the two simple gases are indicative of the weights of their atoms, we should conclude that an atom of azote is to one of oxygen as 6 to 7 nearly; the relative weights of ammonia and water also give countenance to such a ratio. But the best criterion is derived from a comparison of the specific gravities of the compound gases themselves. Nitrous gas has the least specific gravity of any of them; this indicates it to be a binary compound; nitrous oxide and nitric acid are both much heavier; this indicates them to be ternary compounds; and the latter being heavier than the former, indicates that oxygen is heavier than azote, as oxygen is known to abound most in the latter. Let us now see how far the facts already known will corroborate these observations.

According to Cavendish and Davy, who are the best authorities we yet have in regard to these compounds, they are constituted as under:

[2] These gases are now known as nitric oxide (NO), nitrogen dioxide (NO_2), nitrous oxide (N_2O), nitrogen trioxide (N_2O_3), and nitrogen pentoxide (N_2O_5) respectively.

	Sp. gr.	Constitution by weight	Ratios	
Nitrous gas	1.102	46.6 azote + 53.4 Oxy.	6.1 : 7	Davy
		44.2 .... + 55.8 ...	5.5 : 7	
		42.3 .... + 57.7 ...	5.1 : 7	
Nitr. oxide	1.614	63.5 .... + 36.5 ...	2 × 6.1 : 7	
		62 .... + 38 ...	2 × 5.7 : 7	
		61 .... + 39 ...	2 × 5.4 : 7	
Nitric acid	2.444	29.5 .... + 70.5 ...	5.8 : 7 × 2	
		29.6 .... + 70.4 ...	5.9 : 7 × 2	Cavendish
		28 .... + 72 ...	5.4 : 7 × 2	
		25.3 .... + 74.5 ...	4.7 : 7 × 2	

The above table is principally taken from Davy's researches: where two or more results are given under one article, they are derived from different modes of analysis. In the third column are given the ratios of the weights of azote and oxygen in each compound, derived from the preceding column, and reduced to the determined weight of an atom of oxygen, 7. This table corroborates the theoretic views above stated most remarkably. The weight of an atom of azote appears to be between 5.4 and 6.1: and it is worthy of notice, that the theory does not differ more from the experiments than they differ from one another; or, in other words, the mean weight of an atom of azote derived from the above experiments would equally accommodate the theory and the experiments. The mean is 5.6, to which all the others might be reduced. We should then have an atom of nitrous gas to weigh 12.6, consisting of 1 atom of azote and 1 of oxygen; an atom of nitrous oxide to weigh 18.2, consisting of 2 atoms of azote and 1 of oxygen; and an atom of [nitric] acid to weigh 19.6, consisting of 1 atom of azote and 2 of oxygen. Nor has the weight of an atom of oxygen any influence on the theory of these compounds; for, it is obvious that if oxygen were taken 3, or 10, or any other number, still the ratios of azote to oxygen in the compounds would continue the same; the only difference would be, that the weight of an atom of azote would rise or fall in proportion as that of oxygen.

I have been solicitous to exhibit this view of the compounds of azote and oxygen, as derived from the experience of others, rather than from my own; because, not having had any views at all similar to mine, the authors could not have favored them by deducing the above results, if they had not been conformable to actual observation.

❋   ❋   ❋   ❋   ❋   ❋   ❋

In the preceding table, the first two columns, *specific gravity* and *constitution-by-weight,* are data that were available in the current literature to Dalton. The third column of data, *ratios,* represents the results of calculations by Dalton using the *constitution-by-weight* data. For example consider the first row of data. Instead of expressing composition as 46.6% azote and 53.4% oxygen for nitrous gas, the parts of azote per unit weight of oxygen could be calculated,

$$\frac{46.6 \text{ units of weight of azote}}{53.4 \text{ units of weight of oxygen}} = \frac{.87 \text{ units of weight of azote}}{1 \text{ unit of weight of oxygen}}.$$

This value of .87 units of weight of azote to 1 unit of weight of oxygen can be converted into units of weight of azote per 7 units of weight of oxygen:

$$\frac{.87 \text{ units of weight of azote}}{1 \text{ unit of weight of oxygen}} \times 7 \text{ units of weight of oxygen} =$$

$$6.1 \text{ units of weight of azote.}$$

This is the ratio recorded by Dalton in the third column. It is merely another way of expressing the constitution-by-weight data.

Now if 7 is the weight of the oxygen atom as determined by Dalton from water and if the atomic constitution of the " atoms " of nitrous gas is NO, the weight of the azote atom as determined from this single calculation is 6.1. Dalton actually assigns the value of 5.6 to the azote atom, the average of all the results, the deviations from 5.6 being laid to experimental errors.

Proceeding as above for the first row of data on nitrous oxide which contains 63.5 parts of azote to 36.5 parts of oxygen, Dalton finds

$$\frac{12.2 \text{ units of weight of azote}}{7 \text{ units of weight of oxygen}}$$

or

$$\frac{2 \times 6.1 \text{ units of weight of azote}}{7 \text{ units of weight of oxygen}}.$$

We can also write the weights of nitrogen and oxygen in units of atomic weights (7 for oxygen and 6.1 for nitrogen),

$$\frac{2 \text{ atoms of azote}}{1 \text{ atom of oxygen}}.$$

Thus there are two atoms of azote to one atom of oxygen and the atomic constitution of the " atoms " of nitrous oxide is N_2O.

Note that all of the above are merely different ways of reporting the same thing, composition by weight. In fact, Dalton quite often in this chapter transforms percentage data to ratio data and occasionally one set of ratio data to other sets of ratio data, as explained above.

The nitric acid data is treated in the same way, and Dalton finds for the first row of data on nitric acid

$$\frac{5.8 \text{ parts of azote}}{2 \times 7 \text{ parts of oxygen}}.$$

Accepting here 5.8 as the weight of the azote atom, the atomic constitution of the " atoms " of nitric acid must be NO_2.

The treatment of the data revealed the existence of the law of multiple proportions: *When two elements unite to form more than one compound, the weights of one element that combine with a fixed weight of the other element in the different compounds are in the ratio of small whole num-bers.* Thus in the case above of the three oxides of nitrogen, the approximate ratio of the weights of nitrogen combined with a fixed weight of oxygen in nitrous oxide, nitrous gas, and nitric acid are respectively 4 : 2 : 1 as can be easily verified.

The law of multiple proportions lay embedded but not recognized in the literature at Dalton's time because of the convention of reporting analyses in percentage compositions. Dalton's treatment of the data revealed the law. Once the probable existence of the law had been indicated, chemists were quick to discover other examples of the law when two substances reacted to produce more than one compound. Brief reflection will show that the law of multiple proportions is implied by Dalton's atomic theory and thus constitutes a verification of it.

Section 3
Oxygen with Carbone

There are two compounds of oxygen and carbone, both elastic fluids; the one goes by the name of *carbonic acid*, the other *carbonic oxide*; and it appears by the most accurate analyses, that the oxygen in the former is just double what it is in the latter for a given weight of carbone. Hence, we infer that one is a binary, and the other a ternary compound; but it must be enquired which of the two is the binary, before we can proceed according to system. The weight of an atom of carbone or charcoal, has not yet been investigated. Of the two compounds, carbonic acid is that which has been longest known, and the proportion of its elements more generally investigated. It consists of nearly 28 parts of charcoal by weight, united to 72 of oxygen. Now as the weight of an atom of oxygen has been determined already to be 7; we shall have the weight of an atom of carbone = 2.7, supposing carbonic acid a binary compound; but 5.4, if we suppose it a ternary compound.

Carbonic acid is of greater specific gravity than carbonic oxide; and on that account, it may be presumed to be the ternary or more complex [compound]. It must, however, be allowed, that this circumstance is rather an indication than a proof of the fact. The element of charcoal may be so light, that two atoms of it with one of oxygen, may be specifically lighter than one with one. But there are certain considerations which incline us to believe, that the element of charcoal is not much inferior to oxygen in weight. Oils, alcohol, ether, wood, &c. are compounds into which hydrogen and charcoal principally enter; these are a little lighter than water, a compound of hydrogen and oxygen. Though charcoal in a state of extreme division is readily sublimed by heat, it does not assume the form of a permanently elastic fluid, which one would expect of a very light element. Besides, carbonic acid is the highest degree of oxidation of which charcoal is susceptible, as far as we know; this rarely happens under two atoms of oxygen. Carbonic acid is easily resolved by electric shocks into oxygen and carbonic oxide; but carbonic oxide does not appear to be resolved in the same mode into charcoal and carbonic acid, which one might expect from a triple compound. One of the most common ways of obtaining carbonic oxide, is to decompose carbonic acid by some substance possessing affinity for oxygen; now, oxygen may be abstracted from a body possessing two atoms of it more easily than from one possessing only one. On all these accounts, there can scarcely be a doubt that carbonic oxide is a binary, and carbonic acid a ternary compound.

*　　*　　*　　*　　*　　*　　*

Dalton then goes on to discuss carbonic oxide, its properties, preparation, and composition. Dalton and his contemporaries used an indirect method to determine the composition of carbonic oxide. The composition of carbonic acid, produced by the direct combination of carbon and oxygen, had been determined many times and was found to be 72% oxygen and 28% carbon by weight. Hence by combining a known weight of carbonic oxide with a known weight of oxygen to produce carbonic acid of known composition, it was possible to calculate the weights of carbon and oxygen in the carbonic oxide.

Another experimental method for determining the composition of carbonic oxide employed by Dalton and his contemporaries is as follows. Carbonic oxide burns readily in the air to produce carbonic acid just as it does in oxygen. First a known volume or weight of carbonic oxide is burned in a known amount of air (amount of air more than sufficient to burn all the oxide) in a closed container. The product of the combustion is carbonic acid mixed with the excess oxygen and unchanged nitrogen of the air. This volume is noted. This mixture of gases is washed with lime water, calcium oxide dissolved in water, which has the property of removing the carbonic acid from the gas mixture. This volume is noted. The decrease in volume due to the lime water treatment is equal to the volume of carbonic acid that is produced. Next the remaining mixture of nitrogen and oxygen gases is treated with nitrous gas. Nitrous gas has the property of reacting with oxygen to produce an oxide of nitrogen that is soluble in water. The effect of this step is to remove the oxygen from the gaseous mixture. Hence the decrease in volume that occurs in this step equals the volume of oxygen that was in excess. The original volume of oxygen in the air is known from the composition of the air which is 20% oxygen and 80% nitrogen by volume. This volume, less the oxygen in excess, gives the amount of oxygen consumed in the reaction. All volumes of course are measured at the same temperature and pressure. Schematically:

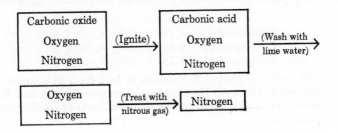

The volumes can be converted to weights by means of specific gravity data. So we have a known weight of carbonic oxide plus a known weight of oxygen producing a known weight of carbonic acid. Since the percentage composition of carbonic acid is known, the percentage composition of carbonic oxide can be determined.

STUDY QUESTIONS

1. Dalton states that Monge in 1783 had produced .25 lb of water by the combustion of hydrogen gas. Accepting Dalton's relation of 7 parts oxygen to 1 part hydrogen by weight in water, the amount of oxygen in pounds consumed in Monge's combustion was approximately

    (1) .18   (2) .16   (3) .03   (4) .22   (5) .7.

2. Dalton, Humboldt, and Gay-Lussac noted that the generally accepted figures for the composition of water (85 parts oxygen and 15 parts of hydrogen by weight) were probably in error due to the presence of water vapor in the hydrogen and oxygen burned to produce water. Previous workers had noted (Fourcroy et al.) that .15 lb of what they took for pure hydrogen required .85 lb of oxygen to produce 1 lb of water. This gives a combining ratio of approximately 5.7 parts of oxygen to one of hydrogen. Assuming that the .15 lb of hydrogen was actually 20% by weight water vapor and the oxygen was pure oxygen, the combining ratio would be approximately

    (1) 6 to 1   (2) 3.5 to 1   (3) 7 to 1   (4) 8 to 1   (5) 5 to 1.

3. Dalton, accepting the combining ratio of 7 parts oxygen to 1 of hydrogen by weight and assuming the water " atom " as binary (the only compound of the two elements he knew), arrived at the relative weights of the oxygen and hydrogen atoms as 7 to 1. If the water " atom " were quaternary, consisting of 3 atoms of hydrogen and 1 of oxygen, the relative weight of the oxygen atom to the hydrogen atom would be

    (1) 14 to 1   (2) 4.7 to 1   (3) 21 to 1   (4) 14 to 2   (5) 7 to 3.

4. If 20 measures of oxygen and 2 of hydrogen (by volume) are ignited by an electric spark to form water, the following measure remains as surplus:

    (1) No surplus   (2) 1 of hydrogen   (3) 18 of oxygen
    (4) 6 of oxygen   (5) 19 of oxygen.

    5–10. Consider the following data:
    Two elements A and B combine to form three gaseous compounds with specific gravities and percentage compositions as follows:

	S.G.	*% Comp.*
Compound I	*1.10*	*60% A, 40% B*
Compound II	*1.54*	*43% A, 57% B*
Compound III	*1.76*	*75% A, 25% B*

    The atomic weight of B is known to be 8 from its compounds with hydrogen. These are the only known compounds of A and B. Follow Dalton in using specific gravity as an indicator of relative weights of particles.

5. The ratios of the weights of A with fixed weight of B in Compounds I, II, and III respectively are

    (1) 4 : 2 : 1   (2) 1 : 4 : 2   (3) 1 : 2 : 4   (4) 4 : 1 : 2   (5) 2 : 1 : 4.

6. The atomic weight of A is

    (1) 6   (2) 15   (3) 3   (4) 12   (5) 9.

7. The combining ratio by weight of A to B in Compound I is

    (1) 12 : 8   (2) 12 : 6   (3) 6 : 8   (4) 24 : 8   (5) 3 : 4.

8. The combining ratio by weight of A to B in Compound II is

    (1) 12 : 8   (2) $12 : 2 \times 8$ (3) $2 \times 12 : 8$ (4) $2 \times 12 : 2 \times 8$
    (5) 1 : 2.

9. The combining ratio by weight of A to B in Compound III is

    (1) $12 : 2 \times 8$ (2) 12 : 8   (3) 2 : 1   (4) $2 \times 12 : 2 \times 8$
    (5) $2 \times 12 : 8$.

10. Subsequently another compound of A and B is discovered which consists of 50% A and 50% B. The atomic composition of its " atoms " is

    (1) AB_3 (2) A_3B (3) A_3B_2 (4) A_2B_3 (5) A_2B_5.

11. The composition of carbonic oxide is assumed by Dalton to be

    (1) CO (2) C_2O (3) CO_2 (4) C_2O_2 (5) C_2O_3.

12. The composition of carbonic acid is assumed by Dalton to be

    (1) CO (2) C_2O (3) CO_2 (4) C_2O_2 (5) C_2O_3.

13. Carbonic acid was found on analysis to be 28% carbon and 72% oxygen. If the composition of carbonic acid is CO_2, the atomic weight of carbon is (assume with Dalton that $O = 7$)

    (1) 1   (2) 28   (3) 12   (4) 5.4   (5) 2.7.

14. Consider the following data:
Sixty-four hundredths (.64) pound of carbonic oxide combine with .36 pound of oxygen to produce 1 pound of carbonic acid. From these data and the known percentage composition of the carbonic acid, calculate the percentage of oxygen in carbonic oxide.

    (1) 56%   (2) 66%   (3) 36%   (4) 50%   (5) 32%.

15–17. In an experiment, 3 measures by volume of carbonic oxide are fired with 10 measures by volume of air (80% nitrogen, 20% oxygen by volume). Assume that 10 measures of the oxide require 5 measures of pure oxygen in burning and that 10 measures of carbonic acid are produced.

15. After firing the above mixture the volume would be

    (1) 13 meas.   (2) 10 meas.   (3) 11.5 meas.   (4) 10.5 meas.
    (5) 11.0 meas.

16. After washing the resulting mixture with lime water to remove the carbonic acid, the volume would be

    (1) 13 meas.   (2) 10.5 meas.   (3) 7 meas.   (4) 8.5 meas.
    (5) 9.5 meas.

17. After supplying a small portion of nitrous gas to the residuum remaining (following the treatment in problem 16) to remove the oxygen, the volume would be

    (1) 13 meas. (2) 7 meas. (3) 10.5 meas. (4) 9 meas.
    (5) 8 meas.

18. According to the law of multiple proportions *when two elements unite to form more than one compound, the weights of one element that combine with a fixed weight of the other element in the different compounds are in the ratio of small whole numbers.* Considering the crudeness of the analyses of Dalton and his contemporaries, would the law have been detectable if the portion of the law that reads " small whole numbers " was replaced by " large whole numbers "?

26

Gay-Lussac's Law of Reacting Volumes

● Dalton's atomic theory was accepted by most chemists because the laws of definite, multiple, and equivalent proportions were readily explainable in terms of its postulates. But there were a minority which included some outstanding chemists who opposed the theory. The chief weakness singled out for attack was Dalton's seven rules. As has been noted these rules were the bridge between experimental data on one hand and relative atomic weights on the other. An obvious weakness was the rule that if only one compound of two elements was known it was to be assumed binary. Even if it is granted that if only one compound of two elements exists it must be the simplest possible, there is no assurance that in cases where only one is known that subsequently another compound of the two elements might not be discovered or prepared and that this compound might not itself be binary.

Further objective evidence relating to chemical reactions was needed that might furnish a clue to the relative number of atoms involved in a particular reaction. Such evidence was furnished by the French chemist Joseph Louis Gay-Lussac (Fig. 26-1), who was born in 1778 in the province of Haute Vienne. His father was a judge whose original family name had been Gay, but who had added the Lussac from the name of a small estate which he owned. Gay-Lussac was graduated from the École Polytechnique in Paris and became Berthollet's assistant. His early researches were mostly physical, and included a verification of the earlier work of Charles on the expansion of gases with increasing temperatures. Since he was interested in both terrestrial magnetism and the composition of the atmosphere, he made two notable balloon ascents. On August 24, 1804 he reached an altitude of 13,000 feet and on September 16 of the same year he reached an altitude of 23,000 feet. He found no difference in the composition of the atmosphere over this range of altitudes.

In 1805 he went on a scientific excursion through Switzerland, Italy, and Germany with Alexander von Humboldt. During this year he read a

Figure 26-1. *J. L. Gay-Lussac (1778–1850).*

paper in which he established that one volume of oxygen combined with two volumes of hydrogen when water was formed. Gay-Lussac was elected to membership in the French Academy in 1806. Two years later, in 1808, he became professor of physics at the Sorbonne. However, at about this time his interest began to turn from physics to chemistry. In 1809, he became professor of chemistry at the École Polytechnique. In the same year he published the paper "Memoir on the Combination of Gaseous Substances with Each Other" which will be excerpted in this chapter.

Gay-Lussac's findings in this memoir are a logical extension of his earlier work with Humboldt on the volume relations in the formation of water. The contents of this memoir are today summarized as Gay-Lussac's law of reacting volumes. The law applies only to gaseous substances involved in a chemical reaction, these gaseous substances being either reactants or products or both. In the conclusion of his memoir, Gay-Lussac states his law essentially as follows: *In a reaction involving two or more gaseous substances, if the volume of the gaseous substance occupying the least volume is designated by unity, the volumes of the remaining gaseous substances are small integral multiples of this least volume.* All volumes are understood to be measured at the same temperature and pressure. No statement is made relative to the volumes of any liquids or solids which may be present as reactants and products in the reaction.[1]

---

[1] Subsequent to Gay-Lussac's memoir, gaseous reactions of the type

2 vol. A + 3 vol. B → a compound

were discovered. To include such cases, as well as the examples noted by Gay-Lussac, the law is now stated: *In a reaction involving two or more gaseous substances, the ratios of the volumes of the gases may be expressed in small whole numbers.*

Following the appearance of this paper, he worked almost entirely in chemistry, collaborating mostly with Louis Jacques Thenard. He investigated the process of fermentation and studied the compounds of boron, chlorine, iodine, and the cyanides. He invented improved methods for manufacturing sulphuric and oxalic acids. He wrote 148 papers.

Gay-Lussac was also active in political life. He was elected deputy in the French legislature for Haute Vienne in 1831. He became professor of chemistry at the Jardin des Plantes in 1832 after resigning his position at the Sorbonne. He was created a Peer of France in 1839. In his last years he regretted that death would take him from the world just as many discoveries were being made that only hinted at still greater discoveries yet to come. He died in Paris in 1850.

In considering his paper "Memoir on the Combination of Gaseous Substances with Each Other," it is obvious that as much experimental evidence as possible must be gathered to support a proposed law in science. The only basis of an empirical scientific law is experimental, and it is the mustering of experimental support that occupies most of the paper. Several types of experimental evidence are cited.

The evidence that is most obvious and the simplest to understand is that obtained by direct observation in the laboratory of chemical reactions involving two or more gases to see if the relative volumes involved satisfy the law. This Gay-Lussac does in several cases, although it is not always possible or convenient to use this direct method.

In some cases there may be data already in existence in the literature which make it possible to calculate the volume relations that would occur in a reaction without the necessity of actually performing the experiment. Also some compounds are not formed readily by the direct combination of elements. However it may be possible, with suitable data, to calculate the relative volumes of the elements that would enter into combination. Thus in addition to direct observation he utilizes three calculation procedures to furnish evidence for his law. These procedures all revolve around three types of data: percentage compositions of compounds, specific gravities of gases, and relative volumes of gases.

The first of these indirect procedures is as follows. Suppose two gases A and B react to yield a compound C.

$$A \text{ (gas)} + B \text{ (gas)} \rightarrow C.$$

Gay-Lussac assumes that the relative volumes of A and B are such that they obey his law. He then looks up or determines the specific gravities of A and B and with the assumed volume relationships he calculates what the percentage composition by weight of C should be in terms of A and B. If the calculated value agrees with the experimental percentage composition of C, the assumed volume relations must have been correct. Gay-Lussac does this in his discussion of the neutral carbonate of ammonia in the portion of his paper cited in this chapter, where his line of reasoning is essentially as follows. Suppose the law is true and the neutral carbonate of ammonia is formed from equal volumes of the gases carbonic acid and ammonia. Then taking the known specific gravities of carbonic acid and ammonia, one can calculate what the percentage composition of the salt should be in terms of carbonic acid and ammonia and can compare this percentage composition with the actual analysis of the salt. If the two percentage compositions agree within the limits of experimental error, the original supposition that equal volumes of the two gases are involved is correct and another verification of the law is obtained.

Supposition: 1 volume of carbonic acid + 1 volume of ammonia
$\rightarrow$ the neutral carbonate of ammonia

Specific gravity of carbonic acid = 1.570
Specific gravity of ammonia = .6163.

Consider a volume of air sufficient to weigh 1 pound.[2] Then from the definition of specific gravity the weight of an equal volume of carbonic acid gas under the same conditions is 1.570 pounds and of the same volume of ammonia is .6163 pound. If the above supposition regarding volumes is correct it would also be true that

1.570 lb of carbonic acid + .6163 lb of ammonia
$\rightarrow$ 2.1863 lb of neutral carbonate of ammonia.

With these weight relations it is possible to calculate the percentage composition of the salt in terms of carbonic acid and ammonia.

For carbonic acid,

$$\frac{1.570 \text{ lb of carbonic acid} \times 100}{2.1863 \text{ lb of salt}} = 71.81\% \text{ carbonic acid.}$$

Actual analysis of the compound, as Gay-Lussac notes, gives a result of 73.34% carbonic acid and 26.66% ammonia. This is very close to the above values, and, if the salt were formed by direct combination of the gases, the volumes of the two gases would be approximately equal. Gay-Lussac claims that if allowances are made for experimental errors they would be equal and his law is verified.

Another method is to start with the experimentally determined composition of a compound in terms of the gases that react to yield it and with the known specific gravities of these component gases. From these data it is possible to calculate the relative volumes of the component gases that react to yield the compound, and it may be noted if these calculated volumes are in agreement with the law. This method is just the reverse of the method discussed above and is the manner in which Gay-Lussac treats Davy's data on the oxides of nitrogen.

---

[2] Any units of weight may be used, since all that is important is the relative weights involved and the specific gravities give these. Actually it is not necessary to choose any particular units of weight.

The third method applies to a gaseous product produced by the reaction of gases. Thus:

$$\text{A (gas)} + \text{B (gas)} \rightarrow \text{C (gas)}.$$

The first step is the same as that previously discussed in the case of the neutral carbonate of ammonia. Using the assumed relative volumes of A and B and their known specific gravities, the weight of C produced can be obtained, and then from the weight of C and its assumed volume, a value of the specific gravity of C may be calculated. If this calculated specific gravity agrees with the actual specific gravity of C, the volume relations of A, B, and C assumed in accordance with the law must be correct. An example of this procedure is used in the discussion of ammonia quoted from Gay-Lussac.

It should of course be realized that in pursuing these various methods to obtain support for his law Gay-Lussac was able to obtain only approximate confirmation, since the relative volumes observed or calculated were in general not small whole numbers. This is to be expected, of course, of any general statement based on experimental observations, since experimental observations are never " exact " and observations of volumes of gases are particularly subject to errors because of slight temperature and pressure changes, slight solubilities of gases in water, et cetera. In all cases he did find that the ratios of the volumes were approximately expressible in small whole numbers and ascribed the departure from small whole numbers to the inevitable experimental errors. It was largely a matter of personal judgment, in view of the techniques of the time, as to what extent it was justifiable to round off experimental figures to obtain a desired result. It will be noted later that Dalton, although the same data were available to him as to Gay-Lussac, denied the existence of Gay-Lussac's law.

Gay-Lussac in discussing the " great law of chemical affinity " makes an important observation that the view has been held that there must be an overall volume decrease as a mixture of elementary gases reacts to produce a gaseous product, due to the approximation (coming together) of the atoms of the elementary gases. For example, if the gases A and B react to yield the gaseous product C, it had been assumed that the gas C would occupy a less volume than the mere mixture of A and B. However he cites several experiments where this is observed not to be true. Note that this is in direct contradiction to Dalton's rules 5 and 6: " A binary compound should be specifically heavier than the mixture of its two ingredients . . ."

The reader is not to attach any modern significance to Gay-Lussac's use of the term " molecule " which was from the Latin and means a small mass. Gay-Lussac's molecule is synonymous with Dalton's atom of an element or " atom " of a compound. Also in Gay-Lussac's usage of the terms " subsalt " and " neutral salt," no more significance should be attached to them than Gay-Lussac does in the paper to be considered. Workers prior to Gay-Lussac had observed that some acids in reacting with bases formed two different compounds or salts. The salt resulting from the reaction of the lesser quantity of acid relative to a fixed amount of base was designated the subsalt and the other salt was designated the neutral salt. If only one salt is formed from an acid and base, it is called a neutral salt.

MEMOIR ON THE COMBINATION OF
GASEOUS SUBSTANCES WITH EACH OTHER [3]
by Joseph Louis Gay-Lussac

Substances, whether in the solid, liquid, or gaseous state, possess properties which are independent of the force of cohesion; but they also possess others which appear to be modified by this force (so variable in its intensity), and which no longer follow any regular law. The same pressure applied to all solid or liquid substances would produce a diminution of volume differing in each case, while it would be equal for all elastic fluids. Similarly, heat expands all substances; but the dilatations of liquids and solids have hitherto presented no regularity, and it is only those of elastic fluids which are equal and independent of the nature of each gas. The attraction of the molecules in solids and liquids is, therefore, the cause which modifies their special properties; and it appears that it is only when the attraction is entirely destroyed, as in gases, that bodies under similar conditions obey simple and regular laws. At least, it is my intention to make known some new properties in gases, the effects of which are regular, by showing that these substances combine amongst themselves in very simple proportions, and that the contraction of volume which they experience on combination also follows a regular law. I hope by this means to give a proof of an idea advanced by several very distinguished chemists — that we are perhaps not far removed from the time when we shall be able to submit the bulk of chemical phenomena to calculation.

It is a very important question in itself, and one much discussed amongst chemists, to ascertain if compounds are formed in all sorts of proportions. M. Proust, who appears first to have fixed his attention on this subject, is of opinion that the metals are susceptible of only two degrees of oxidation, a *minimum* and a *maximum;* but led away by this seductive theory, he has seen himself forced to entertain principles contrary to physics in order to reduce to two oxides all those which the same metal sometimes presents. M. Berthollet thinks, on the other hand — reasoning from general considerations and his own experiments — that compounds are always formed in very variable proportions, unless they are determined by special causes, such as crystallisation, insolubility, or elasticity. Lastly, Dalton has advanced the idea that compounds of two bodies are formed in such a way that one atom of the one unites with one, two, three, or more atoms of the other. It would follow from this mode of looking at compounds that they are formed in constant proportions, the existence of intermediate bodies being excluded, and in this respect Dalton's theory would resemble that of M. Proust; but M. Berthollet has already strongly opposed it in

[3] *Mémoires de la Société d'Arcueil,* II (1809), pp. 207–234. Translated in Alembic Club Reprint, No. 4, The University of Chicago Press, 1902. Portions of the Alembic Club reprint, pages 8–24, are reproduced here.

the Introduction he has written to Thomson's Chemistry, and we shall see that in reality it is not entirely exact. Such is the state of the question now under discussion; it is still very far from receiving its solution, but I hope that the facts which I now proceed to set forth, facts which had entirely escaped the notice of chemists, will contribute to its elucidation.

Suspecting, from the exact ratio of 100 [volumes] of oxygen to 200 [volumes] of hydrogen, which M. Humboldt and I had determined for the proportions of water, that other gases might also combine in simple ratios [by volume], I have made the following experiments. I prepared fluoboric, muriatic, and carbonic gases, and made them combine successively with ammonia gas. 100 parts of muriatic gas saturate precisely 100 parts of ammonia gas, and the salt which is formed from them is perfectly neutral, whether one or other of the gases is in excess. Fluoboric gas, on the contrary, unites in two proportions with ammonia gas. When the acid gas is put first into the graduated tube, and the other gas is then passed in, it is found that equal volumes of the two condense, and that the salt formed is neutral. But if we begin by first putting the ammonia gas into the tube, and then admitting the fluoboric gas in single bubbles, the first gas will then be in excess with regard to the second, and there will result a salt with excess of base, composed of 100 of fluoboric gas and 200 of ammonia gas. If carbonic gas is brought into contact with ammonia gas, by passing it sometimes first, sometimes second into the tube, there is always formed a sub-carbonate composed of 100 parts of carbonic gas and 200 of ammonia gas. It may, however, be proved that neutral carbonate of ammonia would be composed of equal volumes of each of these components. M. Berthollet, who has analyzed this salt, obtained by passing carbonic gas into the sub-carbonate, found that it was composed of 73.34 parts by weight of carbonic gas and 26.66 of ammonia gas. Now, if we suppose it to be composed of equal volumes of its components, we find from their known specific gravity, that it contains by weight

> 71.81 of carbonic acid,
> 28.19 of ammonia,
> ‾‾‾‾‾‾‾
> 100.0

a proportion differing only slightly from the preceding.

If the neutral carbonate of ammonia could be formed by the mixture of carbonic gas and ammonia gas, as much of one gas as of the other would be absorbed; and since we can only obtain it through the intervention of water, we must conclude that it is the affinity of this liquid which competes with that of the ammonia to overcome the elasticity of the carbonic acid, and that the neutral carbonate of ammonia can only exist through the medium of water.

Thus we may conclude that muriatic, fluoboric, and carbonic acids take exactly their own volume of ammonia gas to form neutral salts, and that the last two take twice as much to form *subsalts*. It is very remarkable to see acids so different from one another neutralize a volume of ammonia gas equal to their own; and from this we may suspect that if all acids and all alkalies could be obtained in the gaseous state, neutrality would result from the combination of equal volumes of acid and alkali.

❄   ❄   ❄   ❄   ❄   ❄   ❄

We might even now conclude that gases combine with each other in very simple ratio; but I shall still give some fresh proofs.

According to the experiments of M. Amédée Berthollet, ammonia is composed of

100 of nitrogen,
300 of hydrogen,

by volume.

I have found (1st vol. of the Société d'Arcueil) that sulphuric acid is composed of

100 of sulphurous gas,
50 of oxygen gas.

When a mixture of 50 parts of oxygen and 100 of carbonic oxide (formed by the distillation of oxide of zinc with strongly calcined charcoal) is inflamed, these two gases are destroyed and their place taken by 100 parts of carbonic acid gas. Consequently carbonic acid may be considered as being composed of

100 of carbonic oxide gas,
50 of oxygen gas.

Davy, from the analysis of various compounds of nitrogen with oxygen, has found the following proportions by weight: —

	Nitrogen	Oxygen
Nitrous oxide	63.30	36.70
Nitrous gas	44.05	55.95
Nitric acid	29.50	70.50

Reducing these proportions to volumes we find: —

	Nitrogen	Oxygen
Nitrous oxide	100	49.5
Nitrous gas	100	108.9
Nitric acid	100	204.7

The first and the last of these proportions differ only slightly from 100 to 50, and 100 to 200; it is only the second which diverges somewhat from 100 to 100. The difference, however, is not very great, and is such as we might expect in experiments of this sort; and I have assured myself that it is actually nil.

❋   ❋   ❋   ❋   ❋   ❋   ❋

We may then admit the following numbers for the proportions by volume of the compounds of nitrogen with oxygen: —

	Nitrogen	Oxygen
Nitrous oxide	100	50
Nitrous gas	100	100
Nitric acid	100	200

❋   ❋   ❋   ❋   ❋   ❋   ❋

Thus it appears evident to me that gases always combine in the simplest proportions when they act on one another; and we have seen in reality in all the preceding examples that the ratio of combinations is 1 to 1, 1 to 2, or 1 to 3. It is very important to observe that in considering weights there is no simple and finite relation between the elements of any one compound; it is only when there is a second compound between the same elements that the new proportion of the element that has been added is a multiple of the first quantity. Gases, on the contrary, in whatever proportions they may combine, always give rise to compounds whose elements by volume are multiples of each other.

Not only, however, do gases combine in very simple proportions, as we have just seen, but the apparent contraction of volume which they experience on combination has also a simple relation to the volume of the gases, or at least to that of one of them.

I have said, following M. Berthollet, that 100 parts of carbonic oxide gas, prepared by distilling oxide of zinc and strongly calcined charcoal, produce 100 parts of carbonic gas on combining with 50 of oxygen. It follows from this that the apparent contraction of the two gases is precisely equal to the volume of oxygen gas added.

❋   ❋   ❋   ❋   ❋   ❋   ❋

Ammonia gas is composed of three parts by volume of hydrogen and one of nitrogen, and its density compared to air is 0.596. But if we suppose the apparent contraction to be half of the whole volume, we find 0.594 for the density. Thus it is proved, by this almost perfect concordance, that the apparent contraction of its elements is precisely half the total volume or rather double the volume of the nitrogen.

❋   ❋   ❋   ❋   ❋   ❋   ❋

We see, then, from these various examples, that the contraction experienced by two gases on combination is in almost exact relation with their volume, or rather with the volume of one of them. Only very slight differences exist between the densities of compounds obtained by calculation and those given by experiment, and it is probable that, on undertaking new researches, we shall see them vanish entirely.

Recalling the great law of chemical affinity, that every combination involves an approximation of the elementary molecules, it is difficult to conceive why carbonic oxide gas should be lighter than oxygen. Indeed, that is the principal reason which had led M. Berthollet to assume the existence of hydrogen in this gas, and thus explain its low density. But it seems to me that the difficulty arises from supposing that the approximation of the elementary molecules is represented in gases by the diminution of volume which they suffer on combination. This supposition is not always true, and we might cite several gaseous combinations, the constituent molecules of which would be brought very close together, although there is not only no diminution of volume, but even a dilatation. Such, for example, is nitrous gas, whether we consider it as being formed directly from nitrogen and oxygen, or from nitrous oxide and oxygen. In the first case, there is no diminution of volume; and in the second, there would be dilatation, for 100 parts of nitrous oxide and 50 of oxygen would produce 200 of nitrous gas. We know too that carbonic gas represents an exactly equal volume of oxygen, and that the affinity which unites its elements is very powerful. Nevertheless, if we admitted an immediate relation between the condensation of the elements and the condensation of volume, we should conclude, contrary to experiment, that there is no condensation. Otherwise it would be necessary to suppose that if carbon were in the gaseous state it would combine in equal volumes (or in any other proportion) with oxygen, and that the apparent condensation would then be equal to the whole volume of the gaseous carbon. But if we make this supposition for carbonic acid, we may also make it for carbonic oxide, by assuming, for instance, that 100 parts of gaseous carbon would produce 100 parts of the gas on combining with 50 parts of oxygen. However it may stand with these suppositions, which only serve to make it conceivable that oxygen can produce a compound lighter than itself by combining with a solid substance, we must admit, as a truth founded on a great number of observations, that the condensation of the molecules of two combining substances, in particular of two gases, has no immediate relation to the condensation of volume, since we often see that whilst one is very great the other is very small or even nil.

The observation that the gaseous combustibles combine with oxygen in the simple ratios of 1 to 1, 1 to 2, 1 to ½, can lead us to determine the density of the vapours of combustible substances, or at least to approximate closely to that determination. For if we suppose all combustible substances to be in the gaseous state, a specified volume of each would absorb an equal volume of oxygen, or twice as much, or else half; and as we know the proportion of oxygen taken up by each combustible substance in the solid or liquid state, it is sufficient to convert the oxygen into volumes and also the combustible, under the condition that its vapour shall be equal to the volume of oxygen, or else double or half this value. For example, mercury is susceptible of two degrees of oxidation, and we may compare the first one to nitrous oxide. Now, according to MM. Fourcroy and Thenard, 100 parts of mercury absorb 4.16 [parts by weight of oxygen], which reduced to gas would occupy a space of 8.20. These 100 parts of mercury reduced to vapour should therefore occupy twice the space, viz., 16.40. We thence conclude that the density of mercury vapour is 12.01 greater than that of oxygen, and that the metal on passing from the liquid to the gaseous state assumes a volume 961 times as great.[4]

*   *   *   *   *   *   *

Conclusion

I have shown in this Memoir that the compounds of gaseous substances with each other are always formed in very simple ratios, so that representing one of the terms by unity, the other is 1, or 2, or at most 3. These ratios by volume are not observed with solid or liquid substances, nor when we consider weights, and they form a new proof that it is only in the gaseous state that substances are in the same circumstances and obey regular laws. It is remarkable to see

---

[4] The analogy here is that it is known that

1 volume of nitrogen + ½ volume of oxygen → nitrous oxide.

Gay-Lussac is comparing the oxide of mercury to nitrous oxide and states that if mercury existed as a gas then the reaction would be:

1 volume of mercury + ½ volume of oxygen → oxide of mercury.

Then the volume of mercury, if it existed as a gas, would be twice that of the volume of oxygen with which it combines, viz. $2 \times 8.20 = 16.40$.

that ammonia gas neutralizes exactly its own volume of gaseous acids; and it is probable that if all acids and alkalies were in the elastic state, they would all combine in equal volumes to produce neutral salts. The capacity of saturation of acids and alkalies measured by volume would then be the same, and this might perhaps be the true manner of determining it. The apparent contraction of volume suffered by gases on combination is also very simply related to the volume of one of them, and this property likewise is peculiar to gaseous substances.

STUDY QUESTIONS

1. What " regular laws " do gases obey that liquids and solids do not? What are the reasons for this regular behavior according to Gay-Lussac?
2. Consider two graduated tubes each containing 100 measures of ammonia gas; into the first tube muriatic gas is passed and into the second fluoboric gas. The following represents the volumes of muriatic gas and fluoboric gas reacting respectively:

   (1) 100; 100   (2) 100; 50   (3) 200; 100   (4) 100; 200   (5) 50; 100.

3. Assume that a neutral salt, if it could be produced directly from A and B, would require equal volumes of A and B. If the specific gravity of A is 2.3 and that of B is 1.5, the percentages of A and B respectively in the neutral salt would be calculated to be approximately

   (1) 55; 45   (2) 23; 77   (3) 40; 60   (4) 61; 39   (5) 50; 50.

4. A set of data of the type that could have been utilized by Gay-Lussac would be the following: A and B, both gases, form three compounds of percentage composition as follows:

   Compound I   23.1% A; 76.9% B
   Compound II   37.5% A; 62.5% B
   Compound III   54.5% A; 45.5% B
      Specific Gravity of A = .75
      Specific Gravity of B = 1.25

   Hint: Assume a given weight, say 100 lbs., of the compound formed in each case.
   The volumes of B necessary to react with 100 measures of A to form Compounds I, II, and III respectively are approximately

   (1) 50; 200; 100   (2) 200; 100; 50   (3) 200; 50; 100
   (4) 200; 200; 100   (5) 100; 50; 200.

5. Assume, with Gay-Lussac, that when nitrogen and hydrogen react to yield ammonia the relative volumes are,

   1 vol. nitrogen + 3 vol. hydrogen → 2 vol. ammonia

   Suppose the specific gravity of hydrogen is .0695 and that of nitrogen is .972. What would be the calculated value of the specific gravity of ammonia if the assumed volumes are correct?

   (1) .570   (2) .632   (3) .616   (4) .590   (5) .598.

6. Two gases (elementary or compounded) combine to produce a third gas. Which of the following statements might be applicable?

a. There is a decrease in volume on combination.
b. There is an increase in volume on combination.
c. There is no change in volume on combination.
The correct choice is

(1) a   (2) b   (3) c   (4) a and c   (5) a, b, and c.

7. Use the method that Gay-Lussac used in calculating the density of mercury vapor relative to oxygen to calculate the specific gravity of magnesium vapor from the following data: 6 parts by weight of magnesium combine with 8 parts by weight of oxygen to form the only known compound of the two elements. Hence the oxide is analogous to nitrous gas (1 vol. oxygen + 1 vol. nitrogen → 2 vol. nitrous gas). The specific gravity of oxygen is 1.11. The specific gravity that magnesium would exhibit in the vapor state according to Gay-Lussac is

(1) .833   (2) 1.66   (3) 8.88   (4) .425   (5) 1.11.

8–11. The figures obtained by Berthollet for the composition of ammonia (100 measures by volume of nitrogen with 300 measures by volume of hydrogen) cited by Gay-Lussac were obtained by decomposing ammonia into nitrogen and hydrogen by means of electrical discharge. Typical data in such an experiment would be as follows. Initially there are 100 measures of ammonia in the eudiometer. An electrical discharge is applied to the eudiometer for several hours and the volume is observed to increase to 166 measures. The 166 measures consist of unchanged ammonia, nitrogen, and hydrogen. Upon shaking the mixture of gases with muriatic acid to remove the unchanged ammonia, the 166 measures are reduced to 130 measures.

8. The amount of ammonia (in measures) that decomposed is

(1) 36.0   (2) 130   (3) 166   (4) 30.0   (5) 64.0.

9. The ammonia upon decomposition into nitrogen and hydrogen has increased in volume by a ratio of

(1) 2.03 : 1   (2) 3.00 : 1   (3) 2.50 : 1   (4) 2.00 : 1
(5) no increase.

10. If the decomposed gas consists of 25.2% by volume of nitrogen and 74.8% of hydrogen, then for each 100 measures of nitrogen contained in ammonia there are how many measures of hydrogen?

(1) 200   (2) 203   (3) 300   (4) 297   (5) 100.

11. Allowing for experimental errors, Gay-Lussac would expect 100 measures of nitrogen and 300 measures of hydrogen to yield how many measures of ammonia on combining?

(1) 400   (2) 200   (3) 100   (4) 300   (5) 800.

12. Studies of the various properties of gases have often been the first step in major breakthroughs to a more intimate knowledge of the structure of matter. The first steps in determining the *structure* of atoms came from a study of electrical discharges through gases (see Chapter 38) at the latter part of the 19th century. Can you give a reason why the properties of gases have often been the means of a deeper insight into the structure of matter?

13. Recall Boyle's and Charles' laws which you have probably studied previously. To what practical use could these laws be put relative to the subject matter considered in this chapter?

14. Direct determination of the density or specific gravity of a gas by weighing a known volume was at Gay-Lussac's time and also today fraught with many experimental difficulties. Can you think of an alternate method of determining the weight of a volume of gas? (Hint, most gases can be prepared from solid and/or liquid reactants.)

27

Avogadro's Hypotheses

● Gay-Lussac's law is a concise statement regarding the relationships that exist between the volumes of the gases in reactions involving two or more gases. Gay-Lussac believed that the statement was supported by a sufficient number of observations to warrant its acceptance as a universal statement or law applicable to all such gaseous reactions. Viewed as such it may contain a clue to the atomic constitution of the compounded " atoms " of a compound that is formed from gaseous reactants and thus help in forming a link between the constitution-by-weight data of a compound and the desired relative atomic weights of the atoms of the elements that go to form the compound. This clue to the atomic constitution, if it exists, could then play the same role that Dalton assigned to his seven rules.

The nature of the clue is obvious when the statement of Gay-Lussac's law and the postulates of Dalton's atomic theory are applied to one and the same gaseous reaction. On the one hand we have, according to the postulates of Dalton's atomic theory, that compounded " atoms " consist of small integral numbers of the constituent atoms. Gay-Lussac's law, on the other hand, states that at the same temperature and pressure the ratios of the volumes of gases involved in a chemical reaction are small whole numbers. Combining Dalton's theory and Gay-Lussac's law, there must exist a simple integral relationship between the number of atoms (in the case of elemental gases or vapors) or compounded " atoms " (in the case of compound gases or vapors) in equal volumes of different gases at the same temperature and pressure. For example, suppose that in a reaction involving gaseous reactants and a gaseous product, in accordance with Gay-Lussac's law, the relative volumes are

100 meas. elementary gas A + 100 meas. elementary gas B

→ 100 meas. compound gas C.

If we assume that the atomic constitution of the "atoms" of C is AB, it follows that the equal volumes of A and B must contain the same number of atoms and that there are the same number of "atoms," AB, in the equal volume of C. However if the atomic constitution of the "atoms" of C is A_2B, the 100 measures of A must contain twice as many atoms as the 100 measures of B, and the 100 measures of C must contain the same number of "atoms," A_2B, as the 100 measures of B.

Now, *a priori* we do not know the atomic constitution of the compounded "atoms." What we would like to be able to do is carry out the above process in reverse. This could be done if we knew the relationship between the number of atoms, in the case of elements, or "atoms," in the case of compounds, in equal volumes of different gases or vapors. Inasmuch as a simple integral relationship between the number of atoms or "atoms" in equal volumes of different gases or vapors must exist, if Gay-Lussac's law is true and Dalton's hypotheses are accepted, it is reasonable as a first trial guess to make the simplest assumption; that is, equal volumes of all gases or vapors contain the same number of atoms or "atoms" at the same temperature and pressure.

It may appear strange that the tentative assumption is extended to include the "atoms" of compounds. But this would appear to be justifiable when it is recalled that Gay-Lussac's law includes the volumes of compounds in the gaseous or vapor state, and furthermore the volumes of gases or vapors of compounds show the same behavior under temperature and pressure changes as do gases of the elements.

Such an assumption of "equal-volumes-equal-numbers" combined with the postulates of Dalton's theory, however, often leads to a conclusion that is incompatible with experimental data. In the case of a gaseous or vapor compound formed from gaseous reactants, the specific gravity of the gaseous or vapor compound should always be greater than that of either of the reactants. For the "atom" of the compound, being composed of two or more atoms, is heavier than either of the reactant atoms, and according to the assumption, equal volumes of different gases or vapors contain the same number of atoms or "atoms." But it is experimentally observed that the specific gravity of the gaseous or vapor compound is not always greater than that of either of the reactants. As an example, the specific gravity of water vapor is less than the specific gravity of oxygen, although water is formed from the combination of hydrogen and oxygen.

The contradiction that arises can also be stated in terms of relative volumes instead of specific gravities. The predicted volume of the product, on the basis of equal-volumes-equal-numbers, does not agree with the experimentally observed volume, but is greater. As an example consider the relative volumes involved in the formation of water vapor from hydrogen and oxygen. The volume relations observed are

1 vol. oxygen + 2 vol. hydrogen → 2 vol. water vapor.

But applying the equal-volumes-equal-numbers assumption to the hydrogen and oxygen we have

1 atom oxygen + 2 atoms hydrogen → 1 "atom" water,

and we would predict that the volume of the water vapor should be equal to that of the oxygen and not be double it as is actually observed.

An alternate procedure is to accept the assumption of equal-volumes-equal-numbers of atoms, elementary or compound, and attempt to reconcile it with the experimental data. But this procedure leads to a contradiction of one of the basic postulates of Dalton's theory, the indivisibility of the atoms. Thus in the case of water it is experimentally observed that

1 vol. oxygen + 2 vol. hydrogen → 2 vol. water vapor.

If equal volumes contain equal numbers of atoms, elementary or compounded, we must have

1 atom oxygen + 2 atoms hydrogen → 2 "atoms" water.

But since the 2 "atoms" of water must be identical and are produced from 1 atom of oxygen, the "atoms" of water must each contain one half of an oxygen atom and the oxygen atom must have split. This contradicts Dalton's postulate of the indivisibility of the atoms.

The formation of water from hydrogen and oxygen as regarded from any of these three aspects leads to a contradiction. And there are other examples similar to water that could be cited.

Dalton rejected the simple integral volumes of Gay-Lussac's law as being only an approximation of the actual volumes. He admitted though that "there is something wonderful in the frequency of the approximation." It will also be recalled that Dalton considered the atoms of different gaseous substances as varying greatly in size and being in contact, and such a view is also incompatible with the equal-volumes-equal-numbers hypothesis.

However if Gay-Lussac's law is true, as subsequent experiments tended to confirm, and we accept Dalton's hypotheses, some simple integral relationship must exist between the numbers of atoms in equal volumes of different gases. If we can discover the relation, and if it is of a general nature, it will lead to a method of determining the atomic constitution of "atoms" and to relative atomic weights.

There are several ways of resolving the difficulty discussed above. One is to restrict the equal-volumes-equal-numbers hypothesis to elemental gases and exclude gases of compounds and make no general statement about the numbers of "atoms" in a certain volume of a compound gas as compared to the number of atoms in an equal volume of an elemental gas. Two examples will make this clear. It is observed experimentally that

2 vol. hydrogen + 1 vol. oxygen → 2 vol. water vapor.

Figure 27-1. *Amadeo Avogadro (1776–1856).*

Interpreting this data on the basis of the restricted equal-volumes-equal-numbers hypothesis:

2 atoms hydrogen + 1 atom oxygen → 1 "atom" water (H_2O)

and the number of " atoms " of H_2O in the two volumes of water vapor is not equal to the number of atoms of hydrogen in 2 volumes of hydrogen, but only half. In the case of the formation of ammonia, it is observed experimentally that

1 vol. nitrogen + 3 vol. hydrogen → 2 vol. ammonia.

This is to be interpreted as

1 atom nitrogen + 3 atoms hydrogen → 1 "atom" ammonia (NH_3)

and the number of " atoms " of NH_3 in the two volumes of ammonia is equal to the number of atoms of nitrogen in one volume of nitrogen. Other examples could be cited, and a solution would be to make no attempt at an all-embracing statement about the number of " atoms " of a compound gas in a given volume as compared to the number of atoms of an elemental gas in the same volume, but simply to accept the relative numbers as dictated by experiment. As will be noted later, Berzelius does just this.

An interpretation that could be placed on Gay-Lussac's law, making it reconcilable with Dalton's atomic hypothesis, was made by the Italian scientist Amadeo Avogadro (Fig. 27-1). Avogadro was born in Turin in 1776. He was educated as a lawyer and took his doctor of law degree in 1796, but he forsook the law to devote himself to the study of mathematics and physics. He began to teach physics at the Royal College at Vercelli in 1806, and he later became professor of mathematical physics at the University of Turin. He lost his position during the revolutionary upsets of 1822, but regained his professorship in 1835. His important work was published in French in 1811 in the French scientific review, *Journal de Physique,* but it went practically unnoticed. Avogadro was a mild and humble man and by all accounts his unflamboyant character was a highly admirable one, but perhaps a temperate personality has some disadvantages. Avogadro was little known or appreciated within his own native Italy, and his fame in other lands was even less. He died in Turin in 1856. The value of his work was not recognized until after 1860.

Avogadro's reconciliation of Gay-Lussac's law and Dalton's hypothesis, contained in his paper of 1811, consisted in the proposal of two kinds of "ultimate" particles of elements where Dalton had envisaged only one.[1] Portions of this paper will be considered in this and the following chapter. Unfortunately Avogadro's paper is difficult reading due to his style and failure to define clearly all terms used. In Section I of his paper when Avogadro speaks of the molecules of a gaseous element, these are to be visualized as the particles, separated by distances that are large compared to their size, that constitute the gas of the element. In this section of the paper there is no discussion of the nature of the particles or molecules of the element. And in this section when he speaks of the compound or composite molecules of a gaseous or vapor compound, these likewise are to be understood as the particles, separated by distances that are large compared to their size, that constitute the gas or vapor of the compound. In Section II he discusses the internal nature or composition of the molecules of elements and explains his concept of the existence of two kinds of "ultimate" particles of elements.

ESSAY ON A MANNER OF DETERMINING THE RELATIVE MASSES OF THE ELEMENTARY MOLECULES OF BODIES, AND THE PROPORTIONS IN WHICH THEY ENTER INTO THESE COMPOUNDS [2]

by Amadeo Avogadro

I

M. Gay-Lussac has shown in an interesting Memoir (Mémoires de la Société d'Arcueil, Tome II.) that gases always unite in very simple proportion by volume, and that when the result of the union is a gas, its volume also is very simply related to those of its components. But the quantitative proportions of substances in compounds seem only to depend on the relative number of molecules which combine, and on the number of composite molecules which result. It must then be admitted that very simple relations also exist between the vol-

---

[1] Ampere in 1814 made a proposal similar to Avogadro's.
[2] *Journal de Physique,* LXXIII, (1811), pp. 58–76. Translated in Alembic Club Reprint, No. 4, The University of Chicago Press, 1902, pp. 28–31.

umes of gaseous substances and the numbers of simple or compound molecules which form them. The first hypothesis to present itself in this connection, and apparently even the only admissible one, is the supposition that the number of integral molecules in any gases is always the same for equal volumes, or always proportional to the volumes. Indeed, if we were to suppose that the number of molecules contained in a given volume was different for different gases, it would scarcely be possible to conceive that the law regulating the distance of molecules could give in all cases relations so simple as those which the facts just detailed compel us to acknowledge between the volume and the number of molecules. On the other hand, it is very well conceivable that the molecules of gases being at such a distance that their mutual attraction cannot be exercised, their varying attraction for caloric may be limited to condensing a greater or smaller quantity around them, without the atmosphere formed by this fluid having any greater extent in the one case than in the other, and, consequently, without the distance between the molecules varying; or, in other words, without the number of molecules contained in a given volume being different. Dalton, it is true, has proposed a hypothesis directly opposed to this, namely, that the quantity of caloric is always the same for the molecules of all bodies whatsoever in the gaseous state, and that the greater or less attraction for caloric only results in producing a greater or less condensation of this quantity around the molecules, and thus varying the distance between the molecules themselves. But in our present ignorance of the manner in which this attraction of the molecules for caloric is exerted, there is nothing to decide us *a priori* in favour of the one of these hypotheses rather than the other; and we should rather be inclined to adopt a neutral hypothesis, which would make the distance between the molecules and the quantities of caloric vary according to unknown laws, were it not that the hypothesis we have just proposed [equal volumes of gases contain equal numbers of molecules] is based on that simplicity of relation between the volumes of gases on combination, which would appear to be otherwise inexplicable.

Setting out from this hypothesis, it is apparent that we have the means of determining very easily the relative masses of the molecules of substances obtainable in the gaseous state, and the relative number of these molecules in compounds; for the ratios of the masses of the molecules are then the same as those of the densities of the different gases at equal temperature and pressure, and the relative number of molecules in a compound is given at once by the ratio of the volumes of the gases that form it. For example, since the numbers 1.10359 and 0.07321 express the densities of the two gases oxygen and hydrogen compared to that of atmospheric air as unity, and the ratio of the two numbers consequently represents the ratio between the masses of equal volumes of these two gases, it will also represent on our hypothesis the ratio of the masses of their molecules. Thus the mass of the molecule of oxygen will be about 15 times that of the molecule of hydrogen, or, more exactly, as 15.074 to 1. In the same way the mass of the molecule of nitrogen will be to that of hydrogen as 0.96913 to 0.07321, that is, as 13, or more exactly 13.238, to 1. On the other hand, since we know that the ratio of the volumes of hydrogen and oxygen in the formation of water is 2 to 1, it follows that water results from the union of each molecule of oxygen with two molecules of hydrogen [if equal volumes contain equal numbers of molecules]. Similarly, according to the proportions by volume established by M. Gay-Lussac for the elements of ammonia, nitrous oxide, nitrous gas, and nitric acid, ammonia will result from the union of one molecule of nitrogen with three of hydrogen, nitrous oxide from one molecule of oxygen with two of nitrogen, nitrous gas from one molecule of nitrogen with one of oxygen, and nitric acid from one of nitrogen with two of oxygen.

II

There is a consideration which appears at first sight to be opposed to the admission of our hypothesis with respect to compound substances. It seems that a molecule composed of two or more elementary molecules should have its mass equal to the sum of the masses of these molecules; and that in particular, if in a compound one molecule of one substance unites with two or more molecules of another substance, the number of compound molecules should remain the same as the number of molecules of the first substance. Accordingly, on our hypothesis when a gas combines with two or more times its volume of another gas, the resulting compound, if gaseous, must have a volume equal to that of the first of these gases. Now, in general, this is not actually the case. For instance, the volume of water in the gaseous state is, as M. Gay-Lussac has shown, twice as great as the volume of oxygen which enters into it, or, what comes to the same thing, equal to that of the hydrogen instead of being equal to that of the oxygen.

Avogadro goes on to say, " But a means of explaining facts of this type in conformity with our equal-volumes-equal-numbers hypothesis presents itself naturally enough. . . ." Then Avogadro gives his second, and with him, original hypothesis. The first hypothesis of equal-volumes-equal-numbers of particles had been entertained by Dalton among others and rejected for reasons already noted. His second hypothesis proposes the existence of two kinds of ultimate particles relative to elements where others had envisaged only one. And as will be seen shortly, Avogadro's concept of two kinds of particles relative to elements removes the objections to the equal-volumes-equal-numbers hypothesis noted in the introduction to this chapter. Avogadro's two particles are today called " atom " and " molecule." Before continuing Avogadro's paper the significance of these two terms will be explained in detail.

Molecule is a *physical* concept. A molecule of an element is the smallest particle of an element that possesses the identical chemical properties of the element. Thus consider a quantity of a certain element, which possesses certain chemical properties by which it can be recognized. Imagine this quantity of element to be halved. Then each half is recognizable by its chemical properties as being the original element, except there is a smaller quantity of it. Now imagine the halving process to be repeated on successive halves many times. Eventually one would arrive at a piece of the element, still having the chemical properties of the original, which if subdivided would yield pieces or particles not having the chemical properties of the original. This last particle, having the identical chemical properties of the original, is called a molecule of the element.[3] The ultimate particles into which the molecule is divisible are the atoms of the element. The atom concept will be defined shortly. It will be recalled that Dalton conceived of the atoms of all elements as indivisible particles possessing the identical chemical properties of the elements in mass. Hence the molecule of an element, as defined above, was not conceived by Dalton. In certain special cases, for example the inert gases and the vapor state of metals, Dalton's atomic concept would be valid. But in general Dalton's atomic concept is not valid.

In addition to molecules of elements there are molecules of compounds. This however is not a new concept, but designates what Dalton called the compounded " atoms " of compounds and hence is merely a change in terminology. Thus the molecule of a compound or Dalton's compounded " atom " of a compound is the smallest particle having the chemical properties of the original compound. Both Avogadro and Dalton conceived of this particle as being divisible, but the division would result in two or more particles differing in chemical properties from the original. However as will be noted shortly, Avogadro's hypothesis results in constitutions different from those of Dalton for the molecules of compounds. In summary then the molecule of an element or compound is the smallest particle having the chemical properties of the original substance, element or compound. Avogadro's statement that equal volumes of gases or vapors at the same temperature and pressure contain the same number of molecules is applicable to both elements and compounds.

The atom is a *chemical* concept. An atom is the smallest particle which maintains its identity and is not altered in chemical reactions; it is not subdivisible in the course of a chemical reaction. It is a building block which simply changes partners in chemical reactions. As an example of the use of the terms " atom " and " molecule," consider a container of oxygen gas at ordinary room temperature and pressure. The smallest particle in the container which still has the identical chemical properties of the oxygen gas is an oxygen molecule which consists of a certain number of oxygen atoms " stuck together." Letting O symbolize the oxygen atom and n be the number of atoms " stuck together " to form the molecule, the symbol for the oxygen molecule might be expressed as O_n. A gas consisting of single unattached oxygen atoms, O, would display different chemical properties from the oxygen gas consisting of O_n molecules. For example in combustion reactions the former would react much more vigorously. However when the oxygen gas undergoes a reaction the molecules of O_n split, and it is these split portions that take part in the reaction. If the ultimate in splitting occurs, O atoms will be produced and these particles

[3] The molecules of certain elements, notably the inert gases, are not subdivisible. However the smallest particle possessing the chemical properties of the element in mass is defined as a molecule.

will take part in the reaction, but are themselves not further subdivisible.

Henceforth when the term atom is used in our discussions it is to be understood as defined above. If there is occasion to use the term atom in the Daltonian sense, it will be referred to as the " Daltonian atom."

Before returning to Avogadro's paper there is a point well worth considering. A perusal of Avogadro's paper indicates an orientation relative to molecules and atoms opposite to what we usually take today. Whereas today we in our thinking generally focus our attention on the chemically ultimate particle, the atom, and its relative weight and move toward the molecule by envisaging a certain number of atoms " stuck together," Avogadro does just the opposite. He focuses his attention on the physical molecule and then descends to the submolecular particles of atoms. This orientation is reflected in his choice of terms, as the submolecular particles into which molecules are divisible are not given a unique name but are generally called elementary molecules.

In the problem of determining relative weights Avogadro devotes his entire attention to determining the relative weights of the molecules. At no time does he make an attempt at or seem particularly interested in determining the number of submolecular particles or atoms in a particular molecule, which would make possible a determination of the relative weights of the submolecular particles or atoms. He states that in all cases with which he is familiar the molecules of elementary gases are at least splittable into two parts so that there are at least two atoms to the molecule. But he explicitly does not rule out the possibility of a subdivision of the molecules into 4, 6, or 8, et cetera, and hence the possibility of tetra-, hexa-, or octa-atomic molecules. As a matter of fact at one point, as will be noted in Chapter 28, he seems to indicate his belief that the oxygen molecule is at least splittable into 4 parts and is tetra-atomic. If the reader will adopt Avogadro's orientation and will view the molecule as the entity to be focussed on, he will be able to follow Avogadro's discussion with greater ease.

Avogadro in discussing the two particles, atom and molecule, does not use clear-cut terminology. He uses only the term molecule, qualified by various adjectives, to designate both the concept of the atom and of the molecule. Therefore in considering the remainder of his paper the modern terms, in italics, have been substituted for Avogadro's original terms.

But a means of explaining facts of this type in conformity with our [equal-volumes-equal-numbers] hypothesis presents itself naturally enough: we suppose, namely, that the *molecules of an elementary* gas whatever (i.e., the molecules which are at such a distance from each other that they cannot exercise their mutual action) are not formed of *an atom*, but are made up of a certain number of these *atoms* united by attraction to form a *molecule*; and further, that when molecules of another substance unite with the former to form a compound molecule, the *molecule of a compound* which should result splits up

into two or more parts . . . ; so that the number of *molecules* of the compound becomes double, quadruple, etc., what it would have been if there had
been no splitting-up, and exactly what is necessary to satisfy the volume of the
resulting gas.*

As an example of Avogadro's hypotheses of equal-volumes-equal-numbers of molecules and splittable molecules, consider the formation of
water vapor from hydrogen and oxygen gas. It is experimentally observed
that the relative volumes, all measured at the same temperature and pressure, are

1 vol. oxygen + 2 vol. hydrogen → 2 vol. water vapor.

First applying his hypothesis of equal-volumes-equal-numbers of molecules and letting there be *n* molecules of oxygen in the one volume of
oxygen,

n molecules oxygen + 2*n* molecules hydrogen → 2*n* molecules water,

or

1 molecule oxygen + 2 molecules hydrogen → 2 molecules water.

Then applying his second hypothesis of splittable molecules, the one molecule of oxygen can enter into the formation of two molecules of water if

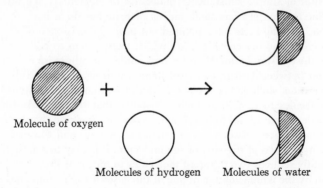

Molecule of oxygen

Molecules of hydrogen   Molecules of water

Figure 27-2. *The formation of a water molecule from hydrogen and oxygen
molecules.*

the oxygen molecule splits into two equal parts (Fig. 27-2). Adopting
Avogadro's orientation one would say that the water molecule is composed of one molecule of hydrogen and one-half molecule of oxygen.

Thus the integral volume relationships of Gay-Lussac's law, Dalton's
atomic theory and the equal-volumes-equal-numbers hypothesis are made
compatible. The fact that water vapor has a smaller specific gravity than

---

* Thus, for example, the . . . molecule of water will be composed of a half-
molecule of oxygen with one molecule, or what is the same thing, two half-molecules
of hydrogen.

oxygen is now understandable. What Dalton had considered to be an addition of hydrogen and oxygen atoms to produce the water molecule is on Avogadro's hypothesis a substitution of a hydrogen molecule for one half of an oxygen molecule. The weight of the entire hydrogen molecule is less than the weight of the half oxygen molecule which it replaces and as a result the water molecule weighs less than the oxygen molecule.

On reviewing the various compound gases most generally known, I only find examples of duplication of the volume relatively to the volume of that one of the constituents which combines with one or more volumes of the other. We have already seen this for water. In the same way, we know that the volume of ammonia gas is twice that of the nitrogen which enters into it. M. Gay-Lussac has also shown that the volume of nitrous oxide is equal to that of the nitrogen which forms part of it, and consequently is twice that of the oxygen. Finally, nitrous gas, which contains equal volumes of nitrogen and oxygen, has a volume equal to the sum of the two constituent gases, that is to say, double that of each of them. Thus in all these cases there must be a division of the molecule into two; but it is possible that in other cases the division might be into four, eight, etc. The possibility of this division of compound molecules might have been conjectured *a priori;* for otherwise the integral molecules [molecules] of bodies composed of several substances with a relatively large number of molecules, would come to have a mass excessive in comparison with the molecules of simple substances [molecules of elements]. We might therefore imagine that nature has some means of bringing them back to the order of the latter, and the facts have pointed out to us the existence of such means. Besides, there is another consideration which would seem to make us admit in some cases the division in question; for how could one otherwise conceive a real combination between two gaseous substances uniting in equal volumes without condensation, such as takes place in the formation of nitrous gas? Supposing the molecules to remain at such a distance that the mutual attraction of those of each gas could not be exercised, we cannot imagine that a new attraction could take place between the molecules of one gas and those of the other. But on the hypothesis of division of the molecule, it is easy to see that the combination really reduces two different molecules to one, and that there would be contraction by the whole volume of one of the gases if each compound molecule did not split up into two molecules of the same nature. M. Gay-Lussac clearly saw that, according to the facts, the diminution of volume of the combination of gases cannot represent the approximation of their elementary molecules. The division of molecules on combination explains to us how these two things may be made independent of each other.

STUDY QUESTIONS

1. The premise or premises that Avogadro cites or assumes in the opening paragraph of his paper are
   a. laws of definite and multiple proportions

    b. Dalton's postulates of the atomic theory

    c. Gay-Lussac's generalization on his observations of the volumes of gases involved in reactions.

The correct choice is

    (1) a   (2) b   (3) c   (4) a and b   (5) a, b, and c.

2. Dalton's " picture " of the gaseous state is

    (1) each molecule of different gases has the same quantity of caloric about it, but the density of the caloric and hence volume of caloric varies due to different molecules having different attractions

    (2) each molecule of different gases has a different quantity of caloric due to greater or lesser attraction resulting in varying densities and varying volumes about each molecule

    (3) each molecule of different gases has a different quantity of caloric due to greater or lesser attraction, but the volume of caloric about each molecule is the same

    (4) each molecule of different gases has the same quantity of caloric about it and the density and hence the volume of caloric about each molecule is the same

    (5) each molecule of different gases has no caloric about it. Due to the great distance between molecules there are no attractive forces between them and each molecule behaves independently.

3. Avogadro's " picture " of the gaseous state is (see question 2)

    (1) 1   (2) 2   (3) 3   (4) 4   (5) 5.

4–5. Consider the following data:
20 volumes of hydrogen react with 10 volumes of gas A to produce a compound.
Specific gravity of hydrogen = 0.0732.
Specific gravity of gas A   = 0.366.

4. The mass of the molecule of gas A relative to the hydrogen molecule is

    (1) .366 : 1   (2) 10 : 1   (3) 2.5 : 1   (4) .5 : 1   (5) 5 : 1.

5. The compound formed results from the union of

    (1) 1 molecule of A with 1 molecule of hydrogen

    (2) 2 molecules of A with 1 molecule of hydrogen

    (3) 1 molecule of A with 2 molecules of hydrogen

    (4) 2 molecules of A with 2 molecules of hydrogen

    (5) 5 molecules of A with 1 molecule of hydrogen.

6. Consider the relative volumes in the following reaction (in light of Avogadro's hypothesis):

½ volume of oxygen reacts with 1 volume of nitrous gas to yield nitric acid. The nitric acid results from the union of

    (1) 1 molecule of oxygen with 2 of nitrous gas

    (2) ½ molecule of oxygen with 2 of nitrous gas

    (3) 1 molecule of oxygen with 1 of nitrous gas

    (4) 2 molecules of oxygen with 1 of nitrous gas

    (5) insufficient data to tell.

7–8. A certain volume of hydrogen weighs 1 lb. A different volume of oxygen under the same conditions weighs 3 lbs.

7. According to Avogadro (use the densities of hydrogen and oxygen, p. 343), the ratio of the volume of hydrogen to that of oxygen is approximately,

(1) 1 : 3   (2) 3 : 1   (3) 5 : 1   (4) 1 : 5   (5) 15 : 1.

8. The ratio of the number of hydrogen molecules to oxygen molecules is

(1) 1 : 3   (2) 3 : 1   (3) 5 : 1   (4) 1 : 5   (5) 15 : 1.

9. Avogadro states that in view of his hypothesis (equal-volumes-equal-numbers) *it would at first sight appear* that if two gases react to yield a product also gaseous, the volume of the gaseous product would be

    (1) equal to the sum of the volumes of the reactants
    (2) equal to the volume of the gaseous reactant having the greatest volume
    (3) equal to one half the sum of the volumes of the reactants
    (4) not necessarily related to the volume of the reactants
    (5) equal to the volume of the gaseous reactant having the least volume.

10. Avogadro notes that in fact this is not true (correct answer to question 9), and in particular that 1 volume of oxygen reacts with 2 volumes of hydrogen to yield how many volumes of water vapor?

(1) 1   (2) 2   (3) 3   (4) negligible   (5) 1½.

11. Avogadro's second hypothesis could be briefly stated as follows: The constituent molecules of a simple or elementary gas are

    (1) monatomic   (2) diatomic   (3) alike in all respects
    (4) polyatomic   (5) indivisible.

12. Consider the following gaseous reaction:
    1 vol. gas A + 2 vol. gas B → 2 vol. product gas C.
    (Gases A and B are assumed elementary.)
    Which one or more of the following statements are correct?
    a. The molecules of gas A are at least divisible into two half molecules of A.
    b. The molecules of gas B are at least divisible into two half molecules of B.
    c. No statement can be made regarding the molecules of A.
    d. No statement can be made regarding the molecules of B.
    The correct choice is

(1) a   (2) b   (3) d   (4) a and d   (5) b and c.

13. Consider the following data:
    1 vol. hydrogen + 1 vol. chlorine → 2 vol. gas called hydrogen chloride.
    From this data it may be deduced that
    a. the hydrogen molecule is at least diatomic
    b. no statement can be made relative to the molecule of hydrogen
    c. the chlorine molecule is at least diatomic
    d. no statement can be made relative to the molecule of chlorine.
    The correct answer is

(1) a   (2) b   (3) c   (4) a and c   (5) d and b.

14. Consider the following data:
    10 cc nitrogen + 30 cc hydrogen → 20 cc ammonia gas.
    From this data it may be deduced that
    a. the hydrogen molecule is at least diatomic

b. no statement can be made relative to the hydrogen molecule
c. the nitrogen molecule is at least diatomic
d. no statement can be made relative to the nitrogen molecule.
The correct answer is

(1) a   (2) a and d   (3) a and c   (4) b and c   (5) b and d.

15. According to Avogadro's concept the molecules of oxygen consist of at least two oxygen atoms (O) " stuck together " (O_2). Does anything strike you as unusual about this concept?

16. Assuming the oxygen molecule exists as O_2, does this indicate the possible existence of a structural aspect to the oxygen atom as opposed to a homogeneous spherical particle concept of the oxygen atom?

28

Avogadro's Calculation of Molecular Weights

● In this last portion of his paper, Avogadro applies his hypothesis of "splittable molecules" to the formation of water, nitrous oxide, ammonia, and other compounds. His theory suggests definite compositions of these molecules which he tries to justify from specific gravity determinations.

ESSAY ON A MANNER OF DETERMINING THE RELATIVE MASSES OF THE ELEMENTARY MOLECULES OF BODIES, AND THE PROPORTIONS IN WHICH THEY ENTER INTO THESE COMPOUNDS (*Continued*) [1]

by Amadeo Avogadro

III

Dalton, on arbitrary suppositions as to the most likely relative number of molecules in compounds, has endeavoured to fix ratios between the masses of the molecules of simple substances. Our hypothesis, supposing it well-founded, put us in a position to confirm or rectify his results from precise data, and, above all, to assign the magnitude of compound molecules according to the volumes of the gaseous compounds, which depend partly on the division of molecules entirely unsuspected by this physicist.

Thus Dalton supposes * that water is formed by the union of hydrogen and oxygen, molecule to molecule. From this, and from the ratio by weight of the two components, it would follow that the mass of the molecule of oxygen would be to that of hydrogen as 7½ to 1 nearly, or, according to Dalton's evaluation, as 6 to 1. [More accurate analysis of water at this time gave the composition as 7½ parts of oxygen to 1 of hydrogen by weight.] This ratio on our hypothesis is, as we saw, twice as great, namely, as 15 to 1. As for the molecule of water, its mass ought to be roughly expressed by $15 + 2 = 17$ (taking

---

[1] Alembic Club Reprint, No. 4. The University of Chicago Press, 1902, pp. 33–36, 51.

* In what follows I shall make use of the exposition of Dalton's ideas given in Thomson's System of Chemistry.

for unity that of hydrogen) [thus Avogadro selects as unity the weight of the hydrogen molecule] if there were no division of the molecule into two; but on account of this division it is reduced to half, 8½, or more exactly 8.537, as may also be found directly by dividing the density of aqueous vapour 0.625 (Gay-Lussac) by the density of hydrogen 0.0732. This mass only differs from 7, that assigned to it by Dalton, by the difference in the values for the composition of water; so that in this respect Dalton's result is approximately correct from the combination of two compensating errors, — the error in the mass of the molecule of oxygen, and his neglect of the division of the molecule.

Using the example cited above we shall note in detail Dalton's and Avogadro's treatments of experimental data. Experimentally, hydrogen and oxygen combine in the following proportions by weight to produce water:

7½ parts oxygen + 1 part hydrogen → 8½ parts water.

Also it is observed that

1 vol. oxygen + 2 vol. hydrogen → 2 vol. water vapor.

Applying his rule of greatest simplicity, Dalton would consider the reaction on the atomic scale as being

1 atom oxygen + 1 atom hydrogen → 1 "atom" water.
O + H → HO.

Then taking cognizance of only the experimental weight relations noted above, he would deduce that the oxygen atom weighed 7½ times as much as the hydrogen atom, and the water "atom" weighed 8½ times as much as the hydrogen atom.

Avogadro on the basis of his equal-volumes-equal-numbers hypothesis would deduce from the experimentally observed volume relations that

1 molecule oxygen + 2 molecules hydrogen → 2 molecules water vapor.

Noting the weight and the volume relations experimentally observed above, he would deduce that the oxygen molecule weighed 15 times as much as the hydrogen molecule, and the water molecule relative to the hydrogen molecule would weigh

$$\frac{1 \text{ molecule oxygen} + 2 \text{ molecules hydrogen}}{2} = \frac{15 + 2}{2} = 8\tfrac{1}{2}.$$

Then Avogadro would observe experimentally whether water vapor was approximately 8½ times as dense as hydrogen.

It is suggested that in Avogadro's following discussion of various other compounds Dalton's and Avogadro's treatments of the data be compared in the above manner.

Dalton supposes that in nitrous gas the combination of nitrogen and oxygen is molecule to molecule: we have seen on our hypothesis that this is actually the case. Thus Dalton would have found the same molecular mass for nitrogen as we have, always supposing that of hydrogen to be unity, if he had not set out from a different value for that of oxygen, and if he had taken precisely the same value for the quantities of the elements in nitrous gas by weight. But by supposing the molecule of oxygen to be less than half what we find, he has been obliged to make that of nitrogen also equal to less than half the value we have assigned to it, viz., 5 instead of 13. As regards the molecule of nitrous gas itself, his neglect of the division of the molecule again makes this result approach ours; he has made it $6 + 5 = 11$, whilst according to us it is about $(15 + 13)/2 = 14$, or more exactly $(15.074 + 13.238)/2 = 14.156$, as we also find by dividing 1.03636, the density of nitrous gas according to Gay-Lussac, by 0.07321. Dalton has likewise fixed in the same manner as the facts have given us, the relative number of molecules in nitrous oxide and in nitric acid, and in the first case the same circumstance has rectified his result for the magnitude of the molecule. He makes it $6 + 2 \times 5 = 16$, whilst according to our method it should be $(15.074 + 2 \times 13.238)/2 = 20.775$, a number which is also obtained by dividing 1.52092, Gay-Lussac's value for the density of nitrous oxide, by the density of hydrogen.

In the case of ammonia, Dalton's supposition as to the relative number of molecules in its composition is on our hypothesis entirely at fault. He supposes nitrogen and hydrogen to be united in it molecule to molecule, whereas we have seen that one molecule of nitrogen unites with three molecules of hydrogen. According to him the molecule of ammonia would be $5 + 1 = 6$: according to us it should be $(13 + 3)/2 = 8$, or more exactly 8.119, as may also be deduced directly from the density of ammonia gas. The division of the molecule, which does not enter into Dalton's calculations, partly corrects in this case also the error which would result from his other suppositions.

All the compounds we have just discussed are produced by the union of one molecule of one of the components with one or more molecules of the other. In nitrous acid we have another compound of two of the substances already spoken of, in which the terms of the ratio between the number of molecules both differ from unity. From Gay-Lussac's experiments (Société d'Arcueil, same volume), it appears that this acid is formed from 1 part by volume of oxygen and 3 of nitrous gas, or, what comes to the same thing, of 3 parts of nitrogen and 5 of oxygen; whence it would follow, on our hypothesis, that its molecule should be composed of 3 molecules of nitrogen and 5 of oxygen, leaving the possibility of division out of account.[2]

[2] Thus it is experimentally observed that

1 vol. oxygen + 3 vol. nitrous gas → nitrous acid.

On the basis of equal-volume-equal-numbers,

1 molecule oxygen + 3 molecules nitrous gas → nitrous acid.

For nitrous gas it is experimentally observed that,

1 vol. oxygen + 1 vol. nitrogen → 2 vol. nitrous gas

or

1 molecule oxygen + 1 molecule nitrogen → 2 molecules nitrous gas.

Hence 3 molecules of nitrous gas are formed from 1½ molecules of nitrogen and 1½ molecules of oxygen. Then

1 molecule oxygen + 3 molecules nitrous gas → nitrous acid

But this mode of combination can be referred to the preceding simpler forms by considering it as the result of the union of 1 molecule of oxygen with 3 of nitrous gas, i.e. with 3 molecules, each composed of a half-molecule of oxygen and a half-molecule of nitrogen, which thus already includes the division of some of the molecules of oxygen which enter into that of nitrous acid. Supposing there to be no other division, the mass of this last molecule would be 57.542, that of hydrogen being taken as unity, and the density of nitrous acid gas would be 4.21267, the density of air being taken as unity. But it is probable that there is at least another division into two, and consequently a reduction of the density to half: we must wait until this density has been determined by experiment.

❋   ❋   ❋   ❋   ❋   ❋   ❋

Avogadro's last statement in the above paragraph seems to indicate that he believes the oxygen and nitrogen molecules are at least divisible into four parts and hence at least tetra-atomic. Thus nitrous acid results from the combination of 1 molecule of oxygen with 3 molecules of nitrous gas. But each molecule of nitrous gas is composed of ½ molecule of nitrogen and ½ molecule of oxygen. Then nitrous acid in turn must be composed of 3 half molecules of nitrogen or 1½ molecules of nitrogen and 2½ molecules of oxygen if there is no further splitting when the nitrous acid molecules and oxygen molecules come together. But if there is a splitting, as Avogadro seems to expect, the resulting molecule of nitrous acid would be composed of ¾ molecule of nitrogen and 1¼ molecules of oxygen. If this were so, then the molecules of nitrogen and oxygen must each be at least divisible into 4 parts and hence tetra-atomic.

In subsequent sections of his paper Avogadro discusses the application of his theory to other specific compounds. In particular he attempts to extend his method, by analogous reasoning, to determine the relative weights of molecules of elements that exist only in the solid state and hence to which his method of relative specific gravities of vapors is not directly applicable. The following relative volumes are observed when carbon, which as an element is known only in the solid state, reacts with gaseous oxygen to form gaseous carbonic acid:

carbon (solid, negligible volume) + 1 volume oxygen
$$\rightarrow 1 \text{ volume carbonic acid.}$$

---

could be written as

1 molecule oxygen + 1½ molecules oxygen + 1½ molecules nitrogen → nitrous acid

or

2½ molecules oxygen + 1½ molecules nitrogen → nitrous acid

or

5 molecules oxygen + 3 molecules nitrogen → nitrous acid.

Thus nitrous acid would be composed of 5 molecules of oxygen and 3 of nitrogen if no subsequent division of the nitrous acid molecule occurs.

Reasoning from analogy to other reactions, Avogadro hypothesizes that if the vapor phase of carbon did exist, the relative volume of the solid carbon in the above reaction would be such that

½ volume carbon vapor + 1 volume oxygen → 1 volume carbonic acid.

By combining the relative weight of the carbon that takes part in the reaction with the assumed relative volume, it is of course possible to calculate the relative weight of the carbon molecule that would exist in such an assumed relative volume.

VIII

It will have been in general remarked on reading this Memoir that there are many points of agreement between our special results and those of Dalton, although we set out from a general principle, and Dalton has only been guided by considerations of detail. This agreement is an argument in favour of our hypothesis, which is at bottom merely Dalton's system furnished with a new means of precision from the connection we have found between it and the general fact established by M. Gay-Lussac. Dalton's system supposes that compounds are made in general in fixed proportions, and this is what experiment shows with regard to the more stable compounds and those most interesting to the chemist. It would appear that it is only combinations of this sort that can take place amongst gases, on account of the enormous size of the molecules which would result from ratios expressed by larger numbers, in spite of the division of the molecules, which is in all probability confined within narrow limits. We perceive that the close packing of the molecules in solids and liquids, which only leaves between the integral molecules distances of the same order as those between the elementary molecules, can give rise to more complicated ratios, and even to combinations in all proportions; but these compounds will be so to speak of a different type from those with which we have been concerned, and this distinction may serve to reconcile M. Berthollet's ideas as to compounds with the theory of fixed proportions.[3]

STUDY QUESTIONS

1. What selection does Avogadro make for unity on his scale of molecular weights? What is the molecular weight of oxygen according to Avogadro on the basis of this selection?

   2–4. Consider the following data:

   (*a*) *10 parts by weight of gas A react with 7.5 parts by weight of oxygen to produce a compound (gaseous) C.*

   (*b*) *1 volume of A reacts with 1 volume of oxygen to produce 2 volumes of the gaseous product C. This is the only known compound of A and oxygen.*

---

[3] "Berthollet's ideas" referred to here is that elements in forming compounds combine in all proportions. See Chapter 23.

Suppose the above data is " exact," so that the only difference in values in the following problems is due to the difference in interpretation of data by Dalton and Avogadro.

(*Note: Take Dalton's atomic weight of oxygen as 7.5, which he would have in 1811 due to more accurate analysis of water then available; 7.5 parts oxygen to 1 of hydrogen.*)

2. The (" atomic ") weight of C according to Dalton would be

   (1) 17.5   (2) 8.75   (3) 35.0   (4) 20.0   (5) none of these.

3. The molecular weight of A according to Avogadro would be

   (1) 10.0   (2) 17.5   (3) 20.0   (4) 5.00   (5) none of these.

4. The molecular weight of C according to Avogadro would be

   (1) 17.5   (2) 8.75   (3) 20.0   (4) 35.0   (5) none of these.

5. If Dalton had used the same experimental data as Avogadro did regarding the formation of ammonia (i.e., 3 parts by weight of hydrogen to 13 of nitrogen) he would have found for the molecular weight of the ammonia:

   (1) 6.00   (2) 8.12   (3) 17.0   (4) 8.00   (5) 5.33.

6. In discussing nitrous acid, Avogadro cites the experiments of Gay-Lussac. If nitrous acid consists of 3 parts of nitrogen and 5 of oxygen by volume and division does occur, then Avogadro would calculate the weight of the nitrous acid molecule (approximately) to be

   (1) 8.00   (2) 117   (3) 75.0   (4) 57.0   (5) 112.

7–11. *Consider the following gaseous reaction:*
   1 volume of element A reacts with 2 volumes of oxygen to produce 2 volumes of a gaseous product C. Analysis of C yields the following: 70% by weight of A and 30% oxygen. C is the only compound of A and oxygen.
   Physical data on oxygen and A:
   Specific gravity of oxygen = 1.11
   Specific gravity of A   = 5.18

7. Dalton using the analysis data and his rule of greatest simplicity would calculate the atomic weight of A to be
   (Assume Dalton's atomic weight of oxygen to be 7.5)

   (1) 7.00   (2) 17.5   (3) 35.0   (4) 70.0   (5) 8.75.

8. Avogadro would calculate the molecular weight of A to be

   (1) 7.00   (2) 17.5   (3) 35.0   (4) 70.0   (5) 8.75.

9. Dalton would calculate the " atomic " weight of C to be

   (1) 70.0   (2) 17.5   (3) 25.0   (4) 50.0   (5) 32.5.

10. Avogadro would calculate the molecular weight of C to be

    (1) 70.0   (2) 17.5   (3) 25.0   (4) 50.0   (5) 32.5.

11. Avogadro would expect the specific gravity of C to be approximately

    (1) 3.70   (2) 1.85   (3) 7.40   (4) 6.30   (5) 3.15.

12. Avogadro states in his conclusion that in obtaining his results he set out from a " general principle," while Dalton was " guided by considerations of detail." Explain Avogadro's meaning here.

13. Consider the relative volumes involved in the three following reactions, all of which Avogadro was familiar with:

2 volumes of hydrogen + 1 volume of oxygen → 2 volumes of water vapor
1 volume of nitrogen + 3 volumes of hydrogen → 2 volumes of ammonia
1 volume of nitrogen + 1 volume of oxygen → 2 volumes of nitrous gas.

What is the smallest degree of submolecularity or atomicity of the molecules of oxygen, nitrogen, and hydrogen that would satisfy the volume relations observed in all three reactions?

29

Chemistry from Avogadro to Cannizzaro

• Avogadro's hypotheses have been seen to yield the same formulas for water and other substances as those that are accepted today, if the simplest degree of atomicity of molecules possible is assumed, so it is to be expected that these hypotheses should loom large in the development of atomic theory. That they do has been obvious, however, only since the latter half of the 19th century, but at the time Avogadro proposed them in 1811 they were ignored by chemists for good reasons.

NEGLECT OF AVOGADRO'S HYPOTHESES

First among these reasons was the novelty of Avogadro's suggestions. It will be recalled that Dalton first proposed his atomic theory in tentative form in 1803 and Dalton's text, from which portions have been quoted, was published in 1808. Avogadro made his proposals in 1811. Most chemists were not yet even thinking in terms of atoms, much less in terms of Avogadro's refinement requiring the existence of two kinds of " ultimate " particles. Also it must be borne in mind that the attempt to determine relative atomic weights was only a small segment of the developments that were occurring in chemistry, since many chemists, for example, were occupied in the field of electrochemistry and with the discovery of new elements.

Furthermore, Avogadro's proposal of the existence of two kinds of " ultimate " particles required the strange behavior that between two like atoms, such as two atoms of oxygen, there must exist some kind of an attractive force, resulting in the formation of an O_2 molecule, but then between two O_2 molecules there must be a repulsive force to explain the tendency of gases to expand. Also as Avogadro admitted there was no way of deciding whether the oxygen molecule was O_4 or O_6 or some other even number of atoms.

Even if Avogadro's proposals had been completely accepted and it was assumed that the molecules of gaseous elements were diatomic, there were only four gaseous elements at the time (hydrogen, oxygen, nitrogen, and chlorine) to which the proposals could be applied directly for the determination of relative atomic weights. Thus there remained the problem of determining the relative atomic weights of the vast majority of chemical elements. Avogadro appreciated this limited applicability and, it will be recalled, sought to extend his proposals to solid elements by use of analogies. Such an extension was only very tenuously supported, and today it is known that it would have led to incorrect atomic weights in many cases. As a matter of fact such a method, often leading to incorrect atomic weights, was subsequently used to some extent.

Finally we shall see in the next chapter that Cannizzaro in 1860 in convincing the majority of chemists of the correctness of Avogadro's hypotheses made use of a large number of easily vaporizable compounds. The most easily vaporizable compounds are organic compounds and these for the most part were still unknown in 1811, and the experimental techniques for determining their relative densities were not in existence. It is perhaps not incorrect to say that Avogadro's hypotheses were ahead of their time, and had to wait for factual chemistry and experimental techniques to catch up before they could be fruitfully applied.

For the foregoing reasons Avogadro was largely ignored in 1811. However, the atomic theory continued to develop along different lines. Although Avogadro's proposals were not accepted, Gay-Lussac's law, which more investigation only further confirmed, occupied a central role.

DEVELOPMENTS BETWEEN 1811 AND 1860

In retrospect the time from 1811 to Cannizzaro's final clarification of the problem of atomic weights in 1860 falls roughly into three periods of approximately equal duration. The first period from 1811 to about 1826 is one in which the determination of atomic weights moved steadily forward utilizing essentially one method for the gaseous elements and several other methods for nongaseous elements. During this period there was no possibility of applying the different methods for gaseous and nongaseous elements to any one element and thus obtaining a cross check. A second period had its beginning in 1826 when Dumas' vapor density studies made it possible to cross check and apply the different methods for gaseous and nongaseous elements to one and the same element. Since the cross check in some cases yielded different values for the atomic weights of a given element, a time of confusion followed. In this period ending about 1845, it was generally felt doubtful if unambiguous relative atomic weights could ever be determined, and chemists generally ceased to write formulas representing atomic constitutions. A final period beginning around 1845 was marked by a gradual return to the atomic theory, due largely to

Figure 29-1. *Jons Jacob Berzelius* (*1779–1848*).

developments in the new field of organic chemistry, and terminated with the eventual clarification furnished by Cannizzaro's proposals in 1860.

In these periods, viewed from a broad perspective, one of the main events that was occurring was the discovery of additional empirical laws that were related to the atomic constitution of matter. In essence these laws furnished criteria whereby atomic constitutions could be assigned to compounds and thus a link could be forged between combining weight data and relative atomic weights. This is the import of Dulong and Petit's law and Mitscherlich's law discovered in the period from 1811 to 1826 which play the same role as Gay-Lussac's law played for Avogadro.

Period 1811–1826

The development of the atomic theory from 1811 to 1826 is dominated by the Swedish chemist Berzelius. If Dalton was the inventor of the atomic theory in chemistry, it was Berzelius who more fully appreciated the implications of the theory for chemistry and carried out most of the necessary painstaking work. After his initial proposals, Dalton contributed little of positive value to the theory. Berzelius (Fig. 29-1) was born in 1779 in Sweden and was educated as a physician, receiving his medical degree from the school at Upsala in 1802. At this time there were no graduate programs in the universities leading to doctors' degrees in the various fields of science and many of the early chemists were educated as physicians.

In 1802 Berzelius was appointed to the faculty of the medical school at Stockholm where he remained for a quarter of a century. As might be expected from his medical background, his early researches were in physiological chemistry. In 1807, however, he became interested in the compositions of compounds and the expression of composition in terms of the atomic theory. Berzelius noted that a necessary prerequisite to the determination of accurate atomic weights was accurate combining weights, and from 1808 to 1818 he analyzed some 2000 compounds, developing many original analytical procedures in the process. This work culminated in his atomic weight tables published in 1818, details of which will be considered shortly.

During his life there was hardly a phase of chemistry in which he did not play a prominent role. Anyone who has taken an elementary laboratory course in chemistry and from the first day has used such indispensable equipment as rubber tubing, wash bottles, filter paper, and water baths, will appreciate something of his influence when it is noted that Berzelius was responsible for introducing all of these and more into the chemistry laboratory.

He published extensively, his writings including over 250 original papers and a handbook that ran through five editions, and for many years he issued an annual report on the progress of chemistry and physics. Many chemists who later became famous went to Sweden to study under him. In his lifetime, he received many honors, among them a barony in 1835. He died in 1848.

Berzelius' Early Contributions to Atomic Theory. One of Berzelius' earliest and most important contributions to atomic theory was contained in a paper published in 1814 in which he also introduced the modern symbols for the elements known at the time. It is worthwhile to consider this paper in some detail as the ideas expressed in it play a central role in what is to follow.

Initially Berzelius expressed the composition of a compound in terms of the relative volumes of the elements that entered into its composition. For example, it was noted experimentally that 1 volume of oxygen reacts with 2 volumes of hydrogen to produce water. Accordingly the composition of water was expressed as $2H + O$, where the symbol O stands for unit volume of oxygen and the symbol H for unit volume of hydrogen and 2H for 2 unit volumes of hydrogen. Later the $2H + O$ was contracted to H_2O, but still with the same significance.

For compounds formed from a solid and a gas he reasoned by analogy as to what the relative volume of the solid would be if it could be brought into the gaseous state and the volume measured at the same temperature and pressure as the other substances involved in the reaction. Thus sulfur, a solid, has many chemical properties similar to oxygen. Like oxygen, sulfur reacts with metals and also forms a compound with hydrogen called hydrogen sulfide. Berzelius reasoned that if sulfur did exist in the gaseous state the relative volumes that would be observed in the formation of hydrogen sulfide would be analogous to the volumes observed in the formation of hydrogen oxide (water) from hydrogen and oxygen. It is observed that

S (solid) + 2 vol. hydrogen → 2 vol. hydrogen sulfide.

If sulfur could be brought into the gaseous state the relative volumes would be

1 vol. sulfur + 2 vol. hydrogen → 2 vol. hydrogen sulfide.

The composition of hydrogen sulfide in terms of volumes would be written as H_2S.

By similar analogous reasoning, Berzelius wrote for carbonic acid gas CO_2 and for the oxides of the metals potassium, sodium, and calcium KO_2, NaO_2, and CaO_2 respectively.

Berzelius in 1818 combined his volume composition views with Dalton's individual particle or atomic views by hypothesizing that equal volumes of *elementary* gases contain equal numbers of atoms. Thus in the case of water it is noted that

1 vol. oxygen + 2 vol. hydrogen → 2 vol. water vapor.

If there are n atoms of oxygen in the volume of oxygen, then there must be $2n$ atoms of hydrogen in the two volumes of hydrogen, and the reaction expressed in terms of atoms becomes

n atoms oxygen + $2n$ atoms hydrogen → n particles water

or

1 atom oxygen + 2 atoms hydrogen → 1 particle water

or

$$O + 2H \rightarrow H_2O,$$

where O now symbolizes an atom of oxygen and H an atom of hydrogen.

The symbolization H_2O for water meant simultaneously to Berzelius that water was composed of 1 volume of oxygen to 2 volumes of hydrogen and that water was composed of 1 atom of oxygen to 2 atoms of hydrogen. Likewise the relative volume composition symbols for other compounds, such as H_2S and NaO_2, translated directly into the relative numbers of atoms entering into the compositions of the compounds.

Note that the n particles of water H_2O must occupy 2 volumes and not 1 volume. That the n particles of water occupied twice the volume occupied by the n particles of hydrogen or oxygen was explained by Berzelius as being because of the greater size of the water particles. In general the relative volume occupied by n particles of a compound was assumed to be determined by the experimental volume observed in the reaction. Thus there was no all-embracing statement that could be made about the relative numbers of particles of compounds in equal volumes.

Only equal volumes of elementary gases contained equal numbers of particles or atoms. In retrospect this assumption seems hardly justifiable inasmuch as gases of both elements and compounds all obey the gas laws.

The Dualistic Theory. Berzelius could not accept Avogadro's postulate of the existence of two kinds of "ultimate" particles of elements, the atom and the polyatomic molecule. That like atoms could exist in combination, constituting the molecule of an element, was contrary to his celebrated dualistic theory of chemical combination that dominated chemical theory for many years.

Berzelius' dualistic theory had its origins in the electrochemical investigations of the time, some of which he had participated in. In 1800 Volta had invented the voltaic cell which is similar to the modern dry cell, and for the first time scientists had a continuous flow of electricity at their disposal for experimentation. One of the immediate fields of investigation was the study of chemical changes that could be caused by electricity (electrolysis). In 1800, two English chemists Nicholson and Carlisle used voltaic cells to decompose water into its elements, hydrogen appearing at the negative electrode and oxygen at the positive electrode. Thus electricity had reversed the formation of water from its elements. Soon after this Davy demonstrated the compound nature of the metallic oxides of some of the light metals, such as sodium and calcium, by the same method. Berzelius, reasoning from these results obtained by electrolysis, proposed his dualistic theory.

Inasmuch as electricity could reverse many chemical changes, it was reasonable to hypothesize that electrical forces were involved in the original combinations of the elements. Berzelius proposed that the atoms that constitute an element each have a net electric charge. In particular, oxygen atoms were assumed to bear a net negative charge and hydrogen atoms a net positive charge, since in the electrolysis of water, oxygen appeared at the positive electrode and hydrogen at the negative electrode. The individual atoms were considered as possessing centers of positive and of negative electricity, the net charge on the atom being determined by the excess of either positive or negative. Chemical combination of hydrogen and oxygen to produce water was assumed to result from the attraction of the positive hydrogen atoms and negative oxygen atoms for each other. "Dualistic" referred to the oppositely charged particles. In combination it was assumed that the charges on the atoms did not exactly neutralize each other because of the fact that the oxygen atom possessed a greater net negative charge than did the hydrogen atom of net positive charge. During electrolysis this combination was broken up by the electrical current from the voltaic cell, permitting oxygen to collect at the positive electrode and hydrogen at the negative electrode. Similarly the combination of other atoms was explained on the basis of attraction of oppositely charged atoms. Thus the combination of iron and oxygen to produce ferrous oxide was because of electrical attraction, and

$$\overset{+}{Fe} + \overset{-}{O} \rightarrow \overset{+}{Fe}O.$$

The FeO combination was assumed to have a residual positive charge due to a larger magnitude of $(+)$ charge on the iron atom. Also the combination of sulfur and oxygen to produce sulfuric acid was

$$\overset{+}{S} + 3\overset{-}{O} \rightarrow \overset{-}{S}O_3.$$

The SO_3 combination was believed to have a net negative charge.

All through this chapter when there are discussions involving atomic constitutions or formulas of a compound, such as FeO and SO_3, it should be borne in mind that such constitutions are to be viewed as tentative only. The problem of atomic constitutions of compounds and atomic weights was not finally solved, of course, until after 1860, the date with which this chapter concludes. However, the formulas for FeO and SO_3 are those accepted today.

The reaction of ferrous oxide, a base,[1] and sulfuric acid to produce the salt ferrous sulfate was considered to be due to the attraction between the oppositely charged complex atomic entities FeO and SO_3.

$$\overset{+}{Fe}O + \overset{-}{S}O_3 \rightarrow \overset{+}{Fe}O \cdot \overset{-}{S}O_3.$$

Thus the ferrous sulfate particle was also of a dual nature, composed of the oppositely charged particles $\overset{+}{Fe}O$ and $\overset{-}{S}O_3$. The attempt was made to represent the particles of all compounds as composed of such pairs of oppositely charged atoms or groups of atoms. Later it will be noted that the attempt was made also to include organic compounds in such a dualistic scheme.

Now it can be seen why Avogadro's proposal of polyatomic molecules of elements was repugnant to Berzelius. He assumed that the atoms of any one element each bore a like net charge and would repel each other making the formation of polyatomic molecules impossible. Eventually the dualistic theory, as we shall note later, was confronted with facts that it could not explain, particularly in the field of organic chemistry, and was finally abandoned about 1840. Thus also this objection to Avogadro's proposals finally disappeared.

Berzelius' Atomic Weight Table of 1818. Berzelius in 1818 published a table (Table 29-1) of atomic weights of 43 elements based on his analysis

---

[1] At this time metallic oxides whose water solutions turned litmus blue were referred to as bases and non-metallic oxides whose water solutions turned litmus red as acids. Today these are called basic and acid anhydrides respectively. The role that water played in acid-base reactions was not appreciated until later and it was assumed to act merely as a solvent.

TABLE 29-1

PORTION OF BERZELIUS' ATOMIC WEIGHT TABLE OF 1818 [2]

Oxygen	O	16.08
Sulfur	S	32.36
Phosphorus	P	63.10
Chlorine	Cl	35.60
Carbon	C	12.11
Nitrogen	N	14.12
Hydrogen	H	1.00
Arsenic	As	151.31
Chromium	Cr	113.68
Silicon	Si	47.68
Mercury	Hg	407.18
Silver	Ag	434.77
Copper	Cu	127.28
Bismuth	Bi	285.29
Lead	Pb	416.40
Tin	Sn	236.53
Iron	Fe	109.12
Zinc	Zn	129.70
Manganese	Mn	114.45
Aluminium	Al	55.06
Magnesium	Mg	50.94
Calcium	Ca	82.36
Sodium	Na	93.58
Potassium	K	158.28

of some 2000 compounds. In arriving at the relative atomic constitutions of the compounds, whereby the combining weight data could be translated into relative atomic weights, he used his special interpretation of Gay-Lussac's law where all the reactants were gaseous, and in the case of compounds formed from one or more nongaseous reactants, he was guided by analogies of the type discussed above for hydrogen sulfide and the metallic oxides. The table is reproduced here on the basis of the atomic weight of hydrogen as 1. Berzelius in his original table took the atomic weight of oxygen as 100.

Note the accuracy of the atomic weights as implied by the number of significant figures. If Berzelius' atomic weights are incorrect due to

[2] From Partington's, A Short History of Chemistry, Macmillan and Co., 1939, London, p. 207.

incorrect molecular compositions, the correct atomic weights are simply integral multiples or integral fractional multiples of the values in the table. Thus in the case of sodium the atomic weight listed is 93.09 based on the assumption that sodium oxide is NaO_2. If later sodium oxide is found to be Na_2O the atomic weight will be 93.09 divided by 4 or 23.27.

Dalton never accepted Berzelius' method of determining atomic weights and continued to rely on the methods cited from his text in Chapters 24 and 25. Gay-Lussac also did not accept the atomic weights and continued to express composition in terms of relative volumes of the reactants as Berzelius did in his paper of 1813. Gay-Lussac did not accept Berzelius' hypothesis of equal volumes containing equal numbers of atoms.

Wurtz, a famous French chemist, states in his text of 1881,[3]

After the ingenious but ignored attempts of Avogadro and Ampère, and the unfruitful efforts of Berzelius, Dalton's conception would have been sentenced to sterility and oblivion, had it not happened that, at the period of which we are speaking [ca. 1818], fresh discoveries and new ideas drew attention to it. We allude to Prout's hypothesis, to the discovery of the law of specific heats and to the discovery of isomorphism.

Prout's Hypothesis. Prout's hypothesis played no direct role in the atomic theory, but it acted as a stimulus to the more accurate determination of atomic weights by Berzelius and other chemists. The hypothesis was rooted in man's ancient desire for a unity in the apparent diversity of matter.

Prout, a London physician, in papers published in 1815–16 attempted to show that the most commonly accepted relative atomic weights of the elements were integral multiples of the atomic weight of hydrogen if the hydrogen atom is assigned the weight of 1. Prout's conclusion was that hydrogen was the primordial matter of which all other matter is composed and that the atoms of the other elements were composed of clusters of the appropriate numbers of atoms of hydrogen. Thus if on this scale the relative atomic weight of oxygen is 16, the oxygen atom was assumed to be composed of a cluster of 16 hydrogen atoms.

At that time the relative atomic weights were too inaccurate to test the hypothesis. This stimulated Berzelius and others to more accurate analysis to make testing of the hypothesis possible. These analyses showed that the relative atomic weights of the elements were not integral multiples of the weight of the hydrogen atom. Thus the hypothesis in the form stated by Prout was disproved, but it had served a useful purpose in stimulating more accurate analytical determinations.

Law of Dulong and Petit. Both Dulong and Petit were professors of physics at the École Polytechnique who became interested in discover-

---

[3] Ad. Wurtz, *The Atomic Theory*, D. Appleton and Co., New York, 1881, p. 48.

ing some connection between the physical properties of elements and the atomic weights of the atoms of the elements. The law that bears their names, as all laws, is based on experiment, and has played a role analogous to Gay-Lussac's law in the development of atomic theory. Both laws furnish criteria by which atomic constitution or formulas can be assigned to compounds and thus accurate combining weight data can be translated into accurate atomic weights. Dulong and Petit did not view their law in this light, but thought that it alone would yield accurate relative atomic weights without the use of combining weights.

This law relates the relative atomic weight of an element to the specific heat of the element. The elements investigated were solids, mostly metals. The *specific heat* of a substance is defined as the ratio of the quantity of heat necessary to raise the temperature of a given mass of the substance 1°F to the quantity of heat necessary to raise the temperature of the same mass of water 1°F. Thus the statement that the specific heat of a substance is .1 means that it takes .1 as much heat to raise the temperature of the substance 1°F as it does to raise the temperature of the same mass of water 1°F.

Dulong and Petit were interested not so much in comparing the specific heats of different elements as they were in comparing the amounts of heat necessary to raise the temperature 1°F of *equal numbers of atoms* of different elements. Thus a sample of iron containing a certain number of atoms requires a certain amount of heat to raise this sample 1°F. How does this amount of heat compare, say, to the amount of heat necessary to raise the temperature 1°F of a sample of copper *containing the same number of atoms* as the iron? If the specific heats of the iron and copper and their relative atomic weights are known, this question can be answered. Assume the atomic weight of iron is 56 and that of the copper is 63. If we consider a sample of iron weighing 56 units and one of copper weighing 63 units, the two samples will contain the same number of atoms since the two weights are in the same ratio as the atomic weights. Then a comparison of the amounts of heat necessary to raise the temperature of the two samples 1°F will be a comparison of the amounts of heat necessary to raise the temperature of *equal numbers of atoms* of iron and copper 1°F. Instead of determining the amounts of heat necessary to raise the temperature 1°F of 56 units of mass of iron and 63 units of mass of copper, it is easier to determine the specific heats of the iron and copper (heat necessary per unit mass per 1°F) and multiply these by the respective atomic weights, 56 for iron and 63 for copper, which gives the desired result. The findings in this specific example were that the quantities of heat necessary to raise the temperature 1°F for the 56 units of mass of iron and the 63 units of mass of copper were approximately the same. Dulong and Petit determined the specific heats of a number of elements which they used together with the relative atomic weights of the elements from the table published by Berzelius in 1818.

Dulong and Petit's findings may be summarized in three ways:

(1) The amount of heat necessary to raise the temperature 1°F of samples of elements containing equal numbers of atoms is the same.

(2) All atoms have the same capacity for heat.

(3) Atomic weight × specific heat = constant.

The constant in (3) is approximately the same for different elements. The law is generally stated and used in the last form.

The path to the conclusions above reached by Dulong and Petit was not as simple and direct as the discussion of the example of copper and iron might seem to indicate. The products of the specific heats of the elements and their atomic weights as reported by Berzelius in his 1818 table yielded numbers that were not the same, but varied widely. In order to make the products of the specific heats and atomic weights yield approximately a constant, Dulong and Petit were forced to use as their atomic weights integral fractions of most of the atomic weights reported by Berzelius. The results obtained by Dulong and Petit and the manner of treating Berzelius' atomic weights to arrive at their atomic weights are summarized in Table 29-2, page 370.

The last column added by Nash to Dulong and Petit's original table indicates the treatment they were forced to give Berzelius' atomic weights in order to obtain atomic weights that would agree with the law they sought, namely, that atomic weight × specific heat = a constant (approximately 6).

Evidently as an "anchor" for their table they relied rather heavily on the atomic weight of sulfur as being 32.19 as reported by Berzelius. There would be some justification for this heavy reliance on sulfur. Many compounds of sulfur were known and by using various analogies, such as that of water and hydrogen sulfide, the formulas of sulfur compounds had become well established. Hence sulfur's atomic weight was known with a greater degree of certainty than existed for most other elements. The product of the atomic weight of sulfur and its specific heat is 6.048. Then evidently for the other elements such fractions of Berzelius' atomic weights for the elements were used which when multiplied by the specific heats of the respective elements yielded approximately 6.048. Note that Dulong and Petit did not determine the specific heats of either hydrogen or oxygen or any gaseous element but only of solids.

As will be noted, most of Dulong and Petit's atomic weights are approximately those accepted today. Two glaring exceptions are tellurium as 64.5 and cobalt as 39.36. The values currently accepted are tellurium 127.61 and cobalt 58.94. The reason that Dulong and Petit found agreement in these two cases with their law was because of compensating er-

TABLE 29-2

PETIT AND DULONG'S TABLE OF SPECIFIC HEATS, ATOMIC WEIGHTS
(CONVERTED TO O = 16), AND THE PRODUCTS OF THESE TWO NUMBERS [4]

Element	Specific heat (relative to water)	Relative weights of the atoms	Products of the weight of each atom multiplied by the corresponding specific heat	Petit and Dulong's "relative weights of the atoms" as derived from Berzelius' 1818 figures [*]
Bismuth	0.0288	212.8	6.128	283.8 × ¾
Lead	.0293	207.2	6.070	414.2 × ½
Gold	.0298	198.9	5.926	397.8 × ½
Platinum	.0314	178.6	5.984	178.4 × 1
Tin	.0514	117.6	6.046	253.3 × ½
Silver	.0557	108.0	6.014	432.5 × ¼
Zinc	.0927	64.5	5.978	129.0 × ½
Tellurium	.0912	64.5	5.880	129.0 × ½
Copper	.0949	63.31	6.008	126.62 × ½
Nickel	.1035	59.0	6.110	118.3 × ½
Iron	.1100	54.27	5.970	108.55 × ½
Cobalt	.1498	39.36	5.896	118.3 × ⅓
Sulfur	.1880	32.19	6.048	32.19 × 1

[*] *This column does not appear in the table given by Petit and Dulong. It has been added to exhibit their (unacknowledged) indebtedness to Berzelius. The figures to the left in this column represent Berzelius' atomic weights which, when they are multiplied by the simple fractions on the right of the column, yield products that are in all cases close to, if not identical with, Petit and Dulong's relative atomic weights, as they are given in the third column of the table.*

rors, their values for the specific heats of these elements being much too high and the values they used for their atomic weights being correspondingly low.

Dulong and Petit were hopeful that their law by itself would furnish a method of determining accurately the relative atomic weights. In their paper they stated,[5]

[4] Quoted from L. K. Nash, *The Atomic-Molecular Theory*, Harvard University Press, 1950, p. 99.

[5] Quoted in Ad. Wurtz, *The Atomic Theory*, D. Appleton and Co., New York, 1881, p. 54.

In fact, the products in question [atomic weight × specific heat], which express the capacities for heat of atoms of different nature, are so nearly the same for all, that we cannot but attribute these very slight differences to inevitable errors, either in the determination of capacities for heat or in the chemical analysis.

In general this proved to be true, but the law was not as exact as they hoped and today we know it is not applicable to elements of low atomic weight.

The potential importance of Dulong and Petit's law to atomic theory should be obvious. The combining weights of a compound can be determined with great accuracy. As has been noted if there is some method of determining the formula of a compound, the accurate combining weights can be translated into accurate atomic weights. The role played by the law is to make it possible to determine the formula of a compound through the approximate atomic weights yielded by the law. Then the combination of formula and accurate combining weights yields accurate atomic weights.

This potential role of the law was not exploited extensively until Cannizzaro's clarification of the atomic theory in 1858. Berzelius in his atomic weight table of 1826 did not rely so heavily on this law as on the principle of isomorphism announced in 1821 by Mitscherlich.

Mitscherlich's Law of Isomorphism.   Mitscherlich was a student of Berzelius and carried out the research that resulted in his law in Berzelius' laboratory. If a saturated solution of a solid substance at high temperature is allowed to cool, the substance generally separates out in small particles, called crystals, of a definite geometrical shape, differing generally only in size. The different crystals of the same substance generally show the same number of faces, and the angles between corresponding faces of the different crystals are the same. As a simple example, sodium chloride crystallizes as cubes consisting of six faces with 90° angles between all adjoining faces.

Prior to Mitscherlich other scientists had noted that different substances often exhibited crystals of similar form. Mitscherlich discovered that different substances that apparently had similar atomic constitutions and formulas, on the basis of Berzelius' determinations, often had the same crystalline form or were isomorphs (equal shape).

The various sodium salts of phosphoric and arsenic acid were the first series of compounds investigated by Mitscherlich. The sodium phosphate salt that today is given the formula $Na_2HPO_4 \cdot 12H_2O$ exhibited a crystalline form similar to that of the sodium arsenate salt that is now written as $Na_2HAsO_4 \cdot 12H_2O$. The same was true of the pair of salts $NaH_2PO_4 \cdot H_2O$ and $NaH_2AsO_4 \cdot H_2O$. Mitscherlich stated,[6]

---

[6] Quoted in J. K. Partington, *A Short History of Chemistry*, Macmillan and Co. Limited, London and St. Martin's Press, Inc., New York, 1st ed., 1939, p. 202.

Every arsenate has its corresponding phosphate, composed according to the same proportions, combined with the same amount of water, and endowed with the same physical properties; in fact the two series of salts differ in no respect except that the radical of the acid in one series is phosphorous, whilst in the other it is arsenic.

Mitscherlich investigated the crystalline form of many other compounds and discovered other cases of isomorphism. From such investigations he stated his law of isomorphism in the tentative form,[7]

From this . . . the result seemed to be generally that certain elements have the property, when combined with an equal number of atoms of one or more common elements, of producing together similar crystal forms, and that in this view, the elements can be divided into certain groups.

Thus arsenic and phosphorous would fall in the same group.

Later the validity of the law was shaken by Mitscherlich's discovery of dimorphism, the crystallization of the same substance in two different crystalline forms. If one substance could crystallize in more than one form, what justification was there in singling out one of the forms and comparing it with the crystalline form of another substance? Mitscherlich felt however that the number of crystalline forms that a single substance could assume were limited and explained the existence of dimorphs on the basis of the atomic theory. He stated,[8]

according to the atomic theory this phenomenon [dimorphism] can easily be understood. Different forms will result whenever the arrangement of the atoms with regard to each other is altered, but the number of separate forms which, according to the assumptions of such a view, can be shown to exist remains very limited.

In view of dimorphism he finally stated his law of isomorphism [9] in the form, " *An equal number of atoms, if they are bound in the same way, produce similar crystal forms, and the crystal form depends not on the nature of the atoms but on the number and method of combination.*"

The influence of this law on Berzelius' revision of his atomic weights of 1818 will be noted shortly. Furthermore, as Wurtz points out in his text *The Atomic Theory*, the law of isomorphism also constitutes a solid support for the atomic theory, as the atomic theory affords precise terms for the enunciation of the law and its understanding.

Berzelius' Table of Atomic Weights of 1826.   Berzelius, in view of the results of the work of Mitscherlich and Dulong and Petit, made modifica-

---

[7] Quoted, Leicester and Klickstein, *Source Book in Chemistry*, McGraw-Hill Book Company, Inc., 1952, p. 307.

[8] Ibid., p. 307.

[9] Ibid., p. 308.

tions in his 1818 table of atomic weights and published a revised table in 1826 and again in 1835 without change (see Table 29-3, page 374). In arriving at this table he still depended upon his view that equal volumes of elemental gases contain equal numbers of atoms and upon the principle of chemical analogy that like substances must have like formulas. In making his revisions he relied heavily on the principle of isomorphism. He noted the cases where his revised atomic weights agreed with Dulong and Petit's law, but in several cases he listed atomic weights which were in disagreement with the law.

As an example of some of the changes, consider the two oxides of chromium which were designated by the names chromic acid and chromium oxide. In his table of 1818, Berzelius had written the formula of the acid as CrO_6 and of the oxide as CrO_3 in arriving at the atomic weight of the chromium. In 1826 he halved the number of oxygen atoms relative to the chromium atom and wrote CrO_3 for the acid. The reason for this change is the fact that chromic acid has certain chemical properties similar to sulfuric acid, and he was fairly certain that sulfuric acid had the formula SO_3. If chromic acid is CrO_3 instead of CrO_6, the number of oxygen atoms per chromium atom in the oxide must also be halved to yield $CrO_{3/2}$ or Cr_2O_3 instead of CrO_3. Thus the atomic weights of chromium in the 1826 table are half those in the table of 1818.

Iron forms two oxides, ferric oxide and ferrous oxide. Ferric oxide is isomorphous with chromic oxide. Thus if chromic oxide is Cr_2O_3, according to the principle of isomorphism, ferric oxide must be Fe_2O_3. With the formula of ferric oxide fixed, ferrous oxide of necessity must be FeO, based on the analytical data.

Also there are oxides of manganese and aluminum which are isomorphous with chromic oxide, so these must be respectively Mn_2O_3 and Al_2O_3. The atomic weights obtained from the analytical data of these oxides on the basis of these formulas agree with the values predicted by the law of Dulong and Petit.

Based on the analogous chemical properties of ferrous oxide, FeO, and silver oxide, Berzelius wrote the formula for silver oxide as AgO, although this formula yielded an atomic weight of silver twice that predicted by the law of Dulong and Petit. Nevertheless Berzelius preferred and reported his value for the atomic weight of silver in spite of the disagreement. Likewise due to chemical similarities of the oxides of lithium, sodium, and potassium with ferrous oxide and silver oxide he wrote as formulas for these oxides LiO, NaO, and KO. These formulas result in atomic weights for the metals that are approximately twice the values accepted today. There are several other disagreements with currently accepted values but as will be noted in the table of 1826 (Table 29-3) reproduced here, most of the atomic weights listed are in close agreement with those accepted today.

In view of this general agreement of Berzelius' values and the modern

TABLE 29-3

BERZELIUS' ATOMIC WEIGHT TABLE OF 1826 [10]

	Symbols	Atomic Weights referred to Hydrogen as 1
Oxygen	O	16.02
Hydrogen	H	1
Carbon	C	12.26
Boron	B	21.82
Phosphorus	P	31.44
Sulphur	S	32.24
Selenium	Se	79.26
Iodine	I	126.56
Bromine	Br	78.40
Chlorine	Cl	35.48
Fluorine	F	18.74
Nitrogen	N	14.18
Potassium	K	78.52
Sodium	Na	46.62
Lithium	L	12.88
Barium	Ba	137.32
Strontium	Sr	87.70
Calcium	Ca	41.04
Magnesium	Mg	25.38
Yttrium	Y	64.50
Glucinum	Gl	53.08
Aluminium	Al	27.44
Thorium	Th	119.30
Zirconium	Zr	67.34
Silicon	Si	44.44
Titanium	Ti	48.66
Tantalum	Ta	184.90
Tungsten	W	189.60
Molybdenum	Mo	95.92
Vanadium	V	137.32
Chromium	Cr	56.38
Uranium	Ur	434.52
Manganese	Mn	55.44
Arsenic	As	75.34
Antimony	Sb	129.24

	Symbols	Atomic Weights referred to Hydrogen as 1
Tellurium	Te	128.50
Bismuth	Bi	142.14
Zinc	Zn	64.62
Cadmium	Cd	111.66
Tin	Sn	117.84
Lead	Pb	207.46
Cobalt	Co	59.14
Nickel	Ni	59.24
Copper	Cu	63.42
Mercury	Hg	202.86
Silver	Ag	216.60
Gold	Au	199.20
Platinum	Pt	197.70
Palladium	Pd	106.72
Rhodium	R	104.40
Iridium	Ir	197.68
Osmium	Os	198.44

values, it may be wondered what reception was accorded Berzelius' 1826 atomic weights by Dalton, Gay-Lussac, and other leading contemporary chemists. At first glance it may seem strange that the majority of chemists rejected these weights and did not use them. The reason for this rejection lay principally in an alternate way of expressing composition by equivalent weights, a method that had been growing in popularity since about 1814. Equivalent weights had one advantage, among others, of being less speculative than atomic weights.

Equivalent Weights. The *equivalent weight* of an element may be defined as the weight of the element that combines with or replaces unit weight of hydrogen in a reaction. If a particular element does not combine directly with or replace hydrogen, its equivalent weight may be determined by noting the weight of the same element that does combine with or replace another element that does react with hydrogen. A few examples will make this clear. Eight units of weight of oxygen combine with a unit weight of hydrogen to form water; hence the equivalent weight of oxygen is eight. Silver does not combine with hydrogen or re-

[10] From Ad. Wurtz, *The Atomic Theory,* D. Appleton and Co., New York, 1881, pp. 62–63.

place hydrogen, but approximately 108 units of weight of silver do combine with 8 units of weight of oxygen (equivalent weight of oxygen) to form silver oxide. Hence the equivalent weight of silver is approximately 108. Also approximately 32 units of weight of zinc combine with 8 units of weight of oxygen, and approximately 32 units of weight of zinc in reacting with an acid will evolve 1 unit of weight of hydrogen. Hence from either observation the equivalent weight of zinc is approximately 32.

One useful characteristic of equivalents is the fact that generally an equivalent weight of one element reacts with or replaces an equivalent weight of another element in a reaction, hence the term "equivalent weights." An example is that approximately 32 units of metallic zinc (the equivalent weight) placed in a solution of silver nitrate will go into solution to form zinc nitrate and 108 units of weight of silver (the equivalent weight) will precipitate out. Because of this aspect of equivalent weights they are still used today in making calculations in gravimetric analysis.

Formulas were written in terms of equivalents. Thus water was written as HO, where the symbol H stood for an equivalent of hydrogen and O for an equivalent of oxygen. No atomic significance was attached to the symbol HO. The concept of equivalents was also extended to compounds.

The compositions of compounds in terms of equivalent weights of elements served to characterize most of the compounds known at the time; each compound had a unique formula in terms of equivalent weights. The compounds that chemists were most familiar with at the time were the inorganic compounds containing elements other than carbon (excepting carbonic oxide and carbonic acid), and a given inorganic compound is composed of a few elements, from the list of many, in simple proportions. Gradually as organic chemistry, the chemistry of compounds of carbon, came to be more fully explored it was discovered that many organic compounds had the same formula in terms of equivalents; that is, each organic compound did not have a unique equivalent formula. This is due to the fact that most organic compounds are composed of carbon and hydrogen, sometimes associated with oxygen. That the use of equivalents did not give unique formulas is one of the dominant reasons for a gradual shift from equivalent weights back to atomic weights, as will be discussed more fully later.

To fully appreciate the popularity of equivalent weights we must place ourselves in the position of the chemists of the time. It must be remembered that at this time atomic weights didn't assume in the minds of chemists the importance they do today. Even if relative atomic weights could have been determined unambiguously, which they couldn't, they possessed no obvious advantage over equivalent weights. At the time chemists were unable to see ahead to the discovery of the periodic properties of the elements and the relation of atomic weights to atomic structure. At that time atomic weights were an end in themselves. Equivalent weights served just as well, and there was nothing speculative in their determination, the only thing necessary for their determination being to observe the weights involved in a reaction.

It should be noted that if one atom always combined with or replaced one atom of another element in a reaction the equivalent weights and atomic weights would be the same. Thus Dalton's rule 1, " When only one combination of two bodies can be obtained, it must be presumed to be a binary one, unless some cause appear to the contrary," makes most of his atomic weights also equivalent weights. In this connection it is to be noted that if two elements reacted to form more than one compound then one of the elements had two equivalent weights. As an example there are two oxides of iron, ferrous oxide and ferric oxide, and if the equivalent weight of oxygen is 8, then in ferrous oxide and ferric oxide there are different weights of iron combined with 8 units of oxygen. This problem was generally solved by designating as the equivalent weight the smaller weight combined with 8 units of oxygen.

By 1826 most chemists preferred equivalent weights over atomic weights as being less speculative. After the work of Dumas, still greater confusion existed as to what value was to be assigned as the atomic weight of an element.

Period 1826–1843

Up to 1826, the problem of determining relative atomic weights had proceeded along two independent lines as reflected in Berzelius' work. One method was used for gaseous elements, utilizing relative gas densities and Berzelius' special interpretation of Gay-Lussac's law, and a different method or methods were used for nongaseous elements, employing chemical analogies, Mitscherlich's law, and the law of Dulong and Petit. The possibility of a cross check whereby the method for gaseous elements and the methods for nongaseous elements might be applied to one and the same element did not exist.

Dumas' Vapor Density Studies. The work of Dumas in 1826 on vapor densities changed this, and it became possible to attempt to determine the atomic weights of various liquid and solid elements in the same way that heretofore had been applicable only to gases. The atomic weights of the solid and liquid elements so determined did not agree with the atomic weights that had been obtained utilizing chemical analogies, Mitscherlich's law, and the law of Dulong and Petit. Dumas' work was a great setback for the atomic theory, and chemists generally despaired of ever determining relative atomic weights.

Dumas was born in Switzerland but did most of his work in Paris. He made many original contributions to chemistry, but the only one that interests us here is his work on vapor densities. His avowed purpose in his own words was, "to replace by definite conceptions the arbitrary data on which nearly the whole of the atomic theory is based." Later, in 1832, he wrote [11]:

Though it is quite easy to establish the ratio in which elements combine, it is very difficult to estimate the actual number of atoms which enter into each of these combinations. Berzelius in his treatise on chemical proportions, which marks so important an epoch in the history of the science . . . was the first to attack this difficult problem in its full scope. Without any rules to guide, he fixed by intuition the atomic weight of each substance, and usually allowed himself to be influenced by analogies which subsequent experience has only tended to confirm. But chemists have always wished that this arbitrary method, so successfully used by Berzelius, might be supplanted by something more fixed, more accessible to all kinds of intellect, and less subject to the capricious modifications of each writer.

Dumas' line of attack was essentially an extension of Avogadro's methods and proposals to elements that under ordinary conditions are liquid or solid but that could be easily converted to the vapor state. Before considering the details of Dumas' extension of Avogadro's work and the results thereof, let us look at a brief description of his experimental method that is still used today.

The solid or liquid element whose vapor density is to be determined is placed in a small glass bulb with a narrow neck. The bulb is then immersed in a bath of a liquid boiling at a sufficiently high temperature to convert the solid or liquid in the bulb to the vapor state. An excess of the element is used so that in being converted into the vapor state, all of the air is swept out of the bulb. Finally, when no more vapor escapes from the narrow neck of the bulb, the vapor of the element is at the pressure of the atmosphere and at the temperature of the boiling liquid in the bath. The neck of the bulb is then sealed, and the bulb is weighed after it has been allowed to cool. This weight is the weight of the bulb plus the weight of the vapor it contains.

Subsequently the weight of the empty bulb (no air) and its volume are determined by methods that don't interest us here. Then the weight of the vapor in the bulb can be determined by the difference of the weight of the bulb plus vapor, and the weight of the empty bulb. The weight of the vapor in the bulb divided by the volume of the bulb gives the weight of the vapor per unit volume, or its density. This density can then be compared to that of hydrogen at the same temperature and pressure and the specific gravity relative to hydrogen gas obtained.

Dumas, in his attempt to determine relative atomic weights from these relative vapor densities, accepted Avogadro's proposals of equal-volumes-equal-numbers of molecules, and the polyatomicity of the molecules of

---

[11] Quoted in Ida Freund's, *The Study of Chemical Composition*, Cambridge University Press, London, 1904, p. 336.

elementary substances. Accepting the equal-volume-equal-numbers hypothesis, the specific gravity of the vapor of a substance relative to hydrogen at the same temperature and pressure gives the weight of the molecule of that substance relative to the hydrogen molecule. Before the relative atomic weights of the substance and hydrogen can be determined, it is necessary to know how many atoms are in the molecule of the substance in question and in the molecule of hydrogen. Here Dumas made an additional proposal of his own that the molecules of all elementary substances in the gaseous or vapor state contain the same number of atoms and, in view of Avogadro's earlier work which indicated that the molecules of hydrogen, oxygen, and nitrogen were at least diatomic, that the molecules of all elementary substances were diatomic. Hence, not only were molecular weights proportional to specific gravities, but since all molecules of elementary substances were assumed to contain the same number of atoms, the atomic weights as well were proportional to the specific gravities.

Comparison of Atomic Weights Obtained by Berzelius and Dumas. Now how did the atomic weights of various solid and liquid elements, determined from such vapor density measurements, compare with the atomic weights obtained by Berzelius for the same solid and liquid elements using the method of Mitscherlich's law, the law of Dulong and Petit, and chemical analogies? Mercury vapor was found to be approximately 100 times as dense as hydrogen at the same temperature and pressure. Hence if the atomic weight of hydrogen is 1, and accepting the hypothesis of equal-volumes-equal-numbers of molecules and the diatomicity of the molecules of elementary substances, the atomic weight of mercury is 100. Since the weight of the hydrogen molecule H_2 is 2 (if the hydrogen atom H is 1) and the weight of the mercury molecule Hg_2 is 200, the weight of the mercury atom Hg is 100. But this does not agree with the value of the atomic weight of mercury of 200 obtained by Berzelius.

Another result from vapor density measurements was that the atomic weight of sulfur was 96 instead of 32 as obtained by Berzelius. Similar anomalous results were obtained for the atomic weights of other elements.

Such incompatible results in turn cast doubt on Berzelius' assumption that equal volumes of the elemental gases, nitrogen, hydrogen, oxygen, and chlorine contain equal numbers of atoms, and thus on the formulas H_2O, NH_3 and HCl that he had obtained for water, ammonia, and hydrogen chloride by using such an assumption. Berzelius in a last ditch attempt to save the equal-volumes-equal-numbers of atoms assumption, stated that it was applicable only to substances that were gaseous at ordinary temperatures and pressures. Such an arbitrary restriction is highly artificial and was unacceptable to other chemists.

Gaudin's Proposal. Gaudin in 1833 pointed out a way of resolving the above difficulties by proposing that equal volumes of different gases and vapors at the same temperature and pressure contain the same number of molecules, but that the molecules of different elements in turn did not necessarily contain the same number of atoms. Assuming the hydrogen molecule is diatomic and the hydrogen atom is assigned the weight 1, the hydrogen molecule has a weight of 2. Since mercury vapor is 100 times as dense as hydrogen gas, the mercury molecule must weigh 100 times as much as the hydrogen molecule ($H_2 = 2$) or 200. But if the mercury molecule consists of a single mercury atom Hg, the atomic weight of mercury is 200 and there is agreement among the various methods for determining the atomic weight of mercury. Similarly the sulfur molecule being 96 times as heavy as the hydrogen molecule must have a molecular weight of 2×96 or 192. Since the atomic weight of sulfur had been determined by Berzelius to be 32 by the combination of methods applicable to solid elements, the sulfur molecule must consist of six atoms, S_6. In a similar manner the other anomalous results of Dumas' work could be explained.

But this was too much for the chemists of the day. It will be recalled that the mere concept of polyatomicity of molecules could not be explained, as it was contrary to the dualistic theory, and now this added requirement that the degree of atomicity of the molecules of different elements was not the same was more than could be accepted.

Furthermore, it should be noted that Dumas' method and Gaudin's proposed reconciliation, even if accepted, do not constitute an advance on the basic problem of determining relative atomic weights. In Gaudin's reconciliation, the crux is Berzelius' atomic weights. Accepting Berzelius' atomic weights, the apparent degree of atomicity of the molecules of vapors of elementary substances can be determined from Dumas' vapor densities of these substances relative to hydrogen gas. What is desired is an unequivocal method of determining the relative atomic weights in the first place.

By the 1830's as has been noted, chemists generally despaired of ever determining relative atomic weights and used equivalent weights almost exclusively in expressing the composition of compounds. But during the 1830's and 1840's, knowledge of the compounds of organic chemistry continued to move forward. This knowledge was eventually to force a return to the problem of atomic weights and of expressing composition in terms of atoms. To these developments in organic chemistry, we now turn.

Period 1843–1860

Developments in organic chemistry during the period of 1820–1860 influenced the atomic-molecular theory in three ways. First many organic compounds are easily vaporizable and hence furnish substances to which, in the vapor state, Avogadro's hypothesis may be applied. Secondly, in an attempt to represent the constitution of organic compounds in a manner that would be consistent with their chemical properties, it was gradually realized that the representation must be in terms of atomic constitution of the molecules of the compounds. To do this the problem of relative atomic weights had to be solved. Thus organic chemistry demanded a solution to the problem of atomic weights and contributed to the means by which a solution was obtained. It is interesting to speculate on how soon the problem of relative atomic weights would have been solved without the existence of compounds of carbon or of compounds of a similar type. And finally organic chemistry contributed to the downfall of Berzelius' dualistic theory, thus removing this objection to polyatomic molecules.

Problem of Organic Formulas.   The solution of the problem of writing formulas representing the constitution of organic compounds consistent with their properties is too involved to be considered in its historical development. However, viewing the problem in retrospect, perhaps we can gain some insight into some of the major developments in organic chemistry that contributed to the solution of the problem of atomic weights.

In organic chemistry there are more compounds of carbon, hydrogen, and oxygen than the number of all the compounds of all of the other elements. Thus it is to be expected that there are many organic compounds that have the same percentage composition. As one example there are a whole series of organic compounds, ethylene, propylene, butylene, et cetera, that are composed of approximately 85.7% carbon and 14.3% hydrogen. If the composition of each of these compounds is represented by a formula in terms of equivalents, as was the usual procedure in inorganic chemistry particularly after 1830, they would all be CH, since the equivalent weights of C and H are 6 and 1. This is just one example among many. Obviously equivalent notation is not suitable for organic compounds, but perhaps representation in terms of the atomic constitution of the molecules would yield a unique formula for each organic compound and would reflect the properties of the compound.

In the attempt to determine unique formulas for organic compounds consistent with their properties, it was gradually realized that there were two additional problems that do not generally occur in the case of formulas for inorganic compounds.

The first step in determining the formulas for both inorganic and organic compounds is to carry out a weight analysis of the compound. Then if the atomic weights of the atoms are known, the composition by weight can be translated into the *relative* number of atoms in the compound. In the case of inorganic compounds the relative number of atoms so obtained is generally the atomic constitution of the molecule or the molecular formula. However, in the case of organic compounds, this is quite often not the case. Thus in the case just cited of ethylene, propylene, and butylene, all are composed of 85.7% carbon and 14.3% hydrogen and therefore must have the same relative atomic constitution. If the atomic weights of carbon and hydrogen are 12 and 1 respectively, in all three compounds there are 2 hydrogen atoms to 1 carbon atom or the relative atomic constitutions are CH_2. Obviously these three different compounds cannot all have the same molecular formula. Evidently, though having the same relative numbers of atoms, they must differ in the *absolute* numbers of atoms.

If the weights of the molecules of ethylene, propylene, and butylene are known, the absolute number of C and H atoms can be determined. The molecular weights of ethylene, propylene, and butylene are respectively 28, 42, and 56. Then since CH_2 weighs 14, the absolute number of atoms in the molecules of ethylene, propylene, and butylene are $(CH_2)_2 = C_2H_4$, $(CH_2)_3 = C_3H_6$, and $(CH_2)_4 = C_4H_8$, and each has a different molecular formula.

The second problem generally peculiar to organic compounds, which was only gradually realized, is that there are organic compounds with markedly different properties that have the same molecular formulas. The difference in properties must be due to the different arrangements of the atoms in the molecules. The determination of the arrangement of the atoms in the molecule of an organic compound results finally in the *structural* formula.

The actual historical development of the knowledge concerning organic compounds did not follow in sequence the logical steps outlined. The nature of the problem became obvious only when viewed in retrospect. Furthermore the attack on the problem of organic formulas was confused in that attempts at solving the molecular formulas were carried on simultaneously with attempts at arranging the atoms in the molecules. We shall consider first a little of the history of the attempts at solving the molecular formulas, ignoring for the present the problem of the structural formulas.

Berzelius' Molecular Organic Formulas. The work on molecular formulas started by Berzelius was carried to a significant conclusion largely by two French chemists Gerhardt and Laurent.

As an illustration of the attempts at determining the molecular formulas of organic compounds, we shall consider in comparative detail the case of the organic acids of vegetable origin. Berzelius attacked the problem of the relative and absolute numbers of atoms of carbon, hydrogen, and oxygen in these compounds as follows. Silver oxide reacts with organic acids to form salts. In the case of acetic acid,

silver oxide + acetic acid → silver acetate (a salt) + water.

Since Berzelius wrote silver oxide as AgO, consistent with his assigning an atomic weight of 216.6 to silver and 16 to oxygen,

$$AgO + acetic\ acid \rightarrow silver\ acetate + water.$$

Berzelius assumed that each molecule of the salt, silver acetate, contained one silver atom. He had made the same assumption for inorganic salts of silver. By analysis he determined the weights of C, H, and O associated with one atom of silver or 216.6 units of weight of silver. These would be the weights of C, H, and O in the acetate. These weights, using his atomic weights of $C = 12.25$, $O = 16.03$ and $H = 1$, could be translated into the numbers of atoms. He found the acetate portion to be $C_4H_6O_4$ and thus silver acetate to be $Ag\,(C_4H_6O_4)$ and acetic acid to be $C_4H_8O_4$. Berzelius also determined what he considered to be the molecular formulas of other organic compounds.

Gerhardt's Molecular Organic Formulas.   In 1839 Gerhardt called attention to the fact that there were a great number of reactions in which two organic substances reacted to form another organic substance with the elimination of water between the two reactants. In 1843, after an extensive study of such reactions, he made a significant observation. He noted that in these reactions, on the basis of Berzelius' organic formulas, two organic molecules in reacting never eliminated a single molecule of water, if water is H_2O as formulated by Berzelius. The number of molecules of water eliminated was always some multiple of two. The same situation also existed for analogous reactions in which some multiple of two molecules of ammonia, NH_3, hydrogen chloride, HCl, and carbonic acid gas, CO_2, were eliminated.

Gerhardt reasoned that among the many such reactions that were known there should be some in which a single molecule of H_2O, NH_3, HCl, or CO_2 was eliminated. This would be the case if Berzelius' organic formulas were halved. Thus acetic acid, as one example, instead of being written as $C_4H_8O_4$ should be written as $C_2H_4O_2$ according to Gerhardt. If Berzelius had halved his atomic weight of silver, using approximately 108 instead of 216, he would have arrived at the same formula, inasmuch as the amounts of C, H, and O associated with 108 units of silver in the analysis of silver acetate are one half that associated with 216 units of silver. Laurent soon followed Gerhardt in halving the generally accepted formulas.

The possible correctness of these "half formulas" of Gerhardt and Laurent is strengthened when it is noted that these formulas, arrived at from a consideration of chemical reactions, are in agreement with Avogadro's hypothesis of equal-volumes-equal-numbers of molecules. Thus two units of weight of hydrogen occupy a certain volume at a given temperature and pressure. A quantity of acetic acid in the vapor state equal to the molecular weight of 60 as calculated on the basis of Gerhardt and Laurent's formula ($C_2H_4O_2$; $C = 12$, $H = 1$, $O = 16$), occupies the same volume at the same temperature and pressure. Similar results were obtained for the other organic substances for which Gerhardt and Laurent had halved the molecular formulas of Berzelius. This supporting evidence minimized the conjectural nature of Avogadro's hypothesis which could now be looked upon as derived from the chemical properties of compounds, since the formula that best explained the chemical reactions of a substance was the same formula that was in agreement with the equal-volumes-equal-numbers-of-molecules hypothesis.

Unfortunately the work of Gerhardt and Laurent was ignored by the majority of contemporary chemists. As a matter of fact due to their views on chemical theory they were ostracized by their contemporaries. However, when Cannizzaro later assigned Avogadro's hypothesis the central role in his method of determining atomic weights, Gerhardt's and Laurent's work could have been cited as reducing the conjectural nature of the hypothesis and giving it almost an experimental foundation.

Problem of Structural Formulas.   The attempts to solve the problem of structural formulas of organic compounds is too complex to be considered in detail here and the final solution occurred only some 15 years after the problem of atomic weights had been solved. Some of the significant high points may be noted, however.

Some appreciation of the magnitude of the problem can be gained by considering the molecular formula of the comparatively simple organic substance acetic acid in the light of what we know today. The molecular formula is $C_2H_4O_2$. Because of the arrangement of the atoms in the molecule, three of the hydrogens are indistinguishable and therefore equivalent, but the fourth has entirely different properties due to its position; the two carbons are not equivalent and the two oxygens are not equivalent.

The problem was somewhat simplified by the fact that certain "chunks" of organic molecules called radicals, C_2H_5, C_6H_5, et cetera, go through many organic reactions unchanged or as units. (Today we know that this is because of the relative stability of the C—H and C—C bonds. The relatively mild conditions of most organic reactions are not sufficient to disrupt these bonds.) The existence of these radicals or units simplified the problem of the arrangement of atoms in a molecule somewhat in the same manner as an attempt to solve a jigsaw puzzle is simplified if certain individual pieces of the puzzle are already assembled in units before an attempt is made to put the whole puzzle together.

The first attempt to systematize the formulas of organic compounds was made by the indefatigable Berzelius. In this attempt he maintained that the results of inorganic chemistry should serve as a guide in studying "the mode of combination of the elements" in organic compounds; he utilized the dualistic theory of the make-up of inorganic compounds. He maintained there was also a two-fold nature to all organic compounds and he wrote all his organic formulas on this basis. He wrote the molecular formula of acetic acid as $C_4H_8O_4$, and its representation in accordance with the dualistic theory was $C_4H_6O_3 + H_2O$; acetic acid was thus a combination of water and what he called anhydrous acetic acid $C_4H_6O_3$. He represented all organic molecules in some such two-fold manner and most other chemists followed suit. It was not until about 1840 that a very important rival view came to be accepted by a majority of chemists.

This rival view, sometimes called the unitary theory, held that the organic molecule must be regarded as a *single* unit or a whole and not as being composed of two coupled groups of atoms. Chemists associated with this change of viewpoint were Dumas and Laurent, some of whose work has already been considered, and the great German organic chemist Liebig. One major piece of experimental evidence responsible for the shift was the preparation by Dumas of chloroacetic acid, which can be obtained by treating acetic acid with chlorine. During the chlorination of acetic acid, hydrogen is replaced by chlorine. The chloroacetic acid that results has almost identical properties to those of the acetic acid. It was inconceivable, on the basis of Berzelius' dualistic theory, that electro-negative chlorine could replace electro-positive hydrogen in a molecule, resulting in a molecule with almost identical properties. As an aside it may be noted that this and other similar experiments resulted in the total collapse of Berzelius' dualistic theory, and hence this objection to polyatomic molecules was removed. Thus from this experiment, and many similar, it began to be realized that an adequate representation of organic molecules that reflected something of their properties required more than the simple juxtaposition of groups of atoms called for by Berzelius' dualistic theory. For example, since in the conversion of acetic acid to the very similar chloroacetic acid the only change had been the substitution of chlorine atoms for hydrogen atoms, it was seen that the important thing was the *arrangement of the individual atoms* in the molecule which in turn was to be looked on as a unit. If this were so, before the problem of arrangement could be finally solved, the problem of numbers of atoms and thus of atomic weights had to be solved once and for all. This shift in view on the make-up of organic molecules was the most important reason that the use of atomic weights became popular again in the 1840's. The resulting focusing of attention on atomic weights culminated finally in the convention at Karlsruhe that we shall consider in the next chapter.

STUDY QUESTIONS

1. Which, if any, of the following statements is true?
   a. Avogadro's proposals (equal-volumes-equal-numbers, and polyatomic molecules) were immediately accepted by most chemists.

b. A drawback to Avogadro's proposals as used for determining atomic weights was the fact that they were applicable only to gaseous substances.

c. Avogadro's proposal necessitated the existence of an attractive force between atoms of the same kind.

The correct answer is

    (1) a   (2) b   (3) c   (4) b and c   (5) none are true.

2. The powerful new tool that became available in 1800 for the investigation of chemical phenomena was

    (1) the chemical balance
    (2) the pneumatic trough
    (3) Dumas' method of determining gas densities
    (4) Dulong and Petit's method of determining specific heats
    (5) the voltaic pile.

3. Which of the following statements are true?

a. Berzelius' dualistic theory was based largely on the phenomenon of electrolysis.

b. According to Berzelius' dualistic theory all chemical compounds owed their stability to the electrical attraction that existed between the oppositely charged particles of which they were composed.

c. The particles of any particular element each bore a like charge according to the dualistic theory.

d. Avogadro's postulate of polyatomic molecules was consistent with the dualistic theory.

The correct answer is

    (1) a and c   (2) b and c   (3) a, b, and c   (4) b, c, and d
    (5) a, c, and d.

4. Berzelius' greatest lasting contribution to the science of chemistry was his

    (1) development of the voltaic pile   (2) discovery of the alkali metals   (3) dualistic theory   (4) formulation of a set of principles whereby formulas of compounds could be determined   (5) accurate determination of combining weights.

5–6. From analysis it is found that 3.969 grams of copper combine with 1 gram of oxygen.

5. If the formula for this oxide of copper is CuO, the atomic weight of copper is

    (1) 3.969   (2) 63.50   (3) 36.79   (4) 127.1   (5) 31.75.

(Take the atomic weight of oxygen as 16.0000, which is the present standard.)

6. If the formula for this oxide of copper is Cu_2O, the atomic weight of copper is

    (1) 3.969   (2) 63.57   (3) 31.75   (4) 127.1   (5) 1.985.

7–8. Berzelius used a combination of several methods to establish the formulas of compounds in order to calculate atomic weights. One of these was volume relations in the case of gaseous reactions. Consider the following gaseous reaction:
    2 vol. element A + 3 vol. element B → 2 vol. compound C.

7. If there are m particles in unit volumes of A and B, Berzelius would conclude that there are how many particles of C formed?

   (1) $1m$ (2) $2m$ (3) $3m$ (4) $2.5m$ (5) none of these.

   What would be the formula of C according to Berzelius?

8. According to Avogadro the number of particles of C would be

   (1) $1m$ (2) $2m$ (3) $3m$ (4) $2.5m$ (5) none of these.

9. In connection with Prout's hypothesis, suppose there is a primordial matter of which all elements are composed, and that the hydrogen atom itself is composed of 2 or 3 or some other finite number of these primordial particles. The atoms of other elements in turn would be composed of a greater number of these particles. Could such a hypothesis be checked by determining the relative weights of atoms?

10. Define specific heat of a substance.

   In order to raise the temperature of 3 lbs. of metal A 6°F there is required 1.8 Btu. The specific heat of the metal is

   (1) 1.8   (2) .3   (3) 5.4   (4) 1   (5) .1.

11. Which one or more of the following are statements of the law of Dulong and Petit?
   a. The specific heat of all elements is the same.
   b. If equal numbers of atoms of different elements are compared, the same amount of heat is required to raise their temperature 1°F.
   c. Specific heat × atomic weight = 6.0 (approximately).
   The answer is

   (1) a   (2) a and c   (3) a and b   (4) b and c   (5) a, b, and c.

12. The specific heat of an element A is found to be .200. The atomic weight of the element according to Dulong and Petit is approximately

   (1) 60   (2) 30   (3) 120   (4) 90   (5) can't tell.

13–15. *The import of the law of Dulong and Petit relative to the atomic theory lies in the following: Combining weights can be accurately determined, and if there were some method of ascertaining the formula of the compound, then atomic weights could be just as accurately determined. Dulong and Petit's law, by giving us an approximate atomic weight, allows us to fix the formula, and then with formula fixed we can use the accurate combining weights to determine accurate atomic weights.*

   Consider the following data: 1.333 grams of B reacts with 1 gram of A to form a compound C.
   Specific heat of B   =   .210.
   The atomic weight of A = 45.00.

13. The approximate atomic weight of B is

   (1) 3.0   (2) 35   (3) 21   (4) 29   (5) 32.

14. The formula of the compound C is

   (1) AB   (2) A_2B (3) AB_2 (4) A_2B_3 (5) A_3B_2.

15. The accurate atomic weight of B is

   (1) 28.57   (2) 29.99   (3) 32.00   (4) 3.00   (5) none of these.

16. In making modifications in his 1818 table of atomic weights to arrive at his 1826 table Berzelius relied most heavily upon

(1) the law of Dulong and Petit
(2) Mitscherlich's law of isomorphism
(3) Prout's hypothesis
(4) the results of Dumas' vapor density studies
(5) the more accurate combining weights available.

17. Which of the following statements are applicable to Dumas' method of determining vapor densities?
   a. The method could be used to ascertain the number of atoms per molecule of vaporized substance.
   b. The method is applicable to liquid or solid substances that could be easily vaporized.
   c. In making calculations from his method, Dumas used the hypothesis that equal volumes contain equal numbers of molecules.
   d. The method is applicable only to elementary substances.
   The correct statements are

   (1) a, b, and c   (2) b, c, and d   (3) a and c   (4) a and b
   (5) b and c.

18–19. A Dumas bulb containing a liquid A is placed in a bath of boiling water. After the liquid is vaporized the bulb is sealed, dried and weighed.

   Weight of bulb plus vapor   = 20.500 gm
   Weight of bulb empty   = 20.000 gm
   Weight of bulb filled with water = 220.00 gm
   Density of water   = 1 gm/1 cc
   Above experiment conducted at atmospheric pressure.

18. The density of the vapor (gm/cc) at 100°C and 1 atmosphere pressure is

   (1) .0025   (2) .0023   (3) .0027   (4) .00200   (5) .0029.

19. The density of hydrogen at the same temperature and pressure is .000065 gm per cc. The particles of liquid in the vapor state are approximately how many times heavier than those of hydrogen?

   (1) 30   (2) 25   (3) 35   (4) 42   (5) 38.

20. The density of phosphorous vapor, as determined by the Dumas method, is found to be .00265 gm per cc at 300°C and 1 atmosphere pressure. The density of hydrogen at the same temperature and pressure is .0000425 gm per cc. Dumas would calculate the atomic weight of phosphorous to be approximately (H = 1):

   (1) 58   (2) 64   (3) 72   (4) 62   (5) 53.

21. The specific heat of phosphorous is .2. According to the law of Dulong and Petit the atomic weight is approximately

   (1) 62   (2) 58   (3) 30   (4) 25   (5) 35.

22. Consider the discrepancy above in problems 20 and 21 as well as that cited in the text (the atomic weight of mercury is 200 from the law of Dulong and Petit and the weight of the mercury particle is 100 times that of hydrogen). Is there any way of resolving these difficulties and at the same time satisfying Avogadro's hypothesis of polyatomic molecules (in particular the diatomicity of the hydrogen molecule)?

23. Suppose by a suitable process a certain hydrocarbon is found to be 1/7 hy-

drogen and 6/7 carbon. What is the relative number of atoms in the compounds? (Take atomic weight of C = 12 and H = 1)

(1) CH   (2) CH_3 (3) CH_2 (4) C_2H (5) C_2H_3.

24. If the molecular weight of the above compound is 70, the molecular formula is

(1) C_6H_{12} (2) C_2H_4 (3) CH_2 (4) C_4H_4 (5) C_5H_{10}.

25. Suppose a certain organic compound has the molecular formula C_2H_6O. What would be the formula determined solely on the basis of analysis?

26–27. An organic acid reacts with silver oxide to yield the silver salt of the acid. Analysis of the silver salt yields the following:
Ag = 55.4%, C = 24.6%, O = 16.4%, and H = 3.60%.

26. If there is one silver atom per molecule of the silver salt, the molecular formula of the salt is

(1) $C_3H_5O_2Ag$ (2) $C_2H_3O_2Ag$ (3) $C_4H_7O_2Ag$ (4) $C_8H_{14}O_4Ag$
(5) $C_{16}H_{28}O_8Ag$.

(Take atomic weights: Ag = 216, C = 12, O = 16, H = 1.)

27. What is the molcular formula of the salt if the atomic weight of the silver is halved?

28. In connection with Gerhardt's work on the molecular formulas that Berzelius had assigned to organic compounds, suppose 12 grams of an organic compound that Berzelius formulated as $C_4H_8O_4$ reacted with 9.2 grams of an organic compound that Berzelius formulated as $C_4H_{12}O_2$ to produce another organic compound with the elimination of 3.6 grams of water. On the basis of Berzelius' formulas, how many molecules of water H_2O are eliminated when 1 molecule of $C_4H_8O_4$ reacted with 1 molecule of $C_4H_{12}O_2$?

(1) 1   (2) 2   (3) 3   (4) 4   (5) ½.

(Take H = 1, O = 16.)

29. What modification would Gerhardt make in Berzelius' formulas?

30. What specific gravity, relative to hydrogen, would Gerhardt expect Berzelius' $C_4O_{12}O_2$ and $C_4H_8O_4$ to have?

31. The hydrocarbon methane has the molecular formula CH_4. By reacting methane with chlorine a series of compounds of molecular formulas CH_3Cl, CH_2Cl_2, $CHCl_3$ can be produced. Upon investigation it is found there is only one compound with the molecular formula CH_3Cl, only one with the molecular formula CH_2Cl_2, and only one with the molecular formula $CHCl_3$. Upon this evidence, what tentative statement or statements can be made about the structural formula of CH_4? Can you propose a tentative structural formula or formulas?

30

The Pamphlet of Cannizzaro

● In 1860, a concerted attack on the problem of atomic weights was launched largely at the instigation of leading organic chemists. On September 3 of that year, the First International Chemical Congress assembled at Karlsruhe, Germany under the chairmanship of Dumas. Nearly every important chemist in the world was in attendance. The conference settled nothing. As the chemists prepared to leave for home in as great confusion of mind as when they had arrived, Angelo Pavesi of the University of Pavia stood at the door and distributed copies of a little pamphlet in Italian written by his friend Stanislao Cannizzaro, professor of chemistry at the University of Genoa. The little pamphlet was entitled *Sunto di un corso di filosofia chimica.* It had originally appeared in the *Nuovo Cimento* in 1858 but had been reprinted at Pisa in 1859.

A copy was given to the German chemist Lothar Meyer. His reactions are best described in his own words [1]:

I also received a copy which I put in my pocket to read on the way home. Once arrived there I read it again repeatedly and was astonished at the clearness with which the little book illuminated the most important points of controversy. The scales seemed to fall from my eyes. Doubts disappeared and a feeling of quiet certainty took their place. If some years later I was myself able to contribute something toward clearing the situation and calming heated spirits no small part of the credit is due to this pamphlet of Cannizzaro. Like me it must have affected many others who attended the convention. The big waves of controversy began to subside, and more and more the old atomic weights of Berzelius came to their own. As soon as the apparent discrepancies between Avogadro's rule and that of Dulong and Petit had been removed by Cannizzaro both were found capable of practically universal application, and so the foundation was laid for determining the valence of the elements, without which the theory of atomic linking could certainly never have been developed.

[1] Quoted in Moore's, *A History of Chemistry,* McGraw-Hill Book Co., 1939, p. 245.

Figure 30-1. *Stanislao Cannizzaro (1826–1910).*

Lothar Meyer made Cannizzaro's views the basis of his influential textbook, *Modernen Theorien der Chemie* which first appeared in 1864.

Stanislao Cannizzaro (Fig. 30-1) was born on July 13, 1826 at Palermo in Sicily. His father was a judge and the Sicilian police chief. With the death of his father in 1836 he entered the Carolino Calasanzio College. After completing his elementary education he entered the University of Palermo in 1841 intending to study medicine. However, he was influenced by Fodera who taught physiology at Palermo, and he began experimental work in chemical physiology. There were no chemical laboratories worthy of the name in Palermo, so Cannizzaro went on to Naples in the fall of 1845. Here he became friendly with the physicist Melloni who recommended Cannizzaro to the chemist Raffaele Piria at the University of Pisa.

Thus Cannizzaro came to the University of Pisa, where two centuries earlier Galileo had studied and had held his first teaching post. Cannizzaro and another young man were the assistants to Piria. Their tasks were to set up Piria's lecture demonstrations and to assist him in his laboratory. Piria was thorough-going and precise. He would not tolerate any slackness from his assistants. The lecture-demonstration equipment had not only to work properly, but it had to look well in addition. Piria and his assistants put in a daily eight hours in his laboratory investigating various vegetable products. His assistants became well trained in carrying out careful laboratory manipulations. Piria, however, would unbend after working hours and freely discuss the chemical problems and procedures involved in the day's work. Cannizzaro credited this uncompromising taskmaster with his own later success as a chemist.

Cannizzaro returned to Sicily at the end of July, 1847 for a vacation period. A revolution broke out in January, 1848 which the fiery young twenty-one year old liberal found much to his liking. He became an artillery officer at Messina. He was elected as the deputy for Francavilla to the Sicilian Parliament at Palermo, where he was its youngest member. With the failure of the revolution in May, 1849 he fled for his life to Marseilles. After some aimless wandering about France he was drawn to Paris toward the end of October. Here a letter from Piria opened the doors of a small laboratory in the Jardin des Plantes. Here he and Cloez prepared cyanamide by the action of ammonia on cyanogen chloride. The joint paper in 1851 which reported the nature of this compound was Cannizzaro's first published work.

Toward the close of 1851 he accepted the position of professor of physical chemistry and mechanics in the National College of Alessandria in northern Italy. He created a small laboratory and, when he was not teaching classes, he carried forward the line of research which he had begun in Paris. It was here that he discovered benzyl alcohol by a reaction which is still called " Cannizzaro's reaction." His vacations were usually spent at Pisa with Piria.

In October of 1855 Cannizzaro became professor of chemistry at the University of Genoa. The new position had both greater prestige and pay, but the laboratory was damp and dark without any conveniences. He equipped a new laboratory on the top floor of the university building so that he could continue his research in organic chemistry. It was at this time that his mind turned to the broader principles of chemistry which culminated in his historic paper, " Sketch for a Course of Chemical Philosophy." Perhaps the inconvenience of his laboratory facilities made theoretical chemistry more appealing to him!

In 1860 Garibaldi and his Thousand landed in Sicily. Within a short time the war was over and Italy began to unite. Cannizzaro had declined a professorship of organic chemistry at the University of Pisa. He had also refused a similar post at the University of Naples. But in October of 1861 his native Sicily asked him to become professor of inorganic and organic chemistry and director of the laboratory of the University of Palermo. As a loyal Sicilian he returned to the same classroom in which he had sat as a student in 1842 only to find that the laboratory that he was to direct was amply housed in a few sparse cabinets. Nevertheless, he remained there ten years training worthy chemists and taking an active part in the life of the university. He served as rector of the University of Palermo for a period.

In 1871 Cannizzaro went to Rome as professor of chemistry and director of the Chemical Institute in the University of Rome. He was made a Senator of the Italian kingdom and took a characteristically active part in public life. He was honored by the scientific societies of the world. He died in 1910 after a full and rich life. Although he wrote about a hundred papers, his great fame was based primarily on the little pamphlet which his friend handed out at the door at the close of the Karlsruhe conference in 1860.

SKETCH OF A COURSE OF CHEMICAL PHILOSOPHY [2]
Given in the Royal University of Genoa
by Stanislao Cannizzaro

I believe that the progress of science made in these last years has confirmed the hypothesis of Avogadro, of Ampère, and of Dumas on the similar constitution of substances in the gaseous state; that is, that equal volumes of these substances, whether simple or compound, contain an equal number of molecules: not however an equal number of atoms, since the molecules of the different substances, or those of the same substance in its different states, may contain a different number of atoms, whether of the same or of diverse nature.

In order to lead my students to the conviction which I have reached myself, I wish to place them on the same path as that by which I have arrived at it — the path, that is, of the historical examination of chemical theories.

I commence, then, in the first lecture by showing how, from the examination of the physical properties of gaseous bodies, and from the law of Gay-Lussac on the volume relations between components and compounds, there arose almost spontaneously the hypothesis alluded to above, which was first of all enunciated by Avogadro, and shortly afterwards by Ampère. Analysing the conception of these two physicists, I show that it contains nothing contradictory to known facts, provided that we distinguish, as they did, molecules from atoms; provided that we do not confuse the criteria by which the number and the weight of the former are compared, with the criteria which serve to deduce the weight of the latter; provided that, finally, we have not fixed in our minds the prejudice that whilst the molecules of compound substances may consist of different numbers of atoms, the molecules of the various simple substances must all contain either one atom, or at least an equal number of atoms.

In the second lecture I set myself the task of investigating the reasons why this hypothesis of Avogadro and Ampère was not immediately accepted by the majority of chemists. I therefore expound rapidly the work and the ideas of those who examined the relationships of the reacting quantities of substances without concerning themselves with the volumes which these substances occupy in the gaseous state; and I pause to explain the ideas of Berzelius, by the influence of which the hypothesis above cited appeared to chemists out of harmony with the facts.

    ✵   ✵   ✵   ✵   ✵   ✵   ✵

From the historical examination of chemical theories, as well as from physical researches, I draw the conclusion that to bring into harmony all the

[2] Translated in Alembic Club Reprint, No. 18. University of Chicago Press, 1911, pp. 1–2; 5–14; 15–18.

branches of chemistry we must have recourse to the complete application of the theory of Avogadro and Ampère in order to compare the weights and the numbers of the molecules; and I propose in the sequel to show that the conclusions drawn from it are invariably in accordance with all physical and chemical laws hitherto discovered.

I begin in the fifth lecture by applying the hypothesis of Avogadro and Ampère to determine the weights of molecules even before their composition is known.

On the basis of the hypothesis cited above, the weights of the molecules are proportional to the densities of the substances in the gaseous state. If we wish the densities of vapours to express the weights of the molecules, it is expedient to refer them all to the density of a simple gas taken as unity, rather than to the weight of a mixture of two gases such as air.

Hydrogen being the lightest gas, we may take it as the unit to which we re-

TABLE 30-1

Names of Substances.	Densities or weights of one volume, the volume of Hydrogen being made = 1, i.e., weights of the molecules referred to the weight of a whole molecule of Hydrogen taken as unity.	Densities referred to that of Hydrogen = 2, i.e., weights of the molecules referred to the weight of half a molecule of Hydrogen taken as unity.
Hydrogen	1	2
Oxygen, ordinary	16	32
Oxygen, electrised	64	128
Sulphur below 1000°	96	192
Sulphur * above 1000°	32	64
Chlorine	35.5	71
Bromine	80	160
Arsenic	150	300
Mercury	100	200
Water	9	18
Hydrochloric Acid	18.25	36.50 †
Acetic Acid	30	60

* This determination was made by Bineau, but I believe it requires confirmation.

† The numbers expressing the densities are approximate: we arrive at a closer approximation by comparing them with those derived from chemical data, and bringing the two into harmony.

fer the densities of other gaseous bodies, which in such a case express the weights of the molecules compared to the weight of the molecule of hydrogen = 1.

Since I prefer to take as common unit for the weights of the molecules and for their fractions, the weight of a half and not of a whole molecule of hydrogen, I therefore refer the densities of the various gaseous bodies to that of hydrogen = 2. If the densities are referred to air = 1, it is sufficient to multiply by 14.438 to change them to those referred to that of hydrogen = 1; and by 28.87 to refer them to the density of hydrogen = 2.

I write the two series of numbers, expressing these weights in the following manner [see preceding Table 30-1].

Whoever wishes to refer the densities to hydrogen = 1 and the weights of the molecules to the weight of half a molecule of hydrogen, can say that the weights of the molecules are all represented by the weight of two volumes.

I myself, however, for simplicity of exposition, prefer to refer the densities to that of hydrogen = 2, and so the weights of the molecules are all represented by the weight of one volume.

From the few examples contained in the table, I show that the same substance in its different allotropic states [existence of a substance in two or more physical forms] can have different molecular weights, without concealing the fact that the experimental data on which this conclusion is founded still require confirmation.

I assume that the study of the various compounds has been begun by determining the weights of the molecules, i.e., their densities in the gaseous state, without enquiring if they are simple or compound.

I then come to the examination of the composition of these molecules. If the substance is undecomposable, we are forced to admit that its molecule is entirely made up by the weight of one and the same kind of matter. If the body is composite, its elementary analysis is made, and thus we discover the constant relations between the weights of its components: then the weight of the molecule is divided into parts proportional to the numbers expressing the relative weights of the components, and thus we obtain the quantities of these components contained in the molecule of the compound, referred to the same unit as that to which we refer the weights of all the molecules. By this method I have constructed the following table [see Table 30-2, page 396].

All the numbers contained in the [following] table are comparable amongst themselves, being referred to the same unit. And to fix this well in the minds of my pupils, I have recourse to a very simple artifice: I say to them, namely, " Suppose it to be shown that the half molecule of hydrogen weighs a millionth of a milligram, then all the numbers of the preceding table become concrete numbers, expressing in millionths of a milligram the concrete weights of the molecules and of their components: the same thing would follow if the common unit had any other concrete value," and so I lead them to gain a clear conception of the comparability of these numbers, whatever be the concrete value of the common unit.

Once this artifice has served its purpose, I hasten to destroy it by explaining how it is not possible in reality to know the concrete value of this unit; but the clear ideas remain in the minds of my pupils whatever may be their degree of mathematical knowledge. I proceed pretty much as engineers do when they

TABLE   30-2

Name of Substance.	Weight of one volume i.e., weight of the molecule referred to the weight of half a molecule of Hydrogen = 1.	Component weights of one volume, i.e., component weights of the molecule, all referred to the weight of half a molecule of Hydrogen = 1.	
Hydrogen	2	2 Hydrogen	
Oxygen, ordinary	32	32 Oxygen	
Oxygen, electrised	128	128 Oxygen	
Sulphur below 1000°	192	192 Sulphur	
Sulphur above 1000° (?)	64	64 Sulphur	
Phosphorus	124	124 Phosphorus	
Chlorine	71	71 Chlorine	
Bromine	160	160 Bromine	
Iodine	254	254 Iodine	
Nitrogen	28	28 Nitrogen	
Arsenic	300	300 Arsenic	
Mercury	200	200 Mercury	
Hydrochloric Acid	36.5	35.5 Chlorine	1 Hydrogen
Hydrobromic Acid	81	80 Bromine	1 Hydrogen
Hydriodic Acid	128	127 Iodine	1 Hydrogen
Water	18	16 Oxygen	2 Hydrogen
Ammonia	17	14 Nitrogen	3 Hydrogen
Arseniuretted Hyd.	78	75 Arsenic	3 Hydrogen
Phosphuretted Hyd.	35	32 Phosphorus	3 Hydrogen
Calomel	235.5	35.5 Chlorine	200 Mercury
Corrosive Sublimate	271	71 Chlorine	200 Mercury
Arsenic Trichloride	181.5	106.5 Chlorine	75 Arsenic
Protochloride of Phosphorus	138.5	106.5 Chlorine	32 Phosphorus
Perchloride of Iron	325	213 Chlorine	112 Iron
Protoxide of Nitrogen	44	16 Oxygen	28 Nitrogen
Binoxide of Nitrogen	30	16 Oxygen	14 Nitrogen
Carbonic Oxide	28	16 Oxygen	12 Carbon
Carbonic Acid	44	32 Oxygen	12 Carbon
Ethylene	28	4 Hydrogen	24 Carbon
Propylene	42	6 Hydrogen	36 Carbon

Acetic Acid, hydrated	60	4 Hydrogen 32 Oxygen 24 Carbon
Acetic Acid, anhydrous	102	6 Hydrogen 48 Oxygen 48 Carbon
Alcohol	46	6 Hydrogen 16 Oxygen 24 Carbon
Ether	74	10 Hydrogen 16 Oxygen 48 Carbon

destroy the wooden scaffolding which has served them to construct their bridges, as soon as these can support themselves. But I fear that you will say, "Is it worth the trouble and the waste of time and ink to tell me of this very common artifice?" I am, however, constrained to tell you that I have paused to do so because I have become attached to this pedagogic expedient, having had such great success with it amongst my pupils, and thus I recommend it to all those who, like myself, must teach chemistry to youths not well accustomed to the comparison of quantities.

Once my students have become familiar with the importance of the numbers as they are exhibited in the preceding table, it is easy to lead them to discover the law which results from their comparison. "Compare," I say to them, "the various quantities of the same element contained in the molecule of the free substance and in those of all its different compounds and you will not be able to escape the following law: *The different quantities of the same element contained in different molecules are all whole multiples of one and the same quantity, which, always being entire, has the right to be called an atom.*"

Thus: —

One molecule of free hydrogen	contains	2 of hydrogen	=	2 × 1
" of hydrochloric acid	"	1 "	=	1 × 1
" of hydrobromic acid	"	1 "	=	1 × 1
" of hydriodic acid	"	1 "	=	1 × 1
" of hydrocyanic acid	"	1 "	=	1 × 1
" of water	"	2 "	=	2 × 1
" of sulphureted hydrogen	"	2 "	=	2 × 1
" of formic acid	"	2 "	=	2 × 1
" of ammonia	"	3 "	=	3 × 1
" of gaseous phosphur- etted hydrogen	"	3 "	=	3 × 1
" of acetic acid	"	4 "	=	4 × 1
" of ethylene	"	4 "	=	4 × 1
" of alcohol	"	6 "	=	6 × 1
" of ether	"	10 "	=	10 × 1

Thus all the various weights of hydrogen contained in the different molecules are integral multiples of the weight contained in the molecule of hydrochloric acid, which justifies our having taken it as common unit of the weights of the atoms and of the molecules. The atom of hydrogen is contained twice in the molecule of free hydrogen.

In the same way it is shown that the various quantities of chlorine existing in different molecules are all whole multiples of the quantity contained in the molecule of hydrochloric acid, that is, of 35.5; and that the quantities of oxygen existing in the different molecules are all whole multiples of the quantity contained in the molecule of water, that is, of 16, which quantity is half of that contained in the molecule of free oxygen, and an eighth part of that contained in the molecule of electrised oxygen (ozone).

Thus: —

One molecule of free oxygen	contains	32	of oxygen	$= 2 \times 16$
" of ozone	"	128	"	$= 8 \times 16$
" of water	"	16	"	$= 1 \times 16$
" of ether	"	16	"	$= 1 \times 16$
" of acetic acid	"	32	"	$= 2 \times 16$
etc. etc.				
One molecule of free chlorine	contains	71	of chlorine	$= 2 \times 35.5$
" of hydrochloric acid	"	35.5	"	$= 1 \times 35.5$
" of corrosive sublimate	"	71	"	$= 2 \times 35.5$
" of chloride of arsenic	"	106.5	"	$= 3 \times 35.5$
" of chloride of tin	"	142	"	$= 4 \times 35.5$
etc. etc.				

In a similar way may be found the smallest quantity of each element which enters as a whole into the molecules which contain it, and to which may be given with reason the name of atom. *In order, then, to find the atomic weight of each element, it is necessary first of all to know the weights of all or of the greater part of the molecules in which it is contained and their composition.*[3]

If it should appear to any one that this method of finding the weights of the molecules is too hypothetical, then let him compare the composition of equal volumes of substances in the gaseous state under the same conditions. He will not be able to escape the following law: *The various quantities of the same element contained in equal volumes either of the free element or of its compounds are all whole multiples of one and the same quantity;* that is, each element has a special numerical value by means of which and of integral coefficients the composition by weight of equal volumes of the different substances in which it is contained may be expressed. Now, since all chemical reactions take place between equal volumes, or integral multiples of them, it is possible to express all chemical reactions by means of the same numerical values and integral coefficients. The law enunciated in the form just indicated is a direct deduction from the facts: but who is not led to assume from this same law that the weights of equal volumes represent the molecular weights, although other

---

[3] Italicizing, the authors'.

proofs are wanting? I thus prefer to substitute in the expression of the law the word molecule instead of volume. This is advantageous for teaching, because, when the vapor densities cannot be determined, recourse is had to other means for deducing the weights of the molecules of compounds. The whole substance of my course consists in this: to prove the exactness of these latter methods by showing that they lead to the same results as the vapour density when both kinds of method can be adopted at the same time for determining molecular weights.

The law above enunciated, called by me the law of atoms, contains in itself that of multiple proportions and that of simple relations between the volumes; which I demonstrate amply in my lecture. After this I easily succeed in explaining how, expressing by symbols the different atomic weights of the various elements, it is possible to express by means of formulae the composition of their molecules and of those of their compounds, and I pause a little to make my pupils familiar with the passage from gaseous volume to molecule, the first directly expressing the fact and the second interpreting it. Above all, I study to implant in their minds thoroughly the difference between molecule and atom. It is possible indeed to know the atomic weight of an element without knowing its molecular weight; this is seen in the case of carbon. A great number of the compounds of this substance being volatile, the weights of the molecules and their composition may be compared, and it is seen that the quantities of carbon which they contain are all integral multiples of 12, which quantity is thus the atom of carbon and expressed by the symbol C; but since we cannot determine the vapour density of free carbon we have no means of knowing the weight of its molecule, and thus we cannot know how many times the atom is contained in it. Analogy does not in any way help us, because we observe that the molecules of the most closely analogous substances (such as sulphur and oxygen), and even the molecules of the same substances in its allotropic states, are composed of different numbers of atoms. We have no means of predicting the vapour density of carbon; the only thing that we can say is that it will be either 12 or an integral multiple of 12 (in my system of numbers).

*   *   *   *   *   *   *

I then discuss whether it is better to express the composition of the molecules of compounds as a function of the molecules of the components, or if, on the other hand, it is better, as I commenced by doing, to express the composition of both in terms of those constant quantities which always enter by whole numbers into both, that is, by means of the atoms. Thus, for example, is it better to indicate in the formula that one molecule of hydrochloric acid contains the weight of half a molecule of hydrogen and half a molecule of chlorine, or that it contains an atom of one and an atom of the other, pointing out at the same time that the molecules of both of these substances consist of two atoms?

Should we adopt the formulae made with symbols indicating the molecules of the elements, then many coefficients of these symbols would be fractional, and the formula of a compound would indicate directly the ratio of the volumes occupied by the components and by the compounds in the gaseous state. This was proposed by Dumas in his classical memoir, "Sur quelques points de la Théorie atomique" (Annales de Chimie et de Physique, tom. 33, 1826).

To discuss the question proposed, I give to the molecules of the elements symbols of a different kind from those employed to represent the atoms, and in this way I compare the formulae made with the two kinds of symbols [see Table 30-3].

TABLE 30-3

Atoms or Molecules.	Symbols of the molecules of the Elements and formulæ made with these symbols.		Symbols of the atoms of the Elements and formulæ made with these symbols.	Nos. expressing their weights.
Atom of Hydrogen	$H\frac{1}{2}$		$= H$ =	1
Molecule of Hydrogen	H		$= H^2$ =	2
Atom of Oxygen	$O\frac{1}{2}$	$= Oz\frac{1}{8}$	$= O$ =	16
Molecule of ordinary Oxygen	O		$= O^2$ =	32
Molecule of electrised Oxygen (Ozone)	Oz		$= O^8$ =	128
Atom of Sulphur	$S\frac{1}{2}$	$= Sa\frac{1}{6}$	$= S$ =	32
Molecule of Sulphur above 1000° (Bineau)	S		$= S^2$ =	64
Molecule of Sulphur below 1000°	Sa		$= S^6$ =	192
" Water	$HO\frac{1}{2}$	$= HOz\frac{1}{8}$	$= H^2O$ =	18
" Sulphuretted Hydrogen	$HS\frac{1}{2}$	$= HSa\frac{1}{6}$	$= H^2S$ =	34

These few examples are sufficient to demonstrate the inconveniences associated with the formulae indicating the composition of compound molecules as a function of the entire component molecules, which may be summed up as follows: —

1°. It is not possible to determine the weight of the molecules of many elements the density of which in the gaseous state cannot be ascertained.

2°. If it is true that oxygen and sulphur have different densities in their different allotropic states, that is, if they have different molecular weights, then their compounds would have two or more formulae according as the quantities of their components were referred to the molecules of one or the other allotropic state.

3°. The molecules of analogous substances (such as sulphur and oxygen) being composed of different numbers of atoms, the formulae of analogous compounds would be dissimilar. If we indicate, instead, the composition of the molecules by means of the atoms, it is seen that analogous compounds contain in their molecules an equal number of atoms.

It is true that when we employ in the formulae the symbols expressing the weights of the molecules, i.e., of equal volumes, the relationship between the volumes of the components and those of the compounds follows directly; but this relationship is also indicated in the formulae expressing the number of atoms; it is sufficient to bear in mind that the atom represented by a symbol is either the entire molecule of the free substance or a fraction of it, that is, it is sufficient to know the atomic formula of the free molecule. Thus, to take an example, it is sufficient to know that the atom of oxygen, O, is one-half of the molecule of ordinary oxygen and an eighth part of the molecule of electrised oxygen — to know that the weight of the atom of oxygen is represented by ½ volume of free oxygen and ⅛ of electrised oxygen. In short, it is easy to accustom students to consider the weights of the atoms as being represented either by a whole volume or by a fraction of a volume, according as the atom is equal to the whole molecule or to a fraction of it. In this system of formulae, those which represent the weights and the composition of the molecules, whether of elements or of compounds, represent the weights and the composition of equal gaseous volumes under the same conditions. The atom of each element is represented by that quantity of it which constantly enters as a whole into equal volumes of the free substance or of its compounds; it may be either the entire quantity contained in one volume of the free substance or a simple sub-multiple of this quantity.

STUDY QUESTIONS

1. Cannizzaro states that he finds no contradictions between Avogadro's hypothesis and the known facts (Dumas' experiments, etc.) if which of the following points are kept in mind?
   a. A distinction must be made between atoms and molecules.
   b. The molecules of all elements must contain the same number of atoms.
   c. A different criterion must be used to determine the relative weights of atoms than that used for determining the weights of molecules.
   d. The molecules of different elements as well as compounds may contain different numbers of atoms.
   e. The molecules of compounds may contain different numbers of atoms, but the molecules of all elements contain only one atom.
   The correct answer is

   (1) a, b, and c   (2) a, c, and d   (3) a, c, and e   (4) b, c, and e
   (5) a and c.

2. Cannizzaro in setting up his scale of relative weights of molecules selects as unity
   (1) the weight of a molecule of hydrogen
   (2) the weight of a molecule of oxygen
   (3) the average weight of the molecules that make up air
   (4) the weight of half a molecule of hydrogen
   (5) none of these.

3. The density of a gas relative to air is 2.50; the density relative to the density of hydrogen taken as 2 is, according to Cannizzaro, approximately

(1) 36.1   (2) 5.00   (3) 72.2   (4) 18.0   (5) 1.25.

4. The weight of 2 liters of hydrogen at a certain temperature and pressure is .20 gm. The weight of 1 liter of gas A at the same temperature and pressure is 1.0 gm. According to Cannizzaro's scale the molecular weight of the molecules of gas A is

(1) 5.0   (2) 10   (3) 20   (4) 14   (5) 29.

5–6. *A problem similar to the problems faced by Cannizzaro in constructing the Table 30-2 might be the following: A compound of tin and chlorine is found upon analysis to be 45.4% tin and 54.6% chlorine. The compound on being brought into the vapor state is found to be 130 times as dense as hydrogen at the same temperature and pressure.*

5. The weight of tin in the molecule of the compound, referred to the weight of half a molecule of hydrogen = 1, is

(1) 45.4   (2) 90.8   (3) 54.0   (4) 118   (5) 236.

6. The weight of chlorine in the molecule of the compound, referred to the weight of half a molecule of hydrogen = 1, is

(1) 54.6   (2) 35.5   (3) 71.0   (4) 109   (5) 142.

7. Suppose half a molecule of hydrogen to weigh 3.7×10^{-27} lb. Then the weight of an ammonia molecule in lb would be

(1) 17×10^{-27} (2) 63×10^{-27} (3) 13×10^{-25}
(4) 8.0×10^{-25} (5) 1.1×10^{-26}.

8. Referring to Table 30-2, the specific gravity of propylene relative to oxygen gas would be

(1) 42.0   (2) 2.62   (3) .660   (4) 1.31   (5) .762.

9. In the light of Cannizzaro's statement, " The different quantities of the same element contained in different molecules are all whole multiples of one and the same quantity, which, always being entire, has the right to be called an atom " (p. 397; this statement contains one of Cannizzaro's most important contributions) and Table 30-2, the probable atomic weights of nitrogen, phosphorus and bromine respectively are

(1) 28, 32, 80   (2) 14, 32, 160   (3) 7, 16, 80   (4) 14, 64, 80
(5) 14, 32, 80.

10–17. *From the following data on the hypothetical element A and five of its compounds, determine the apparent atomic weight of A according to the method of Cannizzaro.*

	% Composition	Density (at same T & P)
Element A in gaseous state		.666 gm/l
Compound I	38.5% A 61.5% O	.866 gm/l
Compound II	12.3% A 87.7% Cl	2.70 gm/l
Compound III	22.0% A 78.0% Cl	1.50 gm/l
Compound IV	55.5% A 44.5% O	1.20 gm/l
Compound V	68.2% A 31.8% N	1.47 gm/l

The density of hydrogen gas (H_2) at the same temperature and pressure is .0666 gm/liter. Atomic weights: O = 16.0, Cl = 35.5, N = 14.0.

10. The atomic weight of A is apparently
    (1) 66.6   (2) 33.3   (3) 20.0   (4) 10.0   (5) 40.0.

11. The formula for compound I is apparently
    (1) AO_2 (2) AO (3) A_2O (4) A_2O_2 (5) A_2O_3.

12. The formula for compound II is apparently
    (1) ACl_2 (2) ACl (3) A_2Cl (4) A_3Cl (5) A_2Cl_3.

13. The formula for compound III is apparently
    (1) ACl_2 (2) ACl (3) A_2Cl (4) A_3Cl (5) A_2Cl_3.

14. The formula for compound IV is apparently
    (1) AO_2 (2) AO (3) A_2O (4) A_2O_2 (5) A_2O_3.

15. The formula for compound V is apparently
    (1) AN_2 (2) AN (3) A_2N (4) A_2N_3 (5) A_3N.

16. When A reacts with one molecule of nitrogen (diatomic) the number of molecules of A required and the number of molecules of compound V produced are respectively
    (1) 1, 1   (2) 3, 1   (3) 2, 3   (4) 3, 2   (5) 1, 3.

17. When A in the gaseous state reacts with unit volume of nitrogen the number of unit volumes of A required and the number of unit volumes of compound V produced are respectively
    (1) 1, 1   (2) 3, 1   (3) 2, 3   (4) 3, 2   (5) 1, 3.

31

Cannizzaro: Atomic Weights and Specific Heats

● In the first part of Cannizzaro's paper considered in the previous chapter, the fundamental ideas are those of Avogadro. Cannizzaro, however, draws a sharp distinction between determining relative molecular weights from specific gravity data according to Avogadro's hypothesis and determining relative atomic weights.

In essence Cannizzaro's procedure in determining the relative atomic weight of, say, the chlorine atom was first to determine the molecular weights from specific gravities of as many gaseous or vaporizable compounds of chlorine as could be prepared. Secondly, he analyzed these compounds and noted the smallest weight of chlorine contained in the molecular weight of the various gaseous compounds of chlorine. This smallest weight was then accepted as the atomic weight of the chlorine atom.

In the latter portions of Cannizzaro's pamphlet considered in this chapter, he first applied the above method to determine the relative atomic weights of several solid and liquid elements that form vaporizable compounds. The atomic weights so obtained were checked against the atomic weights obtained by using the law of Dulong and Petit. Since agreement was found between the two methods, in particular in the case of the relative weight of the mercury atom, the reliability of the atomic weights obtained utilizing the law of Dulong and Petit was strengthened. Then for elements that form no gaseous or vaporizable compounds, such as copper or sodium, Cannizzaro relied entirely on the procedure of using the law of Dulong and Petit. Thus Cannizzaro established a bridge between the two general methods for determining atomic weights, one method applicable to elements that do form gaseous or vaporizable compounds and the other applicable to those elements which do not.

404

SKETCH OF A COURSE OF CHEMICAL PHILOSOPHY (*Continued*) [1]
by Stanislao Cannizzaro

This foundation of the atomic theory having been laid, I begin in the following lecture — the sixth — to examine the constitution of the molecules of the chlorides, bromides, and iodides. Since the greater part of these are volatile, and since we know their densities in the gaseous state, there cannot remain any doubt as to the approximate weights of the molecules, and so of the quantities of chlorine, bromine, and iodine contained in them. These quantities being always integral multiples of the weights of chlorine, bromine, and iodine contained in hydrochloric, hydrobromic, and hydriodic acids, i.e., of the weights of the half molecules, and there can remain no doubt as to the atomic weights of these substances, and thus as to the number of atoms existing in the molecules of their compounds, whose weights and composition are known.

A difficulty sometimes appears in deciding whether the quantity of the other element combined with one atom of these halogens is 1, 2, 3, or n atoms in the molecule; to decide this, it is necessary to compare the composition of all the other molecules containing the same element and find out the weight of this element which constantly enters as a whole. When we cannot determine the vapour densities of the other compounds of the element whose atomic weight we wish to determine, it is necessary then to have recourse to other criteria to know the weights of their molecules and to deduce the weight of the atom of the element. What I am to expound in the sequel serves to teach my pupils the method of employing these other criteria to verify or to determine atomic weights and the composition of molecules. I begin by making them study the following table of some chlorides, bromides, and iodides whose vapour densities are known; I write their formulae, certain of justifying later the value assigned to the atomic weights of some elements existing in the compounds indicated. I do not omit to draw their attention once more to the atomic weights of hydrogen, chlorine, bromine, and iodine being all equal to the weights of half a molecule, and represented by the weight of half a volume, which I indicate in the following table [see Table 31-1]: —

TABLE 31-1

	Symbol.	Weight.
Weight of the atom of Hydrogen or half a molecule represented by the weight of ½ volume.	H	1
Weight of the atom of Chlorine or half a molecule represented by the weight of ½ volume.	Cl	35.5
Weight of the atom of Bromine or half a molecule represented by the weight of ½ volume.	Br	80
Weight of the atom of Iodine or half a molecule represented by the weight of ½ volume.	I	127

[1] Translated in Alembic Club Reprint, No. 18, University of Chicago Press, 1911, pp. 18–27.

These data being given, there follows the table of some compounds of the halogens [see Table 31-2]: —

TABLE 31-2

Names of the Chlorides.	Weights of equal volumes in the gaseous state, under the same conditions, referred to the weight of ½ volume of Hydrogen = 1; i.e., weights of the molecules referred to the weight of the atom of Hydrogen = 1.	Composition of equal volumes in the gaseous state, under the same conditions, i.e., composition of the molecules, the weights of the components being all referred to the weight of the atom of Hydrogen taken as unity, i.e., the common unit adopted for the weights of atoms and of molecules.	Formulae expressing the composition of the molecules or of equal volumes in the gaseous state under the same conditions.
Free Chlorine	71	71 of Chlorine	Cl^2
Hydrochloric Acid	36.5	35.5 of Chlorine 1 of Hydrogen	HCl
Protochloride of Mercury or Calomel	235.5	35.5 of Chlorine 200 of Mercury	HgCl
Bichloride of Mercury or Corrosive Sublimate	271	71 of Chlorine 200 of Mercury	$HgCl^2$
Chloride of Ethyl	64.5	35.5 of Chlorine 5 of Hydrogen 24 of Carbon	C^2H^5Cl
Chloride of Acetyl	78.5	35.5 of Chlorine 3 of Hydrogen 24 of Carbon 16 of Oxygen	C^2H^3OCl
Chloride of Ethylene	99	71 of Chlorine 4 of Hydrogen 24 of Carbon	$C^2H^4Cl^2$
Chloride of Arsenic	181.5	106.5 of Chlorine 75 of Arsenic	$AsCl^3$
Protochloride of Phosphorus	138.5	106.5 of Chlorine 32 of Phosphorus	PCl^3
Chloride of Boron	117.5	106.5 of Chlorine 11 of Boron	BCl^3

   *   *   *   *   *   *   *

I stop to examine the composition of the molecules of the two chlorides and the two iodides of mercury. There can remain no doubt that the protochloride contains in its molecule the same quantity of chlorine as hydrochloric acid, that the bichloride contains twice as much, and that the quantity of mercury contained in the molecules of both is the same. The supposition made by some chemists that the quantities of chlorine contained in the two molecules are equal, and on the other hand that the quantities of mercury are different, is supported by no valid reason. The vapour densities of the two chlorides having been determined, and it having been observed that equal volumes of them contain the same quantity of mercury, and that the quantity of chlorine contained in one volume of the vapour of calomel is equal to that contained in the same volume of hydrochloric acid gas under the same condition, whilst the quantity of chlorine contained in one volume of corrosive sublimate is twice that contained in an equal volume of calomel or of hydrochloric acid gas, the relative molecular composition of the two chlorides cannot be doubtful. The same may be said of the two iodides. Does the constant quantity of mercury existing in the molecules of these compounds, and represented by the number 200, correspond to one or more atoms? The observation that in these compounds the same quantity of mercury is combined with one or two atoms of chlorine or of iodine, would itself incline us to believe that this quantity is that which enters always as a whole into all the molecules containing mercury, namely, the atom; whence Hg = 200.

To verify this, it would be necessary to compare the various quantities of mercury contained in all the molecules of its compounds whose weights and composition are known with certainty. Few other compounds of mercury besides those indicated above lend themselves to this; still there are some in organic chemistry the formulae of which express well the molecular composition; in these formulae we always find $Hg^2 = 200$, chemists having made Hg = 100 and H = 1. This is a confirmation that the atom of mercury is 200 and not 100, no compound of mercury existing whose molecule contains less than this quantity of it. For verification I refer to the law of the specific heat of elements and of compounds.

I call the quantity of heat consumed by the atoms or the molecules the product of their weights into their specific heats. I compare the heat consumed by the atom of mercury with that consumed by the atoms of iodine and of bromine in the same physical state, and find them almost equal, which confirms the accuracy of the relation between the atomic weight of mercury and that of each of the two halogens, and thus also, indirectly, between the atomic weight of mercury and that of hydrogen, whose specific heats cannot be directly compared.

Thus we have —

Name of Substance.	Atomic weight [A].	Specific heat, i.e., heat required to heat unit weight 1° [S].	[S × A], i.e., heat required to heat the atom 1°.
Solid Bromine	80	0.08432	6.74560
Iodine	127	0.05412	6.87324
Solid Mercury	200	0.03241	6.48200

The same thing is shown by comparing the specific heats of the different compounds of mercury. Woestyn and Garnier have shown that the state of combination does not notably change the calorific capacity of the atoms; and since this is almost equal in the various elements, the molecules would require, to heat them 1°, quantities of heat proportional to the number of atoms which they contain. If Hg = 200, that is, if the formulae of the two chlorides and iodides of mercury are HgCl, HgI, HgCl², HgI², it will be necessary that the molecules of the first pair should consume twice as much heat as each separate atom, and those of the second pair three times as much; and this is so in fact, as may be seen in the following table [see Table 31-3]: —

TABLE 31-3

Formulae of the compounds of Mercury	Weights of their molecules = p	Specific heats of unit weight = c	Specific heats of the molecules = p × c	Number of atoms in the molecules = n	Specific heats of each atom = $\dfrac{p \times c}{n}$
HgCl	235.5	0.05205	12.257745	2	6.128872
HgI	327	0.03949	12.91323	2	6.45661
HgCl²	271	0.06889	18.66919	3	6.22306
HgI²	454	0.04197	19.05438	3	6.35146

Thus the weight 200 of mercury, whether as an element or in its compounds, requires to heat it 1° the same quantity of heat as 127 of iodine, 80 of bromine, and almost certainly as 35.5 of chlorine and 1 of hydrogen, if it were possible to compare these two last substances in the same physical state as that in which the specific heats of the above-named substances have been compared.

But the atoms of hydrogen, iodine, and bromine are half their respective molecules: thus it is natural to ask if the weight 200 of mercury also corresponds to half a molecule of free mercury. It is sufficient to look at the table of numbers expressing the molecular weights to perceive that if 2 is the molecular weight of hydrogen, the weight of the molecule of mercury is 200, i.e., equal to the weight of the atom. In other words, one volume of vapour, whether of protochloride or protoiodide, whether of bichloride or of biniodide, contains an equal volume of mercury vapour; so that each molecule of these compounds contains an entire molecule of mercury, which, entering as a whole into all the molecules, is the atom of this substance. This is confirmed by observing that the complete molecule of mercury requires for heating it 1°, the same quantity of heat as half a molecule of iodine, or half a molecule of bromine. It appears to me, then, that I can sustain that what enters into chemical actions is the half molecule of hydrogen and the whole molecule of mercury: both of these quantities are indivisible, at least *in the sphere of chemical actions actually known.* You will perceive that with this last expression I avoid the question if it is possible to divide this quantity further. I do not fail to apprise you that all those who faithfully applied the theory of Avogadro and of Ampère, have arrived at this same result. First Dumas and afterwards Gaudin showed that the molecule of mercury, differing from that of hydrogen, always entered as a whole into compounds. On this account Gaudin called the molecule of mercury monatomic, and that of hydrogen biatomic [that is, the hydrogen molecule consists of two hydrogen atoms, H_2].

＊   ＊   ＊   ＊   ＊   ＊   ＊

In the preceding discussion of the atom and molecule of mercury, Cannizzaro is concerned with two points, the weight of the atom of mercury and the atomic constitution of the molecule of mercury. He deduces that the atomic weight of mercury is 200 from the fact that this is the smallest weight of mercury that enters into the molecules of the various compounds of mercury and from specific heat measurements. The next point is whether this atom of mercury weighing 200 is half a molecule of the free mercury (that is, the atomic constitution of the molecule of free mercury is Hg_2) or it is a whole molecule of free mercury (that is, the atomic constitution of the molecule of free mercury is monatomic, Hg). Vapor density measurements on free mercury (see Table 30-1) indicated that the molecular weight of mercury is 200. Hence Cannizzaro concludes that the atom of mercury is the whole molecule of mercury and the mercury molecule is monatomic. Thus the question of the atomic and molecular weights of mercury which had troubled chemists for years is resolved.

The formulae of the two chlorides of mercury having been demonstrated, I next compare them with that of hydrochloric acid. The atomic formulae indicate that the constitution of the protochloride is similar to that of hydrochloric acid, if we consider the number of atoms existing in the molecules of the two; if, however, we compare the quantities of the components with those which exist in their free molecules, then a difference is perceived. To make this evident I bring the atomic formulae of the various molecules under examination into comparison with the formulae made with the symbols expressing the weights of the entire molecules, placing them in the manner which you see below [Table 31-4, page 410].

The comparison of these formulae confirms still more the preference which we must give to the atomic formulae, which indicate also clearly the relations between the gaseous bodies. It is sufficient to recall that whilst the atoms of chlorine, bromine, iodine, and hydrogen are represented by the weight of ½ volume, the atom of mercury is represented by the weight of a whole volume.

I then come to the examination of the two chlorides of copper. The analogy with those of mercury forces us to admit that they have a similar atomic constitution, but we cannot verify this directly by determining and comparing the weights and the compositions of the molecules, as we do not know the vapour densities of these two compounds.

The specific heats of free copper and of its compounds confirm the atomic constitution of the two chlorides of copper deduced from the analogy with those of mercury. Indeed the composition of the two chlorides leads us to

TABLE 31-4

	Symbols of the molecules of the elements and formulæ of their compounds made with these symbols, i.e., symbols and formulæ representing the weights of equal volumes in the gaseous state.		Symbols of the atoms of the elements, and formulæ of their compounds made with these symbols.		Numbers expressing the corresponding weights.
Atom of Hydrogen	H½	=	H	=	1
Molecule of Hydrogen	H	=	H²	=	2
Atom of Chlorine	Cl½	=	Cl	=	35.5
Molecule of Chlorine	Cl	=	Cl²	=	71
Atom of Bromine	Br½	=	Br	=	80
Molecule of Bromine	Br	=	Br²	=	160
Atom of Iodine	I½	=	I	=	127
Molecule of Iodine	I	=	I²	=	254
Atom of Mercury	Hg	=	Hg	=	200
Molecule of Mercury	Hg	=	Hg	=	200
Molecule of Hydrochloric Acid	H½Cl½	=	HCl	=	36.5
Molecule of Hydrobromic Acid	H½Br½	=	HBr	=	81
Molecule of Hydriodic Acid	H½I½	=	HI	=	128
Molecule of protochloride of Mercury	HgCl½	=	HgCl	=	235.5
Molecule of protobromide of Mercury	HgBr½	=	HgBr	=	280
Molecule of protoiodide of Mercury	HgI½	=	HgI	=	327
Molecule of bichloride of Mercury	HgCl	=	HgCl²	=	271
Molecule of bibromide of Mercury	HgBr	=	HgBr²	=	360
Molecule of biniodide of Mercury	HgI	=	HgI²	=	454

conclude that if they have the formulae $CuCl$, $CuCl^2$, the atomic weight of copper indicated by Cu is equal to 63, which may be seen from the following proportions: —

	Ratio between the components expressed by numbers whose sum = 100.	Ratio between the components expressed by atomic weight.
Protochloride of Copper	36.04 : 63.96	35.5 : 63
	Chlorine Copper	Cl. Cu.
Bichloride of Copper	52.98 : 47.02	71 : 63
	Chlorine Copper	Cl^2. Cu.

Now 63 multiplied by the specific heat of copper gives a product practically equal to that given by the atomic weight of iodine or of mercury into their respective specific heats. Thus:

$$63 \quad \times \quad 0.09515 \quad = 6.$$

Atomic weight   Specific heat
of copper

The same quantity of heat is required to heat the weight of 63 of copper in its compounds through 1°. Thus: —

Formulae of the compounds of Copper.	Weights of their molecules = p.	Specific heats of unit weights = c.	Specific heats of the molecules = p × c.	Number of atoms in the molecules = n	Specific heat of each atom = $\frac{p \times c}{n}$.
CuCl	98.5	0.13827	13.619595	2	6.809797
CuI	190	0.06869	14.0511	2	7.0255

After this comes the question, whether this quantity of copper which enters as a whole into the compounds, the calorific capacity of the atoms being maintained, is an entire molecule or a sub-multiple of it. The analogy of the compounds of copper with those of mercury would make us inclined to believe that the atom of copper is a complete molecule. But having no other proof to confirm this, I prefer to declare that there is no means of knowing the molecular weight of free copper until the vapour density of this substance can be determined.

In the remainder of this section Cannizzaro discusses the halides of various other elements, including sodium, potassium, and silver. Since these metallic elements, like copper, do not form any vaporizable compounds, he relies entirely on specific heat measurements to determine their atomic weights.

This paper of Cannizzaro concludes this section on determining the relative weights of the atoms. Several points are worthy of recapitulation.

What has proven to be an idea of far reaching ramifications, the determination of relative atomic weights, was apparently first conceived by Dalton as merely a possible solution to the comparatively minor problem of the variation of solubility of different gases in water. Although the desirability of determining relative atomic weights first presented itself as a *physical* problem, it was through a *chemical* approach that these relative weights were finally determined.

Dalton in his atomic theory conceived of the existence of only one kind of particle, which he called the " atom," and he applied this concept indiscriminately where we today recognize two particles, the chemical atom and the physical molecule. In order to arrive at his relative atomic weights from the law of definite proportions, Dalton proposed his seven rules. This approach had obvious defects and indicated the need for additional experimental criteria in determining relative atomic weights.

One such additional criterion was discovered by Gay-Lussac in his study of the relative volumes of gases involved in chemical reactions, the results of which are summarized in his law of reacting volumes.

Avogadro first conceived of a possible reconciliation between Dalton's atomic theory and Gay-Lussac's law by proposing the existence of two kinds of ultimate particles, the physical molecule and the chemical atom. For various reasons Avogadro's ideas were not accepted by most chemists, major drawbacks being limited applicability and the difficulty, in the light of Berzelius' dualistic theory, of explaining the combination of two atoms of the same element to form a molecule.

Dumas extended the range of applicability of Avogadro's hypothesis, and with the downfall of the dualistic theory, the objection to polyatomic molecules of the elements disappeared. Gerhardt and Laurent made Avogadro's hypothesis more acceptable, as the formulas derived on the basis of the hypothesis for organic compounds were in agreement with the chemical properties of the compounds. This of course did not explain why the molecules of most elements were polyatomic. In fact, a satisfactory explanation of the polyatomicity of molecules of elements was not obtained until 1925. Finally, Cannizzaro, by his special application of Avogadro's hypothesis for the determination of atomic weights and the demonstration that the atomic weights so obtained were in agreement with those obtained by the method utilizing the law of Dulong and Petit, developed a scheme whereby the atomic weights of all the elements could be determined.

At this time (1858) there was no basis for the determination of the absolute weight of an atom in grams or pounds; all calculations were of relative weights. About 20 years later a rough measurement was obtained of the number of molecules in a given weight of hydrogen and thence the absolute weight of the hydrogen molecule or atom could be calculated. Since the weights of other atoms relative to the hydrogen atom were known, the absolute weights of the other atoms could also be calculated. Today, the number of molecules or atoms in a given weight of an element is known with great accuracy.

The establishment of unambiguous methods for determining relative atomic weights made possible the next major advance in chemistry, the discovery in 1869 of the periodic law by Mendelyeev and Lothar Meyer. According to this law, the properties of the elements are periodic functions of their atomic weights. The existence of this periodicity indicates that there is something repetitious or common in the structures of the various atoms. This line of approach from the chemical properties of matter eventually fused with the studies of the electrical properties to culminate in our modern theories of the structure of matter.

We have noted in our readings only a few of the early experimental observations, such as the laws of definite and multiple proportions and the law of reacting volumes, that indicate the existence of atoms. Subsequent to the period (1800–1860) we have studied, the additional experimental evidence gathered in physics and chemistry for the existence of atoms has continued to grow. Although no one has ever seen an atom, nor ever will, the interlocking experimental evidence that is organized about the atomic concept is almost tantamount to proof of its existence. To abandon the atomic concept would necessitate a complete reorganization of most of the present-day knowledge of physics and chemistry.

STUDY QUESTIONS

1. Suppose that in addition to the two compounds of mercury and chlorine listed in Table 31-3 the following hypothetical compound of the two elements existed:

   Molecular weight from vapor density measurements, 377.5.
   Composition: 200 of Hg; 177.5 of Cl (parts by weight).
   Cannizzaro would deduce its formula to be

   (1) Hg_2Cl (2) $HgCl_3$ (3) Hg_2Cl_3 (4) $HgCl_4$ (5) $HgCl_5$.

   2–4. Suppose there existed the following hypothetical compound of copper and chlorine (data on which is given below) in addition to the two listed in the table on p. 411.

   Analysis: 54.2% Cu; 45.8% Cl

2. The weight of chlorine associated with 63 of copper would be

   (1) 106   (2) 53.2   (3) 35.5   (4) 71.2   (5) 142.

3. Cannizzaro would write the formula of this compound as

   (1) Cu_2Cl (2) $CuCl_3$ (3) Cu_3Cl (4) Cu_2Cl_3 (5) $Cu_1Cl_{1.5}$.

4. Cannizzaro would expect the *specific heat* of this compound to be approximately

  (1) .145 (2) 34.5 (3) 6.80 (4) .290 (5) 6.10.

5. Cannizzaro writes the formulas of the protochloride of copper as $CuCl$ and that of the bichloride of copper as $CuCl_2$. Is he " positive " that this is the constitution of the respective molecules or might they be Cu_2Cl_2 and Cu_2Cl_4 respectively? Does the same problem arise with the chlorides, etc., of mercury?

6. Cannizzaro states, " After this comes the question, whether this quantity of copper (63) which enters as a whole into the compounds, the caloric capacity of the atoms being maintained, is an entire molecule or submultiple of it." If this quantity (63) is an entire molecule, Cannizzaro would expect the specific gravity of copper vapor (if it existed) relative to hydrogen to be

  (1) 126 (2) 31.5 (3) 63.0 (4) .00111 (5) 252.

7–8. Analogous to the problem faced by Cannizzaro in his treatment of the chlorides of copper and the halides of sodium, lithium, potassium, silver, etc., consider the following compound of chlorine and a metal X. Analysis of compound: 79.7% chlorine; 20.3% metal X.
Specific heat of metal X = .249.
Atomic weight of Cl = 35.5.

7. The simplest formula for the compound is

  (1) XCl (2) XCl_2 (3) XCl_3 (4) X_2Cl (5) X_3Cl.

8. The " exact " atomic weight of X is

  (1) 79.7 (2) 54.0 (3) 9.00 (4) 18.0 (5) 27.1.

9–14. Two gaseous oxides of sulfur have the following percentage compositions by weight:
* Oxide I: 50% S; 50% O.*
* Oxide II: 40% S; 60% O.*
* The density of oxide I is less than that of oxide II. The specific heat of sulfur is .18 cal/gm. (Take atomic weight of oxygen as 16.)*

9. On the basis of Dalton's principles, what is the probable atomic weight of sulfur?

  (1) 16 (2) 32 (3) 26 (4) 8 (5) 64.

10. Following Cannizzaro and using the criteria for atomic weights furnished by the law of Dulong and Petit, the atomic weight of sulfur is

  (1) 16 (2) 32 (3) 26 (4) 8 (5) 64.

11. The " atomic heat " of sulfur is

  (1) 6.0 (2) 5.8 (3) 6.1 (4) 7.1 (5) 7.5.

12. The simplest formula for oxide I is (according to Cannizzaro)

  (1) SO (2) S_2O (3) SO_2 (4) SO_3 (5) S_2O_3.

13. The simplest formula for oxide II is (according to Cannizzaro)

  (1) SO (2) S_2O (3) SO_2 (4) SO_3 (5) S_2O_3.

14. If the structure of the molecule I is SO_2, the specific gravity of oxide I in the gaseous state relative to hydrogen gas would be expected to be

    (1) 64   (2) 32   (3) 128   (4) 16   (5) 48.

15. According to Woestyn and Garnier if the specific heat of a certain compound is .0930 and its molecular weight is 200, the number of atoms in the molecule is probably

    (1) 1   (2) 2   (3) 3   (4) 4   (5) 5.

16. Consider two containers of equal volume at the same temperature and pressure, one containing SO_2 (50% S, 50% O) and the other SO_3 (40% S, 60% O). The weight of SO_2 in the first container is 5 lb. The weight of sulfur contained in the SO_3 in the second container is

    (1) not calculable   (2) 1.25 lb   (3) 2.5 lb   (4) 1.5 lb   (5) 1.75 lb.

PART SIX

MOUNTAIN BUILDING

The preceding developments in chemistry, physics, and astronomy helped to lay the foundation for the subsequent growth of certain branches of modern geology. Geology as a science is relatively young. Possibly it is one of the youngest of the sciences because human beings tend to seek after the distant and inaccessible, at the expense of the common and the near at hand. Although geology is young as a science, it is old as an art. The use of various earth materials dates back to the earliest record of man's existence upon the earth. The earliest philosophers speculated upon geological subjects.

Geology is very broad in its scope. Instead of being a single science, it is a group of closely related sciences, such as mineralogy, petrology, volcanology, seismology, paleontology, and structural geology. Some of these are fairly "exact" sciences, based upon mathematical principles and natural laws. Other branches of geology are based to a considerable degree on speculative concepts and contain many unanswered problems, perhaps even unanswerable problems. The question of the formation of mountains which will be considered here is but one of many such difficult problems in geology. There is as yet no complete and fully accepted answer. Instead there are a multitude of possible answers, all theoretical, at least in part. No one hypothesis or theory yet proposed is fully adequate to explain mountain building, yet many of these hypotheses have merit.

Mountains are among the most striking physical features of the earth. It is no wonder that men have speculated about them from the earliest times. The early classification of mountains was based on limited and local observations. There were volcanic mountains, and those produced by the folding of stratified rocks, and then there were those, commonly called composite, which resulted from two or more causes. There were also mountains produced by block faulting, and there were weathered eminences, or residual mountains, which represented the remains of a lofty plateau after a long period of erosion. There were speculations about the mechanism which brought about mountains. Aristotle wrote of " winds escaping from the earth's interior." Strabo thought of " sudden swellings of land beneath the sea " which might elevate the previous ocean bottom to great heights. Somewhat nearer to our own time, A. G. Werner proposed that the major surface features of our earth were sedimentary rocks deposited from a world-wide universal sea. Opposing the views of Werner was James Hutton, who held that the primary source of the crust of the earth was volcanic.

THE BEGINNINGS OF MODERN GEOLOGY

Modern geology begins with careful and comprehensive field work. Detailed structural studies of the Alps and the Pyrenees, for example, provided the basis for important modern theories of mountain origin. These studies were made by a number of geologists, of whom de Saussure (1740–1799) and von Buch (1774–1852) are the most outstanding. De Saussure, a Swiss geologist, was the first to make a detailed study of the Alps. The results of his work were published in four volumes between the years 1779 and 1796. His work represented a monumental effort, for in the progress of his field studies he crossed the whole chain of the Alps fourteen times and made sixteen other traverses from the plains flanking the Alps to their central axis. He did all this work at a time when there were few roads or trails in the mountain regions, when passage over the mountains was very difficult.

De Saussure finally regarded the origin of the Alps as due either (1) to the folding of layers that were originally horizontal or (2) to some force acting upward from below. He believed the first explanation to be the more probable. As to the ultimate causes for the origin of the Alps he hesitated to use the much overused " subterranean fires." In his conclusion he stated that he could devise no general theory that could adequately account for the origin of the Alps, that further studies and observations would be required.

Following de Saussure very closely, von Buch began work in the Alps. Von Buch had been an outstanding student at the Freiberg Mining Academy in Germany, where he studied under A. G. Werner. Werner had taught him that the great folds in the Alps were due to an irregular settling of thick sediments deposited in a universal ocean upon an irregular surface. He soon realized that Werner's explanations for the folds would not suffice. He then reasoned that if there was any general law that governed the structure of the Alps, discovery of it might be possible if parallel cross sections, separated by intervals of considerable distance, were made across the Alps. He proceeded to make such sections on the basis of detailed traverses. At the completion of this phase of his work, von Buch decided he could not obtain the final, complete answer to the problem of the origin of the Alps, but that certainly external forces of compression played a great part in their elevation.

After his initial work in the Alps, von Buch did geological work in Italy, France, Scandinavia, northwestern coastal Africa and adjoining islands, the Hebrides, northern Scotland, northern Ireland, and Germany. He then returned to the Alps for field work which was almost continuous for several years. Through this additional work and his broader field experiences in other areas, von Buch was led to conclude that the Alps [1] " owed their origin to a process of upheaval, due to a force exerted by bodies of volcanic rock beneath the surface, . . . but which here could not find an actual passage to the exterior of the earth owing to the resistance offered by the great thickness of the overlying rocks."

SOME IMPORTANT THEORIES OF MOUNTAIN BUILDING IN THE 19TH AND 20TH CENTURIES

Soon after 1800, theories and hypotheses began to appear to explain the mechanism involved in the origin of mountains. Historical geology came to the forefront. The study of successions of rock layers, called stratigraphy, was carried on everywhere rock layers were exposed. Geological surveys were organized in all civilized countries. Interest in the problem of mountain origin increased throughout the world. Among the many theories and hypotheses that have been advanced since 1800 to explain world-wide mechanisms of mountain building, the following will be considered here:

1. The contraction theory, which postulates a shrinking earth with crustal shortening. This theory is the principal subject matter of Chapter 32 with excerpts from James D. Dana.

2. The geosynclinal theory, which states that the highest mountains occur where thickest sediments had been deposited. The geosynclinal theory is discussed in Chapter 33 with excerpts principally from James Hall.

3. The theory of isostasy, which attempts to explain an apparent tendency for crustal equilibrium in various segments of the earth's crust. Isostasy is the subject matter of Chapters 34 and 35 with quotations from John H. Pratt, George B. Airy, and Clarence E. Dutton.

4. The theory of continental drift, which considers that all continents once " fitted " together in one great land mass that is postulated to have broken apart and " drifted " on a plastic substratum to the present continental positions. If the position of a continent shifted, the friction and resistance to movement on the substratum might conceivably result in the formation of belts of folded mountains.

---

[1] F. D. Adams, *The Birth and Development of the Geological Sciences,* by permission of Dover Publications, Inc., New York, 1938, p. 235.

5. Island-arc (or mountain-arc or structural-arc) theory, which postulates that mountains rise through successive periods (or pulses) of growth from a continental shelf or various other type border areas to form either a single or double island arc, in some cases further evolving into active mountain arcs, and finally to inactive, mature, or old folded mountain ranges.

6. The convection theory, which is based on the supposed transfer of heat within the earth by moving currents. The currents are considered typically to move upward under continental masses and downward beneath ocean basins. According to some proponents the currents drag segments of the crustal materials downward in some boundary regions between continents and ocean basins, resulting in folds and distorted strata and negative gravity zones.[2] The light material may eventually rise isostatically to elevate the folded strata into mountains.

7. The phase-change, or polymorphism theory, which postulates that deep within the earth crystalline solids undergo changes in their atomic or molecular arrangements to become heavier or lighter, as the case may be, depending upon conditions of temperature and pressure. If the change is to denser material, the resulting molecules will occupy less space, consequently allowing for depression; if the change is to less dense, or lighter materials, expansion will occur, contributing to the uplift of mountain masses.

The first three of the above theories were developed for the most part during the latter half of the 19th century. The others have been proposed and developed essentially during the present century. These newer theories are reviewed in Chapter 36.

GEOLOGICAL TIME

The geological time scale included here (Table VI–1) is primarily to aid the reader in determining the relative position in geological time to which certain quotations refer. However it should be realized that terminology relating to geological time has not been very consistent through the years, and that there has been a tendency during the last several decades to increase the length of time allotted to various time divisions. The intervals assigned to each division in the included scale are based largely upon the rate of decay of certain radioactive elements or isotopes of elements. The absolute ages have been compiled mostly from data by the United States Geological Survey and the National Research Council.

---

[2] A commonly used unit of acceleration of gravity is one gal (having a value of one centimeter per second per second and is a modern coinage from Galileo) or milligal, which is one thousandth part of a gal. Values for gravitational acceleration below normal (980.665 gals) are expressed in negative milligals. For example along the inner edge of the oceanic deep near the Celebes, values as low as minus 200 milligals have been observed.

TABLE VI-1

GEOLOGICAL TIME SCALE*

Era	Period	Epoch	Approximate millions of years to beginning of each unit	
	Quaternary	Recent	.01	
		Pleistocene	1	
(5) CENOZOIC	Tertiary	Pliocene	12	
		Miocene	28	
		Oligocene	40	
		Eocene	50	
		Paleocene	60	
(4) MESOZOIC	Cretaceous		130	
	Jurassic		155	
	Triassic		185	
(3) PALEOZOIC	Permian		210	
	Pennsylvanian		235	Carboniferous
	Mississippian		265	
	Devonian		320	
	Silurian		360	
	Ordovician		440	
	Cambrian		520	
(2) PROTEROZOIC	Keweenawan Huronian		1600	Pre-Cambrian time
(1) ARCHEOZOIC	Timiskaming Keewatin		2700±	
COSMIC TIME	Pre Crustal Rocks		4500–5000±	

* From publications of United States Geological Survey and National Research Council

32

The Contraction Theory and Mountain Origin

● For many years previous to the discovery of radio-activity it was commonly accepted as factual that the earth was a cooling body and therefore continually contracting and shrinking. This idea seemed to be all that was needed to explain adequately the folded and faulted mountains of the world, for in accommodating a smaller inner core the more rigid rocks of the crust would crumple much as the peel of an orange crumples when the orange dehydrates.

To whom credit should be given for first mention of the contraction theory is not known. In a paper published in 1847 dealing with contraction as a factor in the origin of the earth's major features, Dana stated in a footnote that he " does not claim to have presented any new principle except it may be the special cause assigned for oceanic depressions." He further stated that the theory of contraction as a cause of the earth's major features dates back at least to the work of Leibnitz (1646–1716). Another author has carried the idea back to Descartes (1596–1650) who considered the possibility of a cooling and shrinking earth, thus accounting for the earth's crumpled crust.

Elie de Beaumont has been credited by some writers as the founder of the contraction theory because of a widely distributed article published in Paris in 1852 in which he postulated that the upheaval of mountains is " a result of the slow and progressive diminution of the volume of the earth." He attributed the loss in volume of the earth to a " dissipation of a part of the heat which the earth held when its crust, now solidified, was in a state of fusion." He held the catastrophist point of view — that all mountains came into existence suddenly, rather than slowly over a long period of time. De Beaumont published his first paper on the contraction theory about 1830.

James D. Dana (Fig. 32-1), born in 1813 at Utica, New York, was probably the greatest proponent of the contraction theory in America. Always greatly interested in science, Dana entered Yale in 1830 where he studied

Figure 32-1. *James D. Dana (1813–1895).*

under Benjamin Silliman, graduating in three years. Dana continued his scientific career by teaching mathematics to naval midshipmen. He returned to Yale in 1836 as an assistant to Professor Silliman in chemistry. During the years 1838–1842 Dana served as a mineralogist and geologist on an expedition under Captain Charles Wilkes. Parts of the next 13 years were spent in writing reports of the expedition.

Dana married the daughter of Professor Silliman in 1844. Two years later he became joint editor and later chief editor of the *American Journal of Science and Arts* which had been founded in 1818 by Professor Silliman. Upon the retirement of Silliman, Dana was appointed Silliman Professor of Natural History and Geology at Yale. He held that position from 1850 until his retirement in 1892.

Dana's bibliography included 214 titles of books and papers, including such monumental works as *Manual of Mineralogy, Manual of Geology,* and *System of Mineralogy.* Dana is probably best known for the latter, a publication which went through many editions and which is still a valuable reference book in mineralogy.

Between the years 1846 and 1879 Dana wrote numerous papers dealing with the origin of mountains and other major earth features, with emphasis upon the contraction theory. Excerpts have been selected from an article dated 1873. This was a major paper in five parts that reviewed the main points of his earlier papers, and brought his views on mountain origin up to date. He also included considerable discussion about the geosynclinal theory. In fact it is Dana who is credited with the coining of the term " geosynclinal," and thus the naming of the theory that was proposed and developed by Hall. Hall's theory is the subject matter of Chapter 33.

ON SOME RESULTS OF THE EARTH'S CONTRACTION FROM COOLING, INCLUDING A DISCUSSION OF THE ORIGIN OF MOUNTAINS, AND THE NATURE OF THE EARTH'S INTERIOR [1]

by James D. Dana

Part I

Preparatory to a discussion of some questions connected with the earth's contraction, I here present a statement of the views which I have entertained with regard to the prominent results of this agency. They first appeared in 1846 and 1847 . . . and were somewhat extended in 1856. . . . The views are as follows:

1. The defining of the continental and oceanic areas began with the commencement of the earth's solidification at surface, . . .

2. The continental areas are the areas of least contraction, and the oceanic basins those of the greatest, the former having earliest had a solid crust. After the continental part was thus stiffened, and rendered comparatively unyielding, the oceanic part went on cooling, solidifying, and contracting throughout; consequently it became depressed, with the sides of the depression somewhat abrupt. The formation of the oceanic basins and continental areas was thus due to " unequal radial contraction."

3. The principal mountain chains are portions of the earth's crust which have been pushed up, and often crumpled or plicated, by the lateral pressure resulting from the earth's contraction.

4. (a) Owing to the lateral pressure from contraction over both the continental and oceanic areas, and to the fact that the latter are the regions of greatest contraction and subsidence, and that their sides pushed, like the ends of an arch, against the borders of the continents, therefore, along these borders, within 300 to 1000 miles of a coast, a continent experienced its profoundest oscillations of level, had accumulated its thickest deposits of rocks, underwent the most numerous uplifts, fractures and plications, had raised its highest and longest mountain chains, and became the scene of the most extensive metamorphic operations, and the most abundant outflows of liquid rock.

And (b) since the most numerous and closest plications, the greatest ranges of volcanoes, the largest regions of igneous eruption and metamorphic action, exist on the *oceanic slope* of the border mountain chains, instead of the continental, therefore the lateral pressure acted most effectively in a direction *from* the ocean.

[1] From *American Journal of Science and Arts,* Series 3, Part I, Vol. 105, and Parts II through VI, Vol. 106, 1873.

(c) Since these border features are vastly grander along that border of a continent which faces the largest ocean, therefore the lateral pressure against the sides of a continent was most effective on the border of the largest oceanic basin, and for the two, the Pacific and Atlantic, was approximately proportioned to the extent of the basins; this being due to the fact that the oceanic were the subsiding areas, that is, those which contracted most, and that the larger area became the most depressed.

5. The oscillations of level that have taken place over the interior of North America, through the geological ages, have in some degree conformed in direction of axis to those of the border regions, all being parts fundamentally of two systems of movements, one dominantly in a direction northwestward or from the Atlantic, and the other northeastward or from the Pacific.

6. Owing to the approximate uniformity of direction in the lateral thrust under these two systems through the successive ages, mountains of *different ages* on the same border, or part of a border, have approximately the *same trend*, and those *of the same age* on the opposite border — Pacific and Atlantic — have in general *a different and nearly transverse trend*. . . .

7. The features of the North American continent were to a great extent defined in pre-Silurian time, the course of the Azoic,[2] from the Great Lakes to Labrador, being that of the Appalachians, and various ridges in the Rocky Mountains foreshadowings of this great chain, and so on in many lines over the continental surface; and thus its adult characteristics were as plainly manifested in its beginnings as are those of a vertebrate in a half-developed embryo.

8. Metamorphism of regions of strata has taken place only during periods of disturbance, or when plication and faults were in progress; all metamorphic regions being regions of disturbed and generally of plicated rocks. . . .

9. The volcanoes of the continental areas are mostly confined to the sea-borders, or the oceanic slope of the border mountain chains, not because of the vicinity of salt water, but because these were the regions of greatest disturbance and fractures through lateral pressure. Volcanoes are indexes of danger, never " safety valves."

10. Earthquakes were a result of sudden fracturings and dislocations proceeding from lateral pressure. . . .

I propose to bring the above principles under consideration with reference to making such changes as may now be necessary.

I take up, first, the question as to whether oscillations of level, that is, subsidences and elevations, have been made by the lateral pressure resulting from contraction, as is assumed in my writings on the subject and those of most other authors; — and how was the lateral thrust from the direction of the oceanic areas made to differ in its results from that from the opposite direction? After which I shall pass to the subjects of metamorphism, igneous eruptions, volcanoes, the earth's interior, and the origin of oceanic basins. . . .

---

[2] The term Azoic was formerly applied to that part of geologic time represented by Pre-Cambrian stratified rocks. Later the term was restricted to Early Pre-Cambrian, or Archeozoic only. The term literally means " devoid of life" and referred to those rocks in which there were no traces of fossil remains. The term is little used in present-day literature.

1. Have subsidences been produced by lateral pressure?

✿   ✿   ✿   ✿   ✿   ✿   ✿

After a lengthy discussion the conclusion is reached that

In the present state of science, then, no adequate cause of subsidence has been suggested apart from the old one of lateral pressure in the contracting material of the globe.

2. Have elevations been produced directly by lateral pressure?

✿   ✿   ✿   ✿   ✿   ✿   ✿

Prof. Le Conte makes the elevation of the mountains real, but, after explaining that the crushing effects of lateral thrust would necessarily cause a lengthening upward of the compressed strata, . . . and thereby produce a large amount of actual elevation, arrives at the view, that there is no permanent elevation beyond what results from crushing. With crushing, in this action, plication is associated; but it should have a larger place than his words seem to give it (in all plication the rocks over a region being pressed into a narrower space, which could be done only by adding to its height), as it has performed ten-fold more work of this kind than crushing.

But are plication and crushing the only methods of producing under lateral pressure, the actual elevations of mountain regions? Is there not real elevation besides?

In the later part of the Post-tertiary or Quaternary era,[3] the region about Montreal was raised nearly 500 feet, as shown by the existence of sea-beaches at that height; and similar evidence proves that the region about Lake Champlain was raised at the same time at least 300 feet, and the coast of Maine 150 to 200 feet. Hence the region raised was large. No crushing or plication of the upper rocks occurred, and none in the under rocks could well have taken place without exhibitions at surface; and this cause, therefore, cannot account for the elevation. The elevated sea-border deposits of the region are in general horizontal. This example is to the point as much as if a mountain had been made by the elevation.[4]

But we have another example on a mountain scale, and one of many. Fossiliferous beds over the higher regions of the Rocky mountains are unquestioned evidence that a large part of this chain has been raised 8,000 to 10,000 feet above the ocean level since the Cretaceous era. The Cretaceous rocks, to which these fossiliferous beds belong, were upturned in the course of the slowly progressing elevation, and so also were part of the Tertiary beds — for the elevation went forward through the larger part, or all, of the Tertiary era. But the local crushing or plication of these beds cannot account for the elevation, and no other crushing among the surface rocks of the mountains can be referred to this era. There may have been a crushing and crumpling of the nether rocks

[3] " Era," as used on this page, would, in present-day writing, be replaced by the term " period." See geological time scale, Table VI-1.

[4] Some of the uplifts in the region here mentioned were later interpreted to be due to isostatic readjustment subsequent to the melting of the Pleistocene glacial ice.

of the mountain. But it must also be admitted that there might have been, under tangential pressure, a bending of the strata without crushing, especially if there is beneath the earth's rind along the continental borders a region or layer of " aqueo-igneous fusion," such as Prof. LeConte recognizes.

In the course of the geological history of the North American continent, there were many oscillations of level in the land. Portions that were raised above the sea-level in one era in another subsided again and sunk beneath it; and Prof. LeConte, in the course of his discussion, admits the existence of an elevated region along the Atlantic border which afterward disappeared. Had the elevation in the case of such oscillations been dependent on plication and crushing beneath, so complete a disappearance afterward would have been very improbable.

Such facts as the above appear to prove that elevatory movements have often been, like those of subsidence, among the direct results of lateral pressure. . . .

3. Kinds and Structure of Mountains.

While mountains and mountain chains all over the world, and low lands, also, have undergone uplifts, in the course of their long history, that are not explained on the idea that all mountain elevating is simply what may come from plication or crushing, the *component parts* of mountain chains, or those simple mountains or mountain ranges that are *the product of one process of making* — may have received, *at the time of their original making*, no elevation beyond that resulting from plication.

This leads us to a grand distinction in orography, hitherto neglected, which is fundamental and of the highest interest in dynamical geology; a distinction between —

1. A simple or *individual* mountain mass or range, which is the result of *one process of making*, like an individual in any process of evolution, and which may be distinguished as a *monogenetic* range, being *one in genesis;* and

2. A composite or *polygenetic* range or chain, made up of two or more monogenetic ranges combined.

The Appalachian chain — the mountain region along the Atlantic border of North America — is a polygenetic chain; it consists, like the Rocky and other mountain chains, of several *monogenetic* ranges, the more important of which are [Fig. 32-2]: 1. The Highland range (including the Blue Ridge or parts of it, and the Adirondacks also, if these belong to the same process of making) pre-Silurian in formation; 2. The Green Mountain range, in western New England and eastern New York, completed essentially after the Lower Silurian era or during its closing period; 3. The Alleghany range, extending from southern New York southwestward to Alabama, and completed immediately after the Carboniferous age. . . .

4. How was the lateral thrust from the direction of the ocean made to differ in its action or results from that from the opposite direction?

The fact of a difference in the effects of the lateral thrust from the opposite directions, the oceanic and continental, is beyond question. The evidence may here be repeated.

The greatest of elevations as well as subsidences, and also of plications and igneous eruptions, have taken place on the continental borders or in their

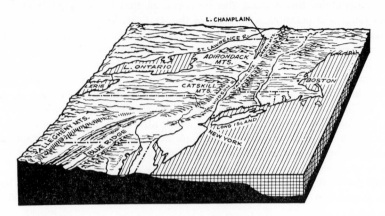

Figure 32-2. *Mountains of Northeastern United States.*

vicinity; they thus show that there is something peculiar along such regions. Again, the border mountains in North America are parallel to the axes of the adjoining oceans; and thereby at right angles, instead of parallel to one another. Again, the folds in the Appalachians are not symmetrical folds, but, instead, have one slope much steeper than the other, proving inequality in the action of lateral pressure from the continental and oceanic directions. Further, the larger ranges of uplifts and effects of heat occur on the *oceanic* slope of the principal border-mountain chain, instead of the continental slope, favoring the view that this lateral thrust was more effective in the direction from the ocean against the continents than in the opposite. Finally, there is the fact that the disturbances or effects of lateral thrust have been *very much the greatest* on the border of the *largest* oceans.

But has this greater effectiveness of lateral thrust from the direction of the ocean been due to a proportionally greater contraction and subsidence of the oceanic crust than the continental — the sinking causing the oceanic arch to press against the sides of the basin. I formerly made this the chief means of mountain lifting; and now, while not giving it so great prominence, I believe it to be a true cause. It is certain that the depressing of the ocean's bed, like the raising of the continental areas, has been in progress through the ages. The great principal rise of the continent and continental mountains took place after the Cretaceous period or during the Tertiary, and some of it even in the Quaternary; and this is almost positive demonstration that the bottoms of the oceans were tending downward cotemporaneously. It is not possible in the nature of contraction that it should have been all accomplished in these basins at the beginning of their existence — a point I shall further illustrate when discussing the nature of the earth's interior. Moreover, the mobile waters that occupy the oceanic depressions would have given important aid in the cooling of the underlying crust. It is to be noted, also, that the distance between the axis of the Appalachians in North America, and the opposite (African) side of the Atlantic is 4000 miles; and that between the axis of the Rocky Mountains and the opposite (Australian) coast of the Pacific is over 7000 miles, while between the axis of the Appalachians in Virginia and that of the Rocky

Mountains in the same latitude, the distance is hardly 1500 miles. Hence the contraction was absolutely greatest over the oceanic areas, independently of any result from special causes; and if the generated pressure were not expended in uplifts over the oceanic areas themselves, it would have been in uplifts on its borders.

In addition to the above advantage which the oceanic areas have had in the making of border oscillations, the lower position of the oceanic crust, and the abruptness with which the sides fall off, give it an opportunity to push beneath the sides of the continents, and this would determine the production of such mountains and just such other effects of pressure, on the continental borders, as actually exist, even if contraction were equable over the globe, that is, were alike in rate over the oceanic and continental areas. It puts the oscillations over the continents inevitably under the direction of the adjoining oceanic crust. The angle of slope of the deepwater sides of the oceanic basin is generally above five degrees.

      ❃   ❃   ❃   ❃   ❃   ❃   ❃

In concluding section 4, Dana wrote

In view of the considerations here presented, I believe there is no occasion to reject the fourth proposition [4(a), near the beginning of the excerpt] but only to modify it as follows:

4(a). Owing to the general contraction of the globe, the greater size of the oceanic than the continental areas, and the greater subsidence from continued contraction over the former than over the latter, and also to the fact that the oceanic crust had the advantage of *leverage*, or, more strictly, of obliquely upward thrust against the borders of the continents, because of its lower position, *therefore*, these borders within 300 to 1,000 miles of the coast, etc.

In section 5, Dana pointed out that mountain making is a very slow process; that "it is necessary to remember that mountain elevation has taken place after immensely long periods of quiet and gentle oscillations."

Section 6 includes a summary of the general system of movements and mountain making on both borders of the North American continent and over the oceanic areas, starting with an enumeration and discussion of the mountain-making periods on the Atlantic border, then on the Pacific border and interior as far as the Rocky Mountains, and ending with a discussion of the record of changes in sea level as determined from island shore lines, especially coral island subsidence.

For the sake of brevity, no excerpts have been taken from Parts II, III, or IV and only a small portion from the conclusion at the end of Part V has been selected. Those parts from which no excerpts were taken deal with the earth's interior, metamorphism, vulcanism, igneous eruptions, and volcanoes and their relations to mountain making, ending with a discussion of the formation of continental plateaus and oceanic depressions. Dana believed that the continental masses have been continents continuously since earliest geologic time.

Part V

Conclusion

❋   ❋   ❋   ❋   ❋   ❋   ❋

The views on mountain-making now sustained suppose the existence, through a large part of geological time, of a thin crust, and of liquid rock beneath that crust so as to make its oscillation possible, and refers the chief oscillations, whether of elevation or of subsidence, to lateral pressure from the contraction of that crust; and this accords with my former view, and with that earlier presented by the clear-sighted French geologist, Prévost.

I hold also, as before, that the prevailing position of mountains on the *borders* of the continents, with the like location of volcanoes and of the greater earthquakes, is due to the fact that the oceanic areas were much the largest, and were the areas of greatest subsidence under the continued general contraction of the globe.

The contraction theory of mountain uplift as expounded by Dana has subsequently been referred to as the " classical " contraction theory, and as such, has been shown by some writers to contain some serious shortcomings. One objection to the classical theory is the fact that not all folded mountains are distributed as would be expected. If the earth were a shrinking body, its circumference should be decreased equally along each and every great circle. It would seem that there should be more than one major east-west mountain chain in the world; it seems improbable that the crust is strong enough in the western hemisphere to transmit forces half way around the earth to produce only one great east-west system, the Alpine-Himalayan system, in the eastern hemisphere.

On the other hand the contraction theory serves as the very foundation for some of the modern theories of mountain uplift. For example, the phase change theory has been referred to as " the contraction theory revived," with its good points included but without its most serious faults.

One of the basic assumptions of the classical contraction theory is the idea that the earth is a cooling body, and that shrinkage is a result of the cooling. But with the realization that radioactive materials are very widespread in the earth's crust, and that heat of radioactivity is constantly being generated, it would seem that the earth's crust may not have been cooling for millions of years, and therefore there would not be uniform crustal shrinkage. The recurrence of ice ages with intervening long periods of world-wide moderate climates would also seem to be contradictory to the idea of a continuously cooling earth.

The contraction theory is not necessarily disproved even if the earth is increasing in heat content as a result of radioactive disintegration. It has been pointed out by one group of investigators [5] that contraction need

[5] Jacobs, Russell, and Wilson, *Physics and Geology*, McGraw-Hill Book Company, Inc., 1959, pp. 353–361.

not depend primarily upon cooling. In fact contraction could have occurred even if the earth were gaining in heat content. The emission of large quantities of material from depth, which would add to the volume of the crust, would be expected to cause contraction of the crust due to the crust having to accommodate a smaller interior.

It has been contended by some that while contraction with shrinkage has not been proved to be the major cause of mountain building, the contraction theory may be regarded as explaining mountain genesis better than any other present theory. No theory yet advanced " provides an account of the development of the earth's surface features comparable to that now possible by using the contraction theory." [6]

STUDY QUESTIONS

1. Of Dana's many contributions to the geological sciences, he is probably best known for his

   (1) geanticlines and geosynclines   (2) extensive research in paleontology   (3) theory on the origin of mountains   (4) research in mineralogy, culminating in publication of *System of Mineralogy*   (5) reports on the Captain Wilkes scientific expedition, on which he was geologist and mineralogist.

2. Contraction as a factor in the genesis of the major features of the earth dates back at least to the work of (*name the earliest listed*)

   (1) Dana   (2) Elie de Beaumont   (3) Leibnitz   (4) Gutenberg   (5) Descartes.

3. One of the strongest objections to the contraction theory followed the discovery of

   (1) the structure of the atom   (2) radioactivity   (3) the fact that there are tensional forces within the earth as well as compressional forces   (4) the very great age of the earth   (5) the fact that many mountains are NOT folded.

4. Dana believed that the existence of continents and ocean basins dates back to the

   (1) time of the first solidified crust   (2) beginning of the Cambrian period   (3) Carboniferous period   (4) time of the earth's earliest existence, perhaps in the gaseous state   (5) early part of the Proterozoic era.

   5–6. These questions are a related pair.

5. Dana has referred to uplift of the region about Montreal, Lake Champlain and the coast of Maine as an example of

   (1) regional tilting
   (2) regional elevation without lateral thrusting and plication

[6] Op. cit., p. 361.

(3) probable intrusive arching
(4) rock expansion through internal heating without the addition of any new materials
(5) a region of unstable rocks.

6. A current explanation (developed subsequent to Dana's writing) is that
  (1) elevation is a direct consequence of the depression of the Great Lake basins
  (2) the region is on the edge of the Canadian Shield, and all shield areas are stable areas of ancient Pre-Cambrian rock
  (3) the uplift naturally followed the disappearance of the vast covering of glacial ice
  (4) that re-elevation naturally follows extensive denudation
  (5) the region had been injected by numerous horizontal intrusions of magma (sills).

7. Select the correct statement or statements.
  According to Dana widespread radial contraction of the earth can account for
  a. the presence in mountainous areas of decreasing rank of metamorphism from the oceanic sides toward the continental interiors
  b. the location of practically all volcanoes and earthquakes
  c. the development of continental masses at elevations above the oceanic basins
  d. the same trend of mountains in North America along both the east coast and the west coast
  e. all permanent elevations in mountainous areas being attributed to crushing with attendant plications.
  The correct answer is
  (1) a and b   (2) b and c   (3) a, b, and c   (4) c and d
  (5) d and e.

8. Select the correct statements.
  Dana believed that the contraction theory could account for
  a. the more massive mountains along the west coast of the United States as compared to the smaller mountains along the east coast
  b. mountains in a general area having the same trend but would not account for mountains in the same area being of different ages
  c. development of plications in mountains and later uplift of the mountainous area
  d. the predominance of symmetrical folds in the Appalachians
  e. the deposition of thick sedimentary layers.
  The correct answer is
  (1) a, b, and c   (2) b, c, and d   (3) c, d, and e   (4) a and c
  (5) b and d.

9. Which one of the following choices is *inconsistent* with Dana's views on the contraction theory?
  (1) The presence of beds containing marine fossils at elevations as great as 10 thousand feet above sea level in the Rocky Mountains is evidence of uplift.
  (2) Because the fossils in the beds in the Rocky Mountains at elevations of 8 to 10 thousand feet above sea level are Cretaceous, clearly an uplift of this amount has occurred since Cretaceous time.

(3) Since the Cretaceous beds in the Rocky Mountains are horizontal, it is probable they were uplifted vertically by the intrusion of magma, and not by compressive forces.

(4) The uplifting of the Rocky Mountains was but one of many oscillations of level in the land surface of North America.

(5) Such elevating of land surfaces as in the Rocky Mountains was probably NOT dependent on plication and crushing of the rocks beneath.

10. According to Dana, continents experienced their greatest changes in level (subsidence or elevation) within 300 to 1000 miles of the coast line. Which of the following were Dana's reasons or explanations for this conclusion?

a. Ocean basins are subject to greater contraction, and therefore greater subsidence than continental masses.

b. Since the oceanic crust is the lower in elevation, it serves as a lever to exert an oblique thrust against the continental borders (lateral pressure).

c. Oceanic basins are subject to greater contraction because they are of so much greater size.

The correct answer is

(1) a and b   (2) b and c   (3) a, b, and c   (4) a and c   (5) c.

11. Because the sharpest folds, greatest volcanoes, and most extensive igneous and metamorphic action upon the rocks occur on the oceanic side of border-zone mountains, Dana concluded that

(1) the rocks were weaker on the oceanic side of the mountains

(2) the ocean floor was thinner and therefore allowed greater amounts of heat to escape to carry on the diastrophic, volcanic, and metamorphic activity

(3) ocean water penetrated to the heated rocks at depth, and the steam thus generated produced the stated results

(4) lateral pressure was more effective on the oceanic side in a direction toward the continental land mass

(5) the thicker rocks on the continental side prevented the escape of the heat and fluids necessary to carry on the diastrophic, volcanic, and other processes.

12. Select the correct statement or statements.

a. The great amount of crustal shrinkage that is known to have occurred is ample to account for all the world's folded mountains.

b. The contraction theory in its classical form adequately accounts for all the compressive forces needed to produce all the folded mountains of the world.

c. The fact that there are both east-west trending and north-south trending folded mountains on almost every continent proves that the earth is a contracting body.

The correct answer is

(1) a and b   (2) b   (3) b and c   (4) c   (5) a and c.

13. In Dana's classification of mountains, what were the principal differences between his polygenetic and monogenetic classes?

14. What was the relative importance of lateral pressure versus vertical pressure in Dana's concept of contraction? Did he distinguish between lateral squeezing from crustal expansion and lateral squeezing from crustal contraction?

15. In 1873 Dana wrote that "formerly" he considered that sinking of the ocean basins caused the oceanic arch to press against the sides of the basin, and this in turn was "the chief means of mountain lifting." By 1873 he still believed this to be a "true cause" of mountain uplift, "while not giving it so great prominence." Can you state or summarize Dana's "chief cause" of mountain uplift in terms of his writings of 1873?

33

The Geosynclinal Theory as an Explanation of Mountain Building

● A geosyncline has been defined as a surface of regional extent subsiding through a long period of time while contained sedimentary and volcanic rocks are accumulating. Geosynclines are most commonly linear, but nonlinear depressions may possess properties that are essentially geosynclinal. Thus the actual geosyncline is simply the surface developed at the base of extensive deposits. The strata deposited on the surface of regional extent are commonly referred to as the geosynclinal prism. (See Fig. 33-1, page 436.)

The deposits are commonly those of shallow water or in some parts even nonmarine, but as subsidence takes place and deposition continues, the surficial materials deposited first may eventually be buried beneath six or eight miles of overlying strata. The form of the geosynclinal surface, then, is a measure of subsidence over a long period of time.

The first man to conceive the idea of geosynclines seems to have been James Hall. The basic ideas in his theory were that " the direction of any mountain chain corresponds with the original line of greatest accumulation, or that line along which the coarser and more abundant sediments were deposited," and that " the elevation of the mountains is of continental origin and not of local origin, or that folding and partial upheaval along mountain chains have nothing to do with the grand elevation." Hall also suggested that downwarping of the sediment-laden trough caused the subcrust beneath the trough to " flow " laterally under the area that supplied the sediments and also under the side of the folded area where the folds die away or end in faults, thus causing these areas to rise. This latter idea was very slow to receive general acceptance.

The Appalachian geosyncline in eastern North America is usually considered the " type " geosyncline. After a detailed study of the Appalachian mountain system had been made, geologists found similar structural and

435

depositional conditions associated with the Alps, Urals, Himalayas, Rockies, Andes, and Ouachitas. In some of these, thicknesses of shallow-water deposits have been measured to total as much as eight miles or more.

Though the association of geosynclines with many mountain ranges is unmistakable, the concept has not been applied to all mountains. Also it is contended by some geologists that there are no typical geosynclines anywhere in the world at present, and that we cannot reconstruct what went on during the development of geosynclines in terms of depositional conditions today. On the other hand others consider the Yellow Sea, off the

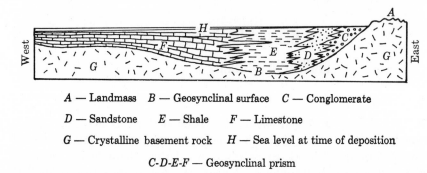

A — Landmass   B — Geosynclinal surface   C — Conglomerate

D — Sandstone   E — Shale   F — Limestone

G — Crystalline basement rock   H — Sea level at time of deposition

C-D-E-F — Geosynclinal prism

Figure 33-1. *Generalized transverse section through an ideal geosyncline showing the geosynclinal prism. In recent years the concept of facies changes has somewhat modified the picture presented above.*

coast of China, to have many characteristics of a geosyncline. This shallow sea receives the great quantities of sediments carried from China by the Yangtze-Kiang and other rivers. The deltas built by these rivers are very comparable to the Devonian delta that has been recognized in the rocks making up the Catskills of New York. Also the great accumulation of sediments in the Barton trough beneath the coastal waters of the Gulf of Mexico very definitely approaches the proportions of a geosynclinal prism.

The date given for the first comparatively clear and concise statement of the geosynclinal concept is 1859, when Hall's ideas were published in Volume III, *Natural History of New York*, " Palæontology," from which an excerpt is given in this chapter. The earliest brief mention of his ideas on accumulation of sediments and formation of mountain chains appeared in a report on the *Geology of Iowa*, about 1856, written when Hall was serving as the first state geologist of Iowa.

Hall presented his ideas to the public in 1857 in Montreal. He was president of the American Association for the Advancement of Science that year, and gave a summary of his concept of the geosynclinal theory in his address as retiring president of the Association. However, he did not use the word " geosyncline "; the naming of the theory was left for Dana, some sixteen years later.

Figure 33-2. *James Hall (1811–1898).*

Hall's AAAS address was not published until about 25 years later. The reason is summed up in a statement by George Merrill, author of *First Hundred Years of American Geology:* " His presidential address to the AAAS in 1857 was so far in advance of his time as to be thought not merely absurd, but mystical, yet today it is recognized as one of the most important contributions to one of the most difficult problems of physical geology."

Hall (Fig. 33-2) was born at Hingham, Massachusetts, near the south shore of Boston Bay in September, 1811, into a family whose lot was that of extreme poverty. As a very small boy he began to collect shells along the seashore. As he studied them his interest grew, this early interest being stimulated by his grammar school teacher.

By the time Hall was 19, he was certain he wanted to become a scientist. Rensselaer Polytechnic Institute at Troy, New York had been newly founded, and it is said that Hall walked approximately 200 miles from Hingham, Massachusetts to Troy to enroll. There he studied under the eminent natural scientist Amos Eaton, who inspired Hall to devote his life's work to the problems of geology.

Hall graduated in 1832. With job prospects for graduates very poor, he obtained a " fill in " job as library assistant at the Institute and assistant to the professor of chemistry. He proved himself rapidly, was appointed assistant professor before the year was out, and earned the rank of full professor within three years.

In 1836, with the establishment of the Geological Survey of New York,

Hall was employed as one of four geologists to study the Adirondack iron ores. His first systematic field work was done in St. Lawrence County at the western Adirondack foothills. The next year he was placed in charge of the survey of the "Fourth Geological District" of New York, in the western part of the state. The Fourth District at the time was described by his superiors as a "level, uninteresting area, good enough for a young man of 25 to tackle." It is remarkable to note that the district, far from being uninteresting, proved to be of such interest to Hall that it gave him his foundation experience. His report on the Fourth District became a classic in geological literature. His interest in the fossils found in the district led him to become an authority in paleontology. Regarding Hall's work in paleontology, Merrill wrote that his publications stand as an "enduring monument to his industry, a record which has never been surpassed and presumably never will be surpassed by another American geologist."

Hall became state geologist of New York and director of the Museum of Natural History at Albany, but the appropriations by the New York state legislature in those days were often inadequate; sometimes he had no working funds at all. Consequently Hall would have to carry on with his own savings, or take work temporarily in other states. It was in such interim periods that he worked for or directed the surveys of Iowa, Ohio, and Wisconsin, and worked with the survey of Canada. The work in these other areas was a blessing in disguise, however, for it gave him a firsthand knowledge of the stratigraphy from east to west and provided the foundation for his geosynclinal concept. To Hall must go the credit, not only of formulating the geosynclinal concept, but also for placing the Paleozoic stratigraphy of eastern North America on a sound scientific basis.

Excerpts from two papers follow, one from Hall dealing with his ideas of the relation between thick sedimentary deposits and the locations of mountains, and the other a critical review of Hall's ideas by Dana.

RELATION OF MOUNTAINS TO DISTRIBUTION OF THICK SEDIMENTARY STRATA [1]

by James Hall

Introduction

❋   ❋   ❋   ❋   ❋   ❋   ❋

The accumulations of the Coal period were the last that have given form and contour to the eastern side of our continent, from the Gulf of St. Lawrence to the Gulf of Mexico. And as we have shown that the great sedimentary deposits of successive periods have followed essentially the same course, parallel to the mountain ranges, we very naturally inquire: What influence has this accumulation had upon the topography of our country? and is the present line

[1] From *Natural History of New York,* "Palæontology," Part I (1859) Vol. III, pp. 66–85.

of mountain elevation, from northeast to southwest, in any manner connected with this original accumulation of sediments?

I have all along shown that the sedimentary deposits are greatly thicker in the eastern than in the western localities, and that for the most part they are extremely poor in calcareous matter; while generally the limestone formations, individually and in the aggregate, are thicker at some distance west of the line of greatest sedimentary accumulations.

An approximate measurement of all the strata along the Appalachian chain gives an aggregate thickness of forty thousand feet, while the same formations in the Mississippi valley measure scarcely four thousand feet; in this, also, are included the Carboniferous limestones, which do not exist in any eastern section.

In the Mississippi valley we have numerous points where the Lower Silurian [2] strata are exposed, and at some points there is a thickness of five hundred feet of the Potsdam sandstone. From this base we follow the series upwards to the top of the mounds, capped by the Niagara limestone; and we there attain an elevation above the Mississippi waters of one thousand feet, which is the whole thickness of the formations from the Potsdam sandstone to the Niagara limestone. The actual measurement of the same set of strata in the Appalachian region would give us more than sixteen thousand feet; and even making large allowances for excess in the measurements, we certainly have, in the Appalachians, more than ten times the thickness of the entire series in the west. Still we have no mountains of this altitude; that is to say, we have no mountains whose altitude equals the actual vertical thickness of the strata composing them.

In the west there has been little or no disturbance, and our highest elevations of land mark essentially the aggregate thickness of the strata which produce the elevation. In the east, though we prove step by step that certain members of the series, with a known thickness, are included in these mountains, the altitude never reaches the aggregate amount of the formations. Reasoning from the facts adduced, and without prejudice or theory, the result certainly does not agree with our anticipations; for on the one hand, we find in a country not mountainous, elevations corresponding essentially to the thickness of the strata; while in a mountainous country, where the strata are immensely thicker, the mountain heights bear no comparative proportion to the thickness of the strata.

We have seen that one simple and intelligible sequence of strata, from the Potsdam sandstone to the end of the Coal measures, covers, with small exceptions, the entire country from the Atlantic slopes to the base of the Rocky mountains; that the same geological formations occupy the mountain chain and the plateau. But while the horizontal strata give their whole elevation to the highest parts of the plain, we find the same beds folded and contorted in

---

[2] It should be noted that the geological time scale commonly used at the time of Hall and Dana showed the lowest rocks of the Lower Silurian to be equivalent to the Cambrian in a present-day time scale. The Potsdam sandstone is now considered Cambrian. The Niagara limestone was considered the lower part of the Upper Silurian, and the Lower Helderberg occupied a place near the top of the Lower Silurian. Niagaran beds are presently considered to be Silurian, and Lower Helderberg beds are Devonian.

the mountain region, and giving to the mountain elevation not one-sixth of their actual measurement.

We are accustomed to believe that mountains are produced by upheaval, folding and plication of the strata; and that from some unexplained cause, these lines of elevation extend along certain directions, gradually dying out on either side, and subsiding at one or each extremity. In these pages, I believe I have shown conclusively that the line of accumulation of sediments has been along the direction of the Appalachian chain; and, with slight variations at different epochs, the course of the current has been essentially the same throughout. The line of our mountain chain, and of the ancient oceanic current which deposited these sediments, is therefore coincident and parallel; or, the line of the greatest accumulation is the line of the mountain chain. In other words, the great Appalachian barrier is due to original deposition of materials, and not to any subsequent action or influence breaking up and dislocating the strata of which it is composed.

To be satisfied of this, it seems only necessary to compare the eastern and western exposures of the formations; for here the valleys, cutting through the rocks of the several groups down to the lower limestones, or to the Potsdam sandstone, present mountain ranges of several thousand feet on either side; while in the valley of the Mississippi, where the strata have thinned, the same denuding action has produced low cliffs or sloping banks of one or two hundred feet in height. Therefore had the country been evenly elevated without metamorphism or folding of the strata, making the lowest palaeozoic rocks the base line, in the States bordering the Atlantic we should have had higher mountains and deeper valleys, wherever the series was complete. At the same time, the great plateau on either side of the Mississippi river would have presented the features it now does, of valleys extending to the Lower Palaeozoic beds, with cliffs of the height represented by the actual thickness of the beds which there constitute the entire series.

The gradual declination of the country westward is due primarily to the thinning out of all the formations which have accumulated with such great force in the Appalachian region. It is also susceptible of proof, that no beds of older date have contributed to elevate the later ones, or to form a part of the mountain chain.

We have in the east one example where the conditions of elevation correspond with those in the Mississippi valley. The Catskill mountains are composed almost entirely of strata in a horizontal or very slightly inclined position; the Hudson-river group, which constitutes a few feet of their elevation at the base, is disturbed, and the succeeding beds lie upon this unconformably. [See Fig. 33-3.] These mountains, therefore, rising to a height of 3800 feet above tidewater, mark in their altitude simply the vertical thickness of the strata.

At this point of our inquiry, several questions of importance present themselves: First, what has been the cause of this folding and plication of the strata; secondly, having been thus folded and plicated, what influence has this action exerted upon the elevation of the parts, or of the whole; and thirdly, what effects are due to the metamorphism which accompanies this mountain chain?

It has been long since shown that the removal of large quantities of sediment from one part of the earth's crust, and its transportation and deposition in another, may not only produce oscillations, but that chemical and dynamical

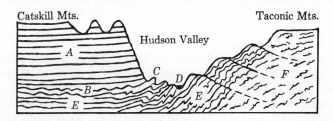

A — Catskill strata, horizontal to slightly inclined   C — Folded ridges
B — Unconformable contact (unconformity)   D — Hudson River
E — Beds of Hudson River Group (disturbed)
F — Mostly schist resulting from metamorphism of early Paleozoic sediments

Figure 33-3. *Diagrammatic cross section across the Hudson Valley from the Catskill to Taconic Mountains as described by Hall. The section shows the position of the contact between the disturbed beds at the base of the Catskill Mountains and the relatively undisturbed beds above the contact. The contact between the two sets of beds marks the unconformity mentioned by Hall. The sketch did not appear in Hall's original publication.*

action are the necessary consequences of large accumulations of sedimentary matter over certain areas. When these are spread along a belt of sea bottom, as originally in the line of the Appalachian chain, the first effect of this great augmentation of matter would be to produce a yielding of the earth's crust beneath, and a gradual subsidence will be the consequence. We have evidence of this subsidence in the great amount of material accumulated; for we cannot suppose that the sea has been originally as deep as the thickness of these accumulations. On the contrary, the evidences from ripplemarks, marine plants, and other conditions, prove that the sea in which these deposits have been successively made was at all times shallow, or of moderate depth. The accumulation, therefore, could only have been made by a gradual or periodical subsidence of the ocean bed; and we may then inquire, what would be the result of such subsidence upon the accumulated stratified sediments spread over the sea bottom?

The line of greatest depression would be along the line of greatest accumulation; and in the direction of the thinning margins of the deposit, the depression would be less. By this process of subsidence, as the lower side becomes gradually curved, there must follow, as a consequence, rents and fractures upon that side; or the diminished width of surface above, caused by this curving below, will produce wrinkles and foldings of the strata. That there may be rents or fractures of the strata beneath is very probable, and into these may rush the fluid or semifluid matter from below, producing trap-dykes; but the folding of strata seems to me a very natural and inevitable consequence of the process of subsidence.

The sinking down of the mass produces a great synclinal axis; and within this axis, whether on a large or small scale, will be produced numerous smaller synclinal and anticlinal axes. [See Fig. 33-4.] And the same is true of every synclinal axis, where the condition of the beds is such as to admit of a careful examination.* I hold, therefore, that it is impossible to have any subsidence along a certain line of the earth's crust, from the accumulation of sediments, without producing the phenomena which are observed in the Appalachian and other mountain ranges.

That this subsidence was periodical, we have the best possible evidence in the unconformability of the Lower Helderberg group upon the Hudson-river group; showing that previous to the deposition of these limestones, there were already foldings and plications, the consequence of a subsidence along the line of accumulation. Subsequently to the deposition of the latter formations, or at

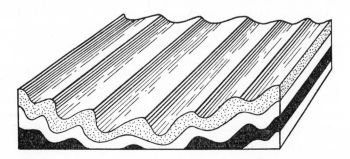

Figure 33-4. *A block diagram of a synclinorium consisting of a series of alternating anticlines and synclines with dominant downward sinking, as described by Hall and named by Dana. The synclinal axes are shown by dashed lines in the bottoms of the downfolds and the anticlinal axes by solid lines at the crests of the upfolds. The sketch was not included in Hall's original publication.*

intervals during their accumulation, there have been other periods of subsidence, and consequently of folding and plication; so that these are not synchronous, nor are they conformable with each other.

This successive accumulation, and the consequent depression of the crust along this line, serves only to make more conspicuous the feature which appears to be the great characteristic, that the range of mountains is the great synclinal axis, and the anticlinals within it are due to the same cause which produced the synclinal; and as a consequence, these smaller anticlinals, and their correspondent synclinals, gradually decline towards the margin of the great synclinal axis, or towards the margin of the zone of depression which corresponds to the zone of greatest accumulation.†

This affords a partial explanation of the fact already observed, that the mountain elevations in the disturbed regions bear in their altitude a much smaller proportion to the actual thickness of the formations, than do the hills

---

* I am indebted to Sir William Logan for this latter suggestion, as the result of his very accurate and extensive observations on the relations of anticlinal and synclinal axes.

† This mode of depression, which is the result of accumulation, and the production of numerous synclinal and anticlinal axes offers a satisfactory explanation, as it appears to me, of the difference of slope on the two sides of the anticlinals which have been so often pointed out as occurring in the Appallachian range, where the dips on one side are uniformly steeper than on the other.

in undisturbed regions. Furthermore it so happens that so soon as disturbance takes place and anticlinals are formed, the beds are weakened at the arching, and become more liable to denuding action. Thus the anticlinals are often worn down to such an extent as to form low grounds or deep valleys; while the synclinal, protected in the downward curving of the beds, remains to form the prominent mountain crest. [See Fig. 33-5.] This is very generally true in many parts of the Appalachian range; and it is only where some heavier or stronger bedded rock occurs, protecting the anticlinals, that they form the higher mountain elevations. Similar features will be observed in other mountain ranges.

Figure 33-5. *Anticlinal valley flanked on either side by synclinal ridges. This figure, while clearly described by Hall, was not included in his original publication.*

It nowhere appears that this folding or plication has contributed to the altitude of the mountains: on the other hand, as I think can be shown, the more extreme this plication, the more it will conduce to the general degradation of the mass, whenever subjected to denuding agencies. The number and abruptness of the foldings will depend upon the width of the zone which is depressed, and the depth of the depression, which is itself dependent on the amount of accumulation.

We have, therefore, this other element of depression to consider, when we compare mountain elevations with the thickness of the original deposition.

It is possible that the suggestion may be made, that if the folding and plication be the result of a sinking or depression of the mass, then these wrinkles would be removed on the subsequent elevation; and the beds might assume, in a degree at least, their original position. But this is not the mode of elevation. The elevation has been one of continental, and not of local origin; and there is no more evidence of local elevation along the Appalachian chain, than there is along the plateau in the west. As it is, a large mass of the matter constituting the sediments of this mountain range still remain below the sea level, as a necessary consequence of the great accumulation; while in the plateau of the west, we have a much greater proportion above the level of the sea.

So far, therefore, as our observation extends, we are able to deduce some general principles in regard to the production of this mountain range. To explain its existence, we are to look to the original accumulation of matter along a certain line or zone, the direction of which will be the direction of the elevation. The line of the existing mountain chain will be the course of the original transporting current. The minor axes or foldings must be essentially parallel to the great synclinal axis and the line of accumulation. The present mountain barriers are but the visible evidences of the deposits upon an ancient ocean bed; while the determining causes of their elevation existed long anterior to the production of the mountains themselves. At no point, nor along any line between the Appalachian and Rocky mountains, could the same forces have produced a mountain chain, because the materials of accumulation were insufficient; and though we may trace what appears to be the gradually subsiding influence of these forces, it is simply in these instances due to the paucity of the material upon which to exhibit its effects. The parallel lines of elevation, on the west of the Appalachians, are evidenced in gentle undulations, with the exception of the Cincinnati axis, which is more important, extending from Lake Ontario to Alabama, and is the last or most western of those parallel to the Appalachian chain.

    ❀   ❀   ❀   ❀   ❀   ❀   ❀

In what I have stated, and in the conclusions drawn, I believe I have controverted no established fact or principle, beyond that of denying the influence of local elevating forces, and the intrusion of ancient or plutonic formations beneath the lines of mountain chains, as ordinarily understood and advocated.[3] In this I believe I am only going back to the views which were long since entertained by geologists relative to mountain elevation. In other respects, the views I have advanced are the legitimate results of observation, and an extension in the application of laws well established and acknowledged in science.

The facts here adduced relative to the strata composing the Appalachian range and their extension to the west and southwest, are all capable of verification; and the deductions hence drawn seem to me perfectly legitimate. I believe, moreover, that this mountain chain, in its component parts, and in its mode of accumulation, and the process by which it has assumed its present position, does not differ materially from other mountain ranges.

DANA'S CONTRIBUTIONS TO THE GEOSYNCLINAL THEORY

James D. Dana took a prominent part in the development of the geosynclinal concept after it was first presented by Hall. In 1866 Dana pointed out that elevation of mountains was left unexplained in Hall's

---

[3] A statement denying the importance of local elevation occurs a few paragraphs earlier; a denial of the influence of plutonic intrusions occurs in a portion of Hall's writings that are not included in this excerpt. On page 75 in Volume III, *Natural History of New York,* Hall wrote ". . . as to a supposed granitic mass or nucleus underlying the strata, it exists only in theory, for we have no positive and tangible evidence of such a nucleus. It is true that in the Appalachian chain there are masses and even considerable areas of what is termed eruptive or intrusive granite; but the existence of such granite furnishes no evidence that it is derived from a primary mass, or that it has been erupted in a state of igneous fusion. Such masses of granite may, indeed, and very probably have been derived from the formation immediately beneath the one on which it rests, and it is almost certainly in all cases a modification of some pre-existing sedimentary rock." The last sentence has an important bearing upon the current problem of granitization.

account of the development of geosynclines.[4] Then in May, 1873 Dana published an analysis of Hall's theory, restated his criticisms of Hall's account, and gave his own contributions to the theory. This report by Dana follows.

ON THE ORIGIN OF MOUNTAINS [5]
by James D. Dana

The remark, that in Professor Hall's theory of the origin of mountains the elevation of mountains is left out, . . . was made by me . . . and not without due consideration. The importance which some still attribute to this theory makes it desirable that its special points should be stated here with more fullness, . . . and that they receive further consideration. The points in the theory, selected out and condensed in the statement from the Introduction to the third volume of Professor Hall's New York Paleontology, are the following:

1. The Paleozoic strata of the Appalachian region bear evidence that they were mostly of shallow water origin.

2. Their great thickness, consequently, was attained through a slowly progressing subsidence, the axis of which was in the direction of the Appalachian chain.

3. This slowly progressing subsidence was occasioned by the weight of the slowly and successively accumulated sediments. The memoir says: "When these [" accumulations of sedimentary matter "] are spread along a sea bottom as originally in the line of the Appalachian chain, the first effect of this augmentation of matter would be to produce a yielding of the earth's crust beneath, and a gradual subsidence would be the consequence."

4. This subsidence produced, as one of its direct results, the extensive folds and faults of the strata characterizing the Appalachian formations. The fact that the folds are generally steepest on the northwest side may also be thus accounted for.

5. The formation of the Appalachians (and so of all mountains) was dependent upon, and the height related to, the thickness of the sedimentary accumulations, of which they are made; and a mountain chain was not a possibility over the Mississippi basin, because there " the materials of accumulation were insufficient."

6. (a) The elevation of the Appalachian mountains was not a result of the process of accumulation, or of the subsidence. (b) The elevation of mountains is, " of continental, and not of local, origin; there is no more evidence of local elevation along the Appalachian chain than there is along the plateau in the west." Again, the chapter says: " It is this ultimate rising of continental masses that I contend for, in opposition to special elevatory movement along the lines of mountain chains." (c) After a continental elevation, the mountain range received its present shape mainly through erosion.

7. Metamorphism requires first large accumulations of rock material; and it went forward in the Appalachian region in consequence of the subsidence. As

---

[4] James D. Dana, " Observations on the Origin of some of the Earth's Features," *Am. Jour. Sci. and Arts* (1866) Vol. 42, pp. 205–211.

[5] *Am. Jour. Sci. and Arts* (1873) Vol. 105, pp. 347–350.

to the causes, Professor Hall says — after alluding to the view of Babbage and Herschel respecting a regular increase of temperature below following an increase in thickness of surface accumulations — " Such an increase of temperature would be much less than that usually supposed necessary for producing metamorphism; and it is extremely doubtful if any portion now exposed to observation ever reached a temperature much above that of boiling water. We must, therefore, look to some other agency than heat ° for the production of the phenomena [of metamorphism] witnessed; and it seems that the prime cause must have existed within the material itself; and that the entire change is due to motion, or fermentation and pressure, aided by a moderate increase of temperature, producing chemical change."

A. The last of these propositions is an expression of the opinion that, in some way not understood, the heat required for metamorphism was generated within the strata that were altered. The effect was restricted by Vose in his Orographic Geology to pressure; but, with each of these authors, this pressure was due to the progressing subsidence referred to in the third proposition.

B. The first two propositions have general acceptation among American geologists.

C. The third and fourth, which are fundamental in the theory, have been shown in my former paper to be, as I believe, physical impossibilities; and LeConte, in his recent article, has further enforced this opinion. The third assumes that the first 500 feet in depth of sediments would press down the crust 500 feet, and so on to the end; but no reason is given why sediments under water should have so immense gravitating power, when the crystalline rocks of the Adirondacks, piled to a height of some thousands of feet *above* the water, had a firm footing close along side of the subsiding region.

But while the weight of accumulating sediments will not cause subsidence, a slow subsidence of a continental region has often been the occasion for thick accumulations of sediments.

D. The fifth proposition announces a relation between the height of the mountains formed over an area, and the thickness of the sedimentary accumulations there previously made, preparatory to the elevation; and it further makes the absence of mountains from a region a consequence of small accumulations.

The relation set forth is a true and important one if taken in the most general way; but the application of it as a strict ratio, or as a universal law, encounters many apparent exceptions. In the Green Mountains of Vermont, the latest rocks of which are Lower Silurian, the conformable Silurian beds constituting them are probably not over half the thickness of those of the Appalachian region in Pennsylvania and Virginia; and yet the average height is greater, although exposed to erosion for a vastly longer time. For most mountain regions we have not the facts needed for the comparison — the thickness of the sediments preceding their formation and the amount of erosion since undergone being

° . . . , Hall observes that the lower beds may be softened by the heat that is received from below in consequence of accumulation above; but this remark is introduced not to make the heat a source of metamorphism, but to give a reason for the rocks yielding and subsiding under accumulating deposits, notwithstanding the property of heat ordinarily to cause expansion.

alike unknown. In some cases of composite mountain masses, like that of the Rocky Mountains, the principle hardly admits of application at all. According to King and others there were 10,000 feet in thickness of Cretaceous deposits laid down in Utah, with coal beds in the upper part of the series proving that subsidence accompanied the deposition; but, while there is evidence of subsequent disturbance in the region, and of the elevation since of a large part of the Rocky Mountain chain, there is, I believe, none that the Utah Cretaceous was raised into mountains overtopping the older ridges of the summit. There are, besides, cases of low plains, like the part of the Patagonian Pampas bordering the Atlantic, where for all that science knows, or ever will know, there may be a great thickness of conformable beds beneath. Again, there are areas now rising, like the coast region of Sweden, where thick accumulations of Tertiary sediments, or of any others since the Paleozoic, are wanting. There are many cases where the highest summits of a region occur at the crossing of two lines of elevation, showing that force has confounded the ratio of height to thickness of sediments, if any such had existed there.

Still, it is evidently a common fact that where mountains have been raised, there, in general, thick accumulations of sediments were previously made; and conversely. But the principle properly stated is — Where mountain ranges have been raised, there, in general, great subsidences, giving opportunity for thick accumulations of sediments, previously occurred; and conversely.

Unless the third and sixth of the above propositions are true, mountains are absent from the Mississippi because no local elevation extensive enough took place there; and no elevation was made, and there were likewise only thin accumulations of sediments, because the region, owing to its interior position, was not within the range of the continental-border oscillations.

E. By the sixth proposition, the influence of erosion in shaping a mountain is recognized, but no provision is made for its elevation — this elevation apart from general a continental elevation being denied. Thus Professor Hall's theory is strictly a " theory of the origin of mountains with the elevation of mountains left out." It accounts for plications by simple subsidence, but supposes the continent to get up high some way — the way not considered — without other plications, or any local uplifts, and on a crust so flexible that it will sink a foot for every foot of sediment added to the surface. The world abounds in cases in which part of the sea-border deposits of a period are now but little away from the old level, while other portions are many thousands of feet above it: e.g., the Cretaceous strata of the United States; and it contains examples of modern rising of land. No principle has been found to explain such facts except that of *local elevation*.

Since, then, the exposition which Professor Hall has made of his views offers nothing in explanation of the elevation of mountains — the event upon which the existence of any mountain depends — and since the only agent of change of level appealed to is one producing subsidence, and this will not work, so that there is no chance from it for the thick accumulations needed, or for the faintest plications or metamorphism, we may with reason pronounce the theory seriously deficient and defective.

Nearly all geologists recognize geosynclines, and the term is a very common one in geological literature. Yet there is not much agreement as to the definition of the term. Some of the uses of the term "geosyncline" include (1) a subsiding surface, (2) a subsiding area of long but narrow extent or (3) the sediments that have been deposited on the subsiding surface. There is even much disagreement as to the origin of a geosynclinal surface, the source of the motivating forces that bring about its development, and the reasons for cessation of its sinking. Likewise the uplift of the trough deposits into folded mountains constitutes a lingering problem.

Attempts have been made to classify geosynclines, or the features that might be called geosynclines, on the basis of the various definitions, in the hope of bringing order out of chaos. Bases for classification that have been used include (1) kind of sediment, (2) sediment source, (3) shape of surface, (4) structural relations, or (5) location. But because terminology has become so massive and cumbersome, there now seems to be a tendency to turn back toward the simplified terminology of Hall and Dana.

STUDY QUESTIONS

1–2. These questions are a related pair.

1. The first man to conceive the idea of geosynclines seems to have been

    (1) James Hutton   (2) James Dana   (3) James Hall
    (4) Elie de Beaumont   (5) Sir William Logan.

2. The man credited with the naming of the geosynclinal theory was

    (1) 1   (2) 2   (3) 3   (4) 4   (5) 5.

3. A geosyncline is commonly defined as

    (1) a surface of regional extent that subsides over a long period of time as a result of deposition on that surface
    (2) a downfold between two geanticlines
    (3) the sedimentary filling of a long but narrow trough
    (4) a down-faulted depression between two upthrown crustal blocks
    (5) the thick mass of sediments that collect near the base of mountains.

4. A certain body of water serves as a resting place for the sediments transported by the Yangtze-Kiang River, and the floor of that body possesses some properties characteristic of a present-day geosyncline. The name of the water body is

    (1) Bay of Bengal   (2) South China Sea   (3) Yellow Sea
    (4) Barton trough   (5) Mediterranean Sea.

5–6. These questions are a related pair.

5. An approximate measurement of all the strata along the Appalachian chain (eastern portion of the Appalachian geosyncline) according to Hall, gives an aggregate thickness, in feet, of about

    (1) 5000   (2) 10,000   (3) 20,000   (4) 30,000   (5) 40,000.

6. These sedimentary strata, traced westward to the Mississippi valley, have an approximate thickness, in feet, of about

  (1) 1000   (2) 2000   (3) 4000   (4) 8000   (5) 16,000.

7. According to Hall, altitudes are greater in the Appalachian region than in the upper Mississippi River valley because

  (1) the Paleozoic sedimentary formations are thicker in the Appalachian region, and decrease in thickness westward
  (2) the Mississippi River has removed vast quantities of materials from its drainage basin, resulting in lower elevations
  (3) the mid-continent area has subsided
  (4) more intense volcanic activity has aided in the uplift of the Appalachian region
  (5) the limestones, present in the Mississippi valley but absent in the east, have been subject to great solutional activity, thus lowering the area to the west.

8. Hall wrote that at no place on a line between the Rocky Mountains and the Appalachians could the same forces which produced these mountains have produced another chain of mountains. His reason for being certain about the above statement was

  (1) the lack of volcanic activity in the area
  (2) the lack of a source area between the Rocky and Appalachian Mountains capable of producing a sufficient volume of sediments
  (3) field observations showed insufficient accumulations of sedimentary deposits
  (4) the fact that the Ohio and Mississippi River system removed the sediments at a rate as great as the rate of regional uplift
  (5) the area is one of crustal sinking due to the weight of the tremendous deposition in the Mississippi valley delta.

9. Even though the sedimentary filling of a geosynclinal trough may be of very great thickness, Hall reasoned that the sediments were originally deposited in water of shallow or intermediate depth because of the

  (1) ripple marks, marine plants, and other shallow-water structures they contained
  (2) nearness of the source of the sediments to their place of deposition
  (3) relatively short period of time required for the filling of the geosyncline
  (4) high oxygen content of the mineral constituents making up the rocks
  (5) relatively unconsolidated character of the sediments.

10. Select the correct statement or statements.
  a. According to Dana progressive subsidence may be brought about by the weight of accumulating sediments; according to Hall this was a physical impossibility.
  b. According to Dana, without exception, mountains could not occur in a region where thick sedimentary deposits were lacking.
  c. According to Dana, where mountains have been uplifted, great subsidences had previously occurred, providing a basin to receive the sediments.
  The correct answer is

  (1) a   (2) a and b   (3) b   (4) b and c   (5) c.

11. Which of the following statements are true?
    a. Hall believed that the folding and plication of the strata in folded mountains took place during uplift of the mountains from a geosyncline.
    b. Hall believed that mountains received their permanent elevations during the folding and plication of the strata.
    c. The presence of narrow, deep-sea trenches reaching depths of thousands of feet below adjacent ocean bottoms represents a condition compatible with Dana's concept concerning the subsidence of geosynclinal areas.
    d. According to Hall the elevation of folded mountains is less than the vertical thicknesses of the beds occurring in the mountains.
    e. Hall believed that great lateral compressive forces acting from outside the geosynclinal areas were the primary cause of metamorphism.
    The correct answer is

    (1) a and b   (2) b and c   (3) c and d   (4) d and e
    (5) a, b, c, and e.

12. According to Hall (select the correct statements)
    a. the presence of unconformities in sediments of folded mountains is evidence of periodical subsidence of geosynclinal materials.
    b. the development of folding and plication at different intervals is evidence of periodical subsidence within a geosyncline.
    c. much of the granite found in the Appalachian chain may not have resulted from intrusion of magma from below.
    d. there are no conditions of elevation in the Appalachians comparable to those in the Mississippi valley.
    e. fracturing and faulting in folded mountains would never occur prior to the uplift of the mountains.
    The correct answer is

    (1) a, b, and c   (2) b, c, and d   (3) c, d, and e   (4) a, c, and e
    (5) a, b, and d.

13. When a great mass of sediments in a geosynclinal trough is depressed, folding and plication of the mass results. When the mass of sediments is subsequently elevated, it might be assumed that the sediments would take their original attitude, that the wrinkles and folds would be removed. The reason that this assumption could NOT be true, according to Hall, is the fact that

    (1) the sediments act as a plastic solid
    (2) the sediments act as viscous liquids
    (3) elevation of the mass is continental in origin, and not local
    (4) faults occur in the sediments and this destroys all original bedding relationships
    (5) elevation is local, so that the effect would be to introduce even more folds and plications superimposed upon the original ones.

14. The basic idea in Hall's geosynclinal theory was that

    (1) local elevating forces were of no significance in raising mountains, only general continental elevation being of importance
    (2) the geosynclinal surface bent downward as a result of the weight of the accumulating sediments
    (3) coarse sediments are characteristic of the deeper parts of geosynclinal areas where thicker deposits accumulated, and limestone and clay are more abundant in the geosynclinal areas where thinner accumulations were laid down

(4) even though the filling of the geosyncline may be very thick, the sediments are all shallow water deposits

(5) the direction of a mountain chain corresponds with the original line along which the coarser and thicker sediments were deposited.

15. Which of the following is a characteristic that Hall pointed out to be generally true in many parts of the Appalachian Mountains?

   (1) Anticlines are worn down to form valleys; the synclines stand out as the ridges or crests of mountains.
   (2) The anticlines generally contain the more resistant rock.
   (3) Since the synclines are the downfolds, they make up the low ground and consequently are more subject to extensive erosion.
   (4) The steeper dips generally occur on the south flanks of the folds.
   (5) The mountain elevations are almost exactly the same as the actual thickness of the beds that make up the mountains.

16. What were Hall's conclusions regarding elevation, structure, and the kind and age of the rocks of the Catskill Mountains? What is meant by the Catskill delta?

17. Can you suggest one or more mountains or ranges of mountains that probably did NOT have a geosynclinal origin?

34

Isostasy and Gravitational Pull of Mountains on the Plumb Line

● Careful mathematical calculations involving specific gravities and altitudes show that mountain masses are not great overloads of rock resting upon the surface of the earth. On the contrary, the mountains tend to be (or become) "in balance" with the surrounding lower land, much like an iceberg is in balance with the water in which it floats. Similarly, the continental masses, composed of materials of lower specific gravity than the rocks making up the sea floors, are considered to be in balance with the heavier but lower oceanic basins (Fig. 34-1). This tendency for balance is termed *isostasy*.

Theoretically, if there was no tendency for the various segments of the earth's crust to remain in balance, there should be no land masses above sea level anywhere in the world at the present time. The average depth of ocean water is nearly 2½ miles; the average height of the continents above sea level is but half a mile. Therefore there is enough water on the earth's surface to cover all land areas to an average depth of several thousand feet. As erosion is relatively rapid, in fact calculated to be rapid enough to lower the entire Mississippi River drainage area a foot in 8 to 10 thousand years, and geologic time has been of very great duration, it would seem that all land areas of the earth should have been eroded to sea level or below, millions of years ago. However, as mountains, and other land areas are eroded, and as the basins and other low areas receive the load of sediments, the eroded lands, according to the isostatic principle, tend to rise and the loaded areas tend to sink. This, essentially, is isostasy in operation.

A French surveying party, including Pierre Bouguer, measured a meridian of arc in Peru between the years 1735 and 1745. Bouguer presented the results of the expedition in a book entitled *Figure de la Terre*, published in Paris in 1749. In this book he gave one of the earliest recorded

452

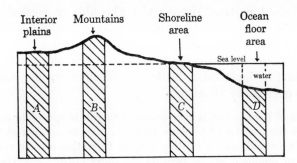

Figure 34-1. *Diagram showing four columns of rock of equal cross-sectional areas: A, under the interior plains; B, under mountains (such as the Blue Ridge in eastern United States); C, at sea level; and D, on the ocean floor. According to the theory of isostasy the weights of the four columns are equal and the columns are " in balance." Balance may be explained by assuming differences in specific gravities in the different columns. In order for column D to be isostatically in balance with the other three columns, the weight of a column of sea water above the rock column is included.*

suggestions that high mountains such as the Andes offer a gravitational attraction that " is much smaller than that expected from the mass of matter represented in those mountains."

In 1770 Maire and Boscovitch,[1] in explaining Bouguer's earlier suggestion, wrote that they believed the mountains were due to thermal expansion of materials at depth, resulting in uplift of the rock layers near the surface. They did not suggest that the uplift was due to any addition of material at depth but instead attributed the uplift to porosity or open space ("vide" or void) compensating for the mass of the mountains above. These men probably were the first to use the term compensate ("compense") in connection with mountain uplift.

The English astronomer Sir John Herschel, son of the discoverer of the planet Uranus, is commonly given credit for outlining a theory to explain the mechanism by which balance may be restored and maintained in the lithosphere. Charles Babbage, an English mathematician, is also commonly given part credit, but the credit belongs to Herschel alone. Probably the confusion resulted from the fact that Herschel's speculations were printed in a book published by Babbage.[2] The appendix of the book contained a letter written by Herschel to Sir Charles Lyell, dated February 20, 1836, in which Herschel clearly set forth his theory. While Babbage had depended upon " pyrometric expansion" or heating effects deep within the earth to account for uplift, and cooling to account for subsidence, Herschel added to that explanation the concept of " mass balance

---

[1] C. Maire and R. J. Boscovitch, *Voyage Astronomique et Géographique*, Paris, 1770, p. 463.
[2] Charles Babbage, *Ninth Bridgewater Treatise*, J. Murray, 2nd Ed., London, 1838.

between adjacent parts of the crust." [3] The idea of vertical expansion through heating emphasized by Babbage was practically the same as that proposed by Maire and Boscovitch sixty-six years earlier.

A short quotation from Herschel's letter to Lyell, along with a copy of the sketch that he included in his letter, will illustrate the clarity of the theory as conceived by Herschel:

Now for a bit of theory. Has it ever occurred to you to speculate on the probable effect of the transfer of pressure from one part to another of the earth's surface by the degradation of existing and the formation of new continents — on the fluid or semifluid matter beneath the outer crust? . . . The elevation of [a] surface due to columnar expansion (which you attribute, in a note, to Babbage,) is in this view inadequate to explain the rise of Scandinavia, or of the Andes, etc. But, in the variation of local pressure due to the transfer of matter by the sea, on the bed of an ocean imperfectly and unequally supported, it seems to me an adequate cause may be found. [Refer to the sketch, Fig. 34-2.]

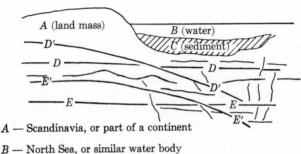

A — Scandinavia, or part of a continent

B — North Sea, or similar water body

C — Sea floor deposits

D — Original ocean floor

E — Semifluid mass at depth below ocean floor

D'— New position of D after adjustment

E' — New position of E after adjustment

Figure 34-2. *Sketch by Herschel to show adjustment between a portion of a continent and an adjacent basin that has received a load of sediments. (Adapted from Babbage, " The Ninth Bridgewater Treatise," J. Murray, Second Edition, London, 1838.)*

Let A be Scandinavia, B the adjacent ocean (the North Sea), C a vast deposit, newly laid on the original bed of the ocean; EEE a semi-fluid, or mixed mass, on which DDD reposes. What will be the effect of the enormous weight

[3] It should be noted that Herschel believed in the effectiveness of the expansive power of heat to uplift an area, but in addition he believed that the inflow of material, squeezed laterally toward regions of lesser weight (therefore lesser pressure) was an equally or even more important factor in uplift.

thus added to the bed DDD (rock being heavier than sea)? Of course, to depress D under it, and to force it down into the yielding mass E, a portion of which will be driven laterally under the continent A, and upheave it. Lay a weight on a surface of soft clay: you depress it below, and raise it around the weight. If the surface of the clay be dry and hard, it will crack in the change of figure. . . .

The removal of matter from above, to below, the sea . . . produces a mechanical subversion of the *equilibrium of pressure*. It also produces a subversion of the equilibrium of temperature. . . . *It must be an excessively slow process*. . . .

The theory received new impetus about 1855, through the efforts of two men, working independently — John H. Pratt, an English clergyman and archdeacon of Calcutta, and George Bedell Airy, an English astronomer. Pratt's observations which aided in development of the principle of isostasy, were based upon the attraction of the Himalaya Mountains upon a plumb line used in a survey in India.

The papers of both men were published simultaneously in volume 145 of the *Philosophical Transactions of the Royal Society of London*, but Pratt's report carried the earlier date. Pratt's paper was dated July 12, 1854, while Airy's paper carried a date line of January 19, 1855.

Neither of the men used the term isostasy. The coining of that term is attributed to Clarence E. Dutton, an American army officer and geologist. Dutton proposed the term in an article published in 1889, an excerpt of which appears in Chapter 35.

In a brief synopsis, the excerpts on isostasy are in the following order:

Pratt; an article completed for publication in 1854, in which he gave his observations, and " discovered " the operation of isostasy in the attraction of the plumb line toward the Himalayas.

Airy; an article completed in 1855, in which he commented upon Pratt's " discovery " and proposed his " hypothesis of crustal balance."

Pratt; an article published in 1864, in which he gave his own theory to account for crustal balance.

Dutton; an article published in 1889, in which he gave the mechanics of operation of the tendency toward crustal equilibrium, and proposed the term isostasy.

ON THE ATTRACTION OF THE HIMALAYA MOUNTAINS, AND OF THE ELEVATED REGIONS BEYOND THEM, UPON THE PLUMB–LINE IN INDIA [4]

by John Henry Pratt, Archdeacon of Calcutta

It is now well known that the attraction of the Himalaya Mountains, and of the elevated regions lying beyond them, has a sensible influence upon the plumb-

[4] From *Philosophical Transactions of the Royal Society of London* (1855) Vol. 145, pp. 53–100. (Dated at Deep River, Cape of Good Hope, July 12, 1854)

line in North India. This circumstance has been brought to light during the progress of the great trigonometrical survey of that country. It has been found by triangulation that the difference of latitude between the two extreme stations of the northern division of the arc, that is, between Kalianpur and Kaliana, is 5°23′42″.294, whereas astronomical observations show a difference of 5°23′37″.058, which is 5″.236 * less than the former. [Fig. 34-3.]

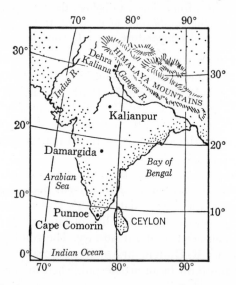

Figure 34-3. *Map showing the relative positions of the stations on the Indian Arc, mentioned by Pratt.*

That the geodetic operations are not in fault appears from this; that two bases, about seven miles long, at the extremities of the arc having been measured with the utmost care, and also the length of the northern base having been computed from the measured length of the southern one, through a chain of triangles stretching along the whole arc, about 370 miles in extent, the difference between the measured and the computed lengths of the northern base was only 0.6 of a foot, an error which would produce, even if wholly lying in the meridian, a difference of latitude no greater than 0″.006.

The difference 5″.236 must therefore be attributed to some other cause than error in the geodetic operations. A very probable cause is the attraction of the superficial matter which lies in such abundance on the north of the Indian arc. This disturbing cause acts in the right direction; for the tendency of the mountain mass must be to draw the lead of the plumb-line at the northern extremity of the arc more to the north than at the southern extremity, which is further removed from the attracting mass. Hence the effect of the attraction will be to lessen the difference of latitude, which is the effect observed. Whether this cause will account for the error in the difference of latitude in *quantity*, as well as in direction, remains to be considered, . . .

---

* This is the difference as stated by Colonel Everest in his work on the Measurement of the Meridional Arc of India, published in 1847.

In Colonel Everest's survey of India (the man for whom Mt. Everest in the Himalaya Mountains was named) the geodetic calculations were adjusted to bring the results of the astronomical and geodetic methods of survey into agreement. Pratt stated that he could see no valid grounds for adjusting the geodetic calculations, but that instead,

It appears to me to be unquestionable that the geodetic operations are in no way sensibly affected by mountain attraction, and therefore need no correction whatever on that account. It is the *astronomical* operation of observing the difference of latitude which requires the correction. That it is here that the correction must be applied appears again in attempting to determine the azimuths of the arc at seven stations *astronomically*. It is only when the plumb-line is brought into use to determine the vertical angles of stars that the effect of attraction becomes sensible; and never in the geodetic calculations, where only horizontal angles or extremely minute vertical angles are observed.

Pratt's paper of 1854 consists of 47 pages, mostly detailed mathematical calculations. Airy referred to the publication as " A paper of great ability."

By calculating the approximate mass of the Himalayas above sea level and computing their average distance from each of several stations, such as Kaliana and Kalianpur, then assuming the Himalayas were an additional load upon an otherwise uniform crust, Pratt was able to calculate the amount that the plumb line should have been deflected toward the mountains at each station (Fig. 34-3). His results showed that at Kaliana the deflection in the meridian should have been 27″.853 and at Kalianpur it should have been 11″.968, a difference of 15″.885, which is more than three times the observed difference of 5″.236 noted by Colonel Everest in his survey of 1847. The difference of 5″.236 of arc would correspond to a distance of about 500 feet of error on the ground. This was an error too great to be explained by surveying errors in a survey so carefully done. If the error were 3 times as great (with the difference of 15″.885), it was certain the error was something other than a surveying error. The discrepancy could best be explained by assuming a deficiency of mass below the Himalayas.

ON THE COMPUTATION OF THE EFFECT OF THE ATTRACTION OF MOUNTAIN–MASSES, AS DISTURBING THE APPARENT ASTRO– NOMICAL LATITUDE OF STATIONS IN GEODETIC SURVEYS [5]

by George Bedell Airy, Astronomer Royal

A paper of great ability has lately been communicated to the Royal Society by Archdeacon Pratt, in which the disturbing effects of the mass of high land northeast of the valley of the Ganges, upon the apparent astronomical latitudes of the principal stations of the Indian Arc of Meridian, are investigated. It is not my intention here to comment upon the mathematical methods used by the author

[5] From *Philosophical Transactions of the Royal Society of London* (1855) Vol. 145, pp. 101–104.

of that paper, or upon the physical measures on which the numerical calculation of his formulæ is based, but only to call attention to the principal result; namely, that the attraction of the mountain-ground, thus computed on the theory of gravitation, is considerably greater than is necessary to explain the anomalies observed. This singular conclusion, I confess, at first surprised me very much.

Yet upon considering the theory of the earth's figure as affected by disturbing causes, with the aid of the best physical hypothesis (imperfect as it must be) which I am able to apply to it, it appears to me, not only that there is nothing surprising in Archdeacon Pratt's conclusion, but that it ought to have been anticipated; and that, instead of a positive attraction of a large mountain mass upon a station at a considerable distance from it, we ought to be prepared to expect no effect whatever, or in some cases even a small negative effect. The reasoning upon which this opinion is founded, inasmuch as it must have some application to almost every investigation of geodesy, may perhaps merit the attention of the Royal Society.

Although the surface of the earth consists everywhere of a hard crust, with only enough water lying upon it to give us everywhere a *couche de niveau* [datum plane], and to enable us to estimate the heights of the mountains in some places, and the depths of the basins in others; yet the smallness of those elevations and depths, the correctness with which the hard part of the earth has assumed the spheroidal form, and the absence of any particular preponderance either of land or of water at the equator as compared with the poles, have induced most physicists to suppose, either that the interior of the earth is now fluid, or that it was fluid when the mountains took their present forms. This fluidity may be very imperfect; it may be mere viscidity; it may even be little more than that degree of yielding which (as is well known to miners) shows itself by changes in the floors of subterraneous chambers at a great depth when their width exceeds 20 or 30 feet; and this yielding may be sufficient for my present explanation. However, in order to present my ideas in the clearest form, I will suppose the interior to be perfectly fluid.

In the accompanying diagram, fig. 1 [Fig. 34-4], suppose the outer circle, as far as it is complete, to represent the spheroidal surface of the earth, conceived to be free from basins or mountains except in one place; and suppose the prominence in the upper part to represent a table-land, 100 miles broad in its smaller horizontal dimension, and two miles high. And suppose the inner circle to represent the concentric spheroidal inner surface of the earth's crust, that inner spheroid being filled with a fluid of greater density than the crust, which, to avoid circumlocution, I will call lava. To fix our ideas, suppose the thickness of

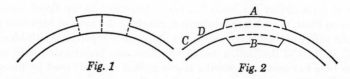

Figure 34-4. *Diagrams which accompany Airy's explanation of his concept of crustal balance, 1855.*

the crust to be ten miles through the greater part of the circumference, and therefore twelve miles at the place of the table-land.

Now I say, that this state of things is impossible; the weight of the table-land would break the crust through its whole depth from the top of the table-land to the surface of the lava, and either the whole or only the middle part would sink into the lava.

        *   *   *   *   *   *   *

We must therefore give up the supposition that the state of things below a table-land of any great magnitude can be represented by such a diagram as fig. 1 [Fig. 34-4]. And we may now inquire what the state of things really must be.

The impossibility of the existence of the state represented in fig. 1 has arisen from the want of a sufficient support of the table-land from below. Yet the table-land does exist in its elevation, and therefore it *is* supported from below. What can the nature of its support be?

I conceive that there can be no other support than that arising from the downward projection of a portion of the earth's light crust into the dense lava; the horizontal extent of that projection corresponding rudely with the horizontal extent of the table-land, and the depth of its projection downwards being such that the increased power of floatation thus gained is roughly equal to the increase of weight above from the prominence of the table-land. It appears to me that the state of the earth's crust lying upon the lava may be compared with perfect correctness to the state of a raft of timber floating upon water; in which, if we remark one log whose upper surface floats much higher than the upper surfaces of the others, we are certain that its lower surface lies deeper in the water than the lower surfaces of the others.

This state of things then will be represented by fig. 2 [Fig. 34-4]. Adopting this as the true representation of the arrangement of masses beneath a table-land, let us consider what will be its effect in disturbing the direction of gravity at different points in its proximity. It will be remarked that the disturbance depends on two actions; the positive attraction produced by the elevated table land [Fig. 34-5]; and the diminution of attraction, or negative attraction, produced by the substitution of a certain volume of light crust (in the lower projection) for heavy lava.

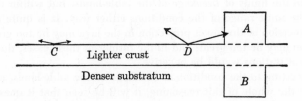

Figure 34-5. At point D, closer to the elevated tableland A, the positive gravitational attraction of A is greater than the negative attraction of the more distant low-density root B. At the distant point C, the two forces are essentially equal.

The diminution of attractive matter below, produced by the substitution of light crust for heavy lava, will be sensibly equal to the increase of attractive matter above. The difference of the negative attraction of one and the positive attraction of the other, as estimated in the direction of a line perpendicular to that joining the centres of attraction of the two masses (or as estimated in a horizontal line), will be proportional to the difference of the inverse cubes of the distances of the attracted point from the two masses.

Suppose then that the point C is at a great distance, where nevertheless the positive attraction of mass A, considered alone, would have produced a very sensible effect on the apparent astronomical latitude, as ten seconds. The effect of the negative attraction of B will be $10'' \times \dfrac{CA^3}{CB^3}$; and the whole effect will be $10'' \times \dfrac{CB^3 - CA^3}{CB^3}$, which probably will be quite insensible.

But suppose that the point D is at a much smaller distance, where the positive attraction of the mass A would have produced the effect n''. The whole effect, by the same formula, will be $n'' \times \dfrac{DB^3 - DA^3}{DB^3}$ or $n'' \times \left(1 - \dfrac{DA^3}{DB^3}\right)$; and as in this case the fraction $\dfrac{DA}{DB}$ is not very nearly equal to 1, there may be a considerable residual disturbing attraction. But even here, and however near to the mountains the station D may be, the real disturbing attraction will be less than found by computing the attraction of the table-land alone.

The general conclusion then is this. In all cases, the real disturbance will be less than that found by computing the effect of the mountains, on the law of gravitation. Near to the elevated country, the part which is to be subtracted from the computed effect is a small proportion of the whole. At a distance from the elevated country, the part which is to be subtracted is so nearly equal to the whole, that the remainder may be neglected as insignificant, even in cases where the attraction of the elevated country itself would be considerable. But in our ignorance of the depth at which the downward immersion of the projecting crust into the lava takes place, we cannot give greater precision to the statement.

In all the latter inferences, it is supposed that the crust is floating in a state of equilibrium. But in our entire ignorance of the *modus operandi* of the forces which have raised submarine strata to the tops of high mountains, we cannot insist on this as absolutely true. We know (from the reasoning above) that it will be so to the limits of *breakage* of the table-lands; but within those limits there may be some range of the conditions either way. It is quite as possible that the immersion of the lower projection in the lava may be too great, as that the elevation may be too great; and in the former of these cases, the attraction on the distant stations would be negative.

Again reverting to the condition of *breakage* of the table-lands, as dominating through the whole of this reasoning, it will be seen that it does not apply in regard to such computations as that of the attraction of Schehallien and the like. It applies only to the computation of the attractions of high tracts of very great horizontal extent, such as those to the north of India.

Dated at Royal Observatory, Greenwich, Jan. 19, 1855.

Let us examine Airy's conclusions in more detail. Consider the elevated land mass (Fig. 34-6) to have a mass M_A, the uniform continuation of the crust beneath this elevation to have a mass M_C and the root of lighter crust extending down into the denser substratum below to have a mass M_B. Also consider an adjacent section of the crust of equal area which would also have a mass M_C and which lies over a section of substratum

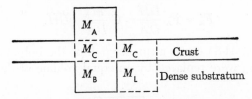

Figure 34-6. *Extension of the low-density crust upward into the tableland M_A and downward in the root M_B. If the tableland and crust are in isostatic equilibrium, the weights of columns of equal area are equal.*

of mass M_L extending down to the same depth as M_B. Then if we apply Archimedes' principle of buoyancy

$$M_A + M_C + M_B = M_C + M_L$$

and

$$M_A = M_L - M_B.$$

In other words, the mass M_A is supported in an elevated position because M_B is lighter than M_L.

We next wish to find the effects of the pulls of these masses on a plumb bob placed at some adjacent point D on the earth's surface (Fig. 34-7).

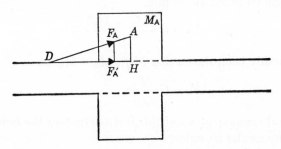

Figure 34-7. *The attraction of M_A for a plumb bob at D is indicated by F_A whose horizontal component is F'_A.*

For convenience assume the plumb bob to have unit mass. Then the force of attraction of M_A for the bob is given by Newton's law of gravitation as

$$F_A = G \frac{M_A}{DA^2}.$$

The horizontal component of this force is represented by F_A' and represents the horizontal sideways pull on the bob. By similar triangles it is obvious that

$$\frac{F_A'}{F_A} = \frac{\overline{DH}}{\overline{DA}}$$

and

$$F_A' = F_A \frac{\overline{DH}}{\overline{DA}} = G \frac{M_A}{\overline{DA}^3} \cdot \overline{DH}.$$

Now M_B (Fig. 34-8) exerts a smaller pull on the bob at D than would be exerted if M_B were replaced by an equal volume of denser rock ma-

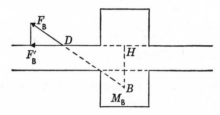

Figure 34-8. *The negative attraction of* M_B *on the plumb bob at* D *is indicated by* F_B. *This negative attraction is the reduction in the force on the bob caused by replacement of the dense substratum by the lighter root* M_B.

terial having a mass M_L. Let us then represent by F_B the *reduction* in the force on the bob caused by replacement of the mass M_L of dense rock material by a less dense root M_B. The reduction in force F_B is then equivalent to a negative gravitational pull.

$$F_B = G \frac{(M_L - M_B)}{\overline{DB}^2}$$

But it has already been shown that $M_L - M_B = M_A$, so

$$F_B = G \frac{M_A}{\overline{DB}^2}.$$

The horizontal component F_B' of this force acting on the bob again may be obtained by similar triangles:

$$\frac{F_B'}{F_B} = \frac{\overline{DH}}{\overline{DB}}$$

and

$$F_B' = F_B \frac{\overline{DH}}{\overline{DB}}$$

$$= G \frac{M_A}{\overline{DB}^3} \cdot \overline{DH}.$$

Following Airy, suppose the deflection of the bob from the vertical caused by the elevation M_A alone is n''. It can be shown that a small deflection n'' is proportional to the horizontal force F_A' causing it. However, the observed deflection is less than n'' due to the negative effect of the lower density of M_B than of M_L. Thus while

$$n'' \propto F_A'$$

and

$$n'' = \text{constant} \cdot F_A',$$

the actually observed deflection N'' is proportional to the difference between the positive pull of M_A and the decreased (negative) pull of M_B because of its lower density.

$$N'' \propto (F_A' - F_B')$$

and

$$N'' = \text{constant} \cdot (F_A' - F_B').$$

Then dividing equations

$$\frac{N''}{n''} = \frac{\text{constant} \cdot (F_A' - F_B')}{\text{constant} \cdot F_A'} = \frac{F_A' - F_B'}{F_A'},$$

and substituting the previously obtained expressions for the forces,

$$N'' = n'' \frac{\dfrac{GM_A\overline{DH}}{\overline{DA}^3} - \dfrac{GM_A\overline{DH}}{\overline{DB}^3}}{\dfrac{GM_A\overline{DH}}{\overline{DA}^3}}$$

$$= n'' \frac{\dfrac{1}{\overline{DA}^3} - \dfrac{1}{\overline{DB}^3}}{\dfrac{1}{\overline{DA}^3}}$$

$$= n''\overline{DA}^3 \left(\frac{1}{\overline{DA}^3} - \frac{1}{\overline{DB}^3}\right)$$

$$= n'' \left(1 - \frac{\overline{DA}^3}{\overline{DB}^3}\right).$$

Now it can be seen that if the observation point D is quite distant from the elevated mass M_A,

$$\overline{DA} = \overline{DB}$$

and

$$N'' = n''(1 - 1) = 0.$$

Thus the effect of an elevated region on a plumb bob is perceptible only when the bob is close enough to the mountain so that the ratio $\overline{DA}/\overline{DB}$ is appreciably different from unity.

STUDY QUESTIONS

1. Select the correct statement or statements.
   a. One of the earliest recorded suggestions that high mountains offer a gravitational attraction, but in quantity *less* than would be expected, considering the mass of the mountains, was published by P. Bouguer.
   b. The man to whom credit is most commonly attributed for the first suggestion that there is a tendency for mass balance in the rocks of the earth's crust (later called isostasy) was J. Herschel.
   c. The first man to propose the term isostasy in his writings to describe a tendency for balance in the segments of the earth's crust was C. Dutton.
   The correct statement is

      (1) a   (2) b   (3) c   (4) a, b, and c   (5) none of the statements.

2. The observations of J. H. Pratt, which helped in the formulation of the principle of isostasy, were based upon

      (1) the attraction of the Himalaya Mountains upon a plumb line in India
      (2) calculations concerning the thicknesses of sedimentary strata in different parts of India
      (3) the behavior of earthquake waves in the deeper zones of the earth
      (4) comparisons of laboratory experiments with field observations
      (5) mathematical calculations, using relative specific gravities of acidic and basic igneous rocks and sediments.

3. Select the correct statement or statements.
   a. The weight of a column of rock of a given cross-sectional area, extending from a zone at a given distance from the earth's center to the earth's surface, whether that surface be located at the top of the highest mountain, at the sea shore, or in the deepest ocean basin, is everywhere precisely the same.
   b. In making a survey of India, Colonel Everest and his party ended with an apparent surveying error of about 5¼ seconds of arc. This would amount to an error in measurement on the ground of approximately 500 feet.
   c. Since Colonel Everest's surveying error was so small, amounting to only a few inches in a mile of horizontal distance, he ignored the error in making his calculations.
   The correct answer is

      (1) a   (2) b   (3) c   (4) a, b, and c   (5) none of the statements.

4. In Airy's hypothesis for crustal balance, the interior of the earth is postulated to be

      (1) a rigid solid   (2) a viscous solid   (3) metallic iron
      (4) a fluid of greater density than the crust
      (5) a fluid of about the same density as an average sediment.

5. Airy stated that his computations dealing with the breakage and sinking of table-lands were applicable

      (1) equally well to plains and continental shelves
      (2) to all mountain regions both large and small
      (3) only to volcanic regions and major earthquake belts

(4) only to high tracts of great horizontal extent

(5) equally as well to narrow linear tracts as to laterally extensive ones.

6. Airy believed that mountain and plateau areas are supported above the surrounding lower lands

(1) by unequal contractions of segments of the crust

(2) by downward projections of light crustal segments into a denser substratum

(3) through the action of underlying volcanic activity

(4) by lateral squeezing of earth segments upward as oceanic segments sink

(5) through fault relationships of adjacent blocks.

7. Regarding the depth to which a plateau crustal segment may project downward into the substratum and remain in balance Airy claimed

(1) a depth about half as great as the height of the mass

(2) a depth equal to the elevation above sea level

(3) the depth is inversely proportional to the cube of the specific gravity

(4) lack of information

(5) that the depth to which all blocks penetrate is uniform.

8. Pratt considered that the apparent error in the survey of India was due to a discrepancy in the astronomical method rather than in the geodetic method. A reason for this conclusion was

(1) precession changed the relative positions of the stars

(2) the dense basaltic lava of the Deccan Plateau of India pulled the plumb bob straight down, and thus reduced the expected deflection of the plumb line toward the Himalayas

(3) the geodetic method is generally far the more accurate

(4) his discovery of an error made in calculating the mass of the Himalayas

(5) that it is the astronomical method that makes use of the plumb line in determining vertical angles of the stars; thus the error was introduced at that operation.

9. Select the statements consistent with Pratt's views on the mountain attraction upon a plumb line.

a. Gravitational attraction by a near-by mountain range has no appreciable effect upon the results of a geodetic survey.

b. The best way to explain a discrepancy between geodetic and astronomical surveys in areas near high mountains is to assume a mass deficiency beneath the mountains.

c. The actual amount of plumb-line deflection can be calculated by subtracting the geodetic readings from the astronomical readings.

The correct answer is

(1) a and b   (2) b and c   (3) a and c   (4) a, b, and c   (5) none of the statements.

10. Select the statements consistent with Airy's views on the mountain attraction upon a plumb line.

a. A large mountain mass several miles from a survey station should not only fail to yield an appreciable positive attraction, but should give *no* attraction or even a small negative effect.

b. The water lying upon the hard crust of the earth gives us a datum plane from which to measure the heights of the mountains and the depths of the oceans.

c. Gravity anomalies depend upon two actions — the positive attraction of the elevated lands and the negative attraction of a certain volume of light crust substituted for heavy material at depth below the elevated lands.

The correct answer is

(1) a and b   (2) b and c   (3) a and c   (4) a, b, and c   (5) none of the statements.

11. According to Airy, the manner in which forces operate within the earth to raise marine strata to mountainous heights is which of the following?

(1) Light materials rise, heavy materials sink.

(2) Forces of volcanic origin inject materials beneath the sea floor being elevated, in a manner similar to a giant hydraulic jack.

(3) Heat within the earth simply causes heavy materials to expand, thus becoming lighter in weight, with a resultant rise in elevation.

(4) Materials do not really rise; elevations are only relative.

(5) The mode of operation of the forces at depth is unknown.

12. In some areas of deep-sea trenches, a negative gravity anomaly exists. Consistent with this information it might be true that

a. the trench has been filled to considerable depth with clastic sediments derived from continental areas

b. the trench has been nearly filled with lava that has been extruded from a considerable depth beneath the ocean basins

c. no sediments have been deposited in the trench.

The correct answer is

(1) a and b   (2) b and c   (3) a and c   (4) a, b, and c   (5) none of the statements.

13. Which of the following might be expected as a future development of a deep-sea trench which is characterized by a negative gravity anomaly?

a. A mountain range would never form within an area occupied by a deep-sea trench.

b. Elevation of the floor of a deep-sea trench might occur in the geologic future.

c. Coarse clastic sediments would continue to accumulate because the sediments would slowly sink after being deposited in the trench.

The correct answer is

(1) a   (2) b   (3) c   (4) a, b, and c   (5) none of the statements.

14. Assume that gravity readings show a large mountainous tract to have a positive gravity anomaly. This observation

(1) would be consistent with Pratt's ideas of isostasy

(2) would be consistent with Airy's concept of isostasy

(3) could result from massive intrusions of granitic materials into the mountainous areas

(4) could result from the presence of denser underlying rocks being elevated to form the bulk of the mountain mass

(5) would indicate the presence of rich veins of valuable ores, such as gold-bearing quartz veins.

15. Which of the following statements are true?
    a. The operations of isostasy might explain the existence of land areas.
    b. The principle of isostasy can explain the present-day rising of land in certain areas that were covered by glacial ice during the Pleistocene epoch.
    c. Isostasy might be a principle that would eliminate Dana's main objection to Hall's theory of mountain building.
    d. Isostasy might conceivably be the principal factor in place of contraction, in the elevation of land areas as conceived by Dana.
    e. Isostasy could be an important factor in the development of peneplains and sub-aerial erosional surfaces throughout the Appalachian and Rocky Mountain areas.
    The correct answer is

    (1) a, b, and c   (2) b, c, and d   (3) c, d, and e   (4) a, b, d, and e
    (5) a, b, c, d, and e.

16. Compare the Maire-Boscovitch conception of crustal balance with that of John Herschel.
17. What was the basis for Pratt's reasoning that Colonel Everest should not have adjusted his geodetic calculations, when his geodetic and astronomical surveys in India did not check, but should have adjusted his astronomical calculations instead?
18. What is Airy's conclusion as to the nature of the support upon which a high plateau rests?
19. What is the basis for Airy's conclusion that the difference of the negative attraction of one mass and the positive attraction of the other will be proportional to the difference of the inverse cubes of the distances of the attracted points from the two masses?

35

Isostasy and Mountain Building

● The previous chapter contained excerpts from writings of Pratt and Airy dealing with the principle of isostasy. The present chapter continues with the same subject, beginning with an article prepared by Pratt about ten years after the writing of the material quoted in Chapter 34.

SPECULATIONS ON THE CONSTITUTION
OF THE EARTH'S CRUST [1]

by John Henry Pratt

The first thing I observe in the results . . . is the very small amount of the resultant deflections at the two extremities of the Indian Arc — Punnoe close to Cape Comorin, [Fig. 34-3] and Kaliana the nearest station to the Himmalaya Mountains; whereas the effect of the Ocean and the Mountains has been shown to be very large. This shows that the effect of variations of density in the crust must be very great, in order to bring about this near compensation. In fact the density of the crust beneath the mountains must be less than that below the plains, and still less than that below the ocean-bed. If solidification from the fluid state commenced at the surface, the amount of contraction in the solid parts beneath the mountain-region has been less than in the parts beneath the sea. In fact, it is this unequal contraction which appears to have caused the hollows in the external surface which have become the basins into which the waters have flowed to form the ocean. As the waters flowed into the hollows thus created, the pressure on the ocean-bed would be increased, and the crust, so long as it was sufficiently thin to be influenced by hydrostatic princi-

[1] From *Proceedings of the Royal Society of London* (1864) Vol. XIII, pp. 272–276. (From a larger work titled " On the degree of uncertainty which Local Attraction, if not allowed for, occasions in the Map of a Country, and in the Mean Figure of the Earth as determined by Geodesy; a Method of obtaining the Mean Figure free from ambiguity by a comparison of the Anglo-Gallic, Russian, and Indian arcs; and Speculations on the Constitution of the Earth's Crust.")

ples of floatation, would so adjust itself that the pressure on any *couche de niveau* of the fluid should remain the same. At the time that the crust first became sufficiently thick to resist fracture under the strain produced by a change in its density — that is, when it first ceased to depend for the elevation or depression of its several parts upon the principles of floatation, the total amount of matter in any vertical prism, drawn down into the fluid below to a given distance from the earth's centre, had been the same through all the previous changes. After this, any further contraction or any expansion in the solid crust would not alter the amount of matter in the vertical prism, except where there was an ocean; in the case of greater contraction under an ocean than elsewhere, the ocean would become deeper and the amount of matter greater, and in case of a less contraction or of an expansion of the crust under an ocean, the ocean would become shallower, or the amount of matter in the vertical prism less than before. It is not likely that expansion and contraction in the solid crust would affect the arrangement of matter in any other way. That changes of level do take place, by the rising and sinking of the surface, is a well-established fact, which rather favours these theoretical considerations. But they receive, I think, great support from the other fact, that the large effect of the ocean at Punnoe and of the mountains at Kaliana almost entirely disappear from the resultant deflections brought out by the calculations. . . . when we get close to the mountain-mass, as at Dehra, which is at the foot of the mountains where they first rise rapidly above the plains, the resultant deflection is very great; the less density of the crust down below the sea-level drawn under the mountain-mass has here a very trifling influence. This is as it should be, if the depth of this less density is considerable; whereas at Kaliana, and stations still further off, the attraction of the mountain-mass above sea-level, and the deficiency of attraction from the crust below that level, would nearly counterbalance each other. Thus, if the thickness of the crust below the plains is 100 miles, and the amount of matter in the crust under the plains equals that of the crust and mountains together in the mountain-region, then the deflections at Kaliana, Kalianpur, and Damargida, instead of being $27''.98$, $12''.05$, $6''.79$, arising from the mountains alone, are reduced to $1''.54$, $-0''.06$, $-0''.06$, which are all insignificant compared with the large deflections caused by the mountains alone.

This theory, that the wide ocean has been collected on parts of the earth's surface where hollows have been made by the contraction and therefore increased density of the crust below, is well illustrated by the existence of a whole hemisphere of water, of which New Zealand is the pole, in stable equilibrium. Were the crust beneath only of the same density as that beneath the surrounding continents, the water would be drawn off by attraction and not allowed to stand in the undisturbed position it now occupies.

I have, in what goes before, supposed that, in solidifying, the crust contracts and grows denser, as this appears to be most natural, though, after the solid mass is formed, it may either expand or contract, according as an accession or diminution of heat may take place. If, however, in the process of solidifying, the mass becomes lighter, the same conclusion will follow — the mountains being formed by a greater degree of expansion of the crust beneath them, and not by a less contraction, than in the other parts of the crust. It may seem at first difficult to conceive how a crust could be formed at all, if in the act of solidification it becomes heavier than the fluid on which it rests; for the equilibrium of the heavy crust floating on a lighter fluid would be unstable, and the crust would sooner or later be broken through, and would sink down into the fluid, which would overflow it. If, however, this process went on perpetually, the descending crust, which was originally formed by a loss of heat radiated from the surface into space, would reduce the heat of the fluid into which it sank, and after a time a thicker crust would be formed than before, and the difficulty of its being broken through would become greater every time a new one was formed. Perhaps the tremendous dislocation of stratified rocks in huge masses with which a traveller in the mountains, especially in the interior of the Himmalaya region, is familiar, may have been brought about in this way. The catastrophes, too, which geology seems to teach have at certain epochs destroyed whole species of living creatures, may have been thus caused, at the same time breaking up the strata in which those species had for ages before been deposited as the strata were formed. These phenomena must now long have ceased to occur, at any rate on a very extensive scale, as . . . investigations on Precession appear to prove that the crust is very thick, . . .

The theory I have proposed, that contraction of the crust has formed the basins in which the sea has settled, can hardly be expected to apply so completely to such confined sheets of water as the Mediterranean south of Spain, and the Gulf of Bothnia. Here there may be an actual deficiency of attracting matter in the water, not altogether compensated for by increased density of the crust below. There hollows may have been formed during the breaking up of the crust and subsequent removal of portions by currents, and not chiefly by the contraction of the crust. Thus the deflections at the stations (1) [Barcelona, Spain] and (12) [Tornea, Lapland] towards the land may be sufficiently accounted for, even if the land about Barcelona and Tornea does not rise sufficiently high to produce them. The deflection at station (2) [Dunkirk, France] is small. It seems probable that even if the North Sea has been produced according to the theory of contraction of the crust, the parts near Dunkirk may have been somewhat hollowed out by the scouring of the tide through the Straits of Dover, so as to give the land, low as it is, every advantage in deflecting the plumb-line south. . . .

The least that can be gathered from the deflections of these coast-stations is, that they present no obstacle to the theory so remarkably suggested by the facts brought to light in India, viz. that mountain-regions and oceans on a large scale have been produced by the contraction of the materials, as the surface of the earth has passed from a fluid state to a condition of solidity — the amount of contraction beneath the mountain-region having been less than that beneath the ordinary surface, and still less than that beneath the ocean-bed, by which process the hollows have been produced into which the ocean has flowed. In fact the testimony of these coast-stations is in some degree directly in favour of the theory, as they seem to indicate, by *excess* of attraction towards the sea, that the contraction of the crust beneath the ocean has gone on increasing in some instances still further since the crust became too thick to be influenced by the principles of floatation, and that an additional flow of water into the increasing hollow has increased the amount of attraction upon stations on its shores.

Murree, Punjab, Aug. 20, 1863.

When Pratt first studied the Himalaya Mountains he suggested that the rock below the Himalayas might be less dense than the rock at a similar depth beneath peninsular India. He proposed that both the Himalayas and the peninsula were "floating" on a deeper plastic substratum of denser material and that the heights of the two surfaces rose above the deeper layer in an inverse proportion to the average densities of the materials making up the two blocks. Thus the high-standing Himalayas are balanced by a deficiency of mass of the materials extending deep into the earth beneath them.

Airy suggested a somewhat different flotation mechanism. He could find no evidence that the density of the material beneath the mountains should be any different from that beneath the peninsula. He considered both blocks to be of the same density, but of unequal thickness. To be sure, the thicker mountain block would rise higher above the surface, but it would also sink deeper into the heavy substratum beneath. Thus, according to Airy the high-standing Himalayas are balanced by a "root" of material lighter than the substratum. This root projects into the substratum and displaces it. This would be similar to the consideration of two icebergs, one with a vertical dimension twice as large as the other; the larger one not only rises higher above water level than the smaller one, but also projects downward deeper into the water.

Thus in summary, Pratt considered different crustal blocks to have different densities and to penetrate to a fluid substratum of uniform surface. Airy considered all crustal blocks to have the same density, but to penetrate to different depths into the fluid substratum, and therefore to stand at different heights above sea level. Figures 35-1 and 35-2 illustrate the two isostatic "pictures."

As a general rule, geologists prefer Airy's hypothesis, because it seems to agree better with what is known or can logically be inferred about the

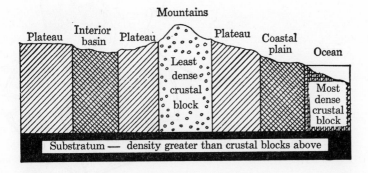

Figure 35-1. *Isostasy after Pratt. Of the crustal segments, Pratt believed the density of the mountain block was the least, the one under the ocean was the greatest, and the others were intermediate. The density of the substratum was believed to be somewhat greater than the most dense crustal block.*

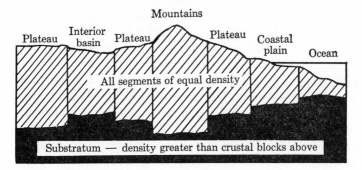

Figure 35-2. *Isostasy after Airy. Airy believed all crustal segments had approximately the same density. The mountain segment was believed to penetrate to a greater depth into the substratum.*

make-up of the earth's crust. However, gravity computations are more commonly made on the basis of Pratt's concept.

The next contribution to the theory of isostasy to be considered was that made by Clarence Dutton (Fig. 35-3), who was born at Wallingford, Connecticut in May, 1841. After attending school at Ellington he com-

Figure 35-3. *Clarence Dutton (1841–1912).*

pleted his formal education at Yale, graduating in 1860. After taking part in the Civil War, he decided to remain in the army, receiving a permanent commission as a lieutenant in the Ordnance Corps. While he was assigned near Troy, New York, he became interested in the controversies James Hall was having relative to his geosynclinal concept. Dutton began to study geology and, upon being transferred to Washington in 1871, met Major John W. Powell, director of the Powell Survey, one of the forerunners of the United States Geological Survey. Through Powell's influence, Dutton was soon released from active duty with the Army to serve as party chief on field surveys in the western part of North America. He remained in geological exploration work for 16 years. It was from field work in this area, the Colorado Plateau in particular, that he arrived at his ideas on the theory of isostasy, and formulated at least a partial explanation of the problem of the uplift of mountains.

The article by Dutton that follows was prepared, as he stated, to fill a vacant half hour on a scientific program sponsored by the Philosophical Society of Washington in 1889. In the article he discussed what he considered to be the three greatest problems in physical geology. One of these problems was the operation of isostasy. The portion of his paper dealing with isostasy follows.

ON SOME OF THE GREATER PROBLEMS
OF PHYSICAL GEOLOGY [2]

ISOSTASY
by Clarence E. Dutton

❁   ❁   ❁   ❁   ❁   ❁   ❁

If the earth were composed of homogeneous matter its normal figure of equilibrium without strain would be a true spheroid of revolution; but if heterogeneous, if some parts were denser or lighter than others, its normal figure would no longer be spheroidal. Where the lighter matter was accumulated there would be a tendency to bulge, and where the denser matter existed there would be a tendency to flatten or depress the surface. For this condition of equilibrium of figure, to which gravitation tends to reduce a planetary body, irrespective of whether it be homogeneous or not, I propose the name *isostasy*. I would have preferred the word isobary, but it is preoccupied. We may also use the corresponding adjective, *isostatic*. An isostatic earth, composed of homogeneous matter and without rotation, would be truly spherical. If slowly rotating it would be a spheroid of two axes. If rotating rapidly within a certain limit, it might be a spheroid of three axes.

But if the earth be not homogeneous — if some portions near the surface be

[2] *Bulletin of the Philosophical Society of Washington,* Judd and Detweiler (1892) Vol. XI, pp. 51–64. (Read before the Society 1889.)

lighter than others — then the isostatic figure is no longer a sphere or spheroid of revolution, but a deformed figure, bulged where the matter is light and depressed where it is heavy. The question which I propose is: How nearly does the earth's figure approach to isostasy?

Mathematical statics alone will not enable us to answer this question with a sufficient degree of approximation. It does, indeed, enable us to fix certain limits to the departure from isostasy which cannot be exceeded. This very problem has been treated with great skill by Prof. George Darwin.

But this problem may be approached from another direction with more satisfactory results. Geology furnishes us with certain facts which enable us to draw a much narrower conclusion. There are several categories of fact to which we may turn. One of the most remarkable is the general fact that where great bodies of strata are deposited they progressively settle down or sink seemingly by reason of their gross mechanical weight, just as a railway embankment across a bog sinks into it. The attention of the earlier Appalachian geologists was called, as soon as they had acquired a fair knowledge of their field, to the surprising fact that the paleozoic strata in that wonderful belt, though tens of thousands of feet in thickness, were all deposited in comparatively shallow water. The paleozoic beds of the Appalachian region have a thickness, ranging from 15000 to over 30000 feet, yet they abound in proofs that when they were deposited their surfaces were the bottom of a shallow sea whose depth could not probably have exceeded a few hundred feet. No conclusion is left us but that sinking went on *pari passu* with the accumulation of the strata. When the geology of the Pacific coast was sufficiently disclosed, the same fact confronted us there. As investigation went on the same fact presented itself over the western mountain region of the United States. One of the most striking cases is the Plateau Country. This great region, nearly 100000 square miles in area, lying in the adjacent parts of Colorado, Utah, New Mexico, and Arizona, discloses from 8000 to 12000 feet of mesozoic and cenozoic strata. Here the proof is abundant that the surface of the strata was throughout that vast stretch of time never more than a few feet from sea level. Again and again it emerged from the water a little way, only to be submerged. At many horizons grew forests which are now represented by those abundant and beautiful fossil woods which of late have become celebrated. In the cretaceous we find many seams and seamlets of coal or carbonaceous shale; but they are included between sandstones which are crossbedded and ripple-marked, or between shales and limestones which abound in the remains of marine mollusca. Here the evidence seems conclusive that the whole subsidence went on at about the same rate as the surface was built up by deposition. In short, it may be laid down as a general rule that where great bodies of sediment have been deposited over extensive areas their deposition has been accompanied by a subsidence of the whole mass.

The second class of facts is even more instructive, and stands in a reciprocal relation to those just mentioned. Wherever broad mountain platforms occur and have been subjected to great erosion the loss of altitude by degradation is made good by a rise of the platform. In the western portion of the United States there occur mountain ranges situated upon broad and lofty platforms from 20 to 60 miles wide and from 50 to 200 miles in length. Some of these platforms contain several mountain ridges. All of them have been enormously eroded, and if the matter removed from them could be replaced it would suffice to build them to heights of eight or ten miles; yet it is incredible that these mountains were ever much loftier than now, and may never have been so lofty. The flanks of these platforms, with the upturned edges of the strata reposing against them or with gigantic faults measuring their immense uplifts, plainly declare to us that they have been slowly pushed upwards as fast as they were degraded by secular erosion.

It seems little doubtful that these subsidences of accumulated deposits and these progressive upward movements of eroded mountain platforms are, in the main, results of gravitation restoring the isostasy which has been disturbed by denudation on the one hand and by sedimentation on the other. The magnitudes of the masses which thus show the isostatic tendency are in some cases no greater than a single mountain platform, less than 100 miles in length, from 20 to 40 miles wide and from 2500 to 3500 feet mean altitude above the surrounding lowlands. From this we may directly infer that in those regions the effective rigidity of the earth is insufficient to uphold a mass so great as one of those platforms if that mass constituted a real deformation of isostasy; and if an equal mass were to be suddenly removed the earth would flow upward from below to fill the hiatus; hence we must look to considerably smaller masses to find a defect of isostasy. It is extremely probable that small or narrow ridges are not isostatic with respect to the country roundabout them. Some volcanic mountains may be expected to be non-isostatic, especially isolated volcanic piles.

    *   *   *   *   *   *   *

The littoral belts upon which sediments are thrown down are coextensive in length with shores. Their widths are no doubt variable, but must often reach a hundred miles or more with considerable thickness, and are not wholly unimportant at much greater distances. The thickness of the deposits may vary much, but may be proportional to the time of accumulation, and here the time is measured by the geologic standard. The gross weight of such masses of sediment must be vast indeed. If there is any viscous yielding at all the problem becomes essentially that of the flowing solid, which is in a large measure governed by hydrostatic laws. The intensity of the force must have a maximum value proportional to the thickness which lies above the isostatic level and also proportional to its specific gravity. The area covered by the deposit enters as a quantity factor, but not as an intensity factor. The greater the area, the greater is the total potential energy of movement without any necessary increase of the intensity of the force. This intensity, being proportional to the thickness of the sediments, may become almost indefinitely great or it may be small. Indeed, it may, and in fact does, become negative when we apply the same statical theory to the movement or stress of the denuded land areas.

But whether these forces are sufficient to produce actual flow is equally dependent upon the rigidity, or, as we may here term it, the viscosity of the masses involved. We have already seen reason to infer that the mean viscosity is not great, being far less than that of the surface rocks alone. Beyond this rather vague statement I perceive no way of assigning a value to the resistance to be overcome.

It remains to inquire what is the resulting direction of motion. The general answer is, towards the direction of least resistance. The specific answer, which must express the direction of least resistance, will, of course, turn upon the configuration of the deposition on the one hand, and of denudation on the other, and also upon the manner in which the rigidity or viscosity varies from place to place. Taking, then, the case of a land area undergoing denudation, its detritus carried to the sea and deposited in a heavy littoral belt, we may regard the weight of each elementary part of the deposited mass as a statical force acting upon a viscous support below. Assuming that we could find a differential expression applicable to each and every element of the mass and a corresponding one for the resistance offered by the viscosity, the integration for the entire mass might give us a series of equipotential surfaces within the mass. The resultant force at any point of any equipotential surface would be normal to that surface. A similar construction may be applied to the adjoining denuded area, in which the defect of isostasy may be treated as so much mass with a negative algebraic sign. The resultants normal to the equipotential surfaces would in this case, also have the negative sign. The effective force tending to produce movement would be the arithmetical sum of the normals or of a single resultant compounded of the two normals. From this construction we may derive a force which tends to push the loaded sea bottoms inward upon the unloaded land horizontally [Fig. 35-4].

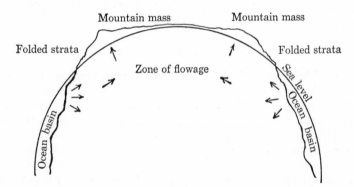

Figure 35-4. *Sketch of a section through the earth showing probable directions of forces as Dutton might have visualized them. The scale of surface features is greatly exaggerated. The sketch was not included in Dutton's original article.*

This gives us a force of the precise kind that is wanted to explain the origin of systematic plications. Long reflection and considerable analysis have satisfied me that it is sufficient both in intensity and in amount unless we assume for the mean viscosity of the superficial and subterranean masses involved in the movement a much greater value than I am disposed to concede. The result is a true viscous flow of the loaded littoral inward upon the unloaded continent.

     ✲   ✲   ✲   ✲   ✲   ✲   ✲

Whatever may have been the cause of these great regional uplifts it in no manner affects the law of isostasy. What the real nature of the uplifting force may be is, to my mind, an entire mystery; but I think we may discern at least one of its attributes, and that is a gradual expansion, or a diminution of the density, of the subterranean magmas. If the isostatic force is operative at all, this expansion is a rigorous consequence; for whenever a rise of the land has taken place one of two things has happened: the region affected has either gained an accession of mass or a mere increase of volume without increase of mass. We know of no cause which could either add to the mass or diminish the density, yet one of the two must surely have happened. But the difference of the two alternatives in respect to consequences is immense. If the increase of volume of an elevated area be due to an accession of matter, the plateau must be hoisted against its own rigidity and also against the statical weight of its entire mass lying above the isostatic level. But if the increase of volume be due to a decrease of density there is no resistance to be overcome in order to raise the surface. Hence I infer that the cause which elevates the land involves an expansion of the underlying magmas, and the cause which depresses it is a shrinkage of the magmas. The nature of the process is, at present, a complete mystery.

In broad terms, the operation of isostasy is generally accepted as fact. In detail, disagreements as to what part isostasy plays in mountain origin and how isostasy operates are very extensive.

W. H. Bucher, in *The Deformation of the Earth's Crust*,[3] gives isostasy as a natural law, as follows: " In an outer shell of limited thickness on the earth, columns of unit area possess approximately the same mass, regardless of the elevation of their surfaces; that is, their densities vary inversely as their heights above a standard surface which lies between fifty and one hundred kilometers [31 to 62 miles] below sea level." Expressed differently, he would say that for any column (see Fig. 34-1) the product of volume and average density is practically a constant.

STUDY QUESTIONS

1. Select the correct statement or statements.
    a. The agent upon which isostasy is dependent for its operation is gravity.
    b. The maximum thickness of the Mesozoic and Cenozoic sedimentary deposits in the Colorado Plateau, according to Dutton, is 12,000 feet.
    c. The sedimentary rocks of the Colorado Plateau are predominantly deep-sea deposits.
    The correct statement is
        (1) a   (2) a and b   (3) b   (4) b and c   (5) c.

2. When isostatic adjustment takes place, the resulting direction of motion is
        (1) downward beneath ocean basins
        (2) upward beneath continental areas

[3] W. H. Bucher, *The Deformation of the Earth's Crust*, Hafner Publishing Company, New York, 1957, p. 24. (Copyright 1933, Princeton University Press.)

(3) toward the direction of greatest gravitational pull

(4) toward the direction of least resistance

(5) uncertain; it depends upon the rigidity or resistance of the substratum.

3. Apparently the views of Pratt and Dana were in agreement in that both men believed the ocean basins were caused by

(1) normal processes of weathering and erosion

(2) a squeezing laterally of dense rock in the plastic state to a new position under the continents

(3) faulting, with the ocean basin areas being depressed

(4) expansive forces originating through radioactivity acting under the continents more than under the ocean basins

(5) unequal contraction of the outer portion of the earth.

4. Select the statements consistent with Dutton's views on isostasy.

a. The littoral deposits are those laid down parallel to the shore line.

b. The widths of the littoral deposits may exceed 100 miles.

c. The thickness of the littoral deposits may be proportional to the length of geologic time during which they accumulated.

The correct answer is

(1) a, b, and c   (2) a and b   (3) b and c   (4) a and c   (5) none of the statements.

5. Which one of the following statements was made by Dutton concerning isostasy and is considered by some geologists to be true?

(1) That changes of level do take place, by the rising and sinking of the surface, is a well-established fact. . .

(2) Where great bodies of strata are deposited, they progressively settle down or sink seemingly by reason of their gross mechanical weight. . .

(3) Since the earth is composed of homogeneous matter its normal figure of equilibrium without strain would be a true sphere.

(4) Theoretically all regions, both great and small, are in isostatic balance.

(5) A rising area should be considered as having positive isostasy and a sinking area negative.

6. Which of the following, as related to isostasy, are true according to Pratt and Dutton?

a. The density of the crust beneath the mountains must be less than that below the plains, but not as low as that below the ocean bed.

b. It appears to be most natural that the crust, in solidifying, contracts and grows denser; but once solidified; it may either become more or less dense depending upon whether heat is lost or added.

c. Since the earth is composed of heterogeneous matter and is rotating on its axis at great speed, there should be a tendency for the denser matter to bulge and the lighter matter to flatten or depress at the surface.

The correct answer is

(1) a   (2) b   (3) c   (4) a, b, and c   (5) none of the statements.

7. Which one (or more) of the following, if any, are compatible with Dutton's views on isostasy?

a. When erosion removes great quantities of sediments from a large area, for example from the Colorado Plateau, the eroded area rises an amount equal to its loss in elevation by the removal of sediments.

b. The rise is commonly rapid and instantaneous, with a minimum of lag between sediment removal and re-elevation.

c. Isostatic balance is generally applicable to any and all areas; for example, if Stone Mountain, near Atlanta, were removed by erosion, the area around Atlanta would be expected to rise at least several inches to compensate for the loss of the mass of the nearby granite mountain.

The correct answer is

(1) a   (2) b   (3) c   (4) a, b, and c   (5) none of the statements.

8. A reason advanced by Dutton for believing that when uplift occurs, such uplift is due to decrease in density of underlying material rather than addition of matter is that

(1) the great force necessary to raise the mass against its own rigidity and weight, in case of addition of matter, need not be necessary in case of decrease in density

(2) the matter of deciding where the additional material comes from is no longer a problem in case of using decrease in density

(3) since the interior of the earth is known to be very hot, decrease in density is readily explainable

(4) the problem of transport of additional material is automatically solved if density decrease is accepted

(5) the accession of matter in any but the liquid or gaseous state is simply too fantastic to consider with any degree of seriousness.

9. When a crust forms on a molten mass of rock, the crust contracts, increases in density, and therefore logically should sink into the molten mass which produced it. Pratt explained the formation of an extensive crust by postulating that

(1) gas bubbles in the molten mass buoy up the crust

(2) the crust forms from mineral crystals which have lower specific gravity while the crystals of greater specific gravity sink deeper into the fluid mass

(3) fragments of the crust break and sink into the fluid mass, thus cooling the fluid, which in time produces an even thicker crust

(4) the crust is held up by lunar and solar tidal attractions

(5) sinking is impossible without thrust faulting because of the curvature of the earth's surface.

10. Which of the following is the *best* statement to emphasize the fundamental difference between the views of Pratt and Airy on isostasy?

(1) Pratt considered isostasy to be applicable on a world wide basis, such as a balance between continents and ocean basins; Airy limited his consideration to balance between mountain masses and lower plains areas.

(2) Airy based his conclusions on mathematical calculations; Pratt based his views purely on physical laws.

(3) The substratum in Airy's hypothesis was considered to be lava; in Pratt's the substratum is a plastic solid of the same density as the surface rocks.

(4) Airy considered all the crustal blocks to be of the same density but the high ones to sink deeper into the substratum; Pratt considered all blocks to penetrate to a uniform depth, but the high blocks to be composed of materials of lower density.

(5) Pratt considered the ocean basins to be deep because the weight of water compressed the basin materials downward; Airy considered the basins to have contracted more than the continents, and the ocean water simply filled the basins because "water seeks its own level."

11. How does Dutton relate the great faults in the Colorado Plateau with isostasy? How would Hall and Dana probably explain faults in the Appalachian Mountains?

12. Contrast the ideas of Dutton, Hall, and Dana concerning the settling of great masses of sediments as a result of their gross mechanical weight.

13. Assume that investigations showed the area of the Mississippi River delta to be characterized by negative gravity anomalies. What would be possible explanations to account for these anomalies?

14. Large areas of continents are said to have risen isostatically. What are some of the events that might have resulted in the necessity for the land to rise in order that isostatic balance be maintained?

36

Some Additional Theories of Mountain Building

● Although many mountain ranges have been subjected to intensive scientific investigations for nearly two centuries, the study of mountain origin still constitutes one of the most fascinating and challenging problems of geology. Of the many modern concepts that have been advanced to account for mountain building, those dealing with continental drift, island arcs, convection currents, and phase changes have been selected for brief consideration in this chapter. As of now, most geologists will agree that no one theory has satisfactorily accounted for mountain building. One geologist or group of geologists may feel that one certain theory more adequately explains mountain origin than another, but geologists from a different school of thought may give considerable preference to an opposing theory, at the same time conceding that neither theory gives a full and complete answer to the problem. One eminent geologist, in writing about the upbuilding of folded mountains, once referred to their formation as " an utterly mysterious process."

In coping with the problems of the origin of mountains, the greatest unknown under any theory is the ultimate origin of the motivating force or forces. Even in the case of volcanic mountains, caused by the build-up of volcanic ejecta and lava, a process that is readily observable, the questions might be asked, What is the force that triggered and carried on the volcanic activity? Did the forces originate in the crust, or in the mantle, or in the earth's core? To answer such questions, there are theories or hypotheses, but as yet no final answers have been attained.

Also it should be remembered that many statements in geology that are commonly considered as " factual" may contain an element of inference, i.e., the " facts " are true only if other supporting ideas are true, and the latter may be based upon a conclusion that has not been, or cannot be, proved. The objectives of a scientific study, however, include not only the

481

description of a certain natural phenomenon, but also its explanation. After a theory or hypothesis has been devised to explain some natural phenomenon, it may at a later date be proved, at least in part, to be in error. Nevertheless a theory serves a useful purpose even if it does no more than to challenge another investigator to devise methods to test its validity. The development and testing of theories or hypotheses constitute a fundamental method in the study and advancement of science.

Before considering some modern mountain-building theories, reference material concerning the earth's interior will be reviewed.

THE INTERIOR OF THE EARTH

As long ago as 1873 James D. Dana proposed that the core of the earth might be composed of iron and nickel. This conclusion of Dana's was arrived at from a study of meteorites. Dana also believed that the deep interior of the earth was in a molten condition. Modern-day seismological evidence indicates the earth's core has very little rigidity. This evidence is based upon the fact that secondary (transverse) earthquake waves are not known to pass through the earth's core. Since fluids are nonrigid and do not transmit transverse earthquake waves, it is commonly assumed that the earth's core is in a liquid state. There is some evidence, though controversial, to suggest that the core of the earth is really a core within a core, and that the inner core might be composed of solid substances surrounded by an outer core in the liquid state (Fig. 36-1).

The inner mantle or "pallasite" layer, as indicated by density calculations and the behavior of earthquake waves, may be a mixture of basic minerals and metallic iron, presumably in a solid state. The propagation of earthquake waves indicates the outer mantle also is solid. This zone is commonly referred to as the "peridotite" zone, and may be a layer predominantly of olivine. This mineral has specific gravity and elastic properties comparable to the properties of the outer mantle. Because olivine contains an abundance of the metallic elements magnesium (abbreviated Ma, although its chemical symbol is Mg) and iron (Fe), the outer mantle sometimes is referred to as the *mafe* zone.

The contact between the mantle and crust is the Mohorovičić discontinuity (or M discontinuity). This seismic discontinuity might be described as marking the base of the crust. Seismic data indicate that the crust has an average thickness of approximately 22 miles under the continents and is divided into three layers, the upper two of which may be partially discontinuous (Fig. 36-2, page 484). The thickness of the crust under ocean floors is thought to be much less, probably not over three or four miles (Fig. 36-3, page 484). The inner layer of the crust is described as the basaltic substratum. Seismically it corresponds to basalt in the speed with which it propagates earthquake waves. Other evidences also

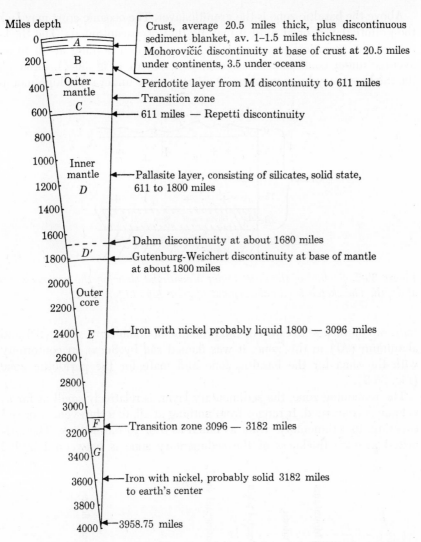

Miles depth

Crust, average 20.5 miles thick, plus discontinuous sediment blanket, av. 1–1.5 miles thickness.
Mohorovičić discontinuity at base of crust at 20.5 miles under continents, 3.5 under oceans

Peridotite layer from M discontinuity to 611 miles
Transition zone
611 miles — Repetti discontinuity

Pallasite layer, consisting of silicates, solid state, 611 to 1800 miles

Dahm discontinuity at about 1680 miles
Gutenburg-Weichert discontinuity at base of mantle at about 1800 miles

Iron with nickel probably liquid 1800 — 3096 miles

Transition zone 3096 — 3182 miles

Iron with nickel, probably solid 3182 miles to earth's center

3958.75 miles

Figure 36-1. *A sector from surface to center of the earth showing the principal zones with thicknesses, inferred from the behavior of earthquake waves and other geophysical data. Scale of thickness in the crustal portion is greatly exaggerated. See Figure 36-2 for an enlargement of the crustal zone A under the continents.*

indicate the presence of widespread basalt within the earth's crust at comparatively shallow depths. Edward Suess, a European geologist, referred to this zone as the *sima* because the probable predominant chemical constituents of the rock are silica (Si) and magnesium (abbreviated Ma). Seismic data indicate that locally the basaltic layer may be thin or discontinuous.

Above the basaltic zone is the granitic layer. The oceanic crust may lack the granitic layer, or at most it may be thin or discontinuous. The thickness of the granitic layer is variable, ranging from nothing at all to an average under continents of some 17 or 18 miles (Fig. 36-2), although the thickness may be as much as 30 miles or more under some high moun-

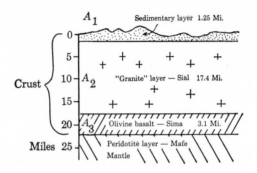

Figure 36-2. *Section of the crust under a continent showing the various zones at depth. The sketch is an enlargement of zone A in Figure 36-1.*

tains or continents. Because of the probable abundance of silica (Si) and aluminum (Al) in this zone, it was named *sial* by Suess, in conformity with the sima for the basaltic zone and mafe for the peridotite zone (Fig. 36-3).

The remaining zone, the sedimentary layer, is relatively small as far as volume is concerned. It ranges from nothing at all, to a thin veneer or soil covering, to sedimentary strata as much as 8 or 10 miles thick. The estimated average thickness of the sedimentary zone is between 1 and 2

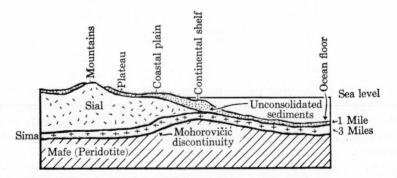

Figure 36-3. *Schematic cross section showing the edge of a continent, somewhat typical of middle eastern United States, and the adjacent ocean to the east, with the inferred layers of the crust. The Mohorovičić discontinuity marks the boundary between the crust and outer mantle.* (After Jacobs, Russell and Wilson, Physics and Geology, *by permission of McGraw-Hill Book Company, 1959.*)

miles, here listed at 1¼ miles (Fig. 36-2), and consists largely of accumulations of waste products of preexisting rocks.

THE THEORY OF CONTINENTAL DRIFT

One of the earliest theories of continental drift was that proposed by an American geologist, F. B. Taylor, and published in 1910.[1] Alfred Wegener, a German meteorologist apparently working independently, put forth his drift theory about 1912. The continental drift theory is commonly attributed to Wegener, apparently because Taylor postulated, as an explanation for the drift, that the moon was acquired by the earth in Cretaceous time. This would cause a sudden, great increase in tides, which in turn would increase the rate of rotation of the earth upon its axis. This part of Taylor's hypothesis was considered so weak that the whole hypothesis has been generally discarded. Although Wegener's hypothesis contained many of the same ideas as Taylor's, Wegener used a slightly different approach, and put forth a theory that has received wide popular acclaim, and still has numerous adherents, although the objections to Wegener's hypothesis are very extensive.

According to this theory the continents are blocks of sial, or light rock, literally floating upon a plastic substratum of denser rock, or sima. In early geologic time the continents were considered to have been a large, probably single, mass. Wegener called this large continent Pangaea. Beginning in late Paleozoic time, Pangaea, through the influence of tidal and centrifugal forces, was postulated to have broken and the fragments, which make up the present continents, were supposed to have drifted to their present positions. The separation was believed to have proceeded slowly at first, but to have speeded up somewhat as geological time progressed, until finally in the Quaternary, Labrador and Newfoundland supposedly separated from Europe, and Greenland was left as a separate block.

Examination of a globe or a world map (Fig. 36-4, page 486) will show that the apparent " fit " of the continents is rather impressive. However it has been pointed out that the conformity should be considered at the edge of the continental shelf, at some 400 to 600 feet in ocean depth, rather than at the present shoreline. The conformity is much less impressive for the edges of the continental shelves than for the present strand lines. Apparent conformity of the land masses on opposite sides of the Atlantic Ocean is much more impressive than along any other opposing shores.

Wegener thought the Andes and Rocky Mountains were formed as a result of continental movement of the Americas westward in response to tidal pull. In his view the folded and uplifted mountains resulted from

[1] Nearly a half century earlier Antonio Snider published the speculative idea that the lands on opposite sides of the Atlantic had once been joined and had drifted apart. But the idea had seemed so fantastic that it was not accepted and was apparently discarded until revived and made into a hypothesis by Taylor and Wegener.

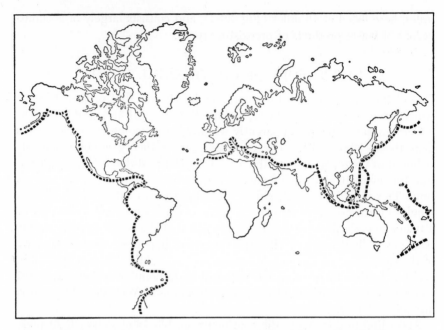

Figure 36-4. *Map showing approximate positions of the major island arc locations of the world.* (*Modified from Jacobs, Russell and Wilson,* Physics and Geology, *by permission of McGraw-Hill Book Company, 1959.*)

resistance or " drag " of the sialic mass against the substratum. According to the hypothesis the mountains were pushed up along the leading edge of the continental blocks. Along the rear sides of the moving blocks there should have been a tendency for a low, " drawing out " leaving such flat shores as the Atlantic coastal plain. Under this concept the island arcs of both the East Indies and West Indies and the mid-Atlantic ridge and other ocean-floor ridges might be considered remnants that failed to glide along with the main masses. As for the Alpine-Himalayan system, Wegener thought that crumpling took place when Europe and Asia moved southward in response to centrifugal force (the force that would require movement equatorward), and collision occurred with the Indian and African masses.

ISLAND–ARC OR MOUNTAIN–ARC THEORY

Much credit for the early work on this theory should go to Edward Suess, a Viennese professor of geology, who made his investigation about the turn of the century. Suess, working in the East Indies, noted that deep marine troughs occur on the convex side of island arcs. He believed that the troughs were characteristic accompaniments of the arc-shaped strings of mountainous islands, that the troughs and mountain arcs were of the same geologic age and represented early stages in mountain building. The two greatest belts where present-day, active mountain arcs occur lie along the margins of the western and northern Pacific and western Atlantic Oceans. These belts lie in the zones of greatest crustal instability, and are included in the world's most active regions of earthquakes and volcanoes (Fig. 36-4).

The island-arc theory largely recognizes a pattern that can be applied to most mountainous areas and to the interpretation of the major surface features of continents. In explaining his theory, Suess postulated the presence of an ancient land mass, which he called Angara Land (essentially the Angara Shield of Asia), which lay to the north and northwest of the present East Indies mountain arcs. Angara was probably an old and rigid land mass, the nucleus of the Asian continent, even before the Cambrian period. Then perhaps through crustal compression, early Asiatic mountains formed around the southern and eastern margins of the Angaran land mass. These were arc shaped, and were simply the first and innermost set of many similar mountain arcs to be uplifted after successive, long passages of time, each new set being formed farther and farther from the center of Angara, each encroaching more and more upon the sea, finally culminating in the great, off-shore island arcs of today. Under the theory these present-day arcs are considered to represent an early phase of mountain building and continuous progressive growth of the continents.

Today the arrangement of an ancient shield (representing the roots of old folded mountain belts), separated from the oceans by landforms, including folded mountains that are progressively younger toward the sea and culminating in off-shore island arcs, is commonly considered as a basic structural pattern of continents. In other words the continents under such a concept are deformed belts of the earth's crust, the ocean areas the undisturbed portion of the earth's crust. Walter H. Bucher, a perceptive student of the earth's crust, has made the statement ". . . it would seem incomprehensible to us that men should ever ask: ' How did the ocean basin come to be? ' Instead we might well be moved to ask: ' How did the continents come to be? ' "

Suess noted that an island arc region is typically made up of several parts: (1) beginning farthest seaward the first element is a deep trough on the convex side of the arc, which Suess called a " foredeep," (2) the next element is a belt of sedimentary deposits, commonly folded, and in the East Indies typically of Tertiary age; and (3) a ridge or series of ridges of progressively older rocks, commonly folded, and containing a zone (4) of volcanic activity, or the volcanic arc (Fig. 36-5). Suess noted that volcanoes never occur in the region of the foredeeps. These several parts, or elements, need not be complete in all island-arc localities, but whether or not the elements are complete, those that do occur are always in the relative order listed above.

Island and mountain arcs may be single or double. If double, the inner arc is the more prominent and commonly contains active volcanoes. A deep trench may mark the position where the outer arc would be expected, if such is not present. If an outer arc is present, it commonly consists of islands composed of sediments that have been folded and uplifted.

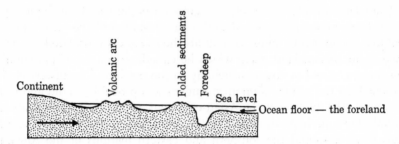

Figure 36-5. *Cross-sectional sketch showing the parts or elements of a typical island arc as described by Suess.*

Figure 36-5 shows the relationships of the island-arc elements as outlined by Suess, and Figure 36-6 indicates the elements of an active single island arc as conceived by some present-day investigators.

The primary arc of volcanic islands rising from fracture zones, and the parallel trough flanking the volcanic islands on the seaward side are the basic elements of an island-arc area. The volcanic islands may continue to

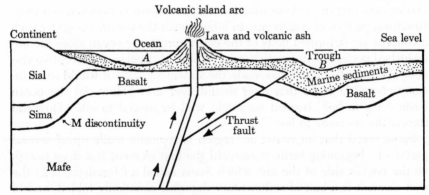

A — An area that may in later geological time be developed into
  secondary mountains.

B — An area that may be uplifted into a sedimentary arc
  as evolution of the island-arc region progresses.

Figure 36-6. *Schematic transverse section through a single island arc.* (Adapted from Jacobs, Russell and Wilson, Physics and Geology, *by permission of McGraw-Hill Book Company, 1959.*)

rise and for long periods of time contribute sediments to the trench as well as toward the mainland. However, the change from volcanic arc to elevated mountains with accompanying development of metamorphic features and formation of large batholiths of intrusive igneous rocks is shrouded with mystery. Again the source of the forces and the prevailing deep-seated conditions challenge some of the most active minds in geological research. A secondary mountain-arc system may form in the areas between the primary volcanic arc and the mainland. This secondary arc is curved in a direction opposite to that of the primary arc. In mountains derived from this arc, sedimentary rocks, commonly consisting of sediments derived from the volcanic arc mixed with materials eroded from the mainland, are compressed and thrust toward the continents. Again, the forces and deep seated conditions responsible for the folding and thrusting in these secondary mountainous areas are conjectural.

To some geologists contraction is the most likely motivating force in developing the primary volcanic arcs, the accompanying trenches, and the evolution of such structural features into mountainous areas. Other possible motivating forces include convection currents and phase changes, concepts to be discussed in the remainder of this chapter.

CONVECTION THEORY AND MOUNTAIN BUILDING

For the most part the convection theory, especially as related to mountain origin, is the product of the last two or three decades. However, the basic principles on which the convection theory is built are much older. For example, as long ago as 1838 thermal convection currents had been postulated to exist within the earth's substratum. W. Hopkins, in his "Researches in Physical Geology," a paper which was transmitted to the Royal Society of London in November 1838 and published in 1839, suggested conduction and convection currents as the two processes by which cooling of the earth takes place. If heat builds up deep within the earth through the action of radioactivity, and if conduction, which is effective principally near the surface, does not remove the heat rapidly enough, convection currents might be expected to form. Such currents would flow very slowly; they are commonly considered to move from a small fraction of an inch to perhaps 2 inches per year. Convection operates best in a large mass of low viscosity and low conductivity where temperature increase with depth is considerable.

Apparently European geologists were the first to postulate that mountain systems can be explained by the action of convection currents within the earth. Among the first to advocate mountain origin by means of convection currents was F. A. Vening Meinesz, a Dutch geodesist. His ideas were based on extensive studies of gravity anomalies, and his results were published in 1934. Vening Meinesz discovered that the island arc areas are zones of negative and positive gravity anomalies.[2] The strong anomalies lie just outside the island chain, and are flanked on both sides by irregular zones of less strong positive anomalies. The narrow zone of negative anomalies has been interpreted by some workers as due to a band of low density sialic material squeezed downward into more dense sima as a result of the movements of convection currents, thus creating a mass

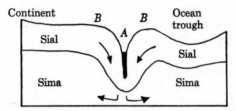

A — Position of strong negative anomalies (possible position for later development of folded sedimentary mountain arc).

B — Locations of positive anomalies.

Figure 36-7. *Section through a tectogene showing the relative positions of the areas of positive and negative gravity anomalies. (After H. H. Hess, " Proceedings, American Philosophical Society," Vol. 79, 1938.)*

deficiency in the earth's crust at that point. Such a crustal down-squeeze has been termed a tectogene (Fig. 36-7). The squeezing downward of the sediments conceivably could cause folding and faulting of the materials. After the convection currents ceased, the low density material should rise in response to isostasy, thus furnishing an explanation for uplift of the area.[3] The tectogene concept can be applied to geosynclinal regions as well as to island-arc areas.

The theory of convection currents was analyzed mathematically in 1935 by the geophysicist C. L. Pekeris. Pekeris showed that convection currents should be expected within the mantle of the earth if there was any radioactivity, and if the earth material has a low viscosity. Currents would be expected to occur whether the material was liquid or plastic. It is thought that in so far as possible the currents would have some symmetry in a regular pattern. Hence Pekeris postulated that the currents within the earth would have somewhat the form as that pictured in Figure 36-8.

Probably the best comprehensive article dealing with the theory was

[2] A deviation, either positive or negative, from the computed theoretical value for gravitational attraction, is termed an anomaly.

[3] According to another explanation, squeezing continues and the light materials at the position of the negative gravity anomaly (Fig. 36-7) are forced to rise, producing folded and overthrust mountains; such mountains make up a sedimentary mountain arc.

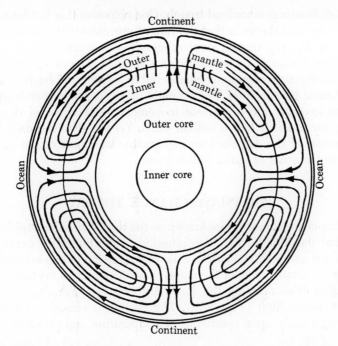

Figure 36-8. *Idealized sketch of convection currents in the earth's mantle, showing upward current direction under continents and downward direction under ocean basins. (Modified from Pekeris and Griggs, " American Journal of Science," Vol. 237, 1939.)*

published in 1939 by the American geophysicist, David Griggs. Griggs constructed models and performed exhaustive experiments. His results seemed to show that by postulating convection currents within the mantle of the earth it is possible to account for the origin and development of a geosyncline, followed by the folding of the geosynclinal prism into low mountains, perhaps as island arcs or mountain arcs such as the present West Indies and East Indies, and finally followed by regional unlift to result in ranges of high mountains. Some earth scientists are reasonably convinced that this very sequence of events can account for such ranges of mountains in the United States as the Appalachians and Rockies, and comparable ranges in other parts of the world.

In summary, convection is a mechanism by which heat is transferred through bodily movement, hot material moving toward a cooler region and losing heat as it moves, and cooler material taking the place of the hot. Convection currents are considered as occurring in pairs, a pair of currents making up a cell (Fig. 36-8). Convection currents might be used to explain the formation of island arcs or their uplift into mountain arcs, and might adequately serve as the motivating force in the uplift of folded mountains from a geosynclinal trough. One objection that has been raised to the convection theory is that the rate of movement usually assigned to these currents, even though slow, ranging perhaps from a fraction of an inch to two inches per year, calls for a span of time much too brief to agree with the time commonly considered to be required for the development of most geosynclines. For example, if an inch per year is assumed to be an average rate of current movement, 40,000 feet of depression could occur in about half a million years. Yet the time required for the development of the Appalachian geosyncline was most of the Paleozoic era, or on the order of half a billion years.

THE PHASE–CHANGE THEORY

The phase-change theory, also known as the theory of polymorphism, proposes that the Mohorovičić discontinuity, at the boundary between the earth's crust and mantle, marks a zone of conversion of one mineral to another by a rearrangement of the atoms to form a different crystalline structure, rather than marking the boundary between layers of completely different composition (Fig. 36-9). The change is considered reversible, depending mainly upon conditions of temperature and pressure.

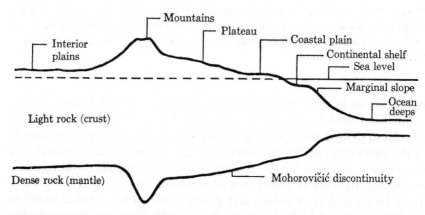

Figure 36-9. *Theoretical profile through a portion of the earth's crust showing the mirror images of the earth's major relief features as projections at the M discontinuity. Light rock material projects downward, thus depressing the M discontinuity under mountains. The reverse is true under major depressions.*

Three types of phase changes have been suggested that would seem to be able to accomplish large scale elevation or depression.

1. Alternate dehydration and hydration of hydrous and anhydrous minerals. For example, the alteration of olivine without water molecules in its molecular structure to serpentine with water of hydration involves a

volume increase of approximately 25 percent.[4] This increase is practically identical to the volume of water added.

2. Alternate melting and recrystallizing of the rock. This would involve volume changes of about 10 percent.

3. Other mineralogical alterations involving substances of the same chemical composition but very different mineralogical composition. As an example [5] of the third type of phase change, the rock eclogite having specific gravity of about 3.3 alters to basalt or gabbro with specific gravity of approximately 2.95. Eclogite and gabbro contain different minerals, but have practically identical chemical composition. The eclogite is the denser rock by about 10 percent. The type of rock at a particular depth limit would be most dependent upon temperature and pressure conditions.

Phase change has been used to explain the uplift of relatively low lands to mountainous heights. The uplift would be the result of the heating of the rocks near the M discontinuity a few degrees or tens of degrees. Upon heating, the phase-change boundary would migrate to greater depth. The dense rock below the discontinuity would invert to lighter rock and the increase in volume would lift the region to higher elevations, becoming mountainous if the heating near the discontinuity was sufficiently great.

Phase change also has been used to explain the development of a geosyncline. As the sediments are transported from high to lower levels, and as they are deposited in any available basin, the first effect of loading would be to increase the pressure at the base of the basin. With this new condition the discontinuity would move upward. As the trough continued to sink it would do so not only because of the increasing sediment load, but also because of the inversion of the light rock to a denser rock of smaller volume. Thus the effect of sediment deposition from a geologically short point of view would be one of sinking; but eventually heat would build up, perhaps from radioactivity in the sediments, coupled with their poor heat-conducting properties, and the sinking effect would tend to cease and uplift to begin. The M discontinuity would cease rising, would reverse and migrate downward. Thus the change in the rocks would be toward less density, with increase in volume, and consequently an uplift of the basin into mountains. Once the mountains were uplifted and erosional forces became active, the discontinuity might continue to migrate very slowly downward, changing the denser rock to light rock, thus keeping the roots supplied with light rock at about the same rate as the mountains were worn down. This process would explain the great age of mountain masses. It has been calculated that at the present rate of erosion, if there were no uplift, all land masses of the earth would be re-

---

[4] H. H. Hess, "Serpentines, Orogeny, and Epeirogeny," Special Paper 62, *Geol. Soc. Amer.*, a Symposium on "Crust of the Earth," A. Poldervaart, Editor (1955) pp. 391–408.

[5] George C. Kennedy, "The Origin of Continents, Mountain Ranges and Ocean Basins," *American Scientist* (1959) Vol. 47, pp. 491–504.

TABLE 36-1[6] COMPARATIVE

MOUNTAIN ORIGINS	CONTRACTION THEORY	GEOSYNCLINAL THEORY	THEORY OF ISOSTASY
Origin of motivating forces (known or postulated)	Force originates largely in the crust through cooling of the earth with consequent shrinkage.	Force once thought to be contractive due to a cooling earth, therefore would be mostly crustal in origin, and compressional. Some now postulate uplift of geosynclinal sediments into mountains to be due to phase change, or due to convection currents, or simply to be an isostatic response.	Force is due to an imbalance or a disturbance in the postulated equilibrium of various segments of the earth's crust.
Adequacy of the force to account for mountain upbuilding	Probably only partially adequate even if the earth *were* a cooling body.	Whatever the force, it has been adequate to elevate the world's greatest mountain masses, commonly conceded to have been of geosynclinal origin.	The forces, wherever and however they operate, have apparently maintained belts of mountains in various portions of the earth throughout decipherable geologic history.
Adequacy of the force to account for folding and/or faulting in elevated areas	Only partially adequate even if the earth *were* a cooling body.	Presumably adequate, and originates in the crust.	In so far as isostasy may be the underlying agency in geosynclinal development, the forces have been adequate to result in the presence of folded mountains.
Adequacy of the force to account for presence of regions of tension and/or compression	Accounts adequately for both the comparative abundance of compressional and scarcity of tensional regions.	Accounts for compression areas adequately; also comparative absence of tensional areas is compatible with the theory.	Accounts adequately for both tension and compression, depending upon whether the segment is rising or sinking.
Primary strong points relative to mountain upbuilding	Provides a logical explanation and adequately accounts for relative scarcity of tensional regions.	Most geologists recognize geosynclines and many consider it obvious that certain mountains originated from uplift and buckling of geosynclinal deposits.	All geologists recognize the existence of a "tendency for balance" even though the balance is imperfect.
Secondary strong points or advantages	Provides a relatively simple explanation for folded mountains, and would operate universally.	Tied with contraction theory provides a fairly simple explanation for folded mountains, though uncertainty must be admitted as to the ultimate "why" and "how."	Provides a ready explanation for the apparent permanence or very long life of land masses despite constant degradation.
Outstanding objections or weaknesses relative to mountain building	Cooling should be continuous, yet mountain building has been cyclic. Distribution of folded mountains does not conform to theory. Calculations of amount of contraction are much too small to account for observable amounts of folding. Horizontal force has acted mostly in one direction within a given range of mountains, but forces arising from cooling would act *equally* in *all* directions.	No agreement on motivating forces. Not known why sinking ceases and mountain uplift begins. Hall's original theory has been described as a "theory of mountains with the mountains left out." Not agreed that there are any typical geosynclines in the process of development anywhere in the world today.	How compensation is achieved is not known, but inferred. The "level" of compensation zone is inferred. Isostasy at best is imperfect, otherwise a peneplain could not form; also probably it is not operative over a small area.

[6] After DeSitter, *Structural Geology*, by permission of McGraw-Hill Book Company, New York, 1959.

CONTINENTAL DRIFT HYPOTHESIS	ISLAND-ARC THEORY	THEORY OF CONVECTION CURRENTS	THEORY OF PHASE CHANGE OR POLYMORPHISM
Forces may be centrifugal acting from pole toward equator and tidal acting westward in the body of the earth due to earth's rotation in an eastward direction on its axis. Forces would be mostly crustal.	Force has been explained as arising from convection currents in the uplifting of sediments into folded mountain arcs. But phase change, or compression through contraction, or operation of isostasy could also be invoked to explain the force.	Motivating force, located in the mantle below the crust, is considered due to both vertical and horizontal thermal gradients, the heat being supplied by radioactivity.	Force is assumed to be somewhere deep within the mantle, and is considered to be due to differences in the earth's temperature and pressure gradients.
Insufficient to account for major mountains, much less adequate to move continental blocks. One geophysicist has calculated the force to be only one millionth of that required for drift.	Probably adequate.	Presumably adequate but theoretically unproved.	Theoretically adequate.
Only partially adequate.	Adequate.	Adequate, but theoretically unproved.	Adequate — the major folds and faults associated with mountain ranges are assumed to be gravitational in origin, though accompanying lateral thrust or other origin is possible.
Theory provides for compression on the leading side and tension in the crust behind the moving block. Adequacy of compression is doubtful, tension inadequately provided for.	Adequately accounts for abundant compression and relatively little tension.	Accounts adequately for compression; absence of tensional regions left unexplained.	Scarcity of tensional regions not adequately explained under gravitational origin of folds and faults; areas of compression adequately explained.
Mountain building is not adequately accounted for.	Attractive in that it combines several problems of mountain building into a single problem. The pattern and arrangement of the world's mountains and their impressive regularity are easily explained.	Large currents, though inferred, are probable; readily explains mountain uplift and accounts adequately for intermittent nature of mountain building.	Phase change explains the long life of mountain regions. Logically explains the uplift of a basin after receiving a geosynclinal prism; explains approximately uniform heat flow from continental and oceanic areas. All phase changes are considered reversible.
Accounts for distribution of organisms, both modern and fossil; adequately explains the striking parallelism of opposite Atlantic shorelines.	Postulates a growing continent, associated with active volcanoes, and possessing gravity anomalies similar to mountain regions. Location of many major earthquakes.	Readily explains the possible formation of a tectogene; readily explains the patterns of distribution of continents and ocean basins needed to carry off heat of radioactivity generated within the earth.	The theory gives new emphasis to the contraction theory. The rocks on both sides of the M discontinuity may be the same; no chemical contrast necessary. No convection currents necessary to transport light material under the continents.
Forces inadequate to account for continental drift. Theory postulates a smooth ocean floor, now known to have great relief. If rocks of the ocean floor are weak enough to permit drift there could be no folding of advancing continents; if rocks of the ocean floor are stronger than those of the continents, there could be no drift. Recent very accurate longitudinal measurements fail to detect even the slightest residual drift.	Theory is incompatible with convection current theory which postulates permanency of continents. The mountains of the world do not lend themselves to as good an arrangement into inner primary and secondary arcs as the theory would require.	Presence of currents, though possible, is not proved — no direct evidence; in fact seismic data cast doubt upon the presence of large scale currents. Assumes permanency of continents which is incompatible with the island-arc postulate of growing continents. With rising currents under continents, the continental centers should be under tension, but there is no evidence of such.	Migration of the M-discontinuity theoretical — not proved.

duced to sea level in something like 25 million years or less. Yet there are geological evidences that there have been land masses continuously for hundreds of millions of years. The phase-change theory has been offered to account for uplift keeping pace with erosion.

Explaining the origin of mountains by the phase-change theory takes care of a weakness of the convection theory, i.e., accounting for the apparent transfer of millions of cubic miles of light rock, the sial, by means of transport by the currents, to keep the continents and mountain masses high above the level of the sima.[7]

What have been described by some investigators as serious objections to the application of the phase-change theory to the origin of mountains from geosynclinal deposits include (1) the fact that the forces are represented as acting mostly vertically, thus making folding and faulting on large scale difficult to explain [8] and (2) the difficulty of visualizing how the discontinuity could be migrating downward under the geosynclinal prism at the same time it was moving upward under the adjacent, rising sediment-source area, and how this opposing relationship could be maintained in close proximity over long periods of geologic time.

It has been stated that the phase-change theory gives new life to the contraction theory with its merits and without most of its weaknesses. The reason for this point of view is that contraction is easily visualized in a given region without a cooling earth. In fact the earth, overall, could be heating, yet through phase change, light rock could be altering to dense rock at the M discontinuity, with consequent contraction resulting in local subsidence.

NOTES ON THE TABLE ON MOUNTAIN ORIGINS

The data in the tabulation (Table 36-1, pages 494 and 495) are from a great many sources, and represent a summary of the results of the work of many different investigators upon the problems of mountain origin. Statements about the adequacy of forces to account for mountain building and about

---

[7] George C. Kennedy, " The Origin of Continents, Mountain Ranges and Ocean Basins," *American Scientist* (1959) Vol. 47, p. 502.

[8] Tectonic experimentation by a group of Russian tectonophysicists, and reported by V. V. Beloussov in the *Bulletin of the Geological Society of America* (1960) Vol. 71, indicates (page 1263) that "folding by general crumpling is a peculiar reaction of stratified masses of the Earth's crust to differential vertical movements of individual blocks. . . . The mechanism of folding by general crumpling is . . . by elongation of the layers with retention of the original area of their occurrence. It is in the stretching of the layers in the crests of rising blocks and in their flow from the elevated block to the relatively depressed rock that this elongation occurs.

" In all cases, the local causes of folding are connected with contrasting vertical movements of blocks of the Earth's crust — a situation peculiar to geosynclines. This is why folding by general crumpling centers in geosynclinal zones." If Beloussov and his associates are correct about the results of their experiments, this first objection not only largely disappears but even strengthens the phase-change theory as the explanation of the forces that provide the vertical differential movements.

the strong points and objections to the various theories most certainly will not meet the approval of all readers. Disagreements can be expected, as evidenced by literally opposing statements in the newest books and periodicals, put out by writers with different viewpoints. Such opposing viewpoints are inevitable since the writers were trained under different schools of thought and gained experience in different geological regions.

CONCLUSIONS REGARDING THE PROBLEM OF ORIGIN OF MOUNTAINS

After considering the principal theories of the origin of mountains and their structures, the conclusion must be reached that the ultimate answer that fits all circumstances regarding the problem has not been found. Some investigators favor one theory and others a different theory. Still others favor a composite theory, consisting of the best points from several existing theories; and finally there are some who favor the idea that one theory may best explain a particular range or ranges of mountains and another theory might well explain types of mountains that appear to be different. Thus, with this apparent confusion relative to mountain origin in mind, let us turn, in Chapter 37, to the method of multiple working hypotheses.

STUDY QUESTIONS

1. The man to whom credit is most commonly attributed for the naming of the sial zone is

   (1) Dana   (2) Hall   (3) Dutton   (4) Suess   (5) Mohorovičić.

2. Select the statement or statements consistent with Dana's ideas about the interior of the earth.
   a. The deep interior of the earth is in a molten state.
   b. Based on a study of earthquake waves, the earth's core has about the same rigidity as steel.
   c. The earth's core, being very dense and rigid, even though hot, readily transmits both transverse and longitudinal earthquake waves.
   The correct answer is

   (1) a   (2) b   (3) c   (4) a and b   (5) a and c.

3. One of the earliest investigators to suggest a causal connection between the folded mountains and the deep oceanic troughs in the West Indies region was

   (1) Wegener   (2) Dana   (3) Mohorovičić   (4) Suess
   (5) Vening Meinesz.

4. Match the following terms and statements.
   A. Tectogene   a. Ancestral land mass (Wegener).
   B. Pangaea   b. Shield area in Asia.

C. Angara   c. A crustal disturbance in which material of low density
                      may be squeezed downward into denser material.
The correct matching is

   (1) Aa, Bb, Cc   (2) Ac, Ba, Cb   (3) Ab, Bc, Ca   (4) Aa, Bc, Cb
   (5) Ac, Bb, Ca.

5. One of the most difficult parts of the problem of mountain origin is

   (1) the ultimate source of the force or forces necessary to trigger and
       carry on the mountain-making processes
   (2) deciding which theory is the correct one
   (3) arriving at the absolute age of the rocks making up the moun-
       tains
   (4) determining whether or not the original rocks making up the
       mountains were deposited on the sea floor
   (5) determining whether the mountains in question were original
       with the origin of the earth, or whether they were secondary.

6. Which of the following statements apply to the Mohorovičić discontinuity?
   a. It marks the boundary between the crust and the mantle of the earth.
   b. It lies under the continents at an average depth close to 22 miles, but
      is located at a much greater depth beneath the ocean floors.
   c. It most commonly occurs near the top of the sial where it was first dis-
      covered by deep drilling.
   The correct answer is

   (1) a and b   (2) b and c   (3) a and c   (4) a   (5) b.

7. Select the statement or statements consistent with the continental drift
   theory.
   a. The original single continent is postulated to have separated into frag-
      ments and floated apart, beginning in late Paleozoic time.
   b. The separation was relatively rapid at first, but has slowed to the
      present-day, imperceptibly slow rate of movement.
   c. The folded Appalachian mountains resulted from westward drift of
      the North American continent in response to the eastward rotation of
      the earth upon its axis.
   The correct answer is

   (1) a   (2) b   (3) c   (4) a, b, and c   (5) a and c.

8. An island-arc region is typically composed of several component parts.
   Beginning farthest seaward, these elements, if all present, occur in which
   of the following sequences?

   (1) Folded and arched sediments, foredeep, volcanic arc, continental
       mass.
   (2) Volcanic arc, islands of folded sediments, foredeep, continent.
   (3) Foreland, foredeep, folded sedimentary islands, ridges of older
       rock with possible volcanic activity, continental mass.
   (4) Volcanic arc, folded arc, foredeep, landmass.
   (5) Foredeep, foreland, volcanic arc, folded arc, continent.

9. Select the statement or statements consistent with the convection theory
   of mountain uplift.
   a. One convincing evidence of proof of the convection theory is the fact
      that the span of time for one cycle of currents from a hot to a cold re-
      gion is about the same as the time required for the development of a
      geosyncline.

b. Convection currents provide the only adequate explanation for the origin and occurrence of island arcs.

c. The heat required to carry on the movement of the convection currents is postulated to be provided by radioactivity.

The correct answer is

(1) a   (2) b   (3) c   (4) a, b, and c   (5) none.

10. Explaining mountain uplift in terms of the phase-change theory involves
   (1) transfer of light material toward the uplift and heavy material away from the uplift
   (2) changes in volume of the affected materials
   (3) the replacing of nonradioactive materials with materials containing radioactive elements
   (4) a cyclic uplift after a long period of subsidence
   (5) the inversion of light rock to heavy rock.

11. Which of the following might logically be considered a phase change?
   a. An anhydrous mineral taking on water of hydration.
   b. The alteration of a basic rock melt (magma) of medium density to one of greater density.
   c. The consolidation of sand grains into a compact sandstone.

   The correct answer is

   (1) a and b   (2) b and c   (3) a and c   (4) a, b, and c   (5) none.

12. Under the continental-drift theory, the Asiatic island arcs as well as those of the West Indies might logically be considered to be
   (1) crumpled masses pushed in front of the major continental block
   (2) batholithic masses that welled up as magma at places where the cracks in the original continental mass occurred
   (3) remnants of the original continental mass that failed to float along with the continental fragments
   (4) chains of volcanic mountains occurring along zones of weakness
   (5) remnants of old mountains that have been sinking since the drift began.

13. In the Appalachian Mountains the Piedmont Plateau is an area of old metamorphic rocks intruded in numerous areas by granite masses. The Valley and Ridge province of the Appalachians is characterized by sedimentary rocks that have been folded and thrust faulted toward the northwest. If it is assumed that the Appalachians at one time occupied the site of an island-arc area, which of the following choices correctly lists the portions of the island-arc area now occupied by the Piedmont Plateau and the Valley and Ridge province respectively?
   (1) Primary volcanic arcs and folded sedimentary islands.
   (2) Foredeep and foreland.
   (3) Ridges of older rock with possible volcanic activity and foredeep.
   (4) Continental mass and foredeep.
   (5) Primary volcanic arc and area between primary volcanic arc and continental mass.

14. Select the correct statements concerning the convection theory.
   a. The convection theory can be used to give a plausible explanation for negative gravity anomalies that occur in areas of deep sea trenches.
   b. The convection theory postulates no forces that might result in uplift of an area.

c. The convection theory can be utilized logically as an aid in explaining the origin of erosional surfaces throughout the Appalachians.

The correct answer is

(1) a and b   (2) b and c   (3) a and c   (4) a, b, and c
(5) none of the statements.

15. Which of the following best explains, under the phase-change theory, the great age of some mountain masses?

    (1) Radioactive disintegration is very slow.
    (2) The downward migration of the discontinuity between light and heavy rock, thus changing dense to light rock, keeps pace with the rate at which the mountains are worn down.
    (3) Individual mountain masses are not as old as they once were thought to be.
    (4) Phase change requires no mechanism of transport for the heavy material that buoys up the mountain mass.
    (5) Phase-change theory assumes (as does the theory of isostasy) that mountains rise more rapidly than they are worn down.

16. Assume that earthquake waves travel at a slower rate beneath mountains than at comparably deep levels in other regions. How could this phenomenon be explained in reference to Pratt's ideas and Airy's ideas on isostasy?

17. Suppose that gravity measurements indicated that basins within continental areas were lighter than should be and mountain ranges heavier than expected. Could such conditions be considered as evidence favoring continental drift or as data opposed to continental drift?

18. Would the conditions stated in Question 17 favor or disfavor the gross mechanical weight of sediments as causing subsidence?

19. What might the presence of positive anomalies over an area of the ocean floor indicate?

37

The Method of Multiple Working Hypotheses

● The situation which we have seen in the theories of mountain building is not uncommon in geology. Whole phalanxes of theories contend with one another. Each theory has its strong features and its strong partisans. Each theory has its weaknesses and its challengers. How then, does a scientist function in such a milieu? One great American geologist, T. C. Chamberlin, has revealed his intellectual processes in a paper written to aid students.

Chamberlin (Fig. 37-1) was born on a farm near Mattoon, Illinois, on September 25, 1843. The family moved to a farm near Beloit, Wisconsin, when he was three years old. His interest in things geological dates back to his early boyhood, when he collected and studied the fossils that could be found on and near his father's farm.

Chamberlin attended Beloit College in Wisconsin, and studied geology, as he said, to see if he could settle the question for himself as to whether or not the earth was created in October, 4004 B.C., as Archbishop Ussher, an Irish churchman, had determined from study of the Scriptures.

Upon completing school, he took an examination and received a teacher's certificate, having felt the desire to teach. He was appointed a high school principal. After two years he took a teaching position in natural sciences at Wisconsin State Normal School. At the age of 30 he was appointed professor of geology at Beloit College, and on the side became assistant state geologist of the newly organized Wisconsin Geological Survey. By 1877 he was made state geologist, and worked largely with Pleistocene glacial problems. His success in solving problems of the Pleistocene earned for him an appointment as director of the glacial division of the United States Geological Survey. In this work he mapped glacial moraines from Montana to the Atlantic coast. While in glacial work, he determined the glacioeolian origin of loess.

At age 43 he was appointed president of the University of Wisconsin. Actually, at the time (1886) the school was still a college, but shortly

Figure 37-1. *Thomas C. Chamberlin (1843–1928).*

thereafter it was made a university. Soon after becoming president, Chamberlin directed an extensive reorganization program. He strengthened the humanities, developed specialized schools in engineering, agriculture, and the sciences, and established a graduate school. He also reorganized the curriculum to provide a program of general education for the first two years, followed by specialization in a major of the student's own choosing during his last two years of undergraduate study.

Chamberlin held the presidency of the University of Wisconsin until 1892, and then resigned to become the first head of the department of geology at the University of Chicago, where he remained until he retired in 1918.

Chamberlin is probably best known for his planetesimal hypothesis of earth origin. He is also remembered as the founder of the *Journal of Geology*, a publication which has been issued continuously since about three months after his arrival on the campus of the University of Chicago.

Although Chamberlin's article, "The Method of Multiple Working Hypotheses," might be considered one of his short, minor works of lesser importance, nevertheless it contains advice that is pertinent and sound, and as useful today as it was in Chamberlin's day. The article was first given as a paper read before the Society of Western Naturalists in 1892. It was then published in a scientific periodical. The response to the talk and to the article was so great that it was deemed advisable to revise and republish the article. This was done as a "Studies for Students" article and it appeared in 1897 in Volume V of the *Journal of Geology*. In revising the article, Chamberlin made it most applicable and most closely related to the student of geological problems. However, his conclusions are applicable to any or all other branches of science.

The entire article follows.

THE METHOD OF MULTIPLE WORKING HYPOTHESES [1]
by T. C. Chamberlin

There are two fundamental modes of study. The one is an attempt to follow by close imitation the processes of previous thinkers and to acquire the results of their investigations by memorizing. It is study of a merely secondary, imitative, or acquisitive nature. In the other mode the effort is to think independently, or at least individually. It is primary or creative study. The endeavor is to discover new truth or to make a new combination of truth or at least to develop by one's own effort an individualized assemblage of truth. The endeavor is to think for one's self, whether the thinking lies wholly in the fields of previous thought or not. It is not necessary to this mode of study that the subject-matter should be new. Old material may be reworked. But it is essential that the process of thought and its results be individual and independent, not the mere following of previous lines of thought ending in predetermined results. The demonstration of a problem in Euclid precisely as laid down is an illustration of the former; the demonstration of the same proposition by a method of one's own or in a manner distinctively individual is an illustration of the latter, both lying entirely within the realm of the known and old.

Creative study however finds its largest application in those subjects in which, while much is known, more remains to be learned. The geological field is preeminently full of such subjects, indeed it presents few of any other class. There is probably no field of thought which is not sufficiently rich in such subjects to give full play to investigative modes of study.

Three phases of mental procedure have been prominent in the history of intellectual evolution thus far. What additional phases may be in store for us in the evolutions of the future it may not be prudent to attempt to forecast. These three phases may be styled the method of the ruling theory, the method of the working hypothesis, and the method of multiple working hypotheses.

In the earlier days of intellectual development the sphere of knowledge was limited and could be brought much more nearly than now within the compass of a single individual. As a natural result those who then assumed to be wise men, or aspired to be thought so, felt the need of knowing, or at least seeming to know, all that was known, as a justification of their claims. So also as a natural counterpart there grew up an expectancy on the part of the multitude that the wise and the learned would explain whatever new thing presented itself. Thus pride and ambition on the one side and expectancy on the other joined hands in developing the putative all-wise man whose knowledge boxed the compass and whose acumen found an explanation for every new puzzle which presented itself. Although the pretended compassing of the entire hori-

[1] *Journal of Geology* (1897) Vol. V, pp. 837–848.

zon of knowledge has long since become an abandoned affectation, it has left its representatives in certain intellectual predilections. As in the earlier days, so still, it is a too frequent habit to hastily conjure up an explanation for every new phenomenon that presents itself. Interpretation leaves its proper place at the end of the intellectual procession and rushes to the forefront. Too often a theory is promptly born and evidence hunted up to fit in afterward. Laudable as the effort at explanation is in its proper place, it is an almost certain source of confusion and error when it runs before a serious inquiry into the phenomenon itself. A strenuous endeavor to find out precisely what the phenomenon really is should take the lead and crowd back the question, commendable at a later stage, " How came this so? " First the full facts, then the interpretation thereof, is the normal order.

The habit of precipitate explanation leads rapidly on to the birth of general theories.* When once an explanation or special theory has been offered for a given phenomenon, self-consistency prompts to the offering of the same explanation or theory for like phenomena when they present themselves and there is soon developed a general theory explanatory of a large class of phenomena similar to the original one. In support of the general theory there may not be any further evidence or investigation than was involved in the first hasty conclusion. But the repetition of its application to new phenomena, though of the same kind, leads the mind insidiously into the delusion that the theory has been strengthened by additional facts. A thousand applications of the supposed principle of levity to the explanation of ascending bodies brought no increase of evidence that it was the true theory of the phenomena, but it doubtless created the impression in the minds of ancient physical philosophers that it did, for so many additional facts seemed to harmonize with it.

For a time these hastily born theories are likely to be held in a tentative way with some measure of candor or at least some self-illusion of candor. With this tentative spirit and measureable candor, the mind satisfies its moral sense and deceives itself with the thought that it is proceeding cautiously and impartially toward the goal of ultimate truth. It fails to recognize that no amount of provisional holding of a theory, no amount of application of the theory, so long as the study lacks in incisiveness and exhaustiveness, justifies an ultimate conviction. It is not the slowness with which conclusions are arrived at that should give satisfaction to the moral sense, but the precision, the completeness and the impartiality of the investigation.

It is in this tentative stage that the affections enter with their blinding influence. Love was long since discerned to be blind and what is true in the personal realm is measurably true in the intellectual realm. Important as the intellectual affections are as stimuli and as rewards, they are nevertheless dangerous factors in research. All too often they put under strain the integrity of the intellectual processes. The moment one has offered an original explanation for a phenomenon which seems satisfactory, that moment affection for his in-

---

* I use the term theory here instead of hypothesis because the latter is associated with a better controlled and more circumspect habit of the mind. This restrained habit leads to the use of the less assertive term hypothesis, while the mind in the habit here sketched more often believes itself to have reached the higher ground of a theory and more often employs the term theory. Historically also I believe the word theory was the term commonly used at the time this method was predominant.

tellectual child springs into existence, and as the explanation grows into a definite theory his parental affections cluster about his offspring and it grows more and more dear to him. While he persuades himself that he holds it still as tentative, it is none the less lovingly tentative and not impartially and indifferently tentative. So soon as this parental affection takes possession of the mind, there is apt to be a rapid passage to the unreserved adoption of the theory. There is then imminent danger of an unconscious selection and of a magnifying of the phenomena that fall into harmony with the theory and support it and an unconscious neglect of phenomena that fail of coincidence. The mind lingers with pleasure upon the facts that fall happily into the embrace of the theory, and feels a natural coldness toward those that assume a refractory attitude. Instinctively there is a special searching-out of phenomena that support it, for the mind is led by its desires. There springs up also unwittingly a pressing of the theory to make it fit the facts and a pressing of the facts to make them fit the theory. When these biasing tendencies set in, the mind rapidly degenerates into the partiality of paternalism. The search for facts, the observation of phenomena and their interpretation are all dominated by affection for the favored theory until it appears to its author or its advocate to have been overwhelmingly established. The theory then rapidly rises to a position of control in the processes of the mind and observation, induction and interpretation are guided by it. From an unduly favored child it readily grows to be a master and leads its author whithersoever it will. The subsequent history of that mind in respect to that theme is but the progressive dominance of a ruling idea. Briefly summed up, the evolution is this: a premature explanation passes first into a tentative theory, then into an adopted theory, and lastly into a ruling theory.

When this last stage has been reached, unless the theory happens perchance to be the true one, all hope of the best results is gone. To be sure truth may be brought forth by an investigator dominated by a false ruling idea. His very errors may indeed stimulate investigation on the part of others. But the condition is scarcely the less unfortunate.

As previously implied, the method of the ruling theory occupied a chief place during the infancy of investigation. It is an expression of a more or less infantile condition of the mind. I believe it is an accepted generalization that in the earlier stages of development the feelings and impulses are relatively stronger than in later stages.

Unfortunately the method did not wholly pass away with the infancy of investigation. It has lingered on, and reappears in not a few individual instances at the present time. It finds illustration in quarters where its dominance is quite unsuspected by those most concerned.

The defects of the method are obvious and its errors grave. If one were to name the central psychological fault, it might be stated as the admission of intellectual affection to the place that should be dominated by impartial, intellectual rectitude alone.

So long as intellectual interest dealt chiefly with the intangible, so long it was possible for this habit of thought to survive and to maintain its dominance, because the phenomena themselves, being largely subjective, were plastic in the hands of the ruling idea; but so soon as investigation turned itself earnestly to an inquiry into natural phenomena whose manifestations are tangible, whose properties are inflexible, and whose laws are rigorous, the defects of the method became manifest and effort at reformation ensued. The first great endeavor was repressive. The advocates of reform insisted that theorizing should be restrained and the simple determination of facts should take its place. The effort was to make scientific study statistical instead of causal. Because theorizing in narrow lines had led to manifest evils theorizing was to be condemned. The reformation urged was not the proper control and utilization of theoretical effort but its suppression. We do not need to go backward more than a very few decades to find ourselves in the midst of this attempted reformation. Its weakness lay in its narrowness and its restrictiveness. There is no nobler aspiration of the human intellect than the desire to compass the causes of things. The disposition to find explanations and to develop theories is laudable in itself. It is only its ill placed use and its abuse that are reprehensible. The vitality of study quickly disappears when the object sought is a mere collocation of unmeaning facts.

The inefficiency of this simply repressive reformation becoming apparent, improvement was sought in the method of the working hypothesis. This has been affirmed to be *the* scientific method. But it is rash to assume that any method is *the* method, at least that it is the ultimate method. The working hypothesis differs from the ruling theory in that it is used as a means of determining facts rather than as a proposition to be established. It has for its chief function the suggestion and guidance of lines of inquiry; the inquiry being made, not for the sake of the hypothesis, but for the sake of the facts and their elucidation. The hypothesis is a mode rather than an end. Under the ruling theory, the stimulus is directed to the finding of facts for the support of the theory. Under the working hypothesis, the facts are sought for the purpose of ultimate induction and demonstration, the hypothesis being but a means for the more ready development of facts and their relations.

It will be observed that the distinction is not such as to prevent a working hypothesis from gliding with the utmost ease into a ruling theory. Affection may as easily cling about a beloved intellectual child when named an hypothesis as if named a theory, and its establishment in the one guise may become a ruling passion very much as in the other. The historical antecedents and the moral atmosphere associated with the working hypothesis lend some good influence however toward the preservation of its integrity.

Conscientiously followed, the method of the working hypothesis is an incalculable advance upon the method of the ruling theory; but it has some serious defects. One of these takes concrete form, as just noted, in the ease with which the hypothesis becomes a controlling idea. To avoid this grave danger, the method of multiple working hypotheses is urged. It differs from the simple working hypothesis in that it distributes the effort and divides the affections. It is thus in some measure protected against the radical defect of the two other methods. In developing the multiple hypotheses, the effort is to bring up into view every rational explanation of the phenomenon in hand and to develop every tenable hypothesis relative to its nature, cause or origin, and to give to all of these as impartially as possible a working form and a due place in the investigation. The investigator thus becomes the parent of a family of hypotheses; and by his parental relations to all is morally forbidden to fasten his affections unduly upon any one. In the very nature of the case, the chief danger that springs from affection is counteracted. Where some of the hypotheses have been already proposed and used, while others are the investigator's own creation, a natural difficulty arises, but the right use of the method requires the impartial adoption of all alike into the working family. The investigator thus at the outset puts himself in cordial sympathy and in parental relations (of adoption, if not of authorship,) with every hypothesis that is at all applicable to the case under investigation. Having thus neutralized so far as may be the partialities of his emotional nature, he proceeds with a certain natural and enforced erectness of mental attitude to the inquiry, knowing well that some of his intellectual children (by birth or adoption) must needs perish before maturity, but yet with the hope that several of them may survive the ordeal of crucial research, since it often proves in the end that several agencies were conjoined in the production of the phenomena. Honors must often be divided between hypotheses. One of the superiorities of multiple hypotheses as a working mode lies just here. In following a single hypothesis the mind is biased by the presumptions of its method toward a single explanatory conception. But an adequate explanation often involves the coordination of several causes. This is especially true when the research deals with a class of complicated phenomena naturally associated, but not necessarily of the same origin and nature, as for example the Basement Complex or the Pleistocene drift. Several agencies may participate not only but their proportions and importance may vary from instance to instance in the same field. The true explanation is therefore necessarily complex, and the elements of the complex are constantly varying. Such distributive explanations of phenomena are especially contemplated and encouraged by the method of multiple hypotheses and constitute one of its chief merits. For many reasons we are prone to refer phenomena to a single cause. It naturally follows that when we find an effective agency present, we are predisposed to be satisfied therewith. We are thus easily led to stop short of full results, sometimes short of the chief factors. The factor we find may not even be the dominant one, much less the full complement of agencies engaged in the accomplishment of the total phenomena under inquiry. The mooted question of the origin of the Great Lake basins may serve as an illustration. Several hypotheses have been urged by as many different students of the problem as the cause of these great excavations. All of these have been pressed with great force and with an admirable array of facts. Up to a certain point we are compelled to go with each advocate. It is practically demonstrable that these basins were river valleys antecedent to the glacial incursion. It is equally demonstrable that there was a blocking up of outlets. We must conclude then that the present basins owe their origin in part to the preexistence of river valleys and to the blocking up of their outlets by drift. That there is a temptation to rest here, the history of the question shows. But on the other hand it is demonstrable that these basins were occupied by great lobes of ice and were important channels of glacial movement. The leeward drift shows much material derived from their bottoms. We cannot therefore refuse assent to the doctrine that the basins owe something to glacial excavation. Still again it has been urged that the earth's crust beneath these basins was flexed downward by the weight of the ice load and contracted by its low temperature and that the basins owe something to crustal deformation. This third cause tallies with certain features not readily explained by the others. And still it is doubtful whether all these combined constitute an adequate explanation of the phenomena. Certain it is, at least, that the measure of participation of each must be determined before a satisfactory elucidation can be reached. The full solution therefore involves not only the recognition of multiple participation but an estimate of the measure and mode of each participation. For this the simultaneous use of a full staff of working hypotheses is demanded. The method of the single working hypothesis or the predominant working hypothesis is incompetent.

In practice it is not always possible to give all hypotheses like places nor does the method contemplate precisely equable treatment. In forming specific plans for field, office or laboratory work it may often be necessary to follow the lines of inquiry suggested by some one hypothesis, rather than those of another. The favored hypothesis may derive some advantage therefrom or go to an earlier death as the case may be, but this is rather a matter of executive detail than of principle.

A special merit of the use of a full staff of hypotheses coordinately is that in the very nature of the case it invites thoroughness. The value of a working hypothesis lies largely in the significance it gives to phenomena which might otherwise be meaningless and in the new lines of inquiry which spring from the suggestions called forth by the significance thus disclosed. Facts that are trivial in themselves are brought forth into importance by the revelation of their bearings upon the hypothesis and the elucidation sought through the hypothesis. The phenomenal influence which the Darwinian hypothesis has exerted upon the investigations of the past two decades is a monumental illustration. But while a single working hypothesis may lead investigation very effectively along a given line, it may in that very fact invite the neglect of other lines equally important. Very many biologists would doubtless be disposed today to cite the hypothesis of natural selection, extraordinary as its influence for good has been, as an illustration of this. While inquiry is thus promoted in certain quarters, the lack of balance and completeness gives unsymmetrical and imperfect results. But if on the contrary all rational hypotheses bearing on a subject are worked coordinately, thoroughness, equipoise, and symmetry are the presumptive results in the very nature of the case.

In the use of the multiple method, the reaction of one hypothesis upon another tends to amplify the recognized scope of each. Every hypothesis is quite sure to call forth into clear recognition new or neglected aspects of the phenomena in its own interests, but oft times these are found to be important contributions to the full deployment of other hypotheses. The eloquent exposition of " prophetic " characters at the hands of Agassiz were profoundly suggestive and helpful in the explication of " undifferentiated " types in the hand of the evolutionary theory.

So also the mutual conflicts of hypotheses whet the discriminative edge of each. The keenness of the analytic process advocates the closeness of differentiating criteria, and the sharpness of discrimination is promoted by the coordinate working of several competitive hypotheses.

Fertility in processes is also a natural sequence. Each hypothesis suggests its own criteria, its own means of proof, its own method of developing the truth; and if a group of hypotheses encompass the subject on all sides, the total outcome of means and of methods is full and rich.

The loyal pursuit of the method for a period of years leads to certain distinctive habits of mind which deserve more than the passing notice which alone can be given them here. As a factor in education the disciplinary value of the method is one of prime importance. When faithfully followed for a sufficient time, it develops a mode of thought of its own kind which may be designated the habit of parallel thought, or of complex thought. It is contra-distinguished from the linear order of thought which is necessarily cultivated in language and mathematics because their modes are linear and successive. The procedure is complex and largely simultaneously complex. The mind appears to become possessed of the power of simultaneous vision from different points of view. The power of viewing phenomena analytically and synthetically at the same time appears to be gained. It is not altogether unlike the intellectual procedure in the study of a landscape. From every quarter of the broad area of the land-scape there come into the mind myriads of lines of potential intelligence which are received and coordinated simultaneously producing a complex impression which is recorded and studied directly in its complexity. If the landscape is to be delineated in language it must be taken part by part in linear succession.

Over against the great value of this power of thinking in complexes there is an unavoidable disadvantage. No good thing is without its drawbacks. It is obvious upon studious consideration that a complex or parallel method of thought cannot be rendered into verbal expression directly and immediately as it takes place. We cannot put into words more than a single line of thought at the same time, and even in that the order of expression must be conformed to the idiosyncrasies of the language. Moreover the rate must be incalcula-bly slower than the mental process. When the habit of complex or parallel thought is not highly developed there is usually a leading line of thought to which the others are subordinate. Following this leading line the difficulty of expression does not rise to serious proportions. But when the method of si-multaneous mental action along different lines is so highly developed that the thoughts running in different channels are nearly equivalent, there is an obvi-ous embarrassment in making a selection for verbal expression and there arises a disinclination to make the attempt. Furthermore the impossibility of express-ing the mental operation in words leads to their disuse in the silent processes of thought and hence words and thoughts lose that close association which they are accustomed to maintain with those whose silent as well as spoken thoughts predominantly run in linear verbal courses. There is therefore a certain predis-position on the part of the practitioner of this method to taciturnity. The rem-edy obviously lies in coordinate literary work.

An infelicity also seems to attend the use of the method with young stu-dents. It is far easier, and apparently in general more interesting, for those of limited training and maturity to accept a simple interpretation or a single theory and to give it wide application, than to recognize several concurrent factors and to evaluate these as the true elucidation often requires. Recalling again for illustration the problem of the Great Lake basins, it is more to the immature taste to be taught that these were scooped out by the mighty power of the great glaciers than to be urged to conceive of three or more great agen-cies working successively in part and simultaneously in part and to endeavor to estimate the fraction of the total results which was accomplished by each of these agencies. The complex and the quantitative do not fascinate the young student as they do the veteran investigator.

The studies of the geologist are peculiarly complex. It is rare that his problem is a simple unitary phenomenon explicable by a single simple cause. Even when it happens to be so in a given instance, or at a given stage of work, the subject is quite sure, if pursued broadly, to grade into some complication or undergo some transition. He must therefore ever be on the alert for mutations and for the insidious entrance of new factors. If therefore there are any advantages in any field in being armed with a full panoply of working hypotheses and in habitually employing them, it is doubtless the field of the geologist.

A striking example of the deleterious effects of a ruling theory is Aristotelianism. Galileo's Simplicio was typical of the Aristotelian Scholastic. He had received from his Master a complete and comprehensive system of his world, its contents, and its mutual interactions. Any phenomenon of the actual world was judiciously pruned or stretched to fit the prescribed system. It was necessary to break these walls if science was to grow. Galileo was one of the first leaders of the assault, to his personal harm but to his undying fame.

Since the downfall of Aristotelianism, our theoretical systems are no longer all-embracing but are limited to domains. The present-day intellectual structures are a patchwork of many theories, often mutually contradictory. As Chamberlin warns, a continuing danger to the healthy growth of science is the undue affection which we sometimes bestow upon a particular theory. One example we have noted is the dualistic theory of Berzelius which was influential in preventing the adoption of the ideas of Avogadro for nearly fifty years. Moreover, there are examples in more recent days of investigators who either consciously or unconsciously selected their data to fit a beloved theory, only later to forfeit their professional standing. The temper of modern science is that any experiment must be repeatable by any competent scientist anywhere and at any time. The scientific conclusion must stand independently of both man and apparatus.

One of the most fruitful methods of science has been that of the working hypothesis. This appears to have been Newton's method in arriving at his law of universal gravitation. Starting with hints of Copernicus and Kepler that the organizing force in the solar system lies within the sun, this force is assumed to be centripetal. Newton then finds that such a force is consistent with orbital motions which satisfy Kepler's second law of equal areas in equal times, and that, moreover, the orbit is a conic section lying within a plane which includes the attracting body at one focus. What is the nature of this attracting force? Newton first turned his attention to the force that must be acting on the moon to cause it to leave its linear path and circle about the earth. A tentative working hypothesis was then formulated that the same force which causes the apple to fall extends out to the orbit of the moon, decreasing inversely as the square of the distance from the center of the earth. A comparison of the distances fallen in a given time by the moon and the apple indicated the soundness of the hypothesis, and the dichotomy of celestial and terrestrial mechanics was finally destroyed. Newton next turned his attention to the satellites of Jupiter and Saturn and to the motions of the planets about the sun. Since in all of these cases Kepler's third law describes the orbits of the satellites and planets, the orbiting bodies behave as if attracted by forces varying inversely as the squares of their distances from the central bodies about which they revolve. Thus, the working hypothesis was further strengthened. Finally, using the second and third laws of motion, Newton showed the attractive force must be proportional to the masses of both objects between which the force was operative, and he proposed his universal law of gravitation — that any two bodies attract each other with a force proportional to the product of the two masses and inversely proportional to the square of the distance between them. Thus a reading of the *Principia* suggests that Newton began with the working hypothesis that some sort of attracting force accounts for the planetary motions. The theoretical and observational consequences of the simplest hypothesis suggested a more detailed hypothesis, which, after testing, led to a still more detailed theory, and so on until the precise statement of the final law.

The fundamental requirement for the method of working hypotheses is a complete and impartial objectivity. One popularly thinks of the ideal scientist as being coldly impersonal in his reasoning. But this is a more or less rare human trait. It is entirely too easy to fall in love with one's own brain children and dangerously favor them. It is for this reason, among others, that Chamberlin commends the method of multiple working hypotheses to his students.

Nevertheless, there appears to be a fundamental difference between the laboratory sciences such as physics and chemistry and the predominately observational sciences like astronomy and geology. It is characteristic that all physicists accept and use Newton's laws of mechanics within their known limitations while it seems at times that two geologists can hardly agree on the most basic mechanisms of the earth. Why should this be? Controversy also initially exists in the laboratory sciences as illustrated by the many different ideas which were held by the chemists about the atomic constitution of substances. But after Cannizzaro's work the chemists of the world generally accepted a common theory and turned their minds to other matters.

Part of the difficulty may be that geology is a comparatively young science. The diversity in geological thought is quite suggestive of the similar variety in chemical outlook in 1700 or in physical views in 1600. And part of the trouble lies purely in the nature of the sciences. Physics and chemistry are investigated by means of controlled experiments performed in the laboratory where all factors except the one being studied can be carefully controlled. Moreover the experiment is repeated until the investigator is satisfied that he has consistent conclusions. The geologist, on the other hand, often cannot experiment or cannot duplicate natural conditions to proper scale in the laboratory. If he is interested in volcanoes, he cannot trigger them off at his will, but can only wait for an eruption which he must then hurry to study. Moreover, he cannot see the really important part of the volcano which lies two to twenty or more miles below the surface. He can only spin a web of conjectures to explain the superficial features that he sees.

Moreover, geology is complex. Chamberlin points out that three different mechanisms were probably at work simultaneously in the formation of the Great Lakes. The wise investigator must keep all possibilities in mind while thinking about geological processes. Thus some men see the mechanism of mountain building as a combination of geosynclines, isostasy, island arcs, and phase change. Others view it as some other synthesis of other theories. Chamberlin's advice of objectivity and multiple working hypotheses seems to make very good sense in geology.

What is the situation in another observational science, such as astronomy? The man who is interested in supernovas cannot explode these stars as he wishes. As with the volcanologist he can observe such events only when they occur. He receives light only from the superficial surface of the star and can only make conjectures as to the all-important internal mechanism. Thus the two observational sciences share some similarities such as multiple working hypotheses, controversy, and contending theories. But in astronomy there seem to be fewer contending theories, a greater number of astronomers who share a common viewpoint, and a tendency for the controversies to ebb and finally to be replaced with a single widely accepted theory. The differences between the two observational sciences might be explained by the greater maturity of astronomy and also perhaps by its greater apparent simplicity! The physical situation in the interior of a star may well be simpler than the physical and chemical situations in the layered earth.

The most productive astronomer, as well as geologist, is generally the more mature investigator with a wide and intimate knowledge, not only of his special field, but of many related fields. He weaves a single theory which integrates the apparently most diverse parts of astronomy. The type of reasoning in modern astronomy is not the linear order of thought which works so well in mathematics and mathematical physics, but a reasoning which moves from the widest possible diversity of observations to a single integrating theory. Moreover, a great deal of statistical reasoning is found in astronomy. This science is concerned with large collections of objects: clusters of stars, galaxies of stars, and clusters of galaxies. Often conclusions cannot be reached from a single measurement, but only from the statistics of tens of thousands of measurements. Thus we draw our conclusions about the structure of our own galaxy from the statistics of thousands upon thousands of stars in ordered classes. Thus it is seen why, due to the differing natures of the laboratory and observational sciences, young men in their twenties such as Newton often reach their pinnacle of achievement in the former, while the great advances in the observational sciences are usually made by older men such as Hutton and Copernicus.

Each area of the physical sciences seems to have its own working methods which fit it best. Thus there is not *one* scientific method but *many*. We can only echo P. W. Bridgman and define the scientific method as simply doing the best that we can do with that with which we have to work.

STUDY QUESTIONS

1. Which one of the following items concerning T. C. Chamberlin is *incorrect?*
   (1) He was born in Illinois but moved to Wisconsin with his father's family at an early age.
   (2) He attended Beloit College in Wisconsin and was later professor of geology at the same school.
   (3) He held several high positions, including state geologist of Wisconsin, president of the University of Wisconsin, director of the glacial division of USGS, and head of the geology department at the University of Chicago.
   (4) He was author of the idea that great glaciers had once spread down across the United States and had scoured out the Great Lake basins.
   (5) He was one of the founders and advocates of a university program of general education.

2. While Chamberlin was working for the United States Geological Survey, he did considerable work on the loess deposits of the upper Mississippi River valley. He determined that much of the loess is
   (1) glacial in origin, but transported and deposited by wind (glacioeolian)
   (2) glaciofluvial in origin   (3) alluvial   (4) lacustrine
   (5) a sedimentary deposit of marine origin.

3. Three phases of mental procedure have been prominent in the history of intellectual evolution, up to the present century, according to Chamberlin. Which of the following are the three phases mentioned by Chamberlin?
   a. The wise-men phase — when a few individuals knew everything, or presumably everything there was to be known.
   b. The method of the ruling theory.
   c. The method of the working hypothesis.
   d. The method of multiple working hypotheses.
   e. The method of the adopted theory.
   f. The method of the tentative theory.
   g. The method of snap judgment or premature explanation.
   The three phases are

   (1) a, b, and c   (2) b, c, and d   (3) c, d, and e   (4) d, e, and f
   (5) e, f, and g.

4. Of the two fundamental modes of study which Chamberlin mentioned, one is an acquisitive or imitative mode — that of pure memorizing. The second mode of study is

    (1) scanning   (2) abstracting   (3) listening to lectures and taking notes

    (4) creative thinking — discovering new truths in either new or old material

    (5) to choose a ruling theory, and discard all extraneous data.

5. Which of the following is *inconsistent* with Chamberlin's statements concerning the development of a ruling theory?

    (1) First the full facts, then the interpretation thereof, is the normal order.

    (2) A premature explanation passes into a tentative theory.

    (3) A tentative theory passes into an adopted theory.

    (4) An adopted theory evolves into a ruling theory.

    (5) Most ruling theories evolve into natural laws.

6. According to Chamberlin's explanation, the principal psychological fault in explaining certain natural phenomena on the basis of a ruling theory is

    (1) that of intellectual affection — i.e., a scientist is commonly prone to explain all related phenomena in terms of his favorite ruling theory

    (2) the fact that a ruling theory excludes the possibility of dual explanations

    (3) the fact that a ruling theory is too indefinite

    (4) the fact that a ruling theory is too subjective

    (5) the fact that a ruling theory fosters a lack of intellectual curiosity.

7. Creative study finds its largest application in those subjects in which

    (1) a great deal remains to be discovered beyond what is already known

    (2) problems can all be solved by laboratory methods

    (3) about everything possible to be determined about such subjects has already been discovered

    (4) books alone are necessary — laboratory supplies are not needed

    (5) the whole outdoors is the field of investigation.

8. The chief function of the working hypothesis, according to Chamberlin, is the

    (1) suggestion and guidance of a procedure designed for the determination of facts

    (2) stating of known facts

    (3) organization of postulates into an orderly sequence

    (4) prominence it gives the scientist who originates it

    (5) solution of a difficult, intangible problem.

9. The method of multiple working hypotheses differs from the simple working hypothesis according to Chamberlin, in

    (1) numbers only ("hypothesis" is singular, "hypotheses" is plural)

    (2) that the multiple method tends to treat all tenable and relevant hypotheses impartially

(3) that the method of multiple working hypotheses is more complex, and generally the more complex means the more nearly correct
(4) degree of perfection, or completion, as far as explaining the facts are concerned
(5) subject matter, principally.

10. The working hypothesis differs from the ruling theory in that the working hypothesis is

(1) shorter and easier to state
(2) more factual and contains fewer scientific "guesses"
(3) closer to becoming a natural law
(4) more nearly the ultimate scientific method
(5) a means of determining facts rather than establishing a postulate.

11. Which of the following were named by Chamberlin as merits, or advantages to be gained, through the use of multiple working hypotheses?
a. Thoroughness.
b. Promotes mental discipline.
c. Promotes a sense of balance in any line of scientific investigation.
The correct answer is

(1) a   (2) b   (3) c   (4) a, b, and c   (5) none.

12. Chamberlin has compared the author or founder of multiple working hypotheses to

(1) the writer of several different kinds of novels
(2) the parent of a family of several members
(3) a scientist who is not sure how to interpret the results of an involved experiment
(4) a person who attacks a problem in the middle and works toward either end
(5) a very methodical person — one who "leaves no stone unturned."

13. Chamberlin wrote that it must be concluded that the present basins of the Great Lakes owe their origin in part to

(1) underground solution of the underlying limestones
(2) the former existence of pre-Pleistocene lake basins in the same general area
(3) the preexistence of river valleys and the blocking of their outlets by glacial drift
(4) the presence of nonresistant rocks, where the basins are located, surrounded by the hard, resistant rocks of the Canadian Shield
(5) the operation of the principle of isostasy.

14. Which of the following were named by Chamberlin as unavoidable disadvantages of the method of multiple working hypotheses?
a. Dims the perspective.
b. Too many "blind alleys."
c. A tendency to elevate one line of thought to which the others are subordinate.
The correct answer is

(1) a   (2) b   (3) c   (4) a, b, and c   (5) none.

15. Since Chamberlin had been a school principal, a college professor and head of a university department, in addition to being a university president, he

knew students very well. Regarding student preferences he made the observation that " the complex and the quantitative do not fascinate the young student as they do the veteran investigator." To illustrate his point, that beginning students preferred simple generalizations over factual details of a geological problem, he referred to the

(1) problem of dolomitization   (2) problem of the Great Lake basins

(3) problem surrounding the disappearance of the dinosaurs

(4) problem concerning the origin of the earth

(5) problem of the cause (or causes) of recurring periods of glaciation.

16. Chamberlin's belief in the method of multiple working hypotheses came about as a result of

(1) his study of multiple origins of loess and glacial drift

(2) his efforts to devise an explanation for the origin of the earth

(3) his recognition that the Great Lakes basins originated through more than one cause

(4) the effort of three of his colleagues to explain the multiple causes of recurring continental glaciation

(5) his determination to end, once and for all, all controversy in earth sciences.

17. Of Chamberlin's many contributions to the geological sciences, he is probably best known for his

(1) planetesimal hypothesis of earth origin

(2) reorganization of the graduate school program at the University of Wisconsin

(3) method of multiple working hypotheses

(4) determination of the glacioeolian origin of loess

(5) success in solving glacial problems of the Pleistocene epoch.

PART SEVEN

THE NATURE OF ELECTRICAL CHARGE

By the middle of the 19th century the atomic nature of matter had been fairly well established, although another half century was to elapse before it would be universally accepted. There had also been some thought given to the possibility that electricity, too, might be corpuscular in nature. Probably one of the first to speculate along these lines was Benjamin Franklin who, about the middle of the 18th century, wrote that electrical matter consists of extremely subtile particles which can permeate all matter with comparative ease.

Faraday's work in electrolysis in the forepart of the 19th century pointed toward a particle nature of electricity. Faraday found that the mass of any given element liberated at an electrode in an electrolytic cell was proportional to the quantity [1] of electricity that had passed through the cell. Thus since the number of atoms liberated was proportional to the quantity of electricity, did it not follow that a given quantity of electricity was associated with each atom and that this quantity was a particle of electricity? Helmholtz said in his Faraday lecture of 1881:

The most startling result of Faraday's law is perhaps this. If we accept the hypothesis that the elementary substances are composed of atoms, we cannot avoid concluding that electricity also, positive as well as negative, is divided into definite elementary portions, which behave like atoms of electricity.

---

[1] Faraday compared quantities of electricity by comparing the deflections of a crude galvanometer when the different quantities were discharged through the galvanometer in short intervals of time. He also used the fact that the steady deflection of the galvanometer caused by a steady current when multiplied by time was also a measure of quantity. Faraday's galvanometer was a magnetic needle pivoted at the center of a vertical coil of wire and free to turn in a horizontal plane. For steady currents through the coil, the amount of the steady deflection of the needle is dependent upon the magnitude of the current. For quick discharges of small quantities of charge through the coil, the maximum "throw" or deflection of the needle is also dependent upon the amount of charge.

517

Following the work of Cannizzaro which made possible the establishment of an unambiguous set of relative atomic weights, the next big advance in the study of the nature of matter was made in 1869 by the Russian chemist Mendelyeev and a year later by the German chemist Lothar Meyer, both of whom noted that if the various elements are listed in order

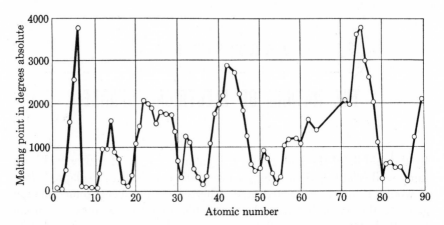

Figure VII-1. *The periodic properties of the elements as illustrated by a plot of atomic numbers versus melting points of the elements. The atomic number of an element is, in general, its position in a list of the elements arranged in order of increasing relative weights. Thus the atomic number of hydrogen is one and of uranium ninety-two.*

of increasing relative weight, elements having essentially the same properties are found periodically in the list (Fig. VII-1). Thus a table of elements, called the periodic table (Table VII-1), could be set up where those elements appearing in the same column or row had the same properties. This table has proved to be one of the most important generalizations in chemistry, and it allowed Mendelyeev to predict with accuracy the physical and chemical properties of specific unknown elements which were subsequently discovered years later.

The periodic table focused interest on the structures of the atoms themselves, since the recurring properties of the various elements seemed

Table VII-1 (opposite page). *Elements in the same column generally have similar properties. Thus the inert gases in the right column do not combine with other atoms and are said to have zero valance. Atoms in column VIIB (fluorine, chlorine, etc.) often exhibit a valence of −1 and thus combine 1 to 1 with atoms in column IA (hydrogen, lithium, etc.) which always have a valence of +1. Two atoms of fluorine (chlorine, etc.) often combine with one atom of an element in column IIA (beryllium, etc.) which always has a valence of +2. The discovery of the electron led to atomic models which gave meaning to these valences or combining abilities.*

Table VII-1. PERIODIC CLASSIFICATION OF THE ELEMENTS

Atomic weight values within parentheses are mass numbers of respective isotopes having longest life or special importance.

	IA	IIA	IIIA	IVA	VA	VIA	VIIA	VIII			IB	IIB	IIIB	IVB	VB	VIB	VIIB	0
1	1 H 1.0080																	2 He 4.003
2	3 Li 6.940	4 Be 9.013											5 B 10.82	6 C 12.011	7 N 14.008	8 O 16.000	9 F 19.00	10 Ne 20.183
3	11 Na 22.991	12 Mg 24.32											13 Al 26.98	14 Si 28.09	15 P 30.975	16 S 32.066	17 Cl 35.457	18 Ar 39.944
4	19 K 39.100	20 Ca 40.08	21 Sc 44.96	22 Ti 47.90	23 V 50.95	24 Cr 52.01	25 Mn 54.94	26 Fe 55.85	27 Co 58.94	28 Ni 58.71	29 Cu 63.54	30 Zn 65.38	31 Ga 69.72	32 Ge 72.60	33 As 74.91	34 Se 78.96	35 Br 79.916	36 Kr 83.8
5	37 Rb 85.48	38 Sr 87.63	39 Y 88.92	40 Zr 91.22	41 Nb 92.91	42 Mo 95.95	43 Tc (99)	44 Ru 101.1	45 Rh 102.91	46 Pd 106.4	47 Ag 107.880	48 Cd 112.41	49 In 114.82	50 Sn 118.70	51 Sb 121.76	52 Te 127.61	53 I 126.91	54 Xe 131.3
6	55 Cs 132.91	56 Ba 137.36	57* La 138.92	72 Hf 178.50	73 Ta 180.95	74 W 183.86	75 Re 186.22	76 Os 190.2	77 Ir 192.2	78 Pt 195.09	79 Au 197.0	80 Hg 200.61	81 Tl 204.39	82 Pb 207.21	83 Bi 209.00	84 Po 210.	85 At (211)	86 Rn 222.
7	87 Fr (223)	88 Ra 226.05	89** Ac 227.0															

Lanthanides:

58 Ce 140.13	59 Pr 140.92	60 Nd 144.27	61 Pm (145)	62 Sm 150.35	63 Eu 152.0	64 Gd 157.26	65 Tb 158.93	66 Dy 162.51	67 Ho 164.94	68 Er 167.27	69 Tm 168.94	70 Yb 173.04	71 Lu 174.99

Actinides:

90 Th 232.05	91 Pa 231.	92 U 238.07	93 Np (237)	94 Pu (239)	95 Am (243)	96 Cm (245)	97 Bk (249)	98 Cf (249)	99 Es (253)	100 Fm (254)	101 Md (256)	102 No (254)	103 Lw (257)

to indicate something repetitious in their structures. It was natural, as a result of the fact that all substances can be electrified by rubbing and of the phenomena of electrolysis, to assume that electrical charges could have something to do with this structure.

In spite of the fact that Faraday's laws had been published about forty years previously, it was not until 1881 that an attempt to evaluate the magnitude of the electrical particle from electrolytic data was reported by G. Johnstone Stoney of Dublin. The value he obtained was about the correct order of magnitude (about one-sixteenth the present value), the error being due at least in part to the fact that the number of atoms per gram of hydrogen was known only roughly at the time. This number was obtained by a crude approximation based on the kinetic theory of gases. This theory was built on a Newtonian mechanical picture which assumed a gas to be composed of elastic particles (molecules) moving with random velocities and exerting pressure by impacts against the walls of the container. To Stoney goes not only the honor of having made the first quantitative determination of the amount of charge associated with each atom but also of naming this charge the *electron*.

The corpuscular nature of electricity was firmly established in 1897 by Sir J. J. Thomson by studying the cathode rays in an evacuated electrical discharge tube. He found that these rays could be deflected in electric as well as magnetic fields, thus showing that electrical and magnetic forces acted on the particles. By applying the basic laws of mechanics proposed by Newton, in this case to subatomic particles instead of planets, Thomson and later Millikan were able to make measurements from which both the charge and mass of the individual corpuscles of electricity could be accurately determined.

38

Electric and Magnetic Fields

● The two similar, although for centuries apparently unrelated, phenomena of electricity and magnetism have been known from the time of the early Greeks. Thales is generally given credit for knowing that if a piece of amber was rubbed with a cloth it would attract light pieces of material such as chaff or pieces of straw and had become "electrified." It has since become known that any two substances when rubbed together, such as one's dry hair and a comb, one's clothing and plastic seat covers, or gasoline sloshing in the tank of a truck, become electrified. Thales also probably knew that certain chunks of iron ore, called lodestones, would exert forces on other lodestones or would attract pieces of iron. This was the phenomenon which is now called magnetism.

Little was done to explore the phenomena of electricity and magnetism until the English physician William Gilbert published his book in 1600, *On the Magnet, Magnetic Bodies, and the Great Magnet, the Earth.* He also discussed amber and its related effects, emphasizing the difference between electrification and magnetism. Concerning both he wrote,

Great has ever been the fame of the lodestone and of amber in the writings of the learned; many philosophers cite the lodestone and also amber whenever, in explaining mysteries, their minds become obfuscated and reason can no farther go.

EARLY EXPERIMENTATION WITH STATIC ELECTRICITY

In the latter part of the 17th century, the German Otto von Guericke made two interesting discoveries: he obtained an electrical spark and he found that electrical charges could exert forces of repulsion as well as attraction, thus indicating that there are two types of electrification and that like charges repel and unlike charges attract. In 1746 the Leyden jar (Fig. 38-1), which is a device for storing electrical charges, was discovered,

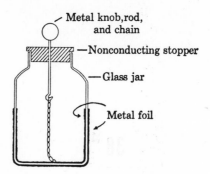

Figure 38-1. *Leyden jar for storing electrical charge. The inner and outer metal foils are given opposite charges.*

thus placing the means at hand for producing much stronger sparks and also electrical shocks. Experimentation with electricity, much of it of a spectacular and popular nature, became widespread both in Europe and the Colonies.

POSITIVE AND NEGATIVE CHARGES; THE ELECTROSCOPE

The nature of electricity was a matter of considerable discussion, some considering it to consist of two kinds of fluids, resinous and vitreous, while others, including Benjamin Franklin, thought it to be a single type of fluid and the two types of electrification to be due to a surplus or de-

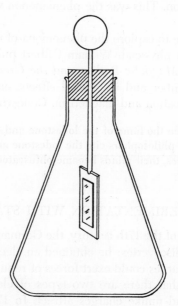

Figure 38-2. *Uncharged electroscope.*

ficiency of this one fluid. Our present terms of positive and negative charge are due to Franklin who associated the term positive with the " vitreous " charge obtained on glass when rubbed with silk. Then a negative or resinous charge is a charge that is the same as that obtained on hard rubber or amber when rubbed with wool. Franklin also demonstrated that the charge obtained from a lightning stroke is of the same nature as that obtained in the laboratory.

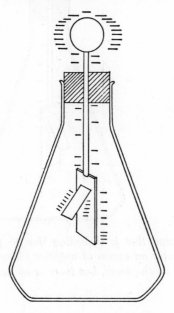

Figure 38-3. *Electroscope that has been charged by touching the knob with a negatively charged rod.*

In addition to the Leyden jar, another device which contributed to the study of electrical charges was the electroscope (Fig. 38-2). One kind of electroscope consists of a glass flask with a stopper made of an insulating material such as sulfur. A metal rod through the stopper has a metal ball on the top and a narrow metal plate at the bottom. Near the top of this metal plate a very thin strip of gold foil is attached. If a charged rod is touched to the knob of the electroscope, the loose end of the gold foil swings away from the metal plate due to the fact that part of the charge given the knob flows down the rod and divides between the metal plate and the foil. The repulsion of like charges causes the gold leaf to diverge (Fig. 38-3). A well-insulated electroscope will hold its charge for several hours. The electroscope need not be touched by the charged rod in order to get the gold leaf to diverge. For example, a negatively charged rod held near the knob will repel negative charges from the knob to the foil and plate which in turn repel each other. The knob would have an excess positive charge, but this distribution of charges would be maintained only so long as the negative rod is held near the knob (Fig. 38-4).

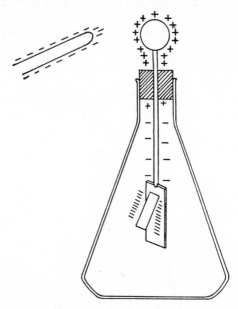

Figure 38-4. *Electroscope that is deflecting due to proximity of negatively charged rod. There is now an excess of negative charge on the leaf and plate and of positive charge on the knob, but there is no net charge on the electroscope.*

COULOMB'S LAW FOR ELECTROSTATIC CHARGES

The first successful attempt at placing the study of electricity on a quantitative basis was made by Charles Coulomb, a French engineer, in 1785. Coulomb designed a delicate torsion balance [1] with which he was able to show that two like charges repel each other (or unlike charges attract) with a force which is directly proportional to the magnitude of each charge and inversely proportional to the square of the distance between them, provided the charges are on small spheres.[2] Thus if the magnitudes of the charges are represented by q_1 and q_2 and the distance between their centers is d, the force F between them is

---

[1] This balance was similar to the one used by Cavendish for measuring gravitational forces. See Figure 22-1 and Shamos, *Great Experiments in Physics*, Holt-Dryden, New York, 1959, p. 73.

[2] Coulomb's experiments were chiefly concerned with establishing the inverse square law of force, and he seemed to take as self-evident the fact that the force was proportional to the magnitude of each charge. That he considered the force proportional to the charge is apparent from the fact that he measured and corrected for leakage of charge that occurred while he was taking measurements.

$$F \propto \frac{q_1 q_2}{d^2}.$$

This proportionality may be written as an equality by introducing a constant of proportionality A. Then Coulomb's law becomes

$$F = A \frac{q_1 q_2}{d^2}.$$

This equation is obviously of the same form as Newton's law of gravitation with the exception that gravitational forces are always attractive while electrical forces may be either attractive or repulsive. Since no unit of quantity of charge has been defined, the above equation may be simplified by arbitrarily setting $A = 1$ when the two charges are in vacuum (or, for practical purposes, in air) and using Coulomb's law for defining unit quantity. Consider two equal, like charges of such magnitude that when placed unit distance apart they repel each other with unit force. Then substituting in Coulomb's law

$$1 = 1 \frac{q \cdot q}{1^2}$$

from which

$$q^2 = 1$$

and

$$q = 1.$$

Thus unit charge may be defined as that charge which when placed unit distance from an equal like charge in vacuum, or air, will repel it with unit force. In defining unit charge in this way, the unit of distance usually taken is the centimeter and the unit of force the dyne. The unit of charge which is thus defined is called the centimeter-gram-second electrostatic unit of charge (abbreviated stat-coulomb). In practice this unit is found to be too small for practical purposes and a much larger unit, the coulomb, is equal to 3×10^9 stat-coulombs.

ELECTRIC FIELDS

Now since any charge q_1 exerts a force on any charge q_2 in the neighborhood of q_1, it is convenient to talk of the region around q_1 as an *electric field*.[3] The field strength will vary in general from point to point in both magnitude and direction and by definition is specified as the force that would be exerted on a unit positive test charge ($q_2 = 1$) placed at the point in question. Faraday carried this idea a little further and represented the electric field around a charge or charges by electric field lines which indicated both the directions and relative strengths of the field at various points. Thus the field around two equal and oppositely charged spheres

---

[3] In a similar manner, the region around a mass is often considered to be a gravitational field, and the pull which causes a body to fall toward the earth may be considered as due to the earth's gravitational field.

would be as shown (Fig. 38-5). The direction of the field lines is from the positive toward the negative sphere, since these are the directions of the forces on a small positive test charge released at various points near the positive sphere. The electric field strength X is greatest near either sphere where the field lines are closest together. The number of field lines is taken everywhere such that the number passing through unit area at

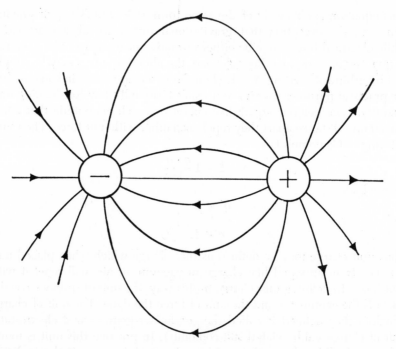

Figure 38-5. *The electric field lines about two equally and oppositely charged spheres.*

right angles to the field is numerically equal to the strength of the field at the position of the unit area. Thus a field strength of 10 at a given point would be represented by 10 lines passing through unit area.

The electric field between two oppositely charged parallel metal plates, called a condenser or capacitor, is also shown (Fig. 38-6). The opposite charges attract each other to the adjacent surfaces of the metal plates and the field is almost entirely limited to the region between the plates. (It is found that metals allow electrical charges to move with comparative ease and are thus called conductors, whereas the non-metals such as sulfur and many compounds such as bakelite do not allow an appreciable movement of charge and are called insulators.) In referring to the diagram of the field between the plates, it is seen that the lines are essentially parallel and hence the field is uniform, having the same strength and direction at various points. Thus if the force on a unit positive charge, the electric field strength, is designated by X, a test charge q placed anywhere between the plates would have a constant force F exerted on it, where

$$F = Xq.$$

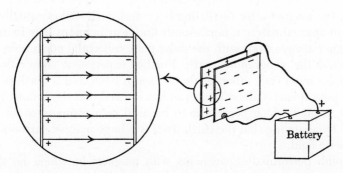

Figure 38-6. *The electric field between two closely-spaced parallel metal plates is essentially uniform except near the edges.*

POTENTIAL DIFFERENCE

If this constant force X exerted on a unit charge between the charged plates is multiplied by the distance d between the plates, the product is called the *potential difference,* or *voltage,* V between the plates.

$$V = Xd.$$

As work is defined as force multiplied by the distance through which the force moves, it is seen that potential difference is the work required to move a unit positive charge from the negative plate across to the positive plate. Usually the unit of work used in electricity is the joule, which is the work performed by a force of one newton [4] acting through a distance of one meter. The joule is equal to approximately three fourths of a foot-pound. The potential difference between two charged plates is thus said to be one volt if one joule of work is required to move one coulomb from one plate to the other against the opposition of the electric field. The one joule of energy is thus transferred to the charge.

COULOMB'S LAW FOR MAGNETIC POLES

Let us now return to a further consideration of magnetic effects. That an unmagnetized bar of iron [5] could be magnetized by putting the iron next to a lodestone and tapping the iron and that such a magnet could be suspended and used for navigational purposes were probably known before

[4] See footnote, p. 234.
[5] It should be noted that while any two substances can be electrified by rubbing, only three of the elements — iron, cobalt, and nickel — and some alloys show appreciable magnetic effects.

the 11th century. A magnetized iron bar or a lodestone, when dipped in iron filings, in general shows magnetic activity at two regions which are called poles. The poles of a bar magnet are usually at the ends. If a small bar magnet is suspended horizontally by a fine thread tied around the middle, the magnet after oscillating back and forth will eventually come to rest in approximately a north-south line. Furthermore it is found that the magnet always stops with the same pole, called the north pole, pointing toward the geographic north. Further experiment shows that two north poles repel each other, as do two south poles, but a north pole and a south pole attract. Gilbert's experiments showed that the action of a suspended magnet which permits it to be used as a compass could be explained by assuming that the earth itself is a huge magnet surrounded by a magnetic field.

Coulomb performed experiments with magnets in which he showed that *two magnetic poles of magnitudes p_1 and p_2 situated a distance d apart exerted forces on each other which were proportional to the strength of each pole and inversely proportional to the square of the distance,* provided the dimensions of the poles were small compared to the distance of separation.[6] Expressed as a proportionality, Coulomb's law for magnetic poles is

$$F \propto \frac{p_1 p_2}{d^2}.$$

This proportionality may be written in equation form as was done with Coulomb's law for electrostatic charges, the constant of proportionality again arbitrarily set equal to unity when the poles are in air, and the equation used for defining unit pole strength.

MAGNETIC FIELDS

As in the case of electrical charges, the region around a magnetic pole may be considered as being a *magnetic field* whose strength and direction at any point are given by the force on a unit north pole placed at the point. Again it is often convenient to represent this field geometrically by magnetic field lines. Thus the field in the neighborhood of a bar magnet is as shown (Fig. 38-7), with the field lines directed from the N pole toward the S pole and the strength of the field H the greatest near the poles where the lines are closest together.

---

[6] Here again Coulomb's experiments dealt principally with determining the manner in which the force between two given poles varied with the distance, and again he took it as self-evident that the force varied directly as the strength of each pole: "The magnetic fluid acts by attraction or repulsion in a ratio compounded directly of the density of the fluid and inversely of the square of the distance. . . . The first part of this proposition does not need to be proved." In performing the experiment, long thin magnets were used to minimize the effects of the poles on the opposite ends of the magnets, since isolated single poles are not known to exist.

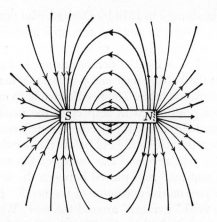

Figure 38-7. *The magnetic field lines about a bar magnet.*

Again suppose we have two magnetic pole faces that are flat and parallel, such as might be obtained by using a large ring-shaped magnet as shown (Fig. 38-8). Between the poles, a nearly uniform magnetic field of strength H would be directed from the N pole face toward the S pole face.

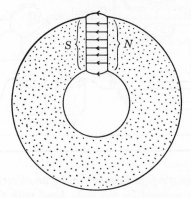

Figure 38-8. *The magnetic field between two closely-spaced parallel pole faces of a magnet is essentially uniform except near the edges.*

ELECTRIC CURRENTS AND MAGNETIC FIELDS

In spite of some similarities in behavior, no relationship was established between the phenomena of electricity and magnetism until Franklin showed that an electrical discharge could affect the magnetization of a magnet or an originally unmagnetized piece of iron. This indicated that *electrical charges in motion* in the discharge produced magnetic effects.

This finding was confirmed in 1819 by Oersted who demonstrated that an electrical current (charges in motion) sets up a magnetic field.

Oersted had been using a battery of voltaic cells in giving a demonstration before a class. Following the demonstration he held the wire carrying a current from the battery near and parallel to a magnetic needle that was on the demonstration table. The needle swung to one side. He moved the wire to various positions with respect to the needle and noted that when the wire was held above the needle the deflection was opposite to that produced when the wire was held below the needle. When the direction of the current was reversed the swing of the needle was also reversed. He noted that materials placed between the wire and the needle had no apparent effect on the deflection of the needle. His conclusion was that the magnetic field "gyrates" around the wire. We now say that the magnetic field lines encircle the wire. The direction of the field lines may be determined by grasping the wire with the right hand, thumb pointing in the direction of the current (direction in which positive charge would move). The fingers then encircle the wire in the direction of the magnetic field lines (Fig. 38-9).

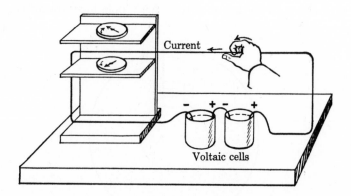

Figure 38-9. *The magnetic field lines set up by an electric current encircle the current. If the wire is grasped by the right hand with the thumb pointing in the direction of the current, the fingers encircle the wire in the same sense as the magnetic field lines.*

MAGNETIC FORCES ON MOVING CHARGES

Since a current or charges in motion set up a magnetic field, a magnetic pole in the neighborhood of a current should have a force exerted on it by the current, and by Newton's third law the current or charges in motion should be urged by an equal and opposite force due to the magnetic pole. The directions of these forces are indicated in the accompanying diagram (Fig. 38-10).

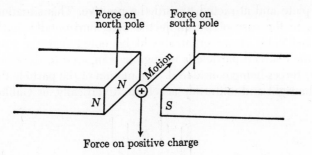

Figure 38-10. *The direction of the force exerted on a positively charged particle shot between the poles of a magnet.*

Subsequently it was shown that an electrical charge e moving with a velocity v at right angles across a magnetic field of strength H experienced a force which was proportional to the strength of the field H, the magnitude of the charge e, and the velocity v. Thus

$$F \propto Hev.$$

By expressing H and e in the so-called electromagnetic system of units, this may be written in equation form with the constant of proportionality equal to unity:

$$F = Hev.$$

This force on the charge e which is moving perpendicularly across the magnetic field is at right angles to its direction of motion and to the magnetic field.

PATHS OF CHARGED PARTICLES IN ELECTRIC AND MAGNETIC FIELDS

To anticipate the experiments described in the next two chapters, let us consider first a negatively charged particle e shot across an electric field between two parallel charged plates (Fig. 38-11). In order for the par-

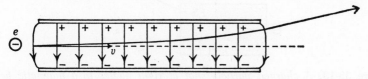

Figure 38-11. *The path of a charged particle shot across an electric field is parabolic.*

ticle to travel unimpeded, the air molecules between the plates must first be removed by a suitable vacuum pump system.

As the negatively charged particle enters the electric field, it will be urged in the opposite direction to the field, i.e., it will be repelled by the negative plate and attracted toward the positive. This situation is quite analogous to the case of the projectile fired horizontally in the earth's gravitational field. However, it should be noted that the gravitational force on the charged particle is negligible compared to the electrical (or magnetic) forces being considered. The motion of the particle then is uniform to the right and uniformly accelerated vertically, as Galileo demon-

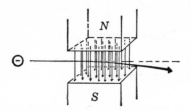

Figure 38-12. *The negative particle shot across the magnetic field is urged up out of the paper.*

strated for a projectile, and the path is parabolic. The vertical acceleration is due to a constant force

$$F = eX$$

where e is the charge on the particle and X is the strength of the electric field between the plates.

Let us next consider the motion of a charged particle as it moves across a magnetic field. If a negative particle is shot across an evacuated region between the poles of a magnet as shown (Fig. 38-12) in the direction of the dotted line, the particle is urged up out of the paper. The path can be better shown by imagining the south pole to be removed and looking into the magnetic field lines as they come out of the N pole face (Fig. 38-13). Since the force $F = Hev$ on the particle is perpendicular to the

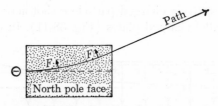

Figure 38-13. *A charged particle shot at right angles to a magnetic field is acted upon by a force which is at right angles to both the field and the velocity and the particle travels in the arc of a circle if the magnetic field is uniform.*

velocity v of the particle, as well as to H, this force is centripetal as defined by Newton, and the path of the particle as it travels across the magnetic field is the arc of a circle if the magnetic field is uniform.

Observation shows that the direction of the force on a charge moving across a magnetic field may be determined by applying an arbitrary left-hand rule. If the thumb and first two fingers of the left hand are all extended at right angles to each other, with the first finger pointing in the direction of the field, second (middle) finger pointing in the direction of a moving positive charge (the direction of the electrical current), then the thumb indicates the direction of the force on the charge. Note that in the case of a moving negative charge, the second finger is pointed in the opposite direction to the motion.

The foregoing principles concerning the motions of charged particles in electric and magnetic fields form the basis for the experiments discussed in the following two chapters.

STUDY QUESTIONS

1. According to Franklin's ideas concerning electrification,
   a. a neutral body contains no electricity
   b. a positively charged body contains more electrical fluid than a negatively charged body
   c. a negatively charged body has a deficiency of electrical fluid.
   The correct answer is

      (1) a   (2) b   (3) c   (4) b and c   (5) a, b, and c.

2. The first person to demonstrate a connection between electricity and magnetism was

      (1) Thales   (2) Coulomb   (3) Franklin   (4) Oersted
      (5) Gilbert.

3. It is found that a light cork ball covered with metal foil (originally uncharged) and suspended by an insulating silk thread is attracted toward a negatively charged rod. This attraction is explained as being due to the metal foil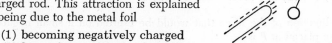
      (1) becoming negatively charged
      (2) becoming positively charged
      (3) being electrically neutral due to the fact it contains no electrical charges
      (4) being electrically neutral, but with a surplus of positive charge on the side near the rod
      (5) being electrically neutral, but with a surplus of negative charge on the side near the rod.

4. The suspended foil-covered cork ball in the previous problem is allowed to touch the charged rod.
      (1) The ball will cling to the charged rod.
      (2) After touching the rod, the ball will drop back to its original position hanging vertically from its support.

(3) The ball will drop away some from the rod, but will still be attracted toward it.

(4) The ball will continue to alternately drop away and then swing back and touch the rod.

(5) The ball will jump away from the rod and remain repelled from the rod so that it hangs on the opposite side of the vertical.

5. A suspended cork ball which has been allowed to touch a negatively charged rod will be
   a. attracted toward a hard rubber rod that has been rubbed with wool
   b. attracted toward a glass rod that has been rubbed with silk
   c. repelled from the silk with which the glass rod had been rubbed.
   The correct completion(s) is (are)

   (1) a   (2) b   (3) c   (4) a and c   (5) b and c.

6–7. Two equal and opposite electrical charges are placed as shown.

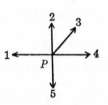

For problems 6–7.

6. The direction of the electric field at a point *P* equidistant from the two charges is

   (1) 1   (2) 2   (3) 3   (4) 4   (5) 5.

7. The direction of the force that would be exerted on a small negative test charge placed at *P* is

   (1) 1   (2) 2   (3) 3   (4) 4   (5) 5.

8–9. A bar magnet is placed as shown.

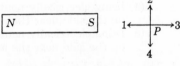

8. The direction of the magnetic field at a point *P* situated on the axis of the magnet is

   (1) 1   (2) 2   (3) 3   (4) 4   (5) none of the preceding.

9. The direction of the force exerted by the magnet on a small positively charged cork ball placed at the point *P* is

   (1) 1   (2) 2   (3) 3   (4) 4   (5) none of the preceding.

10. Assume a uniform magnetic field perpendicular to and into the plane of the paper as shown. A positively charged particle shot into the field as shown would

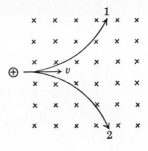

    (1) be bent along path 1
    (2) be bent along path 2
    (3) continue straight ahead along v
    (4) be bent up out of the paper toward you
    (5) be bent back into the paper away from you.

11. A small bar magnet is hung by a fine thread in a uniform magnetic field as shown (looking down). The suspended magnet which is free to move (either rotation or translation) will

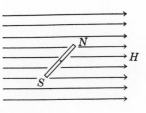

    (1) tend to move (translation) to the right
    (2) tend to move (translation) to the left
    (3) tend to set itself (rotation) parallel to the field
    (4) tend to set itself (rotation) at right angles to the field
    (5) not be affected by the field.

12. A positively charged particle is shot across a uniform electric field as shown. The particle will tend to

    (1) be bent along path 1
    (2) be bent along path 2
    (3) continue straight ahead along v
    (4) be bent up out of the paper toward you
    (5) be bent down into the paper away from you.

13. Point P_2 is twice as far as P_1 from the center of a positively charged sphere as shown. If the electric field strength at P_2 is 20, the electric field strength at P_1 is

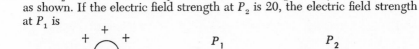

    (1) 10   (2) 20   (3) 40   (4) 80   (5) 5.

14–17. The potential difference between two electrically charged parallel metal plates is 100 volts. The plates are .02 meters apart.

14. The direction of the electric field at point P is

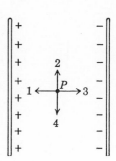

    (1) 1   (2) 2   (3) 3   (4) 4   (5) none of the preceding.

15. The direction of the magnetic field at point P is

    (1) 1   (2) 2   (3) 3   (4) 4   (5) none of the preceding.

16. The strength of the electric field at point P is in volts per meter (newtons per coulomb)

    (1) 50   (2) 2   (3) 5000   (4) 100   (5) 200.

17. The force in newtons that would be exerted on a negative charge of 1.6×10^{-19} coulombs placed at P would be

    (1) 8×10^{-18} to the right   (2) 8×10^{-18} to the left
    (3) 8×10^{-16} to the right   (4) 8×10^{-16} to the left
    (5) 1.6×10^{-17} to the left.

39

The Nature of Cathode Rays

● The line of attack which eventually proved most fruitful in determining the nature of electricity, whether particle or fluid, was a study of electrical discharges through gases. At ordinary pressures, air is an excellent insulator but if sufficiently high voltages are impressed between two electrodes, such as spheres, a spark discharge will result. The voltage required to produce a spark in air at atmospheric pressure is of the order of 30,000 volts per centimeter separation of the near points of the spheres.

The discharge may be studied under varying conditions by sealing electrodes into each end of a glass tube as shown in Figure 39-1. The

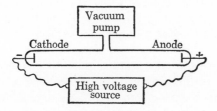

Figure 39-1. *A high voltage gaseous discharge tube. The pressure is reduced by means of the vacuum pump.*

discharge tube is connected to a vacuum pump, and a high voltage of several tens of thousands of volts is applied to the electrodes. As the pressure in the tube is reduced it is found that the voltage to cause a spark discharge is also reduced. The flickering, jagged spark becomes more diffuse (Fig. 39-2) as the pressure is reduced, and when the pressure has been lowered to the order of one hundredth of an atmosphere the gas within the tube glows with a light, called the positive column, whose color is dependent on the particular gas used. The tube under

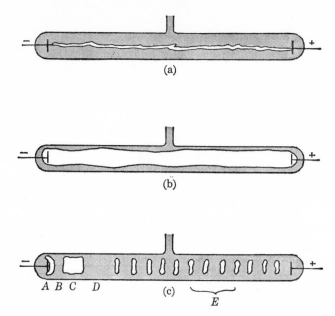

Figure 39-2. *Discharge tube. (a) As the pressure is reduced, a jagged spark occurs between the two electrodes. (b) At a pressure of about one-hundredth of an atmosphere, the spark has become the diffuse positive column, filling the tube. (c) At a pressure of about one-thousandth of an atmosphere, the positive column has receded from the cathode and broken up into disk-like striations E. The cathode is surrounded by the cathode glow A. The Crookes dark space B separates the cathode glow and the negative glow C, which in turn is separated from the striated positive column E by the poorly defined Faraday dark space D. Evacuation of the tube down to about one-hundred-thousandth of an atmosphere causes the Crookes dark space to fill the entire tube.*

these conditions is in the same state as the now common neon sign tube. As the pressure is further reduced the appearance of the tube changes, the positive column breaking into disk-like striations and receding from the cathode, and a clearly defined dark region known as the Crookes dark space extends out from the cathode. By the time the pressure has been reduced to a few thousandths of a millimeter of mercury, corresponding to about one hundred thousandth of an atmosphere, the luminosity of the gas within the tube has disappeared and the Crookes dark space fills the tube. At this stage the glass walls of the discharge tube fluoresce with a pale greenish light whose color is dependent on the nature of the glass.

The fluorescence of the glass was shown by Goldstein in 1876 and by Hittorf to be due to invisible rays, called *cathode rays*, traveling out from the cathode in straight lines, since an obstacle placed in the tube cast a shadow on the end of the tube away from the cathode (Fig. 39-3). It was further observed that the position of this shadow could be made to change by bringing a magnet near the tube. In 1878 Sir William Crookes reported in detail on experiments with discharge tubes.

There were two schools of thought concerning the nature of cathode rays. The English school considered the rays to be charged particles, while the German school considered them to be waves. The deflection of the rays in a magnetic field was considered by the English to be de-

Figure 39-3. *Crookes tube evacuated so that the Crookes dark space fills the entire tube and the glass walls of the tube fluoresce. A hinged mica cross causes a dark shadowlike cross to appear on the end of the tube when the mica is raised.*

cisive proof that the rays were beams of charged particles, but Hertz, who belonged to the German school of thought, explained the deflection as a secondary effect caused by the magnetization of the medium. Also Hertz reasoned that if the rays were charged particles they should also be deflected in an electric field. In an experiment he sent a beam of cathode rays between two charged plates but failed to detect any deflection. He also attempted to see if the rays carried an electrical charge by catching them in a metal cylinder connected to an electroscope, but again he got negative results. Another observation which was difficult to explain on the corpuscular theory was that cathode rays could be gotten out of the discharge tube through a thin but airtight aluminum window.

The arguments against the corpuscular nature of the rays were answered by the results of new experiments. Perrin in 1895 repeated the experiment performed by Hertz and succeeded in collecting a negative charge when a beam of cathode rays struck a metal cylinder. J. J. Thomson suspected that the failure of Hertz to note a deflection in an electric field was due to the fact that the tube Hertz was using was not sufficiently evacuated and that his negative results were due to the gas in the tube becoming an electrical conductor. Subsequent experiments by Thomson using a better vacuum showed his guess to be correct, for when his discharge tube was sufficiently evacuated he was able to measure the deflection caused when the cathode ray beam was shot between two electrically charged plates.

These then were essentially the known facts concerning electrical discharges at reduced pressures when J. J. Thomson reported in 1897 on his

Figure 39-4. *Joseph John Thomson (1856–1940).*

classic experiment on the nature of cathode rays which definitely established the corpuscular nature of electrical charge. The excerpt quoted here is not taken from his original report,[1] which contains considerable detail, but instead is taken from his book on *The Corpuscular Theory of Matter* published in 1907.

Joseph John Thomson (Fig. 39-4) was born near Manchester, England on December 18, 1856, the son of a bookseller who died while Joseph was in college. He entered Owens College in Manchester at the age of 14 and became interested in physics, where with half a dozen other students he worked under an excellent teacher in the physics laboratory in the attic. He published his first paper on electricity while at Owens and won a scholarship to Trinity College at Cambridge.

In mathematics he was very good but by no means a genius. However throughout his life he did mathematical work of merit. He became quite adept at mental calculations and on one occasion left a challenger with a slide rule "at the post." On the other hand, in the laboratory he was quite inadept with his hands and had a helper who performed the manipulation of the apparatus for him, but he was ingenious in designing experimental methods and seeing fruitful avenues of approach.

In 1883 at the age of 27 he was appointed lecturer at Trinity, and was also elected a Fellow of the Royal Society. The following year he was made professor of experimental physics at Cambridge and was placed

---

[1] J. J., Thomson, "Cathode Rays," *Philosophical Magazine* (1897) Vol. 44, Series 5, pp. 293 ff.

in charge of the Cavendish Laboratory which was a signal honor for a man of his age. During the next third of a century, graduate work at Cambridge was expanded and many important advances in physics and many outstanding physicists were developed in the Cavendish Laboratory.

Thomson was a dedicated teacher and gave excellent lectures to elementary students. In the laboratory he took personal interest in each student, whom he visited daily. In spite of his contact with students of superior intellect, he was fully as interested, especially in his later years, with those less generously endowed whom he felt had definite contributions to make to society. He minimized the efficacy of formal lectures in teaching, except for stimulating interest, and considered the most effective situation that of an intelligent teacher using unconventional methods with a small class. He also felt that the personal triumph of the student in the acquisition of knowledge was an essential factor in education. Although generally not a participant, he was keenly interested in sports and probably knew more team statistics, past and present, than anyone else on the campus.

In 1918 Thomson was made Master of Trinity College, but in spite of his broadened duties he maintained connections with the Cavendish Laboratory. He continued as Master until his death in 1940. His highly successful tenure in this position was due to his great intellectual eminence coupled with his all-embracing human interests.

Thomson had wide interests and abilities. He was always interested in plants and gardening and nearly missed a trip to the Franklin Institute in Philadelphia, where he was invited to give a series of talks, because he had not had time to make out his annual order for bulbs for his garden. In financial affairs, he was eminently successful and at his death left a sizable fortune which he had accumulated on the stock market.

Thomson's main contributions to science were his discovery of the elementary charge of electricity, the study of isotopes, and a proposed theory of the structure of the atom. During his lifetime he received over one hundred distinctions, including the Nobel prize in physics in 1906. Professor Bragg, a noted physicist, said of him: " He, more than any other man, was responsible for the fundamental change in outlook which distinguishes the physics of this [20th] century from that of the last."

THE CORPUSCULAR THEORY OF MATTER [2]
by J. J. Thomson

To return to the corpuscular theory. This theory, as I have said, supposes that the atom is made up of positive and negative electricity. A distinctive feature of this theory — the one from which it derives its name — is the peculiar way

[2] London, Archibald Constable & Co. Ltd., 1907, pp. 2–11.

in which the negative electricity occurs both in the atom and when free from matter. We suppose that the negative electricity always occurs as exceedingly fine particles called corpuscles, and that all these corpuscles, whenever they occur, are always of the same size and always carry the same quantity of electricity. Whatever may prove to be the constitution of the atom, we have direct experimental proof of the existence of these corpuscles, and I will begin the discussion of the corpuscular theory with a description of the discovery and properties of corpuscles.

Corpuscles in Vacuum Tubes.

The first place in which corpuscles were detected was a highly exhausted tube through which an electric discharge was passing. When I send an electric discharge through this highly exhausted tube you will notice that the sides of the tube glow with a vivid green phosphorescence. That this is due to something proceeding in straight lines from the cathode — the electrode where the negative electricity enters the tube — can be shown in the following way: the experiment is one made many years ago by Sir William Crookes. A Maltese cross made of thin mica is placed between the cathode and the walls of the tube. You will notice that when I send the discharge through the tube, the green phosphorescence does not now extend all over the end of the tube as it did in the tube without the cross. There is a well-defined cross in which there is no phosphorescence at the end of the tube; the mica cross has thrown a shadow on the tube, and the shape of the shadow proves that the phosphorescence is due to something, travelling from the cathode in straight lines, which is stopped by a thin plate of mica. The green phosphorescence is caused by cathode rays, and at one time there was a keen controversy as to the nature of these rays. Two views were prevalent, one, which was chiefly supported by English physicists, was that the rays are negatively electrified bodies shot off from the cathode with great velocity; the other view, which was held by the great majority of German physicists, was that the rays are some kind of ethereal vibrations or waves.

The arguments in favour of the rays being negatively charged particles are (1) that they are deflected by a magnet in just the same way as moving negatively electrified particles. We know that such particles when a magnet is placed near them are acted upon by a force whose direction is at right angles to the magnetic force, and also at right angles to the direction in which the particles are moving. Thus, if the particles are moving horizontally from east to west, and the magnetic force is horizontal and from north to south, the force acting on the negatively electrified particles will be vertical and downwards.

When the magnet is placed so that the magnetic force is along the direction in which the particle is moving the latter will not be affected by the magnet. By placing the magnet in suitable positions I can show you that the cathode particles move in the way indicated by the theory. The observations that can be made in lecture are necessarily very rough and incomplete; but I may add that elaborate and accurate measurements of the movement of cathode rays under magnetic forces have shown that in this respect the rays behave exactly as if they were moving electrified particles.

The next step made in the proof that the rays are negatively charged particles, was to show that when they are caught in a metal vessel they give up to it a charge of negative electricity. This was first done by Perrin. I have here a modification of his experiment [Fig. 39-5]. A is a metal cylinder with a hole in it. It is placed so as to be out of the way of the rays coming from C, unless they are deflected by a magnet, and is connected with an electroscope. You see that when the rays do not pass through the hole in the cylinder the electroscope does not receive a charge. I now, by means of a magnet, deflect the

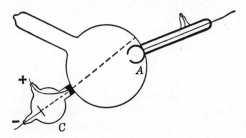

Figure 39-5. *Thomson's discharge tube for demonstrating that cathode rays carry a negative charge.*

rays so that they pass through the hole in the cylinder. You see by the divergence of the gold-leaves that the electroscope is charged, and on testing the sign of the charge we find that it is negative.

Deflection of the Rays by a Charged Body.

If the rays are charged wtih negative electricity they ought to be deflected by an electrified body as well as by a magnet. In the earlier experiments made on this point no such deflection was observed. The reason of this has been shown to be that when the cathode rays pass through a gas they make it a conductor of electricity, so that if there is any appreciable quantity of gas in the vessel through which the rays are passing, this gas will become a conductor of electricity, and the rays will be surrounded by a conductor which will screen them from the effects of electric force just as the metal covering of an electroscope screens off all external electric effects. By exhausting the vacuum tube until there was only an exceedingly small quantity of air left in to be made a conductor, I was able to get rid of this effect and to obtain the electric deflection of the cathode rays. The arrangement I used for this purpose is shown in Fig. 2 [Fig. 39-6]. The rays on their way through the tube pass between two parallel plates, A, B, which can be connected with the poles of a battery of storage cells. The pressure in the tube is very low. You will notice that the rays are very considerably deflected when I connect the plates with the poles of the battery, and that the direction of the deflection shows that the rays are negatively charged.

❀   ❀   ❀   ❀   ❀   ❀   ❀

We have seen that the cathode rays behave under every test that we have applied as if they are negatively electrified particles; we have seen that they

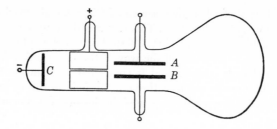

Figure 39-6. *Thomson's discharge tube for measuring the ratio of charge to mass of the cathode ray particles.*

carry a negative charge of electricity and are deflected by electric and magnetic forces just as negatively electrified particles would be.

Hertz showed, however, that the cathode particles possess another property which seemed inconsistent with the idea that they are particles of matter, for he found that they were able to penetrate very thin sheets of metal, for example, pieces of gold-leaf placed between them and the glass, and produce appreciable luminosity on the glass after doing so. The idea of particles as large as the molecules of a gas passing through a solid plate was a somewhat startling one in an age which knew not radium — which does project particles of this size through pieces of metal much thicker than gold-leaf — and this led me to investigate more closely the nature of the particles which form the cathode rays.

The principle of the method used is as follows: When a particle carrying a charge e is moving with the velocity v across the lines of force in a magnetic field, placed so that the lines of magnetic force are at right angles to the motion of the particle, then if H is the magnetic force, the moving particle will be acted on by a force equal to Hev. This force acts in the direction which is at right angles to the magnetic force and to the direction of motion of the particle, so that if the particle is moving horizontally as in the figure and the magnetic force is at right angles to the plane of the paper and towards the reader, then the negatively electrified particle will be acted on by a vertical and upward force. The pencil of rays will therefore be deflected upwards and with it the patch of green phosphorescence where it strikes the walls of the tube. Let now the two parallel plates A and B (Fig. 2) [Fig. 39-6] between which the pencil of rays is moving be charged with electricity so that the upper plate is negatively and the lower plate positively electrified, the cathode rays will be repelled from the upper plate with a force Xe where X is the electric force between the plates. Thus, if the plates are charged when the magnetic field is acting on the rays, the magnetic force will tend to send the rays upwards, while the charge on the plates will tend to send them downwards. We can adjust the electric and magnetic forces until they balance and the pencil of rays passes horizontally in a straight line between the plates, the green patch of phosphorescence being undisturbed. When this is the case, the force Hev due to the magnetic field is equal to Xe — the force due to the electric field — and we have

$$Hev = Xe$$

or

$$v = \frac{X}{H}$$

Thus, if we measure, as we can without difficulty, the values of X and H when the rays are not deflected, we can determine the value of v, the velocity of the particles. The velocity of the rays found in this way is very great; it varies largely with the pressure of the gas left in the tube. In a very highly exhausted tube it may be ⅓ the velocity of light or about 60,000 miles per second; in tubes not so highly exhausted it may not be more than 5,000 miles per second, but in all cases when the cathode rays are produced in tubes their velocity is much greater than the velocity of any other moving body with which we are acquainted. It is, for example, many thousand times the average velocity with which the molecules of hydrogen are moving at ordinary temperatures, or indeed at any temperature yet realised.

Determination of e/m.

Having found the velocity of the rays, let us in the preceding experiment take away the magnetic force and leave the rays to the action of the electric force alone. Then the particles forming the rays are acted upon by a constant vertical downward force and the problem is practically that of a bullet projected horizontally with a velocity v and falling under gravity. We know that in time t the body will fall a depth equal to $\frac{1}{2}at^2$ where a is the vertical acceleration; in our case the vertical acceleration is equal to Xe/m where m is the mass of the particle, the time it is falling is l/v where l is the length of path measured horizontally, and v the velocity of projection. Thus, the depth the particle has fallen when it reaches the glass, i.e., the downward displacement of the patch of phosphorescence where the rays strike the glass, is equal to [3]

$$\frac{1}{2} \frac{Xe}{m} \frac{l^2}{v^2}$$

We can easily measure d the distance the phosphorescent patch is lowered, and as we have found v and X and l are easily measured, we can find e/m from the equation:

$$\frac{e}{m} = \frac{2d\,v^2}{X\,l^2}$$

The results of the determinations of the values of e/m made by this method are very interesting, for it is found that however the cathode rays are produced we always get the same value of e/m for all the particles in the rays. We may, for example, by altering the shape of the discharge tube and the pressure of the gas in the tube, produce great changes in the velocity of the particles, but unless the velocity of the particles becomes so great that they are moving nearly as fast as light, when, as we shall see, other considerations have to be

[3] In deriving this relation, Thomson has assumed that the end of the glass tube (Fig. 39-6) where d is measured is at AB where the cathode rays emerge from between plates. The distance l is then the width of the plates. It is seen that after the cathode particles emerge from the electric field between the plates they will no longer be accelerated and will travel in a straight line.

taken into account, the value of e/m is constant. The value of e/m is not merely independent of the velocity. What is even more remarkable is that it is independent of the kind of electrodes we use and also of the kind of gas in the tube. The particles which form the cathode rays must come either from the gas in the tube or from the electrodes; we may, however, use any kind of substance we please for the electrodes and fill the tube with gas of any kind, and yet the value of e/m will remain unaltered.

This constant value is, when we measure e/m in the C. G. S. system of magnetic units, equal to about 1.7×10^7. If we compare this with the value of the ratio of the mass to the charge of electricity carried by any system previously known, we find that it is of quite a different order of magnitude. Before the cathode rays were investigated the charged atom of hydrogen met with in the electrolysis of liquids was the system which had the greatest known value for e/m, and in this case the value is only 10^4; hence for the corpuscle of the cathode rays the value of e/m is 1,700 times the value of the corresponding quantity for the charged hydrogen atom. This discrepancy must arise in one or other of two ways, either the mass of the corpuscle must be very small compared with that of the atom of hydrogen, which until quite recently was the smallest mass recognised in physics, or else the charge on the corpuscle must be very much greater than that on the hydrogen atom. Now it has been shown by a method which I shall shortly describe that the electric charge is practically the same in the two cases; hence we are driven to the conclusion that the mass of the corpuscle is only about 1/1700 of that of the hydrogen atom. Thus the atom is not the ultimate limit to the subdivision of matter; we may go further and get to the corpuscle, and at this stage the corpuscle is the same from whatever source it may be derived.

Corpuscles very widely distributed.

It is not only from what may be regarded as a somewhat artificial and sophisticated source, viz., cathode rays, that we can obtain corpuscles. When once they had been discovered it was found that they were of very general occurrence. They are given out by metals when raised to a red heat: you have already seen what a copious supply is given out by hot lime. Any substance when heated gives out corpuscles to some extent; indeed, we can detect the emission of them from some substances, such as rubidium and the alloy of sodium and potassium, even when they are cold; and it is perhaps allowable to suppose that there is some emission by all substances, though our instruments are not at present sufficiently delicate to detect it unless it is unusually large.

Corpuscles are also given out by metals and other bodies, but especially by the alkali metals, when these are exposed to light. They are being continually given out in large quantities, and with very great velocities by radio-active substances such as uranium and radium; they are produced in large quantities when salts are put into flames, and there is good reason to suppose that corpuscles reach us from the sun.

The corpuscle is thus very widely distributed, but wherever it is found it preserves its individuality, e/m being always equal to a certain constant value.

The corpuscle appears to form a part of all kinds of matter under the most diverse conditions; it seems natural, therefore, to regard it as one of the bricks of which atoms are built up.

In his study of cathode rays, Thomson had first thought that he was working with charged atoms, but a study of the deflections obtained in magnetic fields indicated that he was dealing with particles having a smaller mass than that of a hydrogen atom. Thus he was led to his most important discovery of a particle of matter smaller than any previously assumed to exist.

STUDY QUESTIONS

1. By the word " corpuscles," Thomson is referring to

    (1) electrons   (2) protons   (3) photons   (4) atoms   (5) at least two of the foregoing.

2. Which one of the following was not observed to be a source of corpuscles?

    (1) Heated lime.   (2) The negative electrode in a Crookes tube. (3) Heated metals. (4) Radioactive substances.   (5) The mica Maltese cross in a discharge tube.

3. From the data obtained in his experiment involving the deflection of cathode rays, Thomson was able to calculate
    a. the velocity of the rays
    b. the charge on one corpuscle
    c. the mass of one corpuscle.
    The correct answer is

    (1) a   (2) b   (3) c   (4) a and b   (5) a, b, and c.

4. In a Crookes tube,
    a. the cathode is connected to the negative terminal of the potential source
    b. free negative charges are repelled from the cathode
    c. the " phosphorescence" of the glass is caused by bombardment by cathode rays.
    The correct answer is

    (1) a   (2) b   (3) c   (4) a and b   (5) a, b, and c.

5. The experiment with the mica Maltese cross in the Crookes tube showed that
    a. cathode rays travel in straight lines
    b. cathode rays travel away from the cathode
    c. the greenish glow of the glass is due to the illumination of the glass by light from the cathode.
    The correct answer is

    (1) a   (2) b   (3) c   (4) a and b   (5) a, b, and c.

6. Thomson showed that cathode rays are negative charges of electricity by
    a. deflecting them in electric fields
    b. deflecting them in magnetic fields
    c. testing their charge with an electroscope.
    The correct answer is

    (1) a   (2) b   (3) c   (4) a and b   (5) a, b, and c.

7–9. *A negative particle is shot with a velocity v across a uniform electric field X between two charged plates as shown. The region between the plates is evacuated.*

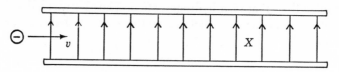

For problems 7–9.

7. The particle will be accelerated toward the
   a. top plate   b. bottom plate   c. right, in the direction of v.
   The correct answer is

   (1) a   (2) b   (3) c   (4) a and c   (5) b and c.

8. The path of the particle across the field will be

   (1) a parabola curving into the paper away from you
   (2) a parabola curving down toward the bottom plate
   (3) a parabola curving up toward the top plate
   (4) an arc of a circle curving up
   (5) an arc of a circle curving down.

9. In order to produce a deflection in the opposite direction to that caused by the electric field, the direction of a magnetic field would need to be

   (1) down, opposite to the electric field
   (2) up, the same direction as the electric field
   (3) perpendicular to the electric field and out of the paper toward you
   (4) perpendicular to the electric field and into the paper away from you
   (5) perpendicular to the electric field and to the right in the direction v.

10. A uniform magnetic field is perpendicular to the paper and directed out toward you. A negative particle is shot into the field in the direction v. As it moves in the field it will

    (1) take path 1   (2) take path 2   (3) continue in direction v
    (4) be bent out of the paper toward you
    (5) be bent into the paper away from you.

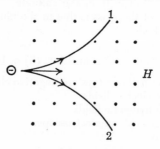

For problem 10.

11. A negative particle is shot between the poles of the magnet as shown in direction v. The force on the particle due to the magnetic field is in direction

    (1) 1   (2) 2   (3) 3   (4) 4   (5) v

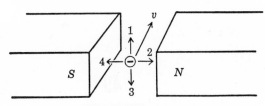

For problem 11.

12. In a Thomson tube (Fig. 39-6) the electric field between plates A and B and the crossed magnetic field are so adjusted that for a particular voltage applied between the cathode C and the adjacent anode, the cathode beam is undeflected. If the voltage between C and the anode is now doubled,
    a. the speed of the cathode rays is increased
    b. the beam will continue to be undeflected
    c. the force on the particles exerted by the electric field between A and B remains unchanged.
    The correct answer is

    (1) a   (2) b   (3) c   (4) a and c   (5) a, b, and c.

13. By comparing the value of e/m for a cathode corpuscle with that for a hydrogen ion, and using other data on their relative charges, Thomson concludes that
    a. both have the same ratio of charge to mass
    b. the charge of the hydrogen ion is about 1700 times that of a corpuscle
    c. the mass of the hydrogen ion is about 1700 times that of a corpuscle.
    The correct answer is

    (1) a   (2) b   (3) c   (4) a, b, and c   (5) none of them.

14. In comparing results for e/m for corpuscles obtained under various experimental conditions, Thomson found that
    a. the value of e/m was roughly proportional to the atomic weight of the cathode emitting the corpuscles
    b. approximately the same value of e/m was always obtained regardless of the source of the corpuscles
    c. all the corpuscles had the same charge, regardless of the source.
    The correct answer is

    (1) a   (2) b   (3) c   (4) a and c   (5) none of them.

15. A corpuscle is shot across a magnetic field. Discuss the effect on the radius of curvature of the path of increasing the velocity of the corpuscle.
16. A corpuscle is shot across an electric field. What effect does the velocity of the particle have on the force exerted by the field? On the curvature of the path?
17. Did Thomson's experiment prove that all cathode rays have the same charge?
18. Derive algebraically the equation given by Thomson for determining e/m.

40

The Charge of the Electron

● The so-called era of modern physics was ushered in during a six-year period at the end of the 19th century by four discoveries, one of which was Thomson's determination of the corpuscular nature of electricity. The others were the discoveries of x-rays in 1895 by Röntgen, of radioactivity in 1896 by Becquerel, and of the discontinuous (quantum) nature of atomic energy changes by Planck in 1900. It is interesting to note that the first three of these were related to experiments that were being carried on with the Crookes discharge tube.

Figure 40-1. *The cloud chamber is a cylindrically-shaped vessel covered on one end with a glass plate. When the piston inserted in the other end is suddenly moved outward, the moist air in the cylinder cools and becomes supersaturated. Water droplets then condense on any electrically charged ions in the cylinder.*

Thomson's experiments with cathode rays had given a numerical value for the ratio of charge to mass for the electron. Obviously the next step was to attempt to determine either the mass or the charge separately, and it was evident that it would necessarily be the charge. As previously noted, Stoney had attempted to make such a determination from electrolytic data. Thomson and others, taking advantage of the newly discovered cloud chamber (Fig. 40-1), made use of the fact that in a region super-

Figure 40-2. *Robert A. Millikan (1868–1953).*

saturated with water vapor, water droplets condense on electrically charged ions. Thus each water droplet carried an electrical charge. Attempts to determine the average charge on each droplet by measuring the total charge on a large known number of droplets was only partially successful.

In 1906, R. A. Millikan in attempting to improve on the cloud-droplet method of measuring the electronic charge, happened on the fact that instead of dealing with a cloud of droplets, where it was becoming apparent the droplets were not equally charged, he could make measurements on a single droplet. It further became obvious to him that he could change the charge on the droplet by one electron at a time. He was thus able to measure the individual charge of a single electron instead of dealing with a statistical average of many charges as was necessary with the cloud of droplets. Continued refinements in experimental method yielded in 1912 a value for the electronic charge e which, after certain corrections are made, is within about one-tenth of one percent of the presently accepted value. A description of this experiment is given in the quoted excerpt.

Robert A. Millikan (Fig. 40-2) was born in Morrison, Illinois in 1868, the son of a small town minister. In 1891 he graduated from Oberlin College, as eventually did his two brothers and three sisters. At the end of his sophomore year, his professor of Greek suggested he teach physics in the preparatory department the following year. Although he had had a short course in physics, he felt he knew little about it, but accepted the position and worked through the material by himself during the summer. It is interesting to note that at this time the only two adequate physics texts available in this country were translations from the French. Millikan developed a keen interest in physics, and after graduation continued on at Oberlin two more years as tutor of physics in the preparatory department. Simultaneously he carried on independent work in physics for which he was awarded the master's degree in 1893. Millikan had an excellent physique and throughout his stay at Oberlin he was acting director of the college gymnasium.

Hoping to get Millikan back to Oberlin as a physics instructor, his teacher of Greek again intervened, and without Millikan's knowledge, sent his credentials and application to Columbia University for a fellowship, which was granted. At that time, physical science in the United States was in its infancy. True, starting with Franklin, there had been a few scientists of note, but in 1893 Millikan was the only graduate student in physics at Columbia and there were only a scattered few physicists in the country. Publication of the first American journal in physics was started that year. This situation was in marked contrast to that on the continent where numerous physicists, chemists, and mathematicians of note were at work.

At Columbia Millikan completed the work for his Ph.D. in 1895 and with borrowed money went to Germany for a year where he studied with several outstanding physicists. He then accepted an appointment at the recently opened University of Chicago where, except for the war years, he remained for twenty-five years. During the first ten of these years his major efforts were spent in teaching and in textbook writing. Like Thomson, he had little use for large lecture sections, except for demonstrations, feeling that the thread of the course should be carried in small laboratory and problem sections.

By 1906 Millikan decided to expend his major energies on research. He was placed in charge of nearly all the graduate students in physics until 1917, when he left for war work. During the war he held a number of positions of high responsibility, returning to Chicago in 1919.

In 1921 he accepted the position of director of the Norman Bridge Laboratory of Physics and the chairmanship of the executive council of the California Institute of Technology at Pasadena, at that time a small struggling institution just getting started. During the next quarter of a century of Millikan's tenure, this unique institution combining the humanities with pure and applied science came to occupy a position of preeminence in the educational world.

Millikan's most noteworthy accomplishments in research were his determination of the electronic charge, an experimental verification of the Einstein photoelectric equation in 1916, and his subsequent work with cosmic rays. The most significant of many honors which he received was the Nobel prize in physics in 1923.

Millikan was a very friendly and humane individual who had a deep interest in the philosophical and religious implications of modern research. He died in California in 1953.

THE ISOLATION OF AN ION, A PRECISION MEASUREMENT OF ITS CHARGE, AND THE CORRECTION OF STOKES'S LAW.[1]

by R. A. Millikan

1. Introduction

In a preceding paper [*] a method of measuring the elementary electrical charge was presented which differed essentially from methods which had been used by earlier observers only in that all of the measurements from which the charge was deduced were made upon one individual charged carrier. This modification eliminated the chief sources of uncertainty which inhered in preceding determinations by similar methods such as those made by Sir Joseph Thomson,[†] H. A. Wilson,[‡] Ehrenhaft [§] and Broglie,[!] all of whom had deduced the elementary charge from the average behavior in electrical and gravitational fields of swarms of charged particles.

The method used in the former work consisted essentially in catching ions by C. T. R. Wilson's method on droplets of water or alcohol, in then isolating by a suitable arrangement a single one of these droplets, and measuring its speed first in a vertical electrical and gravitational field combined, then in a gravitational field alone.[*]

The sources of error or uncertainty which still inhered in the method arose from: (1) the lack of complete stagnancy in the air through which the drop moved; (2) the lack of perfect uniformity in the electrical field used; (3) the gradual evaporation of the drops, rendering it impossible to hold a given drop under observation for more than a minute, or to time the drop as it fell under gravity alone through a period of more than five or six seconds; (4) the assumption of the exact validity of Stokes's law [2] for the drops used. The present

---

[1] *Physical Review* (1911), Vol. 32, p. 349.

[*] Millikan, *Phys. Rev.*, December, 1909, and *Phil. Mag.*, 19, p. 209.

[†] Thomson, *Phil. Mag.*, 46, 1898, p. 528; 48, 1899, p. 547; 5, 1903, p. 346.

[‡] H. A. Wilson, *Phil. Mag.*, 5, 1903, p. 429.

[§] Ehrenhaft, *Phys. Zeit.*, Mai, 1909.

[!] Broglie, *Le Radium*, Juillet, 1909.

[*] In work reported since this paper was first presented, Ehrenhaft (*Phys. Zeit.*, July, 1910) has adopted this vertical-field arrangement so that he also now finds it possible to make all his measurements upon individual charged particles.

[2] The droplets used in this experiment were so small that in falling under the force of gravity or in rising due to the force of the electric field they attained their terminal velocities almost immediately. It will be recalled that Galileo had investigated the effect of the medium on falling bodies and had concluded that a falling body would reach a constant terminal velocity when the speed was such that the resisting force of the medium was equal to the force (gravity) causing the motion. A marble dropped in viscous molasses would reach its terminal velocity almost immediately. In a similar way the viscosity of the air retarded the motion of the droplets with which Millikan was working. Stokes' law, relating the force causing the motion, the viscosity (frictional resistance) of the medium, the radius of the droplet, and the velocity of the droplet are given in Equation (2), page 557. This law had been derived mathematically for a sphere traveling at a fixed velocity through a homogeneous fluid medium.

modification of the method is not only entirely free from all of these limitations, but it constitutes an entirely new way of studying ionization and one which seems to be capable of yielding important results in a considerable number of directions.

With its aid it has already been found possible:

1. To catch upon a minute droplet of oil and to hold under observation for an indefinite length of time one single atmospheric ion or any desired number of such ions between 1 and 150.

2. To present direct and tangible demonstration, through the study of the behavior in electrical and gravitational fields of this oil drop, carrying its captured ions, of the correctness of the view advanced many years ago and supported by evidence from many sources that all electrical charges, however produced, are exact multiples of one definite, elementary, electrical charge, or in other words, that an electrical charge instead of being spread uniformly over the charged surface has a definite granular structure, consisting, in fact, of an exact number of specks, or atoms of electricity, all precisely alike, peppered over the surface of the charged body.

3. To make an exact determination of the value of the elementary electrical charge which is free from all questionable theoretical assumptions and is limited in accuracy only by that attainable in the measurement of the coefficient of viscosity of air.

4. To observe directly the order of magnitude of the kinetic energy of agitation of a molecule, and thus to bring forward new direct and most convincing evidence of the correctness of the kinetic theory of matter.

5. To demonstrate that the great majority, if not all, of the ions of ionized air, of both positive and negative sign, carry the elementary electrical charge.

6. To show that Stokes's law for the motion of a small sphere through a resisting medium breaks down as the diameter of the sphere becomes comparable with the mean free path of the molecules of the medium, and to determine the exact way in which it breaks down.

2. The Method

The only essential modification in the method consists in replacing the droplet of water or alcohol by one of oil, mercury or some other non-volatile substance and in introducing it into the observing space in a new way.

Figure 1 [Fig. 40-3] shows the apparatus used in the following experiments. By means of a commercial " atomizer " A * a cloud of fine droplets of oil is blown with the aid of dust-free air into the dust-free chamber C. One or more of the droplets of this cloud is allowed to fall through a pinhole p into the space between the plates M, N of a horizontal air condenser and the pinhole is then closed by means of an electromagnetically operated cover not shown

---

* The atomizer method of producing very minute but accurately spherical drops for the purpose of studying their behavior in fluid media, was first conceived and successfully carried out in January, 1908, at the Ryerson Laboratory, by Mr. J. Y. Lee, while he was engaged in a quantitative investigation of Brownian movements. His spheres were blown from Wood's metal, wax and other like substances which solidify at ordinary temperatures. Since then the method has been almost continuously in use here, upon this and a number of other problems, and elsewhere upon similar problems.

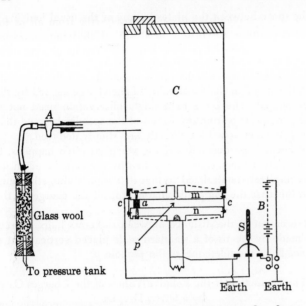

Figure 40-3. *Millikan's oil drop apparatus for measuring the electronic charge.*

in the diagram. If the pinhole is left open air currents are likely to pass through it and produce irregularities. The plates M, N are heavy, circular, ribbed brass castings 22 cm in diameter having surfaces which are ground so nearly to true planes that the error is nowhere more than .02 mm. These planes are held exactly 16 mm apart by means of three small ebonite posts a, held firmly in place by ebonite screws. A strip of thin-sheet ebonite c passes entirely around the plates, thus forming a completely enclosed air space. Three glass windows, 1.5 cm square, are placed in this ebonite strip at the angular positions 0°, 165°, and 180°. A narrow parallel beam of light from an arc lamp enters the condenser through the first window and emerges through the last. The other window serves for observing, with the aid of a short focus telescope placed about 2 feet distant, the illuminated oil droplet as it floats in the air between the plates. The appearance of this drop is that of a brilliant star on a black background. It falls, of course, under the action of gravity, toward the lower plate; but before it reaches it, an electrical field of strength between 3,000 volts and 8,000 volts per centimeter is created between the plates by means of the battery B, and, if the droplet had received a frictional charge of the proper sign and strength as it was blown out through the atomizer, it is pulled up by this field against gravity, toward the upper plate. Before it strikes it the plates are short-circuited by means of the switch S and the time required by the drop to fall under gravity the distance corresponding to the space between the cross hairs of the observing telescope is accurately determined. Then the rate at which the droplet moves up under the influence of the field is measured by timing it through the same distance when the field is on. This operation is repeated and the speeds checked an indefinite number of times, or until the droplet catches an ion from among those which exist normally in air, or which have been produced in the space between the plates by any of the usual ionizing agents like radium or x-rays. The fact that an ion has been caught, and the exact instant at which the event happened is signaled to the observer by the change in the speed of the droplet under the influence of the field. From the sign and magnitude of this change in speed, taken in connection with the constant speed under gravity, the sign and the exact value of the charge carried by the captured ion are determined. The error in a single observation need not exceed one third of one percent. It is from the values of the speeds observed that all of the conclusions above mentioned are directly and simply deduced.

The experiment is particularly striking when, as often happens, the droplet carries but one elementary charge and then by the capture of an ion of opposite sign is completely neutralized so that its speed is altogether unaffected by the field. In this case the computed charge is itself the charge on the captured ion.

The measurement of the distance between the cross hairs, correct to about .01 mm, is made by means of a standard scale placed vertically at exactly the same distance from the telescope as the pinhole p.

3. The Deduction of the Relative Values of the Charges Carried by a Given Droplet

The relations between the apparent mass m of a drop, the charge e_n, which it carries, its speed, v_1 under gravity, and its speed v_2 under the influence of an electrical field of strength F, are given by the simple equation [3]

$$\frac{v_1}{v_2} = \frac{mg}{Fe_n - mg} \quad \text{or} \quad e_n = \frac{mg}{F}\left(\frac{v_1 + v_2}{v_1}\right). \tag{1}$$

This equation involves no assumption whatever save that the speed of the drop is proportional to the force acting upon it, an assumption which is fully and accurately tested experimentally in the following work. Furthermore, equation (1) is sufficient not only for the correct determination of the relative values of all of the charges which a given drop may have through the capture of a larger or smaller number of ions, but it is also sufficient for the establishment of all of the assertions made above, except 3, 4, and 6. However, for the sake of obtaining a provisional estimate of the value of m in equation (1), and therefore of making at once a provisional determination of the absolute values of the charges carried by the drop, Stokes's law will for the present be assumed to be correct, but it is to be distinctly borne in mind that the conclusions just now under consideration are not at all dependent upon the validity of this assumption.

[3] As Galileo pointed out, the net force pulling a body toward the earth when it is first released is the weight (gravitational pull) of the body minus the buoyant force of the fluid medium that is displaced by the body. Thus a droplet is acted upon by an apparent weight which is its true gravitational weight minus the buoyant force (weight) of the displaced air. When this apparent weight is equal to the resisting viscous force of the air the droplet falls at a constant speed which is proportional to the apparent weight. In Equation (1), m is the apparent mass of the droplet which is its true mass minus the mass of air displaced by the droplet. This apparent mass m when multiplied by g, the acceleration of a freely falling body, gives the apparent weight of the droplet in the particular unit (dyne) used by Millikan.

This law in its simplest form states that if μ is the coefficient of viscosity of a medium, x the force acting upon a spherical drop of radius a in that medium, and v the velocity with which the drop moves under the influence of the force, then

$$x = 6\pi\mu a v. \qquad (2)$$

The substitution in this equation of the resulting gravitational force acting on a spherical drop of density σ in a medium of density ρ gives the usual expression for the rate of fall, according to Stokes, of a drop under gravity, viz.,

$$v_1 = \frac{2ga^2}{9\mu}(\sigma - \rho). \qquad (3)$$

The elimination of m from (1) by means of (3), and the further relation $m = \frac{4}{3}\pi a^3(\sigma - \rho)$ gives the charge e_n in the form

$$e_n = \frac{4}{3}\pi \left(\frac{9\mu}{2}\right)^{3/2} \left(\frac{1}{g(\sigma - \rho)}\right)^{1/2} \frac{(v_1 + v_2)v_1^{1/2}}{F}. \qquad (4)$$

It is from this equation that the values of e_n in tables I–XI are obtained.

4. Preliminary Observations upon the Catching of Ions by Oil Drops

Table I presents the record of the observations taken upon a drop which was watched through a period of four and one half hours as it was alternately moved up and down between the cross hairs of the observing telescope under the influence of the field F and gravity G. How completely the errors arising from evaporation, convection currents or any sort of disturbances in the air are eliminated is shown by the constancy during all this time in the value of the velocity under gravity. This constancy was not attained without a considerable amount of experimenting which will be described in section II. It is sufficient here to state that the heating effects of the illuminating arc were eliminated, first by filtering the light through about two feet of water, and second, by shutting off the light from the arc altogether except at occasional instants, when the shutter was opened to see that the star was in place, or to make an observation of the instant of its transit across a cross hair. Further evidence of the complete stagnancy of the air is furnished by the fact that for an hour or more at a time the drop would not drift more than two or three millimeters to one side or the other of the point at which it entered the field.

The observations in Table I [Table 40-1] are far less accurate than many of those which follow, the timing being done in this case with a stopwatch, while many of the later timings were taken with a chronograph. Nevertheless this series is presented because of the unusual length of time over which the drop was observed, and because of the rather unusual variety of phenomena which it presents.

The column headed G shows the successive times in seconds taken by the droplet to fall, under gravity, the distance between the cross hairs. It will be seen that, in the course of the four and one half hours, the value of this time increases very slightly, thereby showing that the drop is very slowly evaporating. Furthermore, there are rather marked fluctuations recorded in the first ten observations which are probably due to the fact that, in this part of the observation, the shutter was open so much as to produce very slight convection currents.

TABLE 40-1

Negative Drop.

Distance between cross-hairs = 1.010 *cm.*
Distance between plates   = 1.600 *cm.*
Temperature   = 24.6°C.
Density of oil at 25°C.   = .8960.
Viscosity of air at 25.2°C.   = .0001836.

	G sec.	F sec.	n	$e_n \times 10^{10}$	$e_1 \times 10^{10}$
	22.8	29.0	7	34.47	4.923
	22.0	21.8	8	39.45	4.931
	22.3	17.2			
G = 22.28	22.4	—			
V = 7950	22.0	17.3	9	44.42	4.936
	22.0	17.3			
	22.0	14.2	10	49.41	4.941
	22.7	21.5	8	39.45	
	22.9	11.0	12	59.12	4.927
	22.4	17.4	9	44.42	
	22.8	14.3	10	49.41	
V = 7920	22.8	12.2			
G = 22.80	22.8	12.3	11	53.92	4.902
	23.0	—			
	22.8	14.2			
F = 14.17	—	—	10	49.41	4.941
	22.8	14.0			
	22.8	17.0			
F = 17.13	—	17.2	9	44.42	4.936
	22.9	17.2			
	22.8	10.9			
F = 10.73	22.8	10.9	12	59.12	4.927
	22.8	10.6			
V = 7900	22.8	12.2	11	53.92	4.902
G = 22.82	22.8	8.7	14	68.65	4.904
F = 6.7	22.7	6.8	17	83.22	4.894
	22.9	6.6			
	22.8	7.2			
	—	7.2			
	—	7.3			
F = 7.25	—	7.2	16	78.34	4.897
	23.0	7.4			
	—	7.3			
	—	7.2			

TABLE 40-1 — *Continued*

	G sec.	F sec.	n	$e_n \times 10^{10}$	$e_1 \times 10^{10}$
$F = \quad 8.65$	22.8 23.1	8.6 8.7	14	68.65	4.904
	23.2 —	9.8 9.8	13	63.68	4.900
$F = \quad 10.63$	23.5 23.4	10.7 10.6	12	59.12	4.927
	23.2	9.6			
	23.0	9.6			
	23.0	9.6			
	23.2	9.5			
$V = 7820$	23.0	9.6	13	63.68	4.900
$G = \quad 23.14$	—	9.4			
$F = \quad 9.57$	22.9	9.6			
	—	9.6			
	22.9	9.6			
	—	10.6	12	59.12	4.927
$F = \quad 8.65$	— 23.4	8.7 8.6	14	68.65	4.904
	23.0	12.3			
$F = \quad 12.25$	23.3	12.2	11	53.92	4.902
	—	12.1			
	23.2	12.4			

Change forced with radium.

	G sec.	F sec.	n	$e_n \times 10^{10}$	$e_1 \times 10^{10}$
$F = \quad 72.10$	23.4	72.4			
	22.9	72.4			
	23.2	72.2	5	24.60	4.920
	23.5	71.8			
	23.0	71.7			
	23.0	39.2	6		
$V = 7800$	23.2	39.2			
$G = \quad 23.22$	—	27.4	7	34.47	
	—	20.7	8	39.38	4.922
	—	26.9 27.2	7	34.47	4.923
	23.3	39.5			
	23.3	39.2	6	29.62	4.937
$F = \quad 39.20$	23.4	39.0			
	23.3	39.1			

(*Table 40-1 continued on next page.*)

TABLE 40-1 — *Continued*

	G sec.	F sec.	n	$e_n \times 10^{10}$	$e_1 \times 10^{16}$
	23.2	71.8	5	24.60	4.920
	23.4	382.5	4		
	23.2	374.0			
	23.4	71.0	5	24.60	4.920
	23.8	70.6			
$V = 7760$	23.4	38.5	6		
$G = \quad 23.43$	23.1	39.2			
	23.5	70.3			
	23.4	70.5			
	23.6	71.2	5	24.60	4.920
	23.4	71.4			
	23.6	71.0			
	23.4	71.4			
	23.5	380.6			
	23.4	384.6			
	23.2	380.0			
$F = \quad 379.6$	23.4	375.4	4	19.66	4.915
	23.6	380.4			
	23.3	374.0			
	23.4	383.6			
	—	39.2			
$F = \quad 39.18$	23.5	39.2	6	29.62	4.937
$V = 7730$	23.5	39.0			
$G = \quad 23.46$	23.4	39.6			
	—	70.8			
$F = \quad 70.65$	—	70.4	5	24.60	4.920
	—	70.6			
	23.6	378.0	4	19.66	
Saw it, here, at end of 305 sec., pick up two negatives.					
	23.6	39.4	6	29.62	4.937
	23.6	70.8	5	24.60	4.920

Mean of all e_1s = 4.917

Differences.

$$24.60 - 19.66 = 4.94$$
$$29.62 - 24.60 = 5.02$$
$$34.47 - 29.62 = 4.85$$
$$39.38 - 34.47 = \underline{4.91}$$
Mean dif. = $\overline{4.93}$

The column headed F is the time of ascent of the drop between the cross hairs under the action of the field. The column headed e_n is the value of the charge carried by the drop as computed from (4). The column headed n gives the number by which the values of the preceding column must be divided to obtain the numbers in the last column. The numbers in the e_n column are in general averages of all the observations of the table which are designated by the same numeral in the n column. If a given observation is not included in the average in the e_n column, a blank appears opposite that observation in the last two columns. On account of the slow change in the value of G, the observations are arranged in groups and the average value of G for each group is placed opposite that group in the first column. The reading of the voltmeter, taken at the mean time corresponding to each group, is labelled V and placed just below or just above the mean G corresponding to that group. The volts were in this case read with a ten-thousand-volt Braun electrometer which had been previously calibrated, but which may in these readings be in error by as much as one percent, though the error in the relative values of the volts will be exceedingly slight. The PD [4] was applied by means of a storage battery. It will be seen from the readings that the potential fell somewhat during the time of observation, the rate of fall being more rapid at first than it was later on.

5. Multiple Relations Shown by the Charges on a Given Drop

Since the original drop in this case was negative, it is evident that a sudden increase in the speed due to the field, that is, a decrease in the time given in column F, means that the drop has caught a negative ion from the air, while a decrease in the speed means that it has caught a positive ion.

If attention be directed, first, to the latter part of the table, where the observations are most accurate, it will be seen that, beginning with the group for which G = 23.43, the time of the drop in the field changed suddenly from 71 sec to 380 sec, then back to 71, then down to 39, then up again to 71, and then up again to 380. These numbers show conclusively that the positive ion caught in the first change, i.e., from 71 to 380, carried exactly the same charge as the negative ion caught in the change from 380 to 71. Or again, that the negative ion caught in the change from 71 to 39, had exactly the same charge as the positive ion caught in the change from 39 to 71.

Furthermore, the exact value of the charge caught in each of the above cases is obtained in terms of mg from the difference in the values of e_n, given by equation (1), and if it be assumed that the value of m is approximately known through Stokes's law, then the approximately correct value of the charge on the captured ion is given by the difference between the values of e_n obtained through equation (4). The mean value of this difference obtained from all the changes in the latter half of Table 1 (see Differences) is 4.93×10^{-10}.

Now it will be seen from the first observation given in the table that the charge which was originally upon this drop and which was obtained, not from the ions in the air, but from the frictional process involved in blowing the spray, was 34.47×10^{-10}. This number comes within one seventh of one per cent of being exactly seven times the charge on the positive, or on the negative, ion caught in the observations under consideration. In the interval between December, 1909, and May, 1910, Mr. Harvey Fletcher and myself took observations in this way upon hundreds of drops which had initial charges varying between the limits 1 and 150, and which were upon as diverse substances as oil, mercury and glycerine and found in every case the original

[4] Potential difference.

charge on the drop an exact multiple of the smallest charge which we found that the drop caught from the air. The total number of changes which we have observed would be between one and two thousand, and *in not one single instance has there been any change which did not represent the advent upon the drop of one definite invariable quantity of electricity, or a very small multiple of that quantity.* These observations are the justification for assertions 1 and 2 of the introduction.

For the sake of exhibiting in another way the multiple relationship shown by the charges on a given drop the data of Table I have been rearranged in the form shown in Table II [Table 40-2].

No more exact or more consistent multiple relationship is found in the data which the chemists have amassed on combining powers, and upon which the atomic theory of matter rests, than is found in tables I to XIII.

TABLE 40-2

n	$4.917 \times n$	Observed Charge	n	$4.917 \times n$	Observed Charge
1	4.917	——	10	49.17	49.41
2	9.834	——	11	54.09	53.92
3	14.75	——	12	59.00	59.12
4	19.66	19.66	13	63.92	63.68
5	24.59	24.60	14	68.84	68.65
6	29.50	29.62	15	73.75	——
7	34.42	34.47	16	78.67	78.34
8	39.34	39.38	17	83.59	83.22
9	44.25	44.42	18	88.51	——

The experimental work of Millikan and Thomson had demonstrated the particle nature of negative electricity, and evidence had been obtained that all matter contained electrons. As mentioned previously, electrolysis and the periodic properties of the elements had focused interest on the structures of the atoms. With the discovery of the electron, one of the building blocks was available for constructing an atomic model, and the first such model was devised by Thomson shortly before Millikan measured the electronic charge. The Thomson model of the atom was composed of electrons embedded in a positive sphere, the arrangement of the electrons being such as to at least partially correlate with the periodic properties of the elements. To quote Thomson [5]:

The Arrangement of Corpuscles in the Atom

We have seen that corpuscles are always of the same kind whatever may be the nature of the substance from which they originate; this, in conjunction with the fact that their mass is much smaller than that of any known atom, suggests that they are a constituent of all atoms; that, in short, corpuscles are an essential part of the structure of the atoms of the different elements. This

[5] J. J. Thomson, *The Corpuscular Theory of Matter*, Archibald Constable & Co. Ltd., London, 1907, p. 103.

consideration makes it important to consider the ways in which groups of corpuscles can arrange themselves so as to be in equilibrium. Since the corpuscles are all negatively electrified, they repel each other, and thus, unless there is some force tending to hold them together, no group in which the distances between the corpuscles is finite can be in equilibrium. As the atoms of the elements in their normal states are electrically neutral, the negative electricity on the corpuscles they contain must be balanced by an equivalent amount of positive electricity; the atoms must, along with the corpuscles, contain positive electricity. The form in which this positive electricity occurs in the atom is at present a matter about which we have very little information. No positively electrified body has yet been found having a mass less than that of an atom of hydrogen. All the positively electrified systems in gases at low pressures seem to be atoms which, neutral in their normal state, have become positively charged by losing a corpuscle. In default of exact knowledge of the nature of the way in which positive electricity occurs in the atom, we shall consider a case in which the positive electricity is distributed in the way most amenable to mathematical calculation, i.e., when it occurs as a sphere of uniform density, throughout which the corpuscles are distributed. The positive electricity attracts the corpuscles to the centre of the sphere, while their mutual repulsion drives them away from it; when in equilibrium they will be distributed in such a way that the attraction of the positive electrification is balanced by the repulsion of the other corpuscles.

Thomson assumed that the lightest atom hydrogen contained one negative corpuscle at the center of an equal (electrically) positive sphere of charge. In building up models for the heavier atoms, he assumed the number of corpuscles to be proportional to the atomic weights and the positive electricity in the enveloping sphere to increase correspondingly. Assuming the corpuscles to lie in a plane, configurations containing one, six, and seventeen corpuscles are shown in Figure 40-4.

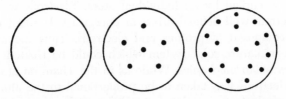

Figure 40-4. *Thomson's distribution of corpuscles, for atoms containing one, six, and seventeen. In atoms containing one to five the corpuscles were in one ring, those containing six to sixteen in two rings, those containing seventeen to thirty-one in three rings, and the number of rings increased to seven for those containing 94 or more corpuscles. Each time a new ring was started at the center, Thomson assumed the chemical properties of the elements would be repeated, thus explaining the periodicity of these properties. Both the inner and outer rings added corpuscles more or less alternately.*

Shortly following Millikan's measurement of the electronic charge, Rutherford working in the Cavendish Laboratory obtained experimental results on the scattering of radioactive radiations which made the Thomson atom untenable. These results indicated that an atom consisted of a relatively small positive nucleus surrounded by negative electrons. This model was put on a quantitative basis by the Danish physicist Bohr. The Rutherford-Bohr model proved to be highly successful in agreeing with spectroscopic data on emitted light and with explaining the periodic

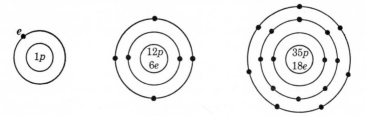

Figure 40-5. *Models of the Bohr atoms for the elements hydrogen, carbon, and chlorine having atomic numbers one, six, and seventeen and atomic weights one, twelve, and thirty-five. New energy levels in the Bohr atom are added at the outside, each starting with one electron. Thus different elements having the same number of electrons (one, two, etc. up to eight) in the outer energy level would have similar properties. An electron transferring from one energy level to fill a vacancy in another level would receive or emit a given amount of energy, called a quantum. Such a quantum might be of visible light, ultraviolet light, or perhaps of x-rays.*

properties of the elements, as well as predicting other phenomena which had not previously been observed. In this model, the positive charge instead of being diffused throughout a sphere was assumed to occur in discrete quantities called protons which were quite minute in size compared to the space occupied by an individual atom. Electrons were assumed to occupy certain well defined orbits or energy levels about the nucleus which was composed of protons and electrons. Thus the arrangement resembled a miniature solar system which could be treated mathematically by Newtonian mechanics. While as in the Thomson atom the total number of electrons was taken to be proportional to the atomic weight, the number of electrons in orbits around the nucleus was assumed to be equal to the atomic number, the position occupied by a given element in the periodic table. The number of protons in the nucleus was assumed to be equal to the atomic weight (Fig. 40-5), and to make the atom electrically neutral, a sufficient number of electrons were assumed to be in the nucleus with the protons.[6]

---

[6] The subsequent discovery in 1934 of the neutron, a particle having the mass of a proton but no charge, caused the revision of the original Bohr atom model so that the number of protons in the nucleus and the number of orbital electrons around the nucleus were each equal to the atomic number, and the desired relative weight of the atom was obtained by adding the proper number of neutrons to the nucleus.

This then was the start of our period of modern physics in which discoveries and developments have happened so rapidly that the specialist in one branch cannot keep up with advances in other branches. The most spectacular of these developments has culminated in the production, both controlled and uncontrolled, of energy from nuclear reactions. Some further insights into our present concepts of the nature of matter will be given in the concluding chapter.

STUDY QUESTIONS

1. Millikan's method of determining e differed from previous methods in that he
   - (1) could see and count the individual charges on the droplets through his telescope
   - (2) used Faraday's laws of electrolysis
   - (3) used oil instead of water droplets
   - (4) obtained his droplets from an atomizer
   - (5) employed both (3) and (4) above.

2. Millikan used oil instead of water droplets because
   - (1) the oil had a lower density and would fall more slowly
   - (2) turbulence did not affect the oil droplets so much
   - (3) water droplets could not be charged
   - (4) the oil evaporated more slowly
   - (5) his research was being financed by an oil company.

3. Falling under the action of the gravitational field alone (metal plates uncharged), the oil droplets
   a. fall with a constant positive acceleration
   b. fall with constant terminal velocities
   c. fall noticeably faster when they carry a charge because they are heavier.
   The correct answer is
   (1) a   (2) b   (3) c   (4) a and c   (5) b and c.

4. A single droplet falling in the oil drop apparatus under the action of gravity alone was observed to fall faster when the electric field was turned on. If the direction of the electric field between the plates was vertically downward, it is probable that
   - (1) the droplet was uncharged after the field was turned on
   - (2) the turning on of the field charged the droplet
   - (3) the droplet had a net positive charge
   - (4) the droplet had a net negative charge
   - (5) nothing can be said about the charge on the droplet.

5. If a droplet is falling at constant speed when the electric field is on and directed vertically down, it is possible that the droplet is

---

Thus chlorine, whose atomic number is seventeen and whose relative weight is approximately thirty-five, was assumed to have seventeen orbital electrons and a nucleus composed of seventeen protons and eighteen neutrons.

a. uncharged   b. negatively charged   c. positively charged.
The correct answer is

(1) a   (2) b   (3) c   (4) a and c   (5) a, b, and c.

6. When a droplet is falling under the action of gravity (no electric field) the net force on the drop is equal to

(1) the weight of the drop
(2) the difference between the weight of the drop and the weight of the displaced air
(3) the sum of the weights of the drop and of the displaced air
(4) the difference between the weight of the drop and the frictional (viscosity) resistance of the air
(5) zero.

7. Assume that in arbitrary force units the weight of a droplet is 1000 and the weight of an equal volume of air is 1. When falling at terminal velocity under gravity only (no electric field), the frictional resistance of the air is

(1) 1   (2) 999   (3) 1000   (4) 1001   (5) 0.

8. If in the previous problem when the electric field is turned on the droplet is observed to cease falling and stand still, the electric force exerted on the droplet is

(1) 1   (2) 999   (3) 1000   (4) 1001   (5) 1999.

9–14. Assume that in arbitrary force units the weight of a droplet is 1000 and the weight of an equal volume of air is 1. When falling under gravity alone the droplet is observed through a telescope to fall 10 divisions in 20 seconds.

9. If when the electric field is turned on in a vertically downward direction, the downward speed of the droplet is reduced to 5 divisions in 20 seconds, the electrical force on the droplet is

(1) 999   (2) 1000   (3) 499.5   (4) 500   (5) 1499.5.

10. The frictional resistance in Prob. 9 is

(1) 999   (2) 1000   (3) 499.5   (4) 500   (5) 1499.5.

11. Is the droplet charged positively or negatively?

12. If when the electric field is turned on in a vertically downward direction, the droplet moves up at a speed of 10 divisions in 20 seconds, the electrical force on the droplet is

(1) 999   (2) 1000   (3) 499.5   (4) 500   (5) 1998.

13. The frictional resistance in Prob. 12 is

(1) 999   (2) 1000   (3) 499.5   (4) 500   (5) 1998.

14. Is the droplet charged positively or negatively?

15. Referring to the data in Table 40-1, it is seen that the time of rise of the droplet is about 380 seconds when the droplet carries 4 electronic charges and is about 21 seconds when carrying 8 electronic charges. If the charge is doubled why isn't the time halved?

16. Was there any appreciable evaporation of the droplet in Table 40-1?

17. Discuss the relative speeds of fall due to gravity of two droplets, one having twice the radius of the other.

18. Derive equation (1).

19. Derive equation (3).

20. Using equations (1), (2), and (3), derive equation (4).

41

Modern Particle Theory

● We have seen in our study of Newton's laws that the future courses of all bodies, not subject to forces, are determined by their present velocities and positions since they continue to move in straight paths with unchanged velocities. Newton's laws also provide the means of calculating the changes in these paths when forces are applied.

Thus it is possible in principle to predict the position of every particle in the universe if we know the initial positions and velocities of all of them and the forces that will act at all future times. How do we determine these forces? In one sense, Newton has not solved the problem of describing the universe but has merely shifted it to one of determining the forces and their nature.

During the period following Newton until about 1920 a great deal of effort was spent trying to understand the nature of these forces. Newton himself showed that the gravitational force exerted on the moon by the earth depended only upon the distance between the two bodies. There are other gravitational forces acting on the moon due to the sun, planets, and even the stars but these all depend upon the positions of these bodies and are quite small relative to that of the earth. According to Newton, the gravitation forces on any body depend only upon the positions and the masses, which are constant, of all the bodies of the universe. Therefore, since we can compute the positions of all bodies for each succeeding second of time by Newton's laws and can determine the gravitational forces from these positions, we could determine, in principle, the precise position of all bodies for any time in the future from the knowledge of their present positions and velocities if gravitation provided the only kind of force. Since all bodies have present positions and velocities whether we know them or not, we say that the future of the universe would be " determined."

Now there are kinds of forces at work other than gravitational. During the 19th century, great strides were made in the study of forces between electrical charges. These studies led to the conclusion that, although the present positions of electrical charges are not sufficient to determine the electrical forces acting upon them at the present instant, their past histories are sufficient. Thus, if all forces were electrical and gravitational in nature, Newton's laws would predict the entire future course of the universe if its past were known. Since the universe has a past whether we know it or not, we again would say that its future is " determined."

As more and more became known of the nature of Newton's forces, it became more and more evident that the trend of scientific investigation was in the direction of proving that the universe runs like a great machine and that its future course is completely determined by its past. This fact had a tremendous impact upon philosophy and religion and led to the development of Deism which pictured God as a great watch maker who created the universe, set it in motion, and left it to run its course. Of course the concept of Deism was entirely unacceptable to most theologians. They could only hope that the then existent trend of science would someday come to a halt and that, in reality, there must exist spiritual forces. This was the state of affairs at the turn of the century in 1900.

In a sense the theologians were correct when they stated that the trend in science toward a determined universe would alter. Rather than discovering spiritual forces, however, modern physics attributes this change in trend to the realization that in dealing with subatomic particles Newton's laws were not always applicable. In the late eighteen hundreds, science began to explore the subatomic region of the universe. Atoms are constructed of very small particles, electrons, neutrons, and protons. It was soon discovered that these small particles do not always behave in the manner predicted by Newton's laws.

In 1900, Max Planck, then forty-two, read a theoretical paper before the German Physical Society on the radiation of energy from hot bodies. To obtain the experimentally known radiation laws he assumed that energy was emitted in discrete bundles, called quanta, where the energy in each bundle was strictly proportional to the frequency of the emitted radiation. The factor of proportionality is now known as Planck's constant in his honor. This was the opening skirmish in the revolution in physics which has occurred during this century. Until 1900 everyone had assumed that energy in a light beam of a given frequency could be made arbitrarily small. Planck assumed that it was emitted in definite packages only and hence could not be made indefinitely small since no fractional quanta were allowed.

While nearly everyone in Planck's audience could see the mathematical efficacy of his assumption, few were willing to account it scientific. Even Planck spent the next several years trying to obtain the same results from some set of less revolutionary postulates. One of the few men who did take Planck seriously was the twenty-six year old Albert Einstein who in 1905 was a Swiss patent office examiner. Einstein adapted the new discontinuous physics to the theory of photoelectric phenomena with eminent success. These phenomena deal with the emission of electrons when light strikes a metal surface. In fact, it was Einstein's theory of the photoelectric effect which won him the Nobel prize in physics rather than his two relativity theories. We have seen that in 1913 the twenty-eight year old Niels Bohr proposed a new theory for the hydrogen atom. His postulates were an extension of Planck's and again made a serious break with the past.

By 1926 the revolution was in full swing. Young men, including among others, Heisenberg, Schroedinger, De Broglie, and Dirac, were challenging the older classical physics which had been founded by Newton and developed by many generations of mathematical physicists. The new postulates of the young men were bold, but their predicted results agreed strikingly well with a myriad of phenomena not previously understood. The new theories were particularly successful in the atomic domain. These successes had their repercussions not only in physics, but in philosophy, religion, and other wide areas of human life.

Let us consider a very common piece of apparatus, a television picture tube, to see how electrons deviate from Newton's laws. When a television tube has been running for some time and is switched off, it may show a bright spot at its center. This spot comes from a very large number of electrons striking the end of the tube, called the screen. As each electron hits, a tiny bright point appears. A large number of such bright points make up the spot.

The construction of an idealized and simplified picture tube is shown in Figure 41-1. Electrons are emitted from a hot filament, pass through

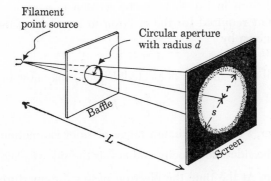

Figure 41-1. *Electrons leaving the point source and traveling through the small circular hole in the baffle would be expected by Newtonian mechanics to travel in straight lines striking the screen within the circular spot of radius r. However some electrons are found to strike farther away within a ring of outer radius* s.

a circular aperture of radius d, and strike the screen somewhere in the spot of radius s. We may neglect gravitation effects because the electrons travel so fast that there is too little time for them to be appreciably deflected. Let us also assume that there are no electrical forces that would cause the electrons to deviate from straight lines as they travel from the filament through the baffle to the screen.

Straight lines drawn from the filament to the screen just passing through the edge of the circular aperture define a region on the screen whose radius r limits the maximum sidewise motion that any electron can make if it strikes the screen and follows Newton's laws. We may say that this maximum distance r has been "determined" by the physical baffle. We should be able to make the size of the spot on the screen as small as desired simply by reducing the radius d of the hole in the baffle.

Experiments similar to the one above, however, have shown that this is not the case. In addition to the uncertainty as to the exact point on the screen where each electron will strike due to the size of the aperture, there is another uncertainty since it is found that the spot is larger than that predicted by Newton's laws. The spot is larger by an amount depending upon the size of the aperture, upon the mass m of the electron, and upon Planck's constant h so that the spot radius s is given by

$$s = r + (hL/mvd) \tag{1}$$

where v is the magnitude of the velocity of the electron, and L is the distance from filament to screen. We see then that s gets very large if d is very small. Planck's constant h is approximately given by

$$h = 6.6 \times 10^{-27} \tag{2}$$

when the lengths involved are measured in centimeters and the mass in grams. It is clear, then, that the mass of the particle must be very small for s to be appreciably different from the r predicted by Newton's laws.

The second term in Eq. (1) can be written in a somewhat different way. The time t required for the electron to travel from the filament to the screen is given by

$$t = L/v. \tag{3}$$

If d is so small that r may be neglected, Eq. (1) may now be rewritten as

$$m \frac{s}{t} d = h. \tag{4}$$

Since, however, s is the maximum range of sidewise motion observed in time t, s/t is the sidewise velocity and $m \frac{s}{t}$ is the sidewise momentum that we may call p. At the time the electron passes the aperture its distance from the center line is known to be within a distance d. Thus we say that the baffle determines the position of the electron to within d and the momentum within p and Eq. (4) becomes

$$pd \text{ is greater than or } = h. \tag{5}$$

Figure 41-2. *Erwin C. Schroedinger (1887–1961).*

The " greater than " takes care of the *r* that can be added to the right hand side according to Eq. (1). This is the famous Heisenberg *uncertainty principle* which, in words, states that "*physical forces* (in our case, the baffle) *can determine the momentum and position of a particle only to the extent that the product of the uncertainty in momentum and uncertainty in position in any direction is greater than or equal to* h."

In terms of the experiment discussed above, there is no way by means of physical objects that we can determine the exact spot on the screen that an electron will strike. Also, for any given experimental arrangement, we are unable to predict exactly where the next electron will strike the screen. Some uncertainty will always remain. In a similar way it is true that, even if we knew all that we could know about the universe at the present time and in the past, *in principle* we could not predict its future course. This implies that, according to present scientific theory, the future course of the universe is not precisely determined from its past although the courses of bodies, so large that we can see them, are determined for a very long time to a very great accuracy. As to whether or not any elements, other than physical, step in to determine the course of future events where the physical leaves off, science has nothing to say. It is, however, the belief of most leading scientists today that a realm of *indeterminacy* exists beyond the control of physical forces.

Erwin Schroedinger (Fig. 41-2) is a good example of the bright young men who brought the new quantum mechanics into flower in the second and third decades of this century. He was born in Vienna on August 12, 1887 and educated at home until the age of eleven. Then he entered the intermediate school in Vienna and went on to study at the University of Vienna from 1906 to 1910. In 1911 Schroedinger became an assistant in the Department of Physics at Vienna, but his academic life was interrupted by World War I. Following the war in 1920, he went to Jena in Germany as an assistant to Max Wien. After only a semester here, he was called to Stuttgart as a professor extraordinary, which is to say an associate professor in the American system. Again after only one semester he was offered and accepted the post of full professor of Breslau.

Schroedinger was moving up rapidly in the academic world. In 1921 he was appointed professor of mathematical physics in the University of Zurich in Switzerland. Here he devised a great deal of the modern wave mechanics, including its fundamental differential equation, which has been named Schroedinger's equation in his honor. In 1928 he succeeded Max Planck as professor of theoretical physics at the University of Berlin.

With the rise of Hitler, Schroedinger left Germany for Oxford in 1933. In the same year he received the Nobel prize "for the discovery of new and fruitful forms of atomic theory," to quote his citation. In 1936 he returned to Austria as a professor in the University of Graz, the south Austrian city in which Kepler had taught three centuries earlier. But the Nazis annexed that country too, so he left for the United States but finally settled in Ireland where he was appointed senior professor in the Dublin Institute for Advanced Studies in 1940. In 1956, after World War II, he returned to the University of Vienna where he himself had studied. He died there on January 4, 1961.

Schroedinger was a very articulate scientist. Throughout his life he gave public addresses, wrote semipopular magazine articles, and produced many small books to inform the educated world as to the meaning and the import of the new physics. Such a work is his paper "What is an Elementary Particle?" which is reproduced here in its entirety.[1]

WHAT IS AN ELEMENTARY PARTICLE?
by E. Schroedinger
1. A Particle Is Not an Individual

Atomism in its latest form is called quantum mechanics. It has extended its range to comprise, besides ordinary matter, all kinds of radiation, including light — in brief, all forms of energy, ordinary matter being one of them. In the present form of the theory the 'atoms' are electrons, protons, photons, mesons, etc. The generic name is elementary particle, or merely particle. The

---

[1] E. Schroedinger, "What Is an Elementary Particle?" By permission of *Endeavor* (1935) Vol. 9, No. 35, pp. 109–116.

term atom has very wisely been retained for chemical atoms, though it has become a misnomer.

This essay deals with the elementary particle, more particularly with a certain feature that this concept has acquired — or rather lost — in quantum mechanics. I mean this: that the elementary particle is not an individual; it cannot be identified, it lacks ' sameness.' The fact is known to every physicist, but is rarely given any prominence in surveys readable by non-specialists. In technical language it is covered by saying that the particles ' obey ' a new-fangled statistics, either Einstein-Bose or Fermi-Dirac statistics. The implication, far from obvious, is that the unsuspected epithet ' this ' is not quite properly applicable to, say, an electron, except with caution, in a restricted sense, and sometimes not at all. My objective here is to explain this point and to give it the thought it deserves. In order to create a foil for the discussion, let me summarize in sections 2–5 what we are usually told about particles and waves in the new physics.

2. Current Views: The Amalgamation of Particles and Waves

Our image of the material world had been made up of two kinds of ' fittings ': waves and particles. The former were instanced mainly, if not exclusively, by Maxwell's waves of electromagnetic energy, comprising such as are used in radio, light, X-rays, and gamma-rays. Material bodies were said to consist of particles. One was also familiar with jets of particles, called corpuscular rays, such as cathode rays, beta-rays, alpha-rays, anode rays, etc. Particles would emit and absorb waves. For instance, cathode rays (electrons), when slowed down by colliding with atoms, emit X-rays. The distinction between particles and waves was, however, considered as clear-cut as that between a violin and its sound. An examinee who alleged cathode rays to be waves, or X-rays to be jets of particles, would have got very bad marks.

In the new setting of ideas the distinction has vanished, because it was discovered that all particles have also wave properties, and *vice versa*. Neither of the two concepts must be discarded, they must be amalgamated. Which aspect obtrudes itself depends not on the physical object, but on the experimental device set up to examine it. A jet of cathode rays, for example, produces in a Wilson cloud chamber discrete tracks of water droplets — curved tracks if there is a magnetic field to deflect the electrons, otherwise straight alignments of droplets. We cannot but interpret them as traces of the paths of single electrons. Yet the same jet, after crossing a narrow tube placed at right angles to it and containing crystal powder, will produce on a photographic plate at some distance behind the tube a pattern of concentric circles. This pattern can be understood in all its details when looked upon as the interference pattern of waves, and in no other way. Indeed, it bears a close resemblance to similarly produced X-ray patterns.

The suspicion arises: are the conical jets that impinge on the photographic plate and form the pattern of circles really cathode rays; are they not perhaps secondary X-rays? The suspicion has to be dismissed, for the whole system of circles can be displaced by a magnet, while X-rays can not; moreover, by putting a lead screen with a small hole in it in the place of the photographic plate, a jetlet can be isolated from one of the conical jets and made to display any of the typical particle characters of cathode rays: it will produce discrete tracks in a cloud chamber; bring about discrete discharges in a Geiger-Müller counter; and charge up a Faraday cage in which it is intercepted.

A vast amount of experimental evidence clinches the conviction that wave characteristics and particle characteristics are never encountered singly, but always in a union; they form different aspects of the same phenomenon, and indeed of all physical phenomena. The union is not a loose or superficial one. It would be quite unsatisfactory to consider cathode rays to consist both of particles and of waves. In the early days of the new theory it was suggested that the particles might be singular spots within the waves, actually singularities in the meaning of the mathematician. The white crests on a moderately rough sea would be a fairly adequate simile. The idea was very soon abandoned. It seems that both concepts, that of waves and that of particles, have to be modified considerably, so as to attain a true amalgamation.

3. Current Views: The Nature of Waves

The waves, so we are told, must not be regarded as quite real waves. It is true that they produce interference patterns — which is the crucial test that in the case of light had removed all doubts as to the reality of the waves. However, we are now told that all waves, including light, ought rather to be looked upon as ‘ probability waves.’ They are only a mathematical device for computing the probability of finding a particle in certain conditions, for instance (in the above example), the probability of an electron hitting the photographic plate within a small specified area. There it is registered by acting on a grain of silver bromide. The interference pattern is to be regarded as a statistical registration of the impinging electrons. The waves are in this context sometimes referred to as guiding waves — guiding or directing the particles on their paths. The guidance is not to be regarded as a rigid one; it merely constitutes a probability. The clear-cut pattern is a statistical result, its definiteness being due to the enormous number of particles.

Here I cannot refrain from mentioning an objection which is too obvious not to occur to the reader. Something that influences the physical behaviour of something else must not in any respect be called less real than the something it influences — whatever meaning we may give to the dangerous epithet ‘ real.’ It is certainly useful to recall at times that all quantitative models or images conceived by the physicist are, epistemologically, only mathematical devices for computing observable events, but I cannot see that this applies more to, say, light-waves than to, say, oxygen molecules.

4. Current Views: The Nature of Particles
(Uncertainty Relation)

As regards the modification required in the concept of a particle, the stress is on Heisenberg's uncertainty relation. The so-called classical mechanics hinged on Galileo's and Newton's discovery that the thing which in a moving body is determined at any instant by the other bodies in its environment is only and precisely its acceleration, or, in mathematical terms, the second derivatives with respect to time of the co-ordinates. The first derivatives, commonly called the velocity, are therefore to be included in the description of the momentary state of the body, together with the co-ordinates themselves which label its momentary place in space or 'whereness' (or ubiety, to use an antiquated but convenient word). Thus, to describe the momentary state of a particle, two independent data were required: its co-ordinates and their first time derivatives, or ubiety and velocity. According to the new theory less is required, and less is obtainable. Either of the two data can be given with arbitrary accuracy, provided that no store is set on the other, but both cannot be known together with absolute precision. One may not even conceive of both as having absolutely sharp values at the same instant. They mutually blur each other, as it were. Broadly speaking, the product of the latitudes of their respective inaccuracies cannot be reduced below a fixed constant. For an electron, this constant happens to be about 1 if the units centimetre and second are used. Thus, if the velocity of an electron is considered sharp with a latitude of only 1 cm/sec, its location has to be considered as blurred within the latitude of 1 cm. The strangeness does not lie in the mere existence of inaccuracies, for the particle might be a thing of vague and changeable extension, within which slightly different velocities prevailed at different spots. Then, however, a sharp location or ubiety would probably entail a sharply defined velocity and *vice versa*. Actually it is just the other way round.

5. Current Views: The Meaning of the Uncertainty Relation

Two links connect this strange and certainly very fundamental statement to other parts of the theory. It can be arrived at by declaring that a particle is equivalent to its guiding wave, and has no characteristics save those indicated by the guiding wave according to a certain code. The code is simple enough. The ubiety is indicated by the extension of the wave, the latitude in the velocity by the range of wave numbers. 'Wave number' is short for reciprocal of the wavelength. Each wave number corresponds to a certain velocity proportional to it. That is the code. It is a mathematical truism that the smaller a wave group, the wider is the (minimum) spread of its wave numbers.

Alternatively, we may scrutinize the experimental procedure for determining either the ubiety or the velocity. Any such measuring device implies a transfer of energy between the particle and some measuring instrument — eventually the observer himself, who has to take a reading. This means an actual physical interference with the particle. The disturbance cannot be arbitrarily reduced, because energy is not exchanged continuously but in portions. We are given to understand that, when measuring one of the two items, ubiety or velocity, we interfere with the other the more violently the higher the precision we aim at. We blur its value within a latitude inversely proportional to the latitude of error allowed in the first.

In both explanations the wording seems to suggest that the uncertainty or lack of precision refers to the attainable knowledge about a particle rather than to its nature. Indeed, by saying that we disturb or change a measurable physical quantity we logically imply that it has certain values before and after our interference, whether we know them or not. And in the first explanation, involving the wave, if we call it a guiding wave how should it guide the particle on its path, if the particle has not got a path? If we say the wave indicates the probability of finding the particle at A, or at B, or at C . . . this seems to imply that the particle is at one, and one only, of these places; and similarly for the velocity. (Actually the wave does indicate both probabilities simultaneously, one by its extension, the other by its wave numbers.) However, the current view does not accept either ubiety or velocity as permanent objective realities. It stresses the word ' finding.' Finding the particle at point A does not imply that it has been there before. We are more or less given to understand that our measuring device has brought it there or ' concentrated ' it at that point, while at the same time we have disturbed its velocity. And this does not imply that the velocity ' had ' a value. We have only disturbed or changed the probability of finding this or that value of the velocity if we measure it. The implications as to ' being ' or ' having ' are misconceptions, to be blamed on language. Positivist philosophy is invoked to tell us that we must not distinguish between the knowledge we can obtain of a physical object and its actual state. The two are one.

6. Criticism of the Uncertainty Relation

I will not discuss here that tenet of positivist philosophy. I fully agree that the uncertainty relation has nothing to do with incomplete knowledge. It does reduce the amount of information attainable about a particle as compared with views held previously. The conclusion is that these views were wrong and we must give them up. We must not believe that the completer description they demanded about what is really going on in the physical world is conceivable, but in practice unobtainable. This would mean clinging to the old view. Still, it does not necessarily follow that we must give up speaking and thinking in terms of what is really going on in the physical world. It has become a convenient habit to picture it as a reality. In everyday life we all follow this habit, even those philosophers who opposed it theoretically, such as Bishop Berkeley. Such theoretical controversy is on a different plane. Physics has nothing to do with it. Physics takes its start from everyday experience, which it continues by more subtle means. It remains akin to it, does not transcend it generically, it cannot enter into another realm. Discoveries in physics cannot in themselves — so I believe — have the authority of forcing us to put an end to the habit of picturing the physical world as a reality.

I believe the situation is this. We have taken over from previous theory the idea of a particle and all the technical language concerning it. This idea is inadequate. It constantly drives our mind to ask for information which has obviously no significance. Its imaginative structure exhibits features which are alien to the real particle. An adequate picture must not trouble us with this disquieting urge; it must be incapable of picturing more than there is; it must refuse any further addition. Most people seem to think that no such picture can be found. One may, of course, point to the circumstantial evidence (which I am sorry to say is not changed by this essay) that in fact none has been found. I can, however, think of some reasons for this, apart from the genuine intricacy of the case. The palliative, taken from positivist philosophy and purporting to be a reasonable way out, was administered fairly early and authoritatively. It seemed to relieve us from the search for what I should call real understanding; it even rendered the endeavour suspect, as betraying an unphilosophical mind — the mind of a child who regretted the loss of its favourite toy (the picture or model) and would not realize that it was gone for ever. As a second point, I submit that the difficulty may be intimately connected with the principal subject of this paper, to which I shall now turn without further delay. The uncertainty relation refers to the particle. The particle, as we shall see, is not an identifiable individual. It may indeed well be that no individual entity can be conceived which would answer the requirements of the adequate picture stated above.

It is not at all easy to realize this lack of individuality and to find words for it. A symptom is that the probability interpretation, unless it is expressed in the most highly technical language of mathematics, seems to be vague as to whether the wave gives information about one particle or about an *ensemble* of particles. It is not always quite clear whether it indicates the probability of finding 'the' particle or of finding 'a' particle, or indicates the likely or average number of particles in, say, a given small volume. Moreover the most popular view on probability tends to obliterate these differences. It is true that exact mathematical tools are available to distinguish between them. A point of general interest is involved, which I will explain. A method of dealing with the problem of many particles was indicated in 1926 by the present writer. The method uses waves in many-dimensional space, in a manifold of 3N dimensions, N being the number of particles. Deeper insight led to its improvement. The step leading to this improvement is of momentous significance. The many-dimensional treatment has been superseded by so-called second quantization, which is mathematically equivalent to uniting into one three-dimensional formulation the cases N = 0, 1, 2, 3 . . . (to infinity) of the many-dimensional treatment. This highly ingenious device includes the so-called new statistics, with which we shall have to deal below in much simpler terms. It is the only precise formulation of the views now held, and the one that is always used. What is so very significant in our present context is that one cannot avoid leaving indeterminate the number of the particles dealt with. It is thus obvious that they are not individuals.

7. The Notion of a Piece of Matter

I wish to set forth a view on matter and the material universe, to which Ernst Mach, Bertrand Russell, and others were led by a careful analysis of concepts. It differs from the popular view. We are, however, not concerned with the psychological origin of the concept of matter but with its epistemological analysis. The attitude is so simple that it can hardly claim complete novelty; some pre-Socratics, including the materialist Democritus, were nearer to it than were the great men who resuscitated science and moulded it during the seventeenth to nineteenth centuries.

According to this view, a piece of matter is the name we give to a continuous string of events that succeed each other in time, immediately successive ones being as a rule closely similar. The single event is an inextricable complex of sensates, of associated memory images, and of expectations associated with the former two. The sensates prevail in the case of an unknown object, say a distant white patch on the road, which might be a stone, snow, salt, a cat or a dog, a white shirt or blouse, a handkerchief. Even so, within the ensuing string of events we usually know from general experience how to discount the changes caused by motions of our own body, in particular of our direction of sight. As soon as the nature of the object is recognized, images and expectations begin to prevail. The latter concern sensations as hard, soft, heavy, flexible, rough, smooth, cold, salty, etc., associated with the image of touching and handling; they also concern spontaneous movements or noises such as barking, mewing, shouting, etc. It should be noted that I am not speaking of our thoughts or considerations about the object, but of what forms part and parcel of our perception of it — of what it is to us. However, the limit is not sharp. As our familiarity with a piece of matter grows, and in particular as we approach its scientific aspect, the range of expectations in regard to it widens, eventually to include all the information science has ascertained, e.g. melting point, solubility, electric conductivity, density, chemical and crystalline structure, and so on. At the same time, the momentary sensational core recedes in relevance the more the object becomes familiar to us, whether by scientific knowledge or by everyday use.

8. Individuality or 'Sameness'

After a certain wealth of association has come to outshine the core of sensates, the latter is no longer needed to keep the complex together. It persists even when the contact of our senses with the object temporarily ceases. And more than that: the complex is latently conserved even when the whole string is interrupted by our turning away from the object to others and forgetting all about it. Indeed, this is not exceptional, but a rule which — since we sometimes sleep — has no exception. But we have adopted the useful device of filling these gaps. We supplement the missing parts of the strings relating to pieces of matter in our nearer and farther surroundings, to cover the periods when we neither watch them nor think of them. When a familiar object re-enters our ken, it is usually recognized as a continuation of previous appearances, as being the same thing. The relative permanence of individual pieces of matter is the most momentous feature of both everyday life and scientific experience. If a familiar article, say an earthenware jug, disappears from your room, you are quite sure somebody must have taken it away. If after a time it reappears, you may doubt whether it really is the same one — breakable objects in such circumstances are often not. You may not be able to decide the issue, but you will have no doubt that the doubtful sameness has an indisputable meaning — that there is an unambiguous answer to your query. So firm is our belief in the continuity of the unobserved parts of the strings!

No doubt the notion of individuality of pieces of matter dates from time immemorial. I suppose animals must have it in some way, and a dog, when seeking for his ball that has been hidden, displays it very plainly. Science has taken it over as a matter of course. It has refined it so as safely to embrace all cases of apparent disappearance of matter. The idea that a log which burns away first turns into fire, then into ashes and smoke, is not alien to the primitive mind. Science has substantiated it; though the appearance in bulk may change, the ultimate constituents of the matter do not. This was (in spite of his occasional scepticism mentioned above) the teaching of Democritus. Neither he nor Dalton doubted that an atom which was originally present in the block of wood is afterwards either in the ashes or in the smoke.

9. The Bearing on Atomism

In the new turn of atomism that began with the papers of Heisenberg and of de Broglie in 1925 such an attitude has to be abandoned. This is the most startling revelation emerging from the ensuing development, and the feature which in the long run is bound to have the most important consequences. If we wish to retain atomism we are forced by observed facts to deny the ultimate constituents of matter the character of identifiable individuals. Up to recently, atomists of all ages, for all I know, had transferred that characteristic from visible and palpable pieces of matter to the atoms, which they could not see or touch or observe singly. Now we do observe single particles; we see their tracks in the cloud chamber and in photographic emulsions; we register the practically simultaneous discharges caused by a single swift particle in two or three Geiger counters placed at several yards' distance from each other. Yet we must deny the particle the dignity of being an absolutely identifiable individual. Formerly, if a physicist were asked what stuff the atoms themselves were made of, he might smile and shirk the answer. If the inquirer insisted on the question whether he might imagine them as small unchangeable bits of ordinary matter, he would get the smiling reply that there was no point in doing so but that it would do no harm. The formerly meaningless question has now gained significance. The answer is definitely in the negative. An atom lacks the most primitive property we associate with a piece of matter in ordinary life. Some philosophers of the past, if the case could be put to them, would say that the modern atom consists of no stuff at all but is pure shape.

10. The Meaning of the New Statistics

We must at last proceed to give the reasons for this change of attitude in a more comprehensible form than at the end of section 6. It rests on the so-called new statistics. There are two of them. One is the Bose-Einstein statistics, whose novelty and relevance were first stressed by Einstein. The other is the Fermi-Dirac statistics, of which the most pregnant expression is Pauli's exclusion principle. I shall try to explain the new statistics, and its relation to the old classical or Boltzmann statistics, to those who have never heard about such things and perhaps may be puzzled by what ' statistics ' means in the context. I shall use an instance from everyday life. It may seem childishly simple, particularly because we have to choose small numbers — actually 2 and 3 — in order to make the arithmetic surveyable. Apart from this, the illustration is completely adequate and covers the actual situation.

Three schoolboys, Tom, Dick, and Harry, deserve a reward. The teacher has two rewards to distribute among them. Before doing so, he wishes to realize for himself how many different distributions are at all possible. This is the only question we investigate (we are not interested in his eventual decision). It is a statistical question: to count the number of different distributions. The point is that the answer depends on the nature of the rewards. Three different kinds of reward will illustrate the three kinds of statistics.

(a) The two rewards are two memorial coins with portraits of Newton and Shakespeare respectively. The teacher may give Newton either to Tom or to Dick or to Harry, and Shakespeare either to Tom or to Dick or to Harry.

Thus there are three times three, that is nine, different distributions (classical statistics).

(b) The two rewards are two shilling-pieces (which, for our purpose, we must regard as indivisible quantities). They can be given to two different boys, the third going without. In addition to these three possibilities there are three more: either Tom or Dick or Harry receives two shillings. Thus there are six different distributions (Bose-Einstein statistics).

(c) The two rewards are two vacancies in the football team that is to play for the school. In this case two boys can join the team, and one of the three is left out. Thus there are three different distributions (Fermi-Dirac statistics).

Let me mention right away the *rewards* represent the particles, two of the same kind in every case; the boys represent states the particle can assume. Thus, 'Newton is given to Dick' means: the particle Newton takes on the state Dick.

Notice that the counting is natural, logical, and indisputable in every case. It is uniquely determined by the nature of the objects: memorial coins, shillings, memberships. They are of different categories. Memorial coins are individuals distinguished from one another. Shillings, for all intents and purposes, are not, but they are still capable of being owned in the plural. It makes a difference whether you have one shilling, or two, or three. There is no point in two boys exchanging their shillings. It does change the situation, however, if one boy gives up his shilling to another. With memberships, neither has a meaning. You can either belong to a team or not. You cannot belong to it twice over.

Experimental evidence proves that statistical counts referring to elementary particles must never follow the pattern (a), but must follow either (b) or (c). Some hold that for all genuinely elementary particles (c) is competent. Such particles, electrons for instance, correspond to membership in a club; I mean to the abstract notion of membership, not to the members. Any person eligible to membership in that club represents a well-defined state an electron can take on. If the person is a member, that means there is an electron in that particular state. According to Pauli's exclusion principle, there can never be more than one electron in a particular state. Our simile renders this by declaring double membership meaningless — as in most clubs it would be. In the course of time the list of members changes, and membership is now attached to other persons: the electrons have gone over into other states. Whether you can, in a loose way, speak of a certain membership going over from Dick to Tom, thence from Tom to Harry, etc., depends on the circumstances. They may suggest this view, or they may not, but never in an absolute fashion. In this our simile is perfect, for it is the same with an electron. Moreover, it is quite appropriate to consider the number of members as fluctuating. Indeed, electrons too are created and annihilated.

The example may seem odd and inverted. One might think, 'Why cannot the people be the electrons and various clubs their states? That would be so much more natural.' The physicist regrets, but he cannot oblige. And this is just the salient point: the actual statistical behaviour of electrons cannot be illustrated by any simile that represents them by identifiable things. That is why it follows from their actual statistical behaviour that they are not identi-fiable things.

The case (b), illustrating Einstein-Bose statistics, is competent for light quanta (photons), *inter alia*. It hardly needs discussion. It does not strike us as so strange for the very reason that it includes light, i.e. electro-magnetic energy; and energy, in prequantum times, had always been thought of in very much the way our simile represents it, viz. as having quantity, but no indi-viduality.

11. Restricted Notion of Identity

The most delicate question is that of the states of, say, an electron. They are, of course, to be defined not classically, but in the light of the uncertainty rela-tion. The rigorous treatment referred to at the end of section 6 is not really based on the notion of 'state of one electron' but on that of 'state of the as-sembly of electrons.' The whole list of members of the club, as it were, has to be envisaged together — or rather several membership lists, corresponding to the several kinds of particles that go to compose the physical system under consideration. I mention this, not to go into details about it, but because, taken rigorously, the club simile has two flaws. First, the possible states of an elec-tron (which we had assimilated to the persons eligible for membership) are not absolutely defined; they depend on the arrangement of the — actual or imagined — experiment. Given this arrangement, the states are well-defined individuals, which the electrons are not. They also form — and this is the sec-ond flaw of the simile — a well-ordered manifold. That is, there is a meaning in speaking of neighbouring states as against such as are farther remote from each other. Moreover, I believe it is true to say that this order can be con-ceived in such a fashion that, as a rule, whenever one occupied state ceases to be occupied, a neighbouring state becomes occupied.

This explains that, in favourable circumstances, long strings of successively occupied states may be produced, similar to those contemplated in sections 7 and 8. Such a string gives the impression of an identifiable individual, just as in the case of any object in our daily surrounding. It is in this way that we must look upon the tracks in the cloud chamber or in a photographic emulsion, and on the (practically) simultaneous discharges of Geiger counters set in a line, which discharges we say are caused by the same particle passing one counter after another. In such cases it would be extremely inconvenient to discard this terminology. There is, indeed, no reason to ban it, provided we are aware that, on sober experimental grounds, the sameness of a particle is not an absolute concept. It has only a restricted significance and breaks down com-pletely in some cases.

In what circumstances this restricted sameness will manifest itself is fairly obvious; namely, when only few states are occupied in the region of the state-manifold with which we are concerned, or, in other words, when the occupied states are not too crowded in that region, or when occupation is a rare event — the terms few, crowded, and rare all referring to the state-manifold. Otherwise, the strings intermingle inextricably and reveal the true situation. In the last section we shall formulate the quantitative condition for the prevailing of re-stricted individuality. Now we ask what happens when it is obliterated.

12. Crowdedness and Wave Aspect

One gains the impression that according as the individuality of the particles is wiped out by crowding, the particle aspect becomes altogether less and less expedient and has to be replaced by the wave aspect. For instance, in the electronic shell of an atom or molecule the crowding is extreme, almost all the states within a certain region being occupied by electrons. The same holds for the so-called free electrons inside a metal. Indeed, in both cases the particle aspect becomes entirely incompetent. On the other hand, in an ordinary gas the molecules are extremely rare in the wide region of states over which they spread. No more than one state in 10,000 or so is occupied. And, indeed, the theory of gases, based on the particle aspect, was able to attain great perfection long before the wave nature of ordinary matter was discovered. (In the last remark I have been speaking of the molecules as if they were ultimate particles; this is legitimate as far as their translatory motion is concerned.)

It is tempting to assign to the two rivals, the particle aspect and the wave aspect, full competences in the limiting cases of extreme ' rarefaction ' and extreme ' crowding ' respectively. This would separate them, as it were, with only some sort of transition required for the intermediate region. This idea is not entirely wrong, but it is also far from correct. One may remember the interference patterns referred to in section 2 in evidence of the wave nature of the electron. They can be obtained with an arbitrarily faint bundle of cathode rays, provided the exposure is prolonged. Thus a typical wave phenomenon is produced here, irrespective of crowding. Another instance is this. A competent theoretical investigation of the collision of two particles, whether of the same or of different kind, has to take account of their wave nature. The results are duly applied to the collisions of cosmic ray particles with atomic nuclei in the atmosphere, both being extremely rarefied in every sense of the word. But perhaps this is trivial; it only means that even an isolated particle, which gives us the illusion of transitory individuality, must yet not be likened to a classical particle. It remains subject to the uncertainty relation, of which the only tolerable image is the guiding wave group.

13. The Condition for the Particle Aspect

The following is the quantitative condition for strings to develop which counterfeit individuals and suggest the particle aspect: the product of the momentum p and the average distance l between neighbouring particles must be fairly large compared with Planck's constant h; thus

$$pl \gg h.$$

(The momentum p — and not the velocity — is the thing we should really have referred to when, in sections 4 and 5, we dealt with the uncertainty relation; p is simply the product of the mass and the velocity, unless the latter is comparable with that of light.)

A large l means a low density in ordinary space. What matters, however, is the density in the manifold of states — or phase space, to use the technical term. That is why the momentum p comes in. It is gratifying to remember that those very obvious strings — visible tracks in the cloud chamber or in the photographic emulsion, and simultaneous discharges of aligned counters — are all produced by particles with comparatively very large momentum.

The above relation is familiar from the theory of gases, where it expresses the condition which must be fulfilled in very good approximation in order that the old classical particle theory of gases should apply in very good approximation. This theory has to be modified according to quantum theory when the temperature is very low and at the same time the density very high, so that the product pl is no longer very large compared with h. This modification is called the theory of degenerate gases, of which the most famous application is that by A. Sommerfeld to the electrons inside a metal; we have mentioned them before as an instance of extreme crowding.

There is the following connection between our relation and the uncertainty relation. The latter allows one at any moment to distinguish a particle from its neighbours by locating it with an error considerably smaller than the average distance l. But this entails an uncertainty in p. On account of it, as the particle moves on, the uncertainty in the location grows. If one demands that it still remain well below l after the particle has covered the distance l, one arrives precisely at the above relation.

But again I must warn of a misconception which the preceding sentences might suggest, viz. that crowding only prevents us from registering the identity of a particle, and that we mistake one particle for the other. The point is that they are not individuals which could be confused or mistaken one for another. Such statements are meaningless.

GLOSSARY

The following statements are intended to aid the reader in understanding terms which in the quotations may be used in a restricted or different sense from current usage, but these statements are not intended as comprehensive definitions.

absolute age (absolute chronology)   Refers to dating of geologic events in years, in contrast to relative chronology or relative age, which refers to dating of geologic events in consecutive order.

acceleration   The rate of change of velocity.

acid   To the chemists of the early 19th century, a nonmetallic oxide whose water solution turned litmus red; now called an acid anhydride.

alchemy   An art which sought to transmute baser metals into gold and to discover an elixir of life.

allotrophy   The property of certain elements of existing in two or more modifications distinct in physical properties.

anomalies   Deviations, either positive or negative, from the computed or theoretical values. Commonly applied to gravitation.

aphelion   The point in the orbit of a planet or comet farthest from the sun.

apogee   The point in a satellite's (moon's) orbit which is farthest from the earth.

apparent astronomical latitudes   Latitudinal readings as determined by astronomical measurements. Adjacent mountains by exerting a sideways pull on the plumb bob could introduce slight errors in measurement.

apparent solar day   The interval of time between successive transits of the same branch of the celestial meridian by the apparent sun.

aqueo-igneous fusion   Refers to melting, or bringing rock matter to at least the plastic-flowage stage, through the combined influence of heat and water.

armillary sphere   An arrangement of marked hoops or rings of the same diameter which represent the circles of the celestial sphere. It can be used with a gnomon as a sundial or it can be used with open sights for measuring the positions of objects on the celestial sphere.

astronomical unit   The average distance between the sun and the earth, which is about 93,000,000 miles.

atom (Dalton)   *See* ultimate particle.

atom (following Avogadro)   The smallest particle which maintains its identity and is not divided during chemical reactions.

atomic weight   The relative weight of an atom as compared to some standard particle. Chemists have used various standards at different times, the more common being the hydrogen atom, the hydrogen molecule, and the oxygen atom.

axiom   A statement which is assumed without proof for the sake of studying the consequences that follow from it.

azote   Nitrogen.

base   To the chemists of the early 19th century, a metallic oxide whose water solution turned litmus blue; now called a basic anhydride.

basement complex   A term commonly applied to the igneous and metamorphic rocks underlying the dominantly sedimentary strata. Typically their structure is complex and their age is Pre-Cambrian.

binary compound (Dalton)   A compound containing two atoms (elementary or compound) in each " atom " of the compound.

block-faulting   Breaking of a land mass into a series of blocks. One block may be elevated or depressed relative to the adjacent block, or to the adjoining region.

caloric   The so-called weightless fluid that was believed to constitute heat.

carbonic acid (Dalton)   One " atom " of carbonic acid is composed of one elementary atom of carbon and two elementary atoms of oxygen. Now called carbon dioxide.

carbonic oxide (Dalton)   One " atom " of carbonic oxide is composed of one elementary atom of carbon and one elementary atom of oxygen. Now called carbon monoxide.

carboniferous age   The age of coal formation; formerly considered the geologic time during the late Paleozoic when land plants flourished, their remains producing extensive beds of coal.

celestial equator   The great circle on the celestial sphere which is exactly half-way between the two celestial poles.

celestial horizon   The circle formed by the intersection with the celestial sphere of one's own horizontal plane.

celestial meridian   The great circle on the celestial sphere which contains the observer's zenith, nadir, and both celestial poles. Upper branch — that half containing the zenith; lower branch — that half containing the nadir.

celestial poles   The two points on the celestial sphere about which it appears to rotate daily.

celestial sphere   The imaginary sphere centered on the earth and having the stars and other celestial objects on its inner surface.

centripetal force   A force acting toward a center. Usually used to designate the force required to pull a moving body from its straight line path so that it moves in a conic section such as a circle or ellipse.

chemical change   A process whereby a certain substance or substances that are recognized by their properties disappear and a new substance or substances with different properties appear.

circumjovial   Circling about Jupiter.

circumpolar   Means " about the pole " and usually is applied to that region of the visible sky where the stars neither rise nor set.

coal measures   Commonly applied in early geological reports to rocks containing coal, particularly those now considered Pennsylvanian in age; to some extent applied also to Permian and Mississippian coal beds.

compound A pure substance containing two or more elements in fixed proportions which may be separated by chemical but not by physical processes.

conic section Any curve produced by cutting a cone with a plane.

conjunction The same position on the celestial sphere as that occupied by the sun.

couche de niveau Literally a datum plane or a base level.

cross-bedded Sedimentary laminations oblique to the main stratifications.

cubit A unit of length equal to the length of the forearm from elbow to the outstretched finger tips.

declination Angular distance north or south of the celestial equator of a celestial body.

(Hall) A " decrease in elevation."

deferent The circle upon which an epicycle moves.

density Mass per unit volume or weight per unit volume, depending on usage.

diurnal motion The apparent daily motion of the celestial sphere about the earth.

dynamics That branch of the science of mechanics which is concerned with the theory of motion. Modern dynamics is concerned with masses, forces, and accelerations.

dyne The unbalanced force that will impart an acceleration of 1 centimeter per second per second to a 1 gram-mass.

eccentric An off-center circle.

ecliptic The apparent annual path of the sun around the celestial sphere.

elastic state A gas.

electrolysis The decomposition of a chemical compound by an electric current.

electro-negative element According to Berzelius' dualistic theory, those elements whose atoms possessed a net negative electrical charge. In modern usage, the term has a different meaning.

element A substance which cannot be further resolved into other substances.

energy The ability to perform work. If due to position, this energy is called potential; if due to motion, it is called kinetic.

ephemeris A table of calculated positions of an astronomical body for various times.

epicycle A circle whose center moves on another circle.

equant That point not at the center of the deferent about which the epicycle moves with uniform rotational motion.

equilibrium A state of zero acceleration; hence of no unbalanced force.

equinox Had the original meaning of " equal nights " meaning that day which had exactly 12 hours of daylight and 12 hours of darkness. However, as vernal or autumnal equinox, it can also mean two particular points on the celestial sphere.

equipotential surface A surface along which the force (gravitational or other) is everywhere constant and at right angles to the surface.

equivalent weight The weight of an element that combines with or replaces the unit weight of hydrogen or its equivalent in a reaction.

ether A hypothetical substance filling all celestial space (the space outside the moon's orbit in Ptolemy's universe).

eudiometer   A graduated glass tube sealed at one end and containing two wire electrodes sealed through the glass wall near the closed end of the tube. Used for passing electrical discharges through gases.

fluxions   The term applied by Newton to the calculus.

force   Recognized by Galileo as that action which produces *changes* in motion, although earlier it was considered that the motion itself was proportional to the force. Defined by Newton as being proportional to the change of momentum. Currently defined as proportional to rate of change of momentum, and so used by Newton upon occasion.

galvanism   Dealing with current electricity.

geodesy   The science dealing with the physical measurements of both the shape and dimensions of the earth.

geosynclinal prism   Sediments deposited in a geosyncline.

glacioeolian   Pertaining to the action of wind upon fine materials deposited by glaciers or by glacial meltwater.

glaciofluvial deposits   Pertaining to deposits of materials laid down by streams of glacial meltwater.

gnomon   A pointer erected to cast a shadow as in the sundial.

heliocentric   With the sun at the center.

Hudson-river group   A term variously used in early geological literature referring to a group of formations (especially of New York state) of upper Ordovician or at least pre-Silurian age.

impetus   To the pre-Galilean physicists, a kind of force put into a moving body which kept it moving by violent motion until the impetus was finally all expended against the resistance to the motion.

impulse   The product of the accelerating force and the time the force acts.

inclined sphere   *See* oblique sphere.

inertia   The invariable property of a body in virtue of which it resists acceleration.

isomorphs   Having the same crystalline shape.

isotopes   Variants of an element, having the same atomic number but slightly different atomic weights.

kinematics   That branch of the science of mechanics which describes motion without any reference to mass or cause.

levity   The tendency of light materials, in which the Greek elements fire and air were presumed to predominate, to rise; the opposite of gravity.

libration of the moon   The apparent " rocking " motion of the moon as viewed from the earth.

littoral belts   The near-shore shallower portion of the ocean as contrasted to the deep-water portion.

local noon   The time of day when the sun crosses the upper branch of the celestial meridian.

lodestone   A naturally magnetized stone of iron ore.

loess   An unstratified, relatively unconsolidated deposit of predominantly silt particles, commonly tan to buff in color, which possesses the property of standing in nearly vertical cliffs. Commonly considered to have been transported and deposited by wind.

Lower Helderberg group   Essentially a group of rock formations of lower Devonian age.

mail An Arabian concept of some quantity added to a body which produced motion of the body.

mass The invariable property of ordinary bodies which is proportional to either their inertias or gravitational attractions for other bodies.

mean solar time The time kept by a fictitious " average sun " which has been defined to give exactly equal " mean solar days."

meridian of arc A given number of degrees of latitude on the surface of the earth measured along a true north-south line.

molecule (following Avogadro) A molecule of a pure substance (element or compound) is the smallest particle of the pure substance that possesses the identical chemical properties of the pure substance.

momentum The modern term for what Newton termed " quantity of motion." It is the product of the mass of the moving object and its velocity.

nadir That unseen point on the celestial sphere which is directly opposite the zenith. This point lies under the feet of the observer.

negative gravity zone An area in which a gravity meter reading is lower than expected, indicating subsurface material of lower than normal density.

nether rocks The deeper or lower-lying rocks, as opposed to " upper."

newton The unbalanced force that will impart an acceleration of 1 meter per second per second to a 1 kilogram-mass.

Niagara limestone Limestone strata considered by Hall to make up the lower part of the upper Silurian formations. Niagaran beds are at present referred to middle Silurian.

nodes of the moon's orbit Two diametrically opposed points on the ecliptic produced by the intersection of the moon's orbit with the ecliptic plane.

oblique sphere (inclined sphere) The celestial sphere as viewed when the celestial equator does not pass through the observer's zenith.

opposition The point on the celestial sphere which is opposite the current position of the sun.

orography A branch of physical science dealing with the study of mountains.

Palaeozoic (Paleozoic) The middle era of geologic time; literally means " ancient life."

parabola The path which a projectile near the earth's surface would follow if air resistance were negligible. A parabola is the curve obtained when a plane cuts a cone parallel to one edge of the cone. When plotted, the equation $y = kx^2$ gives a parabola.

parallax The angle made at an object by the two lines of sight from the ends of a given baseline.

pari passu Literally " little by little "; with equal steps; together with.

perigee The point in a satellite's (moon's) orbit which is closest to the earth.

perihelion The point in an orbit nearest the sun.

perturbation Deviation from the normal or expected due to extraneous causes.

phase (chemical) A homogeneous portion of matter which is visually distinguishable from its surroundings and possesses uniform properties throughout.

phase of the moon The quantity and form of its illuminated disk that is visible.

Pleistocene drift Deposits laid down either by ice or by the meltwater of ice during the last ice age.

plumbline A line with a weight attached used to indicate the vertical at a given place.

plutonic intrusions Rock masses which crystallized deep within the earth from magmas.

Potsdam sandstone Sandstone strata considered in Hall's day to be lower Silurian in age, equivalent to present-day upper Cambrian.

pound-force The unbalanced force that will impart to a one pound-mass an acceleration of 32 feet per second per second.

pound-mass A mass that is the same as the standard one-pound mass that is kept at the Bureau of Standards.

precession of the earth's axis The slow westward rotation of the axis about a line perpendicular to the earth's orbit, the inclination of the axis to this line remaining 23½°. The period of precession is about 26,000 years.

precession of the equinoxes The westward motion of the equinoxes along the celestial equator.

pressure Force exerted per unit of area.

pure substance Matter not further resolvable into components by physical processes and whose properties are invariable under similar physical conditions. May be an element or a compound.

quadrature A position on the celestial sphere along the ecliptic and at right angles to the current position of the sun.

quantity of matter Mass.

quantity of motion Momentum.

quintessence (Aristotle) Fifth element of which the universe beyond the lunar sphere was composed.

reductio ad absurdum The refutation of a proposition by demonstrating the absurd conclusion to which it would inevitably lead when logically developed.

regression of the moon's nodes The westward motion of the moon's nodes along the ecliptic, similar to the precession of the equinoxes, with a period of 18.6 years.

resultant That single vector which is equivalent to two (or more) vectors acting together.

retrograde motion The apparent westward motion of a planet among the stars during part of its path on the celestial sphere.

right sphere The celestial sphere viewed when the celestial equator passes through the observer's zenith.

secular erosion Wearing and removal of rock materials over a long period of time by gradational agents.

sidereal day The interval between successive transits of the same branch of the celestial meridian by a given star.

sidereal period The time required to make one revolution around the earth with respect to the stars.

sidereal year The interval of time between the sun's apparent passage of a given point in the sky and its return to that point.

solution A single homogeneous phase which is either a pure substance or a mixture of pure substances.

specific gravity The ratio of the weight of a body to the weight of an equal volume of a standard substance, generally water. The specific gravity of a gas is often referred to air as a standard. The ratio of the density of a substance to the density of a standard substance is also equal to the specific gravity of the substance.

specific heat   The ratio of the amount of heat required to raise the temperature 1° of a given mass of a substance to the amount of heat required to raise the temperature 1° of an equal mass of water.

speed   The distance traveled per unit of time; the rate of covering distance.

summer and winter solstices   Occur on about June 22 and December 22 when the sun is farthest from the celestial equator. The solstices are the two points on the celestial sphere associated with the positions of the sun on these dates.

synodic period   The time required to make one turn about the earth with respect to the sun.

syzygies   Positions of conjunction and opposition.

ternary compound (Dalton)   A compound containing three atoms (elementary or compounded) in each " atom " of the compound.

thermal gradient   Change in temperature per unit distance.

transit   Upper transit occurs when any given celestial body crosses the upper branch of the celestial meridian. *See also* celestial meridian.

trap-dykes (trap dikes)   Tabular shaped intrusive igneous rock bodies consisting of trap rock and occurring in a discordant relationship with the rocks intruded. " Trap " is an indefinite rock term, frequently applied to diabase, basalt, or other dark igneous intrusions.

traverses   Lines surveyed or mapped across an area or a plot of ground.

tropic   Either of the two circles on the celestial sphere which are parallel to the celestial equator and are either 23½° N (tropic of Cancer) or 23½° S (tropic of Capricorn). Also the corresponding circles on the earth.

tropical year   The interval of time between one vernal equinox and the following one.

ultimate particle (Dalton)   The smallest particle obtained by subdivision of a sample of an element or compound which would still have the chemical properties of the original sample. Synonymously Dalton used the term " atom."

uniform motion   Motion in which equal distances are traversed during any equal time intervals.

vector   An arrow whose length represents the magnitude of a given quantity and whose direction indicates the direction of the quantity.

vector quantity   A quantity having a definite magnitude and a definite direction.

velocity   A vector quantity whose magnitude is speed.

vernal and autumnal equinoxes   Occur on about March 21 and September 23 respectively, when the sun crosses the celestial equator. The vernal equinox marks the zero point on the celestial sphere for measurements corresponding to terrestrial longitude.

versed sine of an arc   The perpendicular distance from the center of the doubled arc to its chord.

violent motion   Any motion other than free fall that is impressed on a body by an extraneous force.

viscidity   Thick or sticky consistency.

vis insita   Inertia.

volcanology   The science dealing with the study of volcanoes and volcanic processes. (Also vulcanology.)

vulcanism   A major earth process dealing with the movements of molten rock materials and the formation of rock bodies as products.

weight   The gravitational attractive force exerted on an object by the earth.

work   The product of the force and the distance through which the force moves in the direction of the force.

zenith   That point on the celestial sphere which is directly overhead of an observer.

zenith distance   The angle between a given point on the celestial sphere and the zenith.

zodiac   That belt of the sky which extends 8° on either side of the ecliptic.

zodiacal constellations   The twelve constellations roughly contained within the belt of the zodiac which are distributed around the celestial sphere.

BIBLIOGRAPHY

A Selected Bibliography for Further Reading

General

BUTTERFIELD, HERBERT. *The Origins of Modern Science*, Macmillan, New York, 1953

DURANT, WILL. *The Story of Civilization*, 7 volumes, Simon and Schuster, New York, 1935–1961

LINDSAY, JEAN (editor). *A Short History of Science*, Doubleday Anchor, Garden City, 1959

SINGER, CHARLES (editor). *A History of Technology*, 5 volumes, Oxford University Press, Oxford and New York, 1954–1958

Greek and Early Science

DREYER, J. L. E. *A History of Astronomy from Thales to Kepler*, Dover Publications, New York, 1953

SARTON, GEORGE. *A History of Science*, 2 volumes, Harvard University Press, Cambridge, 1959

Medieval Science

CLAGETT, MARSHALL. *The Science of Mechanics in the Middle Ages*, The University of Wisconsin Press, Madison, 1959

CROMBIE, A. C. *Medieval and Early Modern Science*, 2 volumes, Doubleday Anchor, Garden City, 1959

The Renaissance of Science in Europe

ARMITAGE, ANGUS. *Copernicus, The Founder of Modern Astronomy*, Thomas Yoseloff, New York and London, 1957

CASPAR, MAX. *Kepler*, translated by C. Doris Hellman, Henry Schuman, New York, 1960

COHEN, I. BERNARD. *The Birth of a New Physics*, Doubleday Anchor, Garden City, 1960

DE SANTILLANA, GIORGIO. *The Crime of Galileo*, The University of Chicago Press, Chicago, 1955

HALL, A. R. *The Scientific Revolution, 1500–1800*, The Beacon Press, Boston, 1956

KOESTLER, ARTHUR. *The Sleepwalkers*, Macmillan, New York, 1959

KUHN, THOMAS S. *The Copernican Revolution*, Modern Library Paperback, Random House, New York, 1959

WOLF, A. *A History of Science, Technology, and Philosophy in the XVI and XVII Centuries*, Macmillan, New York, 1950

The Age of the Enlightenment

ANDRADE, E. N. da C. *Sir Isaac Newton, His Life and Work*, Doubleday Anchor, Garden City, 1958

CONANT, JAMES B. (editor). *Harvard Case Histories in Experimental Science*, Vols. I & II, Harvard University Press, Cambridge, 1957

LEICESTER, H. M. AND KLICKSTEIN, H. S. *A Source Book in Chemistry, 1400–1900*, McGraw-Hill, New York, 1952

PARTINGTON, J. R. *A Short History of Chemistry*, Macmillan, London, 1939

WOLF, A. *A History of Science, Technology, and Philosophy in the XVIII Century*, Macmillan, New York, 1952

Modern Times

ADAMS, FRANK DAWSON. *The Birth and Development of the Geological Sciences*, Williams and Wilkins Company, Baltimore, 1938; Dover Publications, reprint, 1954

BASCOM, WILLARD. *A Hole in the Bottom of the Sea*, Doubleday, Garden City, New York, 1961

FENTON, CARROL LANE AND ADAMS, MILDRED. *Giants of Geology*, Doubleday, Garden City, New York, 1956

MOORE, RUTH. *The Earth We Live On*, Alfred A. Knopf, New York, 1956

SCHROEDINGER, ERWIN C. *Science, Theory, and Man*, Dover Publications, New York, 1957

INDEX

595